STUDY GUIDE
to accompany
McConnell and Brue
MACROECONOMICS

STUDY GUIDE
to accompany
McConnell and Brue
MACROECONOMICS

Sixteenth Edition

WILLIAM B. WALSTAD
PROFESSOR OF ECONOMICS
UNIVERSITY OF NEBRASKA–LINCOLN

ROBERT C. BINGHAM
LATE PROFESSOR OF ECONOMICS
KENT STATE UNIVERSITY

 Irwin

Boston   Burr Ridge, IL   Dubuque, IA   Madison, WI   New York
San Francisco   St. Louis   Bangkok   Bogotá   Caracas   Kuala Lumpur
Lisbon   London   Madrid   Mexico City   Milan   Montreal   New Delhi
Santiago   Seoul   Singapore   Sydney   Taipei   Toronto

**McGraw-Hill
Irwin**

*Study Guide to Accompany Macroeconomics
Principles, Problems, and Policies*

ISBN 0-07-288473-8

Editorial director: Robin Zwettler
Publisher: Gary Burke
Sponsoring editor: Lucille Sutton
Developmental editor: Erin Strathmann
Marketing manager: Martin Quinn
Project manager: Jean Lou Hess
Production supervisor: Rose Hepburn
Director of design: Keith McPherson
Editorial coordinator: Karen Minnich
Editorial assistant: Rebecca Hicks
Compositor: TechBooks
Typeface: Helvetica
Printer: Quebecor World Dubuque, Inc.

http://www.mhhe.com

About the Authors

William B. Walstad is a professor of economics at the University of Nebraska–Lincoln, where he directs the National Center for Research in Economic Education. He received his Ph.D. degree from the University of Minnesota. Professor Walstad has been honored with a Distinguished Teaching Award at Nebraska. He also received the Henry H. Villard Research Award for his published research in economic education. He is the chair of the Committee on Economic Education of the American Economic Association. He coedited *Teaching Undergraduate Economics: A Handbook for Instructors* (McGraw-Hill) and serves as an associate editor of the *Journal of Economic Education.*

Robert C. Bingham was an undergraduate student at DePauw University and obtained M.A. and Ph.D. degrees from Northwestern University. He taught at the University of Nebraska–Lincoln, where he was a colleague of Professor McConnell before moving to Kent State University, from which he retired in 1985. He was the author of several other study guides and supplements for the principles of economics courses.

To
Tammie, Laura, Kristin, Eileen, Clara, and Martha

Contents

How to Use the Study Guide to Learn Economics

This *Study Guide* is designed to help you read and understand Campbell R. McConnell and Stanley L. Brue's textbook, *Macroeconomics*, sixteenth edition. If used properly, a study guide can be a great aid to you for what is probably your first course in economics.

No one pretends that the study of economics is easy, but it can be made easier. Of course, a study guide will not do your work for you, and its use is no substitute for reading the text. You must be willing to read the text, spend time on the subject, and work at learning if you wish to understand economics.

Many students do read their text and work hard on their economics course and still fail to learn the subject. This occurs because principles of economics is a new subject for these students, and they have had no previous experience in learning economics. They want to learn but do not know just how to go about it. Here is where the *Study Guide* can help. Let's first see what the *Study Guide* contains and then how to use it.

■ WHAT THE STUDY GUIDE IS

This *Study Guide* contains 21 chapters to support your learning of each of the 21 textbook chapters in *Macroeconomics*. There are also three more *Study Guide* chapters that support the three **Bonus Web Chapters** for *Macroeconomics*. In addition, the *Study Guide* has a **glossary** and answers to each end-of-chapter **Key Question** in your textbook. This *Study Guide* should give you a complete set of resources to advance your learning of principles of economics.

Each *Study Guide* chapter has 11 sections to give you complete coverage of the textbook material in each chapter. The first five sections identify and explain the basic content and concepts in each chapter.

1. An **introduction** explains what is in the chapter of the text and how it is related to material in earlier and later chapters. It points out topics to which you should give special attention and reemphasizes difficult or important principles and facts.

2. A **checklist** tells you the things you should be able to do when you have finished the chapter.

3. A **chapter outline** shows how the chapter is organized and summarizes briefly the essential points made in the chapter.

4. Selected **hints and tips** for each chapter help you master the material and make connections with any previous discussion of a topic.

5. A list of the **important terms** in the chapter points out what you must be able to define in order to understand the material in the chapter. A definition of each term is in the glossary at the end of the *Study Guide*.

The next six sections of the *Study Guide* allow you to **self-test** your understanding of the chapter material.

6. Fill-in questions (short-answer and list questions) help you learn and remember the important generalizations and facts in the chapter.

7. True–false questions test your understanding of the material in the chapter.

8. Multiple-choice questions also give you a chance to check your knowledge of the chapter content and prepare for this type of course examination.

9. Problems help you learn and understand economic concepts by requiring different skills—drawing a graph, completing a table, or finding relationships—to solve the problems.

10. Short answer and **essay questions** can be used as a self-test, to identify important questions in the chapter and to prepare for examinations.

11. Answers to fill-in questions, problems and projects, true–false questions, and multiple-choice questions are found at the end of each chapter. References to the specific pages in the textbook for each true–false, multiple-choice, and short answer or essay question are also provided.

■ HOW TO STUDY AND LEARN WITH THE HELP OF THE *STUDY GUIDE*

1. *Read and outline.* For best results, quickly read the introduction, outline, list of terms, and checklist in the *Study Guide* before you read the chapter in *Macroeconomics*. Then read the chapter in the text slowly, keeping one eye on the *Study Guide* outline and the list of terms. Highlight the chapter as you read it by identifying the *major and minor* points and by placing *Study Guide* outline numbers or letters (such as I or A or 1 or a) in the margins. When you have completed the chapter, you will have the chapter highlighted, and the *Study Guide* outline will serve as a handy set of notes on the chapter.

2. *Review and reread.* After you have read the chapter in the text once, return to the introduction, outline, and list of terms in the *Study Guide*. Reread the introduction and outline. Does everything there make sense? If not, go back to the text and reread the topics that you do not remember well or that still confuse you. Look at the outline. Try to recall each of the minor topics or points that were contained in the text under each of the major points in the outline. When you come to the list of terms, go over them one by one. *Define or explain each to yourself and then look for the definition of the term either in the text chapter or in the glossar*y. Compare your own definition or explanation with that in the *text or glossary*. The quick way to find the definition of a term in the text is to look in the text index for the page(s) in which that term or concept is mentioned. Make any necessary correction or change in your own definition or explanation.

3. *Test and check answers.* When you have done the above reading and review, you will have a good idea of what is in the text chapter. Now complete the self-test sections of the *Study Guide* to check your understanding.

In doing the self-test, start with the *fill-in, true–false, multiple-choice,* and *problems* sections. Tackle each of these four sections one at a time, using the following procedures: (1) answer as many self-test items as you can without looking in the text or in the answer section of the *Study Guide*; (2) check the text for whatever help you need in answering the items; and (3) consult the answer section of the *Study Guide* for the correct answers and reread any section of the text for which you missed items.

The self-test items in these four sections are not equally difficult. Some will be easy to answer and others will be harder. Do not expect to get them all correct the first time. Some are designed to pinpoint material of importance that you will probably miss the first time you read the text and answering them will get you to read the text again with more insight and understanding.

The *short answer and essay questions* cover the major points in the chapter. For some of the easier questions, all you may do is mentally outline your answer. For the more difficult questions, you may want to write out a brief outline of the answer or a full answer. Do not avoid the difficult questions just because they are more work. Answering these questions is often the most valuable work you can do toward acquiring an understanding of economic relationships and principles.

Although no answers are given in the *Study Guide* to the short answer and essay questions, the answer section does list text page references for each question. You are *strongly* encouraged to read those text pages for an explanation of the question or for better insight into the question content.

4. *Double check.* Before you turn to the next chapter in the text and *Study Guide,* return to the checklist. If you cannot honestly check off each item in the list, you have not learned what the authors of the text and of this *Study Guide* hoped you would learn.

■ BONUS WEB CHAPTERS FOR *MACROECONOMICS*

The *Study Guide* includes chapters to cover the textbook material in the three web-based chapters for *Macroeconomics*: Applications and Extensions of Supply and Demand Analysis (Chapter 3W); The Economics of Developing Countries (Chapter 22W); and Transition Economies: Russia and China (Chapter 23W). These chapters are available for students at www.mcconnell16.com.

■ GLOSSARY

All of the important terms and concepts in *Macroeconomics* are defined and described in the glossary. It is included in the *Study Guide* for easy reference when you see a term or concept you do not know. It will also aid your work on self-test items in the *Study Guide*.

■ ANSWERS TO KEY QUESTIONS IN *ECONOMICS*

Your textbook has end-of-chapter questions that you can work on to further your understanding of economics. Some of these questions are designated as **Key Questions** because they cover important material. The answer to each Key Question is provided in the final part of the *Study Guide*. It is highly recommended that you try to complete these questions for each textbook chapter and then check the correct answers in the *Study Guide*.

■ SOME FINAL WORDS

Perhaps the method of using the *Study Guide* outlined above seems like a lot of work. It is! Study and learning necessarily entail work on your part. This is a fact you must accept if you are to learn economics.

After you have used the *Study Guide* to study three or four chapters, you will find that some sections are more valuable to you than others. Let your own experience determine how you will use it. But do not discontinue use of the *Study Guide* after three or four chapters merely because you are not sure whether it is helping you. **Stick with it.**

■ ACKNOWLEDGMENTS

The late Professor Robert Bingham prepared the first 10 editions of the *Study Guide* to serve as a valuable instructional aid for students. Although Professor Bingham did not participate directly in this revision, his work remains a major contribution.

I also want to acknowledge the other help I received. Campbell McConnell and Stanley Brue offered many insightful comments on the *Study Guide* and encouraged my work. I have also received valuable suggestions and help over the years from Kevin Clark, Loretta Fairchild, Joyce Gleason, Richard Harmstone, Ralph Lewis, Peter Kerr, Ken Rebeck, Dave Rosenbaum, Casey Snyder, Mary Stevenson, and Joshua Stull. Students in my principles of economics classes at the University of Nebraska–Lincoln continue to give me feedback that has improved the *Study Guide* with each edition. Sharon Nemeth has been of invaluable assistance in preparing and proofing the manuscript. Lucille Sutton and Erin Strathmann at McGraw-Hill provided great editorial and production support. In spite of the contributions from others, all responsibility for errors and omissions are mine. And as one final note, users of the *Study Guide* are encouraged to send me comments or suggestions at any time.

William B. Walstad

STUDY GUIDE
to accompany
McConnell and Brue
MACROECONOMICS

CHAPTER 1

The Nature and Method of Economics

Chapter 1 introduces you to economics—the study of how people decide how to use scarce productive resources to satisfy material wants. The purpose of this chapter is to explain the nature of the subject and to describe the methods that economists use to study economic questions.

The first section of the chapter describes the three key features of the *economic perspective.* This perspective first recognizes that all choices involve costs and that these costs must be involved in an economic decision. The economic perspective also incorporates the view that to achieve a goal, people make decisions that reflect their rational self-interest. The third feature considers that people compare marginal benefits against marginal costs when making decisions and will choose the situation where the marginal benefit is greater than the marginal cost. You will develop a better understanding of these features and the meaning of the economic perspective as you read about the economic issues in this book.

As you begin your study of economics, you might be wondering if the work you will do to learn the chapter material is worthwhile. It most certainly is. Knowledge of economics is important because it is essential for well-informed citizenship and has many practical applications to professional and personal decisions.

Economics relies heavily on the scientific method to develop theories and principles to explain the likely effects from human events and behavior. A central part of the economic methodology section focuses on *theoretical economics.* It involves gathering data, creating models, and making generalizations. In essence, economic theories and principles (and related terms such as hypotheses, laws, and models) are generalizations. They are imprecise statements and subject to exceptions because economists cannot easily conduct controlled laboratory experiments to test the validity of the generalizations. Economic theories and principles are simplifications—approximations of a complex world—for analyzing problems and for finding solutions to these problems.

Policy economics develops recommended actions (policies) for addressing an economic problem or advancing an economic goal. It involves stating the goal, considering the policy options, and evaluating the likely outcome. The analysis is based on economic theories and principles, but the choice of an economic policy often depends on the value judgments and weights given to different economic goals. In making a policy recommendation, we move from *economic theory* and *positive economics,* which investigates what is, to *normative economics,* which incorporates subjective views of what ought to be. Many of the apparent disagreements among economists are over normative policy issues and involve deciding which economic goals for our economy are most important in making the case for a policy solution.

Both theoretical economics and policy economics are conducted at two levels. Studies in *macroeconomics* focus on the whole economy, or large segments of it, and investigate such issues as how to increase economic growth, control inflation, or maintain full employment. Studies in *microeconomics* target specific units in the economy, and conduct research on such questions as how prices and output are determined for particular products and how consumers will react to price changes.

Clear thinking about economic questions requires that beginning students avoid many pitfalls. Errors of commission and omission can occur from bias, loaded terminology, imprecise definitions, fallacies of composition, and causation fallacies. Awareness of these pitfalls will help you think more objectively about the economic issues you will read about throughout this book.

■ **CHECKLIST**

When you have studied this chapter you should be able to

☐ Write a formal definition of economics.
☐ Describe the three key features of the economic perspective.
☐ Give applications of the economic perspective.
☐ Give two good reasons for studying economics.
☐ Identify the elements of the scientific method.
☐ Describe theoretical economics.
☐ Distinguish among hypotheses, theories, principles, laws, and models.
☐ Discuss how economic principles are generalizations and abstractions.
☐ Explain the "other things equal" (*ceteris paribus*) assumption and its use in economics.
☐ Define policy economics.
☐ List three steps in economic policymaking.
☐ Identify eight economic goals widely accepted in the United States and many other nations.
☐ Discuss the conflicting or complementary nature of economic goals.
☐ Distinguish between macroeconomics and microeconomics.

☐ Give examples of positive and normative economics.
☐ Identify the five pitfalls to objective thinking when given examples.

■ CHAPTER OUTLINE

1. Economics is concerned with the efficient use of limited productive resources to achieve the maximum satisfaction of economic wants.

2. The *economic perspective* has three interrelated features.

    a. It recognizes that scarcity requires choice and all choices entail a cost.

    b. It views people as rational decision makers who make choices based on their self-interests.

    c. It uses marginal analysis to assess how the marginal costs of a decision compare with the marginal benefits.

3. Citizens in a democracy must understand elementary economics to comprehend the present-day problems of their society and to make intelligent decisions when they vote. Economics is an academic rather than a vocational subject, but a knowledge of it is valuable to business executives, consumers, and workers.

4. Economic methodology relies on the scientific method and includes both theoretical economics and policy economics.

    a. *Theoretical economics* is the gathering and analysis of relevant facts to derive economic principles.

    (1) Hypotheses are propositions that are tested and used to develop economic theories. Highly reliable theories are called principles or laws. Theories, principles, and laws are meaningful statements about economic behavior or the economy that can be used to predict the likely outcome from an economic action or event. Models are created when several economic principles are used to explain or describe reality.

    (2) Each principle or theory is a generalization that shows a tendency or average effect.

    (3) The "other-things-equal" (*ceteris paribus*) assumption is used to limit the influence of other factors when making a generalization.

    (4) Economic principles and theories are abstractions from reality.

    (5) Many economic principles or models can be illustrated graphically.

    b. *Policy economics* is the use of economic principles to develop a course of action to solve economic problems.

    (1) The three steps in creating economic policy are stating the goal, considering the options, and evaluating the results.

    (2) Eight major economic goals are considered important in the United States and many other nations: economic growth, full employment, economic efficiency, price-level stability, economic freedom, economic security, an equitable distribution of income, and a balance of trade. Economic goals can be complementary, or they can conflict and require tradeoffs. The interpretation of economic goals and the setting of priorities can be difficult and cause problems in economic policymaking.

5. Economic analysis is conducted at two levels, and might be positive or normative.

    a. *Macroeconomics* looks at the entire economy or its major aggregates or sectors, such as households, businesses, or government.

    b. *Microeconomics* studies the economic behavior of individuals, particular markets, firms, or industries.

    c. *Positive economics* focuses on facts and is concerned with what is, or the scientific analysis of economic behavior.

    d. *Normative economics* suggests what ought to be and answers policy questions based on value judgments. Most disagreements among economists involve normative economics.

6. Sound reasoning in the study and use of economic principles requires strict application of the rules of logic, in which personal emotions are irrelevant, if not detrimental. The pitfalls beginning students encounter when studying and applying economic principles include the following:

    a. Bias of preconceived beliefs not warranted by facts.

    b. Loaded terminology or the use of terms in a way that appeals to emotion and leads to a nonobjective analysis of the issues.

    c. The definition of terms by economists in ways that may not be the same as the ways in which these terms are more commonly used.

    d. The fallacy of composition or the assumption that what is true of the part is necessarily true of the whole.

    e. Two causation fallacies confuse cause and effect.

    (1) The "after this, therefore because of this fallacy" (*post hoc, ergo propter hoc*) is the mistaken belief that when one event precedes another, the first event is the cause of the second.

    (2) The other fallacy is to confuse correlation with causation. Two factors may be related, but that does not mean that one factor caused the other.

■ HINTS AND TIPS

1. The economic perspective presented in the first section of the chapter has three features related to decision making: scarcity and the necessity of choice, rational self-interest in decision making, and marginal analysis of the costs and benefits of decisions. Although these features may seem strange to you at first, they are central to the economic thinking used to examine decisions and problems throughout the book.

2. The chapter introduces important pairs of terms: theoretical economics and policy economics; microeconomics and macroeconomics; and positive economics and normative economics. Make sure you understand what each pair means.

3. Sound reasoning about economic problems is difficult and requires that you be able to recognize the major pitfalls—loaded terminology, inaccurate definitions, fallacy of composition, *post hoc* fallacy, and confusing correlation with causation. One way to remember these pitfalls is to associate each one with a practical example.

■ **IMPORTANT TERMS**

Note: See Glossary in the back of the book for definitions of terms.

economics	tradeoffs
economic perspective	macroeconomics
utility	aggregate
marginal analysis	microeconomics
scientific method	positive economics
theoretical economics	normative economics
principles	fallacy of composition
generalizations	"after this, therefore because of this" fallacy (*post hoc, ergo propter hoc*)
"other-things-equal" assumption (*ceteris paribus*)	
policy economics	

SELF-TEST

■ **FILL-IN QUESTIONS**

1. Economics is the study of the efficient use of (unlimited, limited) _____ resources to achieve (minimum, maximum) _____ satisfaction of economic wants.

2. The economic perspective recognizes that (resources, scarcity) _____ requires choice and that choice has an opportunity (benefit, cost) _____. "There is no such thing as a free lunch" in economics because scarce resources have (unlimited, alternative) _____ uses.

3. The economic perspective also assumes that people make choices based on their self-interest and that they are (irrational, rational) _____. It also is based on comparisons of the (extreme, marginal) _____ costs and benefits of an economic decision.

4. An understanding of economics is essential if we are to be well-informed (citizens, technicians) _____, and such an understanding has many personal and professional applications even though it is (a vocational, an academic) _____ and not _____ subject.

5. Economics relies on the (model, scientific) _____ method. It involves the gathering of

(facts, theories) _____, and the formulation of (data, hypotheses) _____. These are then tested to develop (facts, theories) _____.

6. The systematic arranging of facts, the interpretation of them, and the drawing of conclusions based on them is called (policy, theoretical) _____ economics.

7. Statements about economic behavior that enable the prediction of the likely effects of certain actions are economic (facts, theories) _____. The most reliable of these, those with strong predictive accuracy, are called (hypotheses, principles) _____. Sometimes they are also called (policies, laws) _____. Simplified representations of how markets or the economy works based on combinations of economic principles are called (policies, models) _____.

8. Economic principles are often imprecise quantitative statements or (fallacies, generalizations) _____ about people's economic behavior, and they necessarily involve (abstractions, distractions) _____ from reality to simplify complex situations.

9. When economists assume that other factors are held constant and do not change when studying an economic relationship, they are using the (*post hoc,* other-things-equal) _____ assumption.

10. The formulation of recommended solutions or remedies for economic problems is referred to as (theoretical, policy) _____ economics.

11. The three steps in the formulation of economic policy are (1) stating the economic (theory, goal) _____, (2) determining the policy (results, options) _____, and (3) implementing and evaluating policy (assumptions, effectiveness) _____.

12. Eight widely accepted economic goals in the United States and many nations are

a. _____

b. _____

c. _____

d. _____

e. _____

f. _____

g. _____

h. _____

13. Increases in economic growth that promote full employment would be an example of a set of (conflicting, complementary) _____ economic goals. Efforts to achieve an equitable distribution of income that at the same time reduce economic efficiency would be an example of a set of (conflicting, complementary) _____ economic goals, indicating that there are (tradeoffs, laws) _____ among economic goals.

14. The study of the total output of the economy or the general level of prices is the subject of (microeconomics, macroeconomics) _____, whereas the study of output in a particular industry or of a particular product is the subject of _____.

15. The collection of specific units that are being added and treated as if they were one unit is an (assumption, aggregate) _____.

16. Two different types of statements can be made about economic topics. A (positive, normative) _____ statement explains what is, by offering a scientific proposition about economic behavior that is based on economic theory and facts, but a _____ statement includes a value judgment about an economic policy or the economy that suggests what ought to be. Many of the reported disagreements among economists usually involve (positive, normative) _____ statements.

17. Holding a preconceived notion, such as thinking that corporate profits are always excessive, is an example of (an aggregate, a bias) _____ pitfall in sound economic thinking.

18. Pitfalls to sound economic thinking can also occur because terminology is (theoretical, loaded) _____ and definitions used by the public are based on (common, scientific) _____ usage.

19. The statement that "What is good for the individual is also good for the group" may not be correct because of the fallacy of (complexity, composition) _____.

20. The person who believes that "washing a car will cause it to rain tomorrow" is expressing an ("other-things-equal," "after this, therefore because of this") _____ fallacy.

■ **TRUE–FALSE QUESTIONS**

Circle T if the statement is true, F if it is false.

1. Economics is the social science concerned with the efficient use of scarce resources to achieve the maximum satisfaction of economic wants. **T F**

2. From the economic perspective, "there is no such thing as a free lunch." **T F**

3. Rational self-interest is the same thing as being selfish. **T F**

4. The economic perspective views individuals or institutions as making rational choices based on the marginal analysis of the costs and benefits of decisions. **T F**

5. Economics is academic and of little value because it does not teach the student how to earn a living. **T F**

6. The scientific method involves the observation of real-world data, the formulation of hypotheses based on the data, and the testing of those hypotheses to develop theories. **T F**

7. Systematically arranging facts, interpreting them, and using them to derive economic principles is called economic analysis. **T F**

8. Economic principles enable us to predict the economic consequences of many human actions. **T F**

9. The most reliable economic theories are often called economic principles or laws. **T F**

10. An economic model is simply an adding up of economic facts about an economic event. **T F**

11. The "other-things-equal" or *ceteris paribus* assumption is made to simplify the reasoning process. **T F**

12. Economic principles, or theories, are abstractions. **T F**

13. The first step in the formulation of an economic policy, the statement of goals, may be occasion for disagreement because different people may have different and conflicting goals to be achieved. **T F**

14. Determining the policy options requires a detailed assessment of the benefits, costs, and political feasibility of alternative policies. **T F**

15. One of the widely (although not universally) accepted economic goals of people in the United States is an equitable distribution of income. **T F**

16. A tradeoff is a situation in which some of one economic goal is sacrificed to obtain some of another economic goal. **T F**

17. Macroeconomic analysis is concerned with the economic activity of specific firms or industries. **T F**

18. Microeconomic analysis is concerned with the performance of the economy as a whole or its major aggregates. **T F**

19. The statement that "the legal minimum wage should be raised to give working people a decent income" is an example of a normative statement. **T F**

20. When value judgments are made about the economy or economic policy, this is called positive economics. **T F**

21. The belief that lending money is always superior to borrowing money is an example of a bias in sound reasoning about economic issues. **T F**

22. The fallacy of composition would be calling profits "excessive" or an unemployed worker "lazy." **T F**

23. If you speak of "capital" to most people, they understand that you are referring to money. The economist, therefore, is obligated to use the term "capital" to mean money. **T F**

24. The *post hoc, ergo propter hoc* fallacy is the belief that "what is true for the individual or part of a group is necessarily true for the group or whole." **T F**

25. A person who concludes that more education increases income may be confusing correlation with causation. **T F**

■ **MULTIPLE-CHOICE QUESTIONS**

Circle the letter that corresponds to the best answer.

1. What statement would best complete a short definition of economics? "Economics is the study of
  (a) how businesses produce goods and services"
  (b) the efficient use of scarce productive resources"
  (c) the equitable distribution of society's income and wealth"
  (d) the printing and circulation of money throughout the economy"

2. The idea in economics that "there is no such thing as a free lunch" means that
  (a) the marginal benefit of such a lunch is greater than its marginal cost
  (b) businesses cannot increase their market share by offering free lunches
  (c) scarce resources have alternative uses or opportunity costs
  (d) consumers are irrational when they ask for a free lunch

3. A major feature of the economic perspective is
  (a) equating rational self-interest with selfishness
  (b) comparing marginal benefits with marginal costs
  (c) the validity of normative economics for decision making
  (d) the recognition of the abundance of economic resources

4. From the economic perspective, when a business decides to employ more workers, the business decision maker has most likely concluded that the marginal
  (a) costs of employing more workers have decreased
  (b) benefits of employing more workers have increased
  (c) benefits of employing more workers are greater than the marginal costs
  (d) costs of employing more workers are not opportunity costs for the business because more workers are needed to increase production

5. Economic analysis that derives economic principles about how individuals behave or institutions act is called
  (a) policy economics
  (b) macroeconomics
  (c) normative economics
  (d) theoretical economics

6. The combination of economic theories or principles into a simplified representation of reality is referred to as an economic
  (a) fact
  (b) law
  (c) model
  (d) hypothesis

7. From the perspective of economists, which of the following would offer the highest degree of confidence for explaining economic behavior
  (a) an assumption
  (b) a speculation
  (c) a correlation
  (d) a principle

8. When economists state that "consumer spending rises when personal income increases," this is an example of
  (a) a generalization
  (b) loaded terminology
  (c) a normative statement
  (d) a fallacy of composition

9. Another term for the assumption that "other things equal" is
  (a) *ceteris paribus*
  (b) the correlation fallacy
  (c) the fallacy of composition
  (d) *post hoc, ergo propter hoc*

10. An economic principle states that the lower the price of a product, the greater the quantity consumers will wish to purchase. This principle is based on the critical assumption that
  (a) economic analysis is normative
  (b) the whole is not greater than the sum of the parts
  (c) economic goals are complementary and not conflicting
  (d) there are no other important changes affecting the demand for the product

11. The three basic steps in economic policymaking are
  (a) gather facts, make abstractions, show findings
  (b) state the goal, determine the options, evaluate results
  (c) create the theory, analyze assumptions, derive conclusions
  (d) form hypotheses, simplify the model, assume other things are equal

12. The production of more goods and services and the development of a higher standard of living would be associated with what economic goal?
  (a) economic security
  (b) economic freedom
  (c) economic growth
  (d) full employment

13. Which economic goal is associated with the idea that we want to get the maximum benefit at the minimum cost from the limited productive resources available?
  (a) economic security
  (b) economic freedom
  (c) economic growth
  (d) economic efficiency

14. Which economic goal would be most abstract and difficult to measure?
  (a) full employment
  (b) economic efficiency
  (c) economic freedom
  (d) price-level stability

15. To say that two economic goals are conflicting means
  (a) it is impossible to quantify both goals
  (b) there is a tradeoff in the achievement of the two goals
  (c) the two goals are not fully accepted as important economic goals
  (d) the attainment of one goal also results in the attainment of the other goal

16. If economic growth tends to produce a more equitable distribution of income among people in a nation, this relationship between the two economic goals appears to be
  (a) deductive
  (b) conflicting
  (c) complementary
  (d) mutually exclusive

17. When we look at the whole economy or its major aggregates, our analysis would be at the level of
  (a) microeconomics
  (b) macroeconomics
  (c) positive economics
  (d) normative economics

18. Which would be studied in microeconomics?
  (a) the output of the entire U.S. economy
  (b) the general level of prices in the U.S. economy
  (c) the output and price of wheat in the United States
  (d) the total number of workers employed in the United States

19. Which is a normative economic statement?
  (a) The consumer price index rose 1.2% last month.
  (b) The unemployment rate of 6.8% is too high.
  (c) The average rate of interest on loans is 4.6%.
  (d) The economy grew at an annual rate of 3.6%.

20. Sandra states that "there is a high correlation between consumption and income." Arthur replies that the correlation occurs because "people consume too much of their income and don't save enough."
  (a) Both Sandra's and Arthur's statements are positive.
  (b) Both Sandra's and Arthur's statements are normative.
  (c) Sandra's statement is positive and Arthur's statement is normative.
  (d) Sandra's statement is normative and Arthur's statement is positive.

21. What pitfall to sound reasoning is reflected in a person's view that corporate profits are always excessive?
  (a) bias
  (b) definition
  (c) the fallacy of composition
  (d) confusing correlation and causation

22. During World War II, the United States used price controls to prevent inflation; some people said this was "a fascist and arbitrary restriction of economic freedom," while others said it was "a necessary and democratic means of preventing ruinous inflation." Both labels are examples of
  (a) economic bias
  (b) loaded terminology
  (c) the fallacy of composition
  (d) the misuse of commonsense definitions

23. If a farmer grows a larger crop one year, he or she will likely receive more income. Therefore, to reason that if all farmers grew larger crops one year they will likely receive more income is an example of
  (a) the after this, therefore because of this fallacy
  (b) the fallacy of composition
  (c) using loaded terminology
  (d) economic bias

24. The government increases its expenditures for road construction equipment, and later the average price of this equipment falls. The belief that the lowered price was the result of the increase in government expenditures is an example of
  (a) the after this, therefore because of this fallacy
  (b) the fallacy of composition
  (c) using loaded terminology
  (d) imprecise definition

25. You observe that more education is associated with more income and conclude that more income leads to more education. This would be an example of
  (a) the fallacy of composition
  (b) confusing correlation and causation
  (c) using the other-things-equal assumption
  (d) the after this, therefore because of this fallacy

■ **PROBLEMS**

1. Use the appropriate number to match the terms with the phrase.

1. economics	5. microeconomics
2. theoretical economics	6. positive economics
3. policy economics	7. normative economics
4. macroeconomics	8. marginal analysis

  a. The formulation of courses of action to bring about desired economic outcomes or to prevent undesired occurrences. _____

  b. The attempt to establish scientific statements about economic behavior; a concern with "what is" rather than "what ought to be." _____

  c. Part of economics that involves value judgments about what the economy should be like or the way the economic world should be. _____

  d. Social science concerned with the efficient use of scarce resources to achieve maximum satisfaction of human material wants. _____

  e. Part of economics concerned with the whole economy or its major sectors. _____

  f. The comparison of additional benefits and additional costs. _____

g. Deriving economic principles from relevant economic facts. _____

h. Part of economics concerned with the economic behavior of individual units such as households, firms, and industries (particular markets). _____

2. News report: "The worldwide demand for wheat from the United States increased and caused the price of wheat in the United States to rise." This is a *specific* instance of a more *general* economic principle. Of which economic *generalization* is this a particular example? _____

_____

_____

3. Following is a list of economic statements. Indicate in the space to the right of each statement whether it is positive (**P**) or normative (**N**). Then, in the last four lines below, write two of your own examples of positive economic statements and two examples of normative economic statements.

a. New York City should control the rental price of apartments. _____

b. Consumer prices rose at an annual rate of 2% last year. _____

c. Most people who are unemployed are just too lazy to work. _____

d. Generally, if you lower the price of a product, people will buy more of that product. _____

e. The profits of drug companies are too large and ought to be used to conduct research on new medicines. _____

f. Government should do more to help the poor. _____

g. _____ __P__

h. _____ __P__

i. _____ __N__

j. _____ __N__

4. Following are five statements. Each is an example of one of the pitfalls frequently encountered in the study of economics. Indicate in the space following each statement the type of pitfall involved.

a. "Investment in stocks and bonds is the only way to build real capital assets." _____

b. "An unemployed worker can find a job if the worker looks diligently and conscientiously for employment; therefore, all unemployed workers can find employment if they are diligent and conscientious in looking for a job." _____

c. McConnell: "Regulation of public utilities in the United States is an immoral and unconscionable interference with the divine right of private property and, as you know, there is no private property in the socialist nations." **Brue:** "It is far from that. You know perfectly well that it is an attempt to limit the unmitigated avarice of mammoth corporations in order, as the Constitution commands, to promote the general welfare of a democratic America." _____

_____

d. "The stock market crash of 1929 was followed by and resulted in 10 years of depression." _____

_____

e. "Be neither a borrower nor lender of money." _____

_____

■ **SHORT ANSWER AND ESSAY QUESTIONS**

1. Define economics in both a less and a more sophisticated way. In your latter definition, explain the meaning of "resources" and "wants."

2. What are the three interrelated features of the economic perspective?

3. What is the economic meaning of the statement "There is no such thing as a free lunch"?

4. What is the difference between rational self-interest and selfishness?

5. How do economists use marginal analysis?

6. What are the principal reasons for studying economics?

7. What are the elements of the scientific method?

8. Define and explain the relationships between economic theory and policy economics.

9. What are the differences and similarities between hypotheses, theories, principles, laws, and models?

10. What is a "laboratory experiment under controlled conditions"? Does the science of economics have any kind of laboratory? Why do economists use the "other-things-equal" assumption?

11. Why are economic principles and models necessarily generalized and abstract?

12. What does it mean to say that economic principles can be used for prediction?

13. What procedure should be followed in formulating sound economic policies?

14. Of the eight economic goals listed in the text, which one would you rank first, second, third, and so on? Would you add any other goals to this list? If the goals of full employment and price-level stability were conflicting, which goal would you prefer? Why? If goals of economic growth and an equitable distribution of income were conflicting, which would you prefer? Why?

15. How can the concept "tradeoffs" be applied to the discussion of economic goals? Give an example.

16. Explain the difference between macroeconomics and microeconomics.

17. Why do economists disagree?

18. What are some current examples of positive economic statements and normative economic statements?

19. Explain each of the following terms:
(a) fallacy of composition
(b) loaded terminology
(c) the *post hoc, ergo propter hoc* fallacy

20. Use an example to describe how correlation differs from causation.

ANSWERS

Chapter 1 The Nature and Method of Economics

FILL-IN QUESTIONS

1. limited, maximum
2. scarcity, cost, alternative
3. rational, marginal
4. citizens, an academic, a vocational
5. scientific, facts, hypotheses, theories
6. theoretical
7. theories, principles, laws, models
8. generalizations, abstractions
9. other-things-equal (or *ceteris paribus*)
10. policy
11. goal, options, effectiveness
12. *a.* economic growth; *b.* full employment; *c.* economic efficiency; *d.* price stability; *e.* economic freedom; *f.* equitable distribution of income; *g.* economic security; *h.* balance of trade (*any order for a–h*)
13. complementary, conflicting, tradeoffs
14. macroeconomics, microeconomics
15. aggregate
16. positive, normative, normative
17. bias
18. loaded, common
19. composition
20. "after this, therefore because of this"

TRUE–FALSE QUESTIONS

1. T, p. 3	**8.** T, pp. 6–7	**15.** T, p. 9	**22.** F, p. 11
2. T, p. 3	**9.** T, pp. 6–7	**16.** T, p. 9	**23.** F, p. 11
3. F, p. 4	**10.** F, pp. 6–7	**17.** F, pp. 9–10	**24.** F, p. 11
4. T, pp. 4–5	**11.** T, pp. 7–8	**18.** F, pp. 9–10	**25.** T, pp. 11–12
5. F, p. 5	**12.** T, p. 8	**19.** T, p. 10	
6. T, p. 6	**13.** T, pp. 8–9	**20.** F, p. 10	
7. F, p. 6	**14.** T, p. 8	**21.** T, p. 10	

MULTIPLE-CHOICE QUESTIONS

1. b, p. 3	**8.** a, p. 7	**15.** b, p. 9	**22.** b, p. 10–11
2. c, pp. 3–4	**9.** a, pp. 7–8	**16.** c, p. 9	**23.** b, p. 11
3. b, pp. 4–5	**10.** d, pp. 7–8	**17.** b, p. 9	**24.** a, p. 11
4. c, pp. 4–5	**11.** b, p. 8	**18.** c, p. 9–10	**25.** b, pp. 11–12
5. d, p. 6	**12.** c, p. 8	**19.** b, p. 10	
6. c, p. 7	**13.** d, p. 9	**20.** c, p. 10	
7. d, p. 7	**14.** c, p. 9	**21.** a, pp. 10–11	

PROBLEMS

1. *a.* 3; *b.* 6; *c.* 7; *d.* 1; *e.* 4; *f.* 8; *g.* 2; *h.* 5
2. An increase in the demand for an economic good will cause the price of that good to rise.
3. *a.* N; *b.* P; *c.* N; *d.* P; *e.* N; *f.* N
4. *a.* definitions; *b.* the fallacy of composition; *c.* loaded terminology; *d.* the after this, therefore because of this fallacy; *e.* bias

SHORT ANSWER AND ESSAY QUESTIONS

1. p. 3	**6.** pp. 5–6	**11.** pp. 7–8	**16.** pp. 9–10
2. pp. 3–4	**7.** p. 6	**12.** pp. 7–8	**17.** p. 10
3. pp. 3–4	**8.** pp. 6–9	**13.** pp. 8–9	**18.** p. 10
4. p. 4	**9.** pp. 6–8	**14.** pp. 8–9	**19.** pp. 10–11
5. p. 4	**10.** pp. 7–8	**15.** p. 9	**20.** pp. 11–12

Graphs and Their Meaning

This appendix introduces graphing in economics. Graphs help illustrate and simplify the economic theories and models presented throughout this book. The old saying that "a picture is worth 1000 words" applies to economics; graphs are the way that economists "picture" relationships between economic variables.

You must master the basics of graphing if these "pictures" are to be of any help to you. This appendix explains how to achieve that mastery. It shows you how to construct a graph from a table with data of two variables, such as income and consumption.

Economists usually, but not always, place the *independent variable* (income) on the horizontal axis and the *dependent variable* (consumption) on the vertical axis of the graph. Once the data points are plotted and a line drawn to connect the plotted points, you can determine whether there is a *direct* or an *inverse relationship* between the variables. Identifying direct and inverse relationships between variables is an essential skill used repeatedly in this book.

Information from data in graphs and tables can be written in an equation. This work involves determining the *slope* and *intercept* from a straight line in a graph or data in a table. Using values for the slope and intercept, you can write a *linear equation* that will enable you to calculate what the dependent variable would be for a given level of the independent variable.

Some graphs used in the book are *nonlinear.* With *nonlinear curves,* the slope of the line is no longer constant throughout but varies as one moves along the curve. This slope can be estimated at a point by determining the slope of a straight line that is drawn tangent to the curve at that point. Similar calculations can be made for other points to see how the slope changes along the curve.

■ **APPENDIX CHECKLIST**

After you have studied this appendix you should be able to

☐ Explain why economists use graphs.
☐ Construct a graph of two variables using the numerical data from a table.
☐ Make a table with two variables from data on a graph.
☐ Distinguish between a direct and an inverse relationship when given data on two variables.
☐ Identify dependent and independent variables in economic examples and graphs.
☐ Describe how economists use the other-things-equal (*ceteris paribus*) assumption in graphing two variables.

☐ Calculate the slope of a straight line between two points when given the tabular data, and indicate whether the slope is positive or negative.
☐ Describe how slopes are affected by the choice of the units of measurement for either variable.
☐ Explain how slopes are related to marginal analysis.
☐ Graph infinite or zero slopes and explain their meaning.
☐ Determine the vertical intercept for a straight line in a graph with two variables.
☐ Write a linear equation using the slope of a line and the vertical intercept; when given a value for the independent variable, determine a value for the dependent variable.
☐ Estimate the slope of a nonlinear curve at a point using a line that is tangent to the curve at that point.

■ **APPENDIX OUTLINE**

1. Graphs illustrate the relationship between variables and give economists and students another way, in addition to verbal explanation, of understanding economic phenomena. Graphs are aids in describing economic theories and models.

2. The construction of a simple graph involves plotting the numerical data of two variables from a table.
   a. Each graph has a *horizontal axis* and a *vertical axis* that can be labeled for each variable and then scaled for the range of the data points that will be measured on the axis.
   b. Data points are plotted on the graph by drawing perpendiculars from the scaled points on the two axes to the place on the graph where the perpendiculars intersect.
   c. A line or curve can then be drawn to connect the points plotted on the graph. If the graph is a straight line, it is *linear.*

3. A graph provides information about relationships between variables.
   a. An upward-sloping line to the right on a graph indicates that there is a positive or *direct relationship* between two variables: an increase in one is associated with an increase in the other; a decrease in one is associated with a decrease in the other.
   b. A downward-sloping line to the right means that there is a negative or *inverse relationship* between the two variables: an increase in one is associated with a decrease in the other; a decrease in one is associated with an increase in the other.

4. Economists are often concerned with determining cause and effect in economic events.

    a. A **dependent variable** changes (increases or decreases) because of a change in another variable.

    b. An **independent variable** produces or "causes" the change in the dependent variable.

    c. In a graph, mathematicians place an independent variable on the horizontal axis and a dependent variable on the vertical axis; economists are more arbitrary about which variable is placed on an axis.

5. Economic graphs are simplifications of economic relationships. When graphs are plotted, usually an implicit assumption is made that all other factors are being held constant. This "other-things-equal" or *ceteris paribus* assumption is used to simplify the analysis so the study can focus on the two variables of interest.

6. The **slope of a straight line** in a two-variable graph is the ratio of the vertical change to the horizontal change between two points.

    a. A *positive* slope indicates that the relationship between the two variables is *direct*.

    b. A *negative* slope indicates that there is an *inverse* relationship between the two variables.

    c. Slopes are affected by the *measurement units* for either variable.

    d. Slopes measure *marginal* changes.

    e. Slopes can be *infinite* (line parallel to vertical axis) or *zero* (line parallel to horizontal axis).

7. The **vertical intercept** of a straight line in a two-variable graph is the point where the line intersects the vertical axis of the graph.

8. The slope and intercept of a straight line can be expressed in the form of a *linear equation,* which is written as $y = a + bx$. Once the values for the intercept (a) and the slope (b) are calculated, then given any value of the independent variable (x), the value of the dependent variable (y) can be determined.

9. The slope of a straight line is constant, but the slope of a **nonlinear curve** changes throughout. To estimate the slope of a nonlinear curve at a point, the slope of a line tangent to the curve at that point is calculated.

■ HINTS AND TIPS

1. This appendix will help you understand the graphs and problems presented throughout the book. Do not skip reading the appendix or working on the self-test questions and problems in this *Study Guide.* The time you invest now will pay off in improved understanding in later chapters. Graphing is a basic skill for economic analysis.

2. Positive and negative relationships in graphs often confuse students. To overcome this confusion, draw a two-variable graph with a positive slope and another two-variable graph with a negative slope. In each graph, show what happens to the value of one variable when there is a change in the value of the other variable.

3. A straight line in a two-variable graph can be expressed in an equation. Make sure you know how to interpret each part of the linear equation.

■ IMPORTANT TERMS

vertical axis	independent variable
horizontal axis	slope of a straight line
direct (positive) relationship	vertical intercept
inverse (negative) relationship	nonlinear curve
	tangent
dependent variable	

SELF-TEST

■ FILL-IN QUESTIONS

1. The relationship between two economic variables can be visualized with the aid of a two-dimensional (graph, matrix) _____, which has (a horizontal, an inverse) _____ axis and a (vertical, direct) _____ axis.

2. Customarily, the (dependent, independent) _____ variable is placed on the horizontal axis and the _____ is placed on the vertical axis. The _____ variable is said to change because of a change in the _____ variables.

3. The vertical and horizontal (scales, ranges) _____ of the graph are calibrated to reflect the _____ of values in the table of data points on which the graph is based.

4. The graph of a straight line that slopes downward to the right indicates that there is (a direct, an inverse) _____ relationship between the two variables. A graph of a straight line that slopes upward to the right tells us that the relationship is (direct, inverse) _____. When the value of one variable increases and the value of the other variable increases, then the relationship is _____; when the value of one increases, while the other decreases, the relationship is _____.

5. When interpreting an economic graph, the "cause" or the "source" is the (dependent, independent) _____ variable and the "effect" or "outcome" is the _____ variable.

6. Other variables, beyond the two in a two-dimensional graph, that might affect the economic relationship are assumed to be (changing, held constant) _____. This assumption is also referred to as the "other-things-equal" assumption or as (*post hoc, ceteris paribus*) _____.

7. The slope of a straight line between two points is defined as the ratio of the (vertical, horizontal) _____ change to the _____ change.

8. When two variables move in the same direction, the slope will be (negative, positive) _____; when the variables move in opposite directions, the slope will be _____.

9. The slope of a line will be affected by the (units of measurement, vertical intercept) _____.

10. The concept of a slope is important to economists because it reflects the (marginal, total) _____ change in one variable on another variable.

11. A graph of a line with an infinite slope is (horizontal, vertical) _____, while a graph of a line with a zero slope is _____.

12. The point at which the slope of the line meets the vertical axis is called the vertical (tangent, intercept) _____.

13. We can express the graph of a straight line with a linear equation that can be written as $y = a + bx$.

    a. a is the (slope, intercept) _____ and b is the _____.

    b. y is the (dependent, independent) _____ variable and x is the _____ variable.

    c. If a were 2, b were 4, and x were 5, then y would be _____. If the value of x changed to 7, then y would be _____. If the value of x changed to 3, then y would be _____.

14. The slope of a (straight line, nonlinear curve) _____ is constant throughout; the slope of a _____ varies from point to point.

15. An estimate of the slope of a nonlinear curve at a certain point can be made by calculating the slope of a straight line that is (tangent, perpendicular) _____ to the point on the curve.

■ **TRUE–FALSE QUESTIONS**

Circle T if the statement is true, F if it is false.

1. Economists design graphs to confuse people. **T F**

2. If the straight line on a two-variable graph slopes downward to the right, then there is a positive relationship between the two variables. **T F**

3. A variable that changes as a consequence of a change in another variable is considered a dependent variable. **T F**

4. Economists always put the independent variable on the horizontal axis and the dependent variable on the vertical axis of a two-variable graph. **T F**

5. *Ceteris paribus* means that other variables are changing at the same time. **T F**

6. In the ratio for the calculation of the slope of a straight line, the vertical change is in the numerator and the horizontal change is in the denominator. **T F**

7. If the slope of the linear relationship between consumption and income was .90, then it tells us that for every $1 increase in income there will be a $.90 increase in consumption. **T F**

8. The slope of a straight line in a two-variable graph will *not* be affected by the choice of the units for either variable. **T F**

9. The slopes of lines measure marginal changes. **T F**

10. Assume in a graph that price is on the vertical axis and quantity is on the horizontal axis. The absence of a relationship between price and quantity would be a straight line parallel to the horizontal axis. **T F**

11. A line with an infinite slope in a two-variable graph is parallel to the horizontal axis. **T F**

12. In a two-variable graph, income is graphed on the vertical axis and the quantity of snow is graphed on the horizontal axis. If income was independent of the quantity of snow, then this independence would be represented by a line parallel to the horizontal axis. **T F**

13. If a linear equation is $y = 10 + 5x$, the vertical intercept is 5. **T F**

14. When a line is tangent to a nonlinear curve, then it intersects the curve at a particular point. **T F**

15. If the slope of a straight line on a two-variable (x, y) graph were .5 and the vertical intercept were 5, then a value of 10 for x would mean that y is also 10. **T F**

16. A slope of -4 for a straight line in a two-variable graph indicates that there is an inverse relationship between the two variables. **T F**

17. If x is an independent variable and y is a dependent variable, then a change in y results in a change in x. **T F**

18. An upward slope for a straight line that is tangent to a nonlinear curve indicates that the slope of the nonlinear curve at that point is positive. **T F**

19. If one pair of x, y points was (13, 10) and the other pair was (8, 20), then the slope of the straight line between the two sets of points in the two-variable graph, with x on the horizontal axis and y on the vertical axis, would be 2. **T F**

20. When the value of **x** is 2, a value of 10 for **y** would be calculated from a linear equation of **y** = −2 + 6**x**.

T F

■ **MULTIPLE-CHOICE QUESTIONS**

Circle the letter that corresponds to the best answer.

1. If an increase in one variable is associated with a decrease in another variable, then we can conclude that the variables are
(a) nonlinear
(b) directly related
(c) inversely related
(d) positively related

2. The ratio of the absolute vertical change to the absolute horizontal change between two points of a straight line is the
(a) slope
(b) vertical intercept
(c) horizontal intercept
(d) point of tangency

3. There are two sets of **x, y** points on a straight line in a two-variable graph, with **y** on the vertical axis and **x** on the horizontal axis. If one set of points was (0, 5) and the other set (5, 20), the linear equation for the line would be
(a) **y** = 5**x**
(b) **y** = 5 + 3**x**
(c) **y** = 5 + 15**x**
(d) **y** = 5 + .33**x**

4. In a two-variable graph of data on the price and quantity of a product, economists place
(a) price on the horizontal axis because it is the independent variable and quantity on the vertical axis because it is the dependent variable
(b) price on the vertical axis because it is the dependent variable and quantity on the horizontal axis because it is the independent variable
(c) price on the vertical axis even though it is the independent variable and quantity on the horizontal axis even though it is the dependent variable
(d) price on the horizontal axis even though it is the dependent variable and quantity on the vertical axis even though it is the independent variable

5. In a two-dimensional graph of the relationship between two economic variables, an assumption is usually made that
(a) both variables are linear
(b) both variables are nonlinear
(c) other variables are held constant
(d) other variables are permitted to change

6. If the slope of a straight line is zero, then the straight line is
(a) vertical
(b) horizontal
(c) upward sloping
(d) downward sloping

Questions 7, 8, 9, and 10 are based on the following four data sets. In each set, the independent variable is in the left column and the dependent variable is in the right column.

(1)		(2)		(3)		(4)	
A	**B**	**C**	**D**	**E**	**F**	**G**	**H**
0	1	0	12	4	5	0	4
3	2	5	8	6	10	1	3
6	3	10	4	8	15	2	2
9	4	15	0	10	20	3	1

7. There is an inverse relationship between the independent and dependent variable in data sets
(a) 1 and 4
(b) 2 and 3
(c) 1 and 3
(d) 2 and 4

8. The vertical intercept is 4 in data set
(a) 1
(b) 2
(c) 3
(d) 4

9. The linear equation for data set 1 is
(a) **B** = 3**A**
(b) **B** = 1 + 3**A**
(c) **B** = 1 + .33**A**
(d) **A** = 1 + .33**B**

10. The linear equation for data set 2 is
(a) **C** = 12 − 1.25**D**
(b) **D** = 12 + 1.25**C**
(c) **D** = 12 − .80**C**
(d) **C** = 12 − .80**D**

Answer Questions 11, 12, 13, and 14 on the basis of the following diagram.

11. The variables **A** and **B** are:
(a) positively related
(b) negatively related
(c) indirectly related
(d) nonlinear

12. The slope of the line is
   (a) .33
   (b) .67
   (c) 1.50
   (d) 3.00

13. The vertical intercept is
   (a) 80
   (b) 60
   (c) 40
   (d) 20

14. The linear equation for the slope of the line is
   (a) $A = 20 + .33B$
   (b) $B = 20 + .33A$
   (c) $A = 20 + .67B$
   (d) $B = 20 + .67A$

Answer Questions 15, 16, and 17 on the basis of the following diagram.

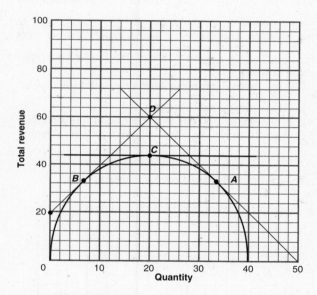

15. The slope of the line tangent to the curve at point **A** is
   (a) 2
   (b) −2
   (c) −1.5
   (d) −0.5

16. The slope of the line tangent to the curve at point **B** is
   (a) −2
   (b) 2
   (c) 3
   (d) 0.5

17. The slope of the line tangent to the curve at point **C** is
   (a) −1
   (b) 1
   (c) 0
   (d) undefined

18. Assume that the relationship between concert ticket prices and attendance is expressed in the equation $P =$ $25 - 1.25Q$, where **P** equals ticket price and **Q** equals concert attendance in thousands of people. On the basis of this equation, it can be said that
   (a) more people will attend the concert when the price is high compared to when the price is low
   (b) if 12,000 people attended the concert, then the ticket price was $10
   (c) if 18,000 people attended the concert, then entry into the concert was free
   (d) an increase in ticket price by $5 reduces concert attendance by 1000 people

19. If you know that the equation relating consumption (**C**) to income (**Y**) is $C = \$7,500 + .2Y$, then
   (a) consumption is inversely related to income
   (b) consumption is the independent variable and income is the dependent variable
   (c) if income is $15,000, then consumption is $10,500
   (d) if consumption is $30,000, then income is $10,000

20. If the dependent variable changes by 22 units when the independent variable changes by 12 units, then the slope of the line is
   (a) 0.56
   (b) 1.83
   (c) 2.00
   (d) 3.27

■ **PROBLEMS**

1. Following are three tables for making graphs. On the graphs, plot the economic relationships contained in each table. Be sure to label each axis of the graph and indicate the unit measurement and scale used on each axis.
   a. Use the table at the top of the next page to graph national income on the horizontal axis and consumption expenditures on the vertical axis below; connect the seven points and label the curve "Consumption." The relationship between income and consumption

is (a direct, an inverse) _____ one and the consumption curve is (an up-, a down-)

_____ sloping curve.

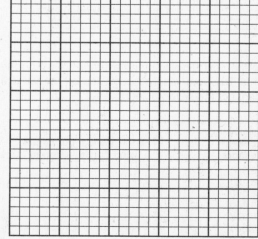

National income, billions of dollars	Consumption expenditures, billions of dollars
$ 600	$ 600
700	640
800	780
900	870
1000	960
1100	1050
1200	1140

b. Use the next table to graph investment expenditures on the horizontal axis and the rate of interest on the vertical axis; connect the seven points and label the curve "Investment." The relationship between the rate of interest and investment expenditures is (a direct, an inverse) _____ one and the investment curve is (an up-, a down-) _____ sloping curve.

Rate of interest, %	Investment expenditures, billions of dollars
8	$220
7	280
6	330
5	370
4	400
3	420
2	430

0

c. Use the next table to graph average salary on the horizontal axis and wine consumption on the vertical axis; connect the seven points.

Average salary, U.S. college professors	Annual per capita wine consumption in liters
$62,000	11.5
63,000	11.6
64,000	11.7
65,000	11.8
66,000	11.9
67,000	22.0
68,000	22.1

0

(1) The average salary of a college professor and wine consumption (are, are not) _____ *correlated*. The higher average salary (is, is not) _____ the *cause* of the greater consumption of wine.

(2) The relationship between the two variables may be purely (coincidental, planned) _____; or, both the higher salaries and the greater consumption of wine may be the result of the higher (taxes, incomes) _____.

2. This question is based on the following graph.

a. Construct a table for points **A–I** from the data shown in the graph.

b. According to economists, price is the (independent, dependent) _____ variable and quantity is the _____ variable.

c. Write a linear equation that summarizes the data.

3. The following three sets of data each show the relationship between an independent variable and a dependent variable. For each set, the independent variable is in the left column and the dependent variable is in the right column.

(1)		(2)		(3)	
A	**B**	**C**	**D**	**E**	**F**
00	10	0	100	0	20
10	30	10	75	50	40
20	50	20	50	100	60
30	70	30	25	150	80
40	90	40	0	200	100

a. Write an equation that summarizes the data for each of the sets (1), (2), and (3).

b. State whether each data set shows a positive or an inverse relationship between the two variables.

c. Plot data sets 1 and 2 on the following graph. Use the same horizontal scale for both sets of independent variables and the same vertical scale for both sets of dependent variables.

0

4. This problem is based on the following graph.

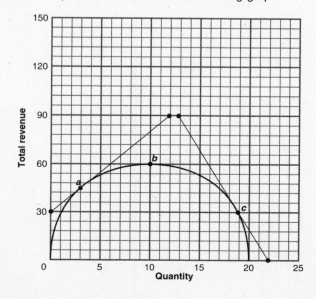

a. The slope of the straight line through point *a* is?

b. The slope of the straight line through point *b* is?

c. The slope of the straight line through point *c* is?

■ **SHORT ANSWER AND ESSAY QUESTIONS**

1. Why do economists use graphs in their work?

2. Give two examples of a graph that illustrates the relationship between two economic variables.

3. What does the slope tell you about a straight line? How would you interpret a slope of 4? A slope of −2? A slope of .5? A slope of −.25?

4. If the vertical intercept increases in value but the slope of a straight line stays the same, what happens to the graph of the line? If the vertical intercept decreases in value, what will happen to the line?

5. How do you interpret a vertical line on a two-variable graph? How do you interpret a horizontal line?

6. When you know that the price and quantity of a product are inversely related, what does this tell you about the slope of a line? What do you know about the slope when the two variables are positively related?

7. Which variable is the dependent and which is the independent in the following economic statement: "A decrease in business taxes had a positive effect on investment spending."

8. How do you tell the difference between a dependent and independent variable when examining economic relationships?

9. Why is an assumption made that all other variables are held constant when we construct a two-variable graph of the price and quantity of a product?

10. How do mathematicians and economists differ at times in how they construct two-dimensional graphs? Give an example.

11. How is the slope of a straight line in a two-variable graph affected by the choice of the units for either variable? Explain and give an example.

12. What is the relationship between the slopes of lines and marginal analysis?

13. Describe a case in which a straight line in a two-variable graph would have an infinite slope and a case in which the slope of a line would be zero.

14. If you know that the equation relating consumption (*C*) to income (*Y*) is $C = 10,000 + 5Y$, then what would consumption be when income is $5000? Construct an income-consumption table for five different levels of income.

15. How do the slopes of a straight line and a nonlinear curve differ? How do you estimate the slope of a nonlinear curve?

ANSWERS

Appendix to Chapter 1 Graphs and Their Meaning

FILL-IN QUESTIONS

1. graph, a horizontal, vertical
2. independent, dependent, dependent, independent
3. scales, ranges
4. an inverse, direct, direct, inverse
5. independent, dependent
6. held constant, *ceteris paribus*
7. vertical, horizontal
8. positive, negative
9. units of measurement
10. marginal
11. vertical, horizontal
12. intercept
13. *a.* intercept, slope; *b.* dependent, independent; *c.* 22, 30, 14
14. straight line, nonlinear curve
15. tangent

TRUE–FALSE QUESTIONS

1. F, p. 15	6. T, p. 17	11. F, pp. 17–18	16. T, p. 17
2. F, p. 16	7. T, pp. 17–18	12. T, pp. 17–18	17. F, pp. 16–17
3. T, p. 16	8. F, p. 17	13. F, p. 18	18. T, pp. 18–19
4. F, p. 16	9. T, p. 17	14. F, p. 19	19. F, p. 17
5. F, p. 17	10. T, pp. 17–18	15. T, p. 18	20. T, p. 18

MULTIPLE-CHOICE QUESTIONS

1. c, p. 16	6. b, pp. 17–18	11. a, p. 16	16. b, pp. 18–19
2. a, p. 17	7. d, p. 16	12. b, p. 17	17. c, pp. 18–19
3. b, p. 18	8. d, p. 18	13. d, p. 18	18. b, p. 18
4. c, p. 16	9. c, p. 18	14. c, p. 18	19. c, p. 18
5. c, p. 17	10. c, p. 18	15. b, pp. 18–19	20. b, p. 17

PROBLEMS

1. *a.* direct, up-; *b.* inverse, down-; *c.* (1) are, is not; (2) coincidental, incomes (standard of living, or similar answer)
2. *a. table below*; *b.* independent, dependent; *c.* $P = 4.00 - .25Q$

Point	Price	Quantity
A	$4.00	0
B	3.50	2
C	3.00	4
D	2.50	6
E	2.00	8
F	1.50	10
G	1.00	12
H	.50	14
I	.00	16

3. *a.* (1) $B = 10 + 2A$; (2) $D = 100 - 2.5C$; (3) $F = 20 + .4E$; *b.* (1) positive; (2) inverse; (3) positive
4. *a.* 5; *b.* 0; *c.* -10

SHORT ANSWER AND ESSAY QUESTIONS

1. p. 15	5. pp. 17–18	9. p. 17	13. pp. 17–18
2. pp. 15–16	6. p. 16	10. p. 16	14. p. 18
3. pp. 17–18	7. p. 16	11. p. 17	15. pp. 18–19
4. pp. 17–18	8. p. 16	12. p. 17	

CHAPTER 2

The Economizing Problem

Chapter 2 explains that the central problem of economics is based on two fundamental facts. First, individuals and institutions have unlimited economic wants. The main purpose of economic activity is to satisfy these wants. Second, economic resources are limited or scarce. It is these resources—land, capital, labor, and entrepreneurial ability—that are used to produce the goods and services that ultimately satisfy these economic wants. The **economizing problem** for both individuals and institutions arises from this continual struggle to decide how best to use limited productive resources to satisfy insatiable economic wants.

Economics is called the science of efficiency. To understand what efficiency means, however, you must first define its two characteristics: **full employment** and **full production.** Full employment means that all productive resources available to the economy are being used. Full production requires that two types of efficiency—allocative and productive—are being achieved. **Allocative efficiency** means that resources are being devoted to the production of the goods and services society most highly values. **Productive efficiency** entails producing this optimal product mix in the least costly way.

The **production possibilities curve** is used in this chapter's tables and graphs to discuss the major concerns of economics. The production possibilities model is a valuable device for illustrating the meaning of many concepts defined in the chapter—scarcity, choice, tradeoffs, opportunity cost, allocative and productive efficiency, unemployment, economic growth, and international trade. It can also be applied to many real economic situations, as you will learn from the examples in the text. This basic economic model is the first and one of the most important ones presented in the text that you will be using to understand the economic world.

Every economy needs to develop an **economic system** to respond to the economizing problem of limited resources and unlimited wants. The two basic types of systems are the *market system* and the *command system.* In the market system there is extensive private ownership of resources and the use of markets and prices to coordinate and direct economic activity. In the command system, there is extensive public ownership of resources and the use of central planning for most economic decision making in the economy. Chapters 3 through 6 explain in greater detail how the U.S. economy uses the market system to respond to the economizing problem.

The **circular flow model** (or diagram) is a device that illustrates for a capitalistic economy the relationship between households and businesses, the flow of money and economic goods and services between households and businesses, their dual role as buyers and sellers, and the two basic types of markets essential to the capitalistic process.

■ **CHECKLIST**

When you have studied this chapter you should be able to

☐ Explain the economizing problem in terms of economic wants and resources.

☐ Identify four types of economic resources.

☐ Describe the resource payments made in return for each economic resource.

☐ Write a definition of economics that incorporates the relationship between resources and wants.

☐ Explain why full employment and full production are necessary for the efficient use of resources.

☐ Distinguish between allocative efficiency and productive efficiency.

☐ State the four assumptions made when a production possibilities table or curve is constructed.

☐ Construct a production possibilities curve when you are given the appropriate data.

☐ Define opportunity cost and utilize a production possibilities curve to explain the concept.

☐ Show how the law of increasing opportunity cost is reflected in the shape of the production possibilities curve.

☐ Explain the economic rationale for the law of increasing opportunity cost.

☐ Use marginal analysis to define allocative efficiency.

☐ Explain how allocative efficiency determines the optimal point on a production possibilities curve.

☐ Use a production possibilities curve to illustrate unemployment and productive inefficiency.

☐ Use the production possibilities curve to illustrate economic growth.

☐ Explain how international trade affects a nation's production possibilities curve.

☐ Give examples and applications of the production possibilities model.

☐ Compare and contrast the market system (capitalism) with the command system (socialism).

☐ Draw the circular flow model, correctly labeling the two markets and the real and money flows between the two sectors in this simplified economy.

■ **CHAPTER OUTLINE**

1. The study of economics rests on the bases of two facts:

   a. Society's material wants are unlimited.

   b. The economic resources that are the ultimate means of satisfying these wants are scarce in relation to the wants.

   (1) Economic resources are classified as land, capital, labor, and entrepreneurial ability. They are called *factors of production*.

   (2) The payments received by those who provide the economy with these four resources are in the form of rental income, interest income, wages, and profits, respectively.

   (3) Because these resources are scarce (or limited), the output that the economy is able to produce is also limited.

2. Economics, then, is the study of how society's scarce resources are used (administered) to obtain the greatest satisfaction of its economic wants. To be efficient in the use of its resources, an economy must achieve both full employment and full production.

   a. *Full employment* means that the economy is using all available resources.

   b. *Full production* means that all resources used for production should contribute to the maximum satisfaction of society's economic wants. Full production implies that there is

   (1) *productive efficiency*, in which the goods and services society desires are being produced in the least costly way.

   (2) *allocative efficiency*, in which resources are devoted to the production of goods and services society most highly values.

   c. The ***production possibilities table*** indicates the alternative combinations of goods and services an economy is capable of producing when it has achieved full employment and productive efficiency.

   (1) The four assumptions usually made when a production possibilities table is constructed are that full employment and productive efficiency, fixed resources, fixed technology, and two products are being considered.

   (2) The table illustrates the fundamental choice every economy must make: what quantity of each good it must sacrifice to obtain more of another good.

   d. The data in the production possibilities table can be plotted on a graph to obtain a production possibilities curve.

   e. The opportunity cost of producing an additional unit of one product is the amount of other products that are sacrificed. The ***law of increasing opportunity costs*** reflects that the opportunity cost of producing an additional unit of a product (the marginal opportunity cost) increases as more of that product is produced.

   (1) The law of increasing opportunity costs results in a production possibilities curve that is concave (from the origin).

   (2) The opportunity cost of producing an additional unit of a product increases as more of the product is pro-

duced because resources are not completely adaptable to alternative uses.

   f. Allocative efficiency means that resources are devoted to the optimal product mix for society. This optimal mix is determined by assessing marginal costs and benefits.

   (1) The marginal-cost curve for a product rises because of the law of increasing opportunity costs; the marginal-benefit curve falls because the consumption of a product yields less and less satisfaction.

   (2) There will be *underallocation* of resources to production of a product when the marginal benefit is greater than the marginal cost, and *overallocation* when the marginal cost is greater than the marginal benefit.

   (3) Allocative efficiency is achieved when the marginal cost of a product equals the marginal benefit of a product.

3. Different outcomes will occur when assumptions underlying the production possibilities model are relaxed.

   a. ***Unemployment.*** The economy may be operating at a point inside the production possibilities curve if the assumption of full employment and productive efficiency no longer holds. In this case, there will be an unemployment of resources and production will not occur in the least costly way.

   b. ***Economic Growth.*** The production possibilities curve can move outward if the assumption of fixed resources or the assumption of no technological change is dropped.

   (1) Economic growth can occur when there is an expansion in the quantity and quality of resources.

   (2) It can increase when there is technological advancement.

   (3) The combination of goods and services an economy chooses to produce today helps determine its production possibilities in the future.

   c. ***Trade.*** International specialization and trade allow a nation to obtain more goods and services than is indicated by its production possibilities curve. The effect on production possibilities is similar to an increase in economic growth.

4. There are many real-world examples and applications of the production possibilities model.

   a. Events leading to unemployment and productive inefficiency may cause nations to operate inside their production possibilities curves. Examples would be the Great Depression in the United States, recessions in different nations, and policies of racial, ethnic, or religious discrimination.

   b. It illustrates tradeoffs and opportunity costs. Controversies over the use of land (for wilderness or production) or decisions over how public funds should be spent (for more criminal justice or more education) are two applications.

   c. The curves can shift. The increase in the number of women in the workforce over the past four decades and their increased productivity have shifted the curve outward for the United States. Similarly, recent advances in technology have shifted the curve outward for the United States.

5. An *economic system* is a set of institutions and a coordinating mechanism to respond to the economizing problem.

　a. The *market system* (capitalism) has extensive private ownership of resources and uses markets and prices to coordinate and direct economic activity. In pure (*laissez-faire*) capitalism there is a limited government role in the economy. In a capitalist economy such as the United States, government plays a large role, but the two characteristics of the market system—private property and markets—dominate.

　b. The *command system* (also called *socialism* or *communism*) is based primarily on extensive public ownership of resources and the use of central planning for most economic decision making. There used to be many examples of command economies (e.g., Soviet Union), but today there are few (e.g., Cuba, North Korea). Most former socialistic nations have been or are being transformed into capitalistic and market-oriented economies.

6. The circular flow model is a device used to clarify the relationships between households and business firms in a market economy. In resource markets, households sell and firms buy resources, and in product markets, the firms sell and households buy products. Households use the incomes they obtain from selling resources to purchase the goods and services produced by the firms, and in the economy there is a real flow of resources and products and a money flow of incomes and expenditures.

■ HINTS AND TIPS

1. Chapter 2 presents many economic definitions and classifications. Spend time learning these definitions now because they will be used in later chapters, and you must know them if you are to understand what follows.

2. The production possibilities graph is a simple and extremely useful economic model. Practice your understanding of it by using it to explain the following economic concepts: scarcity, choice, opportunity cost, the law of increasing opportunity costs, full employment, full production, productive efficiency, allocative efficiency, unemployment, and economic growth.

3. Opportunity cost is always measured in terms of a forgone alternative. From a production possibilities table, you can easily calculate how many units of one product you forgo when you get another unit of a product.

4. In the section on the law of increasing opportunity costs, note the distinction made between two types. The *marginal* opportunity cost measures what is given up to obtain an additional unit. Note too that the size of one unit can vary (e.g., 2 to 3 or 200 to 300). The *total* opportunity cost measures what is given up to obtain a specific number of units (e.g., 3 or 300 units). Review Quick Quiz 2–1 in the text.

■ IMPORTANT TERMS

economizing problem

economic resources

land

capital

investment

labor

entrepreneurial ability

factors of production

full employment

full production

productive efficiency

allocative efficiency

consumer goods

capital goods

production possibilities
　table

production possibilities
　curve

opportunity cost

law of increasing
　opportunity costs

economic growth

economic system

market system

capitalism

command system

resource market

product market

circular flow model

SELF-TEST

■ FILL-IN QUESTIONS

1. The economizing problem arises because society's economic wants are (limited, unlimited) _____ and its economic resources are _____.

2. Consumers want to obtain goods and services that provide satisfaction, or what economists call (resources, utility) "_____." Some wants that meet this objective are considered (capital goods, necessities) _____, while others are considered (investment goods, luxuries) _____.

3. The four types of resources are

　a. _____

　b. _____

　c. _____

　d. _____

4. Both consumer goods and capital goods satisfy human economic wants. The consumer goods satisfy these wants (directly, indirectly) _____, and the capital goods satisfy them _____.

5. The income individuals receive from supplying land or natural resources is (interest, rental) _____ income, whereas the income received from supplying capital goods is _____ income. The income received by individuals who supply labor is (wage, profit) _____ income; the income received from entrepreneurial ability is _____ income.

6. Economics is the social science concerned with the problem of using (unlimited, scarce) _____ resources to attain the maximum fulfillment of society's _____ economic wants.

7. Economic efficiency requires full (employment, allocation) _____ so that all available resources can be used and that there be full (production, distribution) _____ so that the employed resources contribute to the maximum satisfaction of material wants.

8. Full production implies that two types of efficiency are achieved: Resources are devoted to the production of the mix of goods and services society most wants, or there is (allocative, productive) _____ efficiency, and the goods and services will be produced in the least costly way, or there will be _____ efficiency.

9. When a production possibilities table or curve is constructed, four assumptions are made:

    a. _____

    b. _____

    c. _____

    d. _____

10. In a two-product world, the quantity of the other good or service an economy must give up to produce more housing is the opportunity (benefit, cost) _____ of producing the additional housing.

11. The law of increasing opportunity costs explains why the production possibilities curve is (convex, concave) _____ from the origin. The economic rationale for the law is that economic resources (are, are not) _____ completely adaptable to alternative uses.

12. Allocative efficiency is determined by assessing the marginal costs and benefits of the output from the allocation of resources to production.

    a. The marginal cost curve for a product rises because of increasing (satisfaction, opportunity costs) _____, and the marginal benefit curve falls because of less _____ from the additional consumption of a product.

    b. When the marginal benefit is greater than the marginal cost, there will be (over, under) _____-allocation of resources to the production of a product, but when the marginal cost is greater than the marginal benefit, there will be an _____-allocation.

    c. Optimal allocation of resources occurs when the marginal costs of the product output are (greater than, less than, equal to) _____ the marginal benefits.

13. Following is a production possibilities curve for capital goods and consumer goods.

    a. If the economy moves from point **A** to point **B**, it will produce (more, fewer) _____ capital goods and (more, fewer) _____ consumer goods.

    b. If the economy is producing at point **X**, some resources in the economy are either (not available, unemployed) _____ or (underemployed, overemployed) _____.

    c. If the economy moves from point **X** to point **B** (more, fewer) _____ capital goods and (more, fewer) _____ consumer goods will be produced.

    d. If the economy is to produce at point **Y**, there must be (unemployment, economic growth) _____. This can occur because of a resource supply (decrease, increase) _____ or a technological (decline, improvement) _____.

14. Technological advances can shift a nation's production possibilities curve (inward, outward) _____ because the effects lead to (economic growth, unemployment) _____.

15. The more an economy consumes its current production, the (more, less) _____ it will be capable of producing in future years if other things are equal.

16. International specialization and trade enable a nation to obtain (more, less) _____ of a desired good at _____ sacrifice of some other good. The output gains from greater international specialization and trade are the equivalent to economic (growth, decline) _____.

17. The institutional arrangements and coordinating mechanisms used to respond to the economic problem are called (*laissez-faire* capitalism, an economic system) _____.

18. In capitalism, property resources are primarily (publicly, privately) _____ owned. The means used to direct and coordinate economic activity (is central planning, are markets and prices) _____.

19. In a command economy, property resources are primarily (publicly, privately) _____ owned. The coordinating device(s) in this economic system (is central planning, are markets and prices) _____.

20. In the circular flow model,
   a. Households are buyers and businesses are sellers in (product, resource) _____ markets, and businesses are buyers and households are sellers in _____ markets.

   b. The flow of economic resources and finished goods and services is the (money, real) _____ flow, and the flow of income and expenditures is the _____ flow.

■ **TRUE–FALSE QUESTIONS**

Circle T if the statement is true, F if it is false.

1. The conflict between the scarce economic wants of society and its unlimited economic resources gives rise to the economizing problem.　　　　**T　F**

2. The wants with which economics is concerned include only those wants that can be satisfied by goods and services.　　　　**T　F**

3. Money is a resource and is classified as "capital."　　　　**T　F**

4. From the economist's perspective, investment refers to the production and purchase of capital goods.　**T　F**

5. The payment to entrepreneurial ability is interest income.　　　　**T　F**

6. Resources are scarce because society's material wants are unlimited and productive resources are limited.　　　　**T　F**

7. Economic efficiency requires that there be both full employment of resources and full production.　　**T　F**

8. Allocative efficiency means that goods and services are being produced by society in the least costly way.　　　　**T　F**

9. Only allocative efficiency is necessary for there to be full production.　　　　**T　F**

10. Given full employment and full production, it is not possible for an economy capable of producing just two goods to increase its production of both at any one point in time.　　　　**T　F**

11. The opportunity cost of producing antipollution devices is the other goods and services the economy is unable to produce because it has decided to produce these devices.　　　　**T　F**

12. The opportunity cost of producing a good tends to increase as more of it is produced because resources less suitable to its production must be employed.　**T　F**

13. Drawing a production possibilities curve concave to the origin is the geometric way of stating the law of increasing opportunity costs.　　　　**T　F**

14. Economic rationale for the law of increasing opportunity cost is that economic resources are fully adaptable to alternative uses.　　　　**T　F**

15. Allocative efficiency is determined by assessing the marginal costs and benefits of the output from the allocation of resources to production.　　　　**T　F**

16. The marginal-cost curve for a product rises because of increasing satisfaction from the consumption of the product.　　　　**T　F**

17. Economic growth means an increase in the production of goods and services, and is shown by a movement of the production possibilities curve outward and to the right.　　　　**T　F**

18. The more capital goods an economy produces today, the greater will be the total output of all goods it can produce in the future, other things being equal.　**T　F**

19. International specialization and trade permit an economy to overcome the limits imposed by domestic production possibilities and have the same effect on the economy as having more and better resources.　**T　F**

20. The elimination of widespread discrimination based on race, ethnicity, or religion in an economy would move it from a point inside its production possibilities curve toward a point on its curve.　　　　**T　F**

21. Pure capitalism is also called *laissez-faire* capitalism.　　　　**T　F**

22. A command economy is characterized by the private ownership of resources and the use of markets and prices to coordinate and direct economic activity.　　**T　F**

23. Russia and most nations in Eastern Europe have been transforming their economies from a command to market system since the demise of the former Soviet Union.　　　　**T　F**

24. In the circular flow model, households function on the buying side of the resource and product markets.　　　　**T　F**

25. In the circular flow model, there is a *real flow* of economic resources and finished goods and services and a *money flow* of income and consumption expenditures.　　　　**T　F**

■ **MULTIPLE-CHOICE QUESTIONS**

Circle the letter that corresponds to the best answer.

1. Which is the correct match of an economic resource and payment for that resource?
   (a) land and wages

(b) labor and interest income
(c) capital and rental income
(d) entrepreneurial ability and profit

2. An "innovator" is defined as an entrepreneur who
(a) makes basic policy decisions in a business firm
(b) combines factors of production to produce a good or service
(c) invents a new product or process for producing a product
(d) introduces new products on the market or employs a new method to produce a product

3. An economy is efficient when it has achieved
(a) full employment
(b) full production
(c) either full employment or full production
(d) both full employment and full production

4. Allocative and productive efficiency are conditions that best characterize
(a) full employment
(b) full production
(c) traditional economies
(d) command economies

5. When a production possibilities schedule is written (or a production possibilities curve is drawn) in this chapter, four assumptions are made. Which is one of those assumptions?
(a) More than two products are produced.
(b) The state of technology changes.
(c) The economy has both full employment and full production.
(d) The quantities of all resources available to the economy are variable, not fixed.

Answer Questions 6, 7, 8, and 9 based on the following graph for an economy.

6. At point **A** on the production possibilities curve in the above illustration,
(a) wheat production is inefficient
(b) tractor production is inefficient
(c) the economy is employing all its resources
(d) the economy is not employing all its resources

7. Unemployment and productive inefficiency would best be represented in the graph by point
(a) **A**
(b) **B**
(c) **C**
(d) **D**

8. The choice of point **B** over point **A** as the optimal product mix for society would be based on
(a) productive efficiency
(b) full employment of resources
(c) the law of increasing opportunity costs
(d) a comparison of marginal costs and benefits

9. Economic growth could be represented by
(a) a movement from point **A** to point **B**
(b) a movement from point **B** to point **A**
(c) a shift in the production possibilities curve out to point **C**
(d) a shift in the production possibilities curve out to point **D**

10. The production possibilities curve is
(a) concave
(b) convex
(c) linear
(d) positive

11. What is the economic rationale for the law of increasing opportunity cost?
(a) Full production and full employment of resources have not been achieved.
(b) Economic resources are not completely adaptable to alternative uses.
(c) Economic growth is being limited by the pace of technological advancement.
(d) An economy's present choice of output is determined by fixed technology and fixed resources.

12. If there is an increase in the resources available within the economy,
(a) more goods and services will be produced in the economy
(b) the economy will be capable of producing more goods and services
(c) the standard of living in the economy will rise
(d) the technological efficiency of the economy will improve

13. If the production possibilities curve *on the next page* moves from position **A** to position **B,** then
(a) the economy has increased the efficiency with which it produces wheat
(b) the economy has increased the efficiency with which it produces tractors
(c) the economy has put previously idle resources to work
(d) the economy has gone from full employment to less than full employment

14. Which would be the best example of allocative efficiency? When society devoted resources to the production of
- **(a)** slide rules instead of handheld calculators
- **(b)** horse-drawn carriages instead of automobiles
- **(c)** computers with word processors instead of typewriters
- **(d)** long-playing records instead of compact discs

15. Which situation would most likely shift the production possibilities curve for a nation in an outward direction?
- **(a)** deterioration in product quality
- **(b)** reductions in the supply of resources
- **(c)** increases in technological advances
- **(d)** rising levels of discrimination

16. The opportunity cost of a new public stadium is the
- **(a)** money cost of hiring guards and staff for the new stadium
- **(b)** cost of constructing the new stadium in a future year
- **(c)** change in the real estate tax rate to pay off the new stadium
- **(d)** other goods and services that must be sacrificed to construct the new stadium

17. Which situation would most likely cause a nation's production possibilities curve to shift inward?
- **(a)** investing more resources in new plants and equipment
- **(b)** eliminating discrimination based on race and ethnic background
- **(c)** increasing international trade or incurring a trade deficit
- **(d)** going to war with another nation and suffering a major defeat

18. The combination of products in society's production possibilities table that is the most valued or optimal is determined
- **(a)** at the midpoint of the production possibilities table
- **(b)** at the endpoint of the production possibilities table
- **(c)** where the marginal benefits equal marginal costs
- **(d)** where the opportunity costs are maximized

19. The underallocation of resources by society to the production of a product means that the
- **(a)** marginal benefit is greater than the marginal cost
- **(b)** marginal benefit is less than the marginal cost
- **(c)** opportunity cost of production is rising
- **(d)** consumption of the product is falling

Answer Questions 20, 21, and 22 on the basis of the data given in the following production possibilities table.

| | Production possibilities (alternatives) | | | | | |
	A	B	C	D	E	F
Capital goods	100	95	85	70	50	0
Consumer goods	0	100	180	240	280	300

20. The choice of alternative **B** compared with alternative **D** would tend to promote
- **(a)** a slower rate of economic growth
- **(b)** a faster rate of economic growth
- **(c)** increased consumption in the present
- **(d)** central economic planning

21. If the economy is producing at production alternative **D,** the opportunity cost of 40 more units of consumer goods is about
- **(a)** 5 units of capital goods
- **(b)** 10 units of capital goods
- **(c)** 15 units of capital goods
- **(d)** 20 units of capital goods

22. In the table, the law of increasing opportunity costs is suggested by the fact that
- **(a)** greater and greater quantities of consumer goods must be given up to get more capital goods
- **(b)** smaller and smaller quantities of consumer goods must be given up to get more capital goods
- **(c)** capital goods are relatively more scarce than consumer goods
- **(d)** the production possibilities curve will eventually shift outward as the economy expands

23. The private ownership of property resources and use of markets and prices to direct and coordinate economic activity is characteristic of
- **(a)** capitalism
- **(b)** communism
- **(c)** socialism
- **(d)** a command economy

24. The two kinds of markets found in the circular flow model are
- **(a)** real and money markets
- **(b)** real and socialist markets
- **(c)** money and command markets
- **(d)** product and resource markets

25. In the circular flow model, businesses
- **(a)** buy products and resources
- **(b)** sell products and resources
- **(c)** buy products and sell resources
- **(d)** sell products and buy resources

■ **PROBLEMS**

1. Following is a list of resources. Indicate in the space to the right of each whether the resource is land (**LD**), capital (**C**), labor (**LR**), entrepreneurial ability (**EA**), or some combination of these resources.

    a. Fishing grounds in the North Atlantic   _____

    b. A computer in a retail store   _____

    c. Uranium deposits in Canada   _____

    d. An irrigation ditch in Nebraska   _____

    e. Bill Gates in his work in starting Microsoft   _____

    f. The oxygen breathed by human beings   _____

    g. An IBM plant in Rochester, Minnesota   _____

    h. The food on the shelf of a grocery store   _____

    i. A machine in an auto plant   _____

    j. A person who creates new computer software and uses it to start a successful business   _____

    k. A carpenter building a house   _____

2. Following is a production possibilities table for two products, corn and cars. The table is constructed using the usual assumptions. Corn is measured in units of 100,000 bushels and cars in units of 100,000.

Combination	Corn	Cars
A	0	7
B	7	6
C	13	5
D	18	4
E	22	3
F	25	2
G	27	1
H	28	0

    a. Follow the general rules for making graphs (see the appendix to Chapter 1); plot the data from the table on the graph in the next column to obtain a production possibilities curve. Place corn on the vertical axis and cars on the horizontal axis.

    b. Fill in the following table showing the opportunity cost per unit of producing the 1st through the 7th car unit in terms of corn units.

Cars	Cost of production
1st	_____
2nd	_____
3rd	_____
4th	_____
5th	_____
6th	_____
7th	_____

    c. What is the *marginal* opportunity cost of the 3rd car unit in terms of units of corn? _____

    d. What is the *total* opportunity cost of producing 6 car units in terms of units of corn? _____

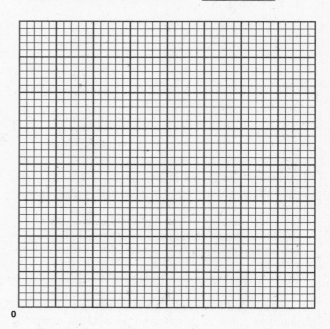

0

3. The following graph is a production possibilities curve. Draw on this graph

    a. a production possibilities curve that indicates greater efficiency in the production of good **A**

    b. a production possibilities curve that indicates greater efficiency in the production of good **B**

    c. a production possibilities curve that indicates an increase in the resources available to the economy

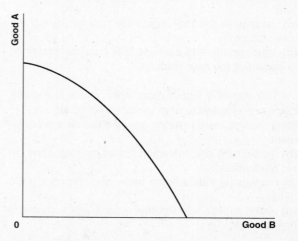

4. Following is a list of 12 economic goods. Indicate in the space to the right of each good whether it is a consumer good (**CON**), a capital good (**CAP**), or that it depends (**DEP**) on who is using it and for what purpose.

    a. An automobile   _____

    b. A tractor   _____

c. A taxicab _____

d. A house _____

e. A factory building _____

f. An office building _____

g. An ironing board _____

h. A refrigerator _____

i. A telephone _____

j. A quart of a soft drink _____

k. A cash register _____

l. A screwdriver _____

5. In the circular flow diagram below, the upper pair of flows (**a** and **b**) represents the resource market and the lower pair (**c** and **d**) the product market.

Supply labels or explanations for each of the four flows:

a. _____

b. _____

c. _____

d. _____

■ SHORT ANSWER AND ESSAY QUESTIONS

1. Explain what the term "economizing problem" means. Why are resources scarce?

2. In what sense are economic wants satiable or insatiable?

3. What are the four economic resources? How is each resource defined?

4. What is the income each economic resource earns?

5. When is a society economically efficient? What does "full production" mean, and how does it differ from "full employment"?

6. Explain why full production implies both allocative efficiency and productive efficiency.

7. What four assumptions are made in drawing a production possibilities curve or schedule?

8. What is opportunity cost? Give an example.

9. What is the law of increasing opportunity cost? Why do costs increase?

10. What determines the optimal product mix for society's production possibilities?

11. How can unemployment be illustrated with the production possibilities curve?

12. What will be the effect of increasing resource supplies on production possibilities?

13. Describe how technological advances will affect the production possibilities curve.

14. Explain the tradeoff between goods for the present and goods for the future and the effect of this tradeoff on economic growth.

15. What qualification does international specialization and trade make for the interpretation of production possibilities?

16. Give examples of how tradeoffs and opportunity costs can be illustrated by the production possibilities curve.

17. Give examples of shifts in the production possibilities curve.

18. The market system and the command system differ in two important ways. Compare and contrast the two economic systems.

19. In the circular flow model, what are the two markets? What roles do households play and what roles do businesses play in each market?

20. In the circular flow model, what are the income flows? What are the expenditure flows?

ANSWERS

Chapter 2 The Economizing Problem

FILL-IN QUESTIONS

1. unlimited, limited
2. utility, necessities, luxuries
3 *a.* land or natural resources, *b.* capital, *c.* labor, *d.* entrepreneurial ability
4. directly, indirectly
5. rental, interest, wage, profit
6. scarce, unlimited
7. employment, production
8. allocative, productive
9. *a.* there is full employment and productive efficiency; *b.* the available supplies of the factors of production are fixed; *c.* technology does not change during the course of the analysis; *d.* the economy produces only two products (any order for *a–d*)
10. cost
11. concave, are not
12. *a.* opportunity costs, satisfaction; *b.* under, over; *c.* equal to
13. *a.* fewer, more; *b.* unemployed, underemployed; *c.* more, more; *d.* economic growth, increase, improvement
14. outward, economic growth
15. less
16. more, less, growth
17. an economic system
18. privately, are markets and prices
19. publicly, is central planning
20. *a.* product, resource; *b.* real, money

TRUE–FALSE QUESTIONS

1. F, pp. 22–23 **8.** F, p. 24   **15.** T, pp. 27–28 **22.** F, pp. 33–34
2. T, pp. 22–23 **9.** F, p. 24   **16.** F, pp. 27–28 **23.** T, pp. 33–34
3. F, p. 23   **10.** T, pp. 25–27 **17.** T, pp. 29–30 **24.** F, pp. 34–35
4. T, p. 23   **11.** T, p. 27   **18.** T, pp. 30–31 **25.** T, pp. 34–35
5. F, pp. 23–24 **12.** T, p. 27   **19.** T, p. 31
6. T, p. 24   **13.** T, p. 27   **20.** T, p. 32
7. T, p. 24   **14.** F, p. 27   **21.** T, p. 33

MULTIPLE-CHOICE QUESTIONS

1. d, pp. 23–24 **8.** d, pp. 27–28 **15.** c, pp. 29–30 **22.** a, p. 27
2. d, pp. 23–24 **9.** d, pp. 29–30 **16.** d, p. 27   **23.** a, p. 33
3. d, p. 24   **10.** a, p. 27   **17.** d, pp. 32–33 **24.** d, pp. 34–35
4. b, p. 24   **11.** b, p. 27   **18.** c, pp. 27–28 **25.** d, pp. 34–35
5. c, p. 25   **12.** b, p. 29   **19.** a, pp. 27–28
6. c, pp. 26–27 **13.** b, pp. 29–31 **20.** b, pp. 30–31
7. c, p. 29   **14.** c, pp. 27–28 **21.** d, p. 27

PROBLEMS

1. *a.* LD; *b.* C; *c.* LD; *d.* C; *e.* EA; *f.* LD; *g.* C; *h.* C; *i.* C; *j.* EA; *k.* LR
2. *b.* 1, 2, 3, 4, 5, 6, 7 units of corn; *c.* 3; *d.* 21
3. *a.* curve will shift outward along good A axis but stay at the same point on good B axis; *b.* curve will shift outward along good B axis but stay at the same point on good A axis; *c.* entire curve will shift outward
4. *a.* DEP; *b.* CAP; *c.* CAP; *d.* DEP; *e.* CAP; *f.* CAP; *g.* DEP; *h.* DEP; *i.* DEP; *j.* DEP; *k.* CAP; *l.* DEP
5. *a.* money income payments (wages, rent, interest, and profit); *b.* services or resources (land, labor, capital, and entrepreneurial ability); *c.* goods and services; *d.* expenditures for goods and services

SHORT ANSWER AND ESSAY QUESTIONS

1. pp. 22–24 **6.** p. 24   **11.** p. 29   **16.** p. 32
2. pp. 22–23 **7.** p. 25   **12.** p. 29   **17.** pp. 32–33
3. p. 23   **8.** p. 27   **13.** pp. 29–30 **18.** pp. 33–34
4. p. 24   **9.** p. 27   **14.** pp. 30–31 **19.** pp. 34–35
5. p. 24   **10.** pp. 27–28 **15.** p. 31   **20.** pp. 34–35

CHAPTER 3

Individual Markets: Demand and Supply

Chapter 3 introduces you to the most fundamental tools of economic analysis: demand and supply. To progress successfully into the later chapters, it is essential that you understand what is meant by demand and supply and how to use these powerful tools.

Demand and supply are simply "boxes" or categories into which all the forces and factors that affect the price and the quantity of a good bought and sold in a competitive market are placed. Demand and supply determine price and quantity exchange, and it is necessary to see *why* and *how* they do this.

Many students never learn to *define* demand and supply. They never learn (1) what an increase or decrease in demand or supply means, (2) the important distinctions between "demand" and "quantity demanded" and between "supply" and "quantity supplied," and (3) the equally important distinctions between a change in demand and a change in quantity demanded, and between a change in supply and a change in quantity supplied.

Having learned these, however, it is no great trick to comprehend the so-called laws of demand and supply. The equilibrium price—that is, the price that will tend to prevail in the market as long as demand and supply do not change—is simply the price at which **quantity demanded** and **quantity supplied** are equal. The quantity bought and sold in the market (the equilibrium quantity) is the quantity demanded and supplied at the equilibrium price. If you can determine the equilibrium price and quantity under one set of demand and supply conditions, you can determine them under any other set.

This chapter includes a brief examination of the factors that determine demand and supply and the ways in which changes in these determinants will affect and cause changes in demand and supply. A graphic method is used in this analysis to illustrate demand and supply, equilibrium price and quantity, changes in demand and supply, and the resulting changes in equilibrium price and quantity. The **demand curve** and the **supply curve** are graphic (or geometric) representations of the same data contained in the schedules of demand and supply.

The application section at the end of the chapter explains government-set prices. When the government sets a legal price in a competitive market, it creates a **price ceiling** or **price floor**. This prevents supply and demand from determining the equilibrium price and quantity of a product that will be provided by a competitive market. As you will learn, the economic consequence of a price ceiling is that it will result in a persistent shortage of the product. An example of a price ceiling would be price controls on apartment rents. A price floor will result in a persistent surplus of a product, and the example given for it is price supports for an agricultural product.

You will use supply and demand over and over. It will turn out to be as important to you in economics as jet propulsion is to the pilot of an airplane: You can't get off the ground without it.

■ CHECKLIST

When you have studied this chapter you should be able to

☐ Define a market.

☐ Define demand and state the law of demand.

☐ Graph the demand curve when you are given a demand schedule.

☐ Explain the difference between individual demand and market demand.

☐ List the major determinants of demand and explain how each one shifts the demand curve.

☐ Distinguish between change in demand and change in the quantity demanded.

☐ Define supply and state the law of supply.

☐ Graph the supply curve when you are given a supply schedule.

☐ List the major determinants of supply and explain how each shifts the supply curve.

☐ Distinguish between change in supply and change in the quantity supplied.

☐ Define surplus and shortage.

☐ Describe how the equilibrium price and quantity are determined in a competitive market.

☐ Determine, when you are given the demand for and the supply of a good, the equilibrium price and the equilibrium quantity.

☐ Predict the effects of changes in demand and supply on equilibrium price and equilibrium quantity and on the prices of substitute and complementary goods.

☐ Explain the meaning of the rationing function of prices.

☐ Explain why violations of the "other-things-equal" assumption may cause confusion about the validity of the laws of demand and supply.

☐ Explain the economic effects of a government-set price ceiling on product price and quantity in a competitive market and give an example.

☐ Describe the economic consequences of a government-set price floor on product price and quantity in a competitive market and supply an example.

■ CHAPTER OUTLINE

1. A market is any institution or mechanism that brings to-gether buyers ("demanders") and sellers ("suppliers") of a particular good or service. This chapter assumes that markets are highly competitive.

2. *Demand* is a schedule of prices and the quantities that buyers would purchase at each of these prices during a selected period of time.

a. As price rises, other things being equal, buyers will purchase smaller quantities, and as price falls they will purchase larger quantities; this is the law of demand.

b. The demand curve is a graphic representation of demand and the law of demand.

c. Market (or total) demand for a good is a summation of the demands of all individuals in the market for that good.

d. The demand for a good depends on the tastes, income, and expectations of buyers; the number of buyers in the market; and the prices of related goods.

e. A change (increase or decrease) in the entire demand schedule and the demand curve is referred to as a *change in demand.* It is the result of a change in one or more of the determinants of demand. For example, an *increase* in the demand for a good may result from an increase in:

(1) *tastes or preferences* for the good;

(2) *the number of buyers* (for the good);

(3) *income* if it is a normal good, but if it is a normal good, it may result from a decrease in income;

(4) *the price of a related good*, but if they are complements, it may result from a decrease in the price of a related good; and

(5) *expectations* of a price increase or a rise in income.

f. A change in demand and a change in the quantity demanded are *not* the same thing.

3. *Supply* is a schedule of prices and the quantities that sellers will sell at each of these prices during some period of time.

a. The supply schedule shows, other things equal, that as the price of the good rises, larger quantities will be offered for sale, and as the price of the good falls, smaller quantities will be offered for sale.

b. The supply curve is a graphic representation of supply and the law of supply; the market supply of a good is the sum of the supplies of all sellers of the good.

c. The supply of a good depends on the techniques used to produce it, the prices of the resources employed in its production, the extent to which it is taxed or subsidized, the prices of other goods that might be produced, the price expectations of sellers, and the number of sellers of the product.

d. A change (increase or decrease) in the entire supply schedule and the supply curve is referred to as a *change in supply.* It is the result of a change in one or more of the determinants of supply. For example, an increase in supply for a good may result from:

(1) a decrease in the *prices of resources* used to make it;

(2) an improvement in the *technology* to produce it;

(3) a fall in *taxes* on it, or an increase in *subsidies* for it;

(4) a decline in the *prices of other goods* that could be produced by firms making it;

(5) an increase or decrease (depending on the market in question) in *expectations* of its higher future prices; and

(6) an increase in the number of sellers of it.

e. A change in supply must be distinguished from a change in quantity supplied.

4. The *market* or *equilibrium price* of a product is that price at which quantity demanded and quantity supplied are equal; the quantity exchanged in the market (the equilibrium quantity) is equal to the quantity demanded and supplied at the equilibrium price.

a. If the price of a product is above the market equilibrium price, there will be a *surplus* or *excess supply.* In this case, the quantity demanded is less than the quantity supplied at that price.

b. If the price of a product is below the market equilibrium price, there will be a *shortage* or *excess demand.* In this case, the quantity demanded is greater than the quantity supplied at that price.

c. The rationing function of prices is the elimination of surpluses and shortages of a product.

d. A change in demand, supply, or both changes both the equilibrium price and the equilibrium quantity in specific ways. (See #4 in "Hints and Tips" section.)

e. When demand and supply schedules (or curves) are drawn up, it is assumed that all the nonprice determinants of demand and supply remain unchanged. This assumption is often stated as "other-things-equal."

5. Supply and demand analysis has many important applications to *government-set prices.*

a. A price ceiling set by government prevents price from performing its rationing function in a market system. It creates a shortage (quantity demanded is greater than the quantity supplied) at the government-set price.

(1) Another rationing method must be found, so government often steps in and establishes one. But all rationing systems have problems because they exclude someone.

(2) Also, a government-set price creates an illegal *black market* for those who want to buy and sell above the government-set price.

(3) One example of a legal price ceiling that creates a shortage would be rent control established in some cities to restrain apartment rents.

b. A *price floor* is a minimum price set by government for the sale of a product or resource. It creates a surplus (quantity supplied is greater than the quantity demanded) at the fixed price. The surplus may induce the government to increase demand or decrease supply to eliminate the surplus. The use of price floors has often been applied to several agricultural products.

■ HINTS AND TIPS

1. This chapter is the most important one in the book. Make sure you spend extra time on it and master the material. If you do, your long-term payoff will be a much easier understanding of the applications in later chapters.

2. One mistake students often make is to confuse **change in demand** with **change in quantity demanded.** A change in demand causes the entire demand curve to *shift,* whereas a change in quantity demanded is simply a *movement* along an existing demand curve.

3. It is strongly recommended that you draw supply and demand graphs as you work on supply and demand problems so you can see a picture of what happens when demand shifts, supply shifts, or both demand and supply shift.

4. Make a chart and related graphs that show the eight possible outcomes from changes in demand and supply. Figure 3–6 in the text illustrates the *four single shift* outcomes:

   (1) **D↑: P↑, Q↑**   (3) **S↑: P↓, Q↑**
   (2) **D↓: P↓, Q↓**   (4) **S↓: P↑, Q↓**

Four shift combinations are described in Table 3–9 of the text. Make a figure to illustrate each combination.

   (1) **S↑, D↓: P↓, Q?**   (3) **S↑, D↑: P?, Q↑**
   (2) **S↓, D↑: P↑, Q?**   (4) **S↓, D↓: P?, Q↓**

5. Make sure you understand the "other-things-equal" assumption described at the end of the chapter. It will help you understand why the law of demand is not violated even if the price and quantity of a product increase over time.

6. Practice always helps in understanding graphs. Without looking at the textbook, draw a supply and demand graph with a **price ceiling** below the equilibrium price and show the resulting shortage in the market for a product. Then, draw a supply and demand graph with a **price floor** above the equilibrium price and show the resulting surplus. Explain to yourself what the graphs show. Check your graphs and your explanations by referring to textbook Figures 3–7 and 3–8 and the related explanations.

■ IMPORTANT TERMS

market	change in quantity demanded
demand	quantity demanded
demand schedule	individual demand
law of demand	total or market demand
diminishing marginal utility	supply
income effect	supply schedule
substitution effect	law of supply
demand curve	quantity supplied
determinants of demand	supply curve
normal good	determinants of supply
inferior good	change in supply
substitute goods	change in quantity supplied
complementary goods	surplus
change in demand	shortage

equilibrium price	price ceiling
equilibrium quantity	price floor
rationing function of prices	

SELF-TEST

■ FILL-IN QUESTIONS

1. A market is the institution or mechanism that brings together buyers or (demanders, suppliers) _____ and sellers or _____ of a particular good or service.

2. The relationship between price and quantity in the demand schedule is (a direct, an inverse) _____ relationship; in the supply schedule the relationship is _____ one.

3. The added satisfaction or pleasure a consumer obtains from additional units of a product decreases as the consumer's consumption of the product increases. This phenomenon is called diminishing marginal (equilibrium, utility) _____.

4. A consumer tends to buy more of a product as its price falls because
  a. The purchasing power of the consumer is increased and the consumer tends to buy more of this product (and of other products); this is called the (income, substitution) _____ effect;
  b. The product becomes less expensive relative to similar products and the consumer tends to buy more of the original product and less of the similar products, which is called the _____ effect.

5. When demand or supply is graphed, price is placed on the (horizontal, vertical) _____ axis and quantity on the _____ axis.

6. The change from an individual to a market demand schedule involves (adding, multiplying) _____ the quantities demanded by each consumer at the various possible (incomes, prices) _____.

7. When the price of one product and the demand for another product are directly related, the two products are called (substitutes, complements) _____; however, when the price of one product and the demand for another product are inversely related, the two products are called _____.

8. When a consumer demand schedule or curve is drawn up, it is assumed that five factors that determine demand are fixed and constant. These five determinants of consumer demand are
  a. _____
  b. _____

c. _____

d. _____

e. _____

9. A decrease in demand means that consumers will buy (larger, smaller) _____ quantities at every price, or will pay (more, less) _____ for the same quantities.

10. A change in income or in the price of another product will result in a change in the (demand for, quantity demanded of) _____ the given product, while a change in the price of the given product will result in a change in the _____ the given product.

11. An increase in supply means that producers will make and be willing to sell (larger, smaller) _____ quantities at every price, or will accept (more, less) _____ for the same quantities.

12. A change in resource prices or the prices of other goods that could be produced will result in a change in the (supply, quantity supplied) _____ of the given product, but a change in the price of the given product will result in a change in the _____.

13. The fundamental factors that determine the supply of any commodity in the product market are

a. _____

b. _____

c. _____

d. _____

e. _____

f. _____

14. If quantity demanded is greater than quantity supplied, price is (above, below) _____ the equilibrium price, and the (shortage, surplus) _____ will cause the price to (rise, fall) _____. If quantity demanded is less than the quantity supplied, price is (above, below) _____ the equilibrium price, and the (shortage, surplus) _____ will cause the price to (rise, fall) _____.

15. The equilibrium price of a product is the price at which quantity demanded is (greater than, equal to) _____ quantity supplied, and there (is, is not) _____ a surplus or a shortage at that price.

16. In the space next to **a–h**, indicate the effect [*increase* (+), *decrease* (−), or *indeterminate* (?)] on equilibrium price (**P**) and equilibrium quantity (**Q**) of each of these changes in demand and/or supply.

	P	**Q**
a. Increase in demand, supply constant	___	___
b. Increase in supply, demand constant	___	___
c. Decrease in demand, supply constant	___	___
d. Decrease in supply, demand constant	___	___
e. Increase in demand, increase in supply	___	___
f. Increase in demand, decrease in supply	___	___
g. Decrease in demand, decrease in supply	___	___
h. Decrease in demand, increase in supply	___	___

17. If supply and demand establish a price for a good so that there is no shortage or surplus of the product, then price is successfully performing its (utility, rationing) _____ function. The price that is set is a market-(changing, clearing) _____ price.

18. To assume that all the determinants of demand and supply do not change is to employ the (marginal utility, other-things-equal) _____ assumption.

19. A price ceiling is the (minimum, maximum) _____ legal price a seller may charge for a product or service, whereas a price floor is the _____ legal price set by government.

20. If a price ceiling is below the market equilibrium price, a (surplus, shortage) _____ will arise in a competitive market, and if a price floor is above the market equilibrium price, a (surplus, shortage) _____ will arise in a competitive market.

■ **TRUE–FALSE QUESTIONS**

Circle T if the statement is true, F if it is false.

1. A market is any arrangement that brings together the buyers and sellers of a particular good or service. **T F**

2. Demand is the amount of a good or service that a buyer will purchase at a particular price. **T F**

3. The law of demand states that as price increases, other things being equal, the quantity of the product demanded increases. **T F**

4. The law of diminishing marginal utility is one explanation of why there is an inverse relationship between price and quantity demanded. **T F**

5. The substitution effect suggests that, at a lower price, you have the incentive to substitute the more expensive product for similar products which are relatively less expensive. **T F**

6. There is no difference between individual demand schedules and the market demand schedule for a product. **T F**

7. In graphing supply and demand schedules, supply is put on the horizontal axis and demand on the vertical axis. **T F**

8. If price falls, there will be an increase in demand. **T F**

9. If consumer tastes or preferences for a product decrease, the demand for the product will tend to decrease. **T F**

10. An increase in income will tend to increase the demand for a product. **T F**

11. When two products are substitute goods, the price of one and the demand for the other will tend to move in the same direction. **T F**

12. If two goods are complementary, an increase in the price of one will tend to increase the demand for the other. **T F**

13. A change in the quantity demanded means that there has been a change in demand. **T F**

14. Supply is a schedule that shows the amounts of a product a producer can make in a limited time period. **T F**

15. An increase in resource prices will tend to decrease supply. **T F**

16. A government subsidy for the production of a product will tend to decrease supply. **T F**

17. An increase in the prices of other goods that could be made by producers will tend to decrease the supply of the current good that the producer is making. **T F**

18. A change in supply means that there is a movement along an existing supply curve. **T F**

19. A surplus indicates that the quantity demanded is less than the quantity supplied at that price. **T F**

20. If the market price of a product is below its equilibrium price, the market price will tend to rise because demand will decrease and supply will increase. **T F**

21. The rationing function of prices is the elimination of shortages and surpluses. **T F**

22. If the supply of a product increases and demand decreases, the equilibrium price and quantity will increase. **T F**

23. If the demand for a product increases and the supply of the product decreases, the equilibrium price will increase and equilibrium quantity will be indeterminant. **T F**

24. Economists often make the assumption of other things equal to hold constant the effects of other factors when examining the relationship between prices and quantities demanded and supplied. **T F**

25. A price ceiling set by government below the competitive market price of a product will result in a surplus. **T F**

■ **MULTIPLE-CHOICE QUESTIONS**

Circle the letter that corresponds to the best answer.

1. The markets examined in this chapter
(a) sell nonstandard or differentiated products
(b) have buyers cooperating to determine prices
(c) are controlled by a single producer
(d) are highly competitive

2. A schedule that shows the various amounts of a product consumers are willing and able to purchase at each price in a series of possible prices during a specified period of time is called
(a) supply
(b) demand
(c) quantity supplied
(d) quantity demanded

3. The reason for the law of demand can best be explained in terms of
(a) supply
(b) complementary goods
(c) the rationing function of prices
(d) diminishing marginal utility

4. Assume that the price of video game players falls. What will most likely happen to the equilibrium price and quantity of video games, assuming this market is competitive?
(a) Price will increase; quantity will decrease.
(b) Price will decrease; quantity will increase.
(c) Price will decrease; quantity will decrease.
(d) Price will increase; quantity will increase.

5. Given the following individuals' demand schedules for product X, and assuming these are the only three consumers of X, which set of prices and output levels below will be on the market demand curve for this product?

Price X	Consumer 1 Q_{dx}	Consumer 2 Q_{dx}	Consumer 3 Q_{dx}
$5	1	2	0
4	2	4	0
3	3	6	1
2	4	8	2
1	5	10	3

(a) ($5, 2); ($1, 10)
(b) ($5, 3); ($1, 18)
(c) ($4, 6); ($2, 12)
(d) ($4, 0); ($1, 3)

6. Which factor will decrease the demand for a product?
(a) a favorable change in consumer tastes
(b) an increase in the price of a substitute good
(c) a decrease in the price of a complementary good
(d) a decrease in the number of buyers

7. The income of a consumer decreases and the consumer's demand for a particular good increases. It can be concluded that the good is
(a) normal
(b) inferior
(c) a substitute
(d) a complement

8. Which of the following could cause a decrease in consumer demand for product X?
(a) a decrease in consumer income
(b) an increase in the prices of goods that are good substitutes for product X
(c) an increase in the price that consumers expect will prevail for product X in the future
(d) a decrease in the supply of product X

9. If two goods are substitutes for each other, an increase in the price of one will necessarily
(a) decrease the demand for the other
(b) increase the demand for the other
(c) decrease the quantity demanded of the other
(d) increase the quantity demanded of the other

10. If two products, A and B, are complements, then
(a) an increase in the price of A will decrease the demand for B
(b) an increase in the price of A will increase the demand for B
(c) an increase in the price of A will have no significant effect on the price of B
(d) a decrease in the price of A will decrease the demand for B

11. If two products, X and Y, are independent goods, then
(a) an increase in the price of X will significantly increase the demand for Y
(b) an increase in the price of Y will significantly increase the demand for X
(c) an increase in the price of Y will have no significant effect on the demand for X
(d) a decrease in the price of X will significantly increase the demand for Y

12. The law of supply states that, other things being constant, as price increases
(a) supply increases
(b) supply decreases
(c) quantity supplied increases
(d) quantity supplied decreases

13. If the supply curve moves from S_1 to S_2 on the graph in the next column, there has been
(a) an increase in supply
(b) a decrease in supply
(c) an increase in quantity supplied
(d) a decrease in quantity supplied

14. A decrease in the supply of a product would most likely be caused by
(a) an increase in business taxes
(b) an increase in consumer incomes
(c) a decrease in resource costs for production
(d) a decrease in the price of a complementary good

15. If the quantity supplied of a product is greater than the quantity demanded for a product, then
(a) there is a shortage of the product
(b) there is a surplus of the product
(c) the product is a normal good
(d) the product is an inferior good

16. If the price of a product is below the equilibrium price, the result will be
(a) a surplus of the good
(b) a shortage of the good
(c) a decrease in the supply of the good
(d) an increase in the demand for the good

Answer Questions 17, 18, and 19 on the basis of the data in the the following table. Consider the following supply and demand schedules for bushels of corn.

Price	Quantity demanded	Quantity supplied
$20	395	200
22	375	250
24	350	290
26	320	320
28	280	345
30	235	365

17. The equilibrium price in this market is
(a) $22
(b) $24
(c) $26
(d) $28

18. An increase in the cost of labor lowers the quantity supplied by 65 bushels at each price. The new equilibrium price would be
(a) $22
(b) $24
(c) $26
(d) $28

19. If the quantity demanded at each price increases by 130 bushels, then the new equilibrium quantity will be
(a) 290
(b) 320
(c) 345
(d) 365

20. A decrease in supply and a decrease in demand will
  (a) increase price and decrease the quantity exchanged
  (b) decrease price and increase the quantity exchanged
  (c) increase price and affect the quantity exchanged in an indeterminate way
  (d) affect price in an indeterminate way and decrease the quantity exchanged

21. An increase in demand and a decrease in supply will
  (a) increase price and increase the quantity exchanged
  (b) decrease price and decrease the quantity exchanged
  (c) increase price and the effect upon quantity exchanged will be indeterminate
  (d) decrease price and the effect upon quantity exchanged will be indeterminate

22. An increase in supply and an increase in demand will
  (a) increase price and increase the quantity exchanged
  (b) decrease price and increase the quantity exchanged
  (c) affect price in an indeterminate way and decrease the quantity exchanged
  (d) affect price in an indeterminate way and increase the quantity exchanged

23. A cold spell in Florida devastates the orange crop. As a result, California oranges command a higher price. Which of the following statements best explains the situation?
  (a) The supply of Florida oranges decreases, causing the supply of California oranges to increase and their price to increase.
  (b) The supply of Florida oranges decreases, causing their price to increase and the demand for California oranges to increase.
  (c) The supply of Florida oranges decreases, causing the supply of California oranges to decrease and their price to increase.
  (d) The demand for Florida oranges decreases, causing a greater demand for California oranges and an increase in their price.

Answer Questions 24, 25, 26, and 27 based on the following graph showing the market supply and demand for a product.

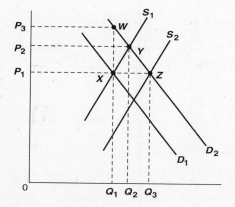

24. Assume that the market is initially in equilibrium where D_1 and S_1 intersect. If there is an increase in the number of buyers, then the new equilibrium would most likely be at point
  (a) W
  (b) X
  (c) Y
  (d) Z

25. Assume that the equilibrium price and quantity in the market are P_2 and Q_2. Which factor would cause the equilibrium price and quantity to shift to P_1 and Q_3?
  (a) an increase in product price
  (b) an increase in demand
  (c) an increase in supply
  (d) a decrease in quantity

26. What would cause a shift in the equilibrium price and quantity from point Z to point X?
  (a) a decrease in production costs and more favorable consumer tastes for the product
  (b) an increase in the number of suppliers and an increase in consumer incomes
  (c) an increase in production costs and decrease in consumer incomes
  (d) an improvement in production technology and decrease in the price of a substitute good

27. Assume that the market is initially in equilibrium where D_1 and S_1 intersect. If consumer incomes increased and the technology for making the product improved, then new equilibrium would most likely be at
  (a) P_1 and Q_1
  (b) P_2 and Q_2
  (c) P_1 and Q_3
  (d) P_3 and Q_1

28. The demand curve and its inverse relationship between price and quantity demanded is based on the assumption of
  (a) other things equal
  (b) changing expectations
  (c) complementary goods
  (d) increasing marginal utility

Questions 29 and 30 relate to the following table that shows a hypothetical supply and demand schedule for a product.

Quantity demanded (pounds)	Price (per pound)	Quantity supplied (pounds)
200	$4.40	800
250	4.20	700
300	4.00	600
350	3.80	500
400	3.60	400
450	3.40	300
500	3.20	200

29. A shortage of 150 pounds of the product will occur if a government-set price is established at
  (a) $3.20
  (b) $3.40
  (c) $3.80
  (d) $4.00

30. If a price floor set by the government is established at $4.20, there will be a
- **(a)** surplus of 300 pounds
- **(b)** shortage of 300 pounds
- **(c)** surplus of 450 pounds
- **(d)** shortage of 450 pounds

■ **PROBLEMS**

1. Using the demand schedule that follows, plot the demand curve on the graph below the schedule. Label the axes and indicate for each axis the units being used to measure price and quantity.

Price	Quantity demanded, 1000 bushels of soybeans
$7.20	10
7.00	15
6.80	20
6.60	25
6.40	30
6.20	35

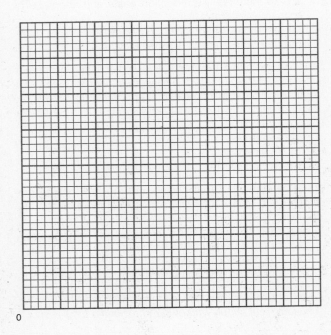

0

a. Plot the following supply schedule on the same graph.

Price	Quantity supplied, 1000 bushels of soybeans
$7.20	40
7.00	35
6.80	30
6.60	25
6.40	20
6.20	15

b. The equilibrium price of soybeans will be $_____.

c. How many thousand bushels of soybeans will be exchanged at this price? _____

d. Indicate clearly on the graph the equilibrium price and quantity by drawing lines from the intersection of the supply and demand curves to the price and quantity axes.

e. If the Federal government supported a price of $7.00 per bushel there would be a (shortage, surplus) _____ of _____ bushels of soybeans.

2. The demand schedules of three individuals (Ellie, Sam, and Lynn) for loaves of bread are shown in the following table. Assuming there are only three buyers of bread, determine and graph the total or market demand schedule for bread.

	Quantity demanded, loaves of bread			
Price	Ellie	Sam	Lynn	Total
$1.50	1	4	0	_____
1.40	3	5	1	_____
1.30	6	6	5	_____
1.20	10	7	10	_____
1.10	15	8	16	_____

3. Following is a demand schedule for bushels of apples. In columns 3 and 4 insert *any* new figures for quantity that represent in column 3 an increase in demand and in column 4 a decrease in demand.

(1) Price	(2) Quantity demanded	(3) Demand increases	(4) Demand decreases
$6.00	400	_____	_____
5.90	500	_____	_____
5.80	600	_____	_____
5.70	700	_____	_____
5.60	800	_____	_____
5.50	900	_____	_____

4. Assume that O'Rourke has, when his income is $100 per week, the demand schedule for good A shown in columns 1 and 2 of the following table and the demand schedule for good B shown in columns 4 and 5. Assume that the prices of A and B are $.80 and $5, respectively.

Demand for A (per week)			Demand for B (per week)		
(1) Price	(2) Quantity demanded	(3) Quantity demanded	(4) Price	(5) Quantity demanded	(6) Quantity demanded
$.90	10	0	$5.00	4	7
.85	20	10	4.50	5	8
.80	30	20	4.00	6	9
.75	40	30	3.50	7	10
.70	50	40	3.00	8	11
.65	60	50	2.50	9	12
.60	70	60	2.00	10	13

a. How much A will O'Rourke buy? _____

How much B? _____

b. Suppose that as a consequence of a $10 increase in O'Rourke's weekly income, the quantities demanded of A become those shown in column 3 and the quantities demanded of B become those shown in column 6.
(1) How much A will he now buy? _____

How much B? _____
(2) Good A is (normal, inferior) _____.
(3) Good B is _____.

5. The market demand for good X is shown in columns 1 and 2 of the following table. Assume the price of X to be $2 and constant.

(1) Price	(2) Quantity demanded	(3) Quantity demanded	(4) Quantity demanded
$2.40	1,600	1,500	1,700
2.30	1,650	1,550	1,750
2.20	1,750	1,650	1,850
2.10	1,900	1,800	2,000
2.00	2,100	2,000	2,200
1.90	2,350	2,250	2,450
1.80	2,650	2,550	2,750

a. If as the price of good Y rises from $1.25 to $1.35, the quantities demanded of good X become those shown in column 3, it can be concluded that X and Y are (substitute, complementary) _____ goods.

b. If as the price of good Y rises from $1.25 to $1.35, the quantities of good X become those shown in column 4, it can be concluded that X and Y are _____

_____ goods.

6. In a local market for hamburger on a given date, each of 300 identical sellers of hamburger has the following supply schedule.

(1) Price	(2) Quantity supplied— one seller, lbs	(3) Quantity supplied— all sellers, lbs
$2.05	150	_____
2.00	110	_____
1.95	75	_____
1.90	45	_____
1.85	20	_____
1.80	0	_____

a. In column 3 construct the market supply schedule for hamburger.
b. Following is the market demand schedule for hamburger on the same date and in the same local market as that given above.

Price	Quantity demanded, lbs
$2.05	28,000
2.00	31,000
1.95	36,000
1.90	42,000
1.85	49,000
1.80	57,000

If the Federal government sets a price on hamburger of $1.90 a pound, the result would be a (shortage, surplus) _____ of _____ pounds of hamburger in this market.

7. Each of the following events would tend to increase or decrease either the demand for or the supply of computer games and, as a result, will increase or decrease the price of these games. In the first blank indicate the effect on demand or supply (increase, decrease); in the second blank, indicate the effect on price (increase, decrease). Assume that the market for computer games is a competitive one.

a. It becomes known that an electronics store is going to have a sale on these games 3 months from now.

_____;

_____

b. The workers who produce the games go on strike

for over 2 months. _____; _____
c. The workers in the industry receive a $2 an hour

wage increase. _____; _____
d. The average price of movie tickets (a substitute)

increases. _____; _____
e. The price of business software, a product also supplied by the computer software producers, rises.

_____; _____

f. It is announced by a private research institute that children who play computer games also improve their

grades in school. _____; _____
g. Because of the use of mass production techniques, the amount of labor necessary to produce a game

decreases. _____; _____

h. The price of computers decreases. _____;

_____
i. The average consumer believes that a shortage of

games is developing in the economy. _____;

_____
j. The Federal government imposes a $5 tax per game on the manufacturers of computer games.

_____; _____

■ **SHORT ANSWER AND ESSAY QUESTIONS**

1. Define demand and the law of demand.

2. Use the diminishing marginal utility concept to explain why the quantity demanded of a product will tend to rise when the price of the product falls.

3. In past decades, the price of coffee in the United States rose significantly as a result of bad weather in coffee-producing regions. Use the income effect and the substitution effect concepts to explain why the quantity of coffee demanded in the United States significantly decreased.

4. What is the difference between individual demand and market demand? What is the relationship between these two types of demand?

5. Explain the difference between an increase in demand and an increase in the quantity demanded.

6. What are the factors that cause a change in demand? Use supply and demand graphs to illustrate what happens to price and quantity when demand increases.

7. How are inferior and normal (or superior) goods defined? What is the relationship between these goods and changes in income?

8. Why does the effect of a change in the price of related goods depend on whether a good is a substitute or complement? What are substitutes and complements?

9. A newspaper reports that "Blue jeans have become even more popular and are now the standard clothing that people wear for both play and work." How will this change affect the demand for blue jeans? What will happen to the price and quantity of blue jeans sold in the market? Explain and use a supply and demand graph to illustrate your answer.

10. Compare and contrast the supply schedule with the demand schedule.

11. Supply does not remain constant for long because the factors that determine supply change. What are these factors? How do changes in them affect supply?

12. Explain the difference between an increase in supply and an increase in the quantity supplied.

13. Describe and illustrate with a supply and demand graph the effect of an increase in supply on price and quantity. Do the same for a decrease in supply.

14. The U.S. Congress passes a law that raises the excise tax on gasoline by $1 per gallon. What effect will this change have on the demand and supply of gasoline? What will happen to gasoline prices and quantity? Explain and use a supply and demand graph to illustrate your answer.

15. What is the relationship between the price of a product and a shortage of the product? What is the relationship between the price of a product and a surplus of the product?

16. Given the demand for and the supply of a commodity, what price will be the equilibrium price of this commodity? Explain why this price will tend to prevail in the market and why higher (lower) prices, if they do exist temporarily, will tend to fall (rise).

17. Analyze the following quotation and explain the fallacies contained in it: "An increase in demand will cause price to rise; with a rise in price, supply will increase and the increase in supply will push price down. Therefore, an increase in demand results in little change in price because supply will increase also."

18. Suppose an industry sells 2000 units of a product at $10 per unit one year, 3000 units at $12 the next year, and 4000 units at $14 the third year. Is this evidence that the law of demand is violated? Explain.

19. What are the consequences of a price ceiling for a product if it is set below the equilibrium price? Illustrate your answer with a graph.

20. What are the economic problems with price floors? How have they been used by government?

ANSWERS

Chapter 3 Individual Markets: Demand and Supply

FILL-IN QUESTIONS

1. demanders, suppliers
2. an inverse, a direct
3. utility
4. *a.* income; *b.* substitution
5. vertical, horizontal
6. adding, prices
7. substitutes, complements
8. *a.* the tastes or preferences of consumers; *b.* the number of consumers in the market; *c.* the money income of consumers; *d.* the prices of related goods; *e.* consumer expectations with respect to future prices, product availability, and income (any order for *a–e*)
9. smaller, less
10. demand for, quantity demanded of
11. larger, less
12. supply, quantity supplied
13. *a.* the technology of production; *b.* resource prices; *c.* taxes and subsidies; *d.* prices of other goods; *e.* price expectations; *f.* the number of sellers in the market (any order for *a–f*)
14. below, shortage, rise, above, surplus, fall
15. equal to, is not
16. *a.* +, +; *b.* −, +; *c.* −, −; *d.* +, −; *e.* ?, +; *f.* +, ?; *g.* ?, −; *h.* −, ?
17. rationing, clearing
18. other-things-equal
19. maximum, minimum
20. shortage, surplus

TRUE–FALSE QUESTIONS

1. T, p. 39	10. T, p. 43	19. T, p. 48
2. F, pp. 40; 44–45	11. T, p. 44	20. F, pp. 48–49
3. F, p. 40	12. F, p. 44	21. T, p. 50
4. T, p. 40	13. F, pp. 44–45	22. F, pp. 50–52
5. F, pp. 40–41	14. F, p. 45	23. T, pp. 50–52
6. F, pp. 41–42	15. T, pp. 46–47	24. T, p. 52
7. F, p. 42	16. F, p. 47	25. F, pp. 52–53
8. F, pp. 42–44	17. T, p. 47	
9. T, p. 43	18. F, pp. 47–48	

MULTIPLE-CHOICE QUESTIONS

1. d, p. 39   **11.** c, p. 44   **21.** c, p. 51
2. b, p. 40   **12.** c, p. 45   **22.** d, p. 52
3. d, pp. 40–41 **13.** a, p. 46   **23.** b, p. 51
4. d, pp. 44; 50 **14.** a, pp. 46–47 **24.** c, pp. 43; 50
5. b, pp. 41–42 **15.** b, p. 48   **25.** c, p. 50
6. d, pp. 43–44 **16.** b, p. 48   **26.** c, pp. 43–44; 46–47; 51
7. b, p. 43   **17.** c, p. 49   **27.** c, pp. 43–44; 46–47; 52
8. a, p. 44   **18.** d, pp. 47; 50 **28.** a, p. 52
9. b, p. 44   **19.** d, pp. 45; 50 **29.** b, p. 53
10. a, p. 44   **20.** d, p. 52   **30.** c, p. 54

PROBLEMS

1. *a.* graph; *b.* 6.60; *c.* 25,000; *d.* graph; *e.* surplus, 20,000
2. Total: 5, 9, 17, 27, 39
3. Each quantity in column 3 is greater than in column 2, and each quantity in column 4 is less than in column 2.
4. *a.* 30, 4; *b.* (1) 20, 7; (2) inferior; (3) normal (superior)

5. *a.* complementary; *b.* substitute
6. *a.* 45,000; 33,000; 22,500; 13,500; 6,000; 0; *b.* shortage, 28,500
7. *a.* decrease demand, decrease price; *b.* decrease supply, increase price; *c.* decrease supply, increase price; *d.* increase demand, increase price; *e.* decrease supply, increase price; *f.* increase demand, increase price; *g.* increase supply, decrease price; *h.* increase demand, increase price; *i.* increase demand, increase price; *j.* decrease supply, increase price

SHORT ANSWER AND ESSAY QUESTIONS

1. p. 40   **8.** p. 44   **15.** p. 48
2. p. 40   **9.** pp. 43; 50   **16.** pp. 48–50
3. p. 41   **10.** pp. 40; 45 **17.** pp. 50–51
4. pp. 41–42   **11.** pp. 46–47   **18.** pp. 50–51
5. pp. 44–45   **12.** pp. 47–48   **19.** pp. 52–53
6. pp. 43–44   **13.** pp. 46; 50–51 **20.** pp. 54–55
7. p. 43   **14.** pp. 47; 50–51

Applications and Extensions of Supply and Demand Analysis

Note: This bonus web chapter is available at the textbook website: www.mcconnell16.com. Go to Chapter 3W at the Student Center.

Chapter 3 Web has two basic purposes. It offers you numerous real-world applications of supply and demand analysis. It also uses supply and demand analysis to provide new insights into the allocation of common resources and economic efficiency.

The first section of the chapter gives you more examples of the effects of **changes in supply and demand** on price and quantity. You will first read about simple changes in which either the demand curve changes or the supply curve changes, but not both. These simple changes result in predictable effects on the price and quantity of a product, such as lettuce or American flags. Then you are given examples, using pink salmon, gasoline, and sushi, of complex changes. In these cases, there is a simultaneous shift in supply and demand. Here the effect of changes in supply and demand on price and quantity will be less certain and will depend on the direction and extent of the changes.

The chapter then extends your understanding of what happens in markets if **pre-set prices** are above or below the equilibrium price. You have already learned that when the government intervenes in a competitive market and sets the price below equilibrium (a price ceiling), it creates a shortage of a product. Similarly, when government sets a price above the equilibrium price (a price floor), it will result in a surplus. As you will learn, shortages and surpluses can also occur in competitive markets when sellers set the price in advance of sales and that pre-set price turns out to be below or above the equilibrium or actual price. The examples given in the text are ticket prices for sporting events that are priced too low or too high by the sellers, resulting in shortages and surpluses.

The third section of the chapter introduces you to a new concept, **nonpriced goods.** These goods or resources are ones that are owned in common by society, such as wildlife, fish, public water, and public land. Although there are no competitive markets or prices, supply and demand analysis can provide insights about the effective use and management of these resources. As you will read, this analysis can explain the plight of buffalo since the 1800s. The text also discusses the alternative methods government uses to ration scarce resources that do not have a market price.

Supply and demand analysis is also used to enhance your understanding of **economic efficiency** in the fourth section of the chapter. This extension requires an explanation of the concepts of **consumer and producer surplus.** Consumer surplus is the difference between the maximum price consumers are willing to pay for a product and the actual price. Producer surplus is the difference between the minimum price producers are willing to accept for a product and the actual price. The chapter also revisits the concept of **allocative efficiency** and explains that it is achieved when the combination of consumer and producer surplus is at a maximum.

Supply and demand analysis is one of the most important means for improving your understanding of the economic world. If you master its use, it will help you explain many events and outcomes in everyday life. This chapter helps you achieve that mastery and understanding.

■ **CHECKLIST**

When you have studied this chapter you should be able to

☐ Explain and graph the effect of an increase in the supply of a product (lettuce) on its equilibrium price and quantity.

☐ Describe and graph the effect of an increase in the demand for a product (American flags) on its equilibrium price and quantity.

☐ Discuss and graph the effects of an increase in the supply of and a decrease in demand for a product (pink salmon) on its equilibrium price and quantity.

☐ Predict and graph the effects of a decrease in the supply of and an increase in the demand for a product (gasoline) on its equilibrium price and quantity.

☐ Explain and graph the effects of an equal increase in the supply of and demand for a product (sushi) on its equilibrium price and quantity.

☐ Discuss and graph how a seller price for a service (Olympic figure skating finals) that is set below the equilibrium price will result in a shortage.

☐ Describe and graph how a seller price for a service (Olympic curling preliminaries) that is set above the equilibrium price will result in a surplus.

☐ Define and give examples of nonpriced goods.

☐ Describe and graph the supply and demand conditions that will result in a shortage of a nonpriced good.

☐ Explain and graph the supply and demand conditions that will result in a surplus of a nonpriced good.

☐ Define consumer surplus and give a graphical example.

☐ Define producer surplus and give a graphical example.

☐ Use consumer surplus and producer surplus to explain how allocative efficiency is achieved in a competitive market.

☐ List the three conditions for achieving allocative efficiency at a quantity level in a competitive market.

☐ Use a supply and demand graph to illustrate efficiency losses when the quantity is greater or less than its equilibrium in a competitive market.

■ **CHAPTER OUTLINE**

1. *Changes in supply and demand* result in changes in the equilibrium price and quantity. The simplest cases are ones where demand changes and supply remains constant, or where supply changes and demand remains constant. More complex cases involve simultaneous changes in supply and demand.

a. *Supply increase.* In a competitive market for lettuce, if a severe freeze destroys a portion of the lettuce crop, then the supply of lettuce will decrease. The decrease in the supply of lettuce, with demand constant, will increase the equilibrium price and decrease the equilibrium quantity.

b. *Demand increase.* In a competitive market for American flags, an increase in patriotism will increase the demand for flags. This increase in demand, with supply remaining the same, will increase the equilibrium price and quantity of flags.

c. *Supply increase and demand decrease.* Over the years, improved fishing techniques and technology contributed to an increase in the supply of pink salmon. Also, an increase in consumer incomes and a lowering of the price of substitute fish contributed to reducing the demand for pink salmon. As a result the price of pink salmon fell. The equilibrium quantity could have increased, decreased, or stayed the same. In this case, the increase in supply was greater than the decrease in demand, so the equilibrium quantity increased.

d. *Demand increase and supply decrease.* An increase in the price of oil, a resource used to produce gasoline, resulted in a decrease in the supply of gasoline. At the same time, rising incomes and a stronger economy created a greater demand for gasoline. This decrease in supply and increase in demand increased the equilibrium price. The equilibrium quantity could have increased, decreased, or stayed the same. In this case, the decrease in supply was less than the increase in demand, so the equilibrium quantity increased.

e. *Demand increase and supply increase.* An increase in the taste for sushi among U.S. consumers resulted in an increase in the demand for this product. At the same time, there was an increase in the number of sushi bars and other food outlets that provide sushi, thus increasing its supply. This increase in both demand and supply increased the equilibrium quantity of sushi. The equilibrium price could have increased, decreased, or stayed the same. In this case, the increase in demand was the same as the increase in supply, so the equilibrium price remained the same.

2. *Pre-set prices* that are set by the seller below or above the equilibrium price can produce shortages and surpluses.

a. If a price is set below the equilibrium price by a seller, then at that pre-set price the quantity demanded is greater than the quantity supplied, resulting in a ***shortage.*** This situation is typical of the market for tickets to Olympic figure skating finals. The shortage of tickets at the pre-set price creates a secondary market (*black market*) for tickets in which buyers bid for tickets held by the initial purchaser. The ticket scalping drives up the price of tickets.

b. If a price is set above the equilibrium price by a seller, then at that pre-set price the quantity demanded is less than the quantity supplied, resulting in a ***surplus.*** This situation is typical of the market for tickets to Olympic curling preliminaries at which there are many empty seats.

3. *Nonpriced goods* (or resources) are ones that are owned in common by society and available for public use. The prices of these goods are essentially zero because they are not bought and sold in markets. Yet, supply and demand analysis can be applied to explain events and situations involving these nonpriced goods.

a. When the demand for a nonpriced good is less than the supply of the good at each and every price across the demand and supply curves, the price of the good will be zero. In this case, the demand and supply curves do not intersect at any positive price. This situation occurred with the buffalo in the pre-railroad era in the United States.

b. With the advent of the railroad and greater hunting of buffalo, the demand for buffalo increased. In graphical terms, the demand curve now intersected the supply curve at a positive equilibrium price, and this price for buffalo would have prevailed if there had been a market. But buffalo was a nonpriced good, so it had a zero price, and at this price a shortage arose. This shortage grew progressively worse as the supply curve shifted left because the buffalo population could not be sustained. Nonpriced goods often get overused.

c. When price is not used as a rationing device, other types of rationing allocate scarce resources. In the case of nonpriced goods such as wildlife or fish sought by hunters or fishers, licenses or quantity limits are used to decrease demand so that it is balanced with the sustainable supply. In some cases, nonpriced goods such as buffalo are being converted to privately owned goods that can be bought and sold in competitive markets.

4. In market transactions, consumers can obtain a beneficial surplus and so can producers.

a. *Consumer surplus* is the difference between the maximum price consumers are willing to pay for a product and the actual (equilibrium) price paid. Graphically, it is the triangular area bounded by the portion of the vertical axis between the equilibrium price and the demand curve intersection, the portion of the demand curve above the equilibrium price, and the horizontal line at the equilibrium price from the vertical axis to the demand curve. Price and consumer surplus are inversely (negatively) related: Higher prices reduce it and lower prices increase it.

b. *Producer surplus* is the difference between the minimum price producers are willing to accept for a product and the actual (equilibrium) price received. Graphically, it is the triangular area bounded by the portion of the vertical axis between the equilibrium price and the supply curve intersection, the portion of the supply curve below the equilibrium price, and the horizontal line at the equilibrium price from the vertical axis to the supply curve. Price and producer surplus are directly (positively) related: Higher prices increase it and lower prices decrease it.

c. The equilibrium quantity shown by the intersection of demand and supply curves reflects *economic efficiency*.

(1) *Productive efficiency* is achieved because production costs are minimized at each quantity level of output.

(2) *Allocative efficiency* is achieved at the equilibrium quantity of output because three conditions are satisfied: Marginal benefit equals marginal cost; maximum willingness to pay equals minimum acceptable price; and the combination of the consumer and producer surplus is at a maximum.

d. If quantity is less than or greater than the equilibrium or most efficient level, there are *efficiency losses.* The efficiency losses reduce the maximum possible size of the combined consumer and producer surplus.

■ HINTS AND TIPS

1. This web chapter offers applications and extensions of Chapter 3 in the textbook, so check your understanding of the corresponding text and web sections: (a) Review the text Chapter 3 section on "Changes in Supply, Demand, and Equilibrium" (pp. 50–52) before reading the web Chapter 3 section on "Changes in Supply and Demand"; and (b) review the text Chapter 3 section on "Application: Government-Set Prices" (pp. 52–55) before reading the web Chapter 3 section on "Pre-Set Prices."

2. Correct terminology is important for mastering supply and demand analysis. You must remember the distinction between a change in demand and a change in quantity demanded or a change in supply and a change in quantity supplied. Consider the case of a single shift in demand with supply staying the same. As the demand curve increases along the existing supply curve, it increases the quantity supplied, but it does not increase supply (which would be a shift in the entire supply curve).

3. The newest concepts in the chapter are those related to consumer surplus and producer surplus. The term "surplus" should not be confused with the previous use related to pre-set prices (when quantity supplied is greater than quantity demanded at a pre-set price). What the consumer surplus refers to is the extra utility or satisfaction that consumers get when they do not have to pay the price they were willing to pay and pay the lower equilibrium price. The producer surplus arises when producers receive an equilibrium price that is above the minimum price that they consider acceptable to selling the product.

4. The concept of allocative efficiency using marginal benefit and marginal cost was first presented in the text, Chapter 2 (pp. 27–28). Review your understanding of this concept in Chapter 2 before reading the web Chapter 3 section on "Efficiency Revisited."

■ IMPORTANT TERMS

nonpriced goods	**producer surplus**
consumer surplus	**efficiency losses**

SELF-TEST

■ FILL-IN QUESTIONS

1. A decrease in the supply of lettuce will result in an equilibrium price that (increases, decreases) _____ and an equilibrium quantity that _____.

2. An increase in the demand for American flags will result in an equilibrium price that (increases, decreases) _____ and an equilibrium quantity that _____.

3. An increase in the supply of pink salmon that is greater than the decrease in the demand for pink salmon will result in an equilibrium price that (increases, decreases, stays the same) _____ and an equilibrium quantity that _____.

4. An increase in the demand for gasoline that is greater than the decrease in the supply of gasoline will result in an equilibrium price that (increases, decreases, stays the same) _____ and an equilibrium quantity that _____.

5. An increase in the demand for sushi that is equal to the increase in the supply of sushi will result in an equilibrium price that (increases, decreases, stays the same) _____ and an equilibrium quantity that _____.

6. If government sets a legal price for a product, a shortage would arise from a price (ceiling, floor) _____ and a surplus would arise from a price _____.

7. If a pre-set price is set by the seller below the equilibrium price it will create a (surplus, shortage) _____, but if a pre-set price is set by the seller above the equilibrium price it will create a _____.

8. A market for tickets to popular sporting events in which buyers bid for tickets held by initial purchasers is referred to as a (primary, secondary) _____ market. In these markets, ticket (destruction, scalping) _____ occurs.

9. Nonpriced goods are resources that are (privately owned, owned in common) _____ and available for taking on (private, public) _____ lands.

10. At a zero price for a nonpriced good, where the quantity available (quantity supplied) is greater than the quantity demanded, there will be a (shortage, surplus) _____, but when the quantity available (quantity supplied) is less than the quantity demanded, there will be a _____.

11. A significant increase in the demand for a nonpriced good will lead to (under-, over-) _____ consumption of the good and (an increase, a decrease) _____ in the sustainable supply of the good.

12. The alternative to using prices and markets to ration nonpriced goods such as fish and game on public lands is to use (scalping, licenses) _____ or set (bonuses, limits) _____ on the number that can be taken.

13. A consumer surplus is the difference between the actual price and the (minimum, maximum) _____ price a consumer is (or consumers are) willing to pay for a product. In most markets, consumers individually or collectively gain more total utility or satisfaction when the actual or equilibrium price they have to pay for a product is (less, more) _____ than what they would have been willing to pay to obtain the product.

14. Consumer surplus and price are (positively, negatively) _____ related. This means that higher prices (increase, decrease) _____ consumer surplus and lower prices _____ it.

15. A producer surplus is the difference between the actual or equilibrium price and the (minimum, maximum) _____ acceptable price a producer is (or producers are) willing to accept in exchange for a product. In most markets, sellers individually or collectively benefit when they sell their product at an actual or equilibrium price that is (less, more) _____ than what they would have been willing to receive in exchange for the product.

16. Producer surplus and price are (positively, negatively) _____ related. This means that higher prices (increase, decrease) _____ producer surplus and lower prices _____ it.

17. When competition forces producers to use the best techniques and combinations of resources to make a product, then (allocative, productive) _____ efficiency is being achieved. When the correct or optimal quantity of output of a product is being produced relative to the other goods and services, then _____ efficiency is being achieved.

18. Points on the demand curve measure the marginal (cost, benefit) _____ of a product whereas points on the supply curve measure the marginal _____ of a product.

19. Allocative efficiency occurs at quantity levels where marginal benefit is (greater than, less than, equal to) _____ marginal cost, maximum willingness to pay by consumers is _____ the minimum acceptable price for producers, and the combined consumer and producer surplus is at a (minimum, maximum) _____.

20. When there is overproduction of a product, there are efficiency (gains, losses) _____ and when there is underproduction there are efficiency _____. In both cases, the combined consumer and producer surplus is (greater than, less than) _____ the maximum that would occur at the efficient quantity of output.

■ **TRUE–FALSE QUESTIONS**

Circle T if the statement is true, F if it is false.

1. An increase in the supply of lettuce decreases its equilibrium price and increases its equilibrium quantity.
T F

2. A decrease in the demand for an American flag increases its equilibrium price and decreases its equilibrium quantity.
T F

3. When demand for American flags increases, there is an increase in the quantity supplied as the equilibrium price rises, but no increase in supply.
T F

4. In the market for pink salmon, the reason that the equilibrium quantity increased was that the increase in supply was greater than the decrease in demand. **T F**

5. In the market for gasoline, the reason that the equilibrium quantity increased was that the increase in demand was less than the decrease in supply. **T F**

6. In the market for sushi, an equal increase in supply and demand will increase the equilibrium price, but have no effect on the equilibrium quantity.　　**T　F**

7. If the government sets a price ceiling below what would be the competitive market price of a product, a shortage of the product will develop.　　**T　F**

8. A price floor set by government will increase the equilibrium price and quantity in a market.　　**T　F**

9. If a seller pre-sets a price that turns out to be below the actual equilibrium price, a shortage will develop in the market.　　**T　F**

10. Ticket scalping often occurs in markets where there is a surplus of tickets.　　**T　F**

11. If a sporting event is not sold out, this indicates that the ticket prices for the event were pre-set above the actual equilibrium price.　　**T　F**

12. A nonpriced good is one that is owned in common by society and available for the taking on public lands.　**T　F**

13. An example of a nonpriced good is cattle that are raised on a cattle ranch.　　**T　F**

14. A nonpriced good has a zero price because demand is less than supply regardless of the price.　　**T　F**

15. Assume that a downsloping demand curve intersects a vertical supply curve. A leftward shift in the supply curve will result in a surplus of a product.　　**T　F**

16. Ways that government rations nonpriced goods are to use licenses and set quantity limits.　　**T　F**

17. Consumer surplus is the difference between the minimum and maximum price a consumer is willing to pay for a good.　　**T　F**

18. Consumer surplus is a utility surplus that reflects a gain in total utility or satisfaction.　　**T　F**

19. Consumer surplus and price are directly or positively related.　　**T　F**

20. The higher the equilibrium price, the greater the amount of consumer surplus.　　**T　F**

21. Producer surplus is the difference between the actual price a producer receives for a product and the minimum price the producer would have been willing to accept for the product.　　**T　F**

22. The higher the actual price, the less the amount of producer surplus.　　**T　F**

23. Competitive markets produce equilibrium prices and quantities that minimize the sum of consumer and producer surpluses.　　**T　F**

24. One of the three conditions for allocative efficiency is that the maximum willingness to pay by consumers is equal to the minimum acceptable price for producers.　　**T　F**

25. Efficiency losses are increases in the combined consumer and producer surplus.　　**T　F**

■ **MULTIPLE-CHOICE QUESTIONS**

Circle the letter that corresponds to the best answer.

1. Bad weather in coffee-producing regions of the world devastated the coffee crop. As a result, coffee prices increased worldwide. Which of the following statements best explains the situation?
 (a) the demand for coffee increased
 (b) the supply of coffee decreased
 (c) the demand for coffee increased and the supply of coffee increased
 (d) the demand for coffee decreased and the supply of coffee decreased

2. Assume that the supply of tomatoes in a competitive market increases. What will most likely happen to the equilibrium price and quantity of tomatoes?
 (a) price will increase; quantity will decrease
 (b) price will decrease; quantity will increase
 (c) price will decrease; quantity will decrease
 (d) price will increase; quantity will increase

3. Assume that the demand for security services increases in a competitive market. What will most likely happen to the equilibrium price and quantity of security services?
 (a) price will increase; quantity will decrease
 (b) price will decrease; quantity will increase
 (c) price will decrease; quantity will decrease
 (d) price will increase; quantity will increase

4. A decrease in the demand for hamburger is more than offset by an increase in its supply. As a result the equilibrium price will
 (a) increase and the equilibrium quantity will decrease
 (b) increase and the equilibrium quantity will increase
 (c) decrease and the equilibrium quantity will decrease
 (d) decrease and the equilibrium quantity will increase

5. A decrease in the supply of oil is more than offset by an increase in its demand. As a result, the equilibrium price will
 (a) increase and the equilibrium quantity will decrease
 (b) increase and the equilibrium quantity will increase
 (c) decrease and the equilibrium quantity will decrease
 (d) decrease and the equilibrium quantity will increase

6. What will happen to the equilibrium quantity and price of a product in a competitive market when there is an equal increase in demand and supply?
 (a) equilibrium quantity and price will both increase
 (b) equilibrium quantity and price will both decrease
 (c) equilibrium quantity will increase and equilibrium price will stay the same
 (d) equilibrium quantity will stay the same and equilibrium price will increase

7. What will happen to the equilibrium quantity and price of a product in a competitive market when the decrease in demand exactly offsets the increase in supply?
 (a) equilibrium quantity will increase and equilibrium price will decrease

(b) equilibrium quantity will decrease and equilibrium price will increase

(c) equilibrium quantity will increase and equilibrium price will stay the same

(d) equilibrium quantity will stay the same and equilibrium price will decrease

8. Which of the following is a correct statement?
(a) price ceilings increase supply
(b) price ceilings create shortages
(c) price floors create shortages
(d) price floors increase demand

9. If a seller sets a price for a product that turns out to be below the equilibrium price, then there will be a
(a) shortage of the product
(b) surplus of the product
(c) price floor for a product
(d) a zero price for the product

10. A surplus means that
(a) demand for a product is greater than the supply
(b) supply of the product is greater than the demand
(c) quantity demanded is less than the quantity supplied at that price
(d) quantity demanded is greater than the quantity supplied at that price

Answer Questions 11, 12, and 13 based on the following graph showing the market supply and demand for a product.

Quantity (in thousands)

11. Given this market, if a seller pre-sets the price at $10, then this action results in a
(a) surplus of 10,000 units
(b) surplus of 80,000 units
(c) shortage of 10,000 units
(d) shortage of 80,000 units

12. Given this market, if a seller pre-sets the price at $30, then this action results in a
(a) surplus of 10,000 units
(b) surplus of 60,000 units
(c) surplus of 70,000 units
(d) shortage of 10,000 units

13. What price will eliminate a surplus or shortage in this market?
(a) $0
(b) $10
(c) $20
(d) $30

14. A market for tickets in which buyers bid for tickets held by initial purchasers rather than the original seller is a
(a) primary market
(b) secondary market
(c) pre-set market
(d) surplus market

15. What are resources called that are owned in common by society and available for the taking on public land?
(a) consumer surplus
(b) producer surplus
(c) nonpriced goods
(d) priced goods

16. A supply and demand graph of the "market" for buffalo in the pre-railroad era would show that
(a) quantity demanded equaled quantity supplied
(b) quantity demanded was greater than quantity supplied
(c) demand was less than supply, so there was a zero price
(d) supply was less than demand, so there was a zero price

17. A supply and demand graph of the "market" for buffalo in the post-railroad era would show that at a zero price
(a) the supply curve was horizontal
(b) the demand curve was vertical
(c) quantity demanded was less than quantity supplied
(d) quantity demanded was greater than quantity supplied

18. Why does government often ration the use of public resources such as fishing and hunting by using licenses and setting limits on quantities or seasons?
(a) to increase the supply of these nonpriced goods
(b) to increase the demand for these nonpriced goods
(c) to decrease the demand for these nonpriced goods
(d) to decrease the supply of these nonpriced goods

19. The difference between the maximum price a consumer is (or consumers are) willing to pay for a product and the actual price is consumer
(a) sovereignty
(b) demand
(c) surplus
(d) utility

20. Katie is willing to pay $50 for a product and Tom is willing to pay $40. The actual price that they have to pay is $30. What is the amount of the consumer surplus for Katie and Tom combined?
(a) $30
(b) $40
(c) $50
(d) $60

21. Given the demand curve, the consumer surplus is
(a) increased by higher prices and decreased by lower prices
(b) decreased by higher prices and increased by lower prices
(c) increased by higher prices but not affected by lower prices
(d) decreased by lower prices, but not affected by higher prices

22. The difference between the actual price that a producer receives (or producers receive) and the minimum acceptable price is producer
(a) cost
(b) wealth
(c) surplus
(d) investment

23. The minimum acceptable price for a product that Juan is willing to receive is $20. It is $15 for Carlos. The actual price they receive is $25. What is the amount of the producer surplus for Juan and Carlos combined?
(a) $10
(b) $15
(c) $20
(d) $25

24. When the combined consumer and producer surplus is at a maximum for a product,
(a) the quantity supplied is greater than the quantity demanded
(b) the market finds alternative ways to ration the product
(c) the market is allocatively efficient
(d) the product is a nonpriced good

25. When the output is greater than the optimal level of output for a product there are efficiency
(a) gains from the underproduction of the product
(b) losses from the underproduction of the product
(c) gains from the overproduction of the product
(d) losses from the overproduction of the product

■ **PROBLEMS**

1. The existing demand and supply schedules are given in columns 1, 2, and 3 of the following table.

Demand and Supply Schedules			New Demand and Supply Schedules		
(1)	(2)	(3)	(4)	(5)	(6)
Price	Quantity demanded	Quantity supplied	Price	Quantity demanded	Quantity supplied
$5.00	10	50	$5.00	____	____
4.00	20	40	4.00	____	____
3.00	30	30	3.00	____	____
2.00	40	20	2.00	____	____
1.00	50	10	1.00	____	____

a. Now the demand *increases* by 10 units at each price and supply *decreases* by 10 units. Enter the new

amounts for quantity demanded and quantity supplied in columns 5 and 6.

b. What was the old equilibrium price? _____

What will be the new equilibrium price? _____

c. What was the old equilibrium quantity? _____

What will be the new equilibrium quantity? _____

2. The demand and supply schedules for a certain product are those given in the following table. Answer the related questions.

Quantity demanded	Price	Quantity supplied
12,000	$10	18,000
13,000	9	17,000
14,000	8	16,000
15,000	7	15,000
16,000	6	14,000
17,000	5	13,000
18,000	4	12,000

a. The equilibrium price of the product is $_____

and the equilibrium quantity is _____.

b. If a seller established a pre-set price of $5 on this product, there would be a (shortage, surplus)

_____ of _____ units.

c. If a seller established a pre-set price of $8, there would be a (shortage, surplus) _____ of

_____ units.

3. Given the following information, calculate the consumer surplus for each individual A to F.

(1) Person	(2) Maximum price willing to pay	(3) Actual price (equilibrium price)	(4) Consumer surplus
A	$25	$12	$_____
B	23	12	_____
C	18	12	_____
D	16	12	_____
E	13	12	_____
F	12	12	_____

4. Given the following information, calculate the producer surplus for each producer A to F.

(1) Person	(2) Maximum acceptable price	(3) Actual price (equilibrium price)	(4) Producer surplus
A	$4	$12	$_____
B	5	12	_____
C	7	12	_____
D	9	12	_____
E	10	12	_____
F	12	12	_____

5. Answer this question based on the following graph showing the market supply and demand for a product. Assume that the output level is Q_1.

a. The area of consumer surplus would be shown by the area _____.

b. The area of producer surplus would be shown by the area _____.

c. The area that maximizes the combined consumer and producer surplus is _____.

d. If the output level is now Q_2, then there are efficiency losses shown by area _____.

e. If the output level is now Q_3, then there are efficiency losses shown by area _____.

■ **SHORT ANSWER AND ESSAY QUESTIONS**

1. Explain, using a supply and demand graph, how a freeze in a vegetable crop will affect the equilibrium price and quantity.

2. In a competitive market, if the supply of a product decreases and demand remains the same, what happens to the quantity demanded?

3. When there are single shifts in the supply or demand curve, you can predict the effects on both equilibrium price and quantity. When there are simultaneous shifts in demand and supply you can make only one prediction of the effects with any certainty. Why?

4. You observe that the equilibrium price has decreased and the equilibrium quantity has increased. What supply and demand conditions would best explain this outcome?

5. If the increase in the demand for gasoline outweighs the decrease in the supply of gasoline, what is the most likely effect on the equilibrium price and quantity? Explain and show your answer with a graph.

6. You observe that the equilibrium quantity has increased but the equilibrium price has stayed the same. What supply and demand conditions would best explain this outcome?

7. What are price ceilings and price floors?

8. What are the consequences if a seller sets a price below the actual equilibrium price?

9. Why do secondary markets arise? Give examples of such markets.

10. Explain, using a supply and demand graph, the situation that arises when there are many unsold tickets to an event. Why does this occur?

11. What are the differences in the characteristics of non-priced and market goods? Give examples of each type.

12. Discuss the plight of the American bison since the 1800s using supply and demand analysis. How did the conditions for the buffalo change from the pre-railroad era to the post-railroad era?

13. What rationing mechanisms are typically used by society to limit consumption of nonpriced goods?

14. Explain using an example how a nonpriced good could be converted to a positively priced good in a private market.

15. How is the consumer surplus related to utility or satisfaction? Explain, using a supply and demand graph.

16. What is the nature of the relationship between prices and consumer surplus?

17. Define, using a supply and demand graph, the meaning of producer surplus.

18. Compare and contrast the relationship between price and consumer surplus and price and producer surplus.

19. Explain the three conditions that exist when there is allocative efficiency.

20. Use consumer and producer surplus to describe efficiency losses in a competitive market. Provide a supply and demand graph to show such losses.

ANSWERS

Chapter 3 Web: Applications and Extensions of Supply and Demand Analysis

FILL-IN QUESTIONS

1. increases, decreases
2. increases, increases
3. decreases, increases
4. increases, increases
5. stays the same, increases
6. ceiling, floor
7. shortage, surplus
8. secondary, scalping
9. owned in common, public
10. surplus, shortage
11. over-, a decrease
12. licenses, limits
13. maximum, less
14. negatively, decrease, increase
15. minimum, more
16. positively, increase, decrease
17. productive, allocative

18. benefit, cost
19. equal to, equal to, maximum
20. losses, losses, less than
Note: Page numbers refer to Chapter 3 Web of the textbook that is available at www.mcconnell16.com.

TRUE–FALSE QUESTIONS

1. T, pp. 2–3	**8.** F, p. 5	**15.** F, p. 7	**22.** F, p. 10
2. F, p. 3	**9.** T, p. 5	**16.** T, p. 8	**23.** F, p. 10
3. T, p. 3	**10.** F, p. 5	**17.** F, p. 8	**24.** T, p. 10
4. T, pp. 3–4	**11.** T, pp. 5–6	**18.** T, pp. 8–9	**25.** F, pp. 10–11
5. F, p. 4	**12.** T, p. 7	**19.** F, p. 9	
6. F, pp. 4–5	**13.** F, pp. 7–8	**20.** F, p. 9	
7. T, p. 5	**14.** T, p. 7	**21.** T, p. 9	

MULTIPLE-CHOICE QUESTIONS

1. b, p. 2	**8.** b, p. 5	**15.** c, p. 7	**22.** c, pp. 9–10
2. b, pp. 2–3	**9.** a, p. 5	**16.** c, p. 7	**23.** b, p. 10
3. d, p. 3	**10.** c, p. 5	**17.** d, pp. 7–8	**24.** c, p. 11
4. d, pp. 3–4	**11.** c, p. 5	**18.** c, p. 8	**25.** d, pp. 11–12
5. b, p. 4	**12.** a, pp. 5–6	**19.** c, pp. 8–9	
6. c, pp. 4–5	**13.** c, pp. 5–6	**20.** a, p. 9	
7. d, pp. 4–5	**14.** b, p. 5	**21.** b, p. 9	

PROBLEMS

1. *a.* column 5 (quantity demanded): 20, 30, 40, 50, 60; column 6 (quantity supplied): 40, 30, 20, 10, 0; *b.* $3.00, $4.00; *c.* 30, 30
2. *a.* $7, 15,000; *b.* shortage, 4000; *c.* surplus, 2000
3. 13, 11, 6, 4, 1, 0
4. 8, 7, 5, 3, 2, 0
5. *a.* abc; *b.* 0ac; *c.* 0bc; *d.* efc; *e.* ghc

SHORT ANSWER AND ESSAY QUESTIONS

1. p. 2	**6.** pp. 4–5	**11.** p. 7	**16.** p. 9
2. p. 2	**7.** p. 5	**12.** pp. 7–8	**17.** p. 9
3. pp. 3–5	**8.** p. 5	**13.** p. 8	**18.** pp. 9–10
4. pp. 3–4	**9.** p. 5	**14.** p. 8	**19.** pp. 10–11
5. p. 4	**10.** p. 6	**15.** pp. 8–9	**20.** pp. 11–12

CHAPTER 4

The Market System

Chapter 4 describes the major characteristics of the market system and offers a detailed explanation of how it works. The first part describes the *ideological* and *institutional* characteristics of the market system. In this system, most of the resources are owned as private property by citizens, who are free to use them as they wish in their own self-interest. Prices and markets express the self-interests of resource owners, consumers, and business firms. Competition regulates self-interest—to prevent the self-interest of any person or any group from working to the disadvantage of the economy and to make self-interests work for the benefit of the entire economy. Government plays an active, but limited, role in a market economy.

Three other characteristics are also found in a market economy. They are the employment of large amounts of *capital goods,* the development of *specialization,* and the *use of money.* Economies use capital goods and engage in specialization because this is a more efficient use of their resources; it results in larger total output and the greater satisfaction of wants. When workers, business firms, and regions within an economy specialize, they become dependent on each other for the goods and services they do not produce for themselves and they must engage in trade. Trade is made more convenient by using money as a medium of exchange.

The second part of Chapter 4 describes the operation of the market system. There are *Four Fundamental Questions* that any economic system must answer in its attempt to use its scarce resources to satisfy its material wants. The four questions or problems are: (1) What will be produced? (2) How will the output be produced? (3) Who is to receive the output? (4) Can the system adapt to change?

The explanation of how the market system finds answers to the Four Fundamental Questions is only an approximation—a simplified version or model—of the methods actually employed by the U.S. economy and other market economies. Yet this simple model, like all good models, contains enough realism to be truthful and is general enough to be understandable. If the aims of this chapter are accomplished, you can begin to understand the market system and methods our economy uses to solve the economizing problem presented in Chapter 2.

■ CHECKLIST

When you have studied this chapter you should be able to

☐ Identify the nine important characteristics of the market system.

☐ Describe the significance of property rights in the market system.

☐ Distinguish between freedom of enterprise and freedom of choice.

☐ Explain why self-interest is a driving force of the market system.

☐ Identify two features of competition.

☐ Explain the roles of markets and prices.

☐ Explain why the market system relies on technology and capital goods, and also why the production of capital goods entails roundabout production.

☐ Discuss how two types of specialization improve efficiency in the market system.

☐ Describe the advantages of money over barter for the exchange of goods and services in a market economy.

☐ Describe the size and role of government in the market system.

☐ List the Four Fundamental Questions to answer about the operation of a market economy.

☐ Explain how a market system determines what goods and services will be produced.

☐ Distinguish between normal profit and economic profit.

☐ Predict what will happen to the price charged by and the output of an expanding and a declining industry, and explain why these events will occur.

☐ Explain how consumer sovereignty and dollar votes work in a market economy.

☐ Describe market restraints on economic freedom.

☐ Explain how goods and services will be produced in a market system.

☐ Find the least costly combination of resources needed for production when given the technological data and the prices of the resources.

☐ Explain how a market system determines who will get the goods and services it produces.

☐ Describe the guiding function of prices to accommodate change in the market system.

☐ Explain how the market system initiates change by fostering technological advances and capital accumulation.
☐ State how the "invisible hand" in the market system tends to promote public or social interests.
☐ List three virtues of the market system.

■ CHAPTER OUTLINE

1. The market system has the following nine characteristics:

a. Private individuals and organizations own and control their property resources by means of the institution of private property.

b. These individuals and organizations possess both the freedom of enterprise and the freedom of choice.

c. Each of them is motivated largely by self-interest.

d. Competition is based on the independent actions of buyers and sellers. They have the freedom to enter or leave markets. This competition spreads economic power and limits its potential abuse.

e. Markets and prices are used to communicate and coordinate the decisions of buyers and sellers.

f. The market system employs complicated and advanced methods of production, new technology, and large amounts of capital equipment to produce goods and services efficiently.

g. It is a highly specialized economy. Human and geographic specializations increase the productive efficiency of the economy.

h. It uses money exclusively to facilitate trade and specialization.

i. Government has an active but limited role.

2. The system of prices and markets and households' and business firms' choices furnish the market economy with answers to **Four Fundamental Questions.**

a. *What goods and services will be produced?* The demands of consumers for products and the desires of business firms to maximize their profits determine what and how much of each product is produced and its price.

b. *How will the goods and services be produced?* The desires of business firms to maximize profits by keeping their costs of production as low as possible guide them to use the most efficient techniques of production and determine their demands for various resources; competition forces them to use the most efficient techniques and ensures that only the most efficient will be able to stay in business.

c. *Who will get the goods and services that are produced?* With resource prices determined, the money income of each household is determined; and with product prices determined, the quantity of goods and services these money incomes will buy is determined.

d. *How will the market system accommodate change?* The market system is able to accommodate itself to changes in consumer tastes, technology, and resource supplies.

(1) The desires of business firms for maximum profits and competition lead the economy to make the appropriate adjustments in the way it uses its resources.

(2) Competition and the desire to increase profits promote better techniques of production and capital accumulation.

3. Competition in the economy compels firms seeking to promote their own interests to promote (as though led by an "invisible hand") the best interests of society as a whole.

a. Competition results in an allocation of resources appropriate to consumer wants, production by the most efficient means, and the lowest possible prices.

b. Three noteworthy merits of the market system are

(1) The *efficient* use of resources

(2) The *incentive* the system provides for productive activity

(3) The personal *freedom* allowed participants as consumers, producers, workers, or investors.

■ HINTS AND TIPS

1. The first section of the chapter describes nine characteristics and institutions of a market system. After reading the section, check your understanding by listing the nine points and writing a short explanation of each one.

2. The section on the "Market System at Work" is both the most important and the most difficult part of the chapter. A market economy must answer *Four Fundamental Questions*. Detailed answers to the four questions are given in this section of the chapter. If you examine each one individually and in the order in which it is presented, you will more easily understand how the market system works. (Actually, the market system finds the answers simultaneously, but make your learning easier for now by considering them one by one.)

3. Be sure to understand the *importance* and *role* of each of the following in the operation of the market system: (1) the guiding function of prices, (2) the profit motive of business firms, (3) the entry into and exodus of firms from industries, (4) the meaning of competition, and (5) consumer sovereignty.

■ IMPORTANT TERMS

private property	economic cost
freedom of choice	normal profit
freedom of enterprise	economic profit
self-interest	expanding industry
competition	declining industry
roundabout production	consumer sovereignty
specialization	dollar votes
division of labor	derived demand
medium of exchange	guiding function of prices
barter	creative destruction
money	"invisible hand"
Four Fundamental Questions	

SELF-TEST

■ FILL-IN QUESTIONS

1. The ownership of property resources by private individuals and organizations is the institution of private (resources, property) _____. The freedom of private businesses to obtain resources and use them to produce goods and services is the freedom of (choice, enterprise) _____, while the freedom to dispose of property or money as a person sees fit is the freedom of _____.

2. Self-interest means that each economic unit attempts to do what is best for itself, but this might lead to an abuse of power in a market economy if it were not directed and constrained by (government, competition) _____. Self-interest and selfishness (are, are not) _____ the same thing in a market economy.

3. Broadly defined, competition is present if two conditions prevail; these two conditions are

a. _____

_____

b. _____

_____

4. In a capitalist economy, individual buyers communicate their demands and individual sellers communicate their supplies in the system of (markets, prices) _____, and the outcomes from economic decisions are a set of product and resource _____ that are determined by demand and supply.

5. Market economies make extensive use of capital goods and engage in roundabout production because it is more (efficient, inefficient) _____ than direct production; they practice specialization and the division of labor because the self-sufficient producer or worker tends to be an _____ one.

6. In market economies money functions chiefly as a medium of (commerce, exchange) _____. Barter between two individuals will take place only if there is a coincidence of (resources, wants) _____.

7. In a market system, government is active, but is assigned (a limited, an extensive) _____ role.

8. List the Four Fundamental Questions every economy must answer.

a. _____

b. _____

c. _____

d. _____

9. A *normal profit* (is, is not) _____ an economic cost because it is a payment that (must, need not) _____ be paid to (workers, entrepreneurs) _____, but an *economic profit* (is, is not) _____ an economic cost because it (must, need not) _____ be paid to them to secure and retain the resources needed by the firm.

10. Pure or economic profit is equal to the total (revenue, cost) _____ of a firm less its total _____.

11. Business firms tend to produce those products from which they can obtain at least a(n) (economic, normal) _____ profit and a maximum _____ profit.

12. If firms in an industry are obtaining economic profits, firms will (enter, leave) _____ the industry; the price of the industry's product will (rise, fall) _____; the industry will employ (more, fewer) _____ resources and produce a (larger, smaller) _____ output; and the industry's economic profits will (increase, decrease) _____ until they are equal to (zero, infinity) _____.

13. Consumers vote with their dollars for the production of a good or service when they (sell, buy) _____ it, and because of this, consumers are said to be (dependent, sovereign) _____ in a market economy. The buying decisions of consumers (restrain, expand) _____ the freedom of firms and resource suppliers.

14. Firms are interested in obtaining the largest economic profits possible, so they try to produce a product in the (most, least) _____ costly way. The most efficient production techniques depend on the available (income, technology) _____ and the (prices, quotas) _____ of needed resources.

15. The market system determines how the total output of the economy will be distributed among its households by determining the (incomes, expenditures) _____ of each household and by determining the (prices, quality) _____ for each good and service produced.

16. In market economies, change is almost continuous in consumer (preferences, resources)

_____, in the supplies of _____, and in technology. To make the appropriate adjustments to these changes, a market economy allows price to perform its (monopoly, guiding) _____ function.

17. The market system fosters technological change. The incentive for a firm to be the first to use a new and improved technique of production or to produce a new and better product is a greater economic (profit, loss) _____, and the incentive for other firms to follow its lead is the avoidance of _____.

18. Technological advance will require additional (capital, consumer) _____ goods, so the entrepreneur uses profit obtained from the sale of _____ goods to acquire (capital, consumer) _____ goods.

19. A market system promotes (unity, disunity) _____ between private and public interests. Firms and resource suppliers seem to be guided by (a visible, an invisible) _____ hand to allocate the economy's resources efficiently.

20. The two *economic* arguments for a market system are that it promotes (public, efficient) _____ use of resources and that it uses (incentives, government) _____ for directing economic activity. The major *noneconomic* argument for the market system is that it allows for personal (wealth, freedom) _____.

■ **TRUE–FALSE QUESTIONS**

Circle T if the statement is true, F if it is false.

1. In a market system, the government owns most of the property resources (land and capital). **T F**

2. Property rights encourage investment, innovation, exchange, maintenance of property, and economic growth. **T F**

3. The freedom of business firms to produce a particular consumer good is always limited by the desires of consumers for that good. **T F**

4. The pursuit of economic self-interest is the same thing as selfishness. **T F**

5. When a market is competitive, the individual sellers of a product are unable to reduce the supply of the product and control its price. **T F**

6. The market system is an organizing mechanism and also a communication network. **T F**

7. The employment of capital to produce goods and services requires that there be "roundabout" production and it is more efficient than "direct" production. **T F**

8. Increasing the amount of specialization in an economy generally leads to the more efficient use of its resources. **T F**

9. One way human specialization can be achieved is through a division of labor in productive activity. **T F**

10. Money is a device for facilitating the exchange of goods and services. **T F**

11. "Coincidence of wants" means that two persons want to acquire the same good or service. **T F**

12. Shells may serve as money if sellers are generally willing to accept them as money. **T F**

13. One of the Four Fundamental Questions is who will control the output. **T F**

14. Business firms try to maximize their normal profits. **T F**

15. Industries in which economic profits are earned by the firms in the industry will attract the entry of new firms. **T F**

16. If firms have sufficient time to enter industries, the economic profits of an industry will tend to disappear. **T F**

17. Business firms are only free to produce whatever they want in any way they wish if they do not want to maximize profits or to minimize losses. **T F**

18. The derived demand of a resource depends on the demands for the products the resource produces. **T F**

19. Resources will tend to be used in those industries capable of earning normal or economic profits. **T F**

20. Economic efficiency requires that a given output of a good or service be produced in the least costly way. **T F**

21. If the market price of resource A decreases, firms will tend to employ smaller quantities of resource A. **T F**

22. Changes in the tastes of consumers are reflected in changes in consumer demand for products. **T F**

23. The incentive that the market system provides to induce technological improvement is the opportunity for economic profits. **T F**

24. The tendency for individuals pursuing their own self-interests to bring about results that are in the best interest of society as a whole is often called the "invisible hand." **T F**

25. A basic economic argument for the market system is that it promotes an efficient use of resources. **T F**

■ **MULTIPLE-CHOICE QUESTIONS**

Circle the letter that corresponds to the best answer.

1. Which is one of the main characteristics of the market system?
  (a) central economic planning

(b) limits on freedom of choice

(c) the right to own private property

(d) an expanded role for government in the economy

2. In the market system, freedom of enterprise means that

(a) businesses are free to produce products that consumers want

(b) consumers are free to buy goods and services that they want

(c) resources are distributed freely to businesses that want them

(d) government is free to direct the actions of businesses

3. The maximization of profit tends to be the driving force in the economic decision making of

(a) entrepreneurs

(b) workers

(c) consumers

(d) legislators

4. How do consumers typically express self-interest?

(a) by minimizing their economic losses

(b) by maximizing their economic profits

(c) by seeking the lowest price for a product

(d) by seeking jobs with the highest wages and benefits

5. Which is a characteristic of competition as economists see it?

(a) a few sellers of all products

(b) the widespread diffusion of economic power

(c) a small number of buyers in product markets

(d) the relatively difficult entry into and exit from industries by producers

6. To decide how to use its scarce resources to satisfy economic wants, capitalism relies on

(a) central planning

(b) monopoly power

(c) markets and prices

(d) command and control

7. The market system is a method of

(a) communicating and coordinating the decisions of consumers, producers, and resource suppliers

(b) making economic decisions by central planning

(c) promoting productive efficiency, but not allocative efficiency

(d) promoting allocative efficiency, but not productive efficiency

8. What is roundabout production?

(a) the division of labor that results from specialization in the production of a good or service

(b) the production and use of capital goods to help make consumer goods

(c) the production of a good and service and the payment for it with money

(d) the production of a consumer good and its sale to consumers

9. When workers specialize in various tasks to produce a commodity, the situation is referred to as

(a) a coincidence of wants

(b) roundabout production

(c) freedom of choice

(d) division of labor

10. In what way does human specialization contribute to an economy's output?

(a) It serves as consumer sovereignty.

(b) It is a process of creative destruction.

(c) It acts like an "invisible hand."

(d) It fosters learning by doing.

11. Which is a prerequisite of specialization?

(a) having a convenient means of exchanging goods

(b) letting government create a plan for the economy

(c) deciding who will get the goods and services in an economy

(d) market restraints on freedom

12. In the market system, the role of government is best described as

(a) nonexistent

(b) significant

(c) extensive

(d) limited

13. Which best defines economic costs?

(a) the difference between economic profit and normal profit

(b) total payments made to secure and retain needed resources

(c) the demand for resources minus the supply of resources

(d) the total revenue plus the total losses of the firm

14. If a business's total economic cost of producing 10,000 units of a product is $750,000 and this output is sold to consumers for $1,000,000, then the firm would earn

(a) a normal profit of $750,000

(b) an economic profit of $750,000

(c) an economic profit of $250,000

(d) a normal profit of $1,750,000

15. If less-than-normal profits are being earned by the firms in an industry, the consequences will be that

(a) lower-priced resources will be drawn into the industry

(b) firms will leave the industry, causing the price of the industry's product to fall

(c) firms will leave the industry, causing the price of the industry's product to rise

(d) the price of the industry's product will fall and thereby cause the demand for the product to increase

16. Which would necessarily result, sooner or later, from a decrease in consumer demand for a product?

(a) a decrease in the profits of firms in the industry

(b) an increase in the output of the industry

(c) an increase in the supply of the product

(d) an increase in the prices of resources employed by the firms in the industry

17. The demand for resources is
  (a) increased when the price of resources falls
  (b) most influenced by the size of government in a capitalist economy
  (c) derived from the demand for the products made with the resources
  (d) decreased when the product that the resources produce becomes popular

Answer Questions 18, 19, and 20 on the basis of the following information.

Suppose 50 units of product X can be produced by employing just labor and capital in the four ways shown below. Assume the prices of labor and capital are $5 and $4, respectively.

	A	B	C	D
Labor	1	2	3	4
Capital	5	3	2	1

18. Which technique is economically most efficient in producing product X?
  (a) A
  (b) B
  (c) C
  (d) D

19. If the price of product X is $1, the firm will realize
  (a) an economic profit of $28
  (b) an economic profit of $27
  (c) an economic profit of $26
  (d) an economic profit of $25

20. Now assume that the price of labor falls to $3 and the price of capital rises to $5. Which technique is economically most efficient in producing product X?
  (a) A
  (b) B
  (c) C
  (d) D

21. Which is the primary factor determining the share of the total output of the economy received by a household?
  (a) the tastes of the household
  (b) the medium of exchange used by the household
  (c) the prices at which the household sells its resources
  (d) ethical considerations in the operation of a market economy

22. If an increase in the demand for a product and a rise in its price cause an increase in the quantity supplied, the size of the industry, and the resources used for production, price is successfully performing its
  (a) guiding function
  (b) roundabout function
  (c) division-of-labor function
  (d) medium-of-exchange function

23. The advent of personal computers and word processing software that eliminated the market for electric typewriters would be an example of

  (a) creative destruction
  (b) the "invisible hand"
  (c) derived demand
  (d) specialization

24. In the market system, if one firm introduces a new and better method of production that enhances the firm's economic profits, other firms will be forced to adopt the new method to
  (a) increase derived demand
  (b) follow rules for roundabout production
  (c) avoid economic losses or bankruptcy
  (d) specialize and divide the labor in an efficient way

25. The chief economic virtue of the competitive market system is that it
  (a) allows extensive personal freedom
  (b) efficiently allocates resources
  (c) provides an equitable distribution of income
  (d) eliminates the need for decision making

■ **PROBLEMS**

1. Use the appropriate number to match the term with the phrase.

1. **invisible hand**	5. **consumer sovereignty**
2. **coincidence of wants**	6. **derived demand**
3. **division of labor**	7. **specialization**
4. **guiding function of prices**	8. **roundabout production**

a. The construction and use of capital goods to aid in the production of consumer goods. _____

b. The ability of price changes to bring about changes in the quantities of products and resources demanded and supplied. _____

c. Using the resources of an individual, a firm, a region, or a nation to produce one (or a few) goods and services. _____

d. The tendency of firms and resource suppliers seeking to further their own self-interest while also promoting the interests of society in a market economy. _____

e. The demand for a resource that depends on the demand for the product it can be used to produce. _____

f. Splitting the work required to produce a product into a number of different tasks that are performed by different workers. _____

g. A situation in which the product the first trader wants to sell is the same as that the second trader wants to buy, and the product the second trader wants to sell is the same as the product the first trader wants to buy. _____

h. Determination by consumers of the types and quantities of goods and services that will be produced in a market economy. _____

2. Assume that a firm can produce product A, product B, *or* product C with the resources it currently employs.

These resources cost the firm a total of $50 per week. Assume, for the purposes of the problem, that the firm's employment of resources cannot be changed. Their market prices, and the quantities of A, B, and C these resources will produce per week are given below. Compute the firm's profit when it produces A, B, or C, and enter these profits in the table below.

Product	Market price	Output	Economic profit
A	$7.00	8	$_____
B	4.50	10	_____
C	.25	240	_____

a. Which product will the firm produce? _____

b. If the price of A rose to $8, the firm would _____

_____

(Hint: You will have to recompute the firm's profit from the production of A.)

c. If the firm were producing A and selling it at a price of $8, what would tend to happen to the number of

firms producing A? _____

_____

3. Suppose that a firm can produce 100 units of product X by combining labor, land, capital, and entrepreneurial ability in three different ways. If it can hire labor at $2 per unit, land at $3 per unit, capital at $5 per unit, and entrepreneurship at $10 per unit, and if the amounts of the resources required by the three methods of producing 100 units of product X are indicated in the table, answer the following questions.

Resource	Method 1	Method 2	Method 3
Labor	8	13	10
Land	4	3	3
Capital	4	2	4
Entrepreneurship	1	1	1

a. Which method is the least expensive way of producing 100 units of X? _____

b. If X sells for 70 cents per unit, what is the economic profit of the firm? $_____

c. If the price of labor should rise from $2 to $3 per unit and if the price of X is 70 cents,

(1) the firm's use of

labor would change from _____ to _____

land would change from _____ to _____

capital would change from _____ to _____
entrepreneurship would not change
(2) the firm's economic profit would change from

$_____ to $_____

■ SHORT ANSWER AND ESSAY QUESTIONS

1. Explain the major characteristics — institutions and assumptions — embodied in a market system.

2. What do each of the following seek if they pursue their own self-interest: consumers, resource owners, and business firms?

3. Explain what economists mean by competition. For a market to be competitive, why is it important that there be buyers and sellers and easy entry and exit?

4. What are the advantages of indirect or roundabout production?

5. How does an economy benefit from specialization and the division of labor?

6. Give an example of how specialization can benefit two separate and diversely endowed geographic regions.

7. What is money? What important function does it perform? Explain how money performs this function and how it overcomes the disadvantages associated with barter.

8. For an item to be useful as money, what is its necessary major characteristic? Can you think of other characteristics that might be favorable?

9. What are the Four Fundamental Questions?

10. In what way do the desires of entrepreneurs to obtain economic profits and avoid losses make consumer sovereignty effective?

11. Why is the ability of firms to enter industries that are prosperous important to the effective functioning of competition?

12. Explain in detail how an increase in the consumer demand for a product will result in more of the product being produced and more resources being allocated to its production.

13. To what extent are firms "free" to produce what they wish by methods that they choose? Do resource owners have freedom to use their resources as they wish?

14. How can the market system adapt to change? How is it done?

15. What is the guiding function of price? Explain how it works.

16. Explain how the market system provides a strong incentive for technological advance.

17. What is "creative destruction"? Give some examples of it.

18. Who "votes" for the production of capital goods, why do they "vote" for capital goods production, and where do they obtain the dollars needed to cast these "votes"?

19. An "invisible hand operates to identify private and public interests." What are private interests and what is the public interest? What is it that leads the economy to operate as if it were directed by an invisible hand?

20. Describe three virtues of the market system.

ANSWERS

Chapter 4 The Market System

FILL-IN QUESTIONS

1. property, enterprise, choice
2. competition, are not
3. *a.* independently acting buyers and sellers operating in markets; *b.* freedom of buyers and sellers to enter or leave these markets
4. markets, prices
5. efficient, inefficient
6. exchange, wants
7. a limited
8. *a.* What goods and services will be produced? *b.* How will the goods and services be produced? *c.* Who will get the goods and services? *d.* How will the system accommodate change?
9. is, must, entrepreneurs, is not, need not
10. revenue, cost
11. normal, economic
12. enter, fall, more, larger, decrease, zero
13. buy, sovereign, restrain
14. least, technology, prices
15. incomes, prices
16. preferences, resources, guiding
17. profit, losses
18. capital, consumer, capital
19. unity, an invisible
20. efficient, incentives, freedom

TRUE–FALSE QUESTIONS

1. F, p. 60	8. T, p. 63	15. T, pp. 65–66
2. T, p. 60	9. T, p. 63	16. T, pp. 65–66
3. T, p. 61	10. T, pp. 63–64	17. T, pp. 66–67
4. F, p. 61	11. F, p. 63	18. T, pp. 66–67
5. T, p. 62	12. T, pp. 63–64	19. T, pp. 66–67
6. T, p. 62	13. F, p. 65	20. T, p. 67
7. T, pp. 62–63	14. F, p. 65	21. F, pp. 67–68
22. T, pp. 67–68		
23. T, pp. 68–69		
24. T, p. 69		
25. T, p. 69		

MULTIPLE-CHOICE QUESTIONS

1. c, p. 60	8. b, p. 63	15. c, p. 66	22. a, p. 68
2. a, p. 61	9. d, p. 63	16. a, p. 66	23. a, pp. 68–69
3. a, p. 61	10. d, p. 63	17. c, pp. 66–67	24. c, pp. 68–69
4. c, p. 61	11. a, p. 63	18. b, p. 67	25. b, p. 69
5. b, p. 62	12. d, p. 64	19. a, pp. 65; 67	
6. c, p. 62	13. b, p. 65	20. d, p. 67	
7. a, p. 62	14. c, p. 65	21. c, pp. 67–68	

PROBLEMS

1. *a.* 8; *b.* 4; *c.* 7; *d.* 1; *e.* 6; *f.* 3; *g.* 2; *h.* 5
2. $6, −$5, $10; *a.* C; *b.* produce A and have an economic profit of $14; *c.* it would increase
3. *a.* method 2; *b.* 15; *c.* (1) 13, 8; 3, 4; 2, 4; (2) 15, 4

SHORT ANSWER AND ESSAY QUESTIONS

1. pp. 60–64	6. p. 63	11. pp. 65–66	16. pp. 68–69
2. p. 61	7. pp. 63–64	12. p. 66	17. pp. 68–69
3. p. 62	8. pp. 63–64	13. pp. 66–67	18. p. 69
4. pp. 62–63	9. p. 65	14. pp. 68–69	19. p. 69
5. p. 63	10. pp. 65–66	15. p. 68	20. p. 69

CHAPTER 5

The U.S. Economy: Private and Public Sectors

The U.S. economy is divided into a private sector and a public sector. The first half of Chapter 5 discusses the private sector—the characteristics of millions of households and business firms. The second half of Chapter 5 describes the public sector—the functions and financing of the Federal, state, and local governments. Learning about these two sectors will give you the basic facts and framework you need for understanding the U.S. economy.

Chapter 5 begins with an examination of the **households** of the economy. Two different distributions of household income are examined. The way in which the total personal income received by all U.S. households is divided among the five types of earned income is called the *functional distribution of income*. The way in which the total personal income received by all households is distributed among the various income classes is called the *personal distribution of income*. Households dispose of the income they receive by spending money on *personal consumption expenditures*, paying *personal taxes*, or allocating funds to *personal saving*.

Businesses in the United States are also a focus of the chapter. It is apparent that what most characterizes U.S. businesses is the differences among firms in size and legal form, as well as in the products they produce. You should note the distinctions between a *proprietorship*, a *partnership*, and a *corporation* and the major advantages and disadvantages of each business form. You will also learn about the principal–agent problem with corporations that can arise from the separation of ownership (the principals) and management (the agents).

Chapter 5 also introduces you to the five basic functions performed by the **government** in the U.S. economy. The chapter does not attempt to list all the specific ways in which government affects the behavior of the economy: Instead, it provides a general classification of the five functions that government performs.

The chapter also returns to the **circular flow model** first presented in Chapter 2. The model has now been modified to include government along with business and household sectors. This addition changes the real and monetary flows in the model.

The facts of **government finance** in the United States are presented in the final sections of Chapter 5. The organization of the discussion is relatively simple. First, the trends for taxes collected and expenditures made by all levels of government—Federal, state, and local—are examined. Second, an explanation is given for the major items on which the Federal government spends its income, the principal taxes it levies to obtain its income,

and the relative importance of these taxes. Third, the chapter closes with a look at the major expenditures and taxes of the state and local governments.

■ CHECKLIST

When you have studied this chapter you should be able to

☐ Define and distinguish between a functional and a personal distribution of income.
☐ State the five sources of personal income in the functional distribution.
☐ List the three uses to which households put their personal incomes and state the relative size of each.
☐ Distinguish among durable goods, nondurable goods, and services in personal consumption expenditures.
☐ Give definitions for a plant, a firm, and an industry.
☐ List the three legal forms of business enterprise.
☐ Report the relative importance of each of the legal forms of business enterprise in the U.S. economy.
☐ State the advantages and disadvantages of the three legal forms of business enterprise.
☐ Identify two hybrid structures for corporations.
☐ Explain the principal–agent problem as it applies to corporations.
☐ List the five economic functions of government in the United States.
☐ Give examples of how government provides the legal framework for the economy.
☐ Define monopoly and explain why government wishes to prevent monopoly and to maintain competition in the economy.
☐ Explain why government redistributes income and list the three principal policies it uses for this purpose.
☐ Define spillover cost and spillover benefit.
☐ Explain why a competitive market fails to allocate resources efficiently when there are spillover costs and benefits.
☐ List two actions government can take to reduce spillover costs.
☐ List three actions government can take to encourage spillover benefits.
☐ Give definitions of a public good and a quasi-public good.
☐ Explain how the government reallocates resources from the production of private goods to the production of public or quasi-public goods.
☐ Describe the stabilization role of government and the two main economic problems it is designed to address.

☐ Explain the qualifications to government's role in the economy.

☐ Draw the circular flow model that includes businesses, households, and government, labeling all the flows and illustrating the role of government.

☐ Explain the difference between government purchases and transfer payments and the effect of each on the composition of national output.

☐ Identify the four largest categories of Federal expenditures.

☐ List the three main sources of Federal tax revenues.

☐ Define and explain the differences between marginal and average tax rates.

☐ Identify the major expenditures by state and local governments.

☐ Describe how state and local governments raise tax revenue.

■ CHAPTER OUTLINE

1. *Households* play a dual role in the economy. They supply the economy with resources, and they purchase the greatest share of the goods and services produced by the economy. They obtain their personal incomes in exchange for the resources they furnish the economy and from the transfer payments they receive from government.

   a. The *functional distribution of income* indicates the way in which total personal income is divided among the five sources of earned income (wages and salaries, proprietors' income, corporate profits, interest, and rents).

   b. The *personal distribution of income* indicates the way in which total personal income is divided among households in different income classes.

2. Households use their incomes to purchase consumer goods, pay taxes, and accumulate savings.

   a. *Personal taxes* constitute a deduction from a household's personal income; what remains after taxes can be either saved or spent.

   b. *Saving* is what a household does not spend of its after-tax income.

   c. Households make *personal consumption expenditures* for durable goods, nondurable goods, and services.

3. The *businesses* of the U.S. economy consist of three major types of entities. A *plant* is a physical structure that produces a product. A *business firm* is an organization that owns and operates plants. (Multiplant firms may be horizontally or vertically integrated, or they may be conglomerates.) An *industry* is a group of firms producing the same or similar goods or services.

4. The three principal *legal forms* of business firms are the *proprietorship, partnership,* and *corporation.*

   a. Each has special characteristics and advantages and disadvantages.

   (1) The *proprietorship* is easy to form, lets the owner be boss, and allows for great freedom. Disadvantages are lack of access to large amounts of financial capital, difficulty of managerial specialization, and the owner's *unlimited liability.*

   (2) The *partnership* is also easy to form and allows for more access to financial capital and permits more managerial specialization. Potential disadvantages are that partners may disagree, there are still limits to financial capital or managerial specialization, continuity of the firm over time is a problem, and partners face unlimited liability.

   (3) The *corporation* can raise financial capital through the sale of stocks and bonds, has *limited liability* for owners, can become large in size, and has an independent life. Chief disadvantages of the corporation are the double taxation of some corporate income, potential for abuse of this legal entity, and legal or regulatory expenses.

   (4) There are also "hybrid" business structures such as the *limited liability company* (LLC) or the *S corporation* that give the advantage of corporations to one or relatively few owners.

   b. Large corporations are a major feature of the U.S. economy. They are also subject to a *principal–agent problem* that arises from the separation of ownership (by stockholders) and control (by corporate executives). This problem can sometimes be overcome by aligning the interests of executives with those of stockholders through stock payment plans.

5. *Government* performs five economic functions.

   a. The first of these functions is to provide the **legal framework and services** that contribute to the effective operation of the market economy.

   b. The second function of government is to **maintain competition** and the control of *monopoly* through regulation and antitrust laws.

   c. Government performs its third function when it **redistributes income** to reduce income inequality. The policies and programs it uses to achieve this objective are transfer payments, market interventions (changing market prices), and taxation.

   d. When government **reallocates resources** it performs its fourth function.

   (1) It reallocates resources to take into account spillovers or externalities.

      (a) Spillover costs are production or consumption costs paid for by a third party without compensation.

      (b) Spillover costs can be discouraged by legislation or specific taxes.

      (c) Spillover benefits are outcomes that benefit third parties without these parties paying for the benefits.

      (d) Spillover benefits can be encouraged by subsidizing consumers, subsidizing producers, or by having government provide the goods (when the benefits are extremely large).

   (2) Government also provides public goods. These goods have the characteristic of *nonrivalry* (benefits are not reduced by consumption) and *nonexcludability* (people cannot be excluded from the benefits).

   (3) Quasi-public goods (e.g., education) are divisible and subject to the exclusion principle, but they often have large spillover benefits, so they are provided by government.

(4) Government levies taxes and uses tax revenues to reallocate income and resources from private uses to public ones (for providing public and quasi-public goods).

e. The fifth function of government is *stabilization* of the economy by controlling inflation and reducing unemployment.

f. The economic role of government is conducted in the context of politics. This process can lead to imperfect and inefficient outcomes.

6. *A circular flow model* that includes the public sector as well as business firms and households in the private sector of the economy reveals that government purchases public goods from private businesses, collects taxes from and makes transfer payments to these firms, purchases labor services from households, collects taxes from and makes transfer payments to these households, and can alter the distribution of income, reallocate resources, and change the level of economic activity by affecting the real and monetary flows in the diagram.

7. *Government finance* is important in the economy. Government spending consists of *purchases* of goods and services and *transfer payments,* but they have different effects on the economy. Purchases are exhaustive because they directly use the economy's resources, while transfers are nonexhaustive. Total government spending is equal to about one-third of domestic output.

8. For the *Federal government,*

a. most spending goes for pensions and income security, national defense, health care, or interest on the public debt.

b. the major sources of revenue are personal income taxes, payroll taxes, and corporate income taxes.

9. For other levels of government,

a. *state governments* depend largely on sales, excise, and personal income taxes, and they spend their revenues on public welfare, education, health care, and highways.

b. *local governments* rely heavily on property taxes; they spend much of the revenue on education.

■ HINTS AND TIPS

1. This chapter is a long one, so do not try to learn everything at once. Break the chapter into its three natural parts and work on each one separately. The first part describes features of the private sector. The second part explains the functions of government. The third part looks at government finance.

2. There are many descriptive statistics about the private and public sectors. Avoid memorizing these statistics. Instead, look for the trends and generalizations that these statistics illustrate about the private or public sector. For example, the discussion of government finance describes recent trends in government expenditures and taxes and indicates the relative importance of taxes and expenditures at each level of government.

■ IMPORTANT TERMS

functional distribution of income

personal distribution of income

personal taxes

personal saving

personal consumption expenditures

durable good

nondurable good

services

plant

firm

industry

sole proprietorship

partnership

corporation

stocks

bonds

limited liability

double taxation

principal–agent problem

monopoly

spillover costs

spillover benefits

public goods

free-rider problem

quasi-public goods

government purchases

transfer payment

personal income tax

marginal tax rate

average tax rate

payroll tax

corporate income tax

sales tax

excise tax

property tax

SELF-TEST

■ FILL-IN QUESTIONS

1. There are approximately 109 million (businesses, households) _____ in the United States. They play a dual role in the economy because they (sell, buy) _____ their resources and _____ most of the total output of the economy.

2. The largest single source of income in the United States is (corporate profits, wages and salaries) _____. It is equal to about (30, 70) _____% of total income.

3. In the United States the poorest (1, 20) _____% of all families receive about 4% of total personal income, and the richest (1, 20) _____% of these families receive about 50% of total personal income.

4. The total income of households is disposed of in three ways: personal _____, personal _____, and personal _____.

5. Households use about 13% of their total income to pay for personal (taxes, consumption expenditures) _____ and about 84% for personal _____.

6. If a product has an expected life of 3 years or more it is a (durable, nondurable) _____ good, whereas if it has an expected life of less than 3 years it is a _____ good.

7. There are millions of business (firms, industries) _____ in the United States. The legal form of the great majority of them is the (sole proprietorship, partnership, corporation) _____, but the legal form that produces almost 90% of the sales of the U.S. economy is the _____.

8. Shares of ownership of corporations are called (stocks, bonds) _____, whereas promises by corporations to repay a loan, usually at a fixed rate of interest, are _____.

9. The liabilities of a sole proprietor and of partners are (limited, unlimited) _____, but the liabilities of stockholders in a corporation are _____.

10. The separation of ownership and control in a corporation may create a (free-rider, principal–agent) _____ problem. In this case, stockholders would be the (riders, principals, agents) _____ and managers would be the _____.

11. List the five economic functions of government.

a. _____

b. _____

c. _____

d. _____

e. _____

12. To control monopoly, the U.S. government has created commissions to (tax, regulate) _____ natural monopolies, and in cases at the local level, government has become an (agent, owner) _____. Government has also enacted (trust, antitrust) _____ laws to maintain competition.

13. The market system, because it is an impersonal mechanism, results in an (equal, unequal) _____ distribution of income. To redistribute income from the upper- to the lower-income groups, the government has provided (transfer, tax) _____ payments, engaged in (military, market) _____ intervention, and used the (income, sales) _____ tax to raise much of its revenues.

14. Government frequently reallocates resources when it finds instances of (market, public) _____ failure. The two major cases of such failure occur when the competitive market system either

a. _____ ;

b. _____

_____

15. Competitive markets bring about an efficient allocation of resources only if there are no (private, spillover) _____ costs or benefits in the consumption and production of a good or service.

16. There is an externality whenever some of the costs of producing a product accrue to people other than the (seller, buyer) _____ or some of the benefits from consuming a product accrue to people other than the _____.

17. a. What two things can government do to make the market reflect spillover costs?

(1) _____

(2) _____

b. What three things can government do to make the market reflect spillover benefits?

(1) _____

(2) _____

(3) _____

18. One characteristic of a public good is (rivalry, nonrivalry) _____ and the other characteristic of a public good is (excludability, nonexcludability) _____. A private firm will not find it profitable to produce a public good because there is a (free-rider, principal–agent) _____ problem.

19. To reallocate resources from the production of private to the production of public and quasi-public goods, government reduces the demand for private goods by (taxing, subsidizing) _____ consumers and then uses the (profits, tax revenue) _____ to buy public or quasi-public goods.

20. To stabilize the economy with less than full employment, government may try to increase total spending by (increasing, decreasing) _____ its expenditures for public goods and services by (increasing, decreasing) _____ taxes, or by (raising, lowering) _____ interest rates. When there are inflationary pressures, the government may try to decrease total spending by (decreasing, increasing) _____ its expenditures for public goods and services, by _____ taxes, or by (raising, lowering) _____ interest rates.

21. An examination of government finance reveals that **a.** since 1960 government *purchases* of goods and services as a percentage of total output (increased, decreased) _____,

b. but government *transfer payments* as a percentage of domestic output since 1960 has (increased, decreased) _____,

c. and the tax revenues required to finance total government spending (purchases plus transfer payments) are today about (30, 70) _____% of domestic output.

d. Government transfer payments are (exhaustive, nonexhaustive) _____, whereas government purchases of goods and services are _____ because they absorb resources.

22. The most important source of revenue for the Federal government is the (personal income, payroll) _____ tax; next in importance is the _____ tax. The three largest categories of Federal expenditures ranked by budget size are (health, national defense, pensions and income security) _____, _____, and _____.

23. Federal income tax rates are progressive, which means that people with (lower, higher) _____ incomes pay a larger percentage of that income as taxes than do persons with _____ incomes. The tax rate paid on an additional unit of income is the (average, marginal) _____ tax rate, while the total tax paid divided by the total taxable income is the _____ tax rate.

24. Many state governments rely primarily on (property, sales and excise) _____ taxes and (personal, corporate) _____ income taxes for their revenue, which they spend mostly on (national defense, public welfare) _____ and (interest, education) _____.

25. At local levels of government the single most important source of revenue is the (income, property) _____ tax and the single most important expenditure is for (public safety, education) _____.

■ **TRUE–FALSE QUESTIONS**

Circle T if the statement is true, F if it is false.

1. The personal distribution of income describes the manner in which society's total personal income is divided among wages and salaries, corporate profits, proprietors' income, interest, and rents.　**T　F**

2. Personal taxes have risen in relative terms since World War II.　**T　F**

3. Most of the personal saving in the U.S. economy is done by those households in the top 10% of its income receivers.　**T　F**

4. *Dissaving* means that personal consumption expenditures exceed after-tax income.　**T　F**

5. A durable good is defined as a good that has an expected life of 3 years or more.　**T　F**

6. A plant is defined as a group of firms under a single management.　**T　F**

7. An industry is a group of firms that produce the same or nearly the same products.　**T　F**

8. Limited liability refers to the fact that all members of a partnership are liable for the debts incurred by one another.　**T　F**

9. The corporate form of organization is the least used by firms in the United States.　**T　F**

10. The corporation in the United States has a tax advantage over other legal forms of business organization.　**T　F**

11. Whether a business firm should incorporate or not depends chiefly on the amount of money capital it must have to finance the enterprise.　**T　F**

12. A limited liability company is like an ordinary partnership for tax purposes, but like a corporation in matters of liability.　**T　F**

13. Bonds are shares of ownership in a corporation.　**T　F**

14. When the interests of the principals are the same as those of agents, there is a free-rider problem.　**T　F**

15. When the Federal government provides for a monetary system, it is doing so primarily to maintain competition.　**T　F**

16. Transfer payments are one means government uses to redistribute income.　**T　F**

17. If demand and supply reflected all the benefits and costs of producing a product, there would be efficient resource use.　**T　F**

18. When there are spillover costs, more resources are allocated to the production of the product and more is produced than is efficient.　**T　F**

19. One way for government to correct for spillover costs from a product is to increase its demand.　**T　F**

20. When there are spillover benefits from a product, there will be an overallocation of resources for its production.　**T　F**

21. One way for government to correct spillover benefits from a product is to subsidize consumers of the product.　**T　F**

22. Nonexcludability means government provides public goods so as to exclude private businesses from providing them.　**T　F**

23. Obtaining the benefits of private goods requires that they be purchased; obtaining benefits from public goods requires only that they be produced. **T F**

24. Government provides homeland defense services because these services have public benefits and because private producers of such services experience the free-rider problem. **T F**

25. When the Federal government takes actions to control unemployment or inflation it is performing the allocative function of government. **T F**

26. Government purchases of goods and services are called nonexhaustive expenditures and government transfer payments are called exhaustive expenditures. **T F**

27. When a government levies taxes and uses the tax revenue to make transfer payments, it shifts resources from the production of private goods to the production of public goods. **T F**

28. The chief source of revenue for the Federal government is the corporate income tax. **T F**

29. If the marginal tax rate is higher than the average tax rate, the average tax rate will fall as income rises. **T F**

30. Property taxes are the largest percentage of the total revenues of local governments. **T F**

■ **MULTIPLE-CHOICE QUESTIONS**

Circle the letter that corresponds to the best answer.

1. The functional distribution for the United States shows that the largest part of the nation's income is
   (a) wages and salaries
   (b) proprietors' income
   (c) corporate profits
   (d) interest and rents

2. The part of after-tax income which is not consumed is defined as
   (a) saving
   (b) capital investment
   (c) wages and salaries
   (d) nondurable goods expenditure

3. If personal consumption expenditures were 80% of income and personal taxes were 8% of income, then personal savings would be
   (a) 8% of income
   (b) 10% of income
   (c) 12% of income
   (d) 88% of income

4. Consumer products that have expected lives of three years or more are
   (a) durable goods
   (b) nondurable goods
   (c) quasi-public goods
   (d) services

5. A firm owns and operates a farm growing wheat, a flour-milling plant, and a plant that bakes and sells bakery products. This firm would best be described as
   (a) a horizontally integrated firm
   (b) a vertically integrated firm
   (c) a conglomerate
   (d) a monopoly

6. Limited liability is associated with
   (a) sole proprietorships
   (b) partnerships
   (c) free-riders
   (d) corporations

7. Which form of business can most effectively raise money capital?
   (a) corporation
   (b) partnership
   (c) proprietorship
   (d) households

8. The separation of ownership and control in a corporation may create
   (a) a principal–agent problem
   (b) a free-rider problem
   (c) a monopoly
   (d) limited liability

9. One major means that government uses to deal with a monopoly is to
   (a) increase the demand for its product
   (b) decrease the supply of its product
   (c) stabilize incomes
   (d) regulate the firm

10. Government redistributes income through
   (a) limited liability
   (b) conglomerates
   (c) transfer payments
   (d) sole proprietorships

11. To redistribute income from high-income to low-income households, government might
   (a) increase transfer payments to high-income and decrease transfer payments to low-income households
   (b) increase the taxes paid by high-income and increase the transfer payments to low-income households
   (c) increase the taxes paid by low-income and decrease the taxes paid by high-income households
   (d) decrease the taxes paid by high-income and decrease the transfer payments to low-income households

12. Which is the best example of a good or service providing the economy with a spillover cost?
   (a) a textbook
   (b) an automobile
   (c) a business suit
   (d) an audit of a business firm's books

13. Which economic situation would result in overallocation of resources to the production of a good?
   (a) spillover benefits
   (b) spillover costs

(c) a free-rider program
(d) inflation

14. How does government correct for spillover benefits?
(a) by taxing consumers
(b) by taxing producers
(c) by subsidizing producers
(d) by separating ownership from control

15. Which is characteristic of public goods?
(a) nonrivalry
(b) excludability
(c) limited liability
(d) spillover costs

16. There is a free-rider problem when people
(a) are willing to pay for what they want
(b) are not willing to pay for what they want
(c) benefit from a good without paying for its cost
(d) want to buy more than is available for purchase in the market

17. Quasi-public goods are goods and services
(a) that are indivisible
(b) that have large spillover costs
(c) that have large spillover benefits
(d) that would not be produced by private producers through the market system

18. In the circular flow model, government provides goods and services and receives net taxes from
(a) colleges and universities
(b) businesses and households
(c) resource and product markets
(d) foreign nations and corporations

19. Which accounts for the largest percentage of all Federal expenditures?
(a) income security
(b) national defense
(c) interest on the public debt
(d) veterans' services

20. Which is the largest source of the tax revenues of the Federal government?
(a) sales and excise taxes
(b) property taxes
(c) payroll taxes
(d) personal income taxes

21. A tax that would most likely alter consumer expenditures on a particular product would be
(a) an excise tax
(b) a payroll tax
(c) a personal income tax
(d) a corporate income tax

22. Which pair represents the chief source of income and the most important type of expenditure of *state* governments?
(a) personal income tax and expenditures for hospitals
(b) personal income tax and expenditures for highways
(c) sales and excise taxes and expenditures for education
(d) sales and excise taxes and expenditures for public safety

23. Which pair represents the chief source of income and the most important type of expenditure of local governments?
(a) property tax and expenditures for highways
(b) property tax and expenditures for education
(c) sales and excise taxes and expenditures for public welfare
(d) sales and excise taxes and expenditures for police, fire, safety, and general government

Questions 24 and 25 are based on the tax table given below. [Note: total tax is for the highest income in that tax bracket.]

Taxable income	Total tax
$ 0	$ 0
30,000	5,000
70,000	15,000
150,000	42,000

24. The marginal tax rate at the $70,000 level of taxable income is
(a) 16.6%
(b) 21.4
(c) 25.0
(d) 28.0

25. The average tax rate at the $150,000 level of taxable income is
(a) 21.4%
(b) 28.0
(c) 31.5
(d) 33.8

■ **PROBLEMS**

1. The following table shows the functional distribution of total income in the United States in a recent year.

	Billions of dollars
Wages and salaries	$4,703
Proprietors' income	545
Corporate profits	804
Interest	450
Rents	148
Total income	6,650

Of the total income about _____% were wages and salaries, and about _____% were corporate profits.

2. Indicate in the space to the right of **a–i** whether these business characteristics are associated with the proprietorship (**PRO**), partnership (**PART**), corporation (**CORP**), two of these, or all three of these legal forms.
a. Red tape and legal expense in obtaining a charter for the firm _____

b. Unlimited liability _____

c. No specialized management _____

d. Has a life independent of its owner(s) _____

e. Double taxation of income _____

f. Greatest ability to acquire funds for the expansion of the firm _____

g. Permits some but not a great degree of specialized management _____

h. Possibility of an unresolved disagreement among several owners of the firm over courses of action

_____

i. The potential for the separation of ownership and control of the business _____

3. Following is a list of various government activities. Indicate in the space to the right of each into which of the five classes of government functions the activity falls. If it falls under more than one of the functions, indicate this.

a. Maintaining an army _____

b. Providing for a system of unemployment compensation _____

c. Establishment of the Federal Reserve Banks _____

_____

d. Providing medical care for government employees _____

e. Establishment of an Antitrust Division in the Department of Justice _____

f. Making it a crime to sell stocks and bonds under false pretenses _____

g. Providing low-cost lunches to school children _____

_____

h. Taxation of beer and wine _____

i. Regulation of organized stock, bond, and commodity markets _____

j. Setting tax *rates* higher for larger incomes than for smaller ones _____

4. The following circular flow diagram includes business firms, households, and the government (the public sector). Also shown are the product and resource markets.

a. Supply a label or an explanation for each of the 12 flows in the model:

(1) _____

(2) _____

(3) _____

(4) _____

(5) _____

(6) _____

(7) _____

(8) _____

(9) _____

(10) _____

(11) _____

(12) _____

b. If government wished to

(1) expand output and employment in the economy, it would increase expenditure flows _____ or _____, decrease net tax flows _____ or _____, or do both;

(2) increase the production of public goods and decrease the production of private goods in the economy, it would increase flows _____ and _____ or _____;

(3) redistribute income from high-income to low-income households, it would (increase, decrease) _____ the net taxes (taxes minus transfers) paid by the former and _____ the net taxes paid by the latter in flow _____.

5. In the following table are several levels of taxable income and hypothetical marginal tax rates for each $1000 increase in income.

Taxable income	Marginal tax rate, %	Tax	Average tax rate, %
$1500		$300	20
2500	22	520	20.8
3500	25	_____	_____
4500	29	_____	_____
5500	34	_____	_____
6500	40	_____	_____

a. At the four income levels compute the tax and the average tax rate.

b. As the marginal tax rate

(1) increases, the average tax rate (increases, decreases, remains constant) _____

_____

(2) decreases, the average tax rate _____

c. This tax is (progressive, regressive) _____ because the average tax rate increases as income (decreases, increases) _____.

■ **SHORT ANSWER AND ESSAY QUESTIONS**

1. Explain the difference between a functional and a personal distribution of income. Rank the five types of earned income in the order of their size.

2. Describe how saving and personal consumption vary across income levels. Which group is most likely to *dissave*?

3. The purchase of what type of consumer goods is largely postponable? Why is this? How is it possible for a family's personal consumption expenditures to exceed its after-tax income?

4. What is the difference between a plant and a firm? Between a firm and an industry?

5. What are the principal advantages and disadvantages of each type of the three legal forms of business organization?

6. Which of the disadvantages of the proprietorship and partnership accounts for the formation of corporations? Explain why it is important.

7. Describe the two different hybrid structures for business.

8. Explain what "separation of ownership and control" of the modern corporation means. What problem does this separation create for stockholders and managers?

9. How does government provide a legal framework and services for the effective operation of the economy?

10. What does the government do to maintain competition?

11. Why does the market system provide some people with lower incomes than it provides others?

12. What is meant by a spillover in general and by a spillover cost and a spillover benefit in particular?

13. How does the existence of spillover costs and benefits affect the allocation of resources and the prices of products?

14. What methods does government use to
(a) redistribute income?
(b) reallocate resources to take account of spillover costs?
(c) reallocate resources to take account of spillover benefits?

15. Distinguish between a private and a public good. Include in your answer an explanation of rivalry, excludability, and the free-rider problem.

16. What basic method does government in the United States use to reallocate resources away from the production of private goods and toward the production of public and quasi-public goods?

17. What is the stability function of government? What are the two economic problems that this function addresses?

18. How does politics affect the economic role of government in the economy?

19. In a circular flow diagram that includes not only business firms and households but also government (or the public sector), what are the four flows of money into or out of the government sector of the economy? Using this diagram, explain how government redistributes income, reallocates resources from the private to the public sector, and stabilizes the economy.

20. What is the present size of government spending and taxation in the U.S. economy?

21. Government expenditures fall into two broad classes: expenditures for goods and services and transfer payments. Explain the difference between these, and give examples of expenditures that fall into each of the two classes.

22. Explain precisely the difference between the marginal tax rate and the average tax rate.

23. Explain how the Federal personal income tax enables the Federal government to perform some of its economic functions.

24. Explain in detail the differences that exist among Federal and state governments in the taxes on which they primarily rely for their revenues and the major purposes for which they use these revenues.

25. What are tax revenue sources and expenditures at the local level?

ANSWERS

Chapter 5 The U.S. Economy: Private and Public Sectors

FILL-IN QUESTIONS

1. households, sell, buy
2. wages and salaries, 70
3. 20, 20
4. consumption, saving, taxes (any order)
5. taxes, consumption expenditures
6. durable, nondurable
7. firms, sole proprietorship, corporation
8. stocks, bonds
9. unlimited, limited
10. principal–agent, principals, agents
11. *a.* provide legal foundation; *b.* maintain competition; *c.* redistribute income; *d.* reallocate resources; *e.* stabilize the economy (any order for *a–e*)
12. regulate, owner, antitrust
13. unequal, transfer, market, income
14. market; *a.* produces the "wrong" amounts of certain goods and services; *b.* fails to allocate any resources to the production of certain goods and services whose production is economically justified
15. spillover
16. seller, buyer

17. *a.* (1) enact legislation, (2) pass special taxes; *b.* (1) subsidize consumers, (2) subsidize suppliers, (3) government financing or production of the product
18. nonrivalry, excludability, free-rider
19. taxing, tax revenue
20. increasing, decreasing, lowering, decreasing, increasing, raising
21. *a.* decreased; *b.* increased; *c.* 30; *d.* nonexhaustive, exhaustive
22. personal income, payroll, pensions and income security, national defense, health
23. higher, lower, marginal, average
24. sales and excise, personal, public welfare, education
25. property, education

TRUE–FALSE QUESTIONS

1. F, pp. 73–74	**9.** F, pp. 76–77	**17.** T, p. 80	**25.** F, pp. 82–83
2. T, p. 74	**10.** F, pp. 77–78	**18.** T, p. 80	**26.** F, p. 84
3. T, p. 74	**11.** T, pp. 77–78	**19.** F, pp. 80–81	**27.** F, pp. 84–85
4. T, p. 74	**12.** T, pp. 77–78	**20.** F, p. 81	**28.** F, pp. 85–86
5. T, p. 75	**13.** F, p. 77	**21.** T, p. 81	**29.** F, p. 86
6. F, p. 75	**14.** F, p. 78	**22.** F, p. 81	**30.** T, p. 87
7. T, p. 76	**15.** F, p. 79	**23.** T, p. 81	
8. F, p. 77	**16.** T, pp. 79–80	**24.** T, p. 81	

MULTIPLE-CHOICE QUESTIONS

1. a, p. 73	**8.** a, p. 78	**15.** a, p. 81	**22.** c, p. 87
2. a, p. 74	**9.** d, p. 79	**16.** c, pp. 81–82	**23.** b, p. 87
3. c, pp. 74–75	**10.** c, pp. 79–80	**17.** c, p. 82	**24.** c, p. 86
4. a, p. 75	**11.** b, pp. 79–80	**18.** b, pp. 83–84	**25.** b, p. 86
5. b, p. 76	**12.** b, p. 80	**19.** a, pp. 85–86	
6. d, p. 77	**13.** b, pp. 80–81	**20.** d, p. 86	
7. a, pp. 77–78	**14.** c, p. 81	**21.** a, p. 87	

PROBLEMS

1. 71, 12
2. *a.* CORP; *b.* PRO and PART; *c.* PRO; *d.* CORP; *e.* CORP; *f.* CORP; *g.* PART; *h.* PART; *i.* CORP
3. *a.* reallocates resources; *b.* redistributes income; *c.* provides a legal foundation and stabilizes the economy; *d.* reallocates resources; *e.* maintains competition; *f.* provides a legal foundation and maintains competition; *g.* redistributes income; *h.* reallocates resources; *i.* provides a legal foundation; *j.* redistributes income
4. *a.* (1) businesses pay costs for resources that become money income for households; (2) households provide resources to businesses; (3) household expenditures become receipts for businesses; (4) businesses provide goods and services to households; (5) government spends money in product market; (6) government receives goods and services from product market; (7) government spends money in resource market; (8) government receives resources from resource market; (9) government provides goods and services to households; (10) government provides goods and services to businesses; (11) businesses pay net taxes to government; (12) households pay net taxes to government; *b.* (1) 5, 7 (either order), 11, 12 (either order); (2) 9, 10, 11 (any order); (3) increase, decrease, 12
5. *a.* tax: $770, 1,060, 1,400, 1,800; average tax rate: 22%, 23.6%, 25.5%, 27.7%; *b.* (1) increases, (2) decreases; *c.* progressive, increases

SHORT ANSWER AND ESSAY QUESTIONS

1. pp. 73–74	**8.** p. 78	**15.** p. 81	**22.** p. 86
2. pp. 74–75	**9.** p. 79	**16.** pp. 81–82	**23.** pp. 85–86
3. p. 75	**10.** p. 79	**17.** pp. 82–83	**24.** pp. 85–87
4. pp. 76–77	**11.** pp. 79–80	**18.** p. 83	**25.** p. 87
5. pp. 76–78	**12.** pp. 80–81	**19.** p. 83	
6. pp. 76–78	**13.** pp. 80–81	**20.** pp. 84–85	
7. p. 78	**14.** pp. 79–80	**21.** p. 84	

CHAPTER 6

The United States in the Global Economy

The United States is linked to the global economy in many ways. As you will learn in the first section of Chapter 6, there are four types of **economic flows** among nations: trade; resource; information and technology; and financial.

The second section explains **why international trade is important** to the United States. In *relative* terms, other nations have exports and imports that are a larger percentage of their GDPs because they often have a small domestic market and a limited resource base. By contrast, the exports and imports of the United States account for a smaller percentage of its GDP because it has a larger domestic market and a more abundant resource base. In *absolute* terms, however, the United States is the world's largest trading nation. Most of the trade is with other industrially advanced nations such as Canada, Japan, and Germany. This volume of trade has grown over the years with expansion of the global economy, the rise of multinational corporations, and the emergence of new trading nations.

In the third section, you learn about the principle of **comparative advantage,** which is the basis for all trade between individuals, regions, and nations. A nation, for example, will specialize in the production of a product for which it has a lower domestic opportunity cost and trade to obtain those products for which its domestic opportunity cost is higher. Thus, specialization and trade increase productivity within a nation and increase a nation's output and standard of living.

Trading in a global economy requires a **foreign exchange market** in which national currencies are exchanged, as you discover in the fourth section. This market is competitive, so the principles of supply and demand that you read about in Chapter 3 apply to it. Changes in supply and demand for currency will affect the price of a national currency. When the U.S. dollar price of another currency has increased, the value of the U.S. dollar has *depreciated* relative to the other currency. Conversely, when the U.S. dollar price of another currency has decreased, the value of the U.S. dollar has *appreciated* in value relative to the other currency.

Government can affect international trade in many ways, as you learn in the fifth section. Governments can impose protective tariffs, import quotas, and nontariff barriers, or they can foster exports through subsidies. The reasons for the interventions are difficult to explain given the strong economic rationale for free trade based on the principle of comparative advantage. Nevertheless, public misunderstanding of the gains from trade, or political considerations designed to protect domestic industries, often lead to government policies that create trade barriers and distort the free flow of products between nations, thus increasing costs for society.

The sixth section discusses **multilateral agreements** among nations and the creation of **free-trade zones** that have been designed to reduce trade barriers and increase world trade. In the United States, the process of gradual tariff reduction began with the Reciprocal Trade Agreements Act of 1934. Since 1947, worldwide multilateral negotiations to reduce trade barriers have been conducted through the General Agreement on Tariffs and Trade (GATT). The Uruguay Round of GATT negotiations established the World Trade Organization (WTO) as GATT's successor. Trade negotiations under the WTO continue in the Doha Round that began in 2001.

The other major development has been the formation of free-trade zones. The European Union (EU), which was originally started in 1958 as the Common Market, is now a trading bloc of 25 European nations. A major accomplishment of the EU, in addition to the reduction of trade barriers among member nations, was the establishment of a common currency (the **euro**) that in 2003 was used by 12 nations. The United States, Canada, and Mexico also established a free-trade zone in 1993 through the North American Free Trade Agreement (NAFTA).

The final section of the chapter briefly explores the issue of the effects of **increased competition in the global economy.** Global competition has certainly changed production practices and employment in U.S. industry. Many U.S. firms have adapted to the changes by increasing productivity to reduce costs, improving product quality, and expanding export markets. Although some firms have failed and domestic jobs have been lost, the benefits of free trade to the economy in the form of lower prices, greater economic efficiency, and a wider variety of products far outweigh any losses.

■ CHECKLIST

When you have studied this chapter you should be able to

☐ Identify the four main categories of economic flows linking nations.

☐ Explain the importance of international trade to the U.S. economy in terms of volume, dependence, trade patterns, and financial linkages.

☐ Describe several factors that have facilitated the rapid growth of international trade since World War II.

☐ Identify the key participating nations in international trade.

☐ Explain the basic principle of comparative advantage based on an individual example.

☐ Compute the comparative costs of production from production possibilities data when you are given an example with cost data for two countries.

☐ Determine which of two countries has a comparative advantage in an example.

☐ Indicate the range in which the terms of trade will be found in an example.

☐ Show the gains from specialization and trade in an example.

☐ Define the main characteristics of the foreign exchange market.

☐ Demonstrate how supply and demand analysis applies to the foreign exchange market.

☐ Distinguish between the appreciation and depreciation of a currency.

☐ Identify four means by which governments interfere with free trade.

☐ Discuss two reasons why governments intervene in international trade.

☐ Give estimates of the cost to society from trade restrictions.

☐ List the major features of the Reciprocal Trade Agreements Act and the General Agreement on Tariffs and Trade (GATT).

☐ Identify the major provisions of the Uruguay round of GATT negotiations.

☐ Describe the World Trade Organization (WTO).

☐ Describe the history, goals, and results from the European Union (EU).

☐ Explain what the euro is and expectations for it.

☐ Explain the features and significance of the North American Free Trade Agreement (NAFTA).

☐ Discuss the effects on increased competition in the global economy on U.S. firms, workers, and consumers.

■ **CHAPTER OUTLINE**

1. Four main categories of *economic flows* link nations: goods and services flows, capital and labor flows, information and technology flows, and financial flows.

2. *Trade is important* and thus warrants special attention.

    a. Although the relative importance of international trade to the United States is less than it is for other nations, it is still vital.

    (1) Exports and imports are about 11–16% of GDP, and the United States is the largest trading nation in the world.

    (2) The U.S. economy depends on international trade for vital raw materials and a variety of finished products.

    (3) There are some patterns in U.S. trade: Most are with industrially advanced nations, with Canada being the largest trade partner; overall imports exceed exports, but the deficits are greatest with Japan, China, and OPEC countries.

    (4) International trade must be financed, and, in the case of the United States, large trade deficits have required the selling of business ownership (securities) to companies in other nations.

    b. Factors facilitating trade since World War II include improvements in transportation and communications technology, and a general decline in tariffs.

    c. The major participants in international trade are the United States, Japan, and the nations of western Europe. Newer participants include many Asian economies—Hong Kong (now part of China), Singapore, South Korea, Taiwan, Malaysia, and Indonesia. China has also emerged as a major trading nation in this region. The collapse of communism in the former Soviet Union and the nations of Eastern Europe significantly changed trade patterns in that region, opened these nations to market forces, and increased international trade.

3. International trade policies have changed over the years with the development of *multilateral agreements* and *free-trade* zones.

    a. United States trade policy has been significantly affected by the *Reciprocal Trade Agreements Act* of 1934. Until 1934, the United States steadily increased tariff rates to protect private interest groups, but since the passage of the 1934 act, tariff rates have been substantially reduced. This act gave the President the authority to negotiate with foreign nations and included *most-favored-nation (MFN) status* clauses.

    b. The *General Agreement on Tariffs and Trade* (GATT) began in 1947. GATT provided equal treatment of all member nations and sought to reduce tariffs and eliminate import quotas by multilateral negotiations. The Uruguay Round of GATT negotiations started in 1986 and was completed in 1993. The major provisions, which will be phased in through 2005, reduce tariffs on products, cut restrictive rules applying to services, phase out quotas on textiles and apparel, and decrease subsidies for agriculture.

    c. The *World Trade Organization* (WTO) was the successor to GATT. It oversees trade agreements and provides a forum for trade negotiations, the latest of which is the *Doha Round*. The WTO works to expand trade and reduce protectionism, but the outcomes can be controversial.

    d. The *European Union* (EU) is an example of a regional free-trade zone or trade bloc among 25 western European nations. It abolished tariffs among member nations and developed common policies on various economic issues, such as the tariffs on goods to and from nonmember nations. The EU has produced freer trade and increased economies of scale for production in its member nations, but such a trading bloc creates trade frictions with nonmember nations like the United States. Many of the EU nations share a common currency—the *euro*.

    e. In 1993, *The North American Free Trade Agreement* (NAFTA) created a free-trade zone covering the United States, Mexico, and Canada. Critics of this agreement fear job losses and the potential for abuse by other nations using Mexico as a base for production. Defenders cite the mutual advantages from freer trade and the fact that increased worldwide investment in Mexico will stimulate growth in that nation and trade with the United States.

4. Increased international trade has resulted in more *global competition.* Most U.S. firms have been able to meet the competitive challenge by lowering production costs, improving products, or using new technology. Some firms and industries have had difficulty remaining competitive and continue to lose market share and employment. Overall, increased trade has produced substantial benefits for U.S. consumers (lower prices and more products) and enabled the nation to make more efficient use of its scarce resources.

■ **HINTS AND TIPS**

1. Comparative advantage is directly related to the opportunity cost concept and production possibilities you learned about in Chapter 2.

   a. A nation has a comparative advantage in the production of a product when it can produce the product at a lower domestic opportunity cost than can a trading partner. A nation will specialize in the production of a product for which it is the low (opportunity) cost producer.

   b. When production possibilities schedules for two nations that trade two products have a constant cost ratio, you can reduce the complicated production possibilities schedules to a 2 × 2 table. Put the two products in the two columns and the two nations in the two rows of the matrix. In each cell of the matrix put the *maximum* of each product that can be produced by that row's nation. Then for each nation, divide the maximum of one product into the maximum amount of the other product to get the domestic opportunity cost of one product in terms of the other.

   c. This last point can be illustrated with an example from problem 2 in this study guide chapter. Lilliput can produce a *maximum* of 40 pounds of apples or 20 pounds of bananas. Brobdingnag can produce a *maximum* of 75 pounds of apples or 25 pounds of bananas. The 2 × 2 matrix would look like this:

	Apples	Bananas
Lilliput	40	20
Brobdingnag	75	25

For Lilliput, the domestic opportunity cost of producing 1 pound of apples is .5 pound of bananas. In Brobdingnag, the domestic opportunity cost of producing 1 pound of apples is .33 pound of bananas. Brobdingnag is the lower (opportunity) cost producer of apples and will specialize in the production of that product. Lilliput is the lower (opportunity) cost producer of bananas, because producing 1 pound of bananas requires giving up 2 pounds of apples, whereas in Brobdingnag producing 1 pound of bananas requires giving up 3 pounds of apples.

2. Foreign exchange rates often confuse students because they can be expressed in two ways: the U.S. dollar price of a unit of foreign currency ($1.56 for 1 British pound), or the amount of foreign currency that can be purchased by one U.S. dollar ($1 can purchase .64 British pound). If you know the exchange rate in one way, you can easily calculate it the other way. Using the information from the first way, dividing $1.56 into 1 British pound gives you the British pound price for 1 U.S. dollar (1/1.56 = .64 of a British pound). Using information from the second way, dividing .64 of a British pound into 1 U.S. dollar gives you the dollar price of a British pound (1/.64 = 1.56). Both ways may be used, although one way may be used more often than the other. Rates for British pounds or Canadian dollars are usually expressed the first way, in terms of U.S. dollars. Rates for the Swiss franc, Japanese yen, or European euro are expressed the second way, per U.S. dollar.

■ **IMPORTANT TERMS**

multinational corporations

comparative advantage

terms of trade

foreign exchange market

exchange rates

depreciation

appreciation

protective tariffs

import quotas

nontariff barriers

export subsidies

Smoot-Hawley Tariff Act

Reciprocal Trade Agreements Act

most-favored-nation clauses

General Agreement on Tariffs and Trade (GATT)

World Trade Organization (WTO)

European Union (EU)

trade bloc

euro

North American Free Trade Agreement (NAFTA)

SELF-TEST

■ **FILL-IN QUESTIONS**

1. List the four major economic flows among nations.

   a. _____

   b. _____

   c. _____

   d. _____

2. The importance of international trade varies by nation. Nations in which exports account for a relatively high percentage of GDP tend to have a (limited, diversified) _____ resource base and domestic market, whereas nations in which exports account for a lower percentage of GDP tend to have a _____ resource base and domestic market. An example of a higher exporting nation would be the (United States, Netherlands) _____, and a lower exporting nation would be the _____ .

3. In relative terms, the imports and exports of the United States amounted to about (11–16, 31–36) _____% of the economy's GDP in 2002. In absolute terms, the United States is the world's (smallest, largest) _____ trading nation.

4. The bulk of the trade of the United States is with (less-developed, industrially advanced) _____ nations. The largest trading partner for the United States is (Canada, Japan) _____. The United States has a large trade deficit with (Canada, Japan) _____.

5. Factors that have helped increase the growth of world trade since World War II include improvement in _____ and _____ technology and a general decline in _____.

6. The top participants in international trade include the _____, _____, and the nations of western Europe. These participants serve as the headquarters for most (national, multinational) _____ corporations and dominate world trade. The economies of Singapore, South Korea, and Taiwan have (increased, decreased) _____ their share of the world trade in recent decades. Another major trading nation in Asia is (China, Thailand) _____.

7. Specialization and trade (increase, decrease) _____ the productivity of a nation's resources and _____ total output more than would be the case without them.

8. When one nation has a lower opportunity cost of producing a product relative to another nation it has a (nontariff barrier, comparative advantage) _____ _____. The amount of one product that must be given up to obtain 1 unit of another product is the (foreign exchange, opportunity cost) _____.

9. When the dollar price of foreign currency increases, there has been a(n) (appreciation, depreciation) _____ in the the value of the dollar. When the dollar price of foreign currency decreases, there has been a(n) _____ in the value of the dollar. For example, if the dollar price of a euro decreases from $1.00 = 1 euro to $0.90 = 1 euro, then it means that there has been a(n) (appreciation, depreciation) _____ in the value of the dollar; but if the dollar price of a euro increases from $0.95 = 1 euro to $1.05 = 1 euro, then it means that there has been a(n) _____ in the value of the dollar.

10. In the market for Japanese yen, an increase in the (demand for, supply of) _____ yen will decrease the dollar price of yen, while an increase in the _____ yen will increase the dollar price of yen. If the dollar price of the yen increases, then Japanese goods imported into the United States will be (more, less) _____ expensive.

11. The major government policies that restrict trade include
a. excise taxes or duties on imported goods that are called _____,
b. limits on the quantities or total value of specific items that may be imported, referred to as _____,
c. licensing requirements, unreasonable standards, and red tape for a product, which are _____,
d. government payments to domestic producers of export goods, known as _____.

12. Governments may intervene in trade between nations because they mistakenly think of (exports, imports) _____ as helpful and _____ as harmful for a national economy. In fact, there are important gains from trade in the form of the extra output obtained from abroad. Trade makes it possible to obtain (exports, imports) _____ at a lower cost than would be the case if they were produced using domestic resources, and the earnings from _____ help a nation pay for these lower cost (exports, imports) _____.

13. Another reason why governments interfere with free trade is based on (private, political) _____ considerations. Groups and industries seek protection from foreign competition through (GATT, tariffs) _____ and import (quotas, subsidies) _____, or other kinds of trade restrictions. The costs of trade protectionism are (clear to, hidden from) _____ consumers in the protected product so there is little opposition to demands for protectionism.

14. Tariffs and quotas (benefit, cost) _____ domestic firms in the protected industries, but _____ domestic consumers in the form of (lower, higher) _____ prices than would be the case if there were free trade. They also (benefit, cost) _____ domestic firms that use the protected goods as inputs in their production processes.

15. Until 1934, the trend of tariff rates in the United States was (upward, downward) _____. The trend has been (upward, downward) _____ since the 1934 passage of the (Smoot-Hawley Tariff, Reciprocal Trade Agreements) _____ Act. This act empowered the President to lower (tariffs, quotas) _____ by up to 50% in return for a reduction in foreign restrictions on U.S. goods and incorporated (quotas, most-favored-nation) _____ clauses in U.S. trade agreements.

16. The three cardinal principles established in the General Agreement on Tariffs and Trade of 1947 are

a. _____

b. _____

c. _____

17. The major provisions of the Uruguay Round of (NAFTA, GATT) _____ negotiations include (exchange rate, tariff) _____ reductions, coverage of legal, financial, and other (goods, services) _____ cuts in agricultural (import quotas, subsidies) _____, and protection of (collective, intellectual) _____ property against piracy. It also created the successor to GATT, called the (Reciprocal, World) _____ Trade Organization.

18. An example of a free-trade zone or trade bloc is the (Western, European) _____ Union.

a. The specific aims of the EU were the abolition of (capital and labor, tariffs and quotas) _____, the establishment of (common, different) _____ tariffs on goods imported from outside the EU, the (restricted, free) _____ movement of capital and labor within the EU, and common policies on other matters.

b. The EU created (small, large) _____ markets and stimulated production that has allowed industries to achieve (higher, lower) _____ costs. The economic effects of the EU on nonmember nations such as the United States are mixed because economic growth in the EU causes U.S. exports to the EU to (decrease, increase) _____ while the tariff barriers cause U.S. exports to _____.

c. The common currency of many of the member nations of the EU is called the (peso, euro) _____.

19. The North American Free Trade Agreement (NAFTA) formed a trade (barrier, bloc) _____ among the United States, Canada, and Mexico. This agreement eliminated (terms of trade, tariffs) _____ among the nations. Critics in the United States said that it would (increase, decrease) _____ jobs, but the evidence shows a(n) _____ in jobs and total output since its passage.

20. Many U.S. firms can (monopolize, compete) _____ and be successful in the global economy; however, some firms that benefited from past trade protection may find it difficult to adjust to global (control, competition) _____ and may go out of business.

■ TRUE–FALSE QUESTIONS

Circle T if the statement is true, F if it is false.

1. For the United States, the volume of international trade has been increasing relatively but not absolutely.   **T F**

2. The U.S. economy's share of world trade has decreased since 1950.   **T F**

3. The United States exports and imports goods and services with a dollar value greater than any other nation in the world.   **T F**

4. The United States is dependent on trade for certain commodities that cannot be obtained in domestic markets.   **T F**

5. Canada is the most important trading partner for the United States in terms of the volume of exports and imports.   **T F**

6. If a person, firm, or region has a comparative advantage in the production of a particular commodity, it should specialize in the production of that commodity.   **T F**

7. If one nation has a comparative advantage in the production of a commodity over another nation, then it has a higher opportunity cost of production relative to the other nation.   **T F**

8. The economic effects of specialization and trade between nations are similar to increasing the quantity of resources or to achieving technological progress.   **T F**

9. The interaction of the demand for, and supply of, Japanese yen will establish the dollar price of Japanese yen.   **T F**

10. An increase in incomes in the United States would tend to cause the dollar price of the Japanese yen to fall.   **T F**

11. When the dollar price of another nation's currency increases, there has been an appreciation in the value of the dollar.   **T F**

12. When the dollar depreciates relative to the value of the currencies of the trading partners of the United States, then goods imported into the United States will tend to become more expensive.   **T F**

13. Export subsidies are government payments to reduce the price of a product to buyers from other nations.   **T F**

14. Nontariff barriers include excise taxes or duties placed on imported goods.   **T F**

15. Through world trade, an economy can reach a point beyond its domestic production possibilities curve. **T F**

16. One reason that trade restrictions get public support is that the alleged benefits of the restrictions are often immediate and clear-cut, but the adverse affects are often obscure and dispersed over the economy. **T F**

17. Tariffs and quotas benefit domestic firms in the protected industries and also help domestic consumers by lowering the prices for those products. **T F**

18. The Smoot-Hawley Tariff Act of 1930 reduced tariffs in the United States to the lowest level ever in an attempt to pull the nation out of the Great Depression. **T F**

19. If the United States concludes a tariff agreement that lowers the tariff rates on goods imported from another nation, the lower tariff rates are then applied to those goods when they are imported from other nations with most-favored-nation (MFN) status. **T F**

20. The World Trade Organization (WTO) is the world's major advocate for trade protectionism. **T F**

21. The members of the European Union (EU) have experienced freer trade since it was formed. **T F**

22. The economic integration of nations creates larger markets for firms within the nations that integrate and makes it possible for these firms and their customers to benefit from the economies of large-scale (mass) production. **T F**

23. The formation of the European Union (EU) may make it more difficult for U.S. firms to compete for European customers with firms located within the Union. **T F**

24. The 1993 North American Free Trade Agreement (NAFTA) includes all Central American nations. **T F**

25. Major U.S. firms are unable to compete in global markets without significant protection from foreign competition. **T F**

■ MULTIPLE-CHOICE QUESTIONS

Circle the letter that corresponds to the best answer.

1. Which nation is the world's leading trading nation in terms of absolute volumes of imports and exports?
   (a) Japan
   (b) China
   (c) Germany
   (d) United States

2. Which nation is our most important trading partner in terms of the quantity of trade volume?
   (a) Japan
   (b) Canada
   (c) Germany
   (d) United Kingdom

3. Which of the following is true?
   (a) Exports as a percentage of GDP are greatest in the United States.

(b) The United States is almost totally dependent on other nations for aircraft, machine tools, and coal.
   (c) Most of the exports and imports trade of the United States is with industrially advanced nations.
   (d) The United States has a trade surplus with Japan.

4. How is most of the trade deficit financed by a nation such as the United States?
   (a) by buying securities or assets from other nations
   (b) by selling securities or assets to other nations
   (c) by borrowing from the Federal government
   (d) by lending to the Federal government

5. Which is one way the United States finances its trade deficit?
   (a) by lending to foreigners
   (b) by selling real assets to foreigners
   (c) by purchasing real assets from foreigners
   (d) by passing protective tariffs on foreign products

6. Which factor has greatly facilitated international trade since World War II?
   (a) greater import quotas
   (b) expanded export subsidies
   (c) increased nontariff barriers
   (d) improved communications

7. Which industrializing nation would be considered one of the new participants in international trade?
   (a) Canada
   (b) Sweden
   (c) Japan
   (d) China

8. Why do nations specialize and engage in trade?
   (a) to protect multinational corporations
   (b) to increase output and income
   (c) to improve communications
   (d) to control other nations

Answer Questions 9, 10, 11, and 12 on the basis of the data given for two regions, Slobovia and Utopia, which have the following production possibilities tables.

SLOBOVIA PRODUCTION POSSIBILITIES TABLE

Product	Production alternatives					
	A	**B**	**C**	**D**	**E**	**F**
Cams	1,500	1,200	900	600	300	0
Widgets	0	100	200	300	400	500

UTOPIA PRODUCTION POSSIBILITIES TABLE

Product	Production alternatives				
	A	**B**	**C**	**D**	**E**
Cams	4,000	3,000	2,000	1,000	0
Widgets	0	200	400	600	800

9. In Slobovia, the comparative cost of
   (a) 1 cam is 3 widgets
   (b) 1 widget is .33 of a cam
   (c) 1 cam is .33 of a widget
   (d) 3 widgets is 1 cam

10. Which of the following statements is *not* true?

(a) Slobovia should specialize in the production of widgets.

(b) Slobovia has a comparative advantage in the production of widgets.

(c) Utopia should specialize in the production of widgets.

(d) Utopia has a comparative advantage in the production of cams.

11. The terms of trade will be

(a) greater than 7 cams for 1 widget

(b) between 7 cams for 1 widget and 5 cams for 1 widget

(c) between 5 cams for 1 widget and 3 cams for 1 widget

(d) less than 3 cams for 1 widget

12. Assume that if Slobovia did not specialize it would produce alternative C and that if Utopia did not specialize it would select alternative B. The gains from specialization are

(a) 100 cams and 100 widgets

(b) 200 cams and 200 widgets

(c) 400 cams and 500 widgets

(d) 500 cams and 400 widgets

13. If the dollar–yen exchange rate is $1 for 110 yen, then a Sony VCR priced at 27,500 yen would cost a U.S. consumer

(a) $200

(b) $250

(c) $275

(d) $300

14. If the equilibrium exchange rate changes so that the dollar price of Japanese yen increases

(a) the dollar has appreciated in value

(b) the dollar has depreciated in value

(c) U.S. citizens will be able to buy more Japanese goods

(d) Japanese citizens will be able to buy fewer U.S. goods

15. A decrease in the United States demand for Japanese goods will

(a) increase the demand for Japanese yen and increase the dollar price of yen

(b) increase the demand for Japanese yen but decrease the dollar price of yen

(c) decrease the demand for Japanese yen and decrease the dollar price of yen

(d) decrease the demand for Japanese yen but increase the dollar price of yen

16. If the exchange rate for one United States dollar changes from 1.0 euro to 1.1 euros, then there has been

(a) an appreciation in the value of the euro

(b) a depreciation in the value of the dollar

(c) a depreciation in the value of the euro

(d) an increase in the price of the euro

17. Which of the following is designed to restrict trade?

(a) GATT

(b) NAFTA

(c) import quotas

(d) multinational corporations

18. Why do governments often intervene in international trade?

(a) to expand a nation's production possibilities

(b) to improve the position of multinational corporations

(c) to protect domestic industries from foreign competition

(d) to increase revenue from tariff duties and excise taxes

19. Tariffs and quotas in a nation benefit domestic

(a) consumers and foreign producers of the protected product

(b) consumers and producers of the protected product

(c) producers of the protected product, but harm domestic consumers of the product

(d) producers and foreign producers of the product

20. Which one of the following specifically empowered the President of the United States to reduce tariff rates up to 50% if other nations would reduce their tariffs on American goods?

(a) the Smoot-Hawley Tariff Act of 1930

(b) the Reciprocal Trade Agreements Act of 1934

(c) the General Agreement on Tariffs and Trade of 1947

(d) North American Free Trade Agreement of 1993

21. Which of the following is characteristic of the General Agreement on Tariffs and Trade? Nations signing the agreement were committed to

(a) the expansion of import quotas

(b) the establishment of a world customs union

(c) the reciprocal increase in tariffs by negotiation

(d) the nondiscriminatory treatment of all member nations

22. One important outcome from the Uruguay Round of GATT was

(a) an increase in tariff barriers on services

(b) establishment of the World Trade Organization

(c) removal of voluntary export restraints in manufacturing

(d) abolishment of patent, copyright, and trademark protection

23. One of the potential problems with the European Union is that

(a) an unregulated free flow of labor and capital may reduce productivity

(b) economies of large-scale production may increase consumer prices

(c) tariffs may reduce trade with nonmember nations

(d) governments may have difficulty covering the shortfall from the elimination of duties and taxes

24. An example of the formation of a trade bloc would be the

(a) Smoot-Hawley Tariff Act

(b) North American Free Trade Agreement

(c) Reciprocal Trade Agreements Act

(d) General Agreement on Tariffs and Trade

25. The increase in global competition has resulted in:
- **(a)** greater inefficiency among U.S. producers
- **(b)** lower quality in the production of goods
- **(c)** the inability of most U.S. firms to compete
- **(d)** lower prices for many consumer goods and services

■ **PROBLEMS**

1. The following problem will help you understand the principle of comparative advantage and the benefits of specialization. A tailor named Hart has the production possibilities table for trousers and jackets as given. He chooses production alternative D.

HART'S PRODUCTION POSSIBILITIES TABLE

Product	Production alternatives					
	A	B	C	D	E	F
Trousers	75	60	45	30	15	0
Jackets	0	10	20	30	40	50

Another tailor, Schaffner, has the following production possibilities table and produces production alternative E.

SCHAFFNER'S PRODUCTION POSSIBILITIES TABLE

Product	Production alternatives						
	A	B	C	D	E	F	G
Trousers	60	50	40	30	20	10	0
Jackets	0	5	10	15	20	25	30

a. To Hart,

(1) the cost of one pair of trousers is _____ jackets

(2) the cost of one jacket is ____ pairs of trousers

b. To Schaffner,

(1) the cost of one pair of trousers is ____ jackets

(2) the cost of one jacket is ____ pairs of trousers

c. If Hart and Schaffner were to form a partnership to make suits,

(1) _____ should specialize in the making of trousers because he can make a pair of trousers at the cost of _____ of a jacket while it costs his partner _____ of a jacket to make a pair of trousers.

(2) _____ should specialize in the making of jackets because he can make a jacket at the cost of _____ pairs of trousers while it costs his partner _____ pairs of trousers to make a jacket.

d. Without specialization, Hart and Schaffner were able to make 50 pairs of trousers and 50 jackets. If each specializes completely in the item in the production in which he has a comparative advantage, their combined production will be _____ pairs of trousers and _____ jackets. Thus the gain from specialization is _____
_____.

e. When Hart and Schaffner come to divide the income of the partnership between them, the manufacture of a pair of trousers should be treated as the equivalent of from _____ to _____ jackets (or a jacket should be treated as the equivalent of from _____ to _____ pairs of trousers).

2. The countries of Lilliput and Brobdingnag have the production possibilities tables for apples and bananas shown below.

Note that the costs of producing apples and bananas are constant in both countries.

LILLIPUT PRODUCTION POSSIBILITIES TABLE

Product (lbs)	Production alternatives					
	A	B	C	D	E	F
Apples	40	32	24	16	8	0
Bananas	0	4	8	12	16	20

BROBDINGNAG PRODUCTION POSSIBILITIES TABLE

Product (lbs)	Production alternatives					
	A	B	C	D	E	F
Apples	75	60	45	30	15	0
Bananas	0	5	10	15	20	25

a. In Lilliput the cost of producing

(1) 8 apples is _____ bananas

(2) 1 apple is _____ bananas

b. In Brobdingnag the cost of producing

(1) 15 apples is _____ bananas

(2) 1 apple is _____ bananas

c. In Lilliput the cost of producing

(1) 4 bananas is _____ apples

(2) 1 banana is _____ apples

d. In Brobdingnag the cost of producing

(1) 5 bananas is _____ apples

(2) 1 banana is _____ apples

e. The cost of producing 1 apple is lower in the country of _____ and the cost of producing 1 banana is lower in the country of _____.

f. Lilliput has a comparative advantage in the production of _____ and Brobdingnag has a comparative advantage in the production of

_____.

g. The information in this problem is not sufficient to determine the exact terms of trade, but the terms of trade will be greater than _____ apples for 1 banana and less than _____ apples for 1 banana. Put another way, the terms of trade will be between _____ bananas for 1 apple and _____ bananas for 1 apple.

h. If neither nation could specialize, each would produce production alternative C. The combined production of apples in the two countries would be _____ apples and the combined production of bananas would be _____ bananas.

(1) If each nation specializes in producing the fruit for which it has a comparative advantage, their combined production will be _____ apples and _____ bananas.

(2) Their gain from specialization will be _____ apples and _____ bananas.

3. Use the following table that shows 10 different currencies and how much of each currency can be purchased with a U.S. dollar.

		Currency per U.S. $		
Country	Currency	Year 1	Year 2	A or D
Brazil	Real	0.85	0.91	_____
Britain	Pound	0.65	0.59	_____
Canada	Dollar	1.41	1.51	_____
Switzerland	Franc	1.33	1.19	_____
Germany	Euro	1.58	1.69	_____
India	Rupee	31.39	34.55	_____
Japan	Yen	100.15	110.23	_____
Mexico	Peso	4.65	5.09	_____
Norway	Krone	6.88	6.49	_____
Thailand	Bhat	25.12	23.22	_____

a. In the far right column of the table, indicate whether the U.S. dollar has appreciated (**A**) or depreciated (**D**) from year 1 to year 2.

b. In year 1, a U.S. dollar would purchase _____ Swiss francs, but in year 2, it would purchase _____ Swiss francs. The U.S. dollar has (appreciated, depreciated) _____ against the Swiss franc from year 1 to year 2.

c. In year 1, a U.S. dollar would purchase _____ Japanese yen, but in year 2, it would purchase _____ Japanese yen. The U.S. dollar has (appreciated, depreciated) _____ against the Japanese yen from year 1 to year 2.

4. This problem asks you to calculate prices based on exchange rates. Use the data in the table for Problem 3 to answer the following items.

a. Using the exchange rates shown for year 1, what would be the U.S. dollar cost for the following products?

(1) Japanese television costing 30,000 yen.

$_____

(2) Swiss scarf costing 200 francs. $_____

(3) Thai artwork costing 3,768 bhats. $_____

(4) German auto costing 79,000 euros. $_____

(5) Mexican silver bracelet costing 1,376 pesos.

$_____

b. Using the exchange rates shown for year 2, what would be the U.S. dollar cost of the following products?
(1) Japanese television costing 30,000 yen.

$_____

(2) Swiss scarf costing 200 francs. $_____

(3) Thai artwork costing 3,768 bhats. $_____

(4) German auto costing 79,000 euros. $_____

(5) Mexican silver bracelet costing 1,376 pesos.

$_____

c. Indicate whether the U.S. dollar cost of each product in 4b has increased (+) or decreased (−) from year 1 to year 2. _____ _____ _____ _____ _____

d. What is the relationship between your answers in 4c to the ones you gave for the corresponding nations in 3a?

(1) When the U.S. dollar *appreciates* in value against a foreign currency, the U.S. dollar cost of a product from that nation will (increase, decrease) _____.

(2) When the U.S. dollar *depreciates* in value against a foreign currency, the U.S. dollar cost of a product from that nation will (increase, decrease) _____.

■ **SHORT ANSWER AND ESSAY QUESTIONS**

1. Describe the four major economic flows that link the United States to other nations.

2. In relative and absolute terms, how large is the volume of the international trade of the United States? What has happened to these figures over the past 40 or so years?

3. What are the principal exports and imports of the U.S. economy? What commodities used in the economy come almost entirely from abroad, and what American industries sell large percentages of their outputs abroad?

4. Which nations are the principal trading partners of the United States? How much of this trade is with the industrially advanced nations and how much of it is with the developing nations of the world?

5. Give several factors that have facilitated trade since World War II.

6. Who are the major participants in international trade? Describe the relative influence of the key players.

7. Use an example of two individuals to describe the basic principle of comparative advantage.

8. What is meant by comparative cost and comparative advantage?

9. Explain how comparative advantage determines the terms of trade between nations.

10. What is the gain for a nation that results from specialization in the production of products for which there is a comparative advantage?

11. Describe the characteristics of a foreign exchange market and of exchange rates. Why is an exchange rate an unusual price?

12. Illustrate with a supply and demand graph how equilibrium is determined in a dollar–yen market. Be sure to label axes and curves.

13. Why might an appreciation of the value of the U.S. dollar relative to the Japanese yen depress the U.S. economy and stimulate the Japanese economy? Why might a government intervene in the foreign exchange market and try to increase or decrease the value of its currency?

14. What are the major trade impediments and subsidies? How do they restrict international trade?

15. Why do governments intervene in international trade and develop restrictive trade policies?

16. What is the cost to society from trade protectionism? Who benefits and who is hurt by trade protectionism?

17. What was the Smoot-Hawley Tariff Act of 1930? What international trade problems are illustrated by this act?

18. Explain the basic provisions of the Reciprocal Trade Agreements Act of 1934.

19. What were the cardinal principles contained in the General Agreement on Tariffs and Trade (GATT)? What were the basic provisions and important results of the Uruguay Round of GATT negotiations?

20. Describe the purpose of the World Trade Organization (WTO). Why is it controversial?

21. What is the European Union? What has it achieved?

22. Discuss the potential effects of the European Union on the trade of the United States.

23. What is the euro and what are its likely economic effects?

24. What is the North American Free Trade Agreement (NAFTA)? What do its critics and defenders say about the agreement?

25. Evaluate the effects of increased global competition on U.S. firms, workers, and consumers.

ANSWERS

Chapter 6 The United States in the Global Economy

FILL-IN QUESTIONS

1. *a.* goods and services flows (trade flows); *b.* capital and labor flows (resource flows); *c.* information and technology flows; *d.* financial flows (any order for *a–d*)
2. limited, diversified, Netherlands, United States
3. 11–16, largest
4. industrially advanced, Canada, Japan
5. transportation, communications (any order), tariffs
6. United States, Japan (any order), multinational, increased, China
7. increase, increase
8. comparative advantage, opportunity cost
9. depreciation, appreciation, appreciation, depreciation
10. supply of, demand for, more
11. *a.* protective tariffs; *b.* import quotas; *c.* nontariff barriers; *d.* export subsidies
12. exports, imports, imports, exports, imports
13. political, tariffs, quotas, hidden from
14. benefit, cost, higher, cost
15. upward, downward, Reciprocal Trade Agreements, tariffs, most-favored-nation
16. *a.* equal, nondiscriminatory treatment of all member nations; *b.* reduction of tariffs by multilateral negotiations; *c.* elimination of import quotas
17. GATT, tariff, services, subsidies, intellectual, World
18. European; *a.* tariffs and quotas, common, free; *b.* large, lower, increase, decrease; *c.* euro
19. bloc, tariffs, decrease, increase
20. compete, competition

TRUE–FALSE QUESTIONS

1. F, p. 92	10. F, pp. 100–101	19. T, pp. 103–104
2. T, p. 92	11. F, pp. 100–101	20. F, p. 104
3. T, p. 92	12. T, pp. 100–101	21. T, pp. 104–105
4. T, pp. 92–93	13. T, p. 102	22. T, p. 105
5. T, p. 94	14. F, p. 102	23. T, p. 105
6. T, pp. 97–99	15. T, p. 102	24. F, p. 105
7. F, pp. 97–99	16. T, p. 102	25. F, pp. 106–107
8. T, pp. 98–99	17. F, pp. 102–103	
9. T, pp. 99–100	18. F, p. 103	

MULTIPLE-CHOICE QUESTIONS

1. d, p. 92	10. c, pp. 97–98	19. c, pp. 101–102
2. b, p. 94	11. c, p. 98	20. b, pp. 103–104
3. c, p. 94	12. a, pp. 98–99	21. d, p. 104
4. b, p. 94	13. b, p. 99	22. b, p. 104
5. b, p. 94	14. b, pp. 100–101	23. c, p. 105
6. d, pp. 95–96	15. c, pp. 100–101	24. b, p. 105
7. d, p. 95	16. c, pp. 100–101	25. d, pp. 106–107
8. b, p. 96	17. c, p. 102	
9. c, pp. 97–98	18. c, p. 102	

PROBLEMS

1. *a.* (1) .67, (2) 1.5; *b.* (1) .5, (2) 2; *c.* (1) Schaffner, .5, .67; (2) Hart, 1.5, 2; *d.* 60, 50, 10 pairs of trousers; *e.* .5, .67, 1.5, 2
2. *a.* (1) 4, (2) .5; *b.* (1) 5, (2) .33; *c.* (1) 8, (2) 2; *d.* (1) 15, (2) 3; *e.* Brobdingnag, Lilliput; *f.* bananas, apples; *g.* 2, 3, .33, .5; *h.* 69, 18, (1) 75, 20, (2) 6, 2
3. *a.* A, D, A, D, A, A, A, D, D; *b.* 1.33, 1.19, depreciated; *c.* 100.15, 110.23, appreciated
4. *a.* (1) 299.55 (2) 150.38 (3) 150 (4) 50,000 (5) 295.91; *b.* (1) 272.16 (2) 168.07 (3) 162.27 (4) 46,745.56 (5) 270.33; *c.* (1) − (2) + (3) + (4) − (5)−; *d.* (1) decrease (2) increase

SHORT ANSWER AND ESSAY QUESTIONS

1. pp. 91–92	10. pp. 98–99	19. p. 104
2. p. 92	11. pp. 99–100	20. p. 104
3. pp. 92–93	12. pp. 100–101	21. pp. 104–105
4. p. 94	13. pp. 100–101	22. p. 105
5. p. 95	14. pp. 101–102	23. p. 105
6. pp. 95–96	15. p. 102	24. p. 105
7. pp. 96–97	16. pp. 102–103	25. pp. 106–107
8. pp. 97–98	17. p. 103	
9. p. 98	18. pp. 103–104	

CHAPTER 7

Measuring Domestic Output and National Income

The subject of Chapter 7 is **national income accounting.** The first measure that you will learn about in the chapter is the **gross domestic product** (GDP). The GDP is an important economic statistic because it provides the best estimate of the total market value of all final goods and services produced by our economy in one year. You will also discover why GDP is a monetary measure that counts only the value of final goods and services and excludes nonproductive transactions such as secondhand sales.

National income accounting involves estimating output, or income, for the nation's society as a whole, rather than for an individual business firm or family. Note that the terms *"output"* and *"income"* are interchangeable because the nation's domestic output and its income are identical. The value of the nation's output equals the total expenditures for this output, and these expenditures become the income of those who have produced this output. Consequently, there are two equally acceptable methods—expenditures or income—for determining GDP.

From an *expenditure* perspective, GDP is composed of four expenditure categories: personal consumption expenditures (**C**), gross private domestic investment (I_g), government purchases (**G**), and net exports (X_n). These expenditures become income for people when they are paid out in the form of employee compensation, rents, interest, proprietors' income, and corporate profits, with adjustments made for indirect business taxes, depreciation, and net foreign factor income earned in the United States. In national income accounting, the amount spent to purchase this year's total output is equal to money income derived from production of this year's output.

This chapter also explains the relationship of GDP to other national accounts. These accounts include *net domestic product* (NDP), *national income* (NI) as derived from NDP, *personal income* (PI), and *disposable income* (DI). The relationship between GDP, NDP, NI, PI, and DI is shown in Table 7.4 of the text. The circular flow using the expenditures and income approaches to GDP are illustrated in Figure 7.3 of the text.

The next to the last section of the chapter shows you how to calculate *real* GDP from *nominal GDP*. This adjustment is important because nominal GDP is measured in monetary units, so if accurate comparisons are to be made for GDP over time, these monetary measures must be adjusted to take account of changes in the price level. A simple example is presented to show how a GDP price index is constructed. The index is then used to adjust *nominal GDP* to obtain *real GDP* and make correct GDP comparisons from one year to the next. The text also provides data for the U.S. economy so you can see why the calculation of real GDP is necessary and how it is used.

The last section of the chapter looks at the shortcomings of GDP as a measure of total output and economic well-being. You will learn about economic factors that are excluded from GDP measurement—nonmarket or illegal transactions, changes in leisure and product quality, differences in the composition and distribution of output, and the environmental effects of GDP production—and how their exclusion can lead to an under- or overstatement of economic well-being. Although national income accounts are not perfect measures of all economic conditions, they are still reasonably accurate and useful indicators of the performance of the national economy.

Chapter 7 is the essential background for Parts 2 and 3 of the text, which explain the history of and the factors that determine the level of domestic output and income in the economy. Chapter 7 is important because it explains the several methods used to measure the performance of the economy in a given year and to make the adjustments necessary to ensure accurate measurements of performance over time.

■ CHECKLIST

When you have studied this chapter you should be able to

☐ Identify three ways national income accounting can be used for economic decision making.

☐ Give a definition of the gross domestic product (GDP).

☐ Explain why GDP is a monetary measure.

☐ Describe how GDP measures value added and avoids multiple counting.

☐ Give examples of two types of nonproduction transactions that are excluded from GDP.

☐ Describe the relationship between the expenditures and income approaches to GDP accounting.

☐ List the three types of expenditures included in personal consumption expenditures (**C**).

☐ Identify three items included in gross private domestic investment (I_g).

☐ Explain why changes in inventories are an investment.

☐ Distinguish between gross and net investment.

☐ Discuss how differences in the amount of net investment affect the production capacity of the economy.

☐ List two components included in government purchases (**G**).

☐ Describe the meaning and calculation of net exports (X_n).

☐ Compute GDP using the expenditures approach when given national income accounting data.

☐ Identify the five income items that make up U.S. national income.

☐ List three things that can happen to corporate profits.

☐ Explain the adjustment of indirect business taxes to national income accounts.

☐ Define consumption of fixed capital and discuss how it affects national income accounts.

☐ Describe the effect of net foreign factor income on national income accounts.

☐ Compute GDP using the income approach when given national income accounting data.

☐ Define net domestic product (NDP).

☐ Show how to derive U.S. national income (NI) from net domestic product (NDP).

☐ Define personal income (PI) in national income accounts.

☐ Explain how to obtain disposable income (DI) from personal income (PI).

☐ Use Figure 7.3 in the text to describe the circular flow model for GDP.

☐ Distinguish between nominal and real GDP.

☐ Construct a price index when given the necessary price and quantity data.

☐ Obtain a price index when given data on nominal and real GDP.

☐ Discuss some real-world factors that affect the GDP price index.

☐ List seven shortcomings of GDP as a measure of total output and economic well-being.

■ **CHAPTER OUTLINE**

1. **National income accounting** consists of concepts that enable those who use them to measure the economy's output, to compare it with past outputs, to explain its size and the reasons for changes in its size, and to formulate policies designed to increase it.

2. The market value of all final goods and services produced in the economy during the year is measured by the **gross domestic product** (GDP).

   a. GDP is a *monetary measure* that is calculated in dollar terms rather than in terms of physical units of output.

   b. To avoid multiple counting, GDP includes only *final* goods and services (goods and services that will not be processed further during the *current* year).

   c. Nonproduction transactions are not included in GDP; purely financial transactions and secondhand sales are therefore excluded.

   d. Measurement of GDP can be accomplished by either the expenditures or the income method, but the same result is obtained by the two methods.

3. Computation of the GDP by the **expenditures approach** requires the summation of the total amounts of the four types of spending for final goods and services.

   a. **Personal consumption expenditures (C)** are the expenditures of households for *durable goods* and *nondurable goods* and for *services*.

   b. **Gross private domestic investment (I_g)** is the sum of the spending by business firms for machinery, equipment, and tools; spending by firms and households for new buildings; and the changes in the inventories of business firms.

   (1) A change in inventories is included in investment because it is the part of the output of the economy that was not sold during the year.

   (2) Investment does not include expenditures for stocks or bonds or for secondhand capital goods.

   (3) Gross investment exceeds net investment by the value of the capital goods worn out during the year. An economy in which net investment is positive is one with an expanding production capacity.

   c. **Government purchases (G)** are the expenditures made by all governments in the economy for products produced by business firms and for resource services from households. They include expenditures the government makes for products and services to provide public services, and spending for social capital (goods with a long lifetime such as highways).

   d. **Net exports (X_n)** in an economy equal the expenditures made by foreigners for goods and services produced in the economy less the expenditures made by the consumers, governments, and investors of the economy for goods and services produced in foreign nations.

   e. In equation form, $C + I_g + G + X_n = GDP$

4. Computation of GDP by the **income approach** requires adding the income derived from the production and sales of final goods and services. The five income items are

   a. Compensation of employees (the sum of wages and salaries *and* wage and salary supplements).

   b. Rents.

   c. Interest (only the interest payments made by business firms are included, and interest payments made by government are excluded).

   d. Proprietors' income (the profits or net income of unincorporated firms).

   e. Corporate profits which are subdivided into

   (1) Corporate income taxes

   (2) Dividends

   (3) Undistributed corporate profits.

   f. Three additions are made to the income side to balance it with expenditures.

   (1) Indirect business taxes are added because they are initially income that later gets paid to government.

   (2) Depreciation, or the consumption of fixed capital, is added because it is initially income to businesses that later gets deducted in calculating profits.

   (3) Net foreign factor income is added because it reflects income from all domestic output regardless of the foreign or domestic ownership of domestic resources.

5. In addition to GDP, **four other national income measures** are important in evaluating the performance of the economy. Each has a distinct definition and can be com-

puted by making additions to or deductions from another measure.

a. NDP is the annual output of final goods and services over and above the capital goods worn out during the year. It is equal to the GDP minus depreciation (consumption of fixed capital).

b. NI is the total income *earned* by U.S. owners of land and capital and by the U.S. suppliers of labor and entrepreneurial ability during the year. It equals NDP *minus* net foreign factor income earned in the United States and *minus* indirect business taxes.

c. PI is the total income *received*—whether it is earned or unearned—by the households of the economy before the payment of personal taxes. It is found by *adding* transfer payments to and *subtracting* social security contributions, corporate income taxes, and undistributed corporate profits from the NI.

d. DI is the total income available to households after the payment of personal taxes. It is equal to PI less personal taxes and also equal to personal consumption expenditures plus personal saving.

e. The relations among the five income–output measures are summarized in Table 7.4.

f. Figure 7.3 is a more realistic and complex circular flow diagram that shows the flows of expenditures and incomes among the households, business firms, and governments in the economy.

6. *Nominal GDP* is the total output of final goods and services produced by an economy in one year multiplied by the market prices when they were produced. Prices, however, change each year. To compare total output over time, nominal GDP is converted to **real GDP** to account for these price changes.

a. There are two methods for deriving *real GDP* from *nominal GDP.* The first method involves computing a **price index.**

(1) This index is a ratio of the price of a market basket in a given year to the price of the same market basket in a base year, with the ratio multiplied by 100.

(2) To obtain real GDP, divide nominal GDP by the price index expressed in hundredths.

b. In the second method, nominal GDP is broken down into prices and quantities for each year. Real GDP is found by using base-year prices and multiplying them by each year's physical quantities. The GDP price index for a particular year is the ratio of nominal to real GDP for that year.

c. In the real world, complex methods are used to calculate the GDP price index. The price index is useful for calculating real GDP. The price index number for a reference period is arbitrarily set at 100.

(1) For years when the price index is below 100, dividing nominal GDP by the price index (in hundredths) inflates nominal GDP to obtain real GDP.

(2) For years when the price index is greater than 100, dividing nominal GDP by the price index (in hundredths) deflates nominal GDP to obtain real GDP.

7. GDP has shortcomings as a measure of total output and economic well-being.

a. It excludes the value of final goods and services not bought and sold in the markets of the economy.

b. It excludes the amount of leisure the citizens of the economy are able to have.

c. It does not record the improvements in the quality of products that occur over the years.

d. It does not measure the market value of the final goods and services produced in the underground sector of the economy.

e. It does not record the pollution costs to the environment of producing final goods and services.

f. It does not measure changes in the composition and the distribution of the domestic output.

g. It does not measure noneconomic sources of well-being.

■ **HINTS AND TIPS**

1. Read through the chapter several times. A careful reading will enable you to avoid the necessity of memorizing. Begin by making sure you know precisely what GDP means and what is included in and excluded from its measurement.

2. Accounting is essentially an adding-up process. This chapter explains in detail and lists the items that must be added to obtain GDP by the *expenditures approach* or *income approach.* It is up to you to learn what to add on the expenditure side and what to add on the income side. Figure 7.1 is an important accounting reference for this task.

3. Changes in the price level have a significant effect on the measurement of GDP. Practice converting nominal GDP to real GDP using a price index. Problems 4 and 5 in this *Study Guide* should help you understand nominal and real GDP and the conversion process.

4. GDP is a good measure of the market value of the output of final goods and services that are produced in an economy in 1 year; however, the measure is not perfect, so you should be aware of its limitations, which are noted at the end of the chapter.

■ **IMPORTANT TERMS**

national income accounting

price level

gross domestic product (GDP)

intermediate goods

final goods

multiple counting

value added

expenditures approach

income approach

personal consumption expenditures (*C*)

gross private domestic investment (*I_g*)

net private domestic investment

government purchases (*G*)

net exports (*X_n*)

national income (NI)

indirect business taxes

consumption of fixed capital (depreciation)

net domestic product (NDP)

personal income (PI)

disposable income (DI)

nominal GDP

real GDP

price index

SELF-TEST

■ FILL-IN QUESTIONS

1. National income accounting is valuable because it provides a means of keeping track of the level of (unemployment, production) _____ in the economy and the course it has followed over the long run and the information needed to make public (policies, payments) _____ that will improve the performance of the economy.

2. Gross domestic product (GDP) measures the total (market, nonmarket) _____ value of all (intermediate, final) _____ goods and services produced in a country (in 1 year, over 2 years) _____.

3. GDP for a country includes goods and services produced (within, outside) _____ its geographic boundaries and (does, does not) _____ treat resources supplied by U.S. citizens differently from resources supplied by citizens of other countries.

4. GDP is a (monetary, nonmonetary) _____ measure that permits comparison of the (relative, absolute) _____ worth of goods and services.

5. In measuring GDP, only (intermediate, final) _____ goods and services are included; if _____ goods and services were included, the accountant would be (over-, under-) _____ stating GDP, or (single, multiple) _____ counting.

6. A firm buys materials for $2000 from other firms in the economy and produces from them a product that sells for $3015. The value added by the firm is ($1015, $2000, $3015) _____.

7. GDP accounting excludes (production, nonproduction) _____ transactions. These include (financial, nonfinancial) _____ transactions such as public or private transfer payments or the sale of securities, and (first-, second-) _____ hand sales.

8. Personal consumption expenditures are the expenditures of households for goods such as automobiles, which are (durable, nondurable) _____, and goods such as food, which are _____, plus expenditures for (housing, services) _____.

9. Gross private domestic investment basically includes the final purchases of (capital, consumer) _____ goods by businesses, all (construction of new, sales of existing) _____ buildings and houses, and changes in (services, inventories) _____.

10. The difference between gross and net private domestic investment is equal to (depreciation, net exports) _____, or the (production, consumption) _____ of fixed capital.

11. If gross private domestic investment is greater than depreciation, net private domestic investment is (positive, negative) _____ and the production capacity of the economy is (declining, expanding) _____.

12. An economy's *net* exports equal its exports (minus, plus) _____ its imports. If exports are less than imports, net exports are (positive, negative) _____, but if exports are greater than imports, net exports are _____.

13. Using the expenditure approach, the GDP equation equals ($NDP + NI + PI, C + I_g + G + X_n$) _____.

14. The compensation of employees in the system of social accounting consists of actual wages and salaries (plus, minus) _____ wage and salary supplements. Salary supplements are the payments employers make to social security or (public, private) _____ insurance programs and to _____ pension, health, and welfare funds.

15. Corporate profits are disposed of in three ways: corporate income (taxes, interest) _____, (depreciation, dividends) _____, and undistributed corporate (taxes, profits) _____.

16. Three adjustments are added to national income to obtain (GDP, DI) _____. They are (direct, indirect) _____ business taxes, the consumption of (variable, fixed) _____ capital, and (gross, net) _____ foreign factor income earned in the United States.

17. Gross domestic product overstates the economy's production because it fails to make allowance for (multiple counting, depreciation) _____ or the need to replace (consumer, capital) _____ goods. When this adjustment is made, the calculations produce (net domestic product, national income) _____.

18. National income is equal to net domestic product (plus, minus) _____ indirect business taxes plus (gross, net) _____ foreign factor income earned in the United States.

19. Personal income equals national income (plus, minus)

_____ transfer payments _____ the sum of social security contributions, corporate income taxes, and undistributed corporate profits.

20. Disposable income equals (national, personal)

_____ income (plus, minus) _____ personal taxes.

21. A GDP that reflects the prices prevailing when the output is produced is called unadjusted or (nominal, real)

_____ GDP, but a GDP figure that is deflated or inflated for price level changes is called adjusted

or _____ GDP.

22. To calculate a price index in a given year, the combined price of a market basket of goods and services in that

year is (divided, multiplied) _____ by the combined price of the market basket in the base year. The

result is then _____ by 100.

23. Real GDP is calculated by dividing (the price index,

nominal GDP) _____ by _____.

24. The price index expressed in hundredths is calculated

by dividing (real, nominal) _____ GDP by

_____ GDP.

25. For several reasons, GDP has shortcomings as a measure of total output or economic well-being.
   a. It does not include the (market, nonmarket)

_____ transactions that result in the production of goods and services or the amount of (work,

leisure) _____ of participants in the economy.
   b. It fails to record improvements in the (quantity, qual-

ity) _____ of the products produced, or the

changes in the (level, composition) _____, and distribution of the economy's total output.
   c. It does not take into account the undesirable effects of GDP production on the (government, environment)

_____ or the goods and services pro-

duced in the (market, underground) _____ economy.

■ **TRUE–FALSE QUESTIONS**

Circle T if the statement is true, F if it is false.

1. National income accounting allows us to assess the performance of the economy and make policies to improve that performance.   **T   F**

2. Gross domestic product measures at their market values the total output of all goods and services produced in the economy during a year.   **T   F**

3. GDP is simply a count of the quantity of output and is not a monetary measure.   **T   F**

4. The total market value of the wine produced in the United States during a year is equal to the number of bottles of wine produced in that year multiplied by the (average) price at which a bottle sold during that year.   **T   F**

5. GDP includes the sale of intermediate goods and excludes the sale of final goods.   **T   F**

6. The total value added to a product and the value of the final product are equal.   **T   F**

7. Social security payments and other public transfer payments are counted as part of GDP.   **T   F**

8. The sale of stocks and bonds is excluded from GDP.   **T   F**

9. In computing gross domestic product, private transfer payments are excluded because they do not represent payments for currently produced goods and services.   **T   F**

10. The two approaches to the measurement of the gross domestic product yield identical results because one approach measures the total amount spent on the products produced by business firms during a year while the second approach measures the total income of business firms during the year.   **T   F**

11. Personal consumption expenditures only include expenditures for durable and nondurable goods.   **T   F**

12. The expenditure made by a household to have a new home built is a personal consumption expenditure. **T   F**

13. In national income accounting, any increase in the inventories of business firms is included in gross private domestic investment.   **T   F**

14. If gross private domestic investment is greater than depreciation during a given year, the economy's production capacity has declined during that year.   **T   F**

15. Government purchases include spending by all units of government on the finished products of business, but exclude all direct purchases of resources such as labor.   **T   F**

16. The net exports of an economy equal its exports of goods and services less its imports of goods and services.   **T   F**

17. The income approach to GDP includes compensation of employees, rents, interest income, proprietors' income, and corporate profits.   **T   F**

18. Indirect business taxes are the difference between gross private domestic investment and net private domestic investment.   **T   F**

19. Net foreign factor income is the difference between the earnings of foreign-owned resources in the United States and the earnings from U.S.-supplied resources abroad.　　**T　F**

20. A GDP that has been deflated or inflated to reflect changes in the price level is called real GDP.　　**T　F**

21. To adjust nominal GDP for a given year to obtain real GDP, it is necessary to multiply nominal GDP by the price index (expressed in hundredths) for that year.　　**T　F**

22. If nominal GDP for an economy is $11,000 billion and the price index is 110, then real GDP is $10,000 billion.　　**T　F**

23. GDP is a precise measure of the economic well-being of society.　　**T　F**

24. The productive services of a homemaker are included in GDP.　　**T　F**

25. The spillover costs from pollution and other activities associated with the production of the GDP are deducted from total output.　　**T　F**

■ MULTIPLE-CHOICE QUESTIONS

Circle the letter that corresponds to the best answer.

1. Which is a primary use for national income accounting?
(a) It provides a basis for assessing the performance of the economy.
(b) It measures economic efficiency in specific industries.
(c) It estimates expenditures on nonproduction transactions.
(d) It analyzes the cost of pollution to the economy.

2. Gross domestic product (GDP) is defined as
(a) personal consumption expenditures and gross private domestic investment
(b) the sum of wage and salary compensation of employees, corporate profits, and interest income
(c) the market value of final goods and services produced within a country in 1 year
(d) the market value of all final and intermediate goods and services produced by the economy in 1 year

3. GDP provides an indication of society's valuation of the relative worth of goods and services because it
(a) provides an estimate of the value of secondhand sales
(b) gives increased weight to security transactions
(c) is an estimate of income received
(d) is a monetary measure

4. To include the value of the parts used in producing the automobiles turned out during a year in gross domestic product for that year would be an example of
(a) including a nonmarket transaction
(b) including a nonproduction transaction
(c) including a noninvestment transaction
(d) multiple counting

5. Which of the following is a public transfer payment?
(a) the sale of a used (secondhand) toy house at a garage sale
(b) the sale of shares of stock in Microsoft Corporation
(c) the Social Security benefits sent to a retired worker
(d) the birthday gift of a check for $50 sent by a grandmother to her grandchild

6. The sale in year 2 of an automobile produced in year 1 would not be included in the gross domestic product for year 2; doing so would involve
(a) including a nonmarket transaction
(b) including a nonproduction transaction
(c) including a noninvestment transaction
(d) public transfer payments

7. The service a babysitter performs when she stays at home with her baby brother while her parents are out and for which she receives no payment is not included in the gross domestic product because
(a) this is a nonmarket transaction
(b) this is a nonproduction transaction
(c) this is a noninvestment transaction
(d) multiple counting would be involved

8. According to national income accounting, money income derived from the production of this year's output is equal to
(a) corporate profits and indirect business taxes
(b) the amount spent to purchase this year's total output
(c) the sum of interest income and the compensation of employees
(d) gross private domestic investment less the consumption of fixed capital

9. Which would be considered an investment according to economists?
(a) the purchase of newly issued shares of stock in Microsoft
(b) the construction of a new computer chip factory by Intel
(c) the resale of stock originally issued by the General Motors Corporation
(d) the sale of a retail department store building by Sears to JCPenney

10. A refrigerator was produced by its manufacturer in year 1, sold to a retailer in year 1, and sold by the retailer to a final consumer in year 2. The refrigerator was
(a) counted as consumption in year 1
(b) counted as savings in year 1
(c) counted as investment in year 1
(d) not included in the gross domestic product of year 1

11. If gross private domestic investment is greater than depreciation, the economy will most likely be
(a) static
(b) expanding
(c) declining
(d) experiencing inflation

12. The annual charge that estimates the amount of capital equipment used up in each year's production is called
(a) indirect business taxes
(b) inventory reduction
(c) depreciation
(d) investment

13. GDP in an economy is $3452 billion. Consumer expenditures are $2343 billion, government purchases are $865 billion, and gross investment is $379 billion. Net exports are
(a) +$93 billion
(b) +$123 billion
(c) −$45 billion
(d) −$135 billion

14. The income approach to GDP sums the total income earned by U.S. resource suppliers, adds net foreign factor income earned in the United States, and also adds two adjustments:
(a) net investment and the consumption of fixed capital
(b) the consumption of fixed capital and indirect business taxes
(c) indirect business taxes and undistributed corporate profits
(d) undistributed corporate profits and financial transactions

15. What can happen to the allocation of corporate profits?
(a) It is paid to proprietors as income.
(b) It is paid to to stockholders as dividends.
(c) It is paid to the government as interest income.
(d) It is retained by the corporation as rents.

Questions 16 through 22 use the national income accounting data given in the following table.

	Billions of dollars
Net private domestic investment	$ 32
Personal taxes	39
Transfer payments	19
Indirect business taxes	8
Corporate income taxes	11
Personal consumption expenditures	217
Consumption of fixed capital	7
U.S. exports	15
Dividends	15
Government purchases	51
Net foreign factor income earned in the U.S.	0
Undistributed corporate profits	10
Social Security contributions	4
U.S. imports	17

16. Gross private domestic investment is equal to
(a) $32 billion
(b) $39 billion
(c) $45 billion
(d) $56 billion

17. Net exports are equal to
(a) −$2 billion
(b) $2 billion
(c) −$32 billion
(d) $32 billion

18. The gross domestic product is equal to
(a) $298 billion
(b) $302 billion
(c) $317 billion
(d) $305 billion

19. Corporate profits are equal to
(a) $15 billion
(b) $25 billion
(c) $26 billion
(d) $36 billion

20. The net domestic product is equal to
(a) $298 billion
(b) $302 billion
(c) $317 billion
(d) $321 billion

21. National income is equal to
(a) $245 billion
(b) $278 billion
(c) $290 billion
(d) $310 billion

22. Personal income is equal to
(a) $266 billion
(b) $284 billion
(c) $290 billion
(d) $315 billion

23. If both nominal gross domestic product and the level of prices are rising, it is evident that
(a) real GDP is constant
(b) real GDP is rising but not so rapidly as prices
(c) real GDP is declining
(d) no conclusion can be drawn concerning the real GDP of the economy on the basis of this information

24. Suppose nominal GDP rose from $500 billion to $600 billion while the GDP price index increased from 125 to 150. The real GDP
(a) remained constant
(b) increased
(c) decreased
(d) cannot be calculated from these figures

25. In an economy, the total expenditure for a market basket of goods in year 1 (the base year) was $4000 billion. In year 2, the total expenditure for the same market basket of goods was $4500 billion. What was the GDP price index for the economy in year 2?
(a) .88
(b) 1.13
(c) 188
(d) 113

26. Nominal GDP is less than real GDP in an economy in year 1. In year 2, nominal GDP is equal to real GDP. In year 3, nominal GDP is slightly greater than real GDP. In year 4, nominal GDP is significantly greater than real GDP. Which year is most likely to be the base year that is being used to calculate the price index for this economy?
(a) 1
(b) 2
(c) 3
(d) 4

27. Nominal GDP was $3774 billion in year 1 and the GDP deflator was 108 and nominal GDP was $3989 in year 2 and the GDP deflator that year was 112. What was real GDP in years 1 and 2, respectively?
(a) $3494 billion and $3562 billion
(b) $3339 billion and $3695 billion
(c) $3595 billion and $3725 billion
(d) $3643 billion and $3854 billion

28. A price index one year was 145, and the next year it was 167. What is the approximate percentage change in the price level from one year to the next as measured by that index?
(a) 12%
(b) 13%
(c) 14%
(d) 15%

29. GDP accounting includes
(a) the goods and services produced in the underground economy
(b) expenditures for equipment to reduce the pollution of the environment
(c) the value of the leisure enjoyed by citizens
(d) the goods and services produced but not bought and sold in the markets of the economy

30. Which is a major reason why GDP is *not* an accurate index of society's economic well-being?
(a) It includes changes in the value of leisure.
(b) It excludes many improvements in product quality.
(c) It includes transactions from the underground economy.
(d) It excludes transactions from the buying and selling of stocks.

■ **PROBLEMS**

1. Following are national income accounting figures for the United States.

	Billions of dollars
Exports	$ 367
Dividends	60
Consumption of fixed capital	307
Compensation of employees	1722
Government purchases	577
Rents	33
Indirect business taxes	255
Gross private domestic investment	437
Corporate income taxes	88
Transfer payments	320
Interest	201
Proprietors' income	132
Personal consumption expenditures	1810
Imports	338
Social Security contributions	148
Undistributed corporate profits	55
Personal taxes	372
Net foreign factor income earned in the U.S.	0

a. In the following table, use any of these figures to prepare an income statement for the economy similar to the one found in Table 7.3 of the text.

Receipts: Expenditures approach		Allocations: Income approach	
Item	Amount	Item	Amount
_____	$_____	_____	$_____
_____	$_____	_____	$_____
_____	$_____	_____	$_____
_____	$_____	_____	$_____
		_____	$_____
		_____	$_____
		_____	$_____
		National income	$_____
		_____	$_____
		_____	$_____
		_____	$_____
Gross domestic product	$_____	Gross domestic product	$_____

b. Use the other national accounts to find

(1) Net domestic product is $_____

(2) National income is $_____

(3) Personal income is $_____

(4) Disposable income is $_____

2. A farmer owns a plot of ground and sells the right to pump crude oil from his land to a crude oil producer. The crude oil producer agrees to pay the farmer $20 a barrel for every barrel pumped from the farmer's land.
a. During one year 10,000 barrels are pumped.

(1) The farmer receives a payment of $_____ from the crude oil producer.

(2) The value added by the farmer is $_____.
b. The crude oil producer sells the 10,000 barrels pumped to a petroleum refiner at a price of $25 a barrel.
(1) The crude oil producer receives a payment of

$_____ from the refiner.
(2) The value added by the crude oil producer is

$_____.
c. The refiner employs a pipeline company to transport the crude oil from the farmer's land to the refinery and pays the pipeline company a fee of $1 a barrel for the oil transported.
(1) The pipeline company receives a payment of

$_____ from the refiner.

(2) The value added by the company is $_____.
d. From the 10,000 barrels of crude oil, the refiner produces 315,000 gallons of gasoline and various by-products which are sold to distributors and gasoline service stations at an average price of $1 per gallon.
(1) The total payment received by the refiner from its

customers is $_____.

(2) The value added by the refiner is $_____.

e. The distributors and service stations sell the 315,000 gallons of gasoline and by-products to consumers at an average price of $1.30 a gallon.

(1) The total payment received by distributors and service stations is $_____.

(2) The value added by them is $_____.

f. The total value added by the farmer, crude oil producer, pipeline company, refiner, and distributors and service stations is $_____, and the market value of the gasoline and by-products (the final good) is $_____.

3. Following is a list of items which may or may not be included in the five income–output measures of the national income accounts (**GDP, NDP, NI, PI, DI**). Indicate in the space to the right of each which of the income–output measures includes this item; it is possible for the item to be included in none, one, two, three, four, or all of the measures. If the item is included in none of the measures, indicate why it is not included.

a. Interest on the national debt _____

_____

b. The sale of a used computer _____
c. The production of shoes that are not sold by the manufacturer _____

d. The income of a dealer in illegal drugs _____
e. The purchase of a share of common stock on the New York Stock Exchange _____
f. The interest paid on the bonds of the General Motors Corporation _____

g. The labor performed by a homemaker _____

h. The labor performed by a paid babysitter _____
i. The monthly check received by a college student from her parents _____

j. The purchase of a new tractor by a farmer _____

k. The labor performed by an assembly line worker in repapering his own kitchen _____

l. The services of a lawyer _____

m. The purchase of shoes from the manufacturer by a shoe retailer _____

n. The monthly check received from the Social Security Administration by a college student whose parents have died _____

o. The rent a homeowner would receive if she did not live in her own home _____

4. Following is hypothetical data for a market basket of goods in year 1 and year 2 for an economy.
a. Compute the expenditures for year 1.

MARKET BASKET FOR YEAR 1 (BASE YEAR)

Products	Quantity	Price	Expenditures
Toys	3	$10	$____
Pencils	5	2	$____
Books	7	5	$____
Total			$____

b. Compute the expenditures for year 2.

MARKET BASKET FOR YEAR 2

Products	Quantity	Price	Expenditures
Toys	3	$11	$____
Pencils	5	3	$____
Books	7	6	$____
Total			$____

c. In the space below, show how you computed the GDP price index for year 2.

_____

5. The following table shows nominal GDP figures for 3 years and the price indices for each of the 3 years. (The GDP figures are in billions.)

Year	Nominal GDP	Price index	Real GDP
1929	$104	121	$____
1933	56	91	$____
1939	91	100	$____

a. Use the price indices to compute the real GDP in each year. (You may round your answers to the nearest billion dollars.) Write answers in the table.
b. Which of the 3 years appears to be the base year?

_____

c. Between
(1) 1929 and 1933 the economy experienced (inflation, deflation) _____.

(2) 1933 and 1939 it experienced _____.
d. The nominal GDP figure
(1) for 1929 was (deflated, inflated, neither) _____

_____.

(2) for 1933 was _____.

(3) for 1939 was _____.
e. The price level

(1) fell by _____ % from 1929 to 1933.

(2) rose by _____ % from 1933 to 1939.

■ **SHORT ANSWER AND ESSAY QUESTIONS**

1. Of what use is national income accounting to economists and policymakers?

2. What is the definition of GDP? How are the values of output produced at a U.S.-owned factory in the United

States and a foreign-owned factory in the United States treated in GDP accounting?

3. Why is GDP a monetary measure?

4. How does GDP accounting avoid multiple counting and exaggeration of the value of GDP?

5. Why does GDP accounting exclude nonproduction transactions?

6. What are the two principal types of nonproduction transactions? List examples of each type.

7. What are the two sides to GDP accounting? What are the meaning and relationship between the two sides?

8. What would be included in personal consumption expenditures by households?

9. How is gross private domestic investment defined?

10. Is residential construction counted as investment or consumption? Explain.

11. Why is a change in inventories an investment?

12. How do you define an expanding production capacity using the concepts of gross private domestic investment and depreciation?

13. What do government purchases include and what do they exclude?

14. How are imports and exports handled in GDP accounting?

15. What are five income components of GDP that add up to national income? Define and explain the characteristics of each component.

16. What are three adjustments made to the income approach to GDP accounting to get it to balance with expenditures? Define and explain the characteristics of each one.

17. Explain how to calculate net domestic product (NDP), national income (NI), personal income (PI), and disposable income (DI).

18. What is the difference between real and nominal GDP? Describe two methods economists use to determine real GDP. Illustrate each method with an example.

19. Describe the real-world relationship between nominal and real GDP in the United States. Explain why nominal GDP may be greater or less than real GDP depending on the year or period selected.

20. Why might GDP not be considered an accurate measure of total output and the economic well-being of society? identify seven shortcomings of GDP.

ANSWERS

Chapter 7 Measuring Domestic Output and National Income

FILL-IN QUESTIONS

1. production, policies
2. market, final, in one year
3. within, does not
4. monetary, relative
5. final, intermediate, over, multiple
6. $1015
7. nonproduction, financial, second
8. durable, nondurable, services
9. capital, construction of new, inventories
10. depreciation, consumption
11. positive, expanding
12. minus, negative, positive
13. $C + I_g + G + X_n$
14. plus, public, private
15. taxes, dividends, profits
16. GDP, indirect, fixed, net
17. depreciation, capital, net domestic product
18. minus, net
19. plus, minus
20. personal, minus
21. nominal, real
22. divided, multiplied
23. nominal GDP, the price index
24. nominal, real
25. *a.* nonmarket, leisure; *b.* quality, composition; *c.* environment, underground

TRUE–FALSE QUESTIONS

1. T, p. 112	**11.** F, p. 115	**21.** F, pp. 124–125
2. F, pp. 112–113	**12.** F, pp. 115–116	**22.** T, pp. 124–125
3. F, p. 113	**13.** T, pp. 115–116	**23.** F, pp. 124–126
4. T, p. 113	**14.** F, p. 116	**24.** F, p. 125
5. F, p. 113	**15.** F, pp. 116–117	**25.** F, p. 126
6. T, p. 113	**16.** T, p. 117	
7. F, pp. 113–114	**17.** T, pp. 117–118	
8. T, p. 114	**18.** F, p. 119	
9. T, p. 114	**19.** T, p. 119	
10. F, pp. 114–115	**20.** T, pp. 123–124	

MULTIPLE-CHOICE QUESTIONS

1. a, p. 112	**11.** b, p. 116	**21.** c, p. 120
2. c, pp. 112–113	**12.** c, p. 116	**22.** b, pp. 120–121
3. d, p. 113	**13.** d, p. 117	**23.** d, pp. 124–125
4. d, p. 113	**14.** b, pp. 117–118	**24.** a, pp. 124–125
5. c, p. 114	**15.** b, p. 118	**25.** d, pp. 123–124
6. b, p. 114	**16.** b, pp. 115–117	**26.** b, pp. 124–125
7. a, pp. 114, 125	**17.** a, p. 117	**27.** a, pp. 124–125
8. b, p. 115	**18.** d, pp. 115–117	**28.** d, p. 124
9. b, pp. 115–116	**19.** d, p. 118	**29.** b, pp. 125–126
10. c, pp. 115–116	**20.** a, p. 120	**30.** b, pp. 125–126

PROBLEMS

1. *a.* See the following table; *b.* (1) 2546, (2) 2291, (3) 2320, (4) 1948

Receipts: Expenditures approach		Allocations: Income approach	
Personal consumption expenditures	$1810	Compensation of employees	$1722
Gross private domestic investment	437	Rents	33
		Interest	201
Government purchases	577	Proprietors' income	132
Net exports	29	Corporate income taxes	88
		Dividends	60
		Undistributed corporate profit	55
		National income	$2291
		Indirect business taxes	255
		Consumption of fixed capital	307
		Net foreign factor income earned in the U.S.	0
Gross domestic product	$2853	Gross domestic product	$2853

2. *a.* (1) 200,000, (2) 200,000; *b.* (1) 250,000, (2) 50,000; *c.* (1) 10,000, (2) 10,000; *d.* (1) 315,000, (2) 55,000; *e.* (1) 409,500, (2) 94,500; *f.* 409,500, 409,500

3. *a.* personal income and disposable income, a public transfer payment; *b.* none, a secondhand sale; *c.* all, represents investment (additions to inventories); *d.* none, illegal production and incomes are not included if not reported; *e.* none, a purely financial transaction; *f.* all; *g.* none, a nonmarket transaction; *h.* all if reported as income, none if not reported; *i.* none, a private transfer payment; *j.* all; *k.* none, a nonmarket transaction; *l.* all; *m.* all, represents additions to the inventory of the retailer; *n.* personal income and disposable income, a public transfer payment; *o.* all, estimate of rental value of owner-occupied homes is included in rents as if it were income and in personal consumption expenditures as if it were payment for a service

4. *a.* 30, 10, 35, 75; *b.* 33, 15, 42, 90; *c.* ($90/$75) 100 = 120

5. *a.* 86, 62, 91; *b.* 1939; *c.* (1) deflation, (2) inflation; *d.* (1) deflated, (2) inflated, (3) neither; *e.* (1) 24.8 (2) 9.9

SHORT ANSWER AND ESSAY QUESTIONS

CHAPTER 8

Introduction to Economic Growth and Instability

The economic health of a nation relies on **economic growth** because it reduces the burden of scarcity. Small differences in real growth rates result in large differences in the standards of living in nations. The first short section of the chapter introduces you to this important concept and identifies the two main sources of growth. It also presents data on the long-term growth record of the United States.

This record has been interrupted by periods of economic instability, a topic that is the major focus of the chapter. The second section of the chapter discusses the **business cycle:** the ups and downs in the employment of labor and real output of the economy that occur over the years. What may not be immediately evident to you, but will become clear as you read this chapter, is that these alternating periods of prosperity and hard times have taken place over a long period in which the trends in real output, employment, and the standard of living have been upward. During this long history booms and busts have occurred quite irregularly; their duration and intensity have been so varied that it is better to think of them as economic instability rather than regular business cycles.

Two principal problems result from the instability of the economy. The first problem is described in the third section of the chapter. Here you will find an examination of the **unemployment** that accompanies a downturn in the level of economic activity in the economy. You will first learn how economists measure the unemployment rate in the economy and the problems they encounter. You will also discover that there are three different kinds of unemployment, and that full employment means that less than 100% of the labor force is employed. You will also find out how unemployment imposes an economic cost on the economy and this cost is unequally distributed among different groups in our society.

The second major problem that results from economic instability is **inflation.** It is examined in the fourth section of the chapter, and also in the following two sections. Inflation is an increase in the general (or average) level of prices in an economy. It does not have a unique cause: It may result from increases in demand, from increases in costs, or from both sources.

Regardless of its cause, inflation may impose a real hardship on different groups in our society as you will learn in the fifth section of the chapter. **Inflation arbitrarily redistributes real income and wealth** in the economy. Unanticipated inflation hurts those on fixed incomes, those who save money, and those who lend money. If inflation is anticipated some of its burden can be reduced, but that depends on whether a group can protect their income with cost-of-living or interest rate adjustments.

Finally, inflation has redistribution effects on the real output of the economy as described in the last section of the chapter. **Cost-push inflation** and **demand-pull inflation** have different effects on output and employment that vary with the severity of the inflation. In the extreme, an economy can experience very high rates of inflation—**hyperinflation**—that can result in its breakdown.

Understanding the basics of economic growth and the twin problems of unemployment and inflation are important because it prepares you for later chapters and the explanations of how the macroeconomy works.

■ CHECKLIST

When you have studied this chapter you should be able to

☐ Define economic growth in two different ways.
☐ Explain why economic growth is an important goal.
☐ Describe how different growth rates affect real domestic output over time.
☐ Identify the two main sources of economic growth and indicate their relative importance.
☐ Describe the growth record of the U.S. economy since 1940, its rates of economic growth since 1950, and several qualifications to this record.
☐ Explain what the business cycle means.
☐ Describe the four phases of a generalized business cycle.
☐ Identify the immediate case of the cyclical changes in the levels of real output and employment.
☐ Explain differences in the way cyclical fluctuations affect industries producing capital and consumer durable goods, and how they affect those producing consumer nondurable goods and services.
☐ Describe how the Bureau of Labor Statistics (BLS) measures the rate of unemployment, and list the two criticisms of their survey data.
☐ Distinguish among frictional, structural, and cyclical types of unemployment, and explain the causes of these three kinds of unemployment.
☐ Define full employment and the full-employment unemployment rate (the natural rate of unemployment).
☐ Identify the economic and noneconomic costs of unemployment.
☐ Define the GDP gap and state Okun's law.
☐ Discuss the unequal burdens of unemployment.

☐ Define inflation and the rate of inflation.

☐ Explain how inflation is measured with the Consumer Price Index.

☐ Make international comparisons of inflation rate and unemployment rate data.

☐ Define demand-pull inflation.

☐ Define cost-push inflation and its relation to per-unit production costs.

☐ Describe the complexities involved in distinguishing between demand-pull and cost-push inflation.

☐ Distinguish between real and nominal income and calculate real income when given data on nominal income and the price level.

☐ List groups that are hurt by and groups that are unaffected or benefit from unanticipated inflation.

☐ Describe how the redistributive effects of inflation are changed when it is anticipated.

☐ Explain the difference between the real and the nominal interest rates.

☐ Make three final points about the redistribution effects of inflation.

☐ Describe the effect of cost-push inflation on real output.

☐ Explain the contrasting views on the effects of demand-pull inflation.

☐ Define hyperinflation and explain its effects on prices and real output.

■ **CHAPTER OUTLINE**

1. **Economic growth** can be defined as an increase in real GDP over some time period. It can also be defined as an increase in real GDP per capita over some time period. This second definition takes into account the size of the population. With either definition, economic growth is calculated as a percentage rate of growth per year.

   a. Economic growth is important because it lessens the burden of scarcity; it provides the means of satisfying economic wants more fully and fulfilling new wants.

   b. One or two percentage point differences in the rate of growth result in substantial differences in annual increases in the economy's output.

   c. Economic growth can be increased by increasing the inputs of resources and by increasing the **productivity** of those inputs. In the United States about one-third of growth comes from more inputs and two-thirds comes from improved productivity.

   d. Over the past 50 years the U.S. economy has an impressive record of economic growth. The growth record may be understated because it does not take into account improvements in product quality or increases in leisure time. The effects of growth on the environment or quality of life could be negative *or* positive.

   e. The growth record of the United States over the past 50 years lagged behind other major nations, but in the past decade it has surged ahead of those nations.

2. Economic growth in the U.S. economy has been interrupted by periods of inflation, recession, or both.

   a. The **business cycle** means alternating periods of prosperity and recession. These recurrent periods of ups and downs in employment, output, and prices are irregular in their duration and intensity, but the typical pattern is **peak, recession, trough,** and **recovery,** to another peak.

   b. Most economists think that changes in the levels of output and employment are largely the result of changes in the level of **total spending** in the economy.

   c. The business cycle affects almost the entire economy, but it does not affect all parts in the same way and to the same degree: The production of capital and consumer durable goods fluctuates more than the production of consumer nondurable goods and services during the cycle, because the purchase of capital and consumer durable goods can be postponed.

3. One of the twin problems arising from economic instability is **unemployment.**

   a. The **unemployment rate** is calculated by dividing the number of persons in the **labor force** who are unemployed by the total number of persons in the labor force. Unemployment data have been criticized for at least two reasons:

   (1) Part-time workers are considered fully employed.

   (2) **Discouraged workers** who have left the labor force are not counted as unemployed.

   b. Full employment does not mean that all workers in the labor force are employed and there is no unemployment; some unemployment is normal. There are at least three types of unemployment.

   (1) **Frictional unemployment** is due to workers searching for new jobs or waiting to take new jobs; this type of unemployment is generally desirable.

   (2) **Structural unemployment** is due to the changes in technology and in the types of goods and services consumers wish to buy; these changes affect the total demand for labor in particular industries or regions.

   (3) **Cyclical unemployment** is due to insufficient total spending in the economy; this type of unemployment arises during the recession phase of the business cycle.

   c. "Full employment" is less than 100% because some frictional and structural unemployment is unavoidable, The **full-employment unemployment rate** or the **natural rate of unemployment** (NRU) is the sum of frictional and structural unemployment, and is achieved when cyclical unemployment is zero (the real output of the economy is equal to its potential output). The natural rate is about 4 to 5% of the labor force. It is not automatically achieved and changes over time.

   d. Unemployment has an economic cost.

   (1) The **GDP** gap is a measure of that cost. It is the difference between actual and potential GDP. When the difference is negative, it means that the economy is underperforming relative to its potential. **Okun's law** predicts that for every 1% the actual unemployment rate exceeds the natural rate of unemployment, there is a negative GDP gap of about 2%.

   (2) This cost is unequally distributed among different groups of workers in the labor force.

   e. Unemployment also has noneconomic costs in the form of social and psychological problems.

f. Unemployment rates differ across nations because of differences in phases of the business cycle and natural rates of unemployment.

4. Over its history, the U.S. economy has experienced not only periods of unemployment but periods of **inflation.**

a. Inflation is an increase in the general level of prices in the economy; a decline in the level of prices is deflation.

b. The primary measure of inflation in the United States is the **Consumer Price Index** (CPI). It compares the prices of a "market basket" of consumer goods in a particular year to the prices for that market basket in a base period, to produce a price index. The rate of inflation from one year to the next is equal to the percentage change in the CPI between the current year and the preceding year. *The rule of 70* can be used to calculate the number of years it will take for the price level to double at any given rate of inflation.

c. The United States has experienced both inflation and deflation, but the past half-century has been a period of inflation. Other industrial nations also experienced inflation.

d. There are at least two causes of inflation. These may operate separately or simultaneously to raise the price level.

(1) **Demand-pull inflation** is the result of excess total spending in the economy.

(2) **Cost-push inflation** is the result of factors that raise **per-unit production costs.** This average cost is found by dividing the total cost of the resource inputs by the amount of output produced. With cost-push inflation, output and employment decline as the price level rises. The major source of this inflation has been supply shock from an increase in the prices of resource inputs.

e. It is difficult to distinguish between demand-pull and cost-push inflation in the real world.

5. Inflation arbitrarily redistributes real income and wealth. It benefits some groups and hurts other groups in the economy.

a. Whether someone benefits or is hurt by inflation is measured by what happens to real income. Inflation injures those whose real income falls and benefits those whose real income rises.

(1) **Real income** is determined by dividing **nominal income** by the price level expressed in hundredths.

(2) The percentage change in real income can be approximated by subtracting the percentage change in the price level from the percentage change in nominal income.

(3) The redistribution effects of inflation depend on whether it is anticipated or unanticipated.

b. **Unanticipated inflation** hurts *fixed-income receivers, savers,* and *creditors* because it lowers the real value of their assets.

c. Unanticipated inflation may not affect or may help *flexible-income receivers.* It helps *debtors* because it lowers the real value of debts to be repaid.

d. When there is **anticipated inflation** people can adjust their nominal incomes to reflect the expected rise in the price level, and the redistribution of income and wealth is lessened. To reduce the effects of inflation on a nominal interest rate, an inflation premium (the expected rate of inflation) is added to the **real interest rate.**

6. Inflation also has an effect on **real output** that varies by the type of inflation and its severity.

a. Cost-push inflation reduces real output, employment, and income.

b. Views of mild demand-pull inflation vary. It may reduce real output, or it may be a necessary by-product of economic growth.

c. *Hyperinflation*—extremely high rates of inflation—can lead to a breakdown of the economy by redistributing income and reducing real output and employment.

■ HINTS AND TIPS

1. Some students get confused by the seemingly contradictory term *full-employment unemployment rate* and related unemployment concepts. Full employment does not mean that everyone who wants to work has a job; it means that the economy is achieving its potential output and has a natural rate of unemployment. Remember that there are three types of unemployment: frictional, structural, and cyclical. There will always be some unemployment arising from frictional reasons (e.g., people searching for jobs) or structural reasons (e.g., changes in industry demand), and these two types of unemployment are "natural" for an economy. When there is cyclical unemployment because of a downturn in the business cycle, the economy is not producing its potential output. Thus, full-employment unemployment rate means that there are no cyclical reasons causing unemployment, only frictional or structural reasons.

2. To verify your understanding of how to calculate the unemployment rate, GDP gap, or inflation rate, do Problems 3, 4, and 5 in this *Study Guide* chapter.

3. Inflation is a rise in the *general* level of prices, not just a rise in the prices of a few products. An increase in product price is caused by supply or demand factors. You now know why the prices for many products rise in an economy. The macroeconomic reasons given in Chapter 8 for the increase in the general level of prices are different from the microeconomic reasons for a price increase that you learned about in Chapter 3.

■ IMPORTANT TERMS

economic growth	labor force
real GDP per capita	unemployment rate
rule of 70	discouraged workers
productivity	frictional unemployment
business cycle	structural unemployment
peak	cyclical unemployment
recession	full-employment rate of
trough	unemployment
recovery	

natural rate of
   unemployment (NRU)

potential output

GDP gap

Okun's law

inflation

Consumer Price Index (CPI)

demand-pull inflation

cost-push inflation

per-unit production costs

nominal income

real income

anticipated inflation

unanticipated inflation

cost-of-living adjustments
   (COLAs)

real interest rate

nominal interest rate

deflation

hyperinflation

SELF-TEST

■ FILL-IN QUESTIONS

1. Economic growth is best measured either by an increase in (nominal, real) _____ GDP over a time period or by an increase in _____ GDP per capita over a time period.

2. A rise in real output per capita (increases, decreases) _____ the standard of living and _____ the burden of scarcity in the economy.

3. Assume an economy has a real GDP of $3600 billion. If the growth rate is 5%, real GDP will increase by ($360, $180) _____ billion next year; but if the rate of growth is only 3%, the annual increase in real GDP will be ($54, $108)_____ billion. A two percentage point difference in the growth rate results in a ($72, $254) _____ billion difference in the annual increase in real GDP.

4. The two main ways that society can increase its real output and income are by increasing outputs of (products, resources) _____ and by increasing the (consumption, productivity) _____ of these inputs.

5. Since 1940, real GDP has increased (fourfold, sixfold) _____ and real GDP per capita has increased almost _____. These figures do not fully account for (better, worse) _____ products and services and (more, less) _____ leisure.

6. The business cycle is a term that encompasses the recurrent ups, or (decreases, increases) _____, and downs, or _____, in the level of business activity in the economy. The order of the four phases of a typical business cycle are peak, (recovery, trough, recession) _____, _____, and _____.

7. Expansion and contraction of the economy affect to a greater extent the production and employment in the consumer (durables, nondurables) _____ and (capital, consumer) _____ goods industries than they do (durable, nondurable) _____ goods and service industries.

8. The unemployment rate is found by dividing the number of (employed, unemployed) _____ persons by the (population, labor force) _____ and (multiplying, dividing)_____ by 100.

9. When workers are searching for new jobs or waiting to start new jobs, this type of unemployment is called (structural, frictional, cyclical) _____, but when workers are laid off because of changes in the consumer demand and technology in industries or regions, this unemployment is called _____; when workers are unemployed because of insufficient total spending in the economy, this type of unemployment is called _____.

10. The full-employment unemployment rate is called the (Okun, natural) _____ rate of unemployment. It is equal to the total of (frictional and structural, cyclical and frictional) _____ unemployment in the economy. It is realized when the (frictional, cyclical) _____ unemployment in the economy is equal to zero and when the actual output of the economy is (less than, equal to) _____ its potential output. When the economy achieves its natural rate of unemployment, the number of job seekers is (greater than, equal to) _____ the number of job vacancies.

11. The GDP gap is equal to the actual GDP (minus, plus) _____ the potential GDP. For every percentage point the unemployment rate rises above the natural rate, there will be a GDP gap of (2, 5) ____%.

12. The burdens of unemployment are borne more heavily by (black, white) _____, (adult, teenage) _____, and (white-collar, blue-collar) _____ workers, and the percentage of the labor force unemployed for 15 or more weeks is much (higher, lower) _____ than the overall unemployment rate.

13. Inflation means (an increase, a decrease) _____ in the general level of (unemployment, prices) _____ in the economy. To calculate the rate of inflation from year 1 to year 2, subtract the price index for year 1 from year 2, then (multiply, divide) _____ the result by the price index for year 1, and _____ by 100.

14. To find the approximate number of years it takes the price level to double, (multiply, divide) _____ 70 by the percentage annual increase in the rate of inflation. This approximation is called (Okun's law, rule of 70) _____.

15. The basic cause of demand-pull inflation is (an increase, a decrease) _____ in total spending beyond the full employment output rate in the economy. Cost-push inflation is explained in terms of factors that raise per-unit (inflation, production) _____ costs. In practice, it is (easy, difficult) _____ to distinguish between the two types of inflation.

16. The amount of goods and services one's nominal income can buy is called (variable, real) _____ income. If one's nominal income rises by 10% and the price level by 7%, the percentage of increase in (variable, real) _____ income would be (1, 2, 3) _____. If nominal income was $60,000 and the price index, expressed in hundredths, was 1.06, then (variable, real) _____ income would be ($56,604, $63,600) _____.

17. Unanticipated inflation hurts those whose nominal incomes are relatively (fixed, flexible) _____, penalizes (savers, borrowers) _____, and hurts (creditors, debtors) _____.

18. The redistributive effects of inflation are less severe when it is (anticipated, unanticipated) _____. Clauses in labor contracts that call for automatic adjustments of workers' incomes from the effects of inflation are called (unemployment benefits, cost-of-living) _____ adjustments.

19. The percentage increase in purchasing power that the lender receives from the borrower is the (real, nominal) _____ rate of interest; the percentage increase in money that the lender receives is the _____ rate of interest. If the nominal rate of interest is 8% and the real interest rate is 5%, then the inflation premium is (8, 5, 3)_____%.

20. Cost-push inflation (increases, decreases) _____ real output. The output effects of demand-pull inflation are (more, less) _____ certain. Some economists argue that mild demand-pull inflation (increases, decreases) _____ real output while others argue that it _____ real output. Economists generally agree that there may be an economic collapse from (hyperproduction, hyperinflation) _____.

■ TRUE–FALSE QUESTIONS

Circle T if the statement is true, F if it is false.

1. The more useful of the two definitions of economic growth for comparing living standards across economies is an increase in real GDP per capita. **T F**

2. Suppose two economies both have GDPs of $500 billion. If the GDPs grow at annual rates of 3% in the first economy and 5% in the second economy, the difference in their amounts of growth in one year is $10 billion. **T F**

3. Increased labor productivity has been more important than increased labor inputs in the growth of the U.S. economy. **T F**

4. Growth rate estimates generally attempt to take into account changes in the quality of goods produced and changes in the amount of leisure members of the economy enjoy. **T F**

5. The U.S. economy has always experienced steady economic growth, price stability, and full employment. **T F**

6. The business cycle is best defined as alternating periods of increases and decreases in the rate of inflation in the economy. **T F**

7. Individual business cycles tend to be of roughly equal duration and intensity. **T F**

8. The unemployment rate is equal to the number of people in the labor force divided by the number of people who are unemployed. **T F**

9. Frictional unemployment is not only inevitable but also partly desirable so that people can voluntarily move to better jobs. **T F**

10. The essential difference between frictionally and structurally unemployed workers is that the former *do not have* and the latter *do have* salable skills. **T F**

11. When the number of people seeking employment is less than the number of job vacancies in the economy, the actual rate of unemployment is less than the natural rate of unemployment, and the price level will tend to rise. **T F**

12. If unemployment in the economy is at its natural rate, the actual and potential outputs of the economy are equal. **T F**

13. An economy cannot produce an actual real GDP that exceeds its potential real GDP. **T F**

14. Unemployment imposes equal burdens on different groups in the economy. **T F**

15. The economy's GDP gap is measured by subtracting its potential GDP from its actual GDP. **T F**

16. The economic cost of cyclical unemployment is the goods and services that are not produced. **T F**

17. Inflation is defined as an increase in the total output of an economy. **T F**

18. From one year to the next, the Consumer Price Index rose from 154.5 to 160.5. The rate of inflation was therefore 6.6%. **T F**

19. If the price level increases by 10% each year, the price level will double every 10 years. **T F**

20. The essence of demand-pull inflation is "too much spending chasing too few goods." **T F**

21. Cost-push inflation explains rising prices in terms of factors that increase per-unit production cost. **T F**

22. A person's real income is the amount of goods and services that the person's nominal (or money) income will enable him or her to purchase. **T F**

23. Whether inflation is anticipated or unanticipated, the effects of inflation on the distribution of income are the same. **T F**

24. Borrowers are hurt by unanticipated inflation. **T F**

25. Hyperinflation may cause economic collapse in an economy by encouraging speculation, hoarding, and decisions based largely on inflationary expectations. **T F**

■ **MULTIPLE-CHOICE QUESTIONS**

Circle the letter that corresponds to the best answer.

1. Which is a benefit of real economic growth to a society?
(a) The society is less able to satisfy new wants.
(b) Everyone enjoys a greater nominal income.
(c) The burden of scarcity increases.
(d) The standard of living increases.

2. If the real output of an economy were to increase from $2000 billion to $2100 billion in 1 year, the rate of growth of real output during that year would be
(a) 1%
(b) 5%
(c) 10%
(d) 50%

3. Which is one of the four phases of a business cycle?
(a) inflation
(b) recession
(c) unemployment
(d) hyperinflation

4. Most economists believe that the immediate determinant of the levels of domestic output and employment is
(a) the price level
(b) the level of total spending
(c) the size of the civilian labor force
(d) the nation's stock of capital goods

5. Production and employment would be least affected by a severe depression in which type of industry?
(a) nondurable consumer goods
(b) durable consumer goods
(c) capital goods
(d) labor goods

6. The unemployment rate in an economy is 8%. The total population of the economy is 250 million, and the size of the civilian labor force is 150 million. The number of employed workers in this economy is
(a) 12 million
(b) 20 million
(c) 138 million
(d) 140 million

7. The labor force includes those who are
(a) less than 16 years of age
(b) in mental institutions
(c) not seeking work
(d) employed

8. The unemployment data collected by the Bureau of Labor Statistics have been criticized because
(a) part-time workers are not counted in the number of workers employed
(b) discouraged workers are not considered a part of the labor force
(c) it covers frictional unemployment, but not cyclical unemployment, which inflates unemployment figures
(d) the underground economy may understate unemployment

9. A worker who loses a job at a petroleum refinery because consumers and business firms switch from the use of oil to the burning of coal is an example of
(a) frictional unemployment
(b) structural unemployment
(c) cyclical unemployment
(d) disguised unemployment

10. A worker who has quit one job and is taking 2 weeks off before reporting to a new job is an example of
(a) frictional unemployment
(b) structural unemployment
(c) cyclical unemployment
(d) disguised unemployment

11. Insufficient total spending in the economy results in
(a) frictional unemployment
(b) structural unemployment
(c) cyclical unemployment
(d) disguised unemployment

12. The full-employment unemployment rate in the economy has been achieved when
(a) frictional unemployment is zero
(b) structural unemployment is zero
(c) cyclical unemployment is zero
(d) the natural rate of unemployment is zero

13. Which has helped decrease the natural rate of unemployment in the United States in recent years?
(a) a smaller proportion of young workers in the labor force
(b) the increased size of benefits for the unemployed
(c) less competition in product and labor markets
(d) more workers covered by unemployment programs

14. Okun's law predicts that when the actual unemployment rate exceeds the natural rate of unemployment by

two percentage points, there will be a negative GDP gap of about
- **(a)** 2% of the potential GDP
- **(b)** 3% of the potential GDP
- **(c)** 4% of the potential GDP
- **(d)** 5% of the potential GDP

15. If the negative GDP gap were equal to 6% of the potential GDP, the actual unemployment rate would exceed the natural rate of unemployment by
- **(a)** two percentage points
- **(b)** three percentage points
- **(c)** four percentage points
- **(d)** five percentage points

16. The burden of unemployment is *least* felt by
- **(a)** white-collar workers
- **(b)** teenagers
- **(c)** blacks
- **(d)** males

17. If the Consumer Price Index was 110 in one year and 117 in the next year, then the rate of inflation from one year to the next was
- **(a)** 3.5%
- **(b)** 4.7%
- **(c)** 6.4%
- **(d)** 7.1%

18. The price of a good has doubled in about 14 years. The approximate annual percentage rate of increase in the price level over this period has been
- **(a)** 2%
- **(b)** 3%
- **(c)** 4%
- **(d)** 5%

19. Only two resources, capital and labor, are used in an economy to produce an output of 300 million units. If the total cost of capital resources is $150 million and the total cost of labor resources is $50 million, then the per-unit production costs in this economy are
- **(a)** $0.67 million
- **(b)** $1.50 million
- **(c)** $2.00 million
- **(d)** $3.00 million

20. If a person's nominal income increases by 8% while the price level increases by 10%, the person's real income
- **(a)** increases by 2%
- **(b)** increases by 18%
- **(c)** decreases by 18%
- **(d)** decreases by 2%

21. If the average level of nominal income is $21,000 and the price level index is 154, the average real income would be about
- **(a)** $12,546
- **(b)** $13,636
- **(c)** $15,299
- **(d)** $17,823

22. Who would be hurt by *unanticipated* inflation?
- **(a)** those living on incomes with cost-of-living adjustments

- **(b)** those who find prices rising less rapidly than their nominal incomes
- **(c)** those who lent money at a fixed interest rate
- **(d)** those who became debtors when prices were lower

23. With no inflation, a bank would be willing to lend a business firm $10 million at an annual interest rate of 8%. But, if the rate of inflation was anticipated to be 6%, the bank would charge the firm an annual interest rate of
- **(a)** 2%
- **(b)** 6%
- **(c)** 8%
- **(d)** 14%

24. Which contributes to cost-push inflation?
- **(a)** an increase in employment and output
- **(b)** an increase in per-unit production costs
- **(c)** a decrease in resource prices
- **(d)** an increase in unemployment

25. If an economy has experienced an inflation rate of over 1000% per year for several years, this economic condition would best be described as
- **(a)** a cost-of-living adjustment
- **(b)** cost-push inflation
- **(c)** hyperinflation
- **(d)** GDP gap

■ **PROBLEMS**

1. Given the hypothetical data in the table below, calculate the annual rates of growth in real GDP and real per capita GDP over the period given. The numbers of real GDP are in billions.

Year	Real GDP	Annual growth in %	Real GDP per capita	Annual growth in %
1	$2,416		$11,785	
2	2,472	_____	11,950	_____
3	2,563	_____	12,213	_____
4	2,632	_____	12,421	_____
5	2,724	_____	12,719	_____
6	2,850	_____	12,948	_____

2. Suppose the real GDP and the population of an economy in seven different years were those shown in the following table.

Year	Population, million	Real GDP, billions of dollars	Per capita real GDP
1	30	$ 9	$ 300
2	60	24	_____
3	90	45	_____
4	120	66	_____
5	150	90	_____
6	180	99	_____
7	210	105	_____

a. How large would the real per capita GDP of the economy be in each of the other six years? Put your figures in the table.

b. What would have been the size of the optimum population of this economy?_____
c. What was the *amount* of growth in real GDP between year 1 and year 2? _____
d. What was the rate of growth in real GDP between year 3 and year 4? _____%

3. The following table gives statistics on the labor force and total employment during year 1 and year 5. Make the computations necessary to complete the table. (Numbers of persons are in thousands.)

	Year 1	Year 5
Labor force	84,889	95,453
Employed	80,796	87,524
Unemployed	_____	_____
Unemployment rate	_____	_____

a. How is it possible that *both* employment and unemployment increased? _____
_____

b. In relative terms, if unemployment increases, employment will decrease. Why? _____
_____

c. Would you say that year 5 was a year of full employment? _____

d. Why is the task of maintaining full employment over the years more than just a problem of finding jobs for those who happen to be unemployed at any given time?

_____
_____

4. Suppose that in year 1 an economy is at full employment, has a potential and actual real GDP of $3000 billion, and has an unemployment rate of 5.5%.
a. Compute the GDP gap in year 1 and enter it in the table that follows.

Year	Actual GDP	Potential GDP	GDP gap
1	$3000.0	$3000	$_____
2	3724.0	3800	_____
3	3712.5	4125	_____

b. The actual and potential real GDPs in years 2 and 3 are also shown in the table. Compute and enter into the table the GDP gaps in these 2 years.

c. In year 2, the actual real GDP is _____% of the potential real GDP. (Hint: Divide the actual real GDP by the potential real GDP and multiply by 100.)

(1) The actual real GDP is _____% less than the potential real GDP.

(2) Using Okun's law, the unemployment rate will rise from 5.5% in year 1 and be _____% in year 2.

d. In year 3 the actual real GDP is _____% of the potential real GDP.

(1) The actual real GDP is _____% less than the potential real GDP.
(2) The unemployment rate, according to Okun's law, will be _____%.

5. The following table shows the price index in the economy at the end of four different years.

Year	Price index	Rate of inflation
1	100.00	
2	112.00	_____%
3	123.20	_____
4	129.36	_____

a. Compute and enter in the table the rates of inflation in years 2, 3, and 4.
b. Employing the rule of 70, how many years would it take for the price level to double at each of these three inflation rates? _____
_____

c. If nominal income increased by 15% from year 1 to year 2, what was the approximate percentage change in real income? _____

d. If nominal income increased by 7% from year 2 to year 3, what was the approximate percentage change in real income? _____

e. If nominal income was $25,000 in year 2, what was real income that year? _____

f. If nominal income was $25,000 in year 3, what was real income that year? _____

g. If the nominal interest rate was 14% to borrow money from year 1 to year 2, what was the approximate real rate of interest over that period? _____

h. If the nominal interest rate was 8% to borrow money from year 3 to year 4, what was the approximate real rate of interest over that period? _____

6. Indicate in the space below each of the following the most likely effect—beneficial (**B**), detrimental (**D**), or indeterminate (**I**)—of unanticipated inflation on these persons:
a. A retired business executive who now lives each month by spending a part of the amount that was saved and deposited in a fixed-rate savings account for a long term.   _____
b. A retired private-school teacher who lives on the dividends received from shares of stock owned.

_____

c. A farmer who borrowed $500,000 from a bank at a fixed rate; the loan must be repaid in the next 10 years. _____

d. A retired couple whose sole source of income is the pension they receive from a former employer. _____

e. A widow whose income consists entirely of interest received from the corporate bonds she owns. _____

f. A public school teacher. _____
g. A member of a union who works for a firm that produces computers. _____

■ **SHORT ANSWER AND ESSAY QUESTIONS**

1. What two ways are used to measure economic growth? Why should the citizens of the United States be concerned with economic growth?

2. What is the relationship between real GDP produced in a year and the quantity of resource inputs and the productivity of those inputs?

3. Describe the growth record of the U.S. economy over the past half century and in the past decade. Compare recent U.S. growth rates with those in other nations.

4. Define the business cycle. Why do some economists prefer the term "business fluctuations" to "business cycle"? Describe the four phases of a business cycle.

5. In the opinion of most economists, what is the immediate determinant or cause of the fluctuations in the levels of output and employment in the economy?

6. Compare the manner in which the business cycle affects output and employment in the industries producing capital and durable goods with the way it affects industries producing nondurable goods and services. What causes these differences?

7. How is the unemployment rate measured in the United States? What criticisms have been made of the method the Bureau of Labor Statistics uses to determine the unemployment rate?

8. Distinguish among frictional, structural, and cyclical unemployment.

9. When is there full employment in the U.S. economy? (Answer in terms of the unemployment rate, the actual and potential output of the economy, and the markets for labor.)

10. What is the natural rate of unemployment? Will the economy always operate at the natural rate? Why is the natural rate subject to revision?

11. What is the economic cost of unemployment, and how is this cost measured? What is the quantitative relation-ship (called Okun's law) between the unemployment rate and the cost of unemployment?

12. What groups in the economy tend to bear the burdens of unemployment? How are women affected by unemployment, and how is the percentage of the labor force unemployed 15 or more weeks related to the unemployment rate in the economy?

13. How does the unemployment rate in the United States compare with the rates for other industrialized nations in recent years?

14. What is inflation, and how is the rate of inflation measured?

15. What has been the experience of the United States with inflation since the 1920s? How does the inflation rate in the United States compare with those of other industrialized nations in recent years?

16. Compare and contrast demand-pull and cost-push types of inflation.

17. What groups benefit from and what groups are hurt by inflation?

18. What is the difference between the effects of unanticipated inflation and the effects of anticipated inflation on the redistribution of real incomes in the economy?

19. What are the effects of cost-push and demand-pull inflation on real output? Are economists in agreement about these effects? Discuss.

20. Explain how the type and severity of inflation influence domestic output.

ANSWERS

Chapter 8 Introduction to Economic Growth and Instability

FILL-IN QUESTIONS

1. real, real
2. increases, decreases
3. $180, $108, $72
4. resources, productivity
5. sixfold, fourfold, better, more
6. increases, decreases, recession, trough, recovery
7. durables, capital, nondurable
8. unemployed, labor force, multiplying
9. frictional, structural, cyclical
10. natural, frictional and structural, cyclical, equal to, equal to
11. minus, 2
12. black, teenage, blue-collar, lower
13. an increase, prices, divide, multiply
14. divide, rule of 70
15. an increase, production, difficult
16. real, real, 3, real, $56,604
17. fixed, savers, creditors
18. anticipated, cost-of-living
19. real, nominal, 3
20. increases, less, increases, decreases, hyperinflation.

TRUE–FALSE QUESTIONS

1. T, p. 132
2. T, pp. 131–132
3. T, p. 132
4. F, p. 133
5. F, p. 133
6. F, pp. 133–134
7. F, pp. 133–134
8. F, pp. 135–136
9. T, pp. 136–137
10. F, pp. 136–137
11. T, pp. 137–138
12. T, pp. 137–138
13. F, p. 138
14. F, pp. 138–139
15. T, p. 138
16. T, p. 138
17. F, p. 141
18. F, pp. 141–142
19. F, pp. 141–142
20. T, p. 142
21. T, p. 143
22. T, p. 144
23. F, pp. 145–146
24. F, pp. 145–146
25. T, p. 148

MULTIPLE-CHOICE QUESTIONS

1. d, p. 132
2. b, pp. 131–132
3. b, p. 134
4. b, p. 135
5. a, p. 135
6. c, p. 136
7. d, p. 136
8. b, p. 136
9. b, pp. 136–137
10. a, pp. 136–137
11. c, p. 137
12. c, pp. 137–138
13. a, p. 138
14. c, p. 138
15. b, p. 138
16. a, pp. 138–140
17. c, p. 141
18. d, pp. 141–142
19. a, p. 143
20. d, p. 144
21. b, p. 144
22. c, pp. 144–145
23. d, p. 146
24. b, p. 147
25. c, p. 148

PROBLEMS

1. *real GDP*: years 1–2 (2.3%); years 2–3 (3.7%); years 3–4 (2.7%); years 4–5 (3.5%); years 5–6 (4.6%); *real GDP per capita*: years 1–2 (1.4%); years 2–3 (2.2%); years 3–4 (1.7%); years 4–5 (2.4%); years 5–6 (1.8%)

2. *a.* 400, 500, 550, 600, 550, 500; *b.* 150 million; *c.* $15 billion; *d.* 46.7%

3. year 1: 4,093, 4.8; year 5: 7,929, 8.3; *a.* the labor force increased more than employment increased; *b.* because unemployment and employment in relative terms are percentages of the labor force and *always* add to 100%, and if one increases the other must decrease; *c.* no economist would argue that the full-employment unemployment rate is as high as 8.3% and year 5 was not a year of full employment; *d.* the number of people looking for work expands

4. *a.* 0; *b.* 76, 412.5; *c.* 98, (1) 2, (2) 6.5; *d.* 90, (1) 10, (2) 10.5

5. *a.* 12, 10, 5; *b.* 5.8, 7, 14; *c.* 3; *d.* −3; *e.* $22,321; *f.* $20,292; *g.* 2; *h.* 3

6. *a.* D; *b.* I; *c.* B; *d.* D; *e.* D; *f.* I; *g.* I

SHORT ANSWER AND ESSAY QUESTIONS

1. pp. 131–132
2. p. 132
3. p. 133
4. pp. 133–134
5. p. 135
6. p. 135
7. pp. 135–136
8. pp. 136–137
9. pp. 137–138
10. pp. 137–138
11. pp. 138–139
12. pp. 138–140
13. p. 140
14. p. 141
15. p. 142
16. pp. 142–143
17. pp. 144–146
18. pp. 144–146
19. pp. 147–148
20. pp. 147–148

CHAPTER 9

Basic Macro Relationships

This chapter introduces you to three basic relationships in the economy: income and consumption, the interest rate and investment, and changes in spending and changes in output. The relationships between these economic "aggregates" are essential building blocks for understanding the macro models that will be presented in the next two chapters.

The first section of Chapter 9 describes the relationship between the largest aggregate in the economy—*consumption.* An explanation of consumption, however, also entails a study of saving because saving is simply the part of disposable income that is not consumed. This section develops the consumption and saving schedules and describes their main characteristics. Other key concepts are also presented: average propensities to consume (APC), and save (APS), marginal propensities to consume (MPC), and save (MPS), and the nonincome determinants of consumption and saving.

Investment is the subject of the next section of the chapter. The purchase of capital goods depends on the rate of return that business firms expect to earn from an investment and on the real rate of interest they have to pay for the use of money. Because firms are anxious to make profitable investments and to avoid unprofitable ones, they undertake all investments that have an expected rate of return greater than (or equal to) the real rate of interest and do not undertake an investment when the expected rate of return is less than the real interest rate. This relationship between the real interest rate and the level of investment spending is an inverse one: the lower the interest rate, the greater the investment spending. It is illustrated by a downsloping *investment demand curve.* As you will learn, this curve can be shifted by five factors that can change the expected rate of return on investment. You will also learn that investment, unlike consumption, is quite volatile and is the most unstable component of total spending in the economy.

The third section of the chapter introduces you to the concept of the *multiplier.* It shows how an initial change in spending for consumption or investment changes real GDP by an amount that is larger than the initial stimulus. You will also learn about the rationale for the multiplier and how to interpret it. The multiplier can be derived from the marginal propensity to consume and the marginal propensity to save. You will have learned about these marginal propensities at the beginning of the chapter and now they are put to further use as you end the chapter.

■ CHECKLIST

When you have studied this chapter you should be able to

☐ Explain how consumption and saving are related to disposable income.
☐ Draw a graph to illustrate the relationship among consumption, saving, and disposable income.
☐ Construct a hypothetical consumption schedule.
☐ Construct a hypothetical saving schedule, and identify the level of break-even income.
☐ Compute the four propensities (APC, APS, MPC, and MPS) when given the necessary data.
☐ State the relationship between the APC and the APS as income increases.
☐ Demonstrate that the MPC is the slope of the consumption schedule and the MPS is the slope of the saving schedule.
☐ Explain each of the five nonincome determinants of consumption and saving.
☐ Explain the difference between a change in the amount consumed (or saved) and a change in the consumption (or saving) schedule.
☐ Explain how the expected rate of return affects investment decisions.
☐ Describe the influence of the real interest rate on an investment decision.
☐ Draw a graph of an investment demand curve for the business sector and explain what it shows.
☐ Explain how each of the five noninterest determinants of investment will shift the investment demand curve.
☐ Give four reasons why investment spending tends to be unstable.
☐ Define the multiplier effect in words, with a ratio, and using an equation.
☐ Make three clarifying points about the multiplier.
☐ Cite two facts on which the rationale for the multiplier is based.
☐ Discuss the relationship between the multiplier and the marginal propensities.
☐ Find the value of the multiplier when you are given the necessary information.
☐ Explain the significance of the multiplier.
☐ Discuss the reasons for the difference between the textbook example for the multiplier and the actual multiplier for the U.S. economy.

■ CHAPTER OUTLINE

1. There is a positive or direct relationship between *consumption* and disposable income (after-tax income) because as disposable income increases so does consumption. *Saving* is disposable income not spent for consumer goods. Disposable income is the most important determinant of both consumption and saving. The relationship among disposable income, consumption, and saving can be shown by a graph with consumption on the vertical axis and disposable income on the horizontal axis. The 45-degree line on the graph would show where consumption would equal disposable income. If consumption is less than disposable income, the difference is saving.

   a. The *consumption schedule* shows the amounts that households plan to spend for consumer goods at various levels of income, given a price level.

   b. The *saving schedule* indicates the amounts households plan to save at different income levels, given a price level.

   c. The average propensity to consume (**APC**) and the average propensity to save (**APS**) and the marginal propensity to consume (**MPC**) and the marginal propensity to save (**MPS**) can be computed from the consumption and saving schedules.

   (1) The APC and the APS are, respectively, the percentages of income spent for consumption and saved, and they sum to 1.

   (2) The MPC and the MPS are, respectively, the percentages of additional income spent for consumption and saved; and they sum to 1.

   (3) The MPC is the slope of the consumption schedule, and the MPS is the slope of the saving schedule when the two schedules are graphed.

   d. In addition to income, there are several other important determinants of consumption and saving. Changes in these nonincome determinants will cause the consumption and saving schedules to change. An increase in spending will shift the consumption schedule upward and a decrease in spending will shift it downward. Similarly, an increase in saving will shift the saving schedule upward and a decrease in saving will shift it downward.

   (1) The amount that households spend and save depends on their amount of *wealth*. If household wealth increases, people will spend more because they think they are wealthier (the wealth effect), and they will save less.

   (2) *Expectations* about the future affect spending and saving decisions. If prices are expected to rise in the future, people will spend more today and save less.

   (3) *Real interest rates* change spending and saving decisions. When real interest rates fall, households tend to consume more, borrow more, and save less.

   (4) The level of *household debt* influences consumption. Increasing debt will increase consumption, but if the debt level gets too high it will decrease consumption, because households have to spend money to pay off loans.

   (5) *Taxation* affects spending and saving. The higher taxes reduce both consumption and saving.

   e. Three other considerations need to be noted:

   (1) A change in the amount consumed (or saved) is not the same thing as a change in the consumption (or saving) schedule.

   (2) Changes in wealth, expectations, and household debt shift consumption and saving schedules in opposite directions; tax changes shift the consumption and saving schedules in the same direction.

   (3) Both consumption and saving schedules tend to be stable over time.

2. The investment decision is a marginal benefit and marginal cost decision that depends on the expected rate of return (*r*) from the purchase of additional capital goods and the real rate of interest (*i*) that must be paid for borrowed funds.

   a. The *expected rate of return* is directly related to the net profits (revenues less operating costs) that are expected to result from an investment. It is the marginal benefit of investment for a business.

   b. The *real rate of interest* is the price paid for the use of money. It is the marginal cost of investment for a business. When the expected real rate of return is greater (less) than the real rate of interest, a business will (will not) invest because the investment will be profitable (unprofitable).

   c. For this reason, the lower (higher) the real rate of interest, the greater (smaller) will be the level of investment spending in the economy; the *investment demand curve* shows this inverse relationship between the real rate of interest and the level of spending for capital goods. The amount of investment by the business sector is determined at the point where the marginal benefit of investment (*r*) equals the marginal cost (*i*).

   d. There are at least five noninterest determinants of investment demand, and a change in any of these determinants will shift the investment demand curve.

   (1) If the *acquisition, maintenance, and operating costs* for capital goods change, then this change in costs will change investment demand. Rising costs decrease investment demand and declining costs increase it.

   (2) Changes in *business taxes* are like a change in costs so they have a similar effect on investment demand as the previous item.

   (3) *An increase in technological progress* will stimulate investment and increase investment demand.

   (4) *The stock of existing capital goods* will influence investment decisions. If the economy is overstocked, there will be a decrease in investment demand, and if the economy is understocked there will be an increase in investment demand.

   (5) *Expectations* of the future are important. If expectations are positive because of more expected sales or profits, there is likely to be an increase in investment demand. Negative expectations will have an opposite effect on investment demand.

   e. Unlike consumption and saving, investment is inherently unstable. Four factors explain this instability.

(1) *Capital goods are durable,* so when they get replaced may depend on the optimism or pessimism of business owners. If owners are more optimistic about the future they will likely spend more to obtain new capital goods.

(2) *Innovation is not regular,* which means that technological progress is highly variable and contributes to instability in investment spending decisions.

(3) *Profit expectations* influence the investment spending of businesses, but profits are highly variable.

(4) *Other expectations* concerning such factors as exchange rates, the state of the economy, and the stock market can create positive or negative expectations that change investment spending.

3. There is a direct relationship between changes in spending and changes in real GDP. The initial change in spending, however, results in an increase in real GDP that is greater than the initial change in spending. This outcome is called the ***multiplier effect.*** The multiplier is the ratio of the change in the real GDP to the initial change in spending. The initial change in spending typically comes from investment spending, but changes in consumption, net exports, or government spending can also have multiplier effects.

a. The multiplier effect occurs because a change in the dollars spent by one person alters the income of another person in the same direction, and because any change in the income of one person will change the person's consumption and saving in the same direction by a fraction of the change in income. For example, assuming a marginal propensity to consume (MPC) of .75, a change in investment spending of $5.00 will cause a change in consumption of $3.75. The change in consumption ($3.75) will become someone else's income in the second round. The process will continue through successive rounds, but the amount of income in each round will diminish by 25 percent because that is the amount saved from each change in income. After all rounds are completed the initial change of $5 in investment spending produces a total of $20 change because the multiplier was 4 (see Table 9.3 in the text).

b. There is a formula for calculating the multiplier. The multiplier is directly related to the marginal propensity to consume (MPC) and inversely related to the marginal propensity to save (MPS). The multiplier is equal to $[1/(1 - MPC)]$. It is also equal to $[1/MPS]$. The significance of the multiplier is that relatively small changes in the spending plans of business firms or households bring about large changes in the equilibrium real GDP.

c. The simple multiplier that has been described differs from the actual multiplier for the economy. In the simple case the only factor that reduced income in successive rounds was the fraction that went to savings. For the domestic economy, there are other leakages from consumption besides saving such as spending on imports and payment of taxes. These factors reduce the value of the multiplier. For the U.S. economy the multiplier is estimated to be about 2.

■ HINTS AND TIPS

1. An important graph in the chapter is the ***consumption schedule*** (see Key Graph 9.2). Know how to interpret it. There are two lines on the graph. The 45-degree reference line shows all points where disposable income equals consumption (there is no saving). The consumption schedule line shows the total amount of disposable income spent on consumption at each and every income level. Where the two lines *intersect,* all disposable income is spent (consumed). At all income levels to the right of the intersection, the consumption line lies below the 45-degree line, and not all disposable income is spent (there is saving). To the left of the intersection, the consumption line lies above the 45-degree line and consumption exceeds disposable income (there is dissaving).

2. Always remember that ***marginal propensities*** sum to 1 (MPC + MPS = 1). The same is true for average propensities (APC + APS = 1). Thus, if you know the value of one marginal propensity (e.g., MPC), you can always figure out the other (e.g., 1 − MPC = MPS).

3. The ***multiplier*** effect is a key concept in this chapter and in the ones that follow, so make sure you understand how it works.

a. The multiplier is simply the ratio of the change in real GDP to the *initial* changes in spending. Multiplying the *initial* change in spending by the *multiplier* gives you the amount of change in real GDP.

b. The multiplier effect works in both positive and negative directions. An *initial* decrease in spending will result in a larger decrease in real GDP, or an *initial* increase in spending will create a larger increase in real GDP.

c. The multiplier is directly related to the marginal propensities. The multiplier equals 1/MPS. The multiplier also equals 1/(1 − MPC).

d. The main reason for the multiplier effect is that the *initial* change in income (spending) induces additional rounds of income (spending) that add progressively less each round as some of the income (spending) gets saved because of the marginal propensity to save (see Table 9.3 of the text).

■ IMPORTANT TERMS

45° (degree) line	**marginal propensity to consume (MPC)**
consumption schedule	
saving schedule	**marginal propensity to save (MPS)**
break-even income	
average propensity to consume (APC)	**wealth effect**
	expected rate of return
average propensity to save (APS)	**investment demand curve**
	multiplier

SELF-TEST

■ FILL-IN QUESTIONS

1. The consumption schedule shows the various amounts that households plan to (save, consume)

_____ at various levels of disposable income, while the saving schedule shows the various amounts that households plan to _____.

2. Both consumption and saving are (directly, indirectly) _____ related to the level of disposable income. At lower levels of disposable income, households tend to spend a (smaller, larger) _____ proportion of this income and save a _____ proportion, but at higher levels of disposable income, they tend to spend a (smaller, larger) _____ proportion of this income and save a _____ proportion. At the break-even income, consumption is (greater than, less than, equal to) _____ disposable income.

3. As disposable income falls, the average propensity to consume (APC) will (rise, fall) _____ and the average propensity to save (APS) will _____.

4. The sum of APC and APS is equal to (0, 1) _____. If the APC is .90, then the APS is (.10, 1) _____.

5. The marginal propensity to consume (MPC) is the change in (consumption, income) _____ divided by the change in _____.

6. The marginal propensity to save (MPS) is the change in (saving, income) _____ divided by the change in _____.

7. The sum of MPC and MPS is equal to (0, 1) _____. If the MPC is .75, then the MPS is (0, .25) _____.

8. The MPC is the numerical value of the slope of the (consumption, saving) _____ schedule, and the MPS is the numerical value of the slope of the _____ schedule.

9. The most important determinants of consumption spending, other than the level of income, are

a. _____

b. _____

c. _____

d. _____

e. _____

10. An increase in the consumption schedule means that the consumption schedule shifts (upward, downward) _____ and a decrease in the consumption schedule means that it will shift _____, and these shifts occur because of a change in one of the non-income determinants. An increase in the amount consumed occurs because of an increase in (income, stability) _____.

11. The investment spending decision depends on the expected rate of (interest, return) _____ and the real rate of _____.

12. The expected rate of return is the marginal (cost, benefit) _____ of investment and the real rate of return is the marginal _____ of investment.

13. If the expected rate of return on an investment is greater than the real rate of interest for the use of money, a business firm will (increase, decrease) _____ its investment spending, but if the expected rate of return is less than the real rate of interest, the firm will _____ its investment spending.

14. The relationship between the real rate of interest and the total amount of investment in the economy is (direct, inverse) _____ and is shown in the investment (supply, demand) _____ curve. This curve shows that if the real rate of interest rises, the quantity of investment will (increase, decrease) _____, but if the real rate of interest falls, the quantity of investment will _____.

15. Five noninterest determinants of investment demand are

a. _____

b. _____

c. _____

d. _____

e. _____

16. The demand for new capital goods tends to be unstable because of the (durability, nondurability) _____ of capital goods, the (regularity, irregularity) _____ of innovation, the (stability, variability) _____ of current and expected profits, and the _____ of expectations.

17. The multiplier is the change in real GDP (multiplied, divided) _____ by an initial change in spending. When the initial change in spending is _____ by the multiplier, the result equals the change in real GDP.

18. The multiplier means that an increase in initial spending may create a multiple (increase, decrease) _____ in real GDP, and also that a decrease in initial spending may create a multiple _____ in real GDP.

19. The multiplier has a value equal to 1 divided by the marginal propensity to (consume, save) _____, which is the same thing as 1 divided by the quantity of 1 minus the marginal propensity to _____.

20. The higher the value of the marginal propensity to consume, the (larger, smaller) _____ the value of the multiplier, but the larger the value of the marginal propensity to save, the _____ the value of the multiplier.

■ TRUE–FALSE QUESTIONS

Circle T if the statement is true, F if it is false.

1. Consumption equals disposable income plus saving.
T F

2. The most significant determinant of the level of consumer spending is disposable income.
T F

3. Historical data suggest that the level of consumption expenditures is directly related to the level of disposable income.
T F

4. Consumption rises and saving falls when disposable income increases.
T F

5. Empirical data suggest that households tend to spend a similar proportion of a small disposable income than of a larger disposable income.
T F

6. The break-even income is the income level at which business begins to make a profit.
T F

7. The average propensity to save is equal to the level of saving divided by the level of consumption.
T F

8. The marginal propensity to consume is the change in consumption divided by the change in income.
T F

9. The slope of the saving schedule is equal to the average propensity to save.
T F

10. An increase in wealth will increase the consumption schedule (shift the consumption curve upward). **T F**

11. An increase in the taxes paid by consumers will decrease both the amount they spend for consumption and the amount they save.
T F

12. Both the consumption schedule and the saving schedule tend to be relatively stable over time. **T F**

13. The real interest rate is the nominal interest rate minus the rate of inflation.
T F

14. A business firm will purchase additional capital goods if the real rate of interest it must pay exceeds the expected rate of return from the investment.
T F

15. An increase in the stock of capital goods on hand will decrease the investment-demand curve.
T F

16. The relationship between the rate of interest and the level of investment spending is called the interest schedule.
T F

17. Investment tends to be relatively stable over time.
T F

18. The irregularity of innovations and the variability of business profits contribute to the instability of investment expenditures.
T F

19. The multiplier is equal to the change in real GDP multiplied by the initial change in spending.
T F

20. The initial change in spending for the multiplier is usually associated with investment spending because of investment's volatility.
T F

21. The multiplier effect works only in a positive direction in changing GDP.
T F

22. The multiplier is based on the idea that any change in income will cause both consumption and saving to vary in the same direction as a change in income and by a fraction of that change in income.
T F

23. The higher the marginal propensity to consume, the larger the size of the multiplier.
T F

24. When it is computed as 1/MPS, the multiplier reflects only the leakage of income into saving.
T F

25. The value of the actual multiplier for the economy will usually be greater than the value of a textbook multiplier because the actual multiplier is based only on the marginal propensity to save.
T F

■ MULTIPLE-CHOICE QUESTIONS

Circle the letter that corresponds to the best answer.

1. Saving equals
 (a) investment plus consumption
 (b) investment minus consumption
 (c) disposable income minus consumption
 (d) disposable income plus consumption

2. As disposable income decreases, *ceteris paribus,*
 (a) both consumption and saving increase
 (b) consumption increases and saving decreases
 (c) consumption decreases and saving increases
 (d) both consumption and saving decrease

3. Households tend to spend a larger portion of
 (a) a small disposable income than a large disposable income
 (b) a large disposable income than a small disposable income
 (c) their disposable income on saving when the rate of return is high
 (d) their saving than their disposable income when the rate of return is low

4. If consumption spending increases from $358 to $367 billion when disposable income increases from $412 to $427 billion, it can be concluded that the marginal propensity to consume is
 (a) 0.4
 (b) 0.6
 (c) 0.8
 (d) 0.9

APC = $\frac{1}{375}$

5. If disposable income is $375 billion when the average propensity to consume is 0.8, it can be concluded that
   (a) the marginal propensity to consume is also 0.8
   (b) the marginal propensity to save is 0.2
   (c) consumption is $325 billion
   (d) saving is $75 billion

6. As the disposable income of the economy increases
   (a) both the APC and the APS rise
   (b) the APC rises and the APS falls
   (c) the APC falls and the APS rises
   (d) both the APC and the APS fall

7. The slope of the consumption schedule or line for a given economy is the
   (a) marginal propensity to consume
   (b) average propensity to consume
   (c) marginal propensity to save
   (d) average propensity to save

Answer Questions 8 and 9 on the basis of the following graph.

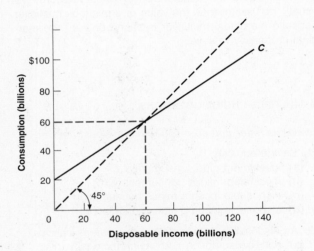

8. This graph indicates that
   (a) consumption decreases after the $60 billion level of disposable income
   (b) the marginal propensity to consume decreases after the $60 billion level of disposable income
   (c) consumption decreases as a percentage of disposable income as disposable income increases
   (d) consumption increases as disposable income decreases

9. If the relevant saving schedule were constructed, one would find that
   (a) the marginal propensity to save is negative up to the $60 billion level of disposable income
   (b) the marginal propensity to save increases after the $60 billion level of disposable income
   (c) saving is zero at the $60 billion level of disposable income
   (d) saving is $20 billion at the $0 level of disposable income

*Answer Questions 10, 11, and 12 on the basis of the following disposable income (**DI**) and consumption (**C**) schedules for a private, closed economy. All figures are in billions of dollars.*

DI	C
$ 0	$ 4
40	40
80	76
120	112
160	148
200	184

10. If plotted on a graph, the slope of the consumption schedule would be
    (a) 0.6
    (b) 0.7
    (c) 0.8
    (d) 0.9

11. At the $160 billion level of disposable income, the average propensity to save is
    (a) 0.015
    (b) 0.075
    (c) 0.335
    (d) 0.925

12. If consumption increases by $5 billion at each level of disposable income, then the marginal propensity to consume will
    (a) change, but the average propensity to consume will not change
    (b) change, and the average propensity to consume will change
    (c) not change, but the average propensity to consume will change
    (d) not change, and the average propensity to consume will not change

13. If the slope of a linear saving schedule decreases, then it can be concluded that
    (a) the MPS has decreased
    (b) the MPC has decreased
    (c) income has decreased
    (d) income has increased

14. An increase in wealth shifts the consumption schedule
    (a) downward and the saving schedule upward
    (b) upward and the saving schedule downward
    (c) downward and the saving schedule downward
    (d) upward and the saving schedule upward

15. Expectations of a recession are likely to lead households to
    (a) increase consumption and saving
    (b) decrease consumption and saving
    (c) decrease consumption and increase saving
    (d) increase consumption and decrease saving

16. Higher real interest rates are likely to
    (a) increase consumption and saving
    (b) decrease consumption and saving
    (c) decrease consumption and increase saving
    (d) increase consumption and decrease saving

17. An increase in taxes shifts the consumption schedule
(a) downward and the saving schedule upward
(b) upward and the saving schedule downward
(c) downward and the saving schedule downward
(d) upward and the saving schedule upward

18. Which relationship is an inverse one?
(a) consumption and disposable income
(b) investment spending and the rate of interest
(c) saving and disposable income
(d) investment spending and GDP

19. A decrease in investment demand would be a consequence of a decline in
(a) the rate of interest
(b) the level of wages paid
(c) business taxes
(d) expected future sales

20. Which would increase investment demand?
(a) an increase in business taxes
(b) an increase in the cost of acquiring capital goods
(c) a decrease in the rate of technological change
(d) a decrease in the stock of capital goods on hand

21. Which best explains the variability of investment?
(a) the predictable useful life of capital goods
(b) constancy or regularities in business innovations
(c) instabilities in the level of profits
(d) business pessimism about the future

22. If there was a change in investment spending of $10 and the marginal propensity to save was .25, then real GDP would increase by
(a) $10
(b) $20
(c) $25
(d) $40

23. If the value of the marginal propensity to consume is 0.6 and real GDP falls by $25, this was caused by a decrease in initial spending of
(a) $10.00
(b) $15.00
(c) $16.67
(d) $20.00

24. If the marginal propensity to consume is 0.67 and initial spending increases by $25, real GDP will
(a) increase by $75
(b) decrease by $75
(c) increase by $25
(d) decrease by $25

25. If in an economy a $150 billion increase in investment spending creates $150 billion of new income in the first round of the multiplier process and $105 billion in the second round, the multiplier and the marginal propensity to consume will be, respectively,
(a) 5.00 and 0.80
(b) 4.00 and 0.75
(c) 3.33 and 0.70
(d) 2.50 and 0.40

■ **PROBLEMS**

1. The following table is a consumption schedule. Assume taxes and transfer payments are zero and that all saving is personal saving.

(GDP = DI)	C	S	APC	APS
$1500	$1540	$_____	1.027	−.027
1600	1620	_____	1.013	−.013
1700	1700	_____	_____	_____
1800	1780	_____	.989	.011
1900	1860	_____	.979	.021
2000	1940	_____	_____	_____
2100	2020	_____	.962	.038
2200	2100	_____	_____	_____

a. Compute saving at each of the eight levels of disposable income and the missing average propensities to consume and to save.
b. The break-even level of disposable income is $_____.
c. As disposable income rises, the marginal propensity to consume remains constant. Between each two GDPs the MPC can be found by dividing $_____ by $_____, and is equal to _____.
d. The marginal propensity to save also remains constant when the GDP rises. Between each two GDPs the MPS is equal to $_____ divided by $_____, or to _____.
e. Plot the consumption schedule, the saving schedule, and the 45-degree line on the graph on the next page.
(1) The numerical value of the slope of the consumption schedule is _____, and the term that is used to describe it is the _____.
(2) If the relevant saving schedule were constructed, the numerical value of the slope of the saving schedule would be _____, and the term that is used to describe it would be the _____.

2. Indicate in the space to the right of each of the following events whether the event will tend to increase (+) or decrease (−) the saving schedule.
a. Development of consumer expectations that prices will be higher in the future _____
b. Gradual shrinkage in the quantity of real assets owned by consumers _____
c. Increase in the volume of consumer indebtedness _____
d. Growing belief that disposable income will be lower in the future _____
e. Expectations that there will be a current shortage of consumer goods _____

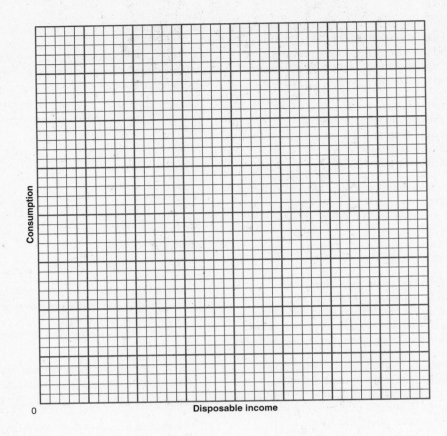

Consumption (vertical axis)

Disposable income (horizontal axis)

0

f. Rise in the actual level of disposable income _____

g. An increase in the financial assets owned by consumers _____

h. Development of a belief by consumers that the Federal government can and will prevent recessions in the future _____

3. The following schedule has eight different expected rates of return, and the dollar amounts of the investment projects expected to have each of these return rates.

Expected rate of return	Investment projects (billions)
18%	$ 0
16	10
14	20
12	30
10	40
8	50
6	60
4	70

a. If the real rate of interest in the economy were 18%, business firms would plan to spend $_____ billion for investment, but if the real interest rate were 16%, they would plan to spend $_____ for investment.

b. Should the real interest rate be 14%, they would still wish to make the investments they were willing to make at real interest rates of 18% and 16%, they would plan to spend an additional $_____ billion for investment, and their total investment would be $_____ billion.

c. If the real rate of interest were 12%, they would make all the investments they had planned to make at higher real interest rates plus an additional $_____ billion, and their total investment spending would be $_____ billion.

d. Complete the following table by computing the amount of planned investment at the four remaining real interest rates.

Real rate of interest	Amount of investment (billions)
18%	$ 0
16	10
14	30
12	60
10	_____
8	_____
6	_____
4	_____

e. Graph the schedule you completed on the following graph. Plot the real rate of interest on the vertical axis and the amount of investment planned at each real rate of interest on the horizontal axis.

0

f. Both the graph and the table show that the relationship between the real rate of interest and the amount of investment spending in the economy is

_____. This means that when the real rate of interest

(1) increases, investment will (increase, decrease)

_____.

(2) decreases, investment will _____.

g. It also means that should we wish to

(1) increase investment, we would need to

_____ the real rate of interest.

(2) decrease investment, we would have to

_____ the real rate of interest.

h. This graph (or table) is the _____ curve.

4. Indicate in the space to the right of the following events whether the event would tend to increase (+) or decrease (−) investment spending.

a. Rising stock market prices _____

b. Development of expectations by business executives that business taxes will be higher in the future

_____

c. Step-up in the rates at which new products and new production processes are being introduced _____

d. Business beliefs that wage rates may be lower in the future and labor and capital are complementary resources _____

e. An expectation of a recession _____

f. A belief that business is "too good" and the economy is due for a period of "slow" consumer demand _____

g. Rising costs in the construction industry _____

h. A rapid increase in the size of the economy's population _____

i. A recent period of a high level of investment spending, which has resulted in productive capacity in excess of the current demand for goods and services _____

5. Assume the marginal propensity to consume is 0.8 and the change in investment is $10. Complete the following table modeled after Table 9.3 in the textbook.

	Change in income	Change in consumption	Change in saving
Increase in gross investment of $10	$ + 10	$_____	$_____
Second round	_____	_____	_____
Third round	_____	_____	_____
Fourth round	_____	_____	_____
Fifth round	_____	_____	_____
All other rounds	16.38	13.10	3.28
Totals	_____	_____	_____

■ **SHORT ANSWER AND ESSAY QUESTIONS**

1. What is the most important determinant of consumer spending and personal saving? What is the relationship between consumer spending and personal saving?

2. Use a graph to illustrate the historical relationship between consumption and disposable income in the U.S. economy. Explain why the slope of the consumption line will be less than the 45-degree reference line.

3. Describe the relationship between consumption and disposable income, called the consumption schedule. Draw a graph of this schedule.

4. Describe the relationship between saving and disposable income, called the saving schedule. Draw a graph of this schedule.

5. Define the two average propensities and the two marginal propensities.

6. Explain briefly how the average propensity to consume and the average propensity to save vary as disposable income varies. Why do APC and APS behave this way? What happens to consumption and saving as disposable income varies?

7. Why do the sum of the APC and the APS and the sum of the MPC and the MPS always equal exactly 1?

8. What is the relationship between MPC and MPS and the slopes of the consumption schedule and saving schedule?

9. Explain briefly and explicitly *how* changes in the five nonincome determinants will affect the consumption schedule and the saving schedule and *why* such changes will affect consumption and saving in the way you have indicated.

10. Which of the five nonincome determinants of consumption will shift the consumption schedule one way and the saving schedule the other way? Which one will shift both the consumption and saving schedules in the same direction?

11. What is the difference between a change in the amount consumed and a change in the consumption schedule? Explain your answer using a graph.

12. Are consumption and saving schedules relatively stable? Explain.

13. Discuss the marginal cost and marginal benefit of an investment decision. How are the marginal cost and the marginal benefit of investment measured?

14. Draw an investment demand curve. Use it to explain why investment spending tends to rise when the real rate of interest falls, and vice versa.

15. Identify and explain how five noninterest determinants of investment spending can increase or decrease the amount of investment. Illustrate the changes with a graph.

16. Why does the level of investment spending tend to be highly unstable? State four reasons.

17. What is the multiplier effect?

18. Give a rationale for the multiplier effect.

19. How is the multiplier effect related to the marginal propensities? Explain in words and equations.

20. How large is the actual multiplier effect? Explain the reasons for the difference between the textbook example of the multiplier and actual multiplier for the economy.

ANSWERS

Chapter 9 Basic Macro Relationships

FILL-IN QUESTIONS

1. consume, save
2. directly, larger, smaller, smaller, larger, equal to
3. rise, fall
4. 1, .10
5. consumption, income
6. saving, income
7. 1, .25
8. consumption, saving
9. *a.* wealth; *b.* expectations; *c.* real interest rate; *d.* level of household debt; *e.* taxation (any order for *a–e*)
10. upward, downward, income
11. return, interest
12. benefit, cost
13. increase, decrease
14. inverse, demand, decrease, increase
15. *a.* the cost of acquiring, maintaining, and operating capital goods; *b.* business taxes; *c.* technological change; *d.* the stock of capital goods on hand; *e.* expectations

16. durability, irregularity, variability, variability
17. divided, multiplied
18. increase, decrease
19. save, consume
20. larger, smaller

TRUE–FALSE QUESTIONS

1. F, p. 152	**10.** T, pp. 156–157	**19.** F, p. 164
2. T, p. 152	**11.** T, p. 157	**20.** T, p. 164
3. T, p. 152	**12.** T, p. 158	**21.** F, p. 164
4. F, pp. 153–154	**13.** T, p. 159	**22.** T, pp. 164–166
5. F, pp. 153–154	**14.** F, pp. 159–160	**23.** T, p. 166
6. F, p. 154	**15.** T, p. 162	**24.** T, pp. 166–167
7. F, pp. 154–156	**16.** F, pp. 160–161	**25.** F, pp. 166–167
8. T, p. 156	**17.** F, pp. 162–164	
9. F, p. 156	**18.** T, pp. 162–164	

MULTIPLE-CHOICE QUESTIONS

1. c, p. 152	**10.** d, pp. 155–156	**19.** d, p. 162
2. d, pp. 152–153	**11.** b, p. 154	**20.** d, p. 162
3. a, pp. 152–153	**12.** c, p. 156	**21.** c, p. 164
4. b, p. 156	**13.** a, p. 156	**22.** d, pp. 164–166
5. d, p. 154	**14.** b, p. 157	**23.** a, pp. 164–166
6. c, p. 154	**15.** c, p. 157	**24.** b, pp. 164–166
7. a, p. 156	**16.** c, p. 157	**25.** c, pp. 164–166
8. c, pp. 155–156	**17.** c, p. 157	
9. c, pp. 155–156	**18.** b, pp. 160–161	

PROBLEMS

1. *a.* S: −40, −20, 0, 20, 40, 60, 80, 100; APC: 1.000, 0.970, 0.955; APS: 0.000, 0.030, 0.045; *b.* 1700; *c.* 80, 100, .8; *d.* 20, 100, .20; *e.* (1) .8, MPC, (2) .2, MPS
2. *a.* −; *b.* +; *c.* −; *d.* +; *e.* −; *f.* none; *g.* −; *h.* −
3. *a.* 0, 10; *b.* 20, 30; *c.* 30, 60; *d.* 100, 150, 210, 280; *f.* inverse, (1) decrease, (2) increase; *g.* (1) lower, (2) raise; *h.* investment-demand
4. *a.* +; *b.* −; *c.* +; *d.* +; *e.* −; *f.* −; *g.* −; *h.* +; *i.* −
5. Change in income: 8.00, 6.40, 5.12, 4.10, 50; Change in consumption: 8.00, 6.40, 5.12, 4.10, 3.28, 40.00; Change in saving: 2.00, 1.60, 1.28, 1.02, 0.82, 10.00

SHORT ANSWER AND ESSAY QUESTIONS

1. p. 152	**8.** p. 156	**15.** pp. 161–162
2. p. 153	**9.** pp. 156–157	**16.** pp. 162–164
3. pp. 153–155	**10.** pp. 157–158	**17.** p. 164
4. pp. 153–155	**11.** pp. 157–158	**18.** pp. 164–165
5. pp. 154–156	**12.** p. 158	**19.** p. 166
6. p. 154	**13.** p. 159	**20.** pp. 166–167
7. pp. 154–156	**14.** pp. 160–161	

CHAPTER 10

The Aggregate Expenditures Model

This chapter develops the first macroeconomic model of the economy presented in the textbook—the **aggregate expenditures model.** You will find out what determines the demand for real domestic output (real GDP) and how an economy achieves an equilibrium level of output.

The chapter begins with some simplifying assumptions and then explains how the investment decisions of individual firms can be used to construct an **investment schedule.** The investment schedule is then combined with the consumption schedule to form an aggregate expenditures schedule that shows the various amounts that will be spent in a private closed economy at each possible output or income level. These aggregate expenditures in tabular or graphical form can be used to find **equilibrium GDP** for this economy. It will be important for you to understand how equilibrium GDP is determined and why this level of output will be produced when you are given information about consumption and investment schedules.

Two other features of this simplified aggregate expenditures model are worth noting. Saving and *actual* investment are always equal because they are defined in exactly the same way: the output of the economy minus its consumption. **Saving** and **planned investment,** however, are equal only when real GDP is at its equilibrium level. When real GDP is *not* at its equilibrium level, saving and planned investment are *not* equal and there are **unplanned changes in inventories.** Equilibrium real GDP is achieved when saving and *planned* investment are equal and there are no unplanned changes in inventories.

From Chapter 10 you will also learn **what causes real GDP to rise and fall** based on changes or additions to aggregate expenditures. The first change that will be discussed is the effect of a change in investment spending on equilibrium real GDP in a closed private economy. The initial change in investment will increase equilibrium real GDP by more than the initial investment stimulus because of the multiplier effect.

The methods used to find the equilibrium real GDP in an open economy (one that exports and imports) is the same one as for a closed economy. The economy will tend to produce a real GDP that is equal to aggregate expenditures. The only difference is that now the aggregate expenditures include not only consumption and investment but also the **net exports** (exports minus imports). An increase in net exports, like an increase in investment, will increase the equilibrium real GDP. A change in net exports also has a multiplier effect on real GDP just like a change in investment.

The section on "Adding the Public Sector" introduces **government taxing and spending** into the analysis of equilibrium real GDP. Government purchases of goods and services add to aggregate expenditures, and taxation reduces the disposable income of consumers, thereby reducing both the amount of consumption and the amount of saving that will take place at any level of real GDP. You will need to know the level of real GDP that will be produced and why.

It is important to be aware that the equilibrium real GDP is not necessarily the real GDP at which full employment is achieved. Aggregate expenditures may be greater or less than the full-employment real GDP. If they are greater, there is an **inflationary gap.** If they are less, there exists a **recessionary gap.** The chapter explains how to measure the size of each gap: the amount by which the aggregate expenditures schedule must change to bring the economy to its full-employment real GDP. Several historical examples are given to help you see the application of recessionary and inflationary gaps.

The aggregate expenditures model is a valuable tool for explaining such economic events as recession, inflation, and economic growth. The model also has limitations. The last section of the chapter describes the major shortcomings and how later chapters in the textbook will address them.

■ CHECKLIST

When you have studied this chapter you should be able to

☐ Describe the simplifying assumptions in this chapter.
☐ Construct an investment schedule showing the relationship between planned investment and GDP.
☐ Combine the consumption and investment schedule to form an aggregate expenditures schedule to explain the equilibrium levels of output, income, and employment in a private closed economy.
☐ Explain why the economy will tend to produce its equilibrium GDP rather than some smaller or larger level of real GDP.
☐ Illustrate graphically equilibrium in an aggregate expenditure model with consumption and investment components.
☐ Explain the relationship between saving and planned investment at equilibrium GDP.

☐ State the conditions for changes in inventories at equilibrium GDP.

☐ Discuss why equilibrium real GDP changes when the aggregate expenditure schedule shifts upward due to an increase in investment spending.

☐ Use the concept of net exports to define aggregate expenditures in an open economy.

☐ Describe the net export schedule and its relationship to real GDP.

☐ Explain what the equilibrium real GDP in an open economy will be when net exports are positive and when net exports are negative.

☐ Find the equilibrium real GDP in an open economy when given the tabular or graphical data.

☐ Give three examples of how circumstances or policies abroad can affect domestic GDP.

☐ List three simplifying assumptions used to add the public sector to the aggregate expenditures model.

☐ Find the equilibrium real GDP in an economy in which the government purchases goods and services when given the tabular or graphical data.

☐ Determine the effect on the equilibrium real GDP when lump-sum taxes are included in the aggregate expenditures model.

☐ Describe the conditions for leakages and injections and unplanned changes in inventories at the equilibrium level of GDP.

☐ Distinguish between the equilibrium real GDP and the full-employment real GDP.

☐ Find the recessionary and the inflationary gaps when you are provided the relevant data.

☐ Apply the concepts of recessionary and inflationary gaps to two historical events in the United States.

☐ Explain five shortcomings of the aggregate expenditures model.

■ **CHAPTER OUTLINE**

1. To simplify the explanation of the **aggregate expenditures model,** it is first assumed that the economy is private and closed, which means there is no international trade or government spending (or taxes). It is also assumed that: Output or income measures are equal (real GDP = disposable income, DI); aggregate output and employment are directly related to aggregate expenditures; and the economy has excess production capacity and unemployed labor, so the price level is constant.

2. The investment decisions of businesses in an economy can be aggregated to form an **investment schedule** that shows the amounts business firms collectively plan to invest at each possible level of GDP. A simplifying assumption is made that investment is independent of disposable income or real GDP.

3. In the aggregate expenditures model, the **equilibrium GDP** is the real GDP at which
   a. aggregate expenditures (consumption plus planned investment) equal real GDP, or
   b. in graphical terms, the aggregate expenditures curve crosses the 45-degree line. The slope of this curve is equal to the marginal propensity to consume.

4. The **investment schedule** indicates what investors plan to do. Actual investment consists of both planned and unplanned investment (unplanned changes in inventories).
   a. At above equilibrium levels of GDP, **saving** is greater than **planned investment,** and there will be unintended or unplanned investment through increases in inventories. At below equilibrium levels of GDP, planned investment is greater than saving, and there will be unintended or unplanned disinvestment through a decrease in inventories.
   b. Equilibrium is achieved when planned investment equals saving and there are no **unplanned changes in inventories.**

5. Changes in investment (or consumption) will cause the equilibrium real GDP to change in the same direction by an amount greater than the initial change in investment (or consumption). The reason for this greater change is due to the **multiplier effect.**

6. In an **open economy** there are **net exports** (X_n), which are defined as exports (X) minus imports (M).
   a. The equilibrium real GDP in an open economy means real GDP is equal to consumption plus investment plus net exports.
   b. The net export schedule will be positive when exports are greater than imports, and negative when imports are greater than exports.
   c. Any increase in X_n will increase the equilibrium real GDP with a multiplier effect. A decrease in X_n will do just the opposite.
   d. In an open economy model, circumstances and policies abroad can affect the U.S. GDP. There can be changes in:
   (1) the level of national incomes abroad;
   (2) tariffs or quotas; and
   (3) exchange rates.

7. Changes in **government spending and tax rates** can affect equilibrium real GDP. This simplified analysis assumes that government purchases do not affect investment or consumption, that taxes are purely personal taxes, and that a fixed amount of taxes are collected regardless of the level of GDP.
   a. **Government purchases** of goods and services add to the aggregate expenditures schedule and increase equilibrium real GDP; an increase in these purchases has a multiplier effect on equilibrium real GDP.
   b. **Taxes** decrease consumption and the aggregate expenditures schedule by the amount of the tax times the **MPC.** They decrease saving by the amount of the tax times the **MPS.** An increase in taxes has a negative multiplier effect on the equilibrium real GDP.
   (1) When government both taxes and purchases goods and services, the equilibrium GDP is the real GDP at which aggregate expenditures (consumption + investment + net exports + government purchases of goods and services) equals real GDP.
   (2) Or from a leakages and injections perspective, the equilibrium GDP is the real GDP at which leakages (saving + imports + taxes) equals injections (investment + exports + government purchases).

(3) At equilibrium real GDP, there are no unplanned changes in inventories.

8. The *equilibrium level of real GDP* may turn out to be an equilibrium that is at less than full employment, at full employment, or at full employment with inflation.

   a. If the equilibrium real GDP is less than the real GDP consistent with full-employment real GDP, there exists a *recessionary gap.* Aggregate expenditures are less than what is needed to achieve full-employment real GDP. The size of the recessionary gap equals the amount by which the aggregate expenditures schedule must increase (shift upward) to increase the real GDP to its full-employment level.

   b. The U.S. recession of 2001 is an example of a recessionary gap as investment spending declined, thus reducing aggregate expenditures.

   c. If aggregate expenditures are *greater* than those consistent with full-employment real GDP, then there is an *inflationary gap.* This gap results from excess spending and will increase the price level, creating demand-pull inflation. The size of the inflationary gap equals the amount by which the aggregate expenditures schedule must decrease (shift downward) if the economy is to achieve full-employment real GDP.

   d. The example of the inflationary gap is the U.S. inflation in the late 1980s during which the economy moved beyond its full-employment output and the price level rose.

9. There are *five limitations* of the aggregate expenditures model: an inability to measure price-level changes or the rate of inflation; no explanation for why demand-pull inflation can occur before the economy reaches its full-employment level of output; no insights into why the economy can expand beyond its full-employment level of real GDP; no coverage of cost-push inflation; and it does not permit "self-correction."

■ **HINTS AND TIPS**

1. Do not confuse the *investment demand curve* for the business sector with the *investment schedule* for an economy. The former shows the inverse relationship between the real interest rate and the amount of total investment by the business sector, whereas the latter shows the collective investment intentions of business firms at each possible level of disposable income or real GDP.

2. The distinction between *actual investment, planned investment,* and *unplanned investment* is important for determining the equilibrium level of real GDP. Actual investment includes both planned and unplanned investment. At any level of real GDP, saving and actual investment will always be equal by definition, but saving and planned investment may not equal real GDP because there may be unplanned investment (unplanned changes in inventories). Only at the equilibrium level of real GDP will saving and planned investment be equal (there is no unplanned investment).

3. There is an important difference between *equilibrium and full-employment real GDP* in the aggregate expenditures model. Equilibrium means no tendency for the economy to change its output (or employment) level. Thus, an economy can experience a low level of output and high unemployment and still be at equilibrium. The *recessionary gap* shows how much aggregate expenditures need to increase, so that when this increase is multiplied by the multiplier, it will shift the economy to a higher equilibrium and to the full-employment level of real GDP. Remember that you multiply the needed increase in aggregate expenditures (the recessionary gap) by the multiplier to calculate the change in real GDP that moves the economy from below to full-employment equilibrium.

■ **IMPORTANT TERMS**

planned investment	unplanned changes in inventories
investment schedule	net exports
aggregate expenditures schedule	lump-sum tax
equilibrium GDP	recessionary gap
leakage	inflationary gap
injection	

SELF-TEST

■ **FILL-IN QUESTIONS**

1. Some simplifying assumptions used in the first part of the chapter are that the economy is (an open, a closed) _____ economy, the economy is (private, public) _____, that real GDP equals disposable (consumption, income) _____, and that an increase in aggregate expenditures will (increase, decrease) _____ real output and employment, but not raise the price level.

2. A schedule showing the amounts business firms collectively intend to invest at each possible level of GDP is the (consumption, investment) _____ schedule. For this schedule, it is assumed that planned (saving, investment) _____ is independent of the level of current disposable income or real output.

3. Assuming a private and closed economy, the equilibrium level of real GDP is determined where aggregate expenditures are (greater than, less than, equal to) _____ real domestic output, consumption plus investment is _____ real domestic output, and the aggregate expenditures schedule or curve intersects the (90-degree, 45-degree) _____ line.

4. A leakage is (an addition to, a withdrawal from) _____ the income expenditure stream, whereas an injection is _____ the income expenditure stream. In this chapter, an example of a leakage is (investment, saving) _____, and an example of an injection is _____.

5. If aggregate expenditures are greater than the real domestic output, saving is (greater than, less than) _____ planned investment, there are unplanned (increases, decreases) _____ in inventories, and real GDP will (rise, fall) _____.

6. If aggregate expenditures are less than the real domestic output, saving is (greater than, less than) _____ planned investment, there are unplanned (increases, decreases) _____ in inventories, and real GDP will (rise, fall) _____.

7. If aggregate expenditures are equal to the real domestic output, saving is (greater than, less than, equal to) _____ planned investment, unplanned changes in inventories are (negative, positive, zero) _____, and real GDP will neither rise nor fall.

8. An upshift in the aggregate expenditures schedule will (increase, decrease) _____ the equilibrium GDP. The upshift in the aggregate expenditures schedule can result from (an increase, a decrease) _____ in the consumption schedule or _____ in the investment schedule.

9. When investment spending increases, the equilibrium real GDP (increases, decreases) _____, and when investment spending decreases, the equilibrium real GDP _____. The changes in the equilibrium real GDP are (greater, less) _____ than the initial changes in investment spending because of the (lump-sum tax, multiplier) _____.

10. In an open economy, a nation's net exports are equal to its exports (plus, minus) _____ its imports. In the open economy, aggregate expenditures are equal to consumption (plus, minus) _____ investment (plus, minus) _____ net exports.

11. What would be the effect, an increase (+) or a decrease (−), of each of the following on an open economy's equilibrium real GDP?

    a. an increase in imports _____

    b. an increase in exports _____

    c. a decrease in imports _____

    d. a decrease in exports _____

    e. an increasing level of national income among trading partners _____

    f. an increase in trade barriers imposed by trading partners _____

    g. a depreciation in the value of the economy's currency _____

12. Increases in public spending will (decrease, increase) _____ the aggregate expenditures schedule and equilibrium real GDP, but decreases in public spending will _____ the aggregate expenditures schedule and equilibrium real GDP.

13. A tax yielding the same amount of tax revenue at each level of GDP is a (lump-sum, constant) _____ tax.

14. Taxes tend to reduce consumption at each level of real GDP by an amount equal to the taxes multiplied by the marginal propensity to (consume, save) _____; saving will decrease by an amount equal to the taxes multiplied by the marginal propensity to _____.

15. In an economy in which government both taxes and purchases goods and services, the equilibrium level of real GDP is the real GDP at which aggregate (output, expenditures) _____ equal(s) real domestic _____, and at which real GDP is equal to consumption (plus, minus) _____ investment (plus, minus) _____ net exports (plus, minus) _____ purchases of goods and services by government.

16. When the public sector is added to the model, the equation for the leakages and injections shows (consumption, investment) _____ plus (imports, exports) _____, plus purchases of goods and services by government equals (consumption, saving) _____ plus (exports, imports) _____ plus taxes.

17. A recessionary gap exists when equilibrium real GDP is (greater, less) _____ than the full-employment real GDP. To bring real GDP to the full-employment level, the aggregate expenditures schedule must (increase, decrease) _____ by an amount equal to the difference between the equilibrium and the full-employment real GDP (multiplied, divided) _____ by the multiplier.

18. The amount by which aggregate spending at the full-employment GDP exceeds the full-employment level of real GDP is (a recessionary, an inflationary)

_____ gap. To eliminate this gap, the aggregate expenditures schedule must (increase, decrease) _____.

19. One limitation of the aggregate expenditures model is that it can explain (cost-push, demand-pull) _____ inflation but not _____ inflation. Another problem is that the model also has no way of measuring the rate of (interest, inflation) _____ because there is no price level.

20. Three other limitations of the aggregate expenditures model are its inability to explain premature (demand-pull, cost-push) _____ inflation, how the economy can expand (to, beyond) _____ the full-employment level of output, and how the economy "self- (inflates," corrects") _____.

■ TRUE–FALSE QUESTIONS

Circle T if the statement is true, F if it is false.

1. The basic premise of the aggregate expenditures model is that the amount of goods and services produced and the level of employment depend directly on the level of total spending. **T F**

2. In the aggregate expenditures model of the economy, the price level is assumed to be constant. **T F**

3. The investment schedule is a schedule of planned investment rather than a schedule of actual investment. **T F**

4. The equilibrium level of GDP is that GDP level corresponding to the intersection of the aggregate expenditures schedule with the 45-degree line. **T F**

5. At levels of GDP below equilibrium, the economy wants to spend at higher levels than the levels of GDP the economy is producing. **T F**

6. At levels of GDP below equilibrium, aggregate expenditures are less than GDP, which causes inventories to rise and production to fall. **T F**

7. Saving is an injection into and investment is a leakage from the income expenditures stream. **T F**

8. Saving and actual investment are always equal. **T F**

9. Saving at any level of real GDP equals planned investment plus unplanned changes in inventories. **T F**

10. The equilibrium level of GDP will change in response to changes in the investment schedule or the consumption schedule. **T F**

11. If there is a decrease in the investment schedule, there will be an upshift in the aggregate expenditures schedule. **T F**

12. Through the multiplier effect, an initial change in investment spending can cause a magnified change in domestic output and income. **T F**

13. The net exports of an economy equal the sum of its exports and imports of goods and services. **T F**

14. An increase in the volume of a nation's exports, other things being equal, will expand the nation's real GDP. **T F**

15. An increase in the imports of a nation will increase the exports of other nations. **T F**

16. A falling level of real output and income among U.S. trading partners enables the United States to sell more goods abroad. **T F**

17. An appreciation of the dollar will increase net exports. **T F**

18. If the MPS were 0.3 and taxes were levied by the government so that consumers paid $20 in taxes at each level of real GDP, consumption expenditures at each level of real GDP would be $14 less. **T F**

19. Equal changes in government spending and taxes do not have equivalent effects on real GDP. **T F**

20. At equilibrium, the sum of leakages equals the sum of injections. **T F**

21. The equilibrium real GDP is the real GDP at which there is full employment in the economy. **T F**

22. The existence of a recessionary gap in the economy is characterized by the full employment of labor. **T F**

23. An inflationary gap is the amount by which the economy's aggregate expenditures schedule must shift downward to eliminate demand-pull inflation and still achieve the full-employment GDP. **T F**

24. The aggregate expenditures model is valuable because it indicates how much the price level will rise when aggregate expenditures are excessive relative to the economy's capacity. **T F**

25. The aggregate expenditures model provides a good explanation for cost-push inflation. **T F**

■ MULTIPLE-CHOICE QUESTIONS

Circle the letter that corresponds to the best answer.

1. The premise of the model in this chapter is that the amount of goods and services produced, and therefore the level of employment, depends
   (a) directly on the rate of interest
   (b) directly on the level of total expenditures
   (c) inversely on the level of disposable income
   (d) inversely on the quantity of resources available

2. If the economy is private, closed to international trade, and government neither taxes nor spends, then real GDP equals
   (a) saving
   (b) consumption
   (c) disposable income
   (d) investment spending

Question 3 is based on the following consumption schedule.

Real GDP	C
$200	$200
240	228
280	256
320	284
360	312
400	340
440	368
480	396

3. If the investment schedule is $60 at each level of output, the equilibrium level of real GDP will be
  (a) $320
  (b) $360
  (c) $400
  (d) $440

4. If real GDP is $275 billion, consumption is $250 billion, and investment is $30 billion, real GDP
  (a) will tend to decrease
  (b) will tend to increase
  (c) will tend to remain constant
  (d) equals aggregate expenditures

5. On a graph, the equilibrium real GDP is found at the intersection of the 45-degree line and the
  (a) saving curve
  (b) consumption curve
  (c) investment demand curve
  (d) aggregate expenditures curve

6. Which is an injection of spending into the income expenditures stream?
  (a) investment
  (b) imports
  (c) saving
  (d) taxes

7. When the economy's real GDP exceeds its equilibrium real GDP,
  (a) leakages equal injections
  (b) planned investment exceeds saving
  (c) there is unplanned investment in the economy
  (d) aggregate expenditures exceed the real domestic output

8. If saving is greater than planned investment
  (a) saving will tend to increase
  (b) businesses will be motivated to increase their investments
  (c) real GDP will be greater than planned investment plus consumption
  (d) aggregate expenditures will be greater than the real domestic output

9. At the equilibrium level of GDP,
  (a) actual investment is zero
  (b) unplanned changes in inventories are zero
  (c) saving is greater than planned investment
  (d) saving is less than planned investment

Answer Questions 10 and 11 on the basis of the following table for a private, closed economy. All figures are in billions of dollars.

Real rate of return	Investment	Consumption	GDP
10%	$ 0	$200	$200
8	50	250	300
6	100	300	400
4	150	350	500
2	200	400	600
0	250	450	700

10. If the real rate of interest is 4%, then the equilibrium level of GDP will be
  (a) $300 billion
  (b) $400 billion
  (c) $500 billion
  (d) $600 billion

11. An *increase* in the real interest rate by 4% will
  (a) increase the equilibrium level of GDP by $200 billion
  (b) decrease the equilibrium level of GDP by $200 billion
  (c) decrease the equilibrium level of GDP by $100 billion
  (d) increase the equilibrium level of GDP by $100 billion

12. Compared with a closed economy, aggregate expenditures and GDP will
  (a) increase when net exports are positive
  (b) decrease when net exports are positive
  (c) increase when net exports are negative
  (d) decrease when net exports are zero

Use the data in the following table to answer Questions 13 and 14.

Real GDP	$C + I_g$	Net exports
$ 900	$ 913	$3
920	929	3
940	945	3
960	961	3
980	977	3
1,000	993	3
1,020	1,009	3

13. The equilibrium real GDP is
  (a) $960
  (b) $980
  (c) $1000
  (d) $1020

14. If net exports are increased by $4 billion at each level of GDP, the equilibrium real GDP would be
  (a) $960
  (b) $980
  (c) $1000
  (d) $1020

15. An increase in the real GDP of an economy will, other things remaining constant,

(a) increase its imports and the real GDPs in other economies

(b) decrease its imports and the real GDPs in other economies

(c) increase its imports and decrease the real GDPs in other economies

(d) decrease its imports and increase the real GDPs in other economies

16. Other things remaining constant, which would increase an economy's real GDP and employment?

(a) an increase in the exchange rate for foreign currencies

(b) the imposition of tariffs on goods imported from abroad

(c) an appreciation of the dollar relative to foreign currencies

(d) an increase in the level of national income among the trading partners for this economy

17. The economy is operating at the full-employment level of output. A depreciation of the dollar will most likely result in

(a) a decrease in exports

(b) an increase in imports

(c) a decrease in real GDP

(d) an increase in the price level

Answer Questions 18 and 19 on the basis of the following diagram.

18. If this were an open economy without a government sector, the level of GDP would be

(a) $100

(b) $170

(c) $240

(d) $310

19. In this graph it is assumed that investment, net exports, and government expenditures

(a) vary directly with GDP

(b) vary inversely with GDP

(c) are independent of GDP

(d) are all negative

Questions 20 and 21 are based on the following consumption schedule.

Real GDP	C
$300	$290
310	298
320	306
330	314
340	322
350	330
360	338

20. If taxes were zero, government purchases of goods and services $10, planned investment $6, and net exports zero, equilibrium real GDP would be

(a) $310

(b) $320

(c) $330

(d) $340

21. If taxes were $5, government purchases of goods and services $10, planned investment $6, and net exports zero, equilibrium real GDP would be

(a) $300

(b) $310

(c) $320

(d) $330

22. The amount by which an economy's aggregate expenditures must shift upward to achieve full-employment GDP is

(a) an injection

(b) a lump-sum tax

(c) a recessionary gap

(d) an unplanned change in inventories

23. If the MPC in an economy is 0.75, government could eliminate a recessionary gap of $50 billion by decreasing taxes by

(a) $33.3 billion

(b) $50 billion

(c) $66.7 billion

(d) $80 billion

24. To eliminate an inflationary gap of $50 in an economy in which the marginal propensity to save is 0.1, it will be necessary to

(a) decrease the aggregate expenditures schedule by $50

(b) decrease the aggregate expenditures schedule by $5

(c) increase the aggregate expenditures schedule by $50

(d) increase the aggregate expenditures schedule by $5

25. One of the limitations of the aggregate expenditures model is that it

(a) fails to account for demand-pull inflation

(b) has no way of measuring the rate of inflation

(c) explains recessionary gaps but not inflationary gaps

(d) gives more weight to cost-push than demand-pull inflation

■ PROBLEMS

1. Following are two schedules showing several GDPs and the level of investment spending (*I*) at each GDP. (All figures are in billions of dollars.)

Schedule number 1		Schedule number 2	
GDP	***I***	**GDP**	***I***
$1850	$90	$1850	$ 75
1900	90	1900	80
1950	90	1950	85
2000	90	2000	90
2050	90	2050	95
2100	90	2100	100
2150	95	2150	105

a. Each schedule is an _____ schedule.
b. When such a schedule is drawn up, it is assumed

that the real rate of interest is _____.
c. In schedule
(1) number 1, GDP and *I* are (unrelated, directly related)

_____.

(2) number 2, GDP and *I* are _____.
d. Should the real rate of interest rise, investment spending at each GDP would (increase, decrease)

_____ and the curve relating GDP and investment spending would shift (upward, downward)

_____.

2. The following table shows consumption and saving at various levels of real GDP. Assume the price level is constant, the economy is closed to international trade, and there is no government, no business savings, no depreciation, and no net foreign factor income earned in the United States.

Real GDP	*C*	*S*	*I_g*	*$C + I_g$*	*UI*
$1300	$1290	$10	$22	$1312	−12
1310	1298	12	22	1320	−10
1320	1306	14	_____	_____	_____
1330	1314	16	_____	_____	_____
1340	1322	18	_____	_____	_____
1350	1330	20	_____	_____	_____
1360	1338	22	_____	_____	_____
1370	1346	24	_____	_____	_____
1380	1354	26	_____	_____	_____
1390	1362	28	22	1384	+6
1400	1370	30	22	1392	+8

a. The next table is an investment demand schedule that shows the amounts investors plan to invest at different rates of interest. Assume the rate of interest is 6%. In the previous table, complete the gross investment, the consumption-plus-investment, and unplanned investment (*UI*) columns, showing unplanned increase in inventories with a + and unplanned decrease in inventories with a −.

0   **Real GDP**

Interest rate	I_g
10%	$ 0
9	7
8	13
7	18
6	22
5	25

b. The equilibrium real GDP will be $ _____.

c. The value of the marginal propensity to consume in this problem is _____, and the value of the marginal propensity to save is _____.

d. The value of the simple multiplier is _____.

e. If the rate of interest should fall from 6% to 5%, investment would (increase, decrease) _____ by $_____; and the equilibrium real GDP would, as a result, (increase, decrease) _____ by $_____.

f. Suppose the rate of interest were to rise from 6% to 7%. Investment would _____ by $_____, and the equilibrium real GDP would _____ by $ _____.

g. Assume the rate of interest is 6%, on the following graph, plot C, $C + I_g$, and the 45-degree line, and indicate the equilibrium real GDP.

3. The second column of the schedule that follows shows what aggregate expenditures (consumption plus investment) would be at various levels of real domestic product in a closed economy.

a. Were this economy to become an open economy, the volume of exports would be a constant $90 billion (column 3), and the volume of imports would be a constant $86 billion (column 4). At each of the seven levels of real GDP (column 1), net exports would be $_____ billion (column 5).

b. Compute aggregate expenditures in this open economy at the seven real GDP levels and enter them in the table (column 6).

c. The equilibrium real GDP in this open economy would be _____ billion.

d. The value of the multiplier in this open economy is equal to _____.

e. A $10 billion increase in

(1) exports would (increase, decrease) _____ the equilibrium real GDP by $_____ billion.

(2) imports would (increase, decrease) _____ the equilibrium real GDP by $_____ billion.

4. Below are consumption schedules.

a. Assume government levies a lump-sum tax of $100. Also assume that imports are $5. Because the marginal propensity to consume in this problem is _____, the imposition of this tax will reduce consumption at all levels of real GDP by $_____. Complete the C_a column to show consumption at each real GDP after this tax has been levied.

Real GDP	C	C_a	$C_a + I_g + X_n + G$
$1500	$1250	$____	$____
1600	1340	____	____
1700	1430	____	____
1800	1520	____	____
1900	1610	____	____
2000	1700	____	____
2100	1790	____	____

b. Suppose that investment is $150, exports are $5, and government purchases of goods and services equal $200. Complete the (after-tax) consumption-plus-investment-plus-net-exports-plus-government-purchases column ($C_a + I_g + X_n + G$).

c. The equilibrium real GDP is $ _____.

d. On the following graph, plot C_a, $C_a + I_g + X_n + G$, and the 45-degree line. Show the equilibrium real GDP. (To answer the questions that follow, it is *not* necessary to recompute C_a, or $C_a + I_g + X_n + G$. They can be answered by using the multipliers.)

(1) Possible levels of real GDP (billions)	(2) Aggregate expenditures, closed economy (billions)	(3) Exports (billions)	(4) Imports (billions)	(5) Net exports (billions)	(6) Aggregate expenditures, open economy (billions)
$ 750	$ 776	$90	$86	$____	$____
800	816	90	86	____	____
850	856	90	86	____	____
900	896	90	86	____	____
950	936	90	86	____	____
1000	976	90	86	____	____
1050	1016	90	86	____	____

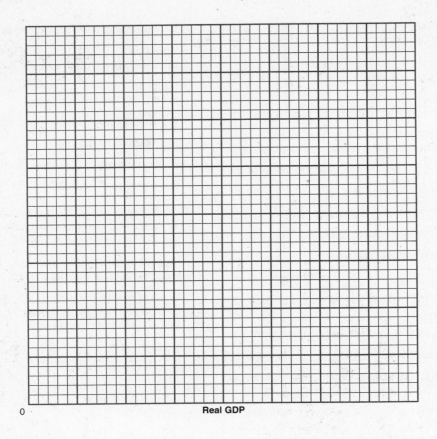

0   **Real GDP**

e. If taxes remained at $100 and government purchases rose by $10, the equilibrium real GDP would (rise, fall) _____ by $ _____.

f. If government purchases remained at $200 and the lump-sum tax increased by $10, the equilibrium real GDP would _____ by $ _____.

g. The combined effect of a $10 increase in government purchases *and* a $10 increase in taxes is to _____ real GDP by $ _____.

5. Here is a consumption schedule for a closed economy. Assume that the level of real GDP at which full employment without inflation is achieved is $590.

Real GDP	C
$550	$520
560	526
570	532
580	538
590	544
600	550
610	556
620	562
630	568

a. The value of the multiplier is _____.

b. If planned investment is $58, the equilibrium nominal GDP is $_____ and exceeds full-employment real GDP by $_____. There is a(n) _____ gap of $_____.

c. If planned investment is $38, the equilibrium real GDP is $_____ and is less than full-employment real GDP by $_____. There is a(n) _____ gap of $_____.

■ **SHORT ANSWER AND ESSAY QUESTIONS**

1. What does it mean that an economy is private and closed?

2. What assumptions are made in this chapter about production capacity, unemployment, and the price level?

3. What is the difference between an investment demand curve and an investment schedule?

4. Why is the equilibrium level of real GDP that level of real GDP at which domestic output equals aggregate expenditures? What will cause real GDP to rise if it is below this level, and what will cause it to fall if it is above this level?

5. Explain what is meant by a leakage and by an injection. Which leakage and which injection are considered in this chapter? Why is the equilibrium real GDP the real GDP at which the leakages equal the injections?

6. Why is it important to distinguish between planned and actual investment in explaining how a private, closed economy achieves its equilibrium level of real GDP?

7. Why does the equilibrium level of real GDP change?

8. How do exports and imports get included in the aggregate expenditures model?

9. What happens to the aggregate expenditures schedule when net exports increase or decrease?

10. Give some examples of international economic linkages affecting the domestic level of GDP.

11. Explain the simplifying assumptions used to include the public sector in the aggregate expenditures model.

12. Describe how government expenditures affect equilibrium GDP.

13. What effect will taxes have on the consumption schedule?

14. Explain why, with government taxing and spending, the equilibrium real GDP is the real GDP at which real GDP equals consumption plus investment plus net exports plus government purchases of goods and services.

15. Use leakages and injections to explain how changes in the different components of aggregate expenditures cause GDP to move to its equilibrium level.

16. Explain what is meant by a recessionary gap.

17. What economic conditions contributed to the recessionary gap in the U.S. economy in 2001?

18. What is an inflationary gap?

19. Why is the U.S. inflation in the late 1980s an example of an inflationary gap?

20. What are the limitations of the demand aggregate expenditures model in terms of the measurement of the price level and treatment of demand-pull and cost-push inflation? Are there other limitations?

ANSWERS

Chapter 10 The Aggregate Expenditures Model

FILL-IN QUESTIONS

1. a closed, private, income, increase
2. investment, investment
3. equal to, equal to, 45-degree
4. a withdrawal from, an addition to, saving, investment
5. less than, decreases, rise
6. greater than, increases, fall
7. equal to, zero
8. increase, an increase, an increase
9. increases, decreases, greater, multiplier
10. minus, plus, plus
11. *a.* −; *b.* +; *c.* +; *d.* −; *e.* +; *f.* −; *g.* +
12. increase, decrease
13. lump-sum
14. consume, save
15. expenditures, output, plus, plus, plus

16. investment, exports, saving, imports
17. less, increase, divided
18. an inflationary, decrease
19. demand-pull, cost-push, inflation
20. demand-pull, beyond, corrects

TRUE–FALSE QUESTIONS

1. T, p. 172	**10.** T, pp. 177–178	**19.** T, pp. 184–185
2. T, p. 172	**11.** F, pp. 177–178	**20.** T, p. 186
3. T, p. 172	**12.** T, p. 178	**21.** F, pp. 186–187
4. T, pp. 175–176	**13.** F, p. 179	**22.** F, p. 186
5. T, pp. 174–175	**14.** T, p. 179	**23.** T, p. 187
6. F, pp. 174–175	**15.** T, p. 179–180	**24.** F, p. 187
7. F, pp. 176–177	**16.** F, p. 181	**25.** F, p. 189
8. T, pp. 176–177	**17.** F, p. 181	
9. T, pp. 176–177	**18.** T, pp. 182–183	

MULTIPLE-CHOICE QUESTIONS

1. b, p. 172	**10.** c, pp. 173–174	**19.** c, pp. 182–183
2. c, p. 172	**11.** b, p. 178	**20.** c, pp. 182–183
3. c, pp. 173–174	**12.** a, p. 179	**21.** b, pp. 182–183
4. b, pp. 174–175	**13.** b, pp. 179–180	**22.** c, p. 186
5. d, pp. 175–176	**14.** c, pp. 179–180	**23.** c, p. 186
6. a, pp. 176–177	**15.** a, p. 181	**24.** a, p. 187
7. c, pp. 176–177	**16.** d, p. 181	**25.** b, p. 187
8. c, pp. 176–177	**17.** d, p. 181	
9. b, pp. 176–177	**18.** c, p. 180	

PROBLEMS

1. *a.* investment; *b.* constant (given); *c.* (1) unrelated, (2) directly related; *d.* decrease, downward

2. *a.* I_g: 22, 22, 22, 22, 22, 22, 22; $C + I_g$: 1,328, 1,336, 1,344, 1,352, 1,360, 1,368, 1,376; *UI*: −8, −6, −4, −2, 0, +2, +4, *b.* 1,360; *c.* 0.8, 0.2; *d.* 5; *e.* increase, 3, increase, 15; *f.* decrease, 4, decrease, 20

3. *a.* $4 (and put $4 in each of the seven net exports values in the table); *b.* $780, 820, 860, 900, 940, 980, 1,020; *c.* $900; *d.* 5; *e.* (1) increase, $50, (2) decrease, $50

4. *a.* 0.9, 90, C_a: 1160, 1250, 1340, 1430, 1520, 1610, 1700; *b.* $C_a + I_g + X_n + G$: 1510, 1600, 1690, 1780, 1870, 1960, 2050; *c.* 1600; *d.* plot graph; *e.* rise, 100; *f.* fall, 90; *g.* raise, 10

5. *a.* 2.5; *b.* 620, 30, inflationary, 12; *c.* 570, 20, recessionary, 8

SHORT ANSWER AND ESSAY QUESTIONS

1. p. 172	**8.** pp. 179–180	**15.** pp. 185–186
2. p. 172	**9.** pp. 179–180	**16.** p. 186
3. p. 173	**10.** p. 181	**17.** pp. 186–187
4. pp. 173–175	**11.** p. 182	**18.** p. 187
5. pp. 176–177	**12.** p. 182	**19.** p. 187
6. pp. 176–177	**13.** p. 183	**20.** pp. 187, 189
7. pp. 177–178	**14.** pp. 182–184	

CHAPTER 11

Aggregate Demand and Aggregate Supply

Chapter 11 introduces another macro model of the economy, one based on aggregate demand and aggregate supply. This model can be used to explain real domestic output and the level of prices at any point in time and to understand what causes output and the price level to change.

The **aggregate demand (AD) curve** is downsloping because of the real balances, interest rate, and foreign purchases effects resulting from changes in the price level. With a downsloping aggregate demand curve, changes in the price level have an inverse effect on the level of spending by domestic consumers, businesses, government, and foreign buyers, and thus on real domestic output, assuming *other things equal*. This change would be equivalent to a movement along an existing aggregate demand curve: A lower price level increases the quantity of real domestic output demanded, and a higher price level decreases the quantity of real domestic output demanded.

The aggregate demand curve can increase or decrease because of a change in one of the nonprice level **determinants of aggregate demand.** The determinants include changes affecting consumer, investment, government, and net export spending. You will learn that underlying each demand determinant are various factors that cause the determinant to change. The size of the change involves two components. For example, if one of these spending determinants increases, then aggregate demand will increase. The change in aggregate demand involves an increase in initial spending plus a multiplier effect that results in a greater change in aggregate demand than the initial change.

The **aggregate supply (AS) curve** shows the relationship between the output of producers and the price level. In the long run, the aggregate supply curve is vertical because the price level does not change production at the full-employment level of output. In the short run, however, the upsloping shape of the aggregate supply curve reflects what happens to per-unit production costs as real domestic output increases or decreases.

You should remember that an assumption has also been made that other things are equal when one moves along an aggregate supply curve. When other things change, the aggregate supply curve can shift. The **determinants of aggregate supply** include changes in input prices, changes in productivity, and changes in the legal and institutional environment for production. As with aggregate demand, you will learn that there are underlying factors that cause these supply determinants to change.

The intersection of the aggregate demand and aggregate supply curves determines **equilibrium real output** and the **equilibrium price level.** Assuming that the determinants of aggregate demand and aggregate supply do not change, there are pressures that will tend to keep the economy at equilibrium. If a determinant changes, then aggregate demand, aggregate supply, or both, can shift.

When **aggregate demand increases,** this will lead to changes in equilibrium real output and the price level. If the economy is operating at full employment, the increase in AD may not have its full multiplier effect on the real GDP of the economy, and it will result in **demand-pull inflation.** There can also be a **decrease in aggregate demand,** but it may reduce output and not the price level. In this case, there can be downward price inflexibility for several reasons, as you will learn in the chapter.

Aggregate supply may increase or decrease. An increase in aggregate supply gives a double bonus for the economy because the price level falls, and output and employment increase. Conversely, a decrease in aggregate supply doubly harms the economy because the price level increases, and output and employment fall, and thus the economy experiences **cost-push inflation.**

The aggregate demand–aggregate supply model is an important framework for determining the equilibrium level of real domestic output and prices in an economy. The model will be used extensively throughout the next eight chapters to analyze how different parts of the economy function.

■ CHECKLIST

When you have studied this chapter you should be able to

☐ Define aggregate demand.
☐ Describe the characteristics of the aggregate demand curve.
☐ Use the real-balances, interest-rate, and foreign purchases effects to explain why the aggregate demand curve slopes downward.
☐ Identify the four major spending determinants of aggregate demand.
☐ Give an example of the effect of the multiplier on changes in aggregate demand.
☐ Explain the four factors that can change the consumer spending determinant.

☐ Explain the two factors that can change the investment spending determinant.

☐ Explain what changes the government spending determinant.

☐ Explain the two factors that can cause changes in the net export spending determinant.

☐ Discuss how the four major spending determinants of aggregate demand (and their underlying factors) can increase or decrease aggregate demand.

☐ Define aggregate supply in both the long run and short run.

☐ Explain why the aggregate supply curve in the long run is vertical.

☐ Explain why the aggregate supply curve in the short run is upsloping.

☐ Identify the three major spending determinants of aggregate supply.

☐ Describe three factors that change the input prices determinant.

☐ Explain what changes the productivity determinant.

☐ Identify two factors that change the legal-institutional environment determinant.

☐ Explain how the three major determinants of aggregate supply (and their underlying factors) can increase or decrease aggregate supply.

☐ Explain why in equilibrium the economy will produce a particular combination of real output and the price level rather than another combination.

☐ Show the effects of an increase in aggregate demand on the real output and the price level and relate the changes to demand-pull inflation.

☐ Illustrate the effects of a decrease in aggregate demand on real output and the price level in the economy and relate the changes to recession and unemployment.

☐ Give five reasons for downward inflexibility of changes in the price level when aggregate demand decreases.

☐ Explain the effects of a decrease in aggregate supply on real output and the price level and relate the changes to cost-push inflation.

☐ Describe the effects of an increase in aggregate supply on real output and the price level and relate the changes in productivity.

■ CHAPTER OUTLINE

1. This chapter introduces the *aggregate demand–aggregate supply model* (AD–AS model). It explains why real domestic output *and* the price level fluctuate in the economy. The chapter begins by explaining the meaning and characteristics of aggregate demand.

    a. *Aggregate demand* is a curve that shows the total quantity of goods and services (real output) that will be purchased (demanded) at different price levels. With aggregate demand there is an inverse or negative relationship between the amount of real output demanded and the price level, so the curve slopes downward.

    b. Three reasons account for the inverse relationship between real output and the price level, and the downward slope of the aggregate demand curve.

    (1) *Real-balances effect:* An increase in the price level decreases the purchasing power of financial assets with a fixed money value, and because those who own such assets are now poorer, they spend less for goods and services. A decrease in the price level has the opposite effects.

    (2) *Interest-rate effect:* With the supply of money fixed, an increase in the price level increases the demand for money, increases interest rates, and as a result reduces those expenditures (by consumers and business firms) that are sensitive to increased interest rates. A decrease in the price level has the opposite effects.

    (3) *Foreign purchases effect:* An increase in the price level (relative to foreign price levels) will reduce U.S. exports because U.S. products are now more expensive for foreigners, and expand U.S. imports because foreign products are less expensive for U.S. consumers. As a consequence, net exports will decrease, which means there will be a decrease in the quantity of goods and services demanded in the U.S. economy as the price level rises. A decrease in the price level (relative to foreign price levels) will have opposite effects.

2. Spending by domestic consumers, businesses, government, and foreign buyers that is independent of changes in the price level are *determinants of aggregate demand.* The amount of changes in aggregate demand involves two components: the amount of the initial change in one of the determinants, and a multiplier effect that multiplies the initial change. These determinants are also called aggregate demand shifts because a change in one of them, other things equal, will shift the entire aggregate demand curve. Figure 11.2 shows the shifts. What follows is a description of each of the four major determinants and underlying factors.

    a. *Consumer spending* can increase or decrease AD. If the price level is constant, and consumers decide to spend more, then AD will increase; if consumers decide to spend less, then AD will decrease. Four factors increase or decrease consumer spending.

    (1) *Consumer wealth:* If the real value of financial asset increases, then consumers will feel wealthier, spend more, and AD increases. If the real value of financial assets falls, consumers will spend less and AD will decrease.

    (2) *Consumer expectations:* If consumers become more optimistic about the future, they will likely spend more and AD will increase. If consumers expect the future to be worse, they will decrease their spending and AD will decrease.

    (3) *Household indebtedness:* If consumers have a high level of debt relative to normal, they may be forced to reduce their spending, thus decreasing AD. Conversely, if the level of debt falls to a more manageable level, they may be able to borrow more money and increase their spending, thus increasing AD.

    (4) *Taxes:* Cuts in taxes increase disposable income and the capacity for consumer spending, thus increasing AD. A rise in taxes decreases disposable income, consumer spending, and AD.

b. *Investment spending* can increase or decrease AD. If the price level is constant, and businesses decide to spend more on investment, then AD will increase. If businesses decide to spend less on investment, then AD will decrease. Three factors increase or decrease investment spending.

(1) *Real interest rates:* A decrease in real interest rates will increase the quantity of investment spending, thus increasing AD. An increase in real interest rates will decrease the quantity of investment spending, thus decreasing AD.

(2) *Expected returns:* If businesses expect higher returns on investments in the future, they will likely increase their investment spending today, so AD will increase. If businesses expect lower returns on investments in the future, they will decrease their investment spending today, and AD will decrease. These expected returns are influenced by expectations about future business conditions, the state of technology, the degree of excess capacity (the amount of unused capital goods), and business taxes.

(a) More positive future expectations, more technological progress, less excess capacity, and lower taxes will increase investment spending and thus increase AD.

(b) Less positive future expectations, less technological progress, more excess capacity, and higher taxes will decrease investment spending and thus decrease AD.

c. *Government spending* has a direct effect on AD, assuming that tax collections and interest rates do not change as a result of the spending. More government spending tends to increase AD and less government spending will decrease AD.

d. *Net export spending* can increase or decrease AD. If the price level is constant and net exports (exports minus imports) should increase, then AD will increase. If net exports are negative, then AD will decrease. Two factors explain the increase or decrease in net export spending.

(1) *National income abroad:* An increase in the national income of other nations will increase the demand for all goods and services, including U.S. exports. If U.S. exports increase relative to U.S. imports, then net exports will increase, and so will AD. A decline in national incomes abroad will tend to reduce U.S. net exports and thus reduces AD.

(2) *Exchange rates:* A depreciation in the value of the U.S. dollar means that U.S. imports should decline because domestic purchases cannot buy as many imports as they used to buy. U.S. exports should increase because foreigners have more purchasing power to buy U.S. products. These events increase net exports, and thus increase AD. An appreciation in the value of the dollar will decrease net exports, and thus decrease AD.

3. *Aggregate supply* is a curve that shows the total quantity of goods and services that will be produced (supplied) at different price levels.

a. In the *long run,* the aggregate supply curve is vertical at the full-employment level of output for the economy because the rise in wages and other inputs will match changes in the price level.

b. In the *short run,* the aggregate supply curve is upsloping because nominal wages and input prices adjust only slowly to changes in the price level. With this curve, an increase in the price level increases real output and a decrease in the price level reduces real output.

4. The *determinants of aggregate supply* that shift the curve include changes in the prices of inputs for production, changes in productivity, and changes in the legal and institutional environment in the economy, as outlined in Figure 11.5.

a. A change in *input prices* for resources used for production will change aggregate supply in the short run. Lower input prices increase AS and higher input prices decrease AS. These input prices are both for domestic and imported resources, and they can be influenced by market power.

(1) *Domestic resource prices* include the prices for labor, capital, and natural resources used for production. If any of these input prices decrease, then AS will decrease because the per-unit cost of production will decrease. When the prices of these domestic factors of production increase, then AS will decrease.

(2) The *prices of imported resources* is the cost of paying for resources imported from other nations. If the value of the dollar appreciates, then it will cost less to pay for imported resources used for production. As a result, per-unit production costs will decrease, and AS will increase. Conversely, if the value of the dollar depreciates, then it will cost more to import resources, so AS will decrease.

(3) A change in the degree of *market power* in resource markets can change resource prices, and thus change AS supply. A more competitive market will tend to decrease resource prices and increase AS. A more monopolistic market will tend to drive up resource prices and decrease AS.

b. As *productivity* improves, per-unit production costs will fall and AS will increase. This outcome occurs because productivity (output divided by input) is the denominator for the formula for per-unit production costs (which is: total input cost divided by productivity). As productivity declines, per-unit production costs will increase, so AS will decrease.

c. Changes in the *legal and institutional environment* for business can affect per-unit production costs and thus AS.

(1) A decrease in *business taxes* is like a reduction in the per-unit cost of production, so it will increase AS. The same effect occurs when there is an increase in *business subsidies.* The raising of taxes or lowering of subsidies for business will increase per-unit production costs and decrease AS.

(2) A decrease in the amount of *government regulation* is similar to a decrease in the per-unit cost of production, so it will increase AS. An increase in government regulation will raise costs, and thus will decrease AS.

5. The *equilibrium domestic output* and the *equilibrium price level* are at the intersection of the aggregate demand and the aggregate supply curves. If the price level were below equilibrium, then producers would supply less real output than was demanded by purchasers. Competition among buyers would bid up the price level and producers would increase their output, until an equilibrium price level and quantity was reached. If the price level were above equilibrium, then producers would supply more real output than was demanded by purchasers. Competition among sellers would lower the price level and producers would reduce their output, until an equilibrium price level and quantity was reached. The aggregate demand and aggregate supply curves can also **shift to change equilibrium.**

   a. An **increase in aggregate demand** would result in an increase in both real domestic output and the price level. An increase in the price level beyond the full-employment level of output is associated with **demand-pull inflation.**

   b. A **decrease in aggregate demand** reduces real output, but it may not decrease the price level. This **price level is inflexible downward** because it is largely influenced by labor costs which account for most of the input prices for the production of many goods and services. There are at least five interrelated reasons for this downward inflexibility of the price level.

   (1) If wages are determined largely by **long-term contracts,** it means that wages cannot be changed in the short run.

   (2) **Morale, effort, and productivity** may be affected by changes in wage rates. Employers may be reluctant to lower wages if they reduce work effort and productivity.

   (3) The **minimum wage** puts a legal floor on the wages for the least skilled workers in the economy.

   (4) Firms are reluctant to change input prices if there are costs related to changing the prices or announcing the change. Such **menu costs** increase the waiting time before businesses make any price changes.

   (5) The fear of starting a **price war** in which firms compete with each other on lowering prices regardless of the cost of production. Such a price war hurts business profits and makes firms reluctant to cut prices for fear of starting one.

   c. A **decrease in aggregate supply** means there will be a decrease in real domestic output (economic growth) and employment along with a rise in the price level, or **cost-push inflation.**

   d. An **increase in aggregate supply** arising from an increase in productivity has the beneficial effects of improving real domestic output and employment while maintaining a stable price level.

■ HINTS AND TIPS

1. Aggregate demand and supply are the tools used to explain what determines the economy's real output and price level. These tools, however, are **different from the demand and supply** used in Chapter 3 to explain what determines the output and price of a *particular* product. Instead of thinking about the quantity of a *particular* good or service demanded or supplied, it is necessary to think

about the total or *aggregate* quantity of all final goods and services demanded (purchased) and supplied (produced). You will have no difficulty with the way demand and supply are used in this chapter once you switch from thinking about a *particular* good or service and its price to the *aggregate* of all final goods and services and their average price.

2. Make a chart showing each of the **determinants** of aggregate demand (see Figure 11.2) and aggregate supply (Figure 11.5). In the chart, state the direction of the change in each determinant, and then state the likely resulting change in AD or AS. For example, if consumer wealth *increases,* then AD *increases.* Or, if imported prices for resources *increase,* then AS *decreases.* This simple chart can help you quickly see in one quick glance all the possible changes in determinants and their likely effects on AD or AS. Problem 2 in this study guide will give you an application for this chart.

3. Make sure you know the difference between a **movement** along an existing aggregate demand or supply curve and a **shift** in (increase or decrease in) an aggregate demand or supply curve. Figures 11.7 and 11.9 illustrate the distinction.

■ IMPORTANT TERMS

aggregate demand–aggregate supply model

aggregate demand (AD)

real-balances effect

interest-rate effect

foreign purchases effect

determinants of aggregate demand

aggregate supply (AS)

long-run aggregate supply curve

short-run aggregate supply curve

determinants of aggregate supply

productivity

equilibrium price level

equilibrium real output

efficiency wages

menu costs

SELF-TEST

■ FILL-IN QUESTIONS

1. Aggregate demand and aggregate supply together determine the equilibrium real domestic (price, output) _____ and the equilibrium _____ level.

2. The aggregate demand curve shows the quantity of goods and services that will be (supplied, demanded) _____ or purchased at various price levels. For aggregate demand, the relationship between real output and the price level is (positive, negative) _____.

3. The aggregate demand curve slopes (upward, downward) _____ because of the (real-balances, consumption) _____ effect, the (profit, interest) _____-rate effect, and the (domestic, foreign) _____ purchases effect.

4. For the aggregate demand curve, an increase in the price level (increases, decreases) _____ the quantity of real domestic output demanded, whereas a decrease in the price level _____ the quantity of real domestic output demanded, assuming other things equal.

5. For the aggregate demand curve, when the price level changes, there is a (movement along, change in) _____ the curve. When the entire aggregate demand curve shifts, there is a change in (the quantity of real output demanded, aggregate demand) _____.

6. List the four factors that may change consumer spending, and thus shift aggregate demand:

a. _____

b. _____

c. _____

d. _____

7. List two major factors that may change investment spending, and thus shift aggregate demand:

a. _____

b. _____

8. If government spending increases, then aggregate demand is likely to (increase, decrease) _____, but if government spending decreases, it is likely to _____.

9. If there is an increase in national income abroad, then net exports spending is most likely to (increase, decrease) _____ and if there is a depreciation of the value of the U.S. dollar, then net exports are likely to _____. When net exports increase, aggregate demand will (increase, decrease) _____.

10. The aggregate supply curve shows the quantity of goods and services that will be (demanded, supplied) _____ or produced at various price levels. As the price level increases, real domestic output (increases, decreases) _____, and as the price level decreases, real domestic output _____. The relationship between the price level and real domestic output supplied is (positive, negative) _____.

11. The basic cause of a decrease in aggregate supply is the (increase, decrease) _____ in per-

unit costs of producing goods and services, and the basic cause of an increase in aggregate supply is the _____ in per-unit costs of production, all other things equal.

12. Aggregate supply shifts may result from:

a. a change in input prices caused by a change in

(1) _____

(2) _____

(3) _____

b. a change in (consumption, productivity) _____

c. a change in the legal and institutional environment caused by a change in

(1) _____

(2) _____

13. The equilibrium real domestic output and price level are found at the (zero values, intersection) _____ of the aggregate demand and the aggregate supply curves. At this price level, the aggregate quantity of goods and services demanded is (greater than, less than, equal to) _____ the aggregate quantity of goods and services supplied. And at this real domestic output, the prices producers are willing to (pay, accept) _____ are equal to the prices buyers are willing to _____.

14. If the price level were below equilibrium, the quantity of real domestic output supplied would be (greater than, less than) _____ the quantity of real domestic output demanded. As a result competition among buyers eliminates the (surplus, shortage) _____ and bids up the price level.

15. If the price level were above equilibrium, the quantity of real domestic output supplied would be (greater than, less than) _____ the quantity of real domestic output demanded. As a result competition among producers eliminates the (surplus, shortage) _____ and lowers the price level.

16. An increase in aggregate demand will (increase, decrease) _____ real domestic output and will _____ the price level. If the economy is initially operating at its full-employment level of output, and aggregate demand increases, it will produce (demand-pull, cost-push) _____ inflation.

17. If aggregate demand decreases, then real domestic output will (increase, decrease) _____. Such a change often produces economic conditions called (inflation, recession) _____ and unemployment (rises, falls) _____.

18. When aggregate demand decreases, the price level is often inflexible (upward, downward) _____. This inflexibility occurs because of wage (contracts, flexibility) _____, workers are paid (efficiency, inefficiency) _____ wages, there is a (maximum, minimum) _____ wage, businesses experience menu (benefits, costs) _____, and there is fear of (price, wage) _____ wars.

19. A decrease in aggregate supply will (increase, decrease) _____ real output and _____ the price level. Such a change in aggregate supply contributes to (demand-pull, cost-push) _____ inflation.

20. An increase in aggregate supply will (increase, decrease) _____ real domestic output and _____ the price level. If aggregate demand increased, the price level would (increase, decrease) _____, but a simultaneous increase in aggregate supply (reinforces, offsets) _____ this change and helps keep the price level stable.

■ **TRUE–FALSE QUESTIONS**

Circle T if the statement is true, F if it is false.

1. Aggregate demand reflects a positive relationship between the price level and the amount of real output demanded. **T F**

2. The explanation for why the aggregate demand curve slopes downward is the same as the explanation for why the demand curve for a single product slopes downward. **T F**

3. A fall in the price level increases the real value of financial assets with fixed money values and, as a result, increases spending by the holders of these assets. **T F**

4. Given a fixed supply of money, a rise in the price level increases the demand for money in the economy and drives interest rates downward. **T F**

5. A rise in the price level of an economy (relative to foreign price levels) tends to increase that economy's exports and to reduce its imports of goods and services. **T F**

6. A movement along a fixed aggregate demand curve is the same as a shift in aggregate demand. **T F**

7. Changes in aggregate demand involve a change in initial spending from one of the determinants and a multiplier effect on spending. **T F**

8. A change in aggregate demand is caused by a change in the price level, *other things equal.* **T F**

9. A fall in excess capacity, or unused existing capital goods, will retard the demand for new capital goods and therefore reduce aggregate demand. **T F**

10. The real-balances effect is one of the determinants of aggregate demand. **T F**

11. A high level of household indebtedness will tend to increase consumption spending and aggregate demand. **T F**

12. Appreciation of the dollar relative to foreign currencies will tend to increase net exports and aggregate demand. **T F**

13. The aggregate supply curve is vertical in the long run at the full-employment level of output. **T F**

14. When the determinants of short-run aggregate supply change, they alter the per-unit production cost and thereby aggregate supply. **T F**

15. A change in the degree of market power or monopoly power held by sellers of resources can affect input prices and aggregate supply. **T F**

16. Productivity is a measure of real output per unit of input. **T F**

17. Per-unit production cost is determined by dividing total input cost by units of output. **T F**

18. At the equilibrium price level, the real domestic output purchased is equal to the real domestic output produced. **T F**

19. An increase in aggregate demand will increase both the price level and the real domestic output. **T F**

20. An increase in aggregate demand is associated with cost-push inflation. **T F**

21. The greater the increase in the price level that results from an increase in aggregate demand, the greater will be the increase in the equilibrium real GDP. **T F**

22. A significant decrease in aggregate demand can result in recession and cyclical unemployment. **T F**

23. Fear of price wars tends to make the price level more flexible rather than less flexible. **T F**

24. A decrease in aggregate supply decreases the equilibrium real domestic output and increases the price level, resulting in cost-push inflation. **T F**

25. An increase in aggregate supply driven by productivity increases can offset the inflationary pressures from an increase in aggregate demand. **T F**

■ **MULTIPLE-CHOICE QUESTIONS**

Circle the letter that corresponds to the best answer.

1. The aggregate demand curve is the relationship between the
(a) price level and what producers will supply
(b) price level and the real domestic output purchased

(c) price level and the real domestic output produced
(d) real domestic output purchased and the real domestic output produced

2. When the price level rises,
(a) the demand for money and interest rates rises
(b) spending that is sensitive to interest-rate changes increases
(c) holders of financial assets with fixed money values increase their spending
(d) holders of financial assets with fixed money values have more purchasing power

3. One explanation for the downward slope of the aggregate demand curve is that a change in the price level results in
(a) a multiplier effect
(b) an income effect
(c) a substitution effect
(d) a foreign purchases effect

4. A sharp decline in the real value of stock prices, which is independent of a change in the price level, would best be an example of
(a) the interest-rate effect
(b) the foreign purchases effect
(c) a change in household indebtedness
(d) a change in real value of consumer wealth

5. The aggregate demand curve will be increased by
(a) a decrease in the price level
(b) an increase in the price level
(c) a depreciation in the value of the U.S. dollar
(d) an increase in the excess capacity of factories

6. The aggregate supply curve is the relationship between the
(a) price level and the real domestic output purchased
(b) price level and the real domestic output produced
(c) price level that producers are willing to accept and the price level purchasers are willing to pay
(d) real domestic output purchased and the real domestic output produced

7. In the long run, the aggregate supply curve is
(a) upsloping
(b) downsloping
(c) vertical
(d) horizontal

8. The short-run aggregate supply curve assumes that
(a) nominal wages respond to changes in the price level
(b) nominal wages do not respond to changes in the price level
(c) the economy is operating at full-employment output
(d) the economy is operating at less than full-employment output

9. If the prices of imported resources increase, then this event would most likely
(a) decrease aggregate supply
(b) increase aggregate supply
(c) increase aggregate demand
(d) decrease aggregate demand

Suppose that real domestic output in an economy is 50 units, the quantity of inputs is 10, and the price of each input is $2. Answer Questions 10, 11, 12, and 13 on the basis of this information.

10. The level of productivity in this economy is
(a) 5
(b) 4
(c) 3
(d) 2

11. The per-unit cost of production is
(a) $0.40
(b) $0.50
(c) $2.50
(d) $3.50

12. If productivity increased such that 60 units are now produced with the quantity of inputs still equal to 10, then per-unit production costs would
(a) remain unchanged and aggregate supply would remain unchanged
(b) increase and aggregate supply would decrease
(c) decrease and aggregate supply would increase
(d) decrease and aggregate supply would decrease

13. All else equal, if the price of each input increases from $2 to $4, productivity would
(a) decrease from $4 to $2 and aggregate supply would decrease
(b) decrease from $5 to $3 and aggregate supply would decrease
(c) decrease from $4 to $2 and aggregate supply would increase
(d) remain unchanged and aggregate supply would decrease

14. If Congress passed much stricter laws to control the air pollution from businesses, this action would tend to
(a) increase per-unit production costs and shift the aggregate supply curve to the right
(b) increase per-unit production costs and shift the aggregate supply curve to the left
(c) increase per-unit production costs and shift the aggregate demand curve to the left
(d) decrease per-unit production costs and shift the aggregate supply curve to the left

15. An increase in business taxes will tend to
(a) decrease aggregate demand but not change aggregate supply
(b) decrease aggregate supply but not change aggregate demand
(c) decrease aggregate demand and decrease aggregate supply
(d) decrease aggregate supply and increase aggregate demand

16. If at a particular price level, real domestic output from producers is less than real domestic output desired by buyers, there will be a
(a) surplus and the price level will rise
(b) surplus and the price level will fall
(c) shortage and the price level will rise
(d) shortage and the price level will fall

Answer Questions 17, 18, and 19 on the basis of the following aggregate demand–aggregate supply schedule for a hypothetical economy.

Real domestic output demanded (in billions)	Price level	Real domestic output supplied (in billions)
$1500	175	$4500
2000	150	4000
2500	125	3500
3000	100	3000
3500	75	2500
4000	50	2000

17. The equilibrium price level and quantity of real domestic output will be
(a) 100 and $2500
(b) 100 and $3000
(c) 125 and $3500
(d) 150 and $4000

18. If the quantity of real domestic output demanded increased by $2000 at each price level, the new equilibrium price level and quantity of real domestic output would be
(a) 175 and $4000
(b) 150 and $4000
(c) 125 and $3500
(d) 100 and $3000

19. Using the original data from the table, if the quantity of real domestic output demanded *increased* by $1500 and the quantity of real domestic output supplied *increased* by $500 at each price level, the new equilibrium price level and quantity of real domestic output would be
(a) 175 and $4000
(b) 150 and $4500
(c) 125 and $4000
(d) 100 and $3500

20. An increase in aggregate demand will increase
(a) the price level and have no effect on real domestic output
(b) the real domestic output and have no effect on the price level
(c) the price level and decrease the real domestic output
(d) both real output and the price level

21. In the aggregate demand–aggregate supply model, an increase in the price level will
(a) increase the real value of wealth
(b) increase the strength of the multiplier
(c) decrease the strength of the multiplier
(d) have no effect on the strength of the multiplier

22. Aggregate demand decreases and real output falls but the price level remains the same. Which factor most likely contributes to downward price inflexibility?
(a) an increase in aggregate supply
(b) the foreign purchases effect
(c) lower interest rates
(d) efficiency wages

23. Menu costs, wage contracts, and fear of price wars are associated with
(a) a price level that is inflexible upward
(b) a price level that is inflexible downward
(c) a domestic output that cannot be increased
(d) a domestic output that cannot be decreased

24. If there were cost-push inflation,
(a) both the real domestic output and the price level would decrease
(b) the real domestic output would increase and rises in the price level would become smaller
(c) the real domestic output would decrease and the price level would rise
(d) both the real domestic output and rises in the price level would become greater

25. An increase in aggregate supply will
(a) increase the price level and real domestic output
(b) decrease the price level and real domestic output
(c) decrease the price level and increase the real domestic output
(d) decrease the price level and have no effect on real domestic output

■ **PROBLEMS**

1. Following is an aggregate supply schedule.

Price level	Real domestic output supplied
250	2100
225	2000
200	1900
175	1700
150	1400
125	1000
100	900

a. Plot this aggregate supply schedule on the graph on the next page.
b. The following table has three aggregate demand schedules.

Price level	Real domestic output demanded			
	(1)	(2)	(3)	(4)
250		1400	1900	500
225		1500	2000	600
200		1600	2100	700
175		1700	2200	800
150		1800	2300	900
125		1900	2400	1000
100		2000	2500	1100

(1) On the graph, plot the aggregate demand curve shown in columns 1 and 2; label this curve **AD₁**. At this level of aggregate demand, the equilibrium real

domestic output is _____ and the equili-

brium price level is _____.
(2) On the same graph, plot the aggregate demand curve shown in columns 1 and 3; label this curve **AD₂**.

The equilibrium real domestic output is _____ and

the equilibrium price level is _____.

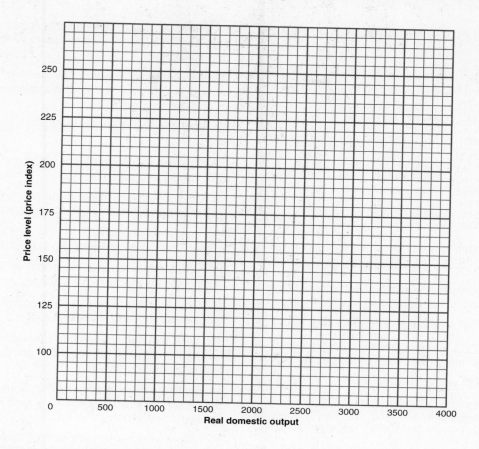

Real domestic output

(3) On the same graph, plot the aggregate demand curve shown in columns 1 and 4; label it **AD₃**. The equilibrium real domestic output is _____

and the equilibrium price level is _____.

2. In the following list, what will most likely happen as a result of each event to (1) aggregate demand (AD); (2) aggregate supply (AS); (3) the equilibrium price level (**P**); and (4) equilibrium real domestic output (**Q**)? Assume that all other things remain constant when the event occurs and that the economy is operating in the intermediate range of the aggregate supply curve. Use the following symbols to indicate the expected effects: **I** = increase, **D** = decrease, **S** = remains the same, and **U** = uncertain.

a. A decrease in labor productivity.

AD_____   AS_____   **P**_____   **Q**_____

b. A fall in the interest rate for business loans.

AD_____   AS_____   **P**_____   **Q**_____

c. Consumer incomes decline as the economy moves into a recession.

AD_____   AS_____   **P**_____   **Q**_____

d. The price of oil on the world market falls to a low level.

AD_____   AS_____   **P**_____   **Q**_____

e. There is an appreciation in the value of the U.S. dollar.

AD_____   AS_____   **P**_____   **Q**_____

3. Following are hypothetical data showing the relationships between the real domestic output and the quantity of input resources needed to produce each level of output.

Output	Input	Productivity		Per-unit cost		
		(1)	(2)	(3)	(4)	(5)
2500	500	___	___	___	___	___
2000	400	___	___	___	___	___
1500	300	___	___	___	___	___

a. In column 1, compute the level of productivity at each level of real domestic output.

b. In column 2, compute the level of productivity if there is a doubling in the quantity of inputs required to produce each level of output.

c. In column 3, compute the per-unit production cost at each level of output if each unit of input costs $15, given the level of productivity in column 1.

d. In column 4, compute the new per-unit production cost at each level of output if each unit of input costs $15, given that there has been a doubling in the required quantity of inputs to produce each level of output as shown in column 2. If this situation occurs, will aggregate supply (decrease, increase, stay the same)?

_____

e. In column 5, compute the new per-unit production cost at each level of output, given that input price is now $10 instead of $15 but the level of productivity stays as it was originally shown in column 1. What will happen to the aggregate supply curve if this situation

occurs? _____

4. Columns 1 and 2 in the table that follows are the aggregate supply schedule of an economy.

(1) Price level	(2) Real GDP	(3) AD$_1$	(4) AD$_2$	(5) AD$_3$	(6) AD$_4$	(7) AD$_5$	(8) AD$_6$
260	2540	940	1140	1900	2000	2090	2390
240	2490	1040	1240	2000	2100	2190	2490
220	2430	1140	1340	2100	2200	2290	2590
200	2390	1240	1440	2200	2300	2390	2690
190	2350	1390	1590	2250	2350	2540	2740
180	2300	1440	1640	2300	2400	2590	2890
160	2200	1540	1740	2400	2500	2690	2990
140	2090	1640	1840	2500	2600	2790	3090
120	1940	1740	1940	2600	2700	2890	3190
100	1840	1840	2040	2700	2800	2990	3290

a. If the aggregate demand in the economy were columns 1 and 3, the equilibrium real GDP would be

_____ and the equilibrium price level would be

_____, and if aggregate demand should increase to that shown in columns 1 and 4, the equilibrium real GDP would increase to _____ and the

price level would _____.
b. Should aggregate demand be that shown in columns 1 and 5, the equilibrium real GDP would be

_____ and the equilibrium price would be

_____, and if aggregate demand should increase by 100 units to that shown in columns 1 and 6,

the equilibrium real GDP would increase to _____

and the price level would rise to _____.
c. If aggregate demand were that shown in columns 1 and 7, the equilibrium real GDP would be

_____ and the equilibrium price level would

be _____, but if aggregate demand increased to that shown in columns 1 and 8, the equilibrium real

GDP would _____ and the price level would

rise to _____.

■ SHORT ANSWER AND ESSAY QUESTIONS

1. What is the aggregate demand curve? Draw a graph and explain its features.

2. Use the interest-rate effect, the real-balances effect, and the foreign purchases effect to explain the relationship between the price level and the real domestic output demanded.

3. Explain the wealth effect and its impact on purchasing power. Give an example.

4. What roles do the expectations of consumers and businesses play in influencing aggregate demand?

5. How is aggregate demand changed by changes in net export spending? What factors cause changes in net export spending?

6. Why is the aggregate supply curve in the long run a vertical curve? Why is output not affected by the price level in the long run?

7. Why does the short-run aggregate supply curve slope upward?

8. Why does a change in the degree of market power affect aggregate supply?

9. Describe how changes in the international economy influence aggregate demand or aggregate supply.

10. How does an increase or decrease in per-unit production costs change aggregate supply? Give examples.

11. How does the legal and institutional environment affect aggregate supply? Give examples.

12. Explain how a change in business taxes affects aggregate demand and aggregate supply.

13. What real domestic output is the equilibrium real domestic output? What will happen to real output if the price level is below equilibrium?

14. What are the effects on the real domestic output and the price level when aggregate demand increases along the aggregate supply curve?

15. What is the relationship between the effect of an increase in aggregate demand on real GDP and the rise in the price level that accompanies it? Discuss it in terms of the multiplier effect.

16. If prices were as flexible downward as they are upward, what would be the effects on real domestic output and the price level of a decrease in aggregate demand?

17. Give reasons why prices in the economy tend to be "sticky" or inflexible in a downward direction in the horizontal range of aggregate supply.

18. What are the effects on the real domestic output and the price level of a decrease in aggregate supply?

19. How does an increase in aggregate supply affect the price level and real output?

20. Using the aggregate demand and aggregate supply concepts, explain the difference between demand-pull and cost-push inflation.

ANSWERS

Chapter 11 Aggregate Demand and Aggregate Supply

FILL-IN QUESTIONS

1. output, price
2. demanded, negative
3. downward, real-balances, interest, foreign
4. decreases, increases
5. movement along, aggregate demand

6. *a.* consumer wealth; *b.* consumer expectations; *c.* household indebtedness; *d.* personal taxes (any order for *a–d*)

7. *a.* interest rates; *b.* expected returns on investment (any order for *a–b*)

8. increase, decrease

9. increase, increase, increase

10. supplied, increases, decreases, positive

11. increase, decrease

12. *a.* (1) domestic resource availability, (2) prices of imported resources, (3) market power (any order for *1–3*); *b.* productivity; *c.* (1) business taxes and subsidies, (2) government regulation (any order for *1–2*)

13. intersection, equal to, accept, pay

14. less than, shortage

15. greater than, surplus

16. increase, increase, demand-pull

17. decrease, recession, rises

18. downward, contracts, efficiency, minimum, costs, price

19. decrease, increase, cost-push

20. increase, decrease, increase, offsets

TRUE–FALSE QUESTIONS

1. F, pp. 193–194	**10.** F, p. 195	**19.** T, p. 203
2. F, p. 194	**11.** F, p. 196	**20.** F, p. 203
3. T, p. 194	**12.** F, p. 197	**21.** F, p. 203
4. F, p. 194	**13.** T, pp. 197–198	**22.** T, pp. 203–204
5. F, pp. 194–195	**14.** T, pp. 198–199	**23.** F, p. 205
6. F, p. 195	**15.** T, p. 200	**24.** T, p. 205
7. T, p. 195	**16.** T, pp. 201–202	**25.** T, pp. 205–206
8. F, p. 195	**17.** T, p. 201	
9. F, pp. 196–197	**18.** T, pp. 201–202	

MULTIPLE-CHOICE QUESTIONS

1. b, p. 193	**10.** a, pp. 200–201	**19.** c, pp. 205–206
2. a, p. 194	**11.** a, pp. 200–201	**20.** d, p. 203
3. d, pp. 194–195	**12.** c, pp. 200–201	**21.** c, p. 203
4. d, p. 196	**13.** d, pp. 200–201	**22.** d, pp. 203–204
5. c, p. 197	**14.** b, p. 201	**23.** b, pp. 204–205
6. b, p. 197	**15.** c, p. 201	**24.** c, p. 205
7. c, pp. 197–198	**16.** c, pp. 201–203	**25.** c, pp. 205–206
8. b, pp. 198–199	**17.** b, p. 202	
9. a, p. 200	**18.** b, p. 202	

PROBLEMS

1. *b.* (1) 1700, 175, (2) 2000, 225, (3) 1000, 125

2. *a. S, D, I, D; b. I, S, I, I; c. D, S, D, D; d. I, I, U, I; e. D, I, D, U*

3. *a.* 5, 5, 5; *b.* 2.5, 2.5, 2.5; *c.* $3, $3, $3; *d.* $6, $6, $6, decrease; *e.* $2, $2, $2, it will increase

4. *a.* 1840, 100, 1940, 120; *b.* 2300, 180, 2350, 190; *c.* 2390, 200, 2490, 240

SHORT ANSWER AND ESSAY QUESTIONS

1. pp. 193–194	**8.** p. 200	**15.** p. 203
2. pp. 194–195	**9.** pp. 197, 200	**16.** pp. 204–205
3. p. 196	**10.** pp. 200–201	**17.** pp. 204–205
4. pp. 196–197	**11.** p. 201	**18.** p. 205
5. p. 197	**12.** pp. 197, 201	**19.** pp. 205–206
6. pp. 197–198	**13.** pp. 201–203	**20.** pp. 203, 205
7. pp. 198–199	**14.** p. 203	

The Relationship of the Aggregate Demand Curve to the Aggregate Expenditure Model

This appendix explains how the aggregate expenditures (AE) model that you learned about in Chapter 10 is related to the aggregate demand (AD) curve that was presented in Chapter 11. There are two short sections to this appendix. The first one focuses on the derivation of the aggregate demand curve from the AE model. The second one explains how shifts in aggregate demand are related to shifts in aggregate expenditures.

Although the aggregate expenditures model is a fixed-price-level model and the aggregate demand–aggregate supply model is a variable-price-level model, there is a close relationship between the two models. The important thing to understand is that prices can be fixed or constant at different levels. The AD curve can be derived from the aggregate expenditures model by letting the price level be constant at different levels. For example, the lower (the higher) the level at which prices are constant in the aggregate expenditures model, the larger (the smaller) will be the equilibrium real GDP in that model of the economy. Various output-price-level combinations can be traced to derive an AD curve that slopes downward, as shown in Figure 1 in the text.

The aggregate demand curve can shift (increase or decrease) because of a change in the nonprice level **determinants of aggregate demand.** The determinants include changes in factors affecting consumer, investment, government, and net export spending. These determinants are similar to the components of the aggregate expenditures model. It is easy to show the relationship between the shifts in the two models. A change in spending will cause a shift (upward or downward) in the aggregate expenditures schedule as shown in Figure 2 in the text. The initial change in spending when multiplied times the multiplier would be equal to the size of the horizontal shift in AD, assuming a constant price level.

■ **CHECKLIST**

When you have studied this appendix you should be able to

☐ Contrast the aggregate expenditures and the aggregate demand–aggregate supply models by comparing the variability of the price level and real GDP.
☐ Use a graph to derive the aggregate demand curve from the aggregate expenditures model.
☐ Explain the effect of a change in a determinant of aggregate demand on aggregate expenditures.

☐ Use a graph to show the relationship between a shift in aggregate expenditures and a shift in aggregate demand.
☐ Discuss how the initial change in spending and the multiplier effect influence the size of the shift in aggregate demand.

■ **CHAPTER OUTLINE**

1. This chapter introduces the **aggregate demand–aggregate supply model** of the economy to explain why real domestic output *and* the price level fluctuate. This model has an advantage over the aggregate expenditures model because it allows the price level to vary (rise and fall) rather than be constant or fixed as in the aggregate expenditures model.

2. The aggregate demand curve can be derived from the intersections of the aggregate expenditures curves and the 45-degree curve. As the price level falls, the aggregate expenditures curve shifts upward and the equilibrium real GDP increases, but as the price level rises, the aggregate expenditures curve shifts downward and the equilibrium real GDP decreases. The inverse relationship between the price level and equilibrium real GDP is the aggregate demand curve. Note that for the aggregate expenditures model,
(1) changes in real balances (wealth) increase or decrease the consumption schedule;
(2) changes in the interest rate increase or decrease the investment schedule; and,
(3) changes in imports or exports affect net exports, which can increase or decrease the net export schedule.

3. If the price level is constant, any change in nonprice-level determinants of consumption and planned investment that shifts the aggregate expenditures curve upward will increase the equilibrium real GDP and shift the AD curve to the right by an amount equal to the initial increase in aggregate expenditures times the multiplier. Conversely, any change in nonprice-level determinants of consumption and planned investment that shifts the aggregate expenditures curve downward will decrease the equilibrium real GDP and shift the AD curve to the left by an amount equal to the initial decrease in aggregate expenditures times the multiplier.

■ HINTS AND TIPS

1. Figure 1 is worth extra study to see the relationship between the quantity (real domestic output) and the price level in both models. The upper panel shows the aggregate expenditures model with aggregate expenditures on the vertical axis and quantity on the horizontal axis. The lower panel shows the aggregate demand model with the price level on the vertical axis and quantity on the horizontal axis. Thus the horizontal axes in both graphs are the same and directly related. The connection between the price levels in each graph is more indirect but they are related nevertheless as shown in Figure 1.

2. Figure 2 shows how shifts are accounted for in each model. A shift upward in aggregate expenditures is the same as a shift outward in aggregate demand. The magnitude of the change in quantity will depend on the multiplier effect, but in both models quantity increases by the same amount.

■ IMPORTANT TERMS

aggregate demand (AD)
determinants of
   aggregate demand

aggregate expenditures
   schedule
multiplier

SELF-TEST

■ FILL-IN QUESTIONS

1. In the aggregate demand–aggregate supply model, the price level is (fixed, variable) _____, but in the aggregate expenditures model, the price level is

_____.

2. In the aggregate expenditures model, a lower price level would (raise, lower) _____ the consumption, investment, and aggregate expenditures curves, and the equilibrium level of real GDP would (rise, fall)

_____.

3. In the aggregate expenditures model, a higher price level would (raise, lower) _____ the consumption, investment, and aggregate expenditures curves, and the equilibrium level of real GDP would (rise, fall)

_____.

4. This relationship between the price level and equilibrium real GDP in the aggregate expenditures model is

(direct, inverse) _____ and can be used to derive the aggregate (demand, supply) _____ curve.

5. If the price level were constant, an increase in the aggregate expenditures curve would shift the aggregate

demand curve to the (right, left) _____ by an amount equal to the upward shift in aggregate expendi-

tures times the (interest rate, multiplier) _____.

A decrease in the aggregate expenditures curve would shift the aggregate demand curve to the (right, left)

_____ by an amount equal to the (upward, downward) _____ shift in aggregate expendi-

tures times the (interest rate, multiplier) _____.

■ TRUE–FALSE QUESTIONS

Circle T if the statement is true, F if it is false.

1. Both the graph of the aggregate demand curve and the aggregate expenditures model show the price level on the vertical axis. **T F**

2. The higher the price level, the smaller the real balances of consumers and the lower the aggregate expenditures schedule. **T F**

3. An increase in the price level will shift the aggregate expenditures schedule upward. **T F**

4. An increase in investment spending will shift the aggregate expenditures curve upward and the aggregate demand curve leftward. **T F**

5. A shift in the aggregate demand curve is equal to the initial change in spending times the multiplier. **T F**

■ MULTIPLE-CHOICE QUESTIONS

Circle the letter that corresponds to the best answer.

1. If the price level in the aggregate expenditures model were lower, the consumption and aggregate expenditures curves would be
   (a) lower, and the equilibrium real GDP would be smaller
   (b) lower, and the equilibrium real GDP would be larger
   (c) higher, and the equilibrium real GDP would be larger
   (d) higher, and the equilibrium real GDP would be smaller

2. In the aggregate expenditures model, a decrease in the price level, other things held constant, will shift the
   (a) consumption, investment, and net exports curves downward
   (b) consumption, investment, and net exports curves upward
   (c) consumption and investment curves upward, but the net exports curve downward
   (d) consumption and net export curves upward, but the investment curve downward

3. An increase in investment spending will
   (a) increase aggregate expenditures and increase aggregate demand
   (b) decrease aggregate expenditures and decrease aggregate demand

(c) increase aggregate expenditures and decrease aggregate demand

(d) decrease aggregate expenditures and increase aggregate demand

4. A decrease in net export spending will shift the

(a) aggregate expenditures schedule upward and the aggregate demand curve rightward

(b) aggregate expenditures schedule upward and the aggregate demand curve leftward

(c) aggregate expenditures schedule downward and the aggregate demand curve rightward

(d) aggregate expenditures schedule downward and the aggregate demand curve leftward

5. An increase in aggregate expenditures shifts the aggregate demand curve to the

(a) right by the amount of the increase in aggregate expenditures

(b) right by the amount of the increase in aggregate expenditures times the multiplier

(c) left by the amount of the increase in aggregate expenditures

(d) left by the amount of the increase in aggregate expenditures times the multiplier

■ **PROBLEMS**

1. Column 1 of the following table shows the real GDP an economy might produce.

(1) Real GDP	(2) $AE_{1.20}$	(3) $AE_{1.00}$	(4) $AE_{0.80}$
$2100	$2110	$2130	$2150
2200	2200	2220	2240
2300	2290	2310	2330
2400	2380	2400	2420
2500	2470	2490	2510
2600	2560	2580	2600

a. If the price level in this economy were $1.20, the aggregate expenditures (AE) at each real GDP would be those shown in column 2 and the equilibrium real GDP would be $_____.

b. If the price level were $1.00, the aggregate expenditures at each real GDP would be those shown in column 3 and the equilibrium real GDP would be $_____.

c. If the price level were $0.80, the aggregate expenditures at each real GDP would be those shown in column 4 and the equilibrium real GDP would be $_____.

d. Show in the following schedule the equilibrium real GDP at each of the three price levels.

Price level	Equilibrium real GDP
$1.20	$____
1.00	____
0.80	____

(1) This schedule is the aggregate (demand, supply) _____ schedule.

(2) The equilibrium real GDP is (directly, inversely) _____ related to the price level.

■ **SHORT ANSWER AND ESSAY QUESTIONS**

1. What do the horizontal axes measure in a graph of the aggregate expenditures model and the aggregate demand curve?

2. Why is there an inverse relationship between aggregate expenditures and the price level? Explain, using real balance, the interest rate, and foreign purchases.

3. Describe how the aggregate demand curve can be derived from the aggregate expenditures model.

4. What is the effect of an increase in aggregate expenditures on the aggregate demand curve? Explain in words and with a graph.

5. What role does the multiplier play in shifting aggregate expenditures and aggregate demand?

ANSWERS

Appendix to Chapter 11 The Relationship of the Aggregate Demand Curve to the Aggregate Expenditures Model

FILL-IN QUESTIONS

1. variable, fixed
2. raise, rise
3. lower, fall
4. inverse, demand
5. right, multiplier, left, downward, multiplier

TRUE–FALSE QUESTIONS

1. F, pp. 211–212
2. T, p. 211
3. F, p. 211
4. F, pp. 211–212
5. T, p. 212

MULTIPLE-CHOICE QUESTIONS

1. c, p. 211
2. b, p. 211
3. a, pp. 211–212
4. d, pp. 211–212
5. b, pp. 211–212

PROBLEMS

1. *a.* 2200; *b.* 2400; *c.* 2600; *d.* 2200, 2400, 2600, (1) aggregate demand, (2) inversely

SHORT ANSWER AND ESSAY QUESTIONS

1. p. 211
2. p. 211
3. pp. 211–212
4. pp. 211–212
5. pp. 211–212

CHAPTER 12

Fiscal Policy

Principles of economics are generalizations about how the economy works. These principles are studied to help devise policies to solve real problems. Over the past 100 years or so, the most serious macroeconomic problems have been those resulting from the swings of the business cycle. Learning what determines the equilibrium level of real output and prices in an economy and what causes them to fluctuate makes it possible to find ways to achieve maximum output, full employment, and stable prices. In short, macroeconomic principles suggest policies to control both recession and inflation in an economy.

As you will discover in Chapter 12, government may use *fiscal policy* to influence the economy's output, employment, and price level. These policies use the Federal government's spending and taxing powers to improve economic conditions. The brief first section of this chapter explains how Congress, in the Employment Act of 1946, committed the Federal government to achieving three goals: economic growth, full employment, and stable prices. This act also established the Council of Economic Advisers (CEA) to advise the president and the Joint Economic Committee (JEC) to advise Congress on national economic policies.

The second section of the chapter discusses *discretionary fiscal policy*, which can be either *expansionary* or *contractionary*. Here you will learn how these fiscal policies affect aggregate demand and the Federal budget. *Expansionary fiscal policy* is used to stimulate the economy and pull it out of a slump or recession. This type of policy can be achieved by increasing government spending, decreasing taxes, or some combination of the two. *Contractionary fiscal policy* is enacted to counter inflationary pressure in the economy. The policy actions taken to dampen inflation include cutting government spending, raising taxes, or a combination of the two. As you will learn, each policy may have a significant effect on aggregate demand and the Federal budget. If the government has a *budget deficit* or *budget surplus,* the way the government finances it may affect the economy's operation as much as the size of the deficit or surplus.

Discretionary fiscal policy requires that Congress take action to change tax rates, transfer payment programs, or purchases of goods and services. *Nondiscretionary fiscal policy* does not require Congress to take any action and is a *built-in stabilizer* for the economy. You should be sure that you understand *why* net taxes increase when the GDP rises and decrease when the GDP falls and *how* this tends to stabilize the economy.

Nondiscretionary fiscal policy by itself may not be able to eliminate any recessionary or inflationary gap that might develop, and discretionary fiscal policy may be necessary if the economy is to produce its full-employment GDP and avoid inflation. The built-in stabilizers make it more difficult to use discretionary fiscal policy to achieve this goal because they create the illusion that the Federal government's policy is expansionary or contractionary when in fact its policy may be just the opposite.

The need to evaluate the direction of fiscal policy has led economists to develop a *full-employment budget* and to distinguish between a *cyclical deficit* and a *full-employment deficit.* This budget analysis enables economists to determine whether Federal fiscal policy is expansionary, contractionary, or neutral, and to determine what policy should be enacted to improve the economy's economic performance. From this budget analysis you will gain insights into the course of U.S. fiscal policy in recent years.

Fiscal policy is not without its problems, criticisms, or complications as you will learn in this section of the chapter. There are timing problems in getting it implemented. There are political considerations in getting it accepted by politicians and voters. If the fiscal policy is temporary rather than permanent it is thought to be less effective. Some economists criticize the borrowing of money by the Federal government for expansionary fiscal policy because they think it will raise interest rates and crowd out investment spending, thus reducing the policy effects. Another complication may arise from aggregate demand shocks from abroad or a net export effect that may increase or decrease the effectiveness of fiscal policy.

The debate over the advisability and effectiveness of discretionary fiscal policy is an ongoing one as will be discussed in the brief concluding section of the chapter. Some economists argue that this policy, with its potential problems and complications, should not be used. Other economists contend that discretionary fiscal policy is a valuable macroeconomic tool for directing economic activity. Perhaps most important in the design of fiscal policy are actions that contribute to the growth of long-run aggregate supply.

■ **CHECKLIST**

When you have studied this chapter you should be able to

☐ State the responsibility imposed on the Federal government by the Employment Act of 1946 and the roles of the CEA and JEC in fulfilling this responsibility.

☐ Distinguish between discretionary and nondiscretionary fiscal policy.

☐ Explain expansionary fiscal policy and the effect of spending and tax policy options on aggregate demand.

☐ Describe contractionary fiscal policy and the effect of spending and tax policy options on aggregate demand.

☐ Explain how the expansionary effect of a budget deficit depends on the method used to finance it.

☐ Describe how the deflationary effect of a budget surplus depends on the method used to finance it.

☐ Assess whether it is preferable to use government spending or taxes to counter recession and reduce inflation.

☐ Define automatic or built-in stabilizers.

☐ Indicate how the built-in stabilizers help to counter recession and inflationary pressures.

☐ Describe the relationship among progressive, proportional, and regressive tax systems and the built-in stability of the economy.

☐ Distinguish between the actual budget and the full-employment budget for evaluating fiscal policy.

☐ Describe recent U.S. fiscal policy using the full-employment budget.

☐ Use the full-employment budget to evaluate the status of discretionary fiscal policy.

☐ Outline three timing problems that may arise with fiscal policy.

☐ Discuss the political considerations affecting fiscal policy.

☐ Explain how policy reversals change the effectiveness of fiscal policy.

☐ Describe how changes in state and local finances may offset fiscal policy at the federal level.

☐ Explain and use a graph to illustrate the crowding-out effect of an expansionary fiscal policy.

☐ State the major criticisms of the crowding-out effect.

☐ Describe two ways that the effectiveness of domestic fiscal policy is complicated by the connection of a national economy with the world economy.

☐ Discuss current thinking on fiscal policy.

■ **CHAPTER OUTLINE**

1. Fiscal policy consists of the changes made by the Federal government in its expenditures and tax receipts to expand or contract the economy. In making these changes, the Federal government may seek to either increase the economy's real output (and employment) or control its rate of inflation.

2. The Employment Act of 1946 set the goals of fiscal policy in the United States and provided for a **Council of Economic Advisers** to the president and the Joint Economic Committee.

3. Fiscal policy is **discretionary** when changes in government spending or taxation by Congress are designed to change the level of real GDP, employment, incomes, or the price level. Specific action needs to be taken by Congress to initiate this discretionary policy, in contrast to nondiscretionary fiscal policy that occurs automatically (see item 4 in the next column).

a. Expansionary fiscal policy is generally used to counteract the negative economic effects of a recession or cyclical downturn in the economy (a decline in real GDP and rising unemployment). The purpose of the policy is to stimulate the economy by increasing aggregate demand. The policy will create a **budget deficit** if the budget was in balance before the policy was enacted. The stimulative effect on the economy from the initial increase in spending from the policy change will be increased by the multiplier effect. Three policy options are used:
(1) an increase in government spending;
(2) a reduction in taxes (which increases consumer spending); or
(3) a combination of an increase in government spending and a tax reduction.

b. Contractionary fiscal policy is a restrictive form of fiscal policy generally used to control demand-pull inflation. The purpose of this policy is to reduce aggregate demand pressures that increase the price level. If the government budget is balanced before the policy is enacted, it will create a **budget surplus.** The contractionary effect on the economy from the initial reduction in spending from the policy will be reinforced by the multiplier effect. Three policy options are used:
(1) a decrease in government spending;
(2) an increase in taxes (which reduces consumer spending); or
(3) a combination of a reduction in government spending and a tax increase.

c. In addition to the size of the budget deficit or surplus, the manner in which government finances its deficit or disposes of its surplus affects the level of total spending in the economy.
(1) To finance a deficit, the government can either borrow money from the public or issue new money to creditors, with the latter action being more expansionary.
(2) Budget surpluses may be used for debt reduction, or the funds may be impounded, with the latter action being more contractionary.

d. Whether government purchases or taxes should be altered to reduce recession and inflation depends on whether an expansion or a contraction of the public sector is desired.

4. In the U.S. economy there are automatic or **built-in stabilizers.** Net taxes revenues (tax revenues minus government transfer payments) are not a fixed amount or lump sum; they automatically increase as the GDP rises and automatically decrease as the GDP falls.

   a. The economic importance of this net tax system is that it serves as a built-in stabilizer of the economy. It reduces purchasing during periods of inflation and expands purchasing during periods of recession.

   b. As GDP increases, the average tax rates will increase in a **progressive tax system,** remain constant in a **proportional tax system,** and decrease in a **regressive tax system;** there is more built-in stability for the economy in progressive tax systems. Built-in stabilizers can only reduce and cannot eliminate economic fluctuations, so discretionary fiscal policy may be needed.

5. To evaluate the direction of discretionary fiscal policy, adjustments need to be made to the actual budget deficits or surpluses.

    a. The *full-employment budget* is a better index than the actual budget of the direction of government fiscal policy because it indicates what the Federal budget deficit or surplus would be if the economy were to operate at full employment. In the case of a budget deficit, the full-employment budget

        (1) removes the *cyclical deficit* that is produced by swings in the business cycle, and

        (2) reveals the size of the *full-employment deficit,* indicating how expansionary the fiscal policy was that year.

    b. U.S. data from the past decade show the years in which fiscal policy was expansionary or contractionary. There were full-employment budget deficits in the early 1990s and full-employment budget surpluses in later years. In 2002 the full-employment budget turned to deficit.

6. Certain *problems, criticisms, and complications* arise in enacting and applying fiscal policy.

    a. There will be problems of timing because it requires time to recognize the need for fiscal policy, to take the appropriate steps in Congress, and for the action taken there to affect output, employment, and the rate of inflation in the economy.

    b. There may be political considerations with fiscal policy that counter the economic effects. Elected officials may cause a *political business cycle* if they lower taxes and increase spending before elections and then do the opposite after elections.

    c. Fiscal policy may be less effective if people think that it may be reversed in the future, thus making the policy temporary rather than permanent.

    d. The fiscal policies of state and local governments can run counter to Federal fiscal policy and offset it.

    e. An expansionary fiscal policy may, by raising the level of interest rates in the economy, reduce (or *crowd out*) investment spending and weaken the effect of the policy on real GDP; but this *crowding-out effect* may be small and can be offset by an expansion in the nation's money supply.

    f. The connection of the domestic economy to a world economy means that fiscal policy may be inappropriate or less effective because of aggregate demand shocks from the world economy and from a *net export effect*. The net export effect may offset an expansionary or contractionary fiscal policy.

        (1) An expansionary fiscal policy may lead to a higher domestic interest rate which causes the dollar to appreciate, and thus net exports (and aggregate demand) decline.

        (2) A contractionary fiscal policy may lead to a lower domestic interest rate which causes the dollar to depreciate, and thus net exports (and aggregate demand) increase.

7. Chapter 12 concludes with a brief review of current thinking about discretionary fiscal policy. Some economists think that fiscal policy is ineffective because of all the potential problems and complications. They recommend the use of monetary policy to guide the economy. Other economists think that fiscal policy can be useful for directing the economy and that it can reinforce or support monetary policy. There is general agreement that fiscal policy should be designed so that its incentives and investments strengthen long-term economic growth.

■ **HINTS AND TIPS**

1. Fiscal policy is a broad concept that covers various taxation and spending policies of the Federal government; it is not limited to one policy. You will need to know the distinctions between the several kinds of fiscal policies. The main difference is between discretionary and nondiscretionary fiscal policies. *Discretionary* fiscal policy is *active* and means that Congress has taken specific actions to change taxes or government spending to influence the economy. It can be *expansionary* or *contractionary.* *Nondiscretionary* fiscal policy is *passive,* or *automatic,* because changes in tax revenues will occur without specific actions by Congress.

2. An increase in government spending that is equal to a cut in taxes will not have an equal effect on real GDP. To understand this point, assume that the MPC is .75, the increase in government spending is $8 billion, and the decrease in taxes is $8 billion. The multiplier would be 4 because it equals $1/(1 - .75)$. The increase in government spending will increase real GDP by $32 billion ($8 billion $\times$ 4). Of the $8 billion decrease in taxes, however, one-quarter of it will be saved ($6 billion $\times$ .25 = $2 billion) and just three-quarters will be spent ($8 billion $\times$ .75 = $6 billion). Thus, the tax cut results in an increase in *initial* spending in the economy of $6 billion, not $8 billion as was the case with the increase in government spending. The tax cut effect on real GDP is $24 billion ($6 billion $\times$ 4), not $32 billion.

3. A large part of the chapter deals with the problems, criticisms, and complications of fiscal policy. Do not miss the big picture and get lost in the details of each problem.

■ **IMPORTANT TERMS**

fiscal policy	progressive tax system
Employment Act of 1946	proportional tax system
Council of Economic Advisers (CEA)	regressive tax system
expansionary fiscal policy	full-employment budget
budget deficit	cyclical deficit
contractionary fiscal policy	political business cycle
budget surplus	crowding-out effect
built-in stabilizer	net export effect

SELF-TEST

■ **FILL-IN QUESTIONS**

  1. The use of fiscal policy to reduce inflation and recession became national economic policy in the

(Employment, Unemployment) _____ Act of 1946. To assist and advise the president, the act established the (Joint Economic Committee, Council of Economic Advisers) _____, and to aid Congress in investigating economic matters, the act established the _____.

2. Policy actions taken by Congress designed to change government spending or taxation are (discretionary, nondiscretionary) _____ fiscal policy, but when the policy takes effect automatically or independently of Congress, then it is _____ fiscal policy.

3. Expansionary fiscal policy is generally designed to (increase, decrease) _____ aggregate demand and thus _____ real GDP and employment in the economy. Contractionary fiscal policy is generally used to (increase, decrease) _____ aggregate demand and _____ the level of prices.

4. Expansionary fiscal policy can be achieved with an increase in (government spending, taxes) _____, a decrease in _____, or a combination of the two; contractionary fiscal policy can be achieved by a decrease in (government spending, taxes) _____, an increase in _____, or a combination of the two.

5. An increase of government spending of $5 billion from an expansionary fiscal policy for an economy might ultimately produce an increase in real GDP of $20 billion. This magnified effect occurs because of the (multiplier, crowding-out) _____ effect.

6. If the Federal budget is balanced and Congress passes legislation supporting an expansionary fiscal policy, then this action is likely to produce a budget (deficit, surplus) _____, but if Congress passes legislation supporting a contractionary fiscal policy, then the action will result in a budget _____.

7. If fiscal policy is to have a countercyclical effect, it probably will be necessary for the Federal government to incur a budget (surplus, deficit) _____ during a recession and a budget _____ during inflation.

8. Of the two principal means available to the Federal government for financing budget deficits, the one that is more expansionary is (borrowing money from the public, creating new money) _____. Of the two principal means available to the Federal government for using funds from a budget surplus, the one that is more contractionary is (impounding funds, debt reduction) _____.

9. Net taxes equal taxes (plus, minus) _____ transfer payments and are called "taxes" in this chapter. In the United States, as GDP increases, tax revenue will (increase, decrease) _____, and as the GDP decreases, tax revenues will _____.

10. Because tax revenues are (directly, indirectly) _____ related to the GDP, the economy has some (artificial, built-in) _____ stability. If the GDP increases, then tax revenue will increase, and the budget surplus will (increase, decrease) _____, thus (stimulating, restraining) _____ the economy when it is needed. When GDP decreases, tax revenues decrease, and the budget deficit (increases, decreases) _____, thus (stimulating, restraining) _____ the economy when it is needed.

11. As GDP increases, the average tax rates will increase with a (progressive, proportional, regressive) _____ tax system, remain constant with a _____ tax system, and decrease with a _____ tax system. With a progressive tax system, there is (more, less) _____ built-in stability for the economy.

12. If there is a deficit in the full-employment budget, then fiscal policy is (contractionary, expansionary) _____ and when there is a surplus in the full-employment budget, then fiscal policy is _____.

13. A deficit produced by swings in the business cycle is (actual, cyclical) _____. When there is a cyclical deficit, the full-employment budget deficit will be (greater, less) _____ than the actual budget deficit.

14. There is a problem of timing in the use of discretionary fiscal policy because of the time between the beginning of a recession or inflation and awareness of it, or (an administrative, an operational, a recognition) _____ lag; the time needed for Congress to adjust fiscal policy, or _____ lag; and the time needed for fiscal policy to take effect, or _____ lag.

15. Political problems arise in the application of discretionary fiscal policy to stabilize the economy because government has (one, several) _____ economic goals, state and local fiscal policies may (reinforce, counter) _____ Federal fiscal policy, and politicians may use fiscal policies in a way that creates (an international, a political) _____ business cycle.

16. Expectations among households and businesses that fiscal policy will be reversed in the future make fiscal policy (more, less) _____ effective. For example, if taxpayers expect a tax cut to be temporary, they may save (more, less) _____ now to pay for a future increase in the tax rate and spend _____ now. As a result, consumption and aggregate demand (increase, decrease) _____.

17. When the Federal government employs an expansionary fiscal policy to increase real GDP and employment in the economy, it usually has a budget (surplus, deficit) _____ and (lends, borrows) _____ in the money market. These actions will (raise, lower) _____ interest rates in the economy and (contract, expand) _____ investment spending. This change in investment spending is the (net export, crowding-out) _____ effect of the expansionary fiscal policy, and it tends to (weaken, strengthen) _____ the influence of the expansionary fiscal policy on real GDP and employment.

18. Fiscal policy is subject to further complications from (independence from, interdependency with) _____ _____ the world economy. For example, the domestic economy can be influenced by aggregate demand (inflation, shocks) _____ from abroad that alter GDP and might reinforce or offset fiscal policy.

19. International trade can also produce a (crowding-out, net export) _____ effect that influences aggregate demand and partially offsets fiscal policy.
  a. When fiscal policy is expansionary, it tends to (increase, decrease) _____ interest rates, which in turn tends to _____ the value of the dollar, (increase, decrease) _____ net exports, and _____ aggregate demand.
  b. When fiscal policy is contractionary, it tends to (increase, decrease) _____ interest rates, which in turn tends to _____ the value of the dollar, (increase, decrease) _____ net exports, and _____ aggregate demand.

20. Current thinking on the advisability and effectiveness of discretionary fiscal policy shows general (agreement, disagreement) _____ about the value of fiscal policy in the short run, and general _____ about evaluating fiscal policy for its contribution to long-run productivity growth.

■ **TRUE–FALSE QUESTIONS**

Circle T if the statement is true, F if it is false.

1. The Council of Economic Advisers was established to give economic advice to Congress. **T F**

2. Discretionary fiscal policy is independent of Congress and left to the discretion of state and local governments. **T F**

3. Expansionary fiscal policy during a recession or depression will create a budget deficit or add to an existing budget deficit. **T F**

4. A decrease in taxes is one of the options that can be used to pursue a contractionary fiscal policy. **T F**

5. To increase initial consumption by a specific amount, government must reduce taxes by more than that amount because some of the tax cut will be saved by households. **T F**

6. A reduction in taxes and an increase in government spending would be characteristic of a contractionary fiscal policy. **T F**

7. Borrowing from the public is the way a budget surplus is financed. **T F**

8. The creation of new money is more expansionary than borrowing from the public as a way of financing deficit spending. **T F**

9. Using a budget surplus to pay off a large public debt may reduce the anti-inflationary impact of the surplus. **T F**

10. The impounding of a budget surplus means that it is used for tax cuts. **T F**

11. Built-in stabilizers are not sufficiently strong to prevent recession or inflation, but they can reduce the severity of a recession or inflation. **T F**

12. The less progressive the tax system, the greater the economy's built-in stability. **T F**

13. The full-employment budget indicates how much government must spend and tax if there is to be full employment in the economy. **T F**

14. The key to assessing discretionary fiscal policy is to observe the change in the full-employment budget. **T F**

15. A full-employment budget surplus is expansionary. **T F**

16. Recognition, administrative, and operational lags in the timing of Federal fiscal policy make fiscal policies more effective in reducing the rate of inflation and decreasing unemployment in the economy. **T F**

17. Economists who see evidence of a political business cycle argue that members of Congress tend to increase taxes and reduce expenditures before elections and to reduce taxes and increase expenditures after elections. **T F**

18. If households expect that a tax cut will be temporary, they are likely to spend more and save less, thus reinforcing the intended effect of the tax cut on aggregate demand.　**T　F**

19. State and local governments' fiscal policies have tended to assist and reinforce the efforts of the Federal government to counter recession and inflation.　**T　F**

20. The fiscal policies of state and local governments are frequently procyclical.　**T　F**

21. The crowding-out effect occurs when an expansionary fiscal policy decreases the interest rate, increases investment spending, and strengthens fiscal policy.　**T　F**

22. Critics contend that the crowding-out effect will be greatest when the economy is in a recession.　**T　F**

23. For a domestic economy, there are gains for specialization and trade but also complications from the interdependency with the world economy.　**T　F**

24. A net export effect may partially offset an expansionary fiscal policy.　**T　F**

25. A net export effect will help the economy achieve the desired objectives of a contractionary fiscal policy.　**T　F**

■ **MULTIPLE-CHOICE QUESTIONS**

Circle the letter that corresponds to the best answer.

1. Which of the following was instrumental in assigning to the Federal government the basic responsibility for promoting economic stability in the U.S. economy?
  (a) the Employment Act of 1946
  (b) the Tax Reform Act of 1986
  (c) Say's law
  (d) Okun's law

2. If the government wishes to increase the level of real GDP, it might reduce
  (a) taxes
  (b) transfer payments
  (c) the size of the budget deficit
  (d) its purchases of goods and services

3. If Congress passes legislation to make a substantial increase in government spending to counter the effects of a severe recession, this would be an example of a
  (a) supply-side fiscal policy
  (b) contractionary fiscal policy
  (c) discretionary fiscal policy
  (d) nondiscretionary fiscal policy

4. Which combination of policies would be the most expansionary?
  (a) an increase in government spending and taxes
  (b) a decrease in government spending and taxes
  (c) an increase in government spending and a decrease in taxes
  (d) a decrease in government spending and an increase in taxes

5. An economy is in a recession and the government decides to increase spending by $4 billion. The MPC is .8.

What would be the full increase in real GDP from the change in government spending?
  (a) $3.2 billion
  (b) $4 billion
  (c) $16 billion
  (d) $20 billion

6. Which combination of fiscal policies would be the most contractionary?
  (a) an increase in government spending and taxes
  (b) a decrease in government spending and taxes
  (c) an increase in government spending and a decrease in taxes
  (d) a decrease in government spending and an increase in taxes

7. Which is a more expansionary way for government to finance a budget deficit?
  (a) borrowing money in the money market
  (b) decreasing government spending
  (c) creating new money
  (d) increasing taxes

8. Which would be the most contractionary use of funds from a budget surplus?
  (a) cutting tax rates
  (b) impounding the funds
  (c) using the funds to retire outstanding government debt
  (d) increasing government spending on social programs

9. When government tax revenues change automatically and in a countercyclical direction over the course of the business cycle, this is an example of
  (a) the political business cycle
  (b) nondiscretionary fiscal policy
  (c) the full-employment budget
  (d) crowding out

10. If the economy is to have built-in stability, when real GDP falls,
  (a) tax revenues and government transfer payments both should fall
  (b) tax revenues and government transfer payments both should rise
  (c) tax revenues should fall and government transfer payments should rise
  (d) tax revenues should rise and government transfer payments should fall

Answer Questions 11, 12, and 13 on the basis of the following diagram.

11. If the slope of the line **T** were steeper, there would be
   (a) more built-in stability for the economy
   (b) less built-in stability for the economy
   (c) no change in the built-in stability for the economy
   (d) the need for more emphasis on discretionary fiscal policy

12. If the slope of the line **T** were flatter, there would be
   (a) larger cyclical deficits produced as GDP moved from Y_3 to Y_2
   (b) smaller cyclical deficits produced as GDP moved from Y_3 to Y_2
   (c) larger full-employment deficits produced as GDP moved from Y_3 to Y_2
   (d) smaller full-employment deficits produced as GDP moved from Y_3 to Y_2

13. Actions by the Federal government to increase the progressivity of the tax system
   (a) flatten the slope of line **T** and increase built-in stability
   (b) flatten the slope of line **T** and decrease built-in stability
   (c) steepen the slope of line **T** and increase built-in stability
   (d) steepen the slope of line **T** and decrease built-in stability

14. With a proportional tax system, as the level of income increases in an economy, the average tax rate will
   (a) increase
   (b) decrease
   (c) remain the same
   (d) either increase or decrease

Use the following table to answer Question 15. The table shows the full-employment budget deficit or surplus as a percentage of GDP over a five-year period.

Year	Deficit (−) Surplus (+)
1	−2.1%
2	−3.0
3	−1.5
4	+0.5
5	+1.0

15. In which year was the fiscal policy expansionary?
   (a) Year 2
   (b) Year 3
   (c) Year 4
   (d) Year 5

16. If the full-employment budget shows a deficit of about $200 billion and the actual budget shows a deficit of about $250 billion over a several-year period, it can be concluded that there is a
   (a) cyclical deficit
   (b) net export effect
   (c) recognition lag
   (d) political business deficit

17. When the actual budget deficit is greater than the full-employment deficit, it can be concluded that
   (a) discretionary fiscal policy is contractionary

   (b) the economy is at less than full employment
   (c) the tax system for the economy is regressive
   (d) the budget surplus has increased

18. If the full-employment deficit as a percentage of GDP is zero one year, and there is a full-employment budget surplus the next year, it can be concluded that
   (a) fiscal policy is expansionary
   (b) fiscal policy is contractionary
   (c) the federal government is borrowing money
   (d) the federal government is lending money

19. The length of time involved for the fiscal action taken by Congress to affect output, employment, or the price level is referred to as the
   (a) administrative lag
   (b) operational lag
   (c) recognition lag
   (d) fiscal lag

20. The crowding-out effect of an expansionary (deficit) fiscal policy is the result of government borrowing in the money market which
   (a) increases interest rates and net investment spending in the economy
   (b) increases interest rates and decreases net investment spending
   (c) decreases interest rates and increases net investment spending
   (d) decreases interest rates and net investment spending

21. The effect of an expansionary fiscal policy on the real GDP of an economy is
   (a) strengthened by the crowding-out effect
   (b) weakened by the crowding-out effect
   (c) reinforced by raising tax rates
   (d) offset by lowering tax rates

22. The crowding-out effect may be
   (a) counteracted by decreasing the supply of money to offset a decrease in the demand for money
   (b) reinforced by decreasing the supply of money to offset a decrease in the demand for money
   (c) reinforced by increasing the supply of money to offset an increase in the demand for money
   (d) counteracted by increasing the supply of money to offset an increase in the demand for money

23. Suppose the United States pursued an expansionary fiscal policy to stimulate its economy and eliminate a recession. The net export effect suggests that net exports would
   (a) decrease, thus decreasing aggregate demand and partially offsetting the fiscal policy
   (b) decrease, thus increasing aggregate demand and partially offsetting the fiscal policy
   (c) increase, thus decreasing aggregate demand and partially offsetting the fiscal policy
   (d) increase, thus increasing aggregate demand and partially reinforcing the fiscal policy

24. Suppose the United States pursued a contractionary fiscal policy to reduce the level of inflation. The net export effect suggests that net exports would

(a) decrease, thus decreasing aggregate demand and partially reinforcing the fiscal policy

(b) decrease, thus increasing aggregate demand and partially offsetting the fiscal policy

(c) increase, thus decreasing aggregate demand and partially reinforcing the fiscal policy

(d) increase, thus increasing aggregate demand and partially offsetting the fiscal policy

25. Current thinking about discretionary fiscal policy among mainstream economists is that it should be designed to

(a) counteract the effects of monetary policy

(b) contribute to long-run economic growth

(c) "fine-tune" the economy in the short run, but not in the long run

(d) control inflationary pressure, but not be used to fight recession

■ **PROBLEMS**

1. Columns 1 and 2 in the following table are an aggregate supply schedule. Columns 1 and 3 are an aggregate demand schedule.

(1) Price level	(2) Real GDP$_1$	(3) AD$_1$	(4) AD$_2$	(5) Real GDP$_2$
220	$ 2390	$ 2100	$ 2200	$ 2490
200	2390	2200	2340	2490
190	2350	2250	2350	2450
180	2300	2300	2400	2400
160	2200	2400	2500	2300

a. The equilibrium real GDP is $_____

and the price level is _____.

b. Suppose the expansionary fiscal policy increases aggregate demand from that shown in columns 1 and 3 to that shown in columns 1 and 4. The price level will

increase to _____, and this rise in the price level

will result in real GDP increasing to $_____.

c. If the expansionary fiscal policy that increased aggregate demand also has supply-side effects and increased aggregate supply from that shown in columns 1 and 2 to that shown in columns 1 and 5, the equi-

librium real GDP would increase to $_____

and the price level would _____.

2. The following table shows seven real GDPs and the net tax revenues of government at each real GDP.

Real GDP	Net tax revenues	Government purchases	Government deficit/surplus
$ 850	$170	$____	$____
900	180	____	____
950	190	____	____
1000	200	____	____
1050	210	____	____
1100	220	____	____
1150	230		

a. Looking at the two columns on the left side of the table, it can be seen that

(1) when real GDP increases by $50, net tax revenues

(increase, decrease) _____ by $_____.

(2) when real GDP decreases by $100, net tax reve-

nues (increase, decrease) _____ by

$_____.

(3) the relationship between real GDP and net tax

revenues is (direct, inverse) _____.

b. Assume the simple multiplier has a value of 10 and that investment spending in the economy decreases by $10.

(1) *If* net tax revenues remained constant, the equilib-

rium real GDP would decrease by $_____.

(2) But when real GDP decreases, net tax revenues also decrease; and this decrease in net tax revenues

will tend to (increase, decrease) _____ the equilibrium real GDP.

(3) And, therefore, the decrease in real GDP brought about by the $10 decrease in investment spending

will be (more, less) _____ than $100.

(4) The direct relationship between net tax revenues

and real GDP has (lessened, expanded) _____ the impact of the $10 decrease in investment spending on real GDP.

c. Suppose the simple multiplier is also 10 and government wishes to increase the equilibrium real GDP by $50.

(1) *If* net tax revenues remained constant, government would have to increase its purchases of goods and ser-

vices by $_____.

(2) But when real GDP rises, net tax revenues also rise, and this rise in net tax revenues will tend to (in-

crease, decrease) _____ the equilibrium real GDP.

(3) The effect, therefore, of the $5 increase in government purchases will also be to increase the equi-

librium real GDP by (more, less) _____ than $50.

(4) The direct relationship between net tax revenues

and real GDP has (lessened, expanded) _____ the effect of the $5 increase in government purchases, and to raise the equilibrium real GDP by $50, the government will have to increase its purchases by (more,

less) _____ than $5.

d. Imagine that the full-employment real GDP of the economy is $1150 and that government purchases of goods and services are $200.

(1) Complete the previous table by entering the government purchases and computing the budget deficit or surplus at each of the real GDPs. (Show a government deficit by placing a minus sign in front of the amount by which expenditures exceed net tax revenues.)

(2) The full-employment surplus equals $_____.
(3) If the economy were in a recession and producing a real GDP of $900, the budget would show a (surplus, deficit) _____ of $_____.
(4) This budget deficit or surplus makes it appear that government is pursuing (an expansionary, a contractionary) _____ fiscal policy, but this deficit or surplus is not the result of a countercyclical fiscal policy but the result of the _____.
(5) If government did not change its net tax *rates,* it could increase the equilibrium real GDP from $900 to the full-employment real GDP of $1150 by increasing its purchases by (approximately) $70. At the full-employment real GDP the budget would show a (surplus, deficit) _____ of $_____.
(6) If government did not change its purchases, it would increase the equilibrium real GDP from $900 to the full-employment real GDP of $1150 by decreasing net tax revenues at all real GDPs by a lump sum of (approximately) $80. The full-employment budget would have a (surplus, deficit) _____ of $_____.

3. a. Complete the table below by computing the average tax rates, given the net tax revenue data in columns 2, 4, and 6. Calculate the average tax rate in percentage to one decimal place (for example, 5.4%).

b. As real GDP increases in column 1, the average tax rate (increases, decreases, remains the same) _____ in column 3, _____ in column 5, and _____ in column 7. The tax system is (progressive, proportional, regressive) _____ in column 2, _____ in column 4, and _____ in column 6.
c. On the graph following the table, plot the real GDP, net tax revenue, and government spending data given in columns 1, 2, 4, 6, and 8. The tax revenue system with the steepest slope is found in column _____, and it is (progressive, proportional, regressive) _____ while the one with the flattest slope is found in column _____, and it is_____.

4. a. Complete the table on the next page by stating whether the direction of discretionary fiscal policy was contractionary (**C**), expansionary (**E**), or neither (**N**) given the hypothetical budget data for an economy.
b. The best gauge of the direction of fiscal policy is the (actual, full-employment) _____ budget deficit or surplus because it removes the (cyclical, actual) _____ component from the discussion of the budget situation.

(1) Real GDP	(2) Net tax revenue	(3) Average tax rate	(4) Net tax revenue	(5) Average tax rate	(6) Net tax revenue	(7) Average tax rate	(8) Government spending
$1000	$100	____%	$100	____%	$100	____%	$120
$1100	120	____	110	____	108	____	120
$1200	145	____	120	____	115	____	120
$1300	175	____	130	____	120	____	120
$1400	210	____	140	____	123	____	120

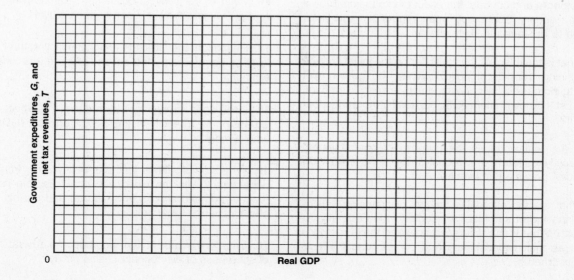

(1) Year	(2) Actual budget deficit (−) or surplus (+)	(3) Full-employment budget deficit (−) or surplus (+)	(4) Direction of fiscal policy
1	−$170 billion	−$130 billion	
2	− 120 billion	− 90 billion	_____
3	+ 40 billion	+ 20 billion	_____
4	− 60 billion	− 50 billion	_____
5	− 120 billion	− 100 billion	_____

c. (1) In what years were there cyclical deficits, and what was the amount of the cyclical deficit in each of those years? _____

_____

(2) In what year was the actual budget surplus greater than the full-employment budget surplus, and by what amount greater? _____

_____

■ **SHORT ANSWER AND ESSAY QUESTIONS**

1. In the Employment Act of 1946, (a) what responsibility was given to the Federal government, (b) what tasks were assigned to the Council of Economic Advisers and the Joint Economic Committee?

2. What is the difference between discretionary fiscal policy and nondiscretionary fiscal policy?

3. What are the Federal government's three options for conducting expansionary or contractionary fiscal policy?

4. Under what economic conditions would expansionary or contractionary fiscal policy be used? What would be the effect on the Federal budget?

5. Compare and contrast the effect of expansionary and of contractionary fiscal policy on aggregate demand. Draw a graph to illustrate the likely effects.

6. What is the effect of the multiplier on the initial change in spending from fiscal policy? When the government wants to increase initial consumption by a specific amount, why must the government reduce taxes by more than that amount?

7. In the real world, is the purpose of contractionary fiscal policy to restore a previously lower price level? How do "sticky" prices affect events?

8. What are the alternative means of financing deficits and disposing of surpluses available to the Federal government? What is the difference between these methods insofar as their expansionary and contractionary effects are concerned?

9. Explain the fiscal policies that would be advocated during a recession and during a period of inflation by those who (a) wish to expand the public sector and (b) wish to contract the size of government.

10. What is a built-in stabilizer? How do the built-in stabilizers work to reduce rises and falls in the level of nominal GDP?

11. What is the economic importance of the direct relationship between tax receipts and GDP?

12. Supply definitions of progressive, proportional, and regressive tax systems. What are the implications of each type of tax system for the built-in stability of the economy?

13. What is the full-employment budget? What was the problem that the use of the full-employment budget was designed to solve?

14. Explain the distinction between a cyclical deficit and full-employment deficit. Which type of deficit provides the best indication of the direction of fiscal policy? Why?

15. Explain the three kinds of time lags that make it difficult to use fiscal policy to stabilize the economy.

16. What is the political business cycle? Explain how it works. Evaluate the likelihood of such a cycle.

17. How might the direction of fiscal policy at the Federal level be countered by the actions of state and local governments?

18. How does crowding out reduce the effect of an expansionary (deficit) fiscal policy on real GDP and employment?

19. What complications for fiscal policy arise from interdependency with the world economy? Explain how aggregate demand shocks from abroad and the net export effect influence fiscal policy.

20. What is the current thinking about the advisability and effectiveness of discretionary fiscal policy?

ANSWERS

Chapter 12 Fiscal Policy

FILL-IN QUESTIONS

1. Employment, Council of Economic Advisers, Joint Economic Committee

2. discretionary, nondiscretionary

3. increase, increase, decrease, decrease

4. government spending, taxes, government spending, taxes

5. multiplier

6. deficit, surplus

7. deficit, surplus

8. creating new money, impounding funds

9. minus, increase, decrease

10. directly, built-in, increase, restraining, increases, stimulating

11. progressive, proportional, regressive, more

12. expansionary, contractionary

13. cyclical, less

14. a recognition, an administrative, an operational

15. several, counter, a political

16. less, more, less, decrease

17. deficit, borrows, raise, contract, crowding-out, weaken

18. interdependency with, shocks

19. net export; *a.* increase, increase, decrease, decrease; *b.* decrease, decrease, increase, increase

20. disagreement, agreement

TRUE–FALSE QUESTIONS

1. F, pp. 214–215	**10.** F, p. 218	**19.** F, p. 224
2. F, p. 215	**11.** T, pp. 218–219	**20.** T, p. 224
3. T, pp. 215–216	**12.** F, pp. 219–220	**21.** F, pp. 224–225
4. F, pp. 216–217	**13.** F, pp. 220–221	**22.** F, pp. 224–225
5. T, p. 216	**14.** T, pp. 221–222	**23.** T, pp. 225–226
6. F, pp. 216–217	**15.** F, pp. 221–222	**24.** T, p. 226
7. F, pp. 217–218	**16.** F, p. 223	**25.** F, p. 226
8. T, p. 218	**17.** T, p. 223	
9. T, p. 218	**18.** F, pp. 223–224	

MULTIPLE-CHOICE QUESTIONS

1. a, p. 214	**10.** c, pp. 218–219	**19.** b, p. 223
2. a, p. 216	**11.** a, pp. 219–220	**20.** b, pp. 224–225
3. c, pp. 215–216	**12.** b, pp. 219–220	**21.** b, pp. 224–225
4. c, pp. 215–216	**13.** c, pp. 219–220	**22.** d, p. 225
5. d, pp. 215–216	**14.** c, pp. 219–220	**23.** a, p. 226
6. d, pp. 216–217	**15.** a, pp. 220–222	**24.** d, p. 226
7. c, pp. 217–218	**16.** a, pp. 220–222	**25.** b, p. 228
8. b, p. 218	**17.** b, pp. 220–222	
9. b, pp. 218–219	**18.** b, pp. 220–222	

PROBLEMS

1. *a.* 2300, 180; *b.* 190, 2350; *c.* 2400, remain constant

2. *a.* increase, $10, (2) decrease, $20, (3) direct; *b.* (1) $100, (2) increase, (3) less, (4) lessened; *c.* (1) $5, (2) decrease, (3) less, (4) lessened, more; *d.* (1) government purchases are $200 at all GDPs, government surplus or deficit: −30, −20, −10, 0, 10, 20, 30, (2) $30, (3) deficit, $20, (4) an expansionary, recession, (5) deficit, $40, (6) deficit, $50

3. *a.* column 3: 10.0, 10.9, 12.1, 13.5, 15.0; column 5: 10.0 at each GDP level; column 7: 10.0, 9.8, 9.6, 9.2, 8.8; *b.* increases, remains the same, decreases; progressive, proportional, regressive; *c.* 2, progressive, 6, regressive

4. *a.* (Year 1–2) contractionary, (Year 2–3) contractionary, (Year 3–4) expansionary, (Year 4–5) expansionary; *b.* full-employment, cyclical; *c.* (1) year 1 ($40 billion), year 2 ($30 billion), year 4 ($10 billion), year 5 ($20 billion), (2) year 3 ($20 billion)

SHORT ANSWER AND ESSAY QUESTIONS

1. pp. 214–215	**8.** pp. 217–218	**15.** p. 223
2. pp. 215, 218	**9.** p. 218	**16.** p. 223
3. pp. 215–217	**10.** pp. 218–219	**17.** p. 224
4. pp. 215–217	**11.** pp. 219–220	**18.** pp. 224–225
5. pp. 215–217	**12.** pp. 219–220	**19.** pp. 225–226
6. pp. 215–216	**13.** pp. 220–221	**20.** p. 228
7. pp. 216–217	**14.** pp. 220–222	

CHAPTER 13

Money and Banking

Chapter 13 explains how the financial system affects the operation of the economy. The chapter is largely descriptive and factual. Pay particular attention to the following: (1) what the money supply is and the function money performs; (2) what gives value to or "backs" money in the United States; (3) how the total demand for money and the money supply together determine the equilibrium rate of interest; and (4) the principal institutions of the U.S. financial system and their functions.

Several points are worth repeating. First, money is whatever performs the three functions of money (*medium of exchange, unit of account, store of value*). In the United States, the supply of money consists largely of the debts (promises to pay) of the Federal Reserve Banks and depository institutions. This money is backed by the willingness to exchange goods and services, *and not by gold.*

Second, the *total demand for money* is made up of a *transactions demand for money* and an *asset demand for money.* Because money is used as a medium of exchange, consumers and business firms wish to hold money for transaction purposes. The quantity of money they demand for this purpose is directly related to the size of the economy's nominal (or money) gross domestic product. This means that when either the price level or the real gross domestic product increases, they will want to have more money on hand to use for transactions.

Money is also used as a store of value that creates an asset demand. Consumers and businesses who own assets may choose to have some of their assets in the form of money (rather than in stocks, bonds, goods, or property). Holding money, however, imposes a cost. This cost is the interest they lose when they own money rather than an interest-earning asset such as a bond. Consumers and businesses will demand less money for asset purposes when the rate of interest (the cost of holding money) is high and demand more money when the rate of interest is low; the quantity of money demanded as an asset is inversely related to the interest rate.

The total demand for money is the sum of the transactions demand and the asset demand. It is affected by both nominal GDP and the rate of interest. The total demand and the supply of money determine interest rates in the *money market.* The inverse relationship between bond prices and interest rates helps this market adjust to shortages or surpluses of money.

Third, the central bank in the United States consists of the 12 *Federal Reserve Banks* and the *Board of Governors* of the *Federal Reserve System* which oversees their operation. These banks, while privately owned by the commercial banks, are operated more or less as agencies of the Federal government. They operate on a not-for-profit basis but are used primarily to regulate the nation's money supply in the best interests of the economy as a whole and secondarily to perform other services for the banks, the government, and the economy. They are able to perform their primary function because they are bankers' banks in which depository institutions (commercial banks and thrifts) can deposit and borrow money. They do not deal directly with the public.

Fourth, these depository institutions accept deposits and make loans, but they also are able to create money by lending checkable deposits. Because they are able to do this, they have a strong influence on the size of the money supply and the value of money. The Federal Reserve Banks exist primarily to regulate the money supply and its value by influencing and controlling the amount of money depository institutions create.

The final section of Chapter 13 discusses recent developments in money and banking, of which three are particularly noteworthy. The relative decline of banks and thrifts and changes in their services have significantly altered the financial services industry. Also, financial markets are now global and more highly integrated than in previous decades. In addition, technological advances have changed the character of money.

■ CHECKLIST

When you have studied this chapter you should be able to

□ List and explain the three functions of money.
□ Give an *M*1 definition of money that explains its two major components.
□ Describe the two major types of institutions offering checkable deposits.
□ Give an *M*2 definition of money and its components.
□ Give an *M*3 definition of money and its components.
□ Distinguish between credit cards and money.
□ Explain why money is debt in the U.S. economy and who holds that debt.
□ State three reasons why currency and checkable deposits are money and have value.
□ Use an equation to explain the relationship between the value of money and the price level, or the purchasing power of money.

☐ Discuss how inflation affects the acceptability of money.

☐ Explain what role government plays in maintaining or stabilizing the value of money.

☐ Give a definition of the transactions demand for money that describes how it varies with nominal GDP.

☐ Give a definition of the asset demand for money that describes how it varies with the rate of interest.

☐ Illustrate graphically how the transactions and asset demands for money combine to form the total demand for money.

☐ Describe the money market and what determines the equilibrium rate of interest.

☐ Explain how changes in nominal GDP and in the money supply affect the interest rate.

☐ Illustrate with an example how disequilibrium in the money market is corrected through changes in bond prices.

☐ Describe the purposes of the Board of Governors and FOMC of the Federal Reserve System.

☐ Explain why the Federal Reserve Banks are central, quasi-public, and bankers' banks.

☐ Discuss the relationship between the Federal Reserve System and commercial banks and thrifts.

☐ List and explain the seven major functions of the Federal Reserve System and indicate which one is most important.

☐ Discuss the reason for the independence of the Federal Reserve System.

☐ Describe five major changes in the financial services industry in the United States in recent years.

■ **CHAPTER OUTLINE**

1. Money is whatever performs the three *basic functions of money.* It is a *medium of exchange* for buying and selling goods and services. It serves as a *unit of account* for measuring the monetary cost of goods and services. It is a *store of value* so money can be used over time.

2. In the U.S. economy, the definition of *money* is whatever is generally used as a medium of exchange and consists of the debts of the Federal government and of commercial banks and other financial institutions.

    a. The narrowly defined money supply is called *M*1 and has two principal components.

    (1) The smaller component is currency: coins which are token money and paper money largely in the form of Federal Reserve Notes.

    (2) The larger and more important component is checkable deposits.

    (3) The two major types of financial institutions offering checkable deposits are *commercial banks* and *thrift institutions.*

    (4) Currency and checkable deposits owned by the Federal government, commercial banks and savings institutions, and the Federal Reserve Banks are not included in *M*1 or in any of the more broadly defined money supplies.

    b. *M*2 is a broader definition of money and includes not only the currency and checkable deposits in *M*1

but such near-monies as noncheckable savings deposits and time deposits in commercial banks and savings institutions. *M*2 includes *M*1 plus noncheckable savings deposits plus small time deposits (less than $100,000) plus money market deposit accounts (MMDA) plus money market mutual funds (MMMF).

    c. *M*3 includes *M*2 plus large time deposits ($100,000 or more). There are advantages to each of the different measures of money, but since *M*1 is included in all the definitions and the principles that apply to it are applicable to the other measures, that narrow definition is used for the textbook discussion unless noted otherwise.

3. The *money supply gets its "backing"* from the ability of the government to keep the value of money stable.

    a. Money is debt or the promise of a commercial bank, a thrift institution, or a Federal Reserve Bank to pay, but these debts cannot be redeemed for anything tangible.

    b. Money has value only because: It is acceptable for the exchange of desirable goods and services; it is *legal tender* (legally acceptable for payment of debts); and it is relatively scarce.

    c. The value of money is inversely related to the price level. Rapid inflation can erode the value of money and public confidence in it.

    d. Money is backed by the confidence the public has that the value of money will remain stable; the Federal government can use monetary and fiscal policy to keep the value of money relatively stable.

4. Business firms and households wish to hold and, therefore, demand money for two reasons.

    a. Because they use money as a medium of exchange, they have a *transactions demand for money* that is directly related to the nominal gross domestic product of the economy.

    b. Because they also use money as a store of value, they have an *asset demand for money* that is inversely related to the rate of interest.

    c. Their *total demand for money* is the sum of the transactions and asset demands.

5. In the *money market,* the demand for money and the supply of money determine the interest rate. Graphically, the demand for money is a downsloping line and the supply of money is a vertical line, and their intersection determines the interest rate. Disequilibrium in this market is corrected by changes in bond prices and their inverse relationship with interest rates.

    a. If there is a decrease in the money supply, there will be a shortage of money and bonds will be sold. The increase in supply of bonds will drive down bond prices, causing interest rates to rise until the shortage is eliminated.

    b. If there is an increase in the money supply, there will be a surplus of money and bonds will be bought. The increased demand for bonds will drive up bond prices, causing interest rates to fall until the surplus is eliminated.

6. The financial sector of the economy is significantly influenced by the **Federal Reserve System** *(the Fed)* and the nation's banks and thrift institutions.

a. The banking system remains centralized and regulated by government because historical problems have led to different kinds of money and the mismanagement of the money supply.

b. The **Board of Governors** of the Fed exercises control over the supply of money and the banking system. The U.S. president appoints the seven members of the Board of Governors.

c. Four important bodies help the Board of Governors establish and conduct policy: the **Federal Open Market Committee (FOMC)**, which establishes policy over the buying and selling of government securities; and three Advisory Councils that provide input from commercial banks, thrift institutions, and consumer-related organizations.

d. The **12 Federal Reserve Banks** of the Fed serve as central banks, quasi-public banks, and bankers' banks.

e. The U.S. banking system contains thousands of commercial banks and thrift institutions that are directly affected by the Fed's decisions.

f. The Fed performs seven functions: issuing currency, setting reserve requirements and holding reserves, lending money to banks and thrifts, collecting and processing checks, serving as the fiscal agent for the Federal government, supervising banks, and controlling the money supply. The last function is the most important.

g. The independence of the Fed protects it from strong political pressure from the U.S. Congress or the president that could lead to poor economic decisions.

7. Three recent developments have affected money and banking and the **financial services industry** in the United States.

a. The number of banks and thrift institutions has declined, partly as a result of bank and thrift mergers. There has also been a convergence in the services offered by different types of financial institutions (banks, insurance companies, etc.).

b. Financial markets are now more globalized and integrated because of advances in computer and communications technologies.

c. The character of money has changed with the shift to the use of **electronic money**.

■ HINTS AND TIPS

1. Most students think of currency as the major component of the money supply, but it is a very small component relative to **checkable deposits.** There are several definitions of the **money supply** that you must know about, from the narrow *M*1 to the broader *M*2 and *M*3.

2. Spend extra time learning how the **total demand for money** is determined (see Figure 13.1 in the text). The total demand for money is composed of the transactions and the asset demands for money. *The transactions de-*

mand for money is influenced by the level of nominal GDP and not affected by the interest rate, so it *is graphed as a vertical line*. The **asset demand for money** is affected by the interest rate, so it *is graphed as a downsloping curve*. The total demand for money is also graphed as a *downsloping curve* because of the influence of the asset demand, but the curve is shifted farther to the right than the asset demand curve because of the influence of the transactions demand.

3. One of the most difficult concepts to understand is the *inverse* relationship between bond prices and interest rates. The simple explanation is that interest yield from a bond is the ratio of the *fixed* annual interest payment to the bond price. The numerator is fixed, but the denominator (bond price) is variable. If the bond price falls, the interest yield on the bond rises because the fixed annual interest payment is being divided by a smaller denominator.

■ IMPORTANT TERMS

medium of exchange	legal tender
unit of account	transactions demand for money
store of value	
*M*1, *M*2, and *M*3	asset demand for money
token money	total demand for money
Federal Reserve Notes	money market
checkable deposits	Federal Reserve System
commercial banks	Board of Governors
thrift institutions	Federal Open Market Committee (FOMC)
near-monies	
savings account	Federal Reserve Banks
money market deposit account (MMDA)	financial services industry
	electronic transactions
time deposits	
money market mutual fund (MMMF)	

SELF-TEST

■ FILL-IN QUESTIONS

1. When money is usable for buying and selling goods and services, it functions as (a unit of account, a store of value, a medium of exchange) _____ _____, but when money serves as a measure of relative worth, it functions as _____, and when money serves as a liquid asset it functions as _____.

2. All coins in circulation in the United States are (paper, token) _____ money, which means that their intrinsic value is (less, greater) _____ than the face value of the coin.

3. Paper money and coins are considered (currency, checkable deposits) _____. One major component of **M**1 is (currency, checkable deposits) _____, and the other major component is _____.

4. **M**2 is equal to (**M**1, **M**3) _____ plus (checkable, noncheckable) _____ savings deposits, (small, large) _____ time deposits, and money market (deposit accounts, mutual funds) _____ and _____.

5. **M**3 is equal to **M**2 plus (small, large) _____ time deposits. These deposits have a face value of (less than $100,000; $100,000 or greater) _____.

6. Credit cards (are, are not) _____ considered money but rather a form of (paper money, loan) _____ from the institution that issued the card.

7. Paper money is the circulating debt of (banks and thrifts, the Federal Reserve Banks) _____ _____, while checkable deposits are the debts of _____. In the United States, currency and checkable deposits (are, are not) _____ backed by gold and silver.

8. Money has value because it is (unacceptable, acceptable) _____ in exchange for products and resources, because it is (legal, illegal) _____ tender, and because it is relatively (abundant, scarce) _____.

9. The value of money varies (directly, inversely) _____ with the price level. To find the value of $1 (multiply, divide) _____ 1 by the price level.

10. Runaway inflation may significantly (increase, decrease) _____ the value of money and _____ its acceptance as a medium of exchange.

11. The transactions demand varies (directly, inversely) _____ with (the rate of interest, nominal GDP) _____, and the asset demand varies (directly, inversely) _____ with (the rate of interest, nominal GDP) _____.

12. The sum of the transactions and asset demands for money is the total (demand, supply) _____ of money, and the intersection of it with the _____ of money determines the equilibrium (interest rate, price level) _____.

13. When the quantity of money demanded exceeds the quantity of money supplied, bond prices (increase, decrease) _____ and interest rates _____. When the quantity of money demanded is less than the quantity of money supplied, bond prices (increase, decrease) _____ and interest rates _____.

14. The Federal Reserve System is composed of the Board of (Control, Governors) _____ that is assisted by the powerful (U.S. Mint, Federal Open Market Committee) _____. There are also (10, 12) _____ Federal Reserve Banks.

15. The Federal Reserve Banks are (private, quasi-public) _____ banks, serve as (consumers', bankers') _____ banks, and are (local, central) _____ banks whose policies are coordinated by the Board of Governors.

16. The workhorses of the U.S. banking system are about 7800 (thrifts, commercial banks) _____ and about 11,800 _____.

17. The seven major functions of the Fed are

a. _____

_____

b. _____

_____

c. _____

_____

d. _____

_____

e. _____

_____

f. _____

_____

g. _____

_____

Of these, the most important function is _____

_____

18. The Congress established the Fed as a(n) (dependent, independent) _____ agency of government. The object was to protect it from political pressure so it could control (taxes, inflation) _____.

19. In the past decade, the number of banks and thrifts (increased, decreased) _____ due to (mergers, inflation) _____ in the financial services industry.

20. Two other recent developments in money and banking are the (localization, globalization) _____ of financial markets and the use of (paper, electronic) _____ transactions.

■ TRUE–FALSE QUESTIONS

Circle T if the statement is true, F if it is false.

1. When the price of a product is stated in terms of dollars and cents, then money is functioning as a unit of account.　　　**T　F**

2. The money supply designated $M1$ is the sum of currency and noncheckable deposits.　　　**T　F**

3. The currency component of $M1$ includes both coins and paper money.　　　**T　F**

4. If a coin is token money, its face value is less than its intrinsic value.　　　**T　F**

5. Both commercial banks and thrift institutions accept checkable deposits.　　　**T　F**

6. The checkable deposits of the Federal government at the Federal Reserve Banks are a component of $M1$.　　　**T　F**

7. $M2$ exceeds $M1$ by the amount of noncheckable savings, small time deposits, and money market deposit accounts and money market mutual funds.　　　**T　F**

8. A *small* time deposit is one that is less than $100,000.　　　**T　F**

9. $M2$ is less than $M3$ by the amount of small time deposits in depository institutions.　　　**T　F**

10. Economists and public officials are in general agreement on how to define the money supply in the United States.　　　**T　F**

11. The major components of the money supply are debts, or promises to pay.　　　**T　F**

12. Currency and checkable deposits are money because they are acceptable to sellers in exchange for goods and services.　　　**T　F**

13. If money is to have a fairly stable value, its supply must be limited relative to the demand for it.　　　**T　F**

14. There is a transactions demand for money because households and business firms use money as a store of value.　　　**T　F**

15. An increase in the price level would increase the transactions demand for money.　　　**T　F**

16. An increase in the nominal GDP, other things remaining the same, will increase both the total demand for money and the equilibrium rate of interest in the economy.　　　**T　F**

17. Bond prices and interest rates are inversely related.　　　**T　F**

18. Members of the Board of Governors of the Federal Reserve System are appointed by the president of the United States and confirmed by the Senate.　　　**T　F**

19. The Federal Open Market Committee (FOMC) is responsible for keeping the stock market open and regulated.　　　**T　F**

20. The Federal Reserve Banks are owned and operated by the U.S. government.　　　**T　F**

21. Federal Reserve Banks are bankers' banks because they make loans to and accept deposits from depository institutions.　　　**T　F**

22. At times, the Fed lends money to banks and thrifts, charging them an interest rate called the *bank and thrift rate*.　　　**T　F**

23. Congress established the Fed as an independent agency to protect it from political pressure so that it can effectively control the money supply and maintain price stability.　　　**T　F**

24. In recent years, banks and thrifts have increased their share of the financial services industry and control of financial assets.　　　**T　F**

25. It is expected that electronic transactions such as the use of smart cards will replace all other means of payment.　　　**T　F**

■ MULTIPLE-CHOICE QUESTIONS

Circle the letter that corresponds to the best answer.

1. Which one is an economic function of money?
 (a) a medium of communications
 (b) a factor of production
 (c) a store of bonds
 (d) a unit of account

2. The largest element of the currency component of $M1$ is
 (a) coins
 (b) gold certificates
 (c) silver certificates
 (d) Federal Reserve Notes

3. Which constitutes the largest element in the $M1$ money supply?
 (a) savings deposits
 (b) small time deposits
 (c) large time deposits
 (d) checkable deposits

4. Checkable deposits are money because they are
 (a) legal tender
 (b) fiat money
 (c) token money
 (d) a medium of exchange

5. The supply of money *M*1 consists almost entirely of the debts of
   (a) the Federal government
   (b) the Federal Reserve Banks
   (c) depository institutions
   (d) the Federal Reserve Banks and depository institutions

Use the following table to answer Questions 6, 7, and 8 about the money supply, given the following hypothetical data for the economy.

Item	Billions of dollars
Checkable deposits	$1775
Small time deposits	345
Currency	56
Large time deposits	1230
Noncheckable savings deposits	945
Money market deposit accounts	256
Money market mutual funds	587

6. The size of the *M*1 money supply is
   (a) $1775
   (b) $1831
   (c) $2176
   (d) $3019

7. The size of the *M*2 money supply is
   (a) $2176
   (b) $3146
   (c) $3964
   (d) $4532

8. The size of the *M*3 money supply is
   (a) $4532
   (b) $5194
   (c) $5339
   (d) $6007

9. Which *best* describes the backing of money in the United States?
   (a) the gold bullion stored in Fort Knox, Kentucky
   (b) the belief of holders of money that it can be exchanged for desirable goods and services
   (c) the willingness of banks and the government to surrender something of value in exchange for money
   (d) the faith and confidence of the public in the ability of government to pay its debts

10. If the price level increases 20%, the value of money decreases
   (a) 14.14%
   (b) 16.67%
   (c) 20%
   (d) 25%

11. To keep the value of money fairly constant, the Federal Reserve
   (a) uses price and wage controls
   (b) controls the money supply
   (c) employs fiscal policy
   (d) buys corporate stock

12. If the dollars held for transactions purposes are, on the average, spent five times a year for final goods and services, then the quantity of money people will wish to hold for transactions is equal to
   (a) five times the nominal GDP
   (b) 20% of the nominal GDP
   (c) five divided by the nominal GDP
   (d) 20% divided by the nominal GDP

13. There is an asset demand for money because money is
   (a) a store of value
   (b) a measure of value
   (c) a medium of exchange
   (d) a standard of deferred payment

14. An increase in the rate of interest would increase
   (a) the opportunity cost of holding money
   (b) the transactions demand for money
   (c) the asset demand for money
   (d) the prices of bonds

Use the table below to answer Questions 15 and 16.

Interest rate	Asset demand (billions)
14%	$100
13	150
12	200
11	250

15. Suppose the transactions demand for money is equal to 10% of the nominal GDP, the supply of money is $450 billion, and the asset demand for money is that shown in the table. If the nominal GDP is $3000 billion, the equilibrium interest rate is
   (a) 14%
   (b) 13%
   (c) 12%
   (d) 11%

16. If the nominal GDP remains constant, an increase in the money supply from $450 billion to $500 billion would cause the equilibrium interest rate to
   (a) rise to 14%
   (b) fall to 11%
   (c) fall to 12%
   (d) remain unchanged

17. The total quantity of money demanded is
   (a) directly related to nominal GDP and the rate of interest
   (b) directly related to nominal GDP and inversely related to the rate of interest
   (c) inversely related to nominal GDP and directly related to the rate of interest
   (d) inversely related to nominal GDP and the rate of interest

18. The stock of money is determined by the Federal Reserve System and does not change when the interest rate changes; therefore the
   (a) supply of money curve is downward sloping
   (b) demand for money curve is downward sloping
   (c) supply of money curve is upward sloping
   (d) supply of money curve is vertical

19. If the legal ceiling on the interest rate was set below equilibrium, the
 (a) quantity of money demanded would be greater than the quantity of money supplied
 (b) quantity of money demanded would be less than the quantity of money supplied
 (c) supply of money would increase and the demand for money would decrease
 (d) demand for money would increase and the supply of money would decrease

20. Which one of the following points would be true?
 (a) Bond prices and the interest rate are directly related.
 (b) A lower interest rate raises the opportunity cost of holding money.
 (c) The supply of money is directly related to the interest rate.
 (d) The total demand for money is inversely related to the interest rate.

Answer Questions 21 and 22 on the basis of the following information: Bond price = $10,000; bond fixed annual interest payment = $1000; bond annual rate of interest = 10%.

21. If the price of this bond decreases by $2500, the interest rate in effect will
 (a) decrease by 1.1 percentage points
 (b) decrease by 1.9 percentage points
 (c) increase by 2.6 percentage points
 (d) increase by 3.3 percentage points

22. If the price of this bond increases by $2000, the interest rate in effect will
 (a) decrease by 1.7 percentage points
 (b) decrease by 2.4 percentage points
 (c) increase by 1.1 percentage points
 (d) increase by 2.9 percentage points

23. The Federal Open Market Committee (FOMC) of the Federal Reserve System is primarily responsible for
 (a) supervising the operation of banks to make sure they follow regulations and monitoring banks so they do not engage in fraud
 (b) handling the Fed's collection of checks and adjusting legal reserves among banks
 (c) setting the Fed's monetary policy and directing the buying and selling of government securities
 (d) acting as the fiscal agent for the Federal government and issuing currency

24. The most important function of the Federal Reserve System is
 (a) issuing currency
 (b) controlling the money supply
 (c) supervising commercial banks
 (d) lending money to banks and thrifts

25. According to the text, which would be a recent development in the banking industry?
 (a) an increase in the number of banks and thrifts
 (b) increased integration of world financial markets

 (c) increased use of coins and currency as a medium of exchange
 (d) an increase in the separation of services offered by financial institutions

■ **PROBLEMS**

1. From the figures in the following table it can be concluded that

Item	Billions of dollars
Small time deposits	$630
Large time deposits	645
Money market deposit accounts	575
Money market mutual funds	425
Checkable deposits	448
Noncheckable savings deposits	300
Currency	170

 a. $M1$ is equal to the sum of $_____ and $_____, so it totals $_____ billion.

 b. $M2$ is equal to $M1$ plus $_____ and $_____ and $_____ and $_____, so it totals $_____ billion.

 c. $M3$ is equal to $M2$ plus $_____, so it totals $_____ billion.

2. Complete the following table that shows the relationship between a percentage change in the price level and the percentage change in the value of money. Calculate the percentage change in the value of money to one decimal place.

Change in price level	Change in value of money
a. *rises* by:	
5%	–_____._____%
10%	–_____._____
15%	–_____._____
20%	–_____._____
25%	–_____._____
b. *falls* by:	
5%	+_____._____%
10%	+_____._____
15%	+_____._____

3. The total demand for money is equal to the transactions plus the asset demand for money.
 a. Assume each dollar held for transactions purposes is spent (on the average) four times per year to buy final goods and services.
 (1) This means that the transactions demand for money will be equal to (what fraction or percent) _____ of the nominal GDP, and, **(2)** if the nominal GDP is $2000 billion, the transactions demand will be $_____ billion.

b. The following table shows the number of dollars demanded for asset purposes at each rate of interest.

(1) Given the transactions demand for money in (a), complete the table.

Interest rate	Amount of money demanded (billions)	
	For asset purposes	Total
16%	$ 20	$_____
14	40	_____
12	60	_____
10	80	_____
8	100	_____
6	120	_____
4	140	_____

(2) On the following graph plot the total demand for money (D_m) at each rate of interest.

c. Assume the money supply (S_m) is $580 billion.

(1) Plot this money supply on the graph.

(2) Using either the graph or the table, the equilibrium rate of interest is _____ %.

d. Should the money supply

(1) increase to $600 billion, the equilibrium interest rate would (rise, fall) _____ to _____ %.

(2) decrease to $540 billion, the equilibrium interest rate would _____ to _____ %.

e. If the nominal GDP

(1) increased by $80 billion, the total demand for money would (increase, decrease) _____ by $_____ billion at each rate of interest and the equilibrium rate of interest would (rise, fall) _____ by _____ %.

(2) decreased by $120 billion, the total demand for money would _____ by $_____ billion at each rate of interest and the equilibrium interest rate would _____ by _____ %.

4. Suppose a bond with no expiration date pays a fixed $500 annually and sells for its face value of $5000.

a. Complete the following table and calculate the interest rate (to one decimal place) that would be obtained from the bond when the bond price is given or calculate the bond price when the interest rate is given.

Bond price	Interest rate
$4000	_____._____%
$_____	11.0
$5000	_____._____
$5500	_____._____
$_____	8.0

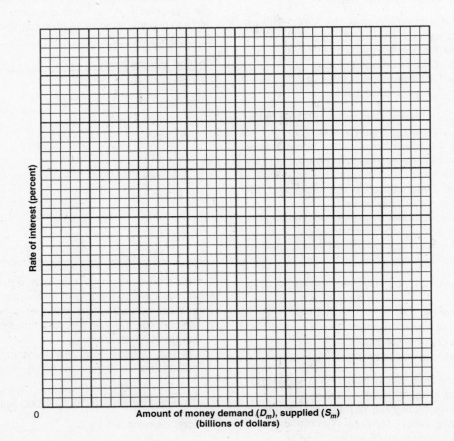

Rate of interest (percent)

Amount of money demand (D_m), supplied (S_m)
(billions of dollars)

b. Based on the results of the table, as the price increases on a bond with a fixed annual payment, the interest yield on the bond (decreases, increases)

_____, but when the price of a bond decreases, the interest yield _____. Given this situation in an economy, you can conclude that a higher price for bonds (increases, decreases)

_____ interest rates and that a lower price for bonds _____ interest rates.

■ SHORT ANSWER AND ESSAY QUESTIONS

1. How would you define money based on its three functions?

2. What are the two components of the *M*1 supply of money in the United States?

3. What are checkable deposits? What are the different types of institutions offering checkable deposits?

4. Are the checkable deposits of government, the Fed, commercial banks, and other financial institutions included in *M*1? Explain.

5. Define *M*2 and *M*3. Explain how they are related.

6. For what reasons are checkable deposits included in the money supply?

7. What backs the money used in the United States? What determines the value of money?

8. Explain the relationship between the value of money and the price level.

9. What must government do if it is to stabilize the value of money?

10. What are the two reasons people wish to hold money? How are these two reasons related to the functions of money?

11. Explain the determinant of each of the two demands for money and how a change in the size of these determinants will affect the amount of money people wish to hold.

12. The rate of interest is a price. Of what good or service is it the price? Explain how demand and supply determine this price.

13. Describe how changes in bond prices correct disequilibrium in the money market. What is the relationship between bond prices and interest rates?

14. Outline the structure of the Federal Reserve System and explain the chief functions of each of the four parts of the system.

15. As briefly as possible, outline the three characteristics of the Federal Reserve Banks and explain the meaning of these characteristics.

16. What are the chief functions the Federal Reserve Banks perform? Explain briefly the meaning of each function. Which of the chief functions is the most important?

17. What are the basic reasons for the independence of the Federal Reserve System?

18. Describe the decline of and consolidation among banks and thrifts in recent years.

19. Discuss the meaning and effects of increased integration of world financial markets.

20. Explain how electronic transactions change the way money is stored and transferred. How do these changes affect banks, thrifts, and the Federal Reserve?

ANSWERS

Chapter 13 Money and Banking

FILL-IN QUESTIONS

1. a medium of exchange, a unit of account, a store of value
2. token, less
3. currency, checkable deposits, currency (either order for the last two)
4. *M*1, noncheckable, small, deposit accounts, mutual funds (either order for the last two)
5. large, $100,000 or greater
6. are not, loan
7. the Federal Reserve Banks, banks and thrifts, are not
8. acceptable, legal, scarce
9. inversely, divide
10. decrease, decrease
11. directly, nominal GDP, inversely, the rate of interest
12. demand, supply, interest rate
13. decrease, increase, increase, decrease
14. Governors, Federal Open Market Committee, 12
15. quasi-public, bankers', central
16. commercial banks, thrifts
17. *a.* issuing currency; *b.* setting reserve requirements and holding reserves; *c.* lending money to banks and thrifts; *d.* collecting and processing checks; *e.* serving as fiscal agent for the Federal government; *f.* bank supervision; *g.* controlling the money supply; controlling the money supply
18. independent, inflation
19. decreased, mergers
20. globalization, electronic

TRUE–FALSE QUESTIONS

1. T, pp. 232–233	10. F, p. 235	19. F, p. 243
2. F, pp. 233–234	11. T, pp. 234–235	20. F, pp. 243–244
3. T, pp. 233–234	12. T, p. 236	21. T, p. 244
4. F, p. 234	13. T, p. 237	22. F, p. 244
5. T, p. 234	14. F, pp. 238–239	23. T, p. 245
6. F, p. 234	15. T, pp. 238–239	24. F, p. 245
7. T, pp. 234–235	16. T, p. 240	25. F, p. 247
8. T, p. 235	17. T, pp. 240–241	
9. F, p. 235	18. T, pp. 242–243	

MULTIPLE-CHOICE QUESTIONS

1. d, pp. 232–233
2. d, pp. 233–234
3. d, pp. 233–234
4. d, p. 234
5. d, p. 236
6. b, pp. 233–234
7. c, pp. 234–235
8. b, p. 235
9. b, p. 236

10. b, p. 237
11. b, p. 237
12. b, pp. 238–239
13. a, pp. 239–240
14. a, pp. 239–240
15. b, pp. 239–240
16. c, pp. 239–240
17. b, p. 240
18. d, p. 240

19. a, pp. 240–241
20. d, pp. 240–241
21. d, p. 241
22. a, p. 241
23. c, p. 243
24. b, pp. 244–245
25. b, p. 247

PROBLEMS

1. *a.* 170, 448 (either order), 618; *b.* 300, 630, 575, 425 (any order), 2548; *c.* 645, 3193

2. *a.* 4.8, 9.1, 13, 16.7, 20; *b.* 5.3, 11.1, 17.6

3. *a.* (1) 1/4 (25%), (2) 500; *b.* (1) 520, 540, 560, 580, 600, 620, 640; *c.* (2) 10; *d.* (1) fall, 8, (2) rise, 14; *e.* (1) increase, 20, rise, 2, (2) decrease, 30, fall, 3

4. *a.* 12.5%, $4545, 10.0%, 9.1%, $6250; *b.* decreases, increases, decreases, increases

SHORT ANSWER AND ESSAY QUESTIONS

1. pp. 232–233
2. pp. 233–234
3. p. 234
4. p. 234
5. pp. 234–235
6. p. 235
7. pp. 236–237

8. p. 237
9. p. 237
10. pp. 238–240
11. pp. 238–240
12. pp. 240–241
13. pp. 240–241
14. pp. 242–244

15. pp. 243–244
16. pp. 244–245
17. p. 245
18. pp. 245–246
19. p. 247
20. p. 247

CHAPTER 14

How Banks and Thrifts Create Money

Chapter 13 explained the institutional structure of banking in the United States today, the functions which banks and the other depository institutions and money perform, and the composition of the money supply. Chapter 14 explains how banks create money—*checkable deposits*—and the factors that determine and limit the money-creating ability of commercial banks. The other depository institutions, such as thrift institutions, also create checkable deposits, but this chapter focuses on the commercial banks to simplify the discussion.

The convenient and simple device used to explain commercial banking operations and money creation is the *balance sheet.* Shown within it are the *assets, liabilities,* and *net worth* of commercial banks. All banking transactions affect this balance sheet. The first step to understanding how money is created is to understand how various simple and typical transactions affect the commercial bank balance sheet.

In reading this chapter you must analyze for yourself the effect of each and every banking transaction discussed on the balance sheet. The important items in the balance sheet are checkable deposits and reserves because *checkable deposits are money.* The ability of a bank to create new checkable deposits is determined by the amount of reserves the bank has. Expansion of the money supply depends on the possession by commercial banks of excess reserves. They do not appear explicitly in the balance sheet but do appear there implicitly because *excess reserves* are the difference between the *actual reserves* and the *required reserves* of commercial banks.

Two cases—the single commercial bank and the banking system—are presented to help you build an understanding of banking and money creation. It is important to understand that the money-creating potential of a single commercial bank differs from the money-creating potential of the entire banking system. It is equally important to understand how the money-creating ability of many single commercial banks is *multiplied* and influences the *money-creating ability* of the banking system as a whole.

Certain assumptions are used throughout most of this chapter to analyze money creation; in certain instances these assumptions may not be completely realistic and may need to be modified. The chapter concludes with a discussion of how the earlier analysis must be modified—but not changed in its essentials—to take into account slightly unrealistic assumptions.

You will also learn that the money-creating actions of banks have a procyclical effect on the economy which needs to be controlled by the Federal Reserve System—a topic discussed in more detail in the next chapter.

■ CHECKLIST

When you have studied this chapter you should be able to

☐ Define the basic items in a bank's balance sheet.
☐ Recount the story of how goldsmiths came to issue paper money and became bankers who created money and held fractional reserves.
☐ Cite two significant characteristics of the fractional reserve banking system today.
☐ Explain the effects of the deposit of currency in a checking account on the composition and size of the money supply.
☐ Define the reserve ratio.
☐ Compute a bank's required and excess reserves when you are given the needed balance-sheet figures.
☐ Explain why a commercial bank is required to maintain a reserve and why a required reserve is not sufficient to protect the depositors from losses.
☐ Indicate how the deposit of a check drawn on one commercial bank and deposited into another will affect the reserves and excess reserves of the two banks.
☐ Show what happens to the money supply when a commercial bank makes a loan (or buys government securities).
☐ Explain what happens to a commercial bank's reserves and checkable deposits after it has made a loan, a check has been written on the newly created checkable deposit and deposited in another commercial bank and cleared, and explain what happens to the reserves and checkable deposits of the commercial bank in which the check was deposited.
☐ Describe what would happen to a commercial bank's reserves if it made loans (or bought government securities) in an amount greater than its excess reserves.
☐ Show what happens to the money supply when a loan is repaid (or a bank sells government securities).
☐ State the money-creating potential of a commercial bank (the amount of money a commercial bank can safely create by lending or buying securities).
☐ Explain how the Federal funds market helps reconcile the goals of profits and liquidity for commercial banks.

☐ State the money-creating potential of the banking system.

☐ Explain how it is possible for the banking system to create an amount of money that is a multiple of its excess reserves when no individual commercial bank ever creates money in an amount greater than its excess reserve.

☐ Compute the size of the monetary multiplier and the money-creating potential of the banking system when you are provided with the necessary data.

☐ Illustrate with an example using the monetary multiplier how money can be destroyed in the banking system.

☐ List the two leakages which reduce the money-creating potential of the banking system.

☐ Explain why there is a need for control of the money supply by the Federal Reserve System.

■ **CHAPTER OUTLINE**

1. The **balance sheet** of the commercial bank is a statement of the **assets, liabilities,** and **net worth** (capital stock) of the bank at a specific time; and in the balance sheet, the bank's assets equal its liabilities plus its net worth.

2. The history of the early goldsmiths illustrates how paper money came into use in the economy. This history also shows how goldsmiths became bankers when they began making loans and issuing money in excess of their gold holdings. The goldsmiths' fractional reserve system is similar to today's fractional banking system, which has two significant characteristics:

 a. Banks can create money in such a system.

 b. Banks are subject to "panics" or "runs" in a **fractional reserve system** and thus need government regulation.

3. By examining the ways the balance sheet of the commercial bank is affected by various transactions, it is possible to understand how a **single commercial bank** in a multibank system can create money.

 a. Once a commercial bank has been founded,

 (1) by selling shares of stock and obtaining cash in return;

 (2) and acquiring the property and equipment needed to carry on the banking business;

 (3) the deposit of cash in the bank does not affect the total money supply; it only changes its composition by substituting checkable deposits for currency in circulation;

 (4) three reserve concepts are vital to an understanding of the money-creating potential of a commercial bank.

 (a) The **required reserves,** which a bank *must* maintain at its Federal Reserve Bank (or as **vault cash**—which can be ignored), equal the reserve ratio multiplied by the checkable deposit liabilities of the commercial bank. (The **reserve ratio** is the ratio of required reserves to a bank's own checkable deposit liabilities.)

 (b) The **actual reserves** of a commercial bank are its deposits at the Federal Reserve Bank (plus the vault cash, which is ignored).

 (c) The **excess reserves** are equal to the actual reserves less the required reserve.

 (5) The writing of a check on the bank and its deposit in a second bank results in a loss of reserves and deposits for the first bank and a gain in reserves and deposits for the second bank.

 b. When a single commercial bank lends or buys government securities, it increases its own deposit liabilities and therefore the supply of money by the amount of the loan or security purchase. But the bank only lends or buys securities in an amount equal to its excess reserves because it fears the loss of reserves to other commercial banks in the economy.

 c. When a single commercial bank receives loan repayments or sells government securities, its deposit liabilities and therefore the supply of money are described by the amount of the loan repayments or securities sale.

 d. An individual commercial bank balances its desire for profits (which result from the making of loans and the purchase of securities) with its desire for liquidity or safety (which it achieves by having excess reserves or vault cash).

 e. The Federal funds market allows banks with excess reserves to lend funds overnight to banks that are short of reserves. The interest rate paid on the overnight loans is the **Federal funds rate.**

4. The ability of a **banking system** composed of many individual commercial banks to lend and to create money is a multiple (greater than 1) of its excess reserves and is equal to the excess reserves of the banking system multiplied by the checkable-deposit (or monetary) multiplier.

 a. The banking system as a whole can do this even though no single commercial bank ever lends an amount greater than its excess reserves because the banking system, unlike a single commercial bank, does not lose reserves.

 b. The **monetary multiplier** is equal to the reciprocal of the required reserve ratio for checkable deposits, and the maximum expansion of checkable deposits is equal to the excess reserves in the banking system times the monetary multiplier.

 c. The potential lending ability of the banking system may not be fully achieved if there are leakages because borrowers choose to hold additional currency or bankers choose to hold excess reserves.

 d. If bankers lend as much as they are able during periods of prosperity and less than they are able during recessions, they add to the instability of the economy. To reduce this instability, the Federal Reserve Banks must control the size of the money supply.

■ **HINTS AND TIPS**

1. Note that several terms are used interchangeably in this chapter: "commercial bank" (or "bank") is sometimes called "thrift institution" or "depository institution."

2. A bank's balance sheet must balance. The bank's assets are either claimed by owners (net worth) or by nonowners (liabilities). **Assets = liabilities + net worth.**

3. Make a running balance sheet in writing for yourself as you read about each of the eight transactions in the text for the Wahoo Bank. Then determine if you understand the material by telling yourself (or a friend) the story for each transaction without using the text.

4. The *maximum amount of checkable-deposit expansion* is determined by multiplying two factors: the excess reserves by the monetary multiplier. Each factor, however, is affected by the required reserve ratio. The monetary multiplier is calculated by dividing 1 by the required reserve ratio. Excess reserves are determined by multiplying the required reserve ratio by the amount of new deposits. Thus, a change in the required reserve ratio will change the monetary multiplier and the amount of excess reserves. For example, a required reserve ratio of 25% gives a monetary multiplier of 4. For $100 in new money deposited, required reserves are $25 and excess reserves are $75. The maximum checkable-deposit expansion is $300 (4 × $75). If the reserve ratio drops to 20%, the monetary multiplier is 5 and excess reserves are $80, so the maximum checkable-deposit expansion is $400. Both factors have changed.

5. Be aware that the monetary multiplier can result in *money destruction* as well as money creation in the banking system. You should know how the monetary multiplier reinforces effects in one direction or the other.

■ IMPORTANT TERMS

balance sheet	excess reserves
fractional reserve banking system	actual reserves
vault cash	Federal funds rate
required reserves	monetary multiplier
reserve ratio	

SELF-TEST

■ FILL-IN QUESTIONS

1. In this chapter, a commercial bank may also be called a (checkable, thrift) _____ institution and a deposit at a bank may also be called a _____ deposit.

2. The balance sheet of a commercial bank is a statement of the bank's (gold account, assets) _____, the claims of the owners of the bank [called (net worth, liabilities) _____], and claims of the nonowners (called _____). This relationship would be written in equation form as:

_____.

3. The banking system used today is a (total, fractional) _____ reserve system, which means that (100%, less than 100%) _____ of the money deposited in a bank is kept on reserve.

4. There are two significant characteristics to the banking system of today.

   a. Banks can create (reserves, money) _____ depending on the amount of _____ they hold.

   b. Banks are susceptible to (panics, regulation) _____ or "runs," and to prevent this situation from happening, banks are subject to government _____.

5. The coins and paper money that a bank has in its possession are (petty, vault) _____ cash or (till, capital) _____ money.

6. When a person deposits cash in a commercial bank and receives a checkable deposit in return, the size of the money supply has (increased, decreased, not changed) _____.

7. The legal reserve of a commercial bank (ignoring vault cash) must be kept on deposit at (a branch of the U.S. Treasury, its district Federal Reserve Bank) _____ _____.

8. The reserve ratio is equal to the commercial bank's (required, gold) _____ reserves divided by its checkable deposits (assets, liabilities) _____.

9. The authority to establish and vary the reserve ratio within limits legislated by Congress is given to the (U.S. Treasury, Fed) _____.

10. If commercial banks are allowed to accept (or create) deposits in excess of their reserves, the banking system is operating under a system of (fractional, currency) _____ reserves.

11. The excess reserves of a commercial bank equal its (actual, required) _____ reserves minus its _____ reserves.

12. The basic purpose for having member banks deposit a legal reserve in the Federal Reserve Bank in their district is to provide (liquidity for, control of) _____ the banking system by the Fed.

13. When a commercial bank deposits a legal reserve in its district Federal Reserve Bank, the reserve is (a liability, an asset) _____ to the commercial bank and _____ to the Federal Reserve Bank.

14. When a check is drawn on Bank X, deposited in Bank Y, and cleared, the reserves of Bank X are (increased, decreased, not changed) _____ and the reserves of Bank Y are _____; deposits in Bank X are (increased, decreased, not changed) _____ and deposits in Bank Y are _____.

15. A single commercial bank in a multibank system can safely make loans or buy government securities equal in amount to the (required, excess) _____ reserves of that commercial bank.

16. When a commercial bank makes a new loan of $10,000, the supply of money (increases, decreases) _____ by $_____, but when a loan is repaid, the supply of money (increases, decreases) _____ by $_____.

17. When a commercial bank sells a $10,000 government bond to a securities dealer, the supply of money (increases, decreases) _____ by $_____, but when a commercial bank buys a $10,000 government bond from a securities dealer, the supply of money (increases, decreases) _____ by $_____.

18. A bank ordinarily pursues two conflicting goals; one goal is the desire to make money, or (profits, liquidity) _____, and the other goal is the need for safety, or _____.

19. When a bank lends temporary excess reserves held at its Federal Reserve Bank to other commercial banks that are temporarily short of legal reserves, it is participating in the (government securities, Federal funds) _____ market. The interest rate paid on these overnight loans is called the (government securities, Federal funds) _____ rate.

20. The monetary multiplier is equal to 1 divided by the (excess, required) _____ reserve ratio.

21. The greater the reserve ratio, the (larger, smaller) _____ the monetary multiplier.

22. The banking system can make loans (or buy government securities) and create money in an amount equal to its (required, excess) _____ reserves multiplied by the (required reserve ratio, monetary multiplier) _____.

23. Assume that the required reserve ratio is 16.67% and the banking system is $6 million short of required reserves. If the banking system is unable to increase its reserves, the banking system must (increase, decrease) _____ the money supply by ($6, $36) _____ million.

24. The money-creating potential of the commercial banking system is lessened by the (addition, withdrawal) _____ of currency from banks and by banks not lending (required, excess) _____ reserves.

25. Commercial banks in the past have kept excess reserves during periods of (prosperity, recession) _____ and have kept few or no excess reserves during periods of _____. By acting this way, they have made the economy (more, less) _____ stable, which has given rise to the need for monetary control by the Federal Reserve System.

■ **TRUE–FALSE QUESTIONS**

Circle T if the statement is true, F if it is false.

1. The balance sheet of a commercial bank shows the transactions in which the bank has engaged during a given period of time. **T F**

2. A commercial bank's assets plus its net worth equal the bank's liabilities. **T F**

3. Goldsmiths increased the money supply when they accepted deposits of gold and issued paper receipts to the depositors. **T F**

4. Modern banking systems use gold as the basis for the fractional reserve system. **T F**

5. Cash held by a bank is sometimes called vault cash. **T F**

6. A commercial bank may maintain its legal reserve either as a deposit in its Federal Reserve Bank or as government bonds in its own vault. **T F**

7. The legal reserve that a commercial bank maintains must equal its own deposit liabilities multiplied by the required reserve ratio. **T F**

8. Legal reserves permit the Board of Governors of the Federal Reserve System to influence the lending ability of commercial banks. **T F**

9. The actual reserves of a commercial bank equal excess reserves plus required reserves. **T F**

10. The reserve of a commercial bank in the Federal Reserve Bank is an asset of the Federal Reserve Bank. **T F**

11. A check for $1000 drawn on Bank X by a depositor and deposited in Bank Y will increase the excess reserves in Bank Y by $1000. **T F**

12. Mary Lynn, a music star, deposits a $30,000 check in a commercial bank and receives a checkable deposit in return; 1 hour later the Manfred Iron and Coal Company borrows $30,000 from the same bank. The money supply has increased $30,000 as a result of the two transactions. **T F**

13. A single commercial bank can safely lend an amount equal to its excess reserves multiplied by the monetary multiplier ratio. **T F**

14. When a borrower repays a loan of $500, either in cash or by check, the supply of money is reduced by $500. **T F**

15. The granting of a $5000 loan and the purchase of a $5000 government bond from a securities dealer by a commercial bank have the same effect on the money supply. **T F**

16. The selling of a government bond by a commercial bank will increase the money supply. **T F**

17. A commercial bank seeks both profits and liquidity, but these are conflicting goals. **T F**

18. The Federal funds rate is the interest rate at which the Federal government lends funds to commercial banks. **T F**

19. The reason that the banking system can lend by a multiple of its excess reserves, but each individual bank can only lend "dollar for dollar" with its excess reserves, is that reserves lost by a single bank are not lost to the banking system as a whole. **T F**

20. The monetary multiplier is excess reserves divided by required reserves. **T F**

21. The maximum checkable-deposit expansion is equal to excess reserves divided by the monetary multiplier. **T F**

22. If the banking system has $10 million in excess reserves and if the reserve ratio is 25%, the system can increase its loans by $40 million. **T F**

23. When borrowers from a commercial bank wish to have cash rather than checkable deposits, the money-creating potential of the banking system is increased. **T F**

24. A desire by banks to hold excess reserves may reduce the size of the monetary multiplier. **T F**

25. There is a need for the Federal Reserve System to control the money supply because profit-seeking banks tend to make changes in the money supply that are pro-cyclical. **T F**

■ **MULTIPLE-CHOICE QUESTIONS**

Circle the letter that corresponds to the best answer.

1. The claims of the owners of the bank against the bank's assets is the bank's
  (a) net worth
  (b) liabilities
  (c) balance sheet
  (d) fractional reserves

2. The fractional reserve system of banking started when goldsmiths began
  (a) accepting deposits of gold for safe storage
  (b) issuing receipts for the gold stored with them
  (c) using deposited gold to produce products for sale to others
  (d) issuing paper money in excess of the amount of gold stored with them

3. When cash is deposited in a demand-deposit account in a commercial bank, there is
  (a) a decrease in the money supply
  (b) an increase in the money supply
  (c) no change in the composition of the money supply
  (d) a change in the composition of the money supply

4. A commercial bank has actual reserves of $9000 and liabilities of $30,000, and the required reserve ratio is 20%. The excess reserves of the bank are
  (a) $3000
  (b) $6000
  (c) $7500
  (d) $9000

5. The primary reason commercial banks must keep required reserves on deposit at Federal Reserve Banks is to
  (a) protect the deposits in the commercial bank against losses
  (b) provide the means by which checks drawn on the commercial bank and deposited in other commercial banks can be collected
  (c) add to the liquidity of the commercial bank and protect it against a "run" on the bank
  (d) provide the Fed with a means of controlling the lending ability of the commercial bank

6. A depositor places $750 in cash in a commercial bank, and the reserve ratio is 33.3%; the bank sends the $750 to the Federal Reserve Bank. As a result, the *reserves* and the *excess reserves* of the bank have been increased, respectively, by
  (a) $750 and $250
  (b) $750 and $500
  (c) $750 and $750
  (d) $500 and $500

7. A commercial bank has no excess reserves until a depositor places $600 in cash in the bank. The bank then adds the $600 to its reserves by sending it to the Federal Reserve Bank. The commercial bank then lends $300 to a borrower. As a consequence of these transactions the size of the money supply has
  (a) not been affected
  (b) increased by $300
  (c) increased by $600
  (d) increased by $900

8. A commercial bank has excess reserves of $500 and a required reserve ratio of 20%; it grants a loan of $1000 to a borrower. If the borrower writes a check for $1000 that is deposited in another commercial bank, the first bank will be short of reserves, after the check has been cleared, in the amount of
  (a) $200
  (b) $500
  (c) $700
  (d) $1000

9. The selling of government bonds by commercial banks is most similar to the
(a) making of loans by banks because both actions increase the money supply
(b) making of loans by banks because both actions decrease the money supply
(c) repayment of loans to banks because both actions decrease the money supply
(d) repayment of loans to banks because both actions increase the money supply

10. A commercial bank sells a $1000 government security to a securities dealer. The dealer pays for the bond in cash, which the bank adds to its vault cash. The money supply has
(a) not been affected
(b) decreased by $1000
(c) increased by $1000
(d) increased by $1000 multiplied by the reciprocal of the required reserve ratio

11. A commercial bank has deposit liabilities of $100,000, reserves of $37,000, and a required reserve ratio of 25%. The amount by which a *single commercial bank* and the amount by which the *banking system* can increase loans are, respectively,
(a) $12,000 and $48,000
(b) $17,000 and $68,000
(c) $12,000 and $60,000
(d) $17,000 and $85,000

12. If the required reserve ratio were 12.5%, the value of the monetary multiplier would be
(a) 5
(b) 6
(c) 7
(d) 8

13. The commercial banking system has excess reserves of $700, makes new loans of $2100, and is just meeting its reserve requirements. The required reserve ratio is
(a) 20%
(b) 25%
(c) 30%
(d) 33.33%

14. The commercial banking system, because of a recent change in the required reserve ratio from 20% to 30%, finds that it is $60 million short of reserves. If it is unable to obtain any additional reserves it must decrease the money supply by
(a) $60 million
(b) $180 million
(c) $200 million
(d) $300 million

15. Only one commercial bank in the banking system has an excess reserve, and its excess reserve is $100,000. This bank makes a new loan of $80,000 and keeps an excess reserve of $20,000. If the required reserve ratio for all banks is 20%, the potential expansion of the money supply is
(a) $80,000
(b) $100,000

(c) $400,000
(d) $500,000

16. The money-creating potential of the banking system is reduced when
(a) bankers choose to hold excess reserves
(b) borrowers choose to hold none of the funds they have borrowed in currency
(c) the Federal Reserve lowers the required reserve ratio
(d) bankers borrow from the Federal Reserve

Use the following balance sheet for the First National Bank to answer Questions 17, 18, 19, 20, and 21. Assume the required reserve ratio is 20%.

Assets		Liabilities and Net Worth	
Reserves	$ 50,000	Checkable deposits	$150,000
Loans	70,000	Capital stock	100,000
Securities	30,000		
Property	100,000		

17. This commercial bank has excess reserves of
(a) $10,000
(b) $20,000
(c) $30,000
(d) $40,000

18. This bank can safely expand its loans by a maximum of
(a) $50,000
(b) $40,000
(c) $30,000
(d) $20,000

19. Using the original bank balance sheet, assume that the bank makes a loan of $10,000 and has a check cleared against it for the amount of the loan; its reserves and checkable deposits will now be
(a) $40,000 and $140,000
(b) $40,000 and $150,000
(c) $30,000 and $150,000
(d) $60,000 and $140,000

20. Using the original bank balance sheet, assume that the bank makes a loan of $15,000 and has a check cleared against it for the amount of the loan; it will then have excess reserves of
(a) $5000
(b) $10,000
(c) $15,000
(d) $20,000

21. If the original bank balance sheet was for the commercial banking *system,* rather than a single bank, loans and deposits could have been expanded by a maximum of
(a) $50,000
(b) $100,000
(c) $150,000
(d) $200,000

Answer Questions 22 and 23 on the basis of the following consolidated balance sheet for the commercial banking system. All figures are in billions. Assume that the required reserve ratio is 12.5%.

Assets		Liabilities and Net Worth	
Reserves	$ 40	Checkable deposits	$200
Loans	80	Capital stock	120
Securities	100		
Property	200		

22. If there is a deposit of $20 billion of new currency into checking accounts in the banking system, excess reserves will increase by
- **(a)** $16.5 billion
- **(b)** $17.0 billion
- **(c)** $17.5 billion
- **(d)** $18.5 billion

23. The maximum amount by which this commercial banking system can expand the supply of money by lending is
- **(a)** $120 billion
- **(b)** $240 billion
- **(c)** $350 billion
- **(d)** $440 billion

24. The excess reserves held by banks tend to
- **(a)** rise during periods of prosperity
- **(b)** fall during periods of recession
- **(c)** rise during periods of recession
- **(d)** fall when interest rates in the economy fall

25. Unless controlled, the money supply will
- **(a)** fall during periods of prosperity
- **(b)** rise during periods of recession
- **(c)** change in a procyclical fashion
- **(d)** change in an anticyclical fashion

■ **PROBLEMS**

1. The following table shows the simplified balance sheet of a commercial bank. Assume that the figures given show the bank's assets and checkable-deposit liabilities *prior to each of the following four transactions*. Draw up the balance sheet as it would appear after each of these transactions is completed and place the balance-sheet figures in the appropriate column. Do *not* use the figures you place in columns **a, b,** and **c** when you work the next part of the problem; start all parts of the problem with the printed figures.

		(a)	(b)	(c)	(d)
Assets:					
Cash	$100	$____	$____	$____	$____
Reserves	200	____	____	____	____
Loans	500	____	____	____	____
Securities	200	____	____	____	____
Liabilities and net worth:					
Checkable deposits	900	____	____	____	____
Capital stock	100	100	100	100	100

a. A check for $50 is drawn by one of the depositors of the bank, given to a person who deposits it in another bank, and cleared (column a).

b. A depositor withdraws $50 in cash from the bank, and the bank restores its vault cash by obtaining $50 in additional cash from its Federal Reserve Bank (column b).

c. A check for $60 drawn on another bank is deposited in this bank and cleared (column c).

d. The bank sells $100 in government bonds to the Federal Reserve Bank in its district (column d).

2. Following are five balance sheets for a single commercial bank (columns 1a–5a). The required reserve ratio is 20%.

a. Compute the required reserves (A), ignoring vault cash, the excess reserves (B) of the bank (if the bank is short of reserves and must reduce its loans or obtain additional reserves, show this by placing a minus sign in front of the amounts by which it is short of reserves), and the amount of new loans it can extend (C).

	(1a)	(2a)	(3a)	(4a)	(5a)
Assets:					
Cash	$ 10	$ 20	$ 20	$ 20	$ 15
Reserves	40	40	25	40	45
Loans	100	100	100	100	150
Securities	50	60	30	70	60
Liabilities and net worth:					
Checkable deposits	175	200	150	180	220
Capital stock	25	20	25	50	50
A. Required reserve	$____	$____	$____	$____	$____
B. Excess reserve	____	____	____	____	____
C. New loans	____	____	____	____	____

b. In the following table, draw up for the individual bank the five balance sheets as they appear after the bank has made the new *loans* that it is capable of making.

	(1b)	(2b)	(3b)	(4b)	(5b)
Assets:					
Cash	$____	$____	$____	$____	$____
Reserves	____	____	____	____	____
Loans	____	____	____	____	____
Securities	____	____	____	____	____
Liabilities and net worth:					
Checkable deposits	____	____	____	____	____
Capital stock	____	____	____	____	____

3. The following table shows several reserve ratios. Compute the monetary multiplier for each reserve ratio and enter the figures in column 2. In column 3 show the maximum amount by which a single commercial bank can increase its loans for each dollar's worth of excess reserves it possesses. In column 4 indicate the maximum amount by which the banking system can increase its loans for each dollar's worth of excess reserves in the system.

(1)	(2)	(3)	(4)
12.5%	$____	$____	$____
16.67	____	____	____
20	____	____	____
25	____	____	____
30	____	____	____
33.33	____	____	____

4. The table at the bottom of the page is the simplified consolidated balance sheet for all commercial banks in the economy. Assume that the figures given show the banks' assets and liabilities *prior to each of the following three transactions* and that the reserve ratio is 20%. Do *not* use the figures you placed in columns 2 and 4 when you begin parts **b** and **c** of the problem; start parts **a, b,** and **c** of the problem with the printed figures.

    a. The public deposits $5 in cash in the banks and the banks send the $5 to the Federal Reserve, where it is added to their reserves. Fill in column 1. If the banking system extends the maximum amount of new loans that it is capable of extending, show in column 2 the balance sheet as it would then appear.

    b. The banking system sells $8 worth of securities to the Federal Reserve. Complete column 3. Assuming the system extends the maximum amount of credit of which it is capable, fill in column 4.

    c. The Federal Reserve lends $10 to the commercial banks; complete column 5. Complete column 6 showing the condition of the banks after the maximum amount of new loans that the banks are capable of making is granted.

■ SHORT ANSWER AND ESSAY QUESTIONS

1. Why does a bank's balance sheet balance?

2. How did the early goldsmiths come to issue paper money and then become bankers?

3. Explain the difference between a 100% and fractional reserve system of banking.

4. What are two significant characteristics of a fractional reserve system of banking?

5. Explain what happens to the money supply when a bank accepts deposits of cash.

6. What are legal reserves? How are they determined? How are legal reserves related to the reserve ratio?

7. Define the meaning of excess reserves. How are they calculated?

8. Explain why bank reserves can be an asset to the depositing commercial bank but a liability to the Federal Reserve Bank receiving them.

9. Do the reserves held by commercial banks satisfactorily protect the bank's depositors? Are the reserves of commercial banks needed? Explain your answers.

10. The owner of a sporting goods store writes a check on his account in a Kent, Ohio, bank and sends it to one of his suppliers who deposits it in his bank in Cleveland, Ohio. How does the Cleveland bank obtain payment from the Kent bank? If the two banks were in Kent and New York City, how would one bank pay the other? How are the excess reserves of the two banks affected?

11. Explain why the granting of a loan by a commercial bank increases the supply of money. Why does the repayment of a loan decrease the supply of money?

12. Why is a single commercial bank able to lend safely only an amount equal to its excess reserves?

13. How does the buying or selling of government securities by commercial banks influence the money supply?

14. Commercial banks seek both profits and safety. Explain how the balance sheet of the commercial banks reflects the desires of bankers for profits and for liquidity.

15. What is the Federal funds rate?

	(1)	(2)	(3)	(4)	(5)	(6)
Assets:						
Cash	$ 50	$____	$____	$____	$____	$____	$____
Reserves	100	____	____	____	____	____	____
Loans	200	____	____	____	____	____	____
Securities	200	____	____	____	____	____	____
Liabilities and net worth:						
Checkable deposits	500	____	____	____	____	____	____
Capital stock	50	50	50	50	50	50	50
Loans for Federal Reserve	0	____	____	____	____	____	____
Excess reserves		____	____	____	____	____	____
Maximum possible expansion of the money supply		____	____	____	____	____	____

16. Discuss how the Federal funds market helps banks reconcile the two goals of profits and liquidity.

17. No one commercial bank ever lends an amount greater than its excess reserves, but the banking system as a whole is able to extend loans and expand the money supply by an amount equal to the system's excess reserves multiplied by the reciprocal of the reserve ratio. Explain why this is possible and how the multiple expansion of deposits and money takes place.

18. What is the monetary multiplier? How does it work?

19. On the basis of a given amount of excess reserves and a given reserve ratio, a certain expansion of the money supply may be possible. What are two reasons why the potential expansion of the money supply may not be fully achieved?

20. Why is there a need for monetary control in the U.S. economy?

ANSWERS

Chapter 14 How Banks and Thrifts Create Money

FILL-IN QUESTIONS

1. thrift, checkable
2. assets, net worth, liabilities, assets = liabilities + net worth
3. fractional, less than 100%
4. *a.* money, reserves; *b.* panics, regulation
5. vault, till
6. not changed
7. its district Federal Reserve Bank
8. required, liabilities
9. Fed
10. fractional
11. actual, required
12. control of
13. an asset, a liability
14. decreased, increased, decreased, increased
15. excess
16. increases, 10,000, decreases, 10,000
17. decreases, 10,000, increases, 10,000
18. profits, liquidity
19. Federal funds, Federal funds
20. required
21. smaller
22. excess, monetary multiplier
23. decrease, $36
24. withdrawal, excess
25. recession, prosperity, less

TRUE–FALSE QUESTIONS

1. F, p. 252	**4.** F, pp. 252–253	**7.** T, pp. 254–255
2. F, p. 252	**5.** T, p. 253	**8.** T, pp. 255–256
3. F, pp. 252–253	**6.** F, pp. 254–255	**9.** T, pp. 254–255

10. F, pp. 256–257	**16.** F, p. 260	**22.** T, p. 263
11. F, pp. 256–257	**17.** T, p. 260	**23.** F, p. 264
12. T, pp. 258–259	**18.** F, p. 260	**24.** T, p. 264
13. F, pp. 258–259	**19.** T, pp. 260–262	**25.** T, p. 264
14. T, p. 259	**20.** F, pp. 262–263	
15. T, pp. 258–260	**21.** F, p. 263	

MULTIPLE-CHOICE QUESTIONS

1. a, p. 252	**10.** b, p. 260	**19.** b, pp. 258–259
2. d, pp. 252–253	**11.** a, pp. 260–262	**20.** a, pp. 258–259
3. d, p. 254	**12.** d, pp. 262–263	**21.** b, pp. 262–263
4. a, p. 255	**13.** d, pp. 262–263	**22.** c, p. 255
5. d, pp. 255–256	**14.** c, pp. 262–263	**23.** a, pp. 262–263
6. b, pp. 256–257	**15.** c, pp. 262–263	**24.** c, p. 264
7. b, pp. 258–259	**16.** a, pp. 262–263	**25.** c, p. 264
8. b, pp. 258–259	**17.** b, p. 255	
9. c, pp. 259–260	**18.** d, pp. 258–259	

PROBLEMS

1. Table

	(a)	(b)	(c)	(d)
Assets:				
Cash	$100	$100	$100	$100
Reserves	150	150	260	300
Loans	500	500	500	500
Securities	200	200	200	100
Liabilities and net worth:				
Checkable deposits	850	850	960	900
Capital stock	100	100	100	100

2. *a.* Table

	(1a)	(2a)	(3a)	(4a)	(5a)
A. Required reserve	$35	$40	$30	$36	$44
B. Excess reserve	5	0	−25	4	1
C. New loans	5	0	*	4	1

b. Table

	(1b)	(2b)	(3b)	(4b)	(5b)
Assets:					
Cash	$ 10	$ 20	$ 20	$ 20	$ 15
Reserves	40	40	25	40	45
Loans	105	100	*	104	151
Securities	50	60	30	70	60
Liabilities and net worth:					
Checkable deposits	180	200	*	184	221
Capital stock	25	20	25	50	50

*If an individual bank is $5 short of reserves it must either obtain additional reserves of $5 by selling loans, securities, or its own IOUs to the reserve bank or contract its loans by $25.

3. Table

(1)	(2)	(3)	(4)
12.50%	$8	$1	$8
16.67	6	1	6
20	5	1	5
25	4	1	4
30	3.33	1	3.33
33.33	3	1	3

4. Table

	(1)	(2)	(3)	(4)	(5)	(6)
Assets:						
Cash	$ 50	$ 50	$ 50	$ 50	$ 50	$ 50
Reserves	105	105	108	108	110	110
Loans	200	220	200	240	200	250
Securities	200	200	192	192	200	200
Liabilities and net worth:						
Checkable deposits	505	525	500	540	500	550
Capital stock	50	50	50	50	50	50
Loans from Federal Reserve	0	0	0	0	10	10
Excess reserves	4	0	8	0	10	0
Maximum possible expansion of the money supply	20	0	40	0	50	0

SHORT ANSWER AND ESSAY QUESTIONS

CHAPTER 15

Monetary Policy

Chapter 15 is the third chapter dealing with money and banking. It explains how the Board of Governors of the Federal Reserve System and the Federal Reserve Banks affect output, income, employment, and the price level of the economy. Central bank policy designed to affect these variables is called **monetary policy,** the goal of which is price-level stability, full employment, and economic growth.

The first half of the chapter explains how the Federal Reserve achieves its basic goal. In this discussion, attention should be paid to the following: (1) the important items on the balance sheet of the Federal Reserve Banks; (2) the three major controls available to the Federal Reserve, and how the employment of these controls can affect the reserves, excess reserves, actual money supply, and money-creating potential of the banking system; (3) the actions the Federal Reserve would take if it were pursuing a **tight money policy** to curb inflation, and the actions it would take if it were pursuing an **easy money policy** to increase economic growth and reduce unemployment; and (4) the relative importance of the three major controls.

Following the examination of "The Tools of Monetary Policy," Professors McConnell and Brue explain how changes in the money supply ultimately affect the economy. They achieve this objective by describing how the demand for money and the supply of money determine the interest rate (in the **money market**), and how the interest rate and the investment demand schedule determine the level of equilibrium GDP. The effects of an easy money policy or a tight money policy in this **cause-effect chain** are illustrated with examples and summarized in Table 15.3. Changes in monetary policy shift aggregate demand across the aggregate supply curve, thus changing real output and the price level.

A major section of the chapter discusses the monetary policy in action. The major strengths are related to its speed and flexibility and isolation from political pressures. In current practice, the Federal Reserve changes monetary policy by adjusting its targets for the **Federal fund rates.** These rates in turn have an effect on other interest rates in the economy, such as the prime interest rate. The Federal Reserve has had many successes during the 1990s and the early 2000s in countering recession by lowering the interest rate and controlling inflation by raising the interest rate.

Monetary policy, however, is not without its problems or complications. There can be lags between the time

actions are taken and the time the monetary policy influences economic activity. Changes in the velocity of money can blunt the effectiveness of monetary policy. Monetary policy can also suffer from cyclical asymmetry by being more influential in controlling inflation than in preventing recession. There have been debates about whether there should be more or less discretion in the conduct of monetary policy and the adoption of inflation targeting. Linkages with the international economy further complicate outcomes because change in monetary policy can affect exchange rates and net exports.

The final section on the "Big Picture" is short but important. Figure 15.4 gives you an overview of the economic factors and government policies that affect aggregate demand and aggregate supply. It summarizes much of the economic theory and policy that have been discussed in this chapter and the eight chapters that preceded it.

■ CHECKLIST

When you have studied this chapter you should be able to

☐ State the fundamental goal of monetary policy.

☐ List the important assets and liabilities of the Federal Reserve Banks.

☐ Identify the three tools of monetary policy.

☐ Explain how the Federal Reserve can expand the money supply by buying government securities from commercial banks and from the public.

☐ Explain how the Federal Reserve can contract the money supply by selling government securities to commercial banks and to the public.

☐ Describe how raising or lowering the reserve ratio can increase or decrease the money supply.

☐ Illustrate how raising or lowering the discount rate can increase or decrease the money supply.

☐ Describe three actions the Fed can take to pursue an easy money policy.

☐ Describe three actions the Fed can take to pursue a tight money policy.

☐ Discuss the relative importance of monetary policy tools.

☐ Draw the demand-for-money and the supply-of-money curves and use them to show how a change in the supply of money will affect the interest rate.

☐ Draw an investment demand curve to explain the effects of changes in the interest rate on investment spending.

☐ Construct an aggregate supply and aggregate demand graph to show how aggregate demand and the equilibrium level of GDP are affected by changes in interest rates and investment spending.

☐ Use a cause-effect chain to explain the links between a change in the money supply and a change in the equilibrium level of GDP when there is an easy money policy and a tight money policy.

☐ List several strengths of monetary policy.

☐ Explain how the Federal Reserve uses monetary policy to change the Federal funds rate.

☐ Describe the relationship between the Federal funds rate and the prime interest rate.

☐ Evaluate monetary policy in the 1990s and 2000s.

☐ Describe three limitations or complications of monetary policy.

☐ Debate whether monetary policy should be largely conducted with discretion or whether there should be inflation targeting.

☐ Explain how the effectiveness of an easy money policy or a tight money policy is influenced by net exports and how these policies affect balance-of-trade deficits.

☐ Summarize the key factors and policies affecting aggregate supply and demand, and the level of output, employment, income, and prices in an economy using Figure 15.4.

■ **CHAPTER OUTLINE**

1. The fundamental *objective of monetary policy* is full employment without inflation. The Federal Reserve can accomplish this objective by exercising control over the amount of excess reserves held by commercial banks, and thereby influencing the size of the money supply and the total level of spending in the economy.

2. By examining the consolidated *balance sheet* and the principal assets and liabilities of the Federal Reserve Banks, an understanding of the ways the Federal Reserve can control and influence the reserves of commercial banks and the money supply can be obtained.

    a. The principal *assets* of the Federal Reserve Banks (in order of size) are U.S. government securities and loans to commercial banks.

    b. Their principal *liabilities* are Federal Reserve Notes, the reserve deposits of commercial banks, and U.S. Treasury deposits.

3. The Federal Reserve Banks use three principal tools (techniques or instruments) to control the reserves of banks and the size of the money supply.

    a. The Federal Reserve can *buy* or *sell government securities* in the open market to change the lending ability of the banking system.

    (1) Buying government securities in the open market from either banks or the public increases the excess reserves of banks.

    (2) Selling government securities in the open market to either banks or the public decreases the excess reserves of banks.

    b. It can *raise or lower the reserve ratio.*

    (1) Raising the reserve ratio decreases the excess reserves of banks and the size of the monetary (checkable-deposit) multiplier.

    (2) Lowering the reserve ratio increases the excess reserves of banks and the size of the monetary multiplier.

    c. It can also *raise* or *lower the discount rate.* Raising the discount rate discourages banks from borrowing reserves from the Fed. Lowering the discount rate encourages banks to borrow from the Fed.

    d. Monetary policy can be easy or tight.

    (1) An *easy money policy* can be implemented by actions of the Federal Reserve to buy government securities in the open market, decrease the discount rate, or decrease the reserve ratio.

    (2) A *tight money policy* can be implemented by actions of the Federal Reserve to sell government securities in the open market, increase the discount rate, or increase the reserve ratio.

    e. Open-market operations is the most important of the three monetary tools because it is the most flexible and direct.

4. Monetary policy affects the *equilibrium GDP* in many ways.

    a. In the *money market,* the demand curve for money and the supply curve of money determine the real interest rate. This rate of interest in turn determines investment spending. Investment spending then affects aggregate demand and the equilibrium levels of real output and prices.

    b. If recession or slow economic growth is a major problem, the Federal Reserve can institute an *easy money policy* that increases the money supply, causing the interest rate to fall and investment spending to increase, thereby increasing aggregate demand and increasing real GDP by a multiple of the increase in investment.

    c. If inflation is the problem, the Federal Reserve can adopt a *tight money policy* that decreases the money supply, causing the interest rate to rise and investment spending to decrease, thereby reducing aggregate demand and inflation.

5. Monetary policy is considered more important and valuable for stabilizing the national economy because of its several advantages over fiscal policy: It is quicker and more flexible, and there is more isolation from political pressure.

    a. The *Federal funds rate,* the interest rate that banks charge each other for overnight loans of excess reserves, has been the recent focus of monetary policy.

    (1) The Federal Reserve can influence the Federal funds rate by buying or selling government bonds. When the Federal Reserve buys bonds, it becomes cheaper for banks to borrow excess reserves overnight because the Federal funds rate falls; conversely, when the Federal Reserve sells bonds, the Federal funds rate rises and it becomes more expensive for banks to borrow funds.

    (2) The *prime interest rate* is the benchmark rate that banks use to decide on the interest rate for loans to

businesses and individuals; it rises and falls with the Federal funds rate.

b. Recent monetary policy has been easy and tight in response to concerns about recession and inflation. In the early 1990s, the Federal Reserve increased excess reserves and reduced interest rates to counter a recession. Interest rates were raised in the mid-1990s to control inflation, but then lowered again in 1998 in response to the financial crisis in southeast Asia. They were raised again in 1999 and 2000, but in 2001 and 2002 the Federal Reserve cut rates to counter an economic slowdown and recession.

c. There are some limitations and complications with monetary policy. It is subject to lags between the time the need for the policy is recognized and the time the policy influences economic activity. Changes in the velocity of money can offset changes in monetary policy. There is a cyclical asymmetry with monetary policy: A tight money policy works better than an easy money policy.

d. Debates over the conduct of monetary policy have focused on the use of management discretion or inflation targeting. Although the Federal Reserve has been successful in recent years with its "artful management" of monetary policy, some economists would like it to adopt inflation targeting, in which the Federal Reserve must specify and be accountable for achieving an inflation target within a range.

e. Monetary policy has international linkages and there is a **net export effect**.

(1) An easy money policy to bring the economy out of recession or slow growth will tend to lower domestic interest rates and cause the dollar to depreciate. In this situation, net exports will increase, thus increasing aggregate demand and reinforcing the effects of the easy money policy.

(2) A tight money policy to reduce inflation will tend to raise domestic interest rates and cause the dollar to appreciate. These events will decrease net exports and reduce aggregate demand, thereby increasing the effects of a tight money policy.

(3) An easy money policy is *compatible* with the goal of correcting a balance-of-trade deficit, but a tight money policy *conflicts* with this economic goal.

6. The *"big picture" of macroeconomics* shows that the equilibrium levels of output, employment, income, and prices are determined by the interaction of aggregate supply and aggregate demand.

a. There are four expenditure components of aggregate demand: consumption, investment, government spending, and net export spending.

b. There are three major components of aggregate supply: the prices of inputs or resources, factors affecting the productivity with which resources are used, and the legal and institutional environment.

c. Fiscal, monetary, or other government policies may have an effect on the components of aggregate demand or supply, which in turn will affect the level of output, employment, income, and prices.

■ HINTS AND TIPS

1. To acquire a thorough knowledge of how the Federal Reserve transactions affect required reserves, excess reserves, the actual money supply, and the potential money supply, carefully study the **balance sheets** that are used to explain these transactions. The items to watch are the reserves and checkable deposits. Be sure that you know why a change is made in each balance sheet, and be able to make the appropriate balance-sheet entries as you trace through the effects of each transaction. Problem 2 in this chapter provides additional practice.

2. You must understand and remember the **cause-effect chain of monetary policy**. The best way to learn it is to draw your own chain (graphs) that shows the links for an easy money policy and a tight money policy as in Figure 15.2. Then check each step for how monetary policy can be used to counter recession or limit inflation using Table 15.3 in the text. Draw another chain for describing monetary policy and the net export effect and check your cause-effect chain against Table 15.4.

3. The section on "monetary policy in action" shows how the theory you have learned has been applied in the real world. In particular, you want to pay attention to how the Federal Reserve uses the Federal funds rate to implement monetary policy, and also learn about the policy successes in recent years to counter recession and limit inflation.

4. The single most important figure for a "big picture" of the macroeconomics part of the textbook is *Figure 15.4*. It reviews and summarizes the determinants of aggregate supply and demand and identifies the key policy variables that have been discussed in this chapter and in Chapters 7–14.

■ IMPORTANT TERMS

monetary policy	tight money policy
open-market operations	Federal funds rate
reserve ratio	prime interest rate
discount rate	inflation targeting
easy money policy	

SELF-TEST

■ FILL-IN QUESTIONS

1. The goal of monetary policy in the United States is to achieve and maintain stability in the (price level, tax level)

_____, a rate of (full, partial) _____ employment in the economy, and economic growth.

2. The two important assets of the Federal Reserve Banks are (Treasury deposits, government securities)

_____ and (reserves of, loans to)

_____ commercial banks. The three major liabilities are (Treasury deposits, government securities) _____, (reserves of, loans to) _____ commercial banks, and (government securities, Federal Reserve Notes) _____.

3. The three tools the monetary authority uses to control the money supply are (open, closed) _____ market operations, changing the (loan, reserve) _____ ratio, and changing the (prime interest, discount) _____ rate.

4. When the Federal Reserve Banks buy government securities in the open market, the reserves of commercial banks will (increase, decrease) _____ and when they sell government securities in the open market, the reserves of commercial banks will _____.

5. If the Federal Reserve Banks were to sell $10 million in government bonds to the *public* and the reserve ratio were 25%, the supply of money would immediately be reduced by $_____, the reserves of commercial banks would be reduced by $_____, and the excess reserves of the banks would be reduced by $_____. But if these bonds were sold to the commercial banks, the supply of money would immediately be reduced by $_____, the reserves of the banks would be reduced by $_____, and the excess reserves of the banks would be reduced by $_____.

6. An increase in the reserve ratio will (increase, decrease) _____ the size of the monetary multiplier and _____ the excess reserves held by commercial banks, thus causing the money supply to (increase, decrease) _____. A decrease in the reserve ratio will (increase, decrease) _____ the size of the monetary multiplier and _____ the excess reserves held by commercial banks, thus causing the money supply to (increase, decrease) _____.

7. If the Federal Reserve Banks were to lower the discount rate, commercial banks would tend to borrow (more, less) _____ from them, and this would (increase, decrease) _____ their excess reserves.

8. To increase the supply of money, the Federal Reserve Banks should (raise, lower) _____ the reserve ratio, (buy, sell) _____ securities in the open market, and/or (increase, decrease) _____ the discount rate.

9. An easy money policy would be characterized by actions of the Federal Reserve to (increase, decrease) _____ the discount rate, _____ reserve ratios, and (buy, sell) _____ government bonds, whereas a tight money policy would include actions taken to (increase, decrease) _____ the discount rate, _____ reserve ratios, and (buy, sell) _____ government bonds.

10. The most effective and most often used tool of monetary policy is a change in (the discount rate, the reserve ratio, open-market operations) _____, and a rarely used tool is a change in _____; an announcement effect is created by a change in _____, but it is relatively weak because banks may not be inclined to borrow even at a lower rate.

11. There is a cause-effect chain of monetary policy.
a. In the money market, the demand for and the supply of money determine the equilibrium rate of (discount, interest) _____.
b. This rate in turn determines the level of (government, investment) _____ spending based on the _____ demand curve.
c. This spending in turn affects aggregate (demand, supply) _____, and the intersection of aggregate supply and demand determine the equilibrium level of real (interest, GDP) _____ and the (discount, price) _____ level.

12. This cause-effect chain can be illustrated with examples.
a. When there is an *increase* in the money supply curve, the real interest rate will (increase, decrease) _____, investment spending will _____, aggregate demand will (increase, decrease) _____, and real GDP will _____.

b. When there is a *decrease* in the money supply curve, the real interest rate will (increase, decrease) _____, investment spending will _____, aggregate demand will (increase, decrease) _____, and real GDP will _____.

13. To eliminate inflationary pressures in the economy, the traditional view holds that the monetary authority should seek to (increase, decrease) _____ the reserves of commercial banks; this would tend to_____ the money supply and to (increase, decrease) _____ the rate of interest, and this in turn would cause investment spending, aggregate demand, and GDP to _____. This action by monetary authorities would be considered (an easy, a tight) _____ money policy.

14. If there were a serious problem with economic growth and unemployment in the economy, the traditional view would be that the Federal Reserve should pursue (an easy, a tight) _____ money policy, in which case the Federal Reserve would (buy, sell) _____ government bonds as a way of (increasing, decreasing) _____ the money supply, and thereby _____ interest rates; these events would have the effect of (increasing, decreasing) _____ investment spending and thus _____ real GDP.

15. An increase in the money supply will shift the aggregate (supply, demand) _____ curve to the (right, left) _____. A decrease in the money supply will shift the aggregate (supply, demand) _____ curve to the (right, left) _____. If the marginal propensity to consume is .75, then the multiplier will be (3, 4) _____, an initial increase in investment of $10 billion will (increase, decrease) _____ aggregate demand by ($30, $40) _____ billion.

16. Monetary policy has strengths. Compared to fiscal policy, monetary policy is speedier and (more, less) _____ flexible, and _____ isolated from political pressure.

17. The interest rate that banks charge one another for overnight loans is the (prime interest, Federal funds) _____ rate, but the rate banks use as a benchmark for setting interest rates on loans is the _____ rate. The (prime interest, Federal funds) _____ rate has been the recent focus of the monetary policy of the Federal Reserve. Since 1990, the Federal Reserve has been successful in countering recession by (raising, lowering) _____ the Federal funds, and it has been successful in limiting inflation by _____ the Federal funds rate.

18. Monetary policy has shortcomings and problems, too.

a. It may be subject to timing (limits, lags) _____ that occur between the time a need is recognized and the policy takes effect.

b. It may be offset when the velocity of money changes in the (same, opposite) _____ direction as the money supply.

c. It may be more effective in counteracting (recession, inflation) _____ than _____.

19. In recent years, there have been calls for the Federal Reserve to focus primarily on the goal of price-level stability and be more accountable for its actions by using (deflation, inflation) _____ targeting. Critics of such a policy contend that the role that it assigns to the Federal Reserve is too (wide, narrow) _____ and that policymakers at the Federal Reserve should have (more, less) _____ discretion over the conduct of monetary policy.

20. An easy money policy (increases, decreases) _____ net exports; a tight money policy _____ net exports. The net export effect from an easy money policy thus (strengthens, weakens) _____ domestic monetary policy, and the net export effect from a tight money policy _____ it. An easy money policy is (compatible, incompatible) _____ with the economic goal of reducing a balance-of-trade deficit, but a tight money policy is _____ with this economic goal.

■ **TRUE–FALSE QUESTIONS**

Circle T if the statement is true, F if it is false.

1. The goal of monetary policy is to lower interest rates.
T F

2. The securities owned by the Federal Reserve Banks are almost entirely U.S. government bonds.
T F

3. If the Federal Reserve Banks buy $15 in government securities from the public in the open market, the effect will be to increase the excess reserves of commercial banks by $15. **T F**

4. When the Federal Reserve sells bonds in the open market, the price of these bonds falls. **T F**

5. A change in the reserve ratio will affect the multiple by which the banking system can create money, but it will not affect the actual or excess reserves of member banks. **T F**

6. If the reserve ratio is lowered, some required reserves are turned into excess reserves.　　　**T　F**

7. When commercial banks borrow from the Federal Reserve Banks, they increase their excess reserves and their money-creating potential.　　　**T　F**

8. If the monetary authority wished to follow a tight money policy, it would sell government bonds in the open market.　　　**T　F**

9. An increase in the required reserve ratio tends to reduce the profits of banks.　　　**T　F**

10. The least effective and least used tool of monetary policy is the open-market operation, in which government securities are bought and sold.　　　**T　F**

11. The equilibrium rate of interest is found at the intersection of the money demand and the money supply curves.　　　**T　F**

12. An increase in the equilibrium GDP will shift the demand-for-money curve to the left and increase the equilibrium interest rate.　　　**T　F**

13. In the cause-effect chain, an easy money policy increases the money supply, decreases the interest rate, increases investment spending, and increases aggregate demand.　　　**T　F**

14. A tight money policy is designed to correct a problem of high unemployment and sluggish economic growth.　　　**T　F**

15. It is generally agreed that fiscal policy is more effective than monetary policy in controlling the business cycle because fiscal policy is more flexible.　　　**T　F**

16. Monetary policy is subject to more political pressure than fiscal policy.　　　**T　F**

17. In recent years, the Federal Reserve has announced its changes in monetary policy by changing its targets for the Federal funds rate.　　　**T　F**

18. The prime interest rate is the rate that banks charge other banks for overnight loans of excess reserves at Federal Reserve banks.　　　**T　F**

19. To increase the Federal funds interest rate, the Federal Reserve buys bonds in the open market to increase the excess reserves of banks.　　　**T　F**

20. Monetary policy is limited by a time lag that occurs from when the problem is recognized to when the policy becomes operational.　　　**T　F**

21. An easy money policy suffers from a "You can lead a horse to water, but you can't make the horse drink" problem.　　　**T　F**

22. Inflation targeting is largely a monetary policy that permits the Federal Reserve to use substantial discretion in managing the economy.　　　**T　F**

23. An easy money policy decreases net exports.　**T　F**

24. A tight money policy will tend to cause the dollar to appreciate.　　　**T　F**

25. A tight money policy is compatible with the goal of correcting a trade deficit.　　　**T　F**

■ **MULTIPLE-CHOICE QUESTIONS**

Circle the letter that corresponds to the best answer.

1. The organization directly responsible for monetary policy in the United States is the
　(a) Internal Revenue Service
　(b) Federal Reserve
　(c) Congress of the United States
　(d) U.S. Treasury

2. The largest single asset in the Federal Reserve Banks' consolidated balance sheet is
　(a) securities
　(b) the reserves of commercial banks
　(c) Federal Reserve Notes
　(d) loans to commercial banks

3. The largest single liability of the Federal Reserve Banks is
　(a) securities
　(b) the reserves of commercial banks
　(c) Federal Reserve Notes
　(d) loans to commercial banks

4. Assume that there is a 20% reserve ratio and that the Federal Reserve buys $100 million worth of government securities. If the securities are purchased from the public, this action has the potential to increase bank lending by a maximum of
　(a) $500 million, but only by $400 million if the securities are purchased directly from commercial banks
　(b) $400 million, but by $500 million if the securities are purchased directly from commercial banks
　(c) $500 million, and also by $500 million if the securities are purchased directly from commercial banks
　(d) $400 million, and also by $400 million if the securities are purchased directly from commercial banks

5. Assuming that the Federal Reserve Banks sell $20 million in government securities to commercial banks and the reserve ratio is 20%, then the effect will be
　(a) to reduce the actual supply of money by $20 million
　(b) to reduce the actual supply of money by $4 million
　(c) to reduce the potential money supply by $20 million
　(d) to reduce the potential money supply by $100 million

6. Lowering the reserve ratio changes
　(a) required reserves to excess reserves
　(b) increases the amount of excess reserves banks must keep
　(c) increases the discount rate
　(d) decreases the discount rate

7. Commercial bank borrowing from the Federal Reserve
(a) is not permitted because of the Federal Reserve Act
(b) is permitted but only for banks that are bankrupt
(c) decreases the excess reserves of commercial banks and their ability to offer credit
(d) increases the excess reserves of commercial banks and their ability to offer credit

8. The economy is experiencing high unemployment and a low rate of economic growth and the Fed decides to pursue an easy money policy. Which set of actions by the Fed would be most consistent with this policy?
(a) buying government securities and raising the reserve ratio
(b) selling government securities and raising the discount rate
(c) buying government securities and lowering the reserve ratio
(d) selling government securities and lowering the discount rate

9. The economy is experiencing inflation and the Federal Reserve decides to pursue a tight money policy. Which set of actions by the Fed would be most consistent with this policy?
(a) buying government securities and lowering the discount rate
(b) buying government securities and lowering the reserve ratio
(c) selling government securities and raising the discount rate
(d) selling government securities and lowering the discount rate

10. Which is the most important control used by the Federal Reserve to regulate the money supply?
(a) changing the reserve ratio
(b) open-market operations
(c) changing the discount rate
(d) changing the Federal funds rate

11. A newspaper headline reads: "Fed Cuts Discount Rate for Third Time This Year." This headline indicates that the Federal Reserve is most likely trying to
(a) reduce inflationary pressures in the economy
(b) increase the Federal funds rate
(c) reduce the cost of credit and stimulate the economy
(d) increase the value of the dollar

12. In the chain of cause and effect between changes in the excess reserves of commercial banks and the resulting changes in output and employment in the economy,
(a) an increase in excess reserves will decrease the money supply
(b) a decrease in the money supply will increase the rate of interest
(c) an increase in the rate of interest will increase aggregate demand
(d) an increase in aggregate demand will decrease output and employment

13. Which is most likely to be affected by changes in the rate of interest?
(a) tax rates
(b) investment spending
(c) government spending
(d) the imports of the economy

Use the following graph to answer Questions 14, 15, and 16.

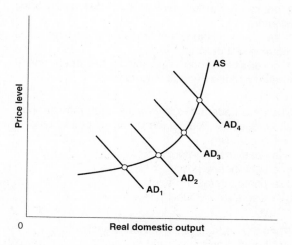

14. A shift from **AD₁** to **AD₂** would be most consistent with
(a) an increase in the prime interest rate by corporations
(b) an increase in the discount rate by the Federal Reserve
(c) the buying of securities by the Federal Reserve
(d) the selling of securities by the Federal Reserve

15. Assume that the Federal Reserve lowers interest rates to increase investment spending. This monetary policy is most likely to shift
(a) **AD₃** to **AD₂**
(b) **AD₃** to **AD₄**
(c) **AD₄** to **AD₃**
(d) **AD₂** to **AD₁**

16. A tight money policy would be most consistent with a shift from
(a) **AD₁** to **AD₂**
(b) **AD₃** to **AD₄**
(c) **AD₄** to **AD₃**
(d) **AD₂** to **AD₃**

17. Assume that monetary policy increases interest rates and results in a decrease in investment spending of $5 billion. If the marginal propensity to consume is .80, then aggregate demand is most likely to
(a) increase by $5 billion
(b) decrease by $25 billion
(c) increase by $25 billion
(d) decrease by $25 billion

18. Which one is considered a *strength* of monetary policy compared to fiscal policy?

(a) cause-effect chain
(b) cyclical asymmetry
(c) isolation from political pressure
(d) effect on changes in the velocity of money

19. The Federal funds rate is the rate that

(a) banks charge for overnight use of excess reserves held at the Federal Reserve banks
(b) banks charge for loans to the most creditworthy customers
(c) the Federal Reserve charges for short-term loans to commercial banks
(d) government bonds are sold in the open-market operations of the Federal Reserve

20. When the Federal Reserve uses open-market operations to reduce the Federal funds rate several times over a year it is pursuing

(a) an easy money policy
(b) a tight money policy
(c) a prime interest rate policy
(d) a discretionary fiscal policy

21. When the Federal Reserve Banks decide to buy government bonds from banks and the public, the supply of reserves in the Federal fund market

(a) increases and the Federal funds rate decreases
(b) decreases and the Federal funds rate decreases
(c) increases and the Federal funds rate increases
(d) decreases and the Federal funds rate increases

22. Assume the Fed creates excess reserves, but the policy does not encourage banks to make loans and thus increase the money supply. This situation is a problem of

(a) tight money
(b) cyclical asymmetry
(c) changes in velocity
(d) targeting the Federal funds rate

23. A tight money policy in the United States is most likely to

(a) increase domestic interest rates and cause the value of the dollar to depreciate
(b) decrease domestic interest rates and cause the value of the dollar to appreciate
(c) increase domestic interest rates and cause the value of the dollar to appreciate
(d) decrease domestic interest rates and cause the value of the dollar to depreciate

24. Which policy combination would tend to reduce net exports?

(a) tight money policy and expansionary fiscal policy
(b) easy money policy and expansionary fiscal policy
(c) tight money policy and contractionary fiscal policy
(d) easy money policy and contractionary fiscal policy

25. A tight money policy that is used to reduce inflation in the domestic economy

(a) is best conducted by reducing the required reserve ratios at commercial banks
(b) increases net exports and the effectiveness of the policy
(c) conflicts with the economic goal of correcting a trade deficit
(d) causes the dollar to depreciate

■ **PROBLEMS**

1. Assume that the following consolidated balance sheet is for all commercial banks. Assume also that the required reserve ratio is 25% and that cash is *not* a part of the commercial banks' legal reserve.

Assets		Liabilities	
Cash	$ 50	Checkable deposits	$400
Reserves	100	Loans from Federal	
Loans	150	Reserve	25
Securities	200	Net worth	75
	$500		$500

a. To *increase* the supply of money by $100, the Fed could (buy, sell) _____ securities worth $_____ in the open market.

b. To *decrease* the supply of money by $50, the Fed could (buy, sell) _____ securities worth $_____ in the open market.

2. Following are the consolidated balance sheets of the Federal Reserve and of the commercial banks. Assume that the reserve ratio for commercial banks is 25%, that cash is *not* a part of a bank's legal reserve, and that the figures in column 1 show the balance sheets of the Federal Reserve and the commercial banks *prior to each of the following five transactions.* Place the new balance sheet figures in the appropriate columns and complete A, B, C, D, and E in these columns. Do *not* use the figures you place in columns 2 through 5 when you work the next part of the problem; start all parts of the problem with the printed figures in column 1.

a. The Federal Reserve Banks sell $3 in securities to the public, which pays by check (column 2).
b. The Federal Reserve Banks buy $4 in securities from the commercial banks (column 3).
c. The Federal Reserve Banks lower the required reserve ratio for commercial banks to 20% (column 4).
d. The U.S. Treasury buys $5 worth of goods from U.S. manufacturers and pays the manufacturers by checks drawn on its accounts at the Federal Reserve Banks (column 5).
e. Because the Federal Reserve Banks have raised the discount rate, commercial banks repay $6 which they owe to the Federal Reserve (column 6).

	(1)	(2)	(3)	(4)	(5)	(6)
Federal Reserve Banks						
Assets:						
Gold certificates	$ 25	$____	$____	$____	$____	$____
Securities	30	____	____	____	____	____
Loans to commercial banks	10	____	____	____	____	____
Liabilities:						
Reserves of commercial banks	50	____	____	____	____	____
Treasury deposits	5	____	____	____	____	____
Federal Reserve Notes	10	____	____	____	____	____
Commercial Banks						
Assets:						
Reserves	$ 50	$____	$____	$____	$____	$____
Securities	70	____	____	____	____	____
Loans	90	____	____	____	____	____
Liabilities:						
Demand deposits	200	____	____	____	____	____
Loans from Federal Reserve	10	____	____	____	____	____
A. Required reserves		____	____	____	____	____
B. Excess reserves		____	____	____	____	____
C. How much has the money supply changed?		____	____	____	____	____
D. How much more can the money supply change?		____	____	____	____	____
E. What is the total of C and D?		____	____	____	____	____

3. On the following graph is the demand-for-money curve that shows the amounts of money consumers and firms wish to hold at various rates of interest (when the nominal GDP in the economy is given).

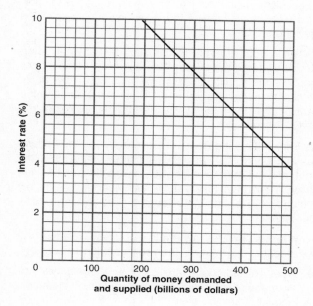

a. Suppose the supply of money is equal to $300 billion. (1) Draw the supply-of-money curve on the above graph. (2) The equilibrium rate of interest in the economy is _____ %.

b. Below is a graph of an investment demand curve which shows the amounts of planned investment at various rates of interest. Given your answer to (2) above, how much will investors plan to spend for capital goods? $_____ billion.

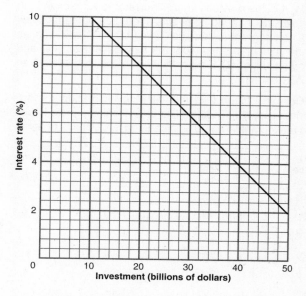

c. The following figure shows the aggregate supply (**AS**) curve in this economy. On the graph, draw an aggregate demand curve (**AD$_1$**) so that it crosses the **AS** in the middle of the curve. Label the price level (**P$_1$**) and output level (**Q$_1$**) associated with the intersection of **AD$_1$** and **AS**.

Real domestic product, GDP

d. Now assume that monetary authorities increase the money supply to $400.

(1) On the money market graph, plot the new money supply curve. The new equilibrium interest rate is

_____ %.

(2) On the investment graph, determine the level of investment spending that is associated with this new

interest rate: $_____ billion. By how much has investment spending increased as a result

of the change in the interest rate? $_____ billion.

(3) Assume that the marginal propensity to consume

is .75. What is the multiplier? _____ By how much will the new investment spending in-

crease aggregate demand? $_____ billion.

(4) On the previous figure, indicate how the change in investment spending affects aggregate demand. Draw a new aggregate demand curve (**AD₂**) so that it crosses the **AS** curve. Also label the new price level (**P₂**) and output level (**Q₂**) associated with the intersection of **AD₂** and **AS.**

4. Columns 1 and 2 of the following table show the aggregate supply schedule. (The price level is a price index, and real domestic output is measured in billions of dollars.)

(1) Price level	(2) Real output	(3) AD₁	(4) AD₂
110	1600	1800	____
120	1700	1700	____
130	1790	1600	____
140	1800	1500	____
150	1940	1400	____
160	2000	1300	____

a. If the aggregate demand schedule were that shown in columns 1 and 3, the equilibrium real domestic

output would be $_____ billion and the price

level would be _____.

b. Now assume that the Federal Reserve took actions to lower the Federal funds rate, and these actions increased investment spending in this economy by $60 billion. Also assume that the marginal propensity to consume in the economy was .8. How much would

aggregate demand increase? $_____ billion

c. In column 4, enter this amount of increase in real domestic output at each price level to define the new **AD** schedule (**AD₂**).

d. What is the new equilibrium real domestic output?

$_____ billion. And the new price level? _____.

■ SHORT ANSWER AND ESSAY QUESTIONS

1. What is the basic goal of monetary policy?

2. What are the important assets and liabilities of the Federal Reserve Banks?

3. Explain how the monetary policy tools of the Federal Reserve Banks would be used to contract the supply of money. How would they be used to expand the supply of money?

4. What is the difference between the effects of the Federal Reserve's buying (selling) government securities in the open market from (to) commercial banks and from (to) the public?

5. Which of the monetary policy tools available to the Federal Reserve is most effective? Why is it more important than other tools?

6. Using three graphs, explain what determines (a) the equilibrium interest rate, (b) investment spending, and (c) the equilibrium GDP. Now use these three graphs to show the effects of a decrease in the money supply upon the equilibrium GDP.

7. Using your answers to Question 6, (a) what determines how large the effect of the decrease in the money supply on the equilibrium GDP will be, and (b) how would the change in the equilibrium GDP affect the demand-for-money curve, the interest rate, investment spending, and the GDP itself?

8. Explain how the Board of Governors and the Federal Reserve Banks can influence income, output, employment, and the price level. In your explanation, employ the following concepts: reserves, excess reserves, the supply of money, the availability of bank credit, and the rate of interest.

9. Why are changes in the rate of interest likely to affect investment spending more than consumption and saving?

10. What are the characteristics of an easy money policy? How does the Federal Reserve implement such policies and what are the effects?

11. What are the characteristics of a tight money policy? How does the Federal Reserve implement such policies and what are the effects?

12. What policies will the Federal Reserve use to counter inflation, or unemployment and recession? Describe the effects on bank reserves, the money supply, interest rates, investment spending, aggregate demand, and real GDP from each policy.

13. What are the major strengths of monetary policy?

14. What happens to the Federal funds rate when the Federal Reserve expands or contracts the money supply through open-market operations?

15. Discuss how monetary policy has been used to counter recession and limit inflation since the 1990s.

16. Why is monetary policy more effective in controlling inflation than in reducing unemployment?

17. Why might a change in velocity reduce the effectiveness of monetary policy?

18. Should monetary policy be "artful management" or should there be inflation targeting? Discuss the advantages and disadvantages of each approach.

19. Explain how the net export effect influences the effectiveness of a tight or an easy money policy.

20. What type of monetary policy would you recommend to correct a balance-of-trade deficit? Why?

ANSWERS

Chapter 15 Monetary Policy

FILL-IN QUESTIONS

1. price level, full
2. government securities, loans to, Treasury deposits, reserves of, Federal Reserve Notes
3. open, reserve, discount
4. increase, decrease
5. 10 million, 10 million, 7.5 million, 0, 10 million, 10 million
6. decrease, decrease, decrease, increase, increase, increase
7. more, increase
8. lower, buy, decrease

9. decrease, decrease, buy, increase, increase, sell
10. open-market operations, the reserve ratio, the discount rate
11. *a.* interest; *b.* investment, investment; *c.* demand, GDP, price
12. *a.* decrease, increase, increase, increase; *b.* increase, decrease, decrease, decrease
13. decrease, decrease, increase, decrease, a tight
14. an easy, buy, increasing, decreasing, increasing, increasing
15. demand, right, demand, left, 4, increase, $40
16. more, more
17. Federal funds, prime interest, Federal funds, lowering, raising
18. lags, opposite, inflation, recession
19. inflation, narrow, more
20. increases, decreases, strengthens, strengthens, compatible, incompatible

TRUE–FALSE QUESTIONS

1. F, p. 268	**10.** F, p. 275	**19.** F, pp. 280–281
2. T, pp. 268–269	**11.** T, pp. 276–277	**20.** T, p. 281
3. F, pp. 270–271	**12.** F, pp. 276–278	**21.** T, pp. 281–282
4. T, pp. 271–272	**13.** T, pp. 276–278	**22.** F, pp. 282–283
5. F, pp. 273–274	**14.** F, p. 279	**23.** F, pp. 283, 286
6. T, p. 274	**15.** F, pp. 279–280	**24.** T, pp. 283, 286
7. T, pp. 274–275	**16.** F, pp. 279–280	**25.** F, pp. 283, 286
8. T, p. 275	**17.** T, p. 280	
9. T, p. 275	**18.** F, pp. 280–281	

MULTIPLE-CHOICE QUESTIONS

1. b, p. 268	**10.** b, p. 275	**19.** a, p. 280
2. a, pp. 268–269	**11.** c, p. 275	**20.** a, pp. 280–281
3. c, pp. 268–269	**12.** b, pp. 276–278	**21.** a, p. 281
4. b, pp. 270–271	**13.** b, pp. 276–278	**22.** b, p. 282
5. d, pp. 271–273	**14.** c, pp. 276–278	**23.** c, pp. 283, 286
6. a, pp. 273–274	**15.** b, pp. 276–278	**24.** a, pp. 283, 286
7. d, pp. 274–275	**16.** c, pp. 276–278	**25.** c, pp. 283, 286
8. c, p. 275	**17.** d, p. 279	
9. c, p. 275	**18.** c, pp. 279–280	

PROBLEMS

1. *a.* buy, 25; *b.* sell, 12 1/2
2. See below

	(2)	(3)	(4)	(5)	(6)
Federal Reserve Banks					
Assets:					
Gold certificates	$ 25	$ 25	$ 25	$ 25	$ 25
Securities	27	34	30	30	30
Loans to commercial banks	10	10	10	10	4
Liabilities:					
Reserves of commercial banks	47	54	50	55	44
Treasury deposits	5	5	5	0	5
Federal Reserve Notes	10	10	10	10	10
Commercial Banks					
Assets:					
Reserves	$ 47	$ 54	$ 50	$ 55	$ 44
Securities	70	66	70	70	70
Loans	90	90	90	90	90
Liabilities:					
Checkable deposits	197	200	200	205	200
Loans from Federal Reserve	10	10	10	10	4
A. Required reserves	49.25	50	40	51.25	50
B. Excess reserves	−2.25	4	10	3.75	−6
C. How much has the money supply changed?	−3	0	0	+5	0
D. How much more can the money supply change?	−9	+16	+50	+15	−24
E. What is the total of C and D?	−12	+16	+50	+20	−24

3. *a.* (2) 8; *b.* 20; *c.* see Figure 15.2 in text; *d.* (1) 6, (2) 30, 10, (3) 4, 40, (4) see Figure 15.2 in text

4. *a.* 1700, 120; *b.* 300 (multiplier of 5 × $60 billion = $300 billion); *c.* 2100, 2000, 1900, 1800, 1700, 1600; *d.* 1800, 140

SHORT ANSWER AND ESSAY QUESTIONS

1. p. 268
2. pp. 268–269
3. pp. 270–275
4. pp. 270–274
5. p. 275
6. pp. 276–278
7. pp. 276–278
8. pp. 276–278
9. p. 278
10. pp. 278–279
11. p. 279
12. pp. 278–279
13. pp. 279–280
14. pp. 280–281
15. p. 281
16. pp. 281–282
17. p. 281
18. pp. 282–283
19. pp. 283, 286
20. pp. 283, 286

Extending the Analysis of Aggregate Supply

Chapter 16 adds to the aggregate demand–aggregate supply (AD–AS) model first introduced in Chapter 11. This addition will give you the analytical tools to improve your understanding of the short-run and long-run relationships between unemployment and inflation.

The major extension to the AD–AS model is the explanation for the **short-run aggregate supply curve** and the **long-run aggregate supply curve.** In the **short run,** nominal wages do not adjust fully as the price level changes, so an increase in the price level increases business profits and real output. In the **long run,** nominal wages are fully responsive to previous changes in the price level, so business profits and employment return to their original levels. Thus, the long-run aggregate supply curve is vertical at the full-employment level of output.

The distinction between the short-run and long-run aggregate supply curves requires a reinterpretation of demand-pull inflation and cost-push inflation. Although **demand-pull inflation** will increase the price level and real output in the short run, once nominal wages increase, the temporary increase in output is gone, but the price level will be higher at the full-employment level of output. **Cost-push inflation** will increase the price level and decrease real output in the short run, but again, once nominal wages fall, output and the price level will return to their original positions. If government policymakers try to counter cost-push inflation by increasing aggregate demand, they may make matters worse by increasing the price level and causing the short-run aggregate supply curve to decrease, thereby setting off an inflationary spiral.

The relationship between inflation and unemployment has been studied for many years. One influential observation, supported by data from the 1950s and 1960s, was embodied in the **Phillips Curve,** which suggested that there was a stable and predictable tradeoff between the rate of inflation and the unemployment rate. During the 1960s, it was thought that this tradeoff could be used for formulating sound monetary and fiscal policy to manage the economy.

The events of the 1970s and early 1980s, however, called into question the shape and stability of the Phillips Curve because the economy was experiencing both higher rates of inflation and unemployment—**stagflation.** The **aggregate supply shocks** of this period shifted the Phillips Curve rightward. When these shocks dissipated in the 1980s, the Phillips Curve began to shift back to its original position. By the end of the 1990s, points on the Phillips Curve were similar to those of the 1960s.

The conclusion to be drawn from studies of the Phillips Curve is that there is *no long-run tradeoff between inflation and unemployment.* In the long run, the downsloping Phillips Curve is actually a vertical line at the natural rate of unemployment. In the short run, if aggregate demand increases and reduces the unemployment rate below its natural rate, the result is only temporary. Eventually, the unemployment rate will return to its natural rate, but at a higher rate of inflation.

Aggregate supply can also be affected by taxation. **Supply-side economics** contends that aggregate supply is important for determining levels of inflation, unemployment, and economic growth. Tax cuts are proposed by supply-siders as a way to create more incentives to work, save, and invest, thus increasing productivity and aggregate supply. The relationship between marginal tax rates and tax revenues is expressed in the **Laffer Curve,** which suggests that cuts in tax rates can increase tax revenues if tax rates are too high for the economy. Critics contend, however, that the incentive effects are small, potentially inflationary, and can have positive or negative effects on tax revenues.

■ CHECKLIST

When you have studied this chapter you should be able to

☐ Give a definition of the short run and long run in macroeconomics.

☐ Distinguish between a change in real wages and a change in nominal wages.

☐ Draw the short-run aggregate supply curve and describe its characteristics.

☐ Explain how the long-run aggregate supply curve is determined.

☐ Draw a graph that illustrates equilibrium in the extended AD–AS model.

☐ Explain demand-pull inflation using the extended AD–AS model and identify its short-run and long-run outcomes.

☐ Describe cost-push inflation using the extended AD–AS model.

☐ Give two generalizations about the policy dilemma for government in dealing with cost-push inflation.

☐ Explain recession and the process of adjustment using the extended AD–AS model.

☐ Draw a Phillips Curve and explain the basic tradeoff it presents.

☐ Define stagflation.

☐ Explain why adverse aggregate supply shocks shifted the Phillips Curve over time.

☐ List events that contributed to the demise of stagflation.

☐ State a generalization about the inflation-unemployment tradeoff in the long run.

☐ Use short-run and long-run Phillips Curves to explain inflation.

☐ Use short-run and long-run Phillips Curves to explain disinflation.

☐ Describe supply-siders' views of the effects of taxation on incentives to work and to save and invest.

☐ Use the Laffer Curve to explain the hypothesized relationship between marginal tax rates and tax revenues.

☐ State three criticisms of the Laffer Curve.

☐ Offer a rebuttal of the criticisms and an evaluation of supply-side economics in the 1980s and 1990s.

■ CHAPTER OUTLINE

1. The aggregate supply curve has short- and long-run characteristics. The short-run curve also shifts because of a change in nominal wages. These factors make the analysis of aggregate supply and demand more complex.

  a. The *short run* is a period in which nominal wages (and other input prices) are unresponsive to changes in the price level. The *long run* is a period in which nominal wages are fully responsive to changes in the price level.

  b. The *short-run aggregate supply curve* is upward sloping: An increase in the price level increases business revenues and profits because nominal wages do not change; in contrast, when the price level decreases, business revenue and profits decline, and so does real output, but nominal wages do not change.

  c. The *long-run aggregate supply curve* is vertical at the potential level of output. Increases in the price level will increase nominal wages and cause a decrease (shift left) in the short-run aggregate supply curve, or declines in the price level will reduce nominal wages and cause an increase (shift right) in the short-run aggregate supply curve. In either case, although the price level changes, output returns to its potential level, and the long-run aggregate supply curve is vertical at the full-employment level of output.

  d. *Equilibrium* in the extended AD–AS model occurs at the price level and output where the aggregate demand curve crosses the long-run aggregate supply curve and also crosses the short-run aggregate supply curve.

2. The extended AD–AS model can be applied to explain conditions of inflation and recession in an economy.

  a. *Demand-pull inflation* will increase (shift right) the aggregate demand curve, which increases the price level and causes a temporary increase in real output. In the long run, workers will realize that their real wages have fallen and will demand an increase in their nominal wages. The short-run aggregate supply curve, which was based on fixed nominal wages, now decreases (shifts left), resulting in an even higher price level with real output returning to its initial level.

  b. *Cost-push inflation* will decrease (shift left) the short-run aggregate supply curve. This situation will increase the price level and temporarily decrease real output, causing a recession. It creates a policy dilemma for government.

  (1) If government takes actions to counter the cost-push inflation and recession by increasing aggregate demand, the price level will move to an even higher level, and the actions may set off an inflationary spiral.

  (2) If government takes no action, the recession will eventually reduce nominal wages, and eventually the short-run aggregate supply curve will shift back to its original position.

  c. If aggregate demand decreases, it will result in a *recession.* If prices and wages are flexible downward, the price level will fall and increase real wages. Eventually, nominal wages will fall to restore the original real wages. This change will increase short-run aggregate supply and end the recession, but not without a long period of high unemployment and lost output.

3. The short- and long-run relationships between inflation and unemployment are important.

  a. If aggregate supply is constant and the economy is operating in the upsloping range of aggregate supply, then the greater the rate of increase in aggregate demand, the higher the rate of inflation (and output) and the lower the rate of unemployment. This inverse relationship between the rate of inflation and unemployment is known as the *Phillips Curve.* In the 1960s, economists thought there was a predictable tradeoff between unemployment and inflation. All society had to do was to choose the combination of inflation and unemployment on the Phillips Curve.

  b. The *aggregate supply shocks* of the 1970s and early 1980s called into question the validity of the Phillips Curve. In that period, the economy experienced *stagflation*—both higher rates of inflation and unemployment. The aggregate supply shocks came from an increase in resource prices (oil), shortages in agricultural production, higher wage demands, and declining productivity. These shocks decreased the short-run aggregate supply curve, which increased the price level and decreased output (and unemployment). These shocks shifted the Phillips Curve to the right or showed there was no dependable tradeoff between inflation and unemployment.

  c. The *demise of stagflation* came in the 1982–1989 period because of such factors as a severe recession in 1981–1982 that reduced wage demands, increased foreign competition that restrained price increases, and a decline in OPEC's monopoly power. The short-run aggregate supply curve increased, and the price level and unemployment rate fell. This meant that the Phillips Curve may have shifted back (left). Recent unemployment–inflation data are now similar to the Phillips Curve of the 1960s.

4. In the *long run,* there is no apparent tradeoff between inflation and unemployment. Any rate of inflation is consistent with the natural rate of unemployment at that time. The long-run Phillips Curve is vertical at the natural rate of unemployment. In the **short run,** there can be a trade-off between inflation and unemployment.

    a. An increase in aggregate demand may temporarily reduce unemployment as the price level increases and profits expand but the actions also set other events into motion.

    (1) The increase in the price level reduces the real wages of workers who demand and obtain higher nominal wages; these actions return unemployment to its original level.

    (2) Back at the original level, there are now higher actual and expected rates of inflation for the economy, so the short-run Phillips Curve has shifted upward.

    (3) The process is repeated if aggregate demand continues to increase. The price level rises as the short-run Phillips Curve shifts upward.

    b. In the long run, the Phillips Curve is stable only as a vertical line at the natural rate of unemployment. After all adjustments in nominal wages to increases and decreases in the rate of inflation, the economy returns to its full-employment level of output and its natural rate of unemployment. There is no tradeoff between unemployment and inflation in the long run.

    c. **Disinflation**—reductions in the inflation rate from year to year—is also explained by the distinction between the short-run and long-run Phillips Curves.

5. **Supply-side economics** views aggregate supply as active rather than passive in explaining changes in the price level and unemployment.

    a. It argues that higher marginal tax rates reduce incentives to work and high taxes also reduce incentives to save and invest. These policies lead to a misallocation of resources, less productivity, and a decrease in aggregate supply. To counter these effects, supply-side economists call for a cut in marginal tax rates.

    b. The **Laffer Curve** suggests that it is possible to lower tax rates and increase tax revenues, thus avoiding a budget deficit because the policies will result in less tax evasion and avoidance.

    c. Critics of supply-side economics and the Laffer Curve suggest that the policy of cutting tax rates will not work because

    (1) It has only a small and uncertain effect on incentives to work (or on aggregate supply).

    (2) It would increase aggregate demand relative to aggregate supply and thus reinforce inflation when there is full employment.

    (3) The expected tax revenues from tax rate cuts depend on assumptions about the economy's position on the Laffer Curve. If tax cuts reduce tax revenues, it will create budget deficits.

    d. Supply-siders argue that the tax cuts under the Reagan administration in the 1980s worked as would be expected: The cut in tax rates increased tax revenue. Critics contend that the reason was that aggregate demand increased as the economy came out of recession and not that aggregate supply increased. There is now general recognition that changes in marginal tax rates change people's behavior, although there is continuing debate about the size of the effect.

■ **HINTS AND TIPS**

1. Chapter 16 is a more difficult chapter because the AD–AS model is extended to include both short-run and long-run effects. Spend extra time mastering this material, but do not try to read everything at once. Break the chapter into its logical sections, and practice drawing each graph.

2. Be sure you understand the distinction between the **short-run and long-run aggregate supply curves.** Then use these ideas to explain demand-pull inflation, cost-push inflation, and recession. Doing problem 2 will be especially helpful.

3. Be sure you understand how adverse **aggregate supply shocks** shift and create stability in the Phillips Curve.

4. Use Figure 16.9 in the text to help you understand why there is a difference in the short-run and long-run relationships between unemployment and inflation. Problem 4 will help your understanding of this complicated graph.

5. The rationales for tax cuts and tax increases have been at the forefront of fiscal policy since the 1980s. This chapter offers a detailed explanation of supply-side economics that has been used to justify the tax cut policies during the past twenty-five years. The last section of the chapter will help you understand the arguments for and against such tax policies that have real-world applications.

■ **IMPORTANT TERMS**

short run	stagflation
long run	aggregate supply shocks
short-run aggregate supply curve	disinflation
long-run aggregate supply curve	supply-side economics
Phillips Curve	Laffer Curve

                     SELF-TEST

■ **FILL-IN QUESTIONS**

1. In an AD–AS model with a stable aggregate supply curve, when the economy is producing in the upsloping portion of the aggregate supply curve, an increase in aggregate demand will (increase, decrease) _____ real output and employment, but a decrease in aggregate supply will _____ real output and employment.

2. In the short run, when the price level changes, nominal wages are (responsive, unresponsive) _____, but in the long run nominal wages are _____. In the short run, the aggregate supply curve is (upsloping, vertical) _____, but in the long run the curve is _____.

3. Demand-pull inflation occurs with a shift in the aggregate demand curve to the (right, left) _____, which will (decrease, increase) _____ the price level and temporarily _____ real output. As a consequence, the (short-run, long-run) _____ aggregate supply curve will shift left because of a rise in (real, nominal) _____ wages, producing a (lower, higher) _____ price level at the original level of real output.

4. Cost-push inflation occurs with a shift in the short-run aggregate supply curve to the (right, left) _____; thus the price level will (increase, decrease) _____ and real output will temporarily _____.

5. If government takes no actions to counter the cost-push inflation, the resulting recession will (increase, decrease) _____ nominal wages and shift the short-run aggregate supply curve back to its original position, yet if the government tries to counter the recession with a(n) _____ in aggregate demand, the price level will move even higher.

6. A recession will occur when there is (an increase, a decrease) _____ in aggregate demand. If the controversial assumption is made that prices and wages are flexible downward, then the price level (rises, falls) _____. Real wages will then (increase, decrease) _____, but eventually nominal wages will _____ and the aggregate supply curve will (increase, decrease) _____ and end the recession.

7. Along the upsloping portion of the short-run aggregate supply curve, the greater the increase in aggregate demand, the (greater, smaller) _____ the increase in the rate of inflation, the _____ the increase in real output, and the (greater, smaller) _____ the unemployment rate.

8. The original Phillips Curve indicates that there will be (a direct, an inverse) _____ relationship between the rate of inflation and the unemployment rate. This means that high rates of inflation will be associated with a (high, low) _____ unemployment rate, or that low rates of inflation will be associated with a _____ unemployment rate.

9. The policy tradeoff based on a stable Phillips Curve was that for the economy to reduce the unemployment rate, the rate of inflation must (increase, decrease) _____, and to reduce the rate of inflation, the unemployment rate must _____.

10. During the 1970s and early 1980s, aggregate (demand, supply) _____ shocks made the Phillips Curve (stable, unstable) _____. These shocks produced (demand-pull, cost-push) _____ inflation that resulted in a simultaneous increase in the inflation rate and the unemployment rate, called (disinflation, stagflation) _____.

11. Several factors contributed to stagflation's demise during the 1982–1989 period. They included
   a. the 1981–1982 (inflation, recession) _____ largely caused by (a tight, an easy) _____ money policy. There was also (increased, decreased) _____ foreign competition and the _____ monopoly power of OPEC.
   b. The effect of these factors (increased, decreased) _____ the short-run aggregate supply curve; thus the inflation rate_____ and the unemployment rate _____.

12. The standard explanation for the Phillips Curve is that during the stagflation of the 1970s, the Phillips Curve shifted (right, left) _____, and during the demise of stagflation from 1982–1989, the Phillips Curve shifted _____. In this view, there is a tradeoff between the unemployment rate and the rate of inflation, but changes in (short-run, long-run) _____ aggregate supply can shift the Phillips Curve.

13. In the long run, the tradeoff between the rate of inflation and the rate of unemployment (does, does not) _____ exist, and the economy is stable at its natural rate of (unemployment, inflation) _____.

14. The Phillips Curve may be downsloping in the (short run, long run) _____, but it is vertical in the _____ at the natural rate of unemployment. A shift in aggregate demand that reduces the unemployment rate in the short run results in the long run in (an increase, a decrease) _____ in the rate of inflation and a return to the natural rate of unemployment.

15. When the actual rate of inflation is higher than the expected rate, profits temporarily (fall, rise) _____ and the unemployment rate temporarily (rises, falls) _____. This case would occur during a period of (inflation, disinflation) _____.

16. When the actual rate of inflation is lower than the expected rate, profits temporarily (fall, rise) _____ and the unemployment rate temporarily (rises, falls)

_____. This case would occur during a period of (inflation, disinflation) _____.

17. It is the view of supply-side economists that high marginal tax rates (increase, decrease) _____ incentives to work, save, invest, and take risks. According to supply-side economists a stimulus for the economy would be a substantial (increase, decrease) _____ in marginal tax rates that would _____ economic growth through (an increase, a decrease) _____ in aggregate supply.

18. The Laffer Curve depicts the relationship between tax rates and (inflation, tax revenues) _____. It is useful for showing how a (cut, rise) _____ in marginal tax rates will increase aggregate supply.

19. In theory, the Laffer Curve shows that as the tax rates increase from 0%, tax revenues will (increase, decrease) _____ to some maximum level, after which tax revenues will _____ as the tax rates increase; or as tax rates are reduced from 100%, tax revenues will (increase, decrease) _____ to some maximum level, after which tax revenues will _____ as tax rates decrease.

20. Criticisms of the Laffer Curve are that the effects of a cut in tax rates on incentives to work, save, and invest are (large, small) _____; that the tax cuts generate an increase in aggregate (demand, supply) _____ that outweigh any increase in aggregate _____ and may lead to inflation when at full employment; and that tax cuts can produce a (gain, loss) _____ in tax revenues that will only add to a budget deficit.

■ TRUE–FALSE QUESTIONS

Circle T if the statement is true, F if it is false.

1. The short run in macroeconomics is a period in which nominal wages are fully responsive to changes in the price level. **T F**

2. The short-run aggregate supply curve has a negative slope. **T F**

3. The long-run aggregate supply curve is vertical because nominal wages eventually change by the same amount as changes in the price level. **T F**

4. Demand-pull inflation will increase the price level and real output in the short run, but in the long run, only the price level will increase. **T F**

5. Cost-push inflation results in a simultaneous increase in the price level and real output. **T F**

6. When the economy is experiencing cost-push inflation, an inflationary spiral is likely to result when the government enacts policies to maintain full employment. **T F**

7. A recession is the result of an increase in the short-run aggregate supply curve. **T F**

8. If the economy is in a recession, prices and nominal wages will presumably fall, and the short-run aggregate supply curve will increase, so that real output returns to its full-employment level. **T F**

9. The Phillips Curve shows an inverse relationship between the rate of inflation and the unemployment rate. **T F**

10. Stagflation refers to a situation in which both the price level and the unemployment rate are rising. **T F**

11. Aggregate supply shocks can cause both higher rates of inflation and higher rates of unemployment. **T F**

12. The data from the 1970s and early 1980s indicated the aggregate supply curve increased. **T F**

13. One explanation of the stagflation of the 1970s and early 1980s was an increase in aggregate demand. **T F**

14. Among the factors that contributed to the demise of stagflation during the 1980s was a recession in 1981 and 1982. **T F**

15. There is no apparent long-run tradeoff between inflation and unemployment. **T F**

16. When the actual rate of inflation is higher than the expected rate, profits temporarily fall and the unemployment rate temporarily rises. **T F**

17. The long-run Phillips Curve is essentially a vertical line at the economy's natural rate of unemployment. **T F**

18. Disinflation is the same as mismeasurement of the inflation rate. **T F**

19. When the actual rate of inflation is lower than the expected rate of inflation, profits temporarily fall and the unemployment rate temporarily rises. **T F**

20. Most economists reject the idea of a short-run trade-off between the unemployment and inflation rates but accept the long-run tradeoff. **T F**

21. Supply-side economists contend that aggregate demand is the only active factor in determining the price level and real output in an economy. **T F**

22. One proposition of supply-side economics is that the marginal tax rates on earned income should be reduced to increase the incentives to work. **T F**

23. Supply-side economists recommend a higher marginal tax rate on interest from saving because no productive work was performed to earn the interest. **T F**

24. The Laffer Curve suggests that lower tax rates will increase the rate of inflation. **T F**

25. A criticism of supply-side economics is that the incentive effects of tax cuts on working and saving are small and have little influence on aggregate supply. **T F**

■ MULTIPLE-CHOICE QUESTIONS

Circle the letter that corresponds to the best answer.

1. For macroeconomics, the short run is a period in which nominal wages
- **(a)** do not fully adjust as the price level stays constant
- **(b)** change as the price level stays constant
- **(c)** do not fully adjust as the price level changes
- **(d)** change as the price level changes

2. Once sufficient time has elapsed for wage contracts to expire and nominal wage adjustments to occur, the economy enters
- **(a)** the short run
- **(b)** the long run
- **(c)** a period of inflation
- **(d)** a period of unemployment

3. A graph of the short-run aggregate supply curve is
- **(a)** downsloping, and a graph of the long-run aggregate supply is upsloping
- **(b)** upsloping, and a graph of the long-run aggregate supply is vertical
- **(c)** upsloping, and a graph of the long-run aggregate supply is downsloping
- **(d)** vertical, and a graph of the long-run aggregate supply is upsloping

4. Assume that initially your nominal wage was $10 an hour and the price index was 100. If the price level increases to 110, then your
- **(a)** real wage has increased to $11.00
- **(b)** real wage has decreased to $9.09
- **(c)** nominal wage has increased to $11.00
- **(d)** nominal wage has decreased to $9.09

5. In the extended AD–AS model, demand-pull inflation occurs because of an increase in aggregate demand that will eventually produce
- **(a)** an increase in real wages, thus a decrease in the short-run aggregate supply curve
- **(b)** an increase in nominal wages, thus an increase in the short-run aggregate supply curve
- **(c)** a decrease in nominal wages, thus a decrease in the short-run aggregate supply curve
- **(d)** an increase in nominal wages, thus a decrease in the short-run aggregate supply curve

6. In the short run, demand-pull inflation increases real
- **(a)** output and decreases the price level
- **(b)** wages and increases nominal wages
- **(c)** output and increases the price level
- **(d)** wages and decreases nominal wages

7. In the long run, demand-pull inflation
- **(a)** decreases real wages

(b) increases the price level
(c) increases the unemployment rate
(d) decreases real output

8. A likely result of the government trying to reduce the unemployment associated with cost-push inflation through stimulative fiscal policy or monetary policy is
- **(a)** an inflationary spiral
- **(b)** stagflation
- **(c)** a recession
- **(d)** disinflation

9. What will occur in the short run if there is cost-push inflation and if the government adopts a hands-off approach to it?
- **(a)** an increase in real output
- **(b)** a fall in unemployment
- **(c)** demand-pull inflation
- **(d)** a recession

10. If prices and wages are flexible, a recession will increase real wages as the price level falls. Eventually, nominal wages will
- **(a)** fall to the previous real wages, and the short-run aggregate supply will increase
- **(b)** rise to the previous real wages, and the short-run aggregate supply will increase
- **(c)** fall to the previous real wages, and the short-run aggregate supply will decrease
- **(d)** rise to the previous real wages, and the short-run aggregate supply will decrease

11. The traditional Phillips Curve is based on the idea that with a constant short-run aggregate supply curve, the greater the increase in aggregate demand
- **(a)** the greater the unemployment rate
- **(b)** the greater the rate of inflation
- **(c)** the greater the increase in real output
- **(d)** the smaller the increase in nominal wages

12. The traditional Phillips Curve shows the
- **(a)** inverse relationship between the rate of inflation and the unemployment rate
- **(b)** inverse relationship between the nominal wage and the real wage
- **(c)** direct relationship between unemployment and demand-pull inflation
- **(d)** tradeoff between the short run and the long run

13. As the unemployment rate falls below its natural rate,
- **(a)** excessive spending produces demand-pull inflation
- **(b)** productivity rises and creates cost-push inflation
- **(c)** the expected rate of inflation equals the actual rate
- **(d)** there is an aggregate supply shock

14. Which would be a factor contributing to stagflation in the 1970s?
- **(a)** a doubling of stock prices
- **(b)** a fivefold increase in productivity
- **(c)** a quadrupling of oil prices by OPEC
- **(d)** a 10% decline in the rate of inflation

15. If there are adverse aggregate supply shocks, with aggregate demand remaining constant, then there will be
   (a) a decrease in the price level
   (b) a decrease in the unemployment rate
   (c) an increase in real output
   (d) an increase in both the price level and the unemployment rate

16. A cause of both higher rates of inflation and higher rates of unemployment would be
   (a) an increase in aggregate demand
   (b) an increase in aggregate supply
   (c) a decrease in aggregate demand
   (d) a decrease in aggregate supply

17. Which would be a factor contributing to the demise of stagflation during the 1982–1989 period?
   (a) a lessening of foreign competition
   (b) a strengthening of the monopoly power of OPEC
   (c) a recession brought on largely by a tight monetary policy
   (d) an increase in regulation of airline and trucking industries

18. The economy is stable only in the
   (a) short run at a high rate of profit
   (b) short run at the natural rate of inflation
   (c) long run at the natural rate of unemployment
   (d) long run at the natural rate of inflation

19. When the actual inflation rate is higher than expected, profits temporarily
   (a) fall and the unemployment rate temporarily falls
   (b) rise and the unemployment rate temporarily falls
   (c) rise and the unemployment rate temporarily rises
   (d) fall and the unemployment rate temporarily rises

20. When the actual rate of inflation is lower than the expected rate, profits temporarily
   (a) fall and the unemployment rate temporarily rises
   (b) rise and the unemployment rate temporarily falls
   (c) rise and the unemployment rate temporarily rises
   (d) fall and the unemployment rate temporarily falls

21. In a disinflation situation, the
   (a) actual rate of inflation is lower than the expected rate, so the unemployment rate will rise to bring the expected and actual rates into balance
   (b) expected rate of inflation is lower than the actual rate, so the unemployment rate will rise to bring the expected and actual rates into balance
   (c) actual rate of inflation is higher than the expected rate, so the unemployment rate will fall to bring the expected and actual rates into balance
   (d) expected rate of inflation is higher than the actual rate, so the unemployment rate will fall to bring the expected and actual rates into balance

22. The long-run Phillips Curve is essentially
   (a) horizontal at the natural rate of unemployment
   (b) vertical at the natural rate of unemployment
   (c) vertical at the natural rate of inflation
   (d) horizontal at the natural rate of inflation

23. Supply-side economists contend that the U.S. system of taxation reduces
   (a) unemployment but causes inflation
   (b) incentives to work, save, and invest
   (c) transfer payments to the poor
   (d) the effects of cost-push inflation

24. Based on the Laffer Curve, a cut in the tax rate from 100% to a point before the maximum level of tax revenue will
   (a) increase the price level
   (b) increase tax revenues
   (c) decrease real output
   (d) decrease the real wages

25. A criticism of tax cuts and supply-side economics made by many economists is that
   (a) the demand-side effects exceed the supply-side effects
   (b) the supply-side effects exceed the demand-side effects
   (c) the demand-side and supply-side effects offset each other
   (d) there are only supply-side effects

■ **PROBLEMS**

1. In columns 1 and 2 of the table on the next page is a portion of a short-run aggregate supply schedule. Column 3 shows the number of full-time workers (in millions) that would have to be employed to produce each of the seven real domestic outputs (in billions) in the short-run aggregate supply schedule. The labor force is 80 million workers and the full-employment output of the economy is

$_____.

   a. If the aggregate demand schedule were that shown in columns 1 and 4,

   (1) the price level would be _____ and the real output would be $_____.

   (2) the number of workers employed would be _____, the number of workers unemployed would be _____ million, and the unemployment rate would be _____%.

   b. If aggregate demand were to increase to that shown in columns 1 and 5 and short-run aggregate supply remained constant,

   (1) the price level would rise to _____ and the real output would rise to $ _____.

   (2) employment would increase by _____ million workers and the unemployment rate would fall to_____%.

   (3) the price level would increase by _____ and the rate of inflation would be _____%.

(1) Price level	(2) Real output supplied	(3) Employment (in millions)	(4) Real output demanded	(5) Real output demanded	(6) Real output demanded
130	$ 800	69	$2300	$2600	$1900
140	1300	70	2200	2500	1800
150	1700	72	2100	2400	1700
160	2000	75	2000	2300	1600
170	2200	78	1900	2200	1500
180	2300	80	1800	2100	1400
190	2300	80	1700	2000	1300

c. If aggregate demand were to decrease to that shown in columns 1 and 6 and short-run aggregate supply remained constant,

(1) the price level would fall to _____

and the real output would fall to $_____.

(2) employment would decrease by _____ compared with situation **a,** and workers and the unemployment rate would rise to _____%.

(3) the price level would decrease and the rate of inflation would be (positive, negative) _____.

2. The following is an aggregate demand and aggregate supply model. Assume that the economy is initially in equilibrium at **AD₁** and **AS₁**. The price level will be _____ and the real domestic output will be _____.

a. If there is demand-pull inflation, then
(1) in the short run, the new equilibrium is at point _____, with the price level at _____ and real output at _____;
(2) in the long run, nominal wages will rise so the aggregate supply curve will shift from _____ to

_____. The equilibrium will be at point _____ with the price level at _____ and real output at _____, so the increase in aggregate demand has only moved the economy along its _____ curve.

b. Now assume that the economy is initially in equilibrium at point **W,** where **AD₁** and **AS₁** intersect. If there is cost-push inflation, then
(1) in the short run, the new equilibrium is at point _____, with the price level at _____ and real output at _____.
(2) if the government tries to counter the cost-push inflation with expansionary monetary and fiscal policy, then aggregate demand will shift from _____ to _____, with the price level becoming _____ and real output _____, but this policy has a trap because the price level has shifted from _____ to _____ and the new level of inflation might shift _____ leftward.
(3) if government does not counter the cost-push inflation, the price level will eventually move to _____ and real output to _____ as the recession reduces nominal wages and shifts the aggregate supply curve from _____ to _____.

c. Now assume that the economy is initially in equilibrium at point **Y,** where **AD₂** and **AS₂** intersect. If there is a recession that reduces investment spending, then
(1) aggregate demand decreases and real output shifts from _____ to _____, and, assuming that prices and wages are flexible downward, the price level shifts from _____ to

_____.
(2) these events cause real wages to (rise, fall) _____, and eventually nominal wages _____ to restore the previous real wages.
(3) when this happens, the short-run aggregate supply curve shifts from _____ to _____ to its new equilibrium at point _____. The

equilibrium price level is _____ and the equi-librium level of output is _____ at the long-run aggregate supply curve _____.

3. The following is a traditional Phillips Curve.

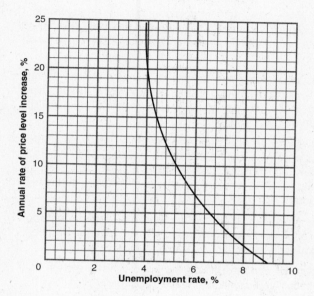

a. At full employment (a 4% unemployment rate) the price level would rise by _____% each year.

b. If the price level were stable (increasing by 0% a year), the unemployment rate would be _____%.

c. Which of the combinations along the Phillips Curve would you choose for the economy? _____ Why would you select this combination? _____

_____

4. Following is a model of short- and long-run Phillips Curves.

a. Suppose you begin at point X_1 and an assumption is made that nominal wages are set on the original expectation that a 3% rate of inflation will continue in the economy.

(1) If an increase in aggregate demand reduces the unemployment rate from 6% to 3%, then the actual rate of inflation will move to _____%. The higher product prices will lift profits of firms and they will hire more workers; thus in the short run the economy will temporarily move to point _____.

(2) If workers demand and receive higher wages to compensate for the loss of purchasing power from higher than expected inflation, then business profits will fall from previous levels and firms will reduce employment; therefore, the unemployment rate will move from point _____ to point _____ on the graph.

The short-run Phillips Curve has shifted from _____ to _____ on the graph.

(3) If aggregate demand continues to increase so that the unemployment rate drops from 6% to 3%, then prices will rise before nominal wages, and output and employment will increase, so that there will be a move from point _____ to point _____ on the graph.

(4) But when workers get nominal wage increases, profits fall, and the unemployment rate moves from point _____ at _____% to point _____ at _____%. The short-run Phillips Curve has now shifted from _____ to _____ on the graph.

(5) The long-run Phillips Curve is the line _____.

b. Suppose you begin at point X_3, where the expected and actual rate of inflation is 9% and the unemployment rate is 6%.

(1) If there should be a decline in aggregate demand because of a recession and if the actual rate of inflation should fall to 6%, well below the expected rate of 9%, then business profits will fall and the unemployment rate will decrease to 9% as shown by the movement from point X_3 to point _____.

(2) If firms and workers adjust their expectation to the 6% rate of inflation, the nominal wages will fall, profits will rise, and the economy will move from point _____ to point _____. The short-run Phillips Curve has shifted from _____ to _____.

(3) If this process is repeated, the long-run Phillips Curve will be traced as line _____.

5. The following is a Laffer Curve.

a. The point of maximum tax revenue is _____. As tax rates decrease from 100% to point **B,** tax revenues will (increase, decrease) _____. As tax rates increase from 0% to point **B,** tax revenues will _____.

b. Supply-side economists would contend that it would be beneficial for government to cut tax rates if they are (below, above) _____ point **B,** whereas critics of supply-side economics contend that it would be harmful for government to cut tax rates if they are _____ point **B.**

■ **SHORT ANSWER AND ESSAY QUESTIONS**

1. What distinguishes the short run from the long run in macroeconomics?

2. Identify the basic difference between a short-run and a long-run aggregate supply curve.

3. Explain what happens to aggregate supply when an increase in the price level results in an increase in nominal wages.

4. Explain how to find equilibrium in the extended AD–AS model.

5. Describe the process of demand-pull inflation in the short run and in the long run.

6. How does demand-pull inflation influence the aggregate supply curve?

7. Describe cost-push inflation in the extended AD–AS model.

8. What two generalizations emerge from the analysis of cost-push inflation? Describe the two scenarios that provide the basis for the generalizations.

9. Describe recession in the extended AD–AS model.

10. What is a Phillips Curve? What two rates are related?

11. Explain how a Phillips Curve with a negative slope may be derived by holding aggregate supply constant and mentally increasing aggregate demand.

12. Were the rates of inflation and of unemployment consistent with the Phillips Curve in the 1960s? What do data on these two rates suggest about the curve since then?

13. What were the aggregate supply shocks to the U.S. economy during the 1970s and early 1980s? How did these shocks affect interpretation of the Phillips Curve?

14. Describe the factors that contributed to stagflation's demise during the 1982–1989 period. What do many economists contend happened to the aggregate supply curve, unemployment, and inflation during this period?

15. How can there be a short-run tradeoff between inflation and unemployment, but no long-run tradeoff? Explain.

16. How can the Phillips Curve be used to explain both inflation and disinflation in the economy?

17. What are the characteristics of the long-run Phillips Curve? How is it related to the natural rate of unemployment?

18. Discuss why supply-side economists contend there are tax disincentives in the economy.

19. Draw and explain a Laffer Curve showing the relationship between tax rates and tax revenues.

20. Outline the three criticisms of the ideas expressed in the depiction of the Laffer Curve.

ANSWERS

Chapter 16 Extending the Analysis of Aggregate Supply

FILL-IN QUESTIONS

1. increase, decrease
2. unresponsive, responsive, upsloping, vertical
3. right, increase, increase, short-run, nominal, higher
4. left, increase, decrease
5. decrease, increase
6. a decrease, falls, increase, decrease, increase
7. greater, greater, smaller
8. an inverse, low, high
9. increase, increase
10. supply, unstable, cost-push, stagflation
11. *a.* recession, a tight, increased, decreased; *b.* increased, decreased, decreased
12. right, left, short-run
13. does not, unemployment
14. short run, long run, an increase
15. rise, falls, inflation
16. fall, rises, disinflation

17. decrease, decrease, increase, an increase
18. tax revenues, cut
19. increase, decrease, increase, decrease
20. small, demand, supply, loss

TRUE–FALSE QUESTIONS

1. F, p. 292	10. T, p. 299	19. T, p. 302
2. F, pp. 293–294	11. T, pp. 299–300	20. F, pp. 300–302
3. T, p. 294	12. F, pp. 299–300	21. F, pp. 302–303
4. T, p. 295	13. F, pp. 299–300	22. T, pp. 302–303
5. F, p. 296	14. T, p. 300	23. F, p. 303
6. T, p. 296	15. T, p. 300	24. F, p. 303
7. F, pp. 296–297	16. F, p. 301	25. T, p. 304
8. T, pp. 296–297	17. T, p. 301	
9. T, pp. 297–298	18. F, p. 302	

MULTIPLE-CHOICE QUESTIONS

1. c, p. 292	10. a, pp. 296–297	19. b, p. 301
2. b, p. 293	11. b, pp. 297–299	20. a, p. 302
3. b, pp. 293–294	12. a, pp. 297–299	21. a, p. 302
4. b, p. 293	13. a, pp. 298–299	22. b, pp. 301–302
5. d, p. 295	14. c, p. 299	23. b, pp. 302–303
6. c, p. 295	15. d, p. 299	24. b, p. 303
7. b, p. 295	16. d, pp. 299–300	25. a, p. 304
8. a, p. 296	17. c, p. 300	
9. d, p. 296	18. c, pp. 300–301	

PROBLEMS

1. 2300; *a.* (1) 160, 2000, (2) 75, 5, 6.25; *b.* (1) 170, 2200, (2) 3, 2.5, (3) 10, 6.25; *c.* (1) 150, 1700, (2) 3, 10, (3) negative
2. P_1, Q_p; *a.* (1) X, P_2, Q_2 (2) AS_1, AS_2, Y, P_3, Q_p, AS_{LR}; *b.* (1) Z, P_2, Q_1, (2) AD_1, AD_2, P_3, Q_p, P_2, P_3, AS_2, (3) P_1, Q_p, AS_2, AS_1; *c.* (1) Q_p, Q_1, P_3, P_2, (2) rise, fall, (3) AS_2, AS_1, W, P_1, Q_p, AS_{LR}
3. *a.* 20; *b.* 9
4. *a.* (1) 6, Y_1, (2) Y_1, X_2, PC_1 PC_2, (3) X_2, Y_2, (4) Y_2, 3, X_3, 6, PC_2, PC_3, (5) PC_{LR}; *b.* (1) Z_2, (2) Z_2, X_2, PC_3, PC_2, (3) PC_{LR}
5. *a.* B, increase, decrease; *b.* above, below

SHORT ANSWER AND ESSAY QUESTIONS

1. pp. 292–293	8. p. 296	15. pp. 300–301
2. pp. 293–294	9. pp. 296–297	16. pp. 300–302
3. p. 293	10. pp. 297–298	17. pp. 300–302
4. p. 294	11. pp. 297–299	18. pp. 302–303
5. p. 295	12. pp. 298–299	19. p. 303
6. p. 295	13. pp. 299–300	20. p. 304
7. p. 296	14. p. 300	

CHAPTER 17

Economic Growth

The United States has an impressive record of economic growth in the past half century. The purpose of this chapter is to explain what factors contributed to this economic growth and the implications for the economy.

The chapter begins by discussing the six main ingredients of economic growth. The four **supply factors** increase the output potential of the economy. Whether the economy actually produces its full potential—that is, whether the economy has both full employment and full production—depends upon two other factors: the level of aggregate demand (the **demand factor**) and the efficiency with which the economy allocates resources (the **efficiency factor**).

The next section of the chapter places the factors contributing to economic growth in graphical perspective with the use of two familiar **economic models.** The production possibilities model was originally presented in Chapter 2 and is now used to discuss how the two major supply factors—labor input and labor productivity—shift the production possibilities curve outward. The second model is the aggregate demand–aggregate supply model that was first explained in Chapter 11 and was discussed in more detail in Chapter 16. Here you learn how both the short-run and the long-run shifts in aggregate supply combined with shifts in aggregate demand (and the factors underlying those shifts) affect the output and the price level.

The **growth record** of the United States has been impressive both in terms of increases in real GDP and in real GDP per capita. What accounts for this long-term economic growth of the United States? First, the size of its labor force has grown. Second and more important, the productivity of the labor force in the United States has increased. The increase in the productivity of labor is the result of technological advances, the expansion of the stock of capital goods in the U.S. economy, the improved education and training of its labor force, economies of scale, the reallocation of resources, and the supportive social, cultural, and political environments.

Increases in productivity have a direct effect on real output, real income, and real wages. A major development in recent years was the doubling in the rate of labor productivity from 1995–2002 compared with that in the 1973–1995 period. This change heralded to some observers that the United States has achieved a **New Economy** that is characterized by advances in technology, more entrepreneurship, increasing returns from resource inputs, and greater global competition. The implications for macroeconomics are significant: faster growth with low inflation,

a reduction in the natural rate of unemployment, and an increase in tax revenues. Whether the economy is in fact "new" remains to be seen because the trend may simply be a short-run upturn in labor productivity and not a long-run outcome.

The last section of the chapter raises an important question: Is more economic growth **desirable and sustainable?** This controversy has two sides. The antigrowth view is based on the pollution problems it creates, its effects on human values, and doubts about whether growth can be sustained. The defense of growth is based in part on its contribution to higher standards of living, improvements in worker safety and the environment, and history of sustainability. After reading this section, you will have to evaluate the advantages and disadvantages of economic growth for the economy.

■ CHECKLIST

When you have studied this chapter you should be able to

☐ Identify four supply factors in economic growth.

☐ Explain the demand factor in economic growth.

☐ Describe the efficiency factor in economic growth.

☐ Show graphically how economic growth shifts the production possibilities curve.

☐ Explain the rationale for an equation for real GDP that is based on labor inputs and labor productivity.

☐ Show that a shift outward in the production possibilities curve is equivalent to a rightward shift in the economy's long-run aggregate supply curve.

☐ Illustrate graphically how economic growth shifts the short-run and long-run aggregate supply curves and the aggregate demand curve.

☐ Describe the average annual growth rates of real GDP and real per capita GDP in the U.S. economy since 1950.

☐ Compare the relative importance of the two major means of increasing the real GDP in the United States.

☐ List the sources of growth in the productivity of labor in the United States and state their relative importance.

☐ Describe the other factors that affect an economy's growth rate.

☐ Explain the relationship between productivity growth and the standard of living.

☐ Describe the growth of labor productivity in the United States since 1973.

☐ Identify the major characteristics of the New Economy.

☐ Discuss how the microchip and information technology have contributed to the New Economy.
☐ Describe the sources of increasing returns and economies of scale within the New Economy.
☐ Explain how the New Economy increases global competition.
☐ Describe three macroeconomic implications from the New Economy.
☐ Offer a skeptical perspective on the New Economy.
☐ Present several arguments against more economic growth.
☐ Make a case for more economic growth.

■ **CHAPTER OUTLINE**

1. The *ingredients of growth* depend on supply, demand, and efficiency factors.

a. *Supply factors* include the quantity and quality of resources (natural, human, and capital) and technology.

b. The *demand factor* influences the level of aggregate demand in the economy that is important for sustaining full employment of resources.

c. The *efficiency factor* affects the efficient use of resources to obtain maximum production of goods and services (productive efficiency) and to allocate them to their highest and best use by society (allocative efficiency).

2. Two familiar *economic models* can be used for the analysis of economic growth.

a. In the *production possibilities model,* economic growth shifts the production possibilities curve outward because of improvement in supply factors. Whether the economy operates on the frontier of the curve or inside the curve depends on the demand factor and efficiency factors.

b. Discussions of growth, however, focus primarily on supply factors. From this perspective, economic growth is obtained by increasing the *labor inputs* and by increasing the *productivity of labor.* This relationship can be expressed in equation terms: real GDP = worker-hours × labor productivity.

c. In the *aggregate demand–aggregate supply model,* economic growth is illustrated by long-run and short-run shifts.

(1) A shift outward in the production possibilities curve is equivalent to a shift rightward in the long-run aggregate supply curve for the economy. In either model, changes in the price level are not important because they do not shift either curve.

(2) The extended AD–AS model takes into account the supply, demand, and efficiency factors. Supply factors shift the long-run aggregate supply curve to the right, and supply and efficiency factors make that curve vertical at the economy's potential output. If the price level increased over time, it would indicate that the rise in potential output was accompanied by a greater shift in aggregate demand.

3. Over the past 50 years, the *rate of growth in real GDP* was about 3.5% annually. The growth rate for real per capita GDP in the United States was about 2.3% annually. These rates increased significantly from 1996–2000, declined significantly in the recession of 2001, and are now starting to return to previous levels.

4. Several factors *account for U.S. economic growth.*

a. The two main factors are increases in quantity of labor (hours of work) and increases in labor productivity. From 1990 to 2002, about two-thirds of this growth was the result of the increased *productivity of labor.* About one-third of the growth was the result of the increased *quantity of labor* employed in the economy.

b. *Technological advance* is combining given amounts of resources in new and innovative ways that result in a larger output. It involves the use of new managerial methods and business organizations that improve production. Technological advance is also embodied in new capital investment that adds to the productive capacity of the economy. It accounted for about 40% of the increase in productivity growth.

c. The *quantity of capital* has expanded with the increase in saving and investment spending in capital goods. This private investment has increased the quantity of each worker's tools, equipment, and machinery. There is also public investment in infrastructure in the United States. The increase in the quantity of capital goods explains about 30% of productivity growth.

d. Increased investment in *human capital* (the training and education of workers) has expanded the productivity of workers, and accounted for about 15% of productivity growth.

e. *Improved allocation of resources* (workers shifting to higher-productivity employment) and *economies of scale* (reductions in the per-unit cost to firms achieved from larger-sized markets) have also expanded the productivity of workers. Together, these factors contribute about 15% to explaining productivity growth.

f. Other factors that are difficult to quantify, such as the *social-cultural-political environment* of the United States, have contributed to economic growth. These factors have fostered growth of the market system under a stable political system and developed positive attitudes towards work, investing, and risk taking.

5. Increases in *productivity growth,* even small ones, can have a substantial effect on average real hourly wages and the standard of living in an economy. From 1973–1995, labor productivity grew by an average of 1.4% annually, but from 1995–2000 it grew by 3.1% annually. This increase indicates there may be a *New Economy.*

a. This New Economy has several characteristics.

(1) It is based on a dramatic rise in entrepreneurship and innovation based on the microchip and information technology.

(2) The new start-up firms often experience increasing returns, which means a firm's output increases by a larger percentage than the increase in its resource inputs. These increasing returns have been achieved by more specialized inputs, the spreading of development costs, simultaneous consumption, the effects of networks, and learning by doing.

(3) The new technology and improvements in communication have increased global competition, thus lowering production costs, restraining price increases, and stimulating innovation to remain competitive.

b. The New Economy has implications for **macroeconomics.**

(1) There can be a faster rate of economic growth with low inflation.

(2) It can lower the natural rate of unemployment.

(3) Tax revenues will increase as economic growth and productivity rise to a higher rate.

c. Questions remain about whether there is a New Economy or just a short upturn in the business cycle. Skeptics wonder whether the five-year increase in productivity growth can be sustained over a longer period of time or whether the economy will return to its long-term trend in productivity. Inflationary pressures can increase in economic boom times. More time may be needed to be sure there is a New Economy.

6. There is an ongoing debate about whether economic growth is desirable and sustainable.

a. The antigrowth view sees several problems: Growth pollutes the environment; may produce more goods and services, but does not create a better life; and doubts remain about whether growth is sustainable at the current rate of resource depletion.

b. The defense of economic growth is based on several considerations: Growth produces a higher standard of living and reduces the burden of scarcity; the technology it creates improves people's lives and can reduce pollution; and it is sustainable because market incentives encourage the use of substitute resources.

■ HINTS AND TIPS

1. Chapter 17 contains very little economics that should be new to you. Chapter 2 introduced you to the production possibilities model that is now discussed in more detail. In Chapters 11 and 16 you learned about the aggregate demand–aggregate supply models that are now used to discuss economic growth. You might review these concepts and models from previous chapters before reading this chapter.

2. Table 17.1 is important if you want to understand the factors that influence economic growth in the United States. The figures in the table indicate the relative importance of each major factor. In the past decade, about two-thirds of U.S. economic growth came from factors affecting increases in labor productivity, and about one-third came from increases in the quantity of labor. Five factors affecting the growth of labor productivity include technological advance, quantity of capital, education and training, economies of scale, and resource allocation.

3. The remaining two sections of the chapter focus on major economics issues about which there is some debate. You will want to evaluate the evidence for and against the idea that there is a "New Economy." You will also want

to understand the advantages and disadvantages of economic growth.

■ IMPORTANT TERMS

economic growth	human capital
supply factor	economies of scale
demand factor	New Economy
efficiency factor	information technology
labor productivity	start-up firm
labor-force participation rate	increasing returns
growth accounting	network effects
infrastructure	learning by doing

SELF-TEST

■ FILL-IN QUESTIONS

1. Economic growth means that real output in the economy (increases, decreases) _____ and produces a standard of living that is (higher, lower) _____ with (more, less) _____ material abundance.

2. The four supply factors in economic growth are

a. _____

b. _____

c. _____

d. _____

3. To realize its growing production potential, a nation must fully employ its expanding supplies of resources, which is the (efficiency, demand) _____ factor in economic growth, and it must also achieve productive and allocative _____, the other factor contributing to economic growth.

4. In the production possibilities model, economic growth increases primarily because of (demand, supply) _____ factors that shift the production possibilities curve to the (left, right) _____; but if there is less than full employment and production, the economy (may, may not) _____ realize its potential.

5. Real GDP of any economy in any year is equal to the quantity of labor employed (divided, multiplied) _____ by the productivity of labor. The quantity of labor is measured by the number of (businesses, hours of labor) _____. Productivity is equal to real GDP per (capita, worker-hour) _____.

6. The quantity of labor employed in the economy in any year depends on the size of the (unemployed, employed)

_____ labor force and the length of the average workweek. The size element depends on the size of the working-age population and the labor-force (unemployment, participation) _____ rate.

7. In the aggregate demand–aggregate supply framework, economic growth is illustrated by an (increase, decrease) _____ in the long-run aggregate supply curve, which is (vertical, horizontal) _____. When the price level also increases, it indicates that the aggregate demand curve has increased (more, less) _____ rapidly than the long-run aggregate supply.

8. Since 1950, real GDP in the United States increased at an annual rate of about (2.3, 3.5) _____% and real GDP per capita increased at an annual rate of about _____%. From 1996–1999, annual growth in real GDP was significantly (higher, lower) _____ than in previous periods and _____ than those in most other industrial nations. Economic growth since 2000 has been (constant, variable) _____ because of a recession and slow economic recovery.

9. The economic growth record of the United States shows that since 1990, the increase in the quantity of labor accounted for (one-third, two-thirds) _____ of economic growth and increases in labor productivity accounted for _____ of economic growth.

10. Factors contributing to labor productivity include

a. technological _____

b. increases in the quantity of _____ and in the quantity available per _____

c. the improved _____ and _____ of workers

d. economies of _____

e. the improved _____ of resources.

11. An increase in the quantity of the capital stock of a nation is the result of saving and (consumption, investment) _____. A key determinant of labor productivity is the amount of capital goods available per (consumer, worker) _____.

12. Infrastructure, such as highways and bridges, is a form of (private, public) _____ investment that complements _____ capital goods.

13. The knowledge and skills that make a productive worker are a form of (physical, human) _____ capital. This type of capital is often obtained through (consumption, education) _____.

14. Reductions in per-unit costs that result from the increase in the size of markets and firms is called (improved resource allocation, economies of scale) _____, but the movement of a worker from a job with lower productivity to one with higher productivity would be an example of _____.

15. Other factors that have led to economic growth in the United States are its social-cultural-political (parties, environment) _____ and (negative, positive) _____ attitudes toward work and risk taking that increase the supply of willing workers and innovative entrepreneurs.

16. An increase in labor productivity will (increase, decrease) _____ real output, real income, and real wages. Assuming an economy has an increase in labor productivity of 1.5%, it will take (28, 47) _____ years for its standard of living to double, but an increase in labor productivity of 2.5% annually will increase its standard of living in _____ years.

17. The characteristics of the New Economy are (advances, declines) _____ in information technology, business firms that experience returns to scale that are (decreasing, increasing) _____, and global competition that is _____.

18. Some implications for macroeconomics in the New Economy include a growth rate that is (faster, slower) _____ with low inflation, a natural rate of unemployment that is (higher, lower) _____, and tax revenues that are _____ because of personal income that is _____.

19. Skeptics of the New Economy argue that the rapid increase in the rate of productivity growth may be a (short-run, long-run) _____ trend that is not sustainable over a _____ period.

20. Critics of economic growth contend that it (cleans up, pollutes) _____ the environment, it (does, does not) _____ solve problems such as poverty and homelessness, and (is, is not) _____ sustainable. Defenders of economic growth say that it creates (less, greater) _____ material abundance, results in a (higher, lower) _____ standard of living, and an efficient and sustainable allocation of resources based on price (discounts, incentives) _____.

■ TRUE–FALSE QUESTIONS

Circle T if the statement is true, F if it is false.

1. Economic growth is measured as either an increase in real GDP or an increase in real per capita GDP. **T F**

2. Changes in the physical and technical agents of production are supply factors for economic growth that enable an economy to expand its potential GDP. **T F**

3. The demand factor in economic growth refers to the ability of the economy to expand its production as the demand for products grows. **T F**

4. An increase in the quantity and quality of natural resources is an efficiency factor for economic growth. **T F**

5. A shift outward in the production possibilities curve is the direct result of improvements in supply factors for economic growth. **T F**

6. The potential output of an economy will not be completely realized unless there is full employment of resources and their efficient use. **T F**

7. The real GDP of an economy in any year is equal to its input of labor divided by the productivity of labor. **T F**

8. The hours of labor input depend on the size of the employed labor force and the length of the average workweek. **T F**

9. One determinant of labor productivity is the quantity of capital goods available to workers. **T F**

10. Supply factors that shift the economy's production possibilities curve outward also cause a leftward shift in its long-run aggregate supply curve. **T F**

11. An increase in economic growth will increase the long-run aggregate supply curve and the short-run aggregate supply curve, but will decrease the aggregate demand curve. **T F**

12. Since 1950, the U.S. data show that the average annual rate of growth was greater for real GDP per capita than for real GDP. **T F**

13. Increased labor productivity has been more important than increased labor inputs in the growth of the U.S. economy since 1990. **T F**

14. The largest factor increasing labor productivity in the U.S. economy has been technological advance. **T F**

15. Public investment in the form of new infrastructure often complements private capital investment. **T F**

16. Education and training contribute to a worker's stock of human capital. **T F**

17. Economies of scale are reductions in per-unit cost that result in a decrease in the size of markets and firms. **T F**

18. The social, cultural, and political environment in the United States has fostered economic growth. **T F**

19. If the rate of growth in labor productivity averages 2.5% a year, it will take about 50 years for the standard of living to double. **T F**

20. The idea of a New Economy is based largely on a slower rate of productivity growth and therefore slower economic growth. **T F**

21. Productivity growth is the basic source of improvements in real wage rates and the standard of living. **T F**

22. More specialized inputs and network effects are two sources of increasing returns and economies of scale in the New Economy. **T F**

23. From a macroeconomic perspective, a New Economy is likely to experience a lower natural rate of unemployment. **T F**

24. Critics of economic growth say that it adds to environmental problems, increases human stress, and exhausts natural resources. **T F**

25. Defenders of economic growth say it is sustainable in the short run, but not in the long run. **T F**

■ MULTIPLE-CHOICE QUESTIONS

Circle the letter that corresponds to the best answer.

1. What is one major measure of economic growth?
 (a) the supply of money
 (b) the demand for money
 (c) nominal GDP per capita
 (d) real GDP per capita

2. A supply factor in economic growth would be
 (a) an increase in the efficient use of resources
 (b) a decline in the rate of resource depletion
 (c) an improvement in the quality of labor
 (d) an increase in consumption spending

3. Which is a demand factor in economic growth?
 (a) an increase in the purchasing power of the economy
 (b) an increase in the economy's stock of capital goods
 (c) more natural resources
 (d) technological progress

Use the following graph to answer Questions 4 and 5.

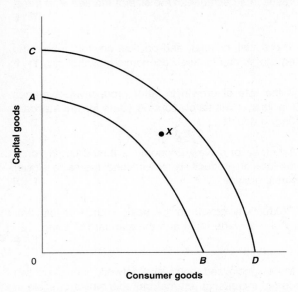

Use the following graph to answer Questions 9 and 10.

4. If the production possibilities curve of an economy shifts from **AB** to **CD**, it is most likely the result of what factor affecting economic growth?
(a) a supply factor
(b) a demand factor
(c) an efficiency factor
(d) an allocation factor

5. If the production possibilities curve for an economy is at **CD** but the economy is operating at point **X**, the reasons are most likely to be because of
(a) supply and environmental factors
(b) demand and efficiency factors
(c) labor inputs and labor productivity
(d) technological progress

6. Total output or real GDP in any year is equal to
(a) labor inputs divided by resource outputs
(b) labor productivity multiplied by real output
(c) worker-hours multiplied by labor productivity
(d) worker-hours divided by labor productivity

7. Assume that an economy has 1000 workers, each working 2000 hours per year. If the average real output per worker-hour is $9, then total output or real GDP will be
(a) $2 million
(b) $9 million
(c) $18 million
(d) $24 million

8. A shift outward of the production possibilities curve would be equivalent to a shift
(a) upward in aggregate demand
(b) downward in aggregate demand
(c) rightward in long-run aggregate supply
(d) leftward in long-run aggregate supply

9. A shift from Q_1 to Q_2 is caused by a shift in the
(a) level of prices
(b) aggregate demand curve
(c) short-run aggregate supply curve
(d) long-run aggregate supply curve

10. Which combination would best explain a shift in the price level from P_1 to P_2 and an increase in real domestic output from Q_1 to Q_2?
(a) an increase in the long-run aggregate supply (AS_1 to AS_2) and in short-run aggregate supply (AD_1 to AD_2).
(b) an increase in aggregate demand (AD_1 to AD_2) and a decrease in long-run aggregate supply (AS_2 to AS_1).
(c) an increase in the long-run aggregate supply (AS_1 to AS_2), an increase in aggregate demand (AD_1 to AD_2), and an increase in short-run aggregate supply (AS_1' to AS_2').
(d) a decrease in the long-run aggregate supply (AS_2 to AS_1), a decrease in aggregate demand (AD_2 to AD_1), and a decrease in short-run aggregate supply (AS_2' to AS_1').

11. The average annual rate of increase in real GDP since 1950 has been about
(a) 1.7%
(b) 2.3%
(c) 3.5%
(d) 4.5%

12. Real GDP per capita in the United States since 1950 grew by an average annual rate of about
(a) 1.1%
(b) 2.3%
(c) 3.5%
(d) 4.5%

13. What is the other major factor that, when combined with the growth of labor productivity, accounts for long-term economic growth in the United States?
(a) an increase in government spending
(b) an increase in the quantity of labor

(c) a decrease in the interest rate

(d) a decrease in personal taxes

14. The factor accounting for the largest increase in the productivity of labor in the United States has been

(a) economies of scale

(b) technological advance

(c) the quantity of capital

(d) the education and training of workers

15. How does a nation typically acquire more capital goods?

(a) by reducing the workweek and increasing leisure

(b) by saving income and using it for capital investment

(c) by increasing government regulation on the capital stock

(d) by reducing the amount of capital goods available per worker

16. An example of U.S. public investment in infrastructure would be

(a) an airline company

(b) a natural gas pipeline

(c) an auto and truck plant

(d) an interstate highway

17. Economists call the knowledge and skills that make a productive worker

(a) the labor-force participation rate

(b) learning by doing

(c) human capital

(d) infrastructure

18. What economic concept would be most closely associated with a situation where a large manufacturer of food products uses extensive assembly lines with computerization and robotics that serve to reduce per-unit costs of production?

(a) economies of scale

(b) sustainability of growth

(c) network effects

(d) simultaneous consumption

19. The decline of discrimination in education and labor markets increased the overall rate of labor productivity in the economy by giving groups freedom to move from jobs with lower productivity to ones with higher productivity. This development would be an example of a(n)

(a) fall in the labor-force participation rate

(b) rise in the natural rate of unemployment

(c) technological advance

(d) improvement in resource allocation

20. If the annual growth in a nation's productivity is 2% rather than 1%, then the nation's standard of living will double in

(a) 25 years

(b) 35 years

(c) 50 years

(d) 70 years

21. The New Economy is described as one with

(a) more tax revenues and more government spending

(b) a faster rate of inflation and fewer specialized inputs

(c) more experienced workers, but fewer available jobs for them

(d) a faster rate of productivity growth and faster economic growth

22. Increasing returns would be a situation where a firm

(a) triples its workforce and other inputs and its output doubles

(b) doubles its workforce and other inputs and its output triples

(c) doubles its workforce and other inputs and its output doubles

(d) quadruples its workforce and other inputs and its output triples

23. Which would be a source of increasing returns and economies of scale within the New Economy?

(a) social environment

(b) noninflationary growth

(c) simultaneous consumption

(d) less specialized inputs

24. A skeptic of the New Economy would argue that it

(a) is based on learning by doing instead of infrastructure

(b) raises tax revenues collected by government

(c) lowers the natural rate of unemployment

(d) is based on a short-run trend

25. Defenders of rapid economic growth say that it

(a) produces an equitable distribution of income

(b) creates common property resources

(c) leads to higher living standards

(d) spreads costs of development

■ **PROBLEMS**

1. The table below shows the quantity of labor (measured in hours) and the productivity of labor (measured in real GDP per hour) in a hypothetical economy in three different years.

Year	Quantity of labor	Productivity of labor	Real GDP
1	1000	$100	$ _____
2	1000	105	_____
3	1100	105	_____

a. Compute the economy's real GDP in each of the three years and enter them in the table.

b. Between years 1 and 2, the quantity of labor remained constant, but

(1) the productivity of labor increased by _____%, and

(2) as a consequence, real GDP increased by _____%.

c. Between years 2 and 3, the productivity of labor remained constant, but

(1) the quantity of labor increased by _____%, and

(2) as a consequence, real GDP increased by

_____%.

d. Between years 1 and 3

(1) real GDP increased by _____%, and

(2) this rate of increase is approximately equal to the sum of the rates of increase in the _____ and the _____ of labor.

2. In the table below, indicate how many years it will take to double the standard of living (Years) in an economy given different annual rates of growth in labor productivity.

Productivity	Years
1.0%	_____
1.4	_____
1.8	_____
2.2	_____
2.6	_____
3.0	_____

What can you conclude about the importance of small changes in the growth rate of productivity on the standard of living?

3. In the first graph below, show an increase in economic growth using a hypothetical production possibilities curve. In the second graph in the next column, show what that increase would mean in terms of the extended aggregate demand and aggregate supply models.

0

0

■ **SHORT ANSWER AND ESSAY QUESTIONS**

1. What is economic growth and how is it measured?

2. What are the six basic ingredients of economic growth? What are the essential differences between the supply, demand, and efficiency factors?

3. How does economic growth affect production possibilities? What demand and efficiency assumptions are necessary to achieve maximum productive potential?

4. What is the relationship between the real GDP produced in any year and the quantity of labor employed and labor productivity?

5. What determines the number of hours worked each year?

6. Identify and describe the factors that determine labor productivity.

7. Describe how economic growth can be illustrated in an aggregate demand–aggregate supply framework. What has happened to aggregate demand compared to long-run aggregate supply when the price level and real domestic output both increase?

8. What has been the growth record of the U.S. economy over the past half-century?

9. What have been the sources of the growth of the real output in the United States?

10. What changes have occurred in the size of the U.S. population and labor force since 1960? What factor has slowed the rate of growth of the former, and what factor has speeded the growth of the latter?

11. What is technological advance, and why are technological advance and capital formation closely related processes?

12. What is the relationship between investment and the stock of capital? What is the connection between increases in the capital stock and the rate of economic growth?

13. What increases the "quality" or human capital of labor? How is this quality usually measured? What are some of the problems with this path to improving the quality of the labor force?

14. Explain the relationship between productivity growth and the New Economy.

15. Discuss how the microchip and information technology contributed to the New Economy.

16. Describe at least four sources of increasing returns and economies of scale within the New Economy.

17. Identify and explain three macroeconomic implications from the New Economy.

18. Is the New Economy too good to be true? Present the skeptic's case.

19. What arguments are made against economic growth in the United States?

20. How can economic growth be defended? What are the reasons given to support this type of growth?

ANSWERS

Chapter 17 Economic Growth

FILL-IN QUESTIONS

1. increases, higher, more
2. *a.* quantity and quality of natural resources; *b.* quantity and quality of human resources; *c.* the supply or stock of capital goods; *d.* technology (any order for *a–d*)
3. demand, efficiency
4. supply, right, may not
5. multiplied, hours of labor, worker-hour
6. employed, participation
7. increase, vertical, more
8. 3.5, 2.3, higher, higher, variable
9. one-third, two-thirds
10. *a.* advance; *b.* capital, worker; *c.* education, training (either order); *d.* scale; *e.* allocation
11. investment, worker
12. public, private
13. human, education
14. economies of scale, improved resource allocation
15. environment, positive
16. increase, 47, 28

17. advances, increasing, increasing
18. faster, lower, higher, higher
19. short-run, long-run
20. pollutes, does not, is not, greater, higher, incentives

TRUE–FALSE QUESTIONS

1. T, p. 308	10. F, pp. 310–311	19. F, p. 317
2. T, p. 308	11. F, pp. 310–312	20. F, p. 317
3. F, pp. 308–309	12. F, p. 312	21. T, p. 317
4. F, p. 309	13. T, p. 313	22. T, pp. 317–318
5. T, pp. 309–310	14. T, pp. 313–314	23. T, p. 319
6. T, p. 309	15. T, p. 314	24. T, pp. 320–321
7. F, p. 310	16. T, pp. 314–315	25. F, p. 321
8. T, p. 310	17. F, p. 315	
9. T, p. 310	18. T, p. 316	

MULTIPLE-CHOICE QUESTIONS

1. d, p. 308	10. c, pp. 310–312	19. d, p. 316
2. c, p. 308	11. c, p. 312	20. b, p. 317
3. a, pp. 308–309	12. b, p. 312	21. d, p. 317
4. a, p. 309	13. b, p. 313	22. b, pp. 317–318
5. b, p. 309	14. b, p. 313	23. c, pp. 317–318
6. c, p. 310	15. b, p. 314	24. d, p. 319
7. c, p. 310	16. d, p. 314	25. c, p. 321
8. c, pp. 310–311	17. c, pp. 314–315	
9. d, pp. 310–312	18. a, p. 315	

PROBLEMS

1. *a.* 100,000, 105,000, 115,500; *b.* (1) 5, (2) 5; *c.* (1) 10, (2) 10; *d.* (1) 15.5, (2) quantity, productivity
2. 70, 50, 39, 31, 27, 23. Small changes make a large difference in the number of years it takes for the standard of living to double in an economy, especially at very low rates of growth in productivity.
3. See Figure 17.3 and Figure 17.4 in the text.

SHORT ANSWER AND ESSAY QUESTIONS

1. p. 308	8. p. 312	15. p. 317
2. pp. 308–309	9. pp. 312–313	16. pp. 317–318
3. pp. 309–310	10. p. 313	17. p. 319
4. p. 310	11. pp. 313–314	18. pp. 319–320
5. p. 310	12. p. 314	19. pp. 320–321
6. p. 310	13. pp. 314–315	20. p. 321
7. pp. 310–312	14. pp. 316–317	

Deficits, Surpluses, and the Public Debt

Over the years the United States accumulated a public debt that now totals about $6.2 trillion. This debt increased because of annual budget deficits. In recent years, these budget deficits were replaced by budget surpluses. Now budget deficits have returned. This chapter looks at the data and issues affecting these three fiscal concepts and explains their significance for the U.S. economy.

The Federal government can operate with a budget deficit, a budget surplus, or a balanced budget during a year. Any budget surplus or deficit affects the size of the *public debt* (often called the national debt). *Budget deficits* increase the public debt and *budget surpluses* decrease it. After defining these basic terms, the chapter discusses three budget philosophies. Be aware that the budget philosophy the Federal government adopts has a significant effect on the level of the public debt, and also on output, employment, and the price level in the economy.

Three major factors—wars, recessions, and lack of fiscal discipline—have contributed to increases in the public debt since 1940. The size of the public debt is placed into perspective by: (1) comparing it (and interest payments on the debt) to the size of the economy (GDP); (2) looking at the sizes of the public debt in other industrial nations; (3) describing who owns the debt; and (4) explaining how Social Security affects its calculation.

The two middle sections of the chapter examine the economic implications or *consequences of the public debt.* These economic problems do not include bankrupting the Federal government because the government can meet its obligations by refinancing and taxation. Nor does the public debt simply shift the economic burden to future generations because the public debt is a public credit for the many people who hold that debt in the form of U.S. securities. Rather, the public debt and payment of interest on the debt contribute to important problems: increased inequality in income, reduced incentives for work and production, decreased standard of living when part of the debt is paid to foreigners, and less capital investment.

The crowding out of investment in plant and equipment in the United States is probably the most serious of the problems. You should understand how crowding out works and how it may impose a burden on future generations by reducing the growth of the nation's capital stock. Whether it does impose a burden on future generations depends on the uses of government spending. If it is used for public investment that increases the future productive capacity of the economy and complements private in-

vestment spending, then this government spending can reduce the net burden on future generations.

The final section of the chapter discusses the recent historical record of budget deficits and surpluses in the United States. As the economy moved from deficits at the beginning of the 1990s to surpluses at the end of the 1990s, the public debate focused on what to do with these *budget surpluses.* The merits and drawbacks of three options were considered—paying down the public debt, cutting taxes, and increasing government spending for various programs. Now the focus has shifted back to budget deficits. As you will learn, they returned because of an economic downturn, a stock market decline, tax cuts without offsetting cuts in government spending, and increased government spending for the war on terrorism.

■ **CHECKLIST**

When you have studied this chapter you should be able to

☐ Define a budget deficit, budget surplus, and the public debt.

☐ Explain how budget deficits, budget surpluses, and the public debt are related.

☐ Describe three major philosophies about the budget.

☐ Explain how an annually balanced budget works and what its economic effects would be.

☐ State the rationale for a cyclically balanced budget.

☐ Explain how functional finance operates as a budget philosophy.

☐ Identify the three principal causes of the public debt and discuss their relative importance.

☐ Describe the quantitative aspects of the public debt and interest payments since 1940.

☐ Compare the relative size of the public debt of the United States to those of other industrial nations.

☐ State who owns the public debt.

☐ Explain how Social Security affects the size of the federal budget.

☐ Give two reasons why a large public debt will not bankrupt the government.

☐ Discuss whether the public debt imposes a burden on future generations.

☐ List four substantive issues related to the public debt.

☐ State the effect of the public debt on income distribution.

☐ Explain how the public debt affects incentives.

☐ Compare the effects of ownership of the debt by whether it is owned by U.S. or foreign citizens or institutions.

☐ Describe the crowding-out effect from a public debt.

☐ Give two qualifications to the argument for a crowding-out effect.

☐ Describe the transition from budget deficits to budget surpluses to budget deficits since 1990.

☐ Evaluate three policy options for the use of budget surpluses.

☐ Discuss the legislative actions and national events that contributed to a return to budget deficits in recent years.

■ **CHAPTER OUTLINE**

1. A **budget deficit** of the Federal government is the amount by which its expenditures are greater than its revenues in a given year. A **budget surplus** is just the opposite: the amount by which government revenues are greater than government expenditures in a given year. The **public debt** at any time is the sum of the Federal government's previous annual deficits, minus any annual surpluses.

2. If the Federal government uses fiscal policy to combat recession and inflation, its budget is not likely to be balanced in any particular year. The government may adopt one of three **budget philosophies.** Any of these philosophies will affect employment, real output, and the price level of the economy.

   a. Proponents of an **annually balanced budget** would have government expenditures and tax revenues equal in every year. Such a budget is pro- rather than countercyclical; but conservative economists favor it to prevent the expansion of the public sector (and the contraction of the private sector) of the economy without the increased payment of taxes by the public.

   b. Those who advocate a **cyclically balanced budget** propose matching surpluses (in years of prosperity) with deficits (in depression years) to stabilize the economy, but there is no assurance that the surpluses will equal the deficits over the years.

   c. Advocates of **functional finance** contend that deficits, surpluses, and the size of the debt are of minor importance and that the goal of full employment without inflation should be achieved regardless of the effects of the necessary fiscal policies on the budget and the size of the public debt.

3. Any government deficit increases the size of the public debt. The public debt has grown substantially since 1940.

   a. There are three basic **causes of the debt:**

   (1) *Wars* require increased Federal borrowing to finance the war effort.

   (2) *Recessions* result in budget deficits because of the built-in stability of the economy (tax revenues fall and domestic spending rises).

   (3) *Lack of fiscal discipline*, such as a cut in tax rates without offsetting reductions in expenditures or a lack of control over increased government spending, will contribute to budget deficits.

   b. The public debt in 2002 was about $6.2 trillion, an increase of $5.3 trillion from 1980.

   (1) The size of the debt as a percentage of the economy's GDP was much less in 2002 than in 1950 even though the absolute size of the debt rose substantially over that period.

   (2) Many industrial nations have public debts as a percentage of GDP that are similar to or greater than that of the United States.

   (3) Since the 1970s the interest payments on the debt rose significantly because of increases in the size of the debt and higher interest rates. Interest payments as a percentage of the economy's GDP also grew dramatically. This latter percentage reflects the level of taxation required to pay interest on the public debt. It is now about 1.6% of GDP.

   (4) About four-tenths (43%) of the public debt is owed to government agencies and the Federal Reserve Banks. About six-tenths (57%) is owed to others, including 18% owed to foreign citizens, firms, and governments.

   (5) The **Social Security trust fund** currently generates more revenue than expenditures for the federal government. This situation decreases budget deficits and increases budget surpluses.

4. The **false contentions** about a large debt are that it will eventually bankrupt the government and that borrowing to finance expenditures passes the cost on to future generations.

   a. The debt **cannot bankrupt** the government because the government

   (1) need not reduce the debt and can refinance it, and

   (2) has the constitutional authority to levy taxes to pay the debt.

   b. The burden of the debt **cannot be shifted to future generations** because U.S. citizens and institutions hold most of the debt. Repayment of any portion of the principal and the payment of interest on it does not reduce the wealth or purchasing power in the United States because it would be paid to U.S. citizens and institutions.

5. The public debt does create real and potential problems in the economy.

   a. The payment of interest on the debt probably increases the extent of **income inequality.**

   b. The payment of taxes to finance these interest payments may **reduce incentives** to bear risks, to innovate, to invest, and to save, and therefore slow economic growth in the economy.

   c. The portion of the debt that is externally held (by foreign citizens and institutions) requires the repayment of principal and the payment of interest to foreign citizens and institutions. This repayment would **transfer to foreigners** a part of the real output of the U.S. economy.

   d. An increase in government spending may impose a burden on future generations by **crowding out** private investment spending, and thus reducing the future stock of capital goods.

(1) If government spending is financed by increased public debt, the increased borrowing of the Federal government will raise interest rates and reduce private investment spending. Future generations will inherit a smaller stock of capital goods.

(2) The burden imposed on future generations is lessened if the increase in government expenditures is for worthwhile public investment that increases the production capacity of the economy. This public investment can also complement and stimulate private investment spending that increases the future capital stock.

6. The growth or shrinkage in the public debt will depend on the size of budget deficits and budget surpluses in future years.

a. In the 1990s, Federal budget deficits were the focus of fiscal policy because of the large size of these deficits early in the decade. In 1993, the Deficit Reduction Act increased individual and corporate tax rates (and gasoline excise taxes) to increase government revenues, and it required that government spending be held to its 1993 nominal level. Strong economic growth later in the decade also increased tax revenues. By 2000, there were growing surpluses in the Federal budget, a remarkable turnaround.

b. In the early 2000s, debate over the Federal budget turned to what to do with the annual **surpluses.** Three basic options were discussed.

(1) The Federal government could use the surpluses to **reduce the public debt.** The advantage of this option was that it would reduce public borrowing from credit markets and thus lower interest rates. In turn, the lower rates would stimulate more private investment spending, adding to the capital stock and contributing to economic growth (a reverse crowding-out effect). The annual interest saving could also be used to bolster the Social Security trust fund.

(2) **Tax cuts** could be used to reduce budget surpluses. This option returns money to taxpayers who were responsible for creating the surpluses. Tax cuts also help maintain consumer spending and saving for the economy, which can be especially important in times of recession or slow economic growth.

(3) Surpluses could pay for **new government spending** on desired programs in such areas as health care, education, or national defense.

c. In 2002, the budget moved from surplus to deficit because of legislative actions and unexpected events that reduced tax revenues and increased government spending.

(1) In 2001, the Economic Growth and Tax Relief Reconciliation Act that cut marginal tax rates was passed.

(2) A recession in 2001 and the stock market decline in 2002 reduced tax revenues as incomes fell and increased government spending.

(3) The terrorist attacks of September 11, 2001, increased government spending for homeland security and national defense to conduct a war on terror.

(4) More tax cuts were passed in 2003 to help stimulate the sluggish economy.

■ HINTS AND TIPS

1. Make sure you know the difference between the **public debt** and the **budget deficit.** These two negative fiscal terms are often confused.

2. The best way to gauge the public debt and budget deficit is to calculate each one as a **percentage of real GDP.** The absolute size of the public debt or the budget deficit is *not* a good indicator of whether it causes problems for the economy.

3. Try to understand the real rather than the imagined problems caused by the public debt. The debt will not cause the country to go bankrupt, nor will it be a burden on future generations. Carefully read the sections on the false issues and the real issues.

■ IMPORTANT TERMS

public debt	functional finance
U.S. securities	Social Security trust fund
annually balanced budget	external public debt
cyclically balanced budget	public investments

■ FILL-IN QUESTIONS

1. If the Federal government has a budget deficit in any year, then its expenditures are (less, greater) _____ than its revenues, but if it has a budget surplus, then its expenditures are _____ than its revenues in that year.

2. The public debt is equal to the sum of the Federal government's past budget (deficits, surpluses) _____ minus its budget _____.

3. An annually balanced budget is (pro-, counter-) _____ cyclical because governments would have to (raise, lower) _____ taxes and _____ their purchases of goods and services during a recession.

4. A cyclically balanced budget designed to ensure full employment without inflation would mean that during recession, government would incur (deficits, surpluses) _____, and during periods of strong economic growth it would incur _____, with the deficits and surpluses offsetting each other over the business cycle.

5. The budget philosophy that has as its main goal the achievement of full employment without inflation is (external debt, functional finance) _____. It regards budget deficits and increases in the public debt as of (primary, secondary) _____ importance.

6. The principal causes of the public debt are the expense of paying for (wars, inflation) _____, changes in the economy such as (a recession, an expansion) _____, and tax rate (cuts, increases) _____ without offsetting reductions in government expenditures.

7. There are several quantitative aspects to the public debt.

    a. The most meaningful way to measure the public debt is relative to (interest rates, GDP)_____, and in 2002 it was (21, 59) _____ % of this figure.

    b. In 2002 the public debt as a percentage of GDP was (higher, lower) _____ in Japan and Italy and _____ in Finland and Australia.

    c. Of the public debt, Federal government agencies and the Federal Reserve hold about (43, 57) _____%, and commercial banks, financial institutions, state and local governments, and individuals and institutions here and abroad hold about _____ %.

    d. Most of the public debt is (internal, external) _____ because foreigners hold only about (9, 18) _____% of the public debt.

8. In the Social Security trust fund, current tax revenues are (greater, less) _____ than benefit payouts to retirees. This trust fund, therefore, creates a (deficit, surplus) _____ that (adds to, subtracts from) _____ the size of a Federal budget surplus.

9. The possibility that the Federal government will go bankrupt is a false issue. It does not need to reduce its debt; it can retire maturing U.S. securities by (taxing, refinancing) _____ them. The government can also pay its debts by increasing (interest, tax) _____ rates.

10. If the public debt is held domestically, then for U.S. taxpayers it is (a liability, an asset) _____ and for U.S. citizens and institutions owning the U.S. debt securities, it is _____.

11. The public debt and the payment of interest on it may (increase, decrease) _____ income inequality in the economy and _____ the incentives to work, take risks, save, and invest in the economy.

12. The public debt is a burden on an economy if it is held by (foreigners, U.S. citizens) _____.

13. A public debt imposes a burden on future generations if the borrowing done to finance an increase in government expenditures results in (an increase, a decrease) _____ in interest rates, _____ in investment spending, and _____ in the stock of capital goods for future generations.

14. The size of the burden from the crowding out of private investment is lessened if government expenditures are used to finance worthwhile (increases, decreases) _____ in physical and human capital that contribute to the productive capacity of the economy, or if they (encourage, discourage) _____ more private investment that complements the public investment.

15. In the 1990s, Federal budget deficits and the growing public debt were the main focus of (monetary, fiscal) _____ policy. To reduce these deficits, in 1993 personal and corporate tax rates were (increased, decreased) _____ and future government spending was _____ by limiting it to the level of 1993 nominal spending. The robust economic growth later in the decade (increased, decreased) _____ tax revenues and helped create a budget (surplus, deficit) _____ for the first time since 1969.

16. One proposed option for the use of the budget surpluses was to (increase, decrease) _____ the public debt, which would _____ interest rates and _____ private investment spending. The economic benefit of this type of policy is that there would be a (direct, reverse) _____ crowding-out effect.

17. A second option for the use of budget surpluses was for tax rates to be (raised, lowered) _____ so that money could be returned to the public and improve incomes in the event of a recession.

18. Arguments were also made to use the budget surpluses for new programs that would (increase, decrease) _____ government spending. This spending would be used for education, health care, and infrastructure projects that would (help, hurt) _____ society and (weaken, strengthen) _____ the economy over the long term.

19. In 2002, the budget moved from (deficit, surplus) _____ to _____. A factor contributing to this development was cuts in (spending, taxes) _____ in 2001, and in 2003 there were additional cuts in _____.

20. An economic downturn in 2001 and a stock market decline in 2002 contributed to the return of budget (surpluses, deficits) _____. As a result of these events tax revenues (increased, decreased) _____, and government spending _____ to counter the downturn. Also, the costs of more homeland security and the financing of a war on terrorism led to (increased, decreased) _____ government spending.

■ TRUE–FALSE QUESTIONS

Circle T if the statement is true, F if it is false.

1. If there is a Federal budget surplus, then government revenues are less than its expenditures. **T F**

2. The public debt is the total accumulation of the deficits, minus any surpluses, that the Federal government has incurred over time. **T F**

3. An annually balanced budget is economically neutral in its effects on the economy. **T F**

4. A cyclically balanced budget is pro-cyclical, not countercyclical. **T F**

5. Proponents of functional finance argue that a balanced budget, whether it is balanced annually or over the business cycle, is of minor importance when compared with the objective of full employment without inflation. **T F**

6. A major reason for the increase in the public debt since 1940 was the government spending associated with financing wartime expenditures. **T F**

7. When national income declines during a recession, tax revenues automatically increase and increase the public debt. **T F**

8. An example of lack of fiscal discipline contributing to the public debt would be tax cuts without offsetting cuts in government spending. **T F**

9. The public debt as a percentage of GDP is higher in the United States than in most other industrial nations. **T F**

10. Interest payments as a percentage of GDP reflect the level of taxation (average tax rate) required to service the public debt. **T F**

11. Most of the public debt is held by Federal government agencies and the Federal Reserve. **T F**

12. In the Federal budget, surpluses obtained from Social Security are treated as an offset to current government spending. **T F**

13. A large public debt will bankrupt the Federal government because it can refinance the debt or increase taxes to pay it. **T F**

14. The public debt is also a public credit. **T F**

15. The payment of interest on the public debt probably increases income inequality. **T F**

16. The additional taxes needed to pay the interest on the public debt increase incentives to work, save, invest, and bear risks. **T F**

17. Selling U.S. securities to foreigners to finance increased expenditures by the Federal government imposes a burden on future generations. **T F**

18. Citizens and institutions of foreign countries hold about 90 percent of the U.S. public debt. **T F**

19. The crowding-out effect is caused by a rise in interest rates resulting from an increase in government borrowing to finance government expenditures. **T F**

20. The crowding-out effect increases the investment-demand curve and investment in private capital goods. **T F**

21. If government spending is for public investments that increase the capital stock, then this spending can increase the future production capacity of the economy. **T F**

22. At the beginning of the 1990s there were budget surpluses, but by the end of the decade there were budget deficits. **T F**

23. Advocates for using budget surpluses to pay down the debt say these actions will reduce interest rates, increase private investment, and thus eventually increase economic growth. **T F**

24. Those individuals who argue for a cut in tax rates as the best use of the budget surpluses justify this option in part based on its beneficial effect on household incomes and consumption in the economy. **T F**

25. The factors contributing to a return to annual budget deficits in 2002 include increases in marginal tax rates and reduction in government spending. **T F**

■ MULTIPLE-CHOICE QUESTIONS

Circle the letter that corresponds to the best answer.

1. The public debt is the sum of all previous
(a) expenditures of the Federal government
(b) budget deficits of the Federal government
(c) budget deficits minus any budget surpluses of the Federal government
(d) budget surpluses less the current budget deficit of the Federal government

2. If there is a budget surplus in a given year, it means that
(a) government expenditures are greater than revenues
(b) government revenues are greater than expenditures
(c) the size of the public debt is increasing
(d) the economy is experiencing a recession

3. Which would involve reducing government expenditures and increasing tax rates during a recession?
(a) functional finance
(b) a cyclically balanced budget policy
(c) an annually balanced budget policy
(d) a policy employing built-in stability

4. A cyclically balanced budget philosophy is
(a) pro-cyclical
(b) countercyclical
(c) functional finance
(d) economically neutral

5. What three factors largely explain why the public debt has increased since 1940?
(a) interest payments on the public debt, spending for Social Security, and depreciation of the dollar
(b) deficit spending to finance wars, effects of automatic stabilizers on the budget during recessions, and lack of fiscal discipline
(c) deficit spending caused by depressions, borrowing funds from other nations, and increased government spending to cover health care problems
(d) interest payments on the public debt, government spending for welfare programs, and the crowding out of investment spending

6. To place the public debt in perspective based on the wealth and productive capacity of the economy, it is more meaningful to
(a) examine its absolute size
(b) calculate the interest payments on the debt
(c) measure it relative to the gross domestic product
(d) compare it to imports, exports, and the trade deficit

7. According to many economists, the primary burden of the debt is the
(a) absolute size of the debt for the economy
(b) annual interest charges from bonds sold to finance the public debt
(c) deficit arising from a decline in exports and increase in imports
(d) government spending that the public debt finances for the economy

8. The public debt of the United States as a percentage of its GDP is
(a) larger than all other industrial nations
(b) smaller than all other industrial nations
(c) less than all other industrial nations except Japan
(d) greater than some industrial nations but less than others

9. In 2002, about what percentage of GDP in the form of taxes did the Federal government have to collect to service the public debt?
(a) 2%
(b) 22%
(c) 55%
(d) 91%

10. Foreign individuals and institutions held about what percentage of the public debt in 2002?
(a) 5%
(b) 9%
(c) 18%
(d) 34%

11. If there is a surplus for the Social Security trust fund in a given year, then this Social Security surplus will increase
(a) a Federal budget deficit that year
(b) a Federal budget surplus that year
(c) interest payments on the public debt
(d) holdings of U.S. securities by foreigners

12. A major reason that a public debt cannot bankrupt the Federal government is because the Federal government has
(a) an annually balanced budget
(b) the Social Security trust fund
(c) the power to levy taxes
(d) a strong military defense

13. Incurring an internal debt to finance a war does not pass the cost of the war on to future generations because
(a) the opportunity cost of the war was borne by the generation that fought it
(b) the government need not pay interest on internally held debts
(c) there is never a need for government to refinance the debt
(d) wartime inflation reduces the relative size of the debt

14. Which would be a consequence of the retirement of the internally held (U.S.-owned) portion of the public debt?
(a) a reduction in the nation's productive capacity
(b) a reduction in the nation's standard of living
(c) a redistribution of the nation's wealth among its citizens
(d) a decrease in aggregate demand in the economy

15. Which is an important consequence of the public debt of the United States?
(a) It decreases the need for U.S. securities.
(b) It transfers a portion of the U.S. output to foreign nations.
(c) It reduces the income inequality in the United States.
(d) It leads to greater saving at every level of disposable income.

16. Greater interest charges on the public debt can lead to
(a) fewer purchases of U.S. securities by foreigners
(b) more private investment spending in the economy
(c) lower taxes, and thus greater incentives to work and invest
(d) higher taxes, and thus reduced incentives to work and invest

17. The crowding-out effect of borrowing to finance an increase in government expenditures
(a) reduces current spending for private investment
(b) increases the privately owned stock of real capital
(c) reduces the economic burden on future generations
(d) increases incentives to innovate

18. The crowding-out effect from government borrowing is reduced when
   (a) interest rates are rising
   (b) the economy is operating at full employment
   (c) government spending improves human capital in the economy
   (d) private investment spending can substitute for government spending

19. During the early 1990s, Federal deficits and the growing public debt and the legislative efforts to control them were the main focus of
   (a) unemployment policy
   (b) inflation policy
   (c) monetary policy
   (d) fiscal policy

20. Deficits in the early 1990s were primarily increased by
   (a) an increase in spending for Social Security
   (b) a recession and a bailout of the savings and loan industry
   (c) an increased demand by foreigners for government securities
   (d) an easy money policy of the Federal Reserve

21. The Deficit Reduction Act of 1993 was legislation passed by Congress and signed by President Clinton. It was designed to
   (a) decrease tax rates on personal income, but increase corporate income taxes
   (b) increase taxes on personal income and hold all government spending to 1993 nominal levels
   (c) use fiscal policy to stimulate the sluggish U.S. economy and reduce the rate of unemployment in 1993
   (d) coordinate fiscal policy with the monetary policy of the Federal Reserve to achieve a budget balance by the year 2010

22. One option considered for the use of budget surpluses is to
   (a) decrease tax rates
   (b) decrease government spending
   (c) increase the public debt by borrowing
   (d) decrease spending for Social Security

23. The primary economic benefit from using budget surpluses to help pay off the public debt would be
   (a) a reverse crowding-out effect
   (b) a cyclically balanced budget
   (c) an increase in the number of government securities
   (d) a decrease in the size of the Social Security trust fund

24. One reason that budget deficits returned to the U.S. economy in 2002 was because of
   (a) cost-push inflation
   (b) an economic downturn
   (c) less government spending
   (d) a reduction in interest rates

25. The 2001 and 2003 tax acts passed by the U.S. Congress and signed into law by President Bush had the immediate effect of
   (a) increasing marginal tax rates and decreasing tax revenues
   (b) decreasing marginal tax rates and increasing tax revenues
   (c) increasing marginal tax rates and increasing tax revenues
   (d) decreasing marginal tax rates and decreasing tax revenues

■ **PROBLEMS**

1. The following table gives data on the public debt and the GDP for selected 5-year periods from 1961–2001. Data for the public debt and the GDP are in billions of dollars.

Year	Debt	GDP	Debt/GDP
1961	$ 296.1	$ 545.7	_____ %
1966	329.3	789.3	_____
1971	424.1	1128.6	_____
1976	653.5	1823.9	_____
1981	1028.7	3131.3	_____
1986	2125.3	4452.9	_____
1991	3665.3	5986.2	_____
1996	5224.8	7813.2	_____
2001	5807.5	10082.2	_____

a. Calculate the ratio of the public debt to GDP expressed as a percentage of GDP. Enter the numbers into the last column of the table.
b. On the graph below, plot the year on the horizontal axis and plot the public debt as a percentage of GDP on the vertical axis.

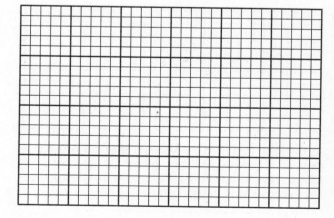

c. Explain what happened to the public debt as a percentage of GDP from 1961–2001.

_____

_____

_____

2. The following table gives data on interest rates and investment demand (in billions of dollars) in a hypothetical economy.

Interest rate	I_{d1}	I_{d2}
10%	$250	$300
8	300	350
6	350	400
4	400	450
2	450	500

a. Use the I_{d1} schedule. Assume that the government needs to finance a budget deficit and this public borrowing increases the interest rate from 4% to 6%. How much crowding out of private investment will occur?

b. Now assume that the deficit is used to improve the capital stock of the economy and that, as a consequence, the investment-demand schedule changes from I_{d1} to I_{d2}. At the same time, the interest rate rises from 4% to 6% as the government borrows money to finance the deficit. How much crowding out of private investment will occur in this case?

c. Graph the two investment-demand schedules on the next graph and show the difference between the two events. Put the interest rate on the vertical axis and the quantity of investment demanded on the horizontal axis.

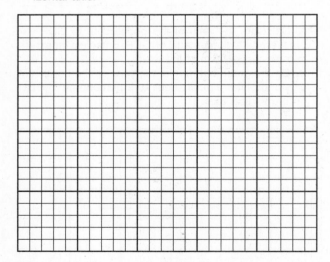

3. Columns 1 and 2 in the following table are investment-demand schedules and show planned investment (I) at different rates of interest (i). Assume the marginal propensity to consume in the economy is 0.8.

(1) i	(2) I	(3) I'
.08	$115	$125
.07	140	150
.06	165	175
.05	190	200
.04	215	225

a. If the Federal government were to spend an additional $20 for goods and services, the equilibrium real GDP would (increase, decrease) _____ by $_____.

b. If the Federal government had obtained the additional $20 by
(1) increasing taxes by $20, the equilibrium real GDP would have (increased, decreased) _____ by a total of $_____;
(2) borrowing $20 in the money market and this borrowing had increased the interest rate from 5% to 6%, (a) planned investment spending would have (increased, decreased) _____ by $_____, (b) the equilibrium real GDP would have _____ by $_____, and (c) the net effect of the increased government spending of the $20 borrowed in the money market would have been to _____ the equilibrium real GDP by $_____.

c. But if the government deficit spending had improved the nation's capital stock and shifted the investment-demand schedule to the one shown in columns 1 and 3 in the preceding table, the total effect of the increased government spending of the $20 borrowed in the money market would have been to (increase, decrease) _____ the equilibrium real GDP by $_____.

■ SHORT ANSWER AND ESSAY QUESTIONS

1. What is the difference between the (Federal) budget deficit and surplus?

2. How are budget deficits and surpluses related to the public debt?

3. Explain why an annually balanced budget is not neutral and how it can intensify, rather than reduce, the tendencies for GDP to rise and fall.

4. How does a cyclically balanced budget philosophy differ from the philosophy of functional finance? Why do advocates of functional finance argue that budget deficits and a mounting national debt are of secondary importance?

5. What have been the three basic causes of the public debt since 1940?

6. How big is the public debt of the United States absolutely and relative to the GDP? How large are the interest payments on this debt absolutely and relative to the GDP?

7. What has happened to the relative size of the debt and the interest payments from 1980–1995 and then from 1995–2002? What explains these changes?

8. Who owns the public debt? What percentage is held by the two major groups? What percentage of the public debt is held by foreigners?

9. Why can't the public debt result in the bankruptcy of the Federal government? What two actions can the government take to prevent bankruptcy?

10. If most of the public debt was owned by American citizens and institutions, and the government decided to pay off the debt, what would happen?

11. Was the increase in the cost of the public debt that resulted from World War II a burden borne by the wartime generation or future generations? Explain.

12. How do the public debt and the payment of interest on this debt affect the distribution of income?

13. What effects does the public debt have on incentives to work, to save, or to assume risk in the economy?

14. What are the economic implications of the portion of the public debt held by foreigners?

15. How does the public debt crowd out private investment and impose a burden on future generations?

16. Does it matter to future generations whether increases in government spending are financed by taxation or increased public debt?

17. What two qualifications might lessen the crowding-out effect on the size of the economic burden that has shifted to future generations?

18. What has been the history of budget deficits and surpluses in recent years? What fiscal policies did the government adopt to eliminate the budget deficits?

19. What are three options for the use of budget surpluses? State a rationale for each option.

20. What legislative actions and national events contributed to the return to budget deficits in recent years?

ANSWERS

Chapter 18 Deficits, Surpluses, and the Public Debt

FILL-IN QUESTIONS

1. greater, less
2. deficits, surpluses
3. pro-, raise, lower
4. deficits, surpluses
5. functional finance, secondary
6. wars, a recession, cuts
7. *a.* GDP, 59; *b.* higher, lower; *c.* 43, 57; *d.* internal, 18
8. greater, surplus, adds to
9. refinancing, tax

10. a liability, an asset
11. increase, decrease
12. foreigners
13. an increase, a decrease, a decrease
14. increases, encourage
15. fiscal, increased, decreased, increased, surplus
16. decrease, decrease, increase, reverse
17. lowered
18. increase, help, strengthen
19. surplus, deficit, taxes, taxes
20. deficits, decreased, increased, increased

TRUE–FALSE QUESTIONS

1. F, p. 325	**10.** T, p. 328	**19.** T, p. 331
2. T, p. 325	**11.** F, pp. 328–329	**20.** F, p. 331
3. F, p. 326	**12.** T, p. 329	**21.** T, p. 331
4. F, p. 326	**13.** F, pp. 329–330	**22.** F, p. 332
5. T, p. 326	**14.** T, p. 330	**23.** T, p. 333
6. T, p. 327	**15.** T, p. 330	**24.** T, p. 333
7. F, p. 327	**16.** F, p. 330	**25.** F, pp. 333–335
8. T, p. 327	**17.** T, pp. 330–331	
9. F, p. 328	**18.** F, p. 330	

MULTIPLE-CHOICE QUESTIONS

1. c, p. 325	**10.** c, p. 329	**19.** d, p. 332
2. b, p. 325	**11.** b, p. 329	**20.** b, p. 332
3. c, p. 326	**12.** c, pp. 329–330	**21.** b, p. 332
4. b, p. 326	**13.** a, p. 330	**22.** a, p. 333
5. b, p. 327	**14.** c, p. 330	**23.** a, p. 333
6. c, p. 328	**15.** b, pp. 330–331	**24.** b, pp. 334–335
7. b, p. 328	**16.** d, p. 330	**25.** d, pp. 333–335
8. d, p. 328	**17.** a, p. 331	
9. a, p. 328	**18.** c, p. 331	

PROBLEMS

1. *a.* 54, 42, 38, 37, 33, 48, 61, 69, 58; *b.* graph; *c.* The debt as a percentage of GDP fell from 1961 to 1981 and then rose substantially from 1981 to 1996. It has fallen since 1996.
2. *a.* $50 billion; *b.* none; *c.* graph
3. *a.* increase, 100; *b.* (1) increased, 20, (2) (a) decreased, 25, (b) decreased, 125, (c) decrease, 25; *c.* increase, 25

SHORT ANSWER AND ESSAY QUESTIONS

1. p. 325	**8.** pp. 328–329	**15.** p. 331
2. p. 325	**9.** pp. 329–330	**16.** pp. 330–331
3. p. 326	**10.** p. 330	**17.** p. 331
4. p. 326	**11.** p. 330	**18.** p. 332
5. p. 327	**12.** p. 330	**19.** p. 333
6. pp. 327–328	**13.** p. 330	**20.** pp. 333–335
7. pp. 327–328	**14.** pp. 330–331	

Disputes over Macro Theory and Policy

Now that you understand the basic theory and models of the macro economy, you are ready to learn about different perspectives on how the economy functions and the major disputes in macro theory and policy.

Economics has always been an arena in which conflicting theories and policies oppose each other. This field of intellectual combat, in major engagements, has seen Adam Smith do battle with the defenders of a regulated economy. It witnessed the opposition of Karl Marx to the orthodox economics of his day. In the 1930s, it saw John Maynard Keynes oppose the classical economists. Around the major engagements have been countless minor skirmishes between opposing viewpoints. Out of these major and minor confrontations have emerged not winners and losers, but the advancement of economic theory and the improvement of economic policy.

Chapter 19 sets the foundation for understanding the modern debates by comparing **classical economics** and **Keynesianism** in terms of macroeconomic theory. The now familiar aggregate demand–aggregate supply model is used to illustrate the classical view that aggregate supply is vertical and. aggregate demand relatively stable. Keynesians, however, saw aggregate supply as being horizontal (to full-employment output), aggregate demand as being highly unstable, and a need for government intervention to stabilize the macro economy.

The chapter then turns to the first of three major questions: **What causes macro instability in the economy?** Four different perspectives on the issues are given. First, from the Keynesian-based *mainstream* view, this instability arises primarily from volatility in investment that shifts aggregate demand or from occasional shocks to aggregate supply. Second, *monetarists* focus on the money supply and assume that the competitive market economy has a high degree of stability, except when there is inappropriate monetary policy. The monetarist analysis is based on the equation of exchange and the assumption that the velocity of money is stable. Changes in the money supply, therefore, directly affect the level of nominal GDP. Third, *real-business-cycle* theorists see instability as coming from the aggregate supply side of the economy and from real factors that affect the long-term growth rather than monetary factors that affect aggregate demand. Fourth, some economists think that macroeconomic instability is the result of *coordination failures* that do not permit people to act jointly to determine the optimal level of output, and that the equilibrium in the economy changes as expectations change.

The next question the chapter discusses is: **Does the economy self-correct its macro instability?** The view of new classical economics is that internal mechanisms in the economy allow it to self-correct. The two variants of this new classical perspective are based on *monetarism* and the *rational expectations theory (RET)*. Monetarists think the economy will self-correct to its long-run level of output, although there can be short-run changes in the price level and real output. The rational expectations theory suggests that the self-correction process is quick and does not change the price level or real output, except when there are price-level surprises.

By contrast, mainstream economists contend that the downward inflexibility of wages limits the self-correction mechanisms in the economy. Several explanations are offered for this inflexibility. There can be long-term wage contracts that support wages. Firms may also pay an efficiency wage to encourage work effort, reduce turnover, and prevent shirking. Firms may also be concerned about maintaining the support and teamwork of key workers (insiders), so they do not cut wages even when other workers (outsiders) might be willing to accept a lower wage.

The different perspectives on macro instability and self-correction set the stage for discussion of the third and final question: **Should the macro economy be guided by policy rules or discretion?** To restrict monetary policy, monetarists and rational expectations economists call for a monetary rule that would have monetary authorities allow the money supply to grow in proportion to the long-term growth in the productive capacity of the economy. Both monetarists and rational expectations economists also oppose the use of fiscal policy, and a few call for a balanced budget requirement to limit the use of discretionary fiscal policy.

Mainstream economists see value in discretionary monetary and fiscal policies. They suggest that a monetary rule would be ineffective in achieving growth and would destabilize the economy. A balanced-budget requirement would also have a pro-cyclical effect that would reinforce recessionary or inflationary tendencies in the economy. And, since government has taken a more active role in the economy, the historical record shows that discretionary monetary and fiscal actions have reduced macro instability.

As was the case in the past, macroeconomic theory and policy have changed because of the debates among economists. The disputes among mainstream economists, monetarists, rational expectationists, and real-business-cycle theorists have produced new insights about how the macro economy operates. In particular, it is now recognized that "money matters" and that the money supply has a significant effect on the economy. More attention is also being given to the influence of people's expectations on policy and coordination failures in explaining macroeconomic events. The disputes in macroeconomics in the past half-century forced economists to reconsider previous conclusions and led to the incorporation of new ideas about macro theory and policy into mainstream thinking.

■ **CHECKLIST**

When you have studied this chapter you should be able to

☐ Compare and contrast the classical and Keynesian views of the aggregate demand curve and the aggregate supply curve.

☐ Describe the mainstream view of stability in the macro economy and the two potential sources of instability.

☐ Explain the monetarist view of stability in the macro economy.

☐ Write the equation of exchange and define each of the four terms in the equation.

☐ Explain why monetarists think the velocity of money is relatively stable.

☐ Write a brief scenario that explains what monetarists believe will happen to change the nominal GDP and will happen to V (velocity of money) when M (money supply) is increased.

☐ Discuss the monetary causes of instability in the macro economy.

☐ Describe the real-business-cycle view of stability in the macro economy.

☐ Give noneconomic and macroeconomic examples of the coordination failures view of stability in the macro economy.

☐ Use a graph to explain the new classical view of self-correction in the macro economy.

☐ Discuss the differences between the monetarist and rational expectations views on the speed of adjustment for self-correction in the macro economy.

☐ State the two basic assumptions of the rational expectations theory (RET).

☐ Use a graph to explain how RET views unanticipated and fully anticipated changes in the price level.

☐ Describe the mainstream view of self-correction in the macro economy.

☐ Give two reasons why there may be downward wage inflexibility.

☐ State three reasons why a higher wage might result in greater efficiency.

☐ Use ideas from the insider–outsider theory to explain the downward inflexibility of wages.

☐ State why monetarists think there should be a monetary rule, and illustrate the rationale using aggregate demand and aggregate supply models.

☐ Describe how monetarists and new classical economists view the effectiveness of fiscal policy.

☐ Offer a mainstream defense of a discretionary stabilization policy and a critique of a monetary rule and balanced-budget requirement.

☐ Describe the possible reasons for increased stability in the macro economy in the past half-century.

☐ Summarize the three alternative views on issues affecting the macro economy.

■ **CHAPTER OUTLINE**

1. *Classical economics* and *Keynesian economics* can be compared by examining their aggregate demand–aggregate supply models of the economy.
    a. In the *classical model,*
    (1) the aggregate supply curve is *vertical* at the economy's full-employment output, and a decrease in aggregate demand will lower the equilibrium price level and have no effect on the real output (or employment) in the economy because of Say's law and flexible, responsive prices and wages.
    (2) the aggregate demand curve slopes downward because (with a fixed money supply in the economy) a fall in the price level increases the purchasing power of money and enables consumers and business firms to purchase a larger real output. Aggregate demand will be reasonably stable if the nation's monetary authorities maintain a constant supply of money to accommodate long-term growth.
    b. In the *Keynesian model,*
    (1) the aggregate supply curve is *horizontal* at the current price level, and a decrease in aggregate demand will lower the real output (and employment) in the economy and have no effect on the equilibrium price level because of the downward inflexibility of prices and wages.
    (2) aggregate demand is viewed as being *unstable* over time, even if the supply of money is held constant, partly because of fluctuations in investment spending. A decline in aggregate demand decreases real domestic output but has no effect on the price level, thereby causing output to stay permanently below the full-employment level.

2. There are four different views among economists on *instability* in the macro economy.
    a. The *mainstream view* is Keynesian-based and holds that instability in the economy arises from
    (1) the volatility in investment spending that makes aggregate demand unstable, and
    (2) occasional aggregate supply shocks which cause cost-push inflation and recession.
    b. *Monetarism* focuses on the money supply. Monetarists think markets are highly competitive and that government intervention destabilizes the economy.
    (1) In monetarism, the equation of exchange is $MV = PQ$, where M is the money supply, V the velocity of money, P the price level, and Q the quantity of goods and services produced.
    (2) Monetarists think that velocity is relatively stable or that the quantity of money demanded is a stable

percentage of GDP (GDP/**M** is constant). If velocity is stable, there is a predictable relationship between **M** and nominal GDP (= **PQ**). An increase in **M** will leave firms and households with more money than they wish to have, so they will increase spending and boost aggregate demand. This causes nominal GDP and the amount of money they wish to hold to rise until the demand for money is equal to **M** and nominal GDP/**M** = **V**.

(3) Monetarists view macroeconomic instability as a result of inappropriate monetary policy. An increase in the money supply will increase aggregate demand, output, and the price level; it will also reduce unemployment. Eventually, nominal wages rise to restore real wages and real output, and the unemployment rate falls back to its natural level at long-run aggregate supply.

c. Real-business-cycle theory sees macroeconomic instability as being caused by real factors influencing aggregate supply instead of monetary factors causing shifts in aggregate demand. Changes in technology and resources will affect productivity and thus the long-run growth rate of aggregate supply.

d. A fourth view of instability in the macro economy attributes the reasons to **coordination failures**. These failures occur when people are not able to coordinate their actions to achieve an optimal equilibrium. A self-fulfilling prophecy can lead to a recession because if households and firms expect it, they individually cut back on spending and employment. If, however, they were to act jointly, they could take actions to counter the recession expectations to achieve an optimal equilibrium.

3. Economists also debate the issue of whether the macro economy self-corrects.

a. New classical economics, based on monetarism and a rational expectations theory, says the economy may deviate from full-employment output, but it eventually returns to this output level because there are self-corrective mechanisms in the economy.

(1) Graphically, if aggregate demand increases, it temporarily raises real output and the price level. Nominal wages rise and productivity falls, so short-run aggregate supply decreases, thus bringing the economy back to its long-run output level.

(2) There is disagreement about the speed of adjustment. The monetarists adopt the adaptive expectations view that there will be a slower, temporary change in output but that in the long run it will return to its natural level. Other new classical economists adopt the **rational expectations theory** (RET) view that there will be a rapid adjustment with little or no change in output. RET is based on two assumptions: People understand how the economy works so that they quickly anticipate the effect on the economy of an economic event, and all markets in the economy are so competitive that equilibrium prices and quantities quickly adjust to changes in policy.

(3) In RET, unanticipated price-level changes, called price-level surprises, cause short-run changes in real output because they cause misperceptions about the economy among workers and firms.

(4) In RET, fully anticipated price-level changes do not change real output even in the short run because workers and firms anticipate and counteract the effects of the changes.

b. The **mainstream view** of self-correction suggests that price and wages may be inflexible downward in the economy.

(1) Graphically, a decrease in aggregate demand will decrease real output but not the price level because nominal wages will not decline and cause the short-run aggregate supply curve to shift right.

(2) Downward wage inflexibility primarily arises because of wage contracts and the legal minimum wage, but they may also occur from efficiency wages and insider–outsider relationships, according to new Keynesian economics.

(3) An **efficiency wage** minimizes the firm's labor cost per unit of output but may be higher than the market wage. This higher wage may result in greater efficiency because it stimulates greater work effort, requires less supervision costs, and reduces job turnover.

(4) **Insider–outsider relationships** may also produce downward wage inflexibility. During a recession, outsiders (who are less essential to the firm) may try to bid down wages to try to keep their jobs, but the firm may not lower wages because it does not want to alienate insiders (who are more essential to the firm) and disrupt the cooperative environment in the firm needed for production.

4. The debates over macro policy also focus on the need for **policy rules or discretion**.

a. Monetarists and new classical economists argue for policy rules to reduce government intervention in the economy. They believe this intervention causes macroeconomic instability.

(1) In regard to monetary policy, monetarists such as Milton Friedman have proposed a monetary rule that the money supply be increased at the same annual rate as the potential annual rate of increase in the real GDP. A monetary rule would shift aggregate demand rightward to match a shift in the long-run aggregate supply curve that occurs because of economic growth, thus keeping the price level stable over time. More recently economists have advocated inflation targeting as an alternative to a Friedman-type monetary rule.

(2) Monetarists and new classical economists question the value of fiscal policy, and some would like to see a balanced Federal budget over time. An expansionist fiscal policy will tend to crowd out investment and cause only a temporary increase in output. RET economists also think that fiscal policy is ineffective and that people will anticipate it and their acts will counteract its intended effects.

b. Mainstream economists think that discretionary fiscal and monetary policy can be effective and are opposed to a monetary rule and a balanced-budget requirement.

(1) They see the velocity of money as relatively unstable and a loose link between changes in the money supply and aggregate demand. This means that a mon-

etary rule might produce too great a shift in aggregate demand (and demand-pull inflation) or too small a shift (and deflation) to match the shift in aggregate supply. Such a rule would contribute to price instability, not price stability.

(2) They support the use of fiscal policy during a recession or to counter growing inflation. Fiscal policy, however, should be reserved for those situations where monetary policy is relatively ineffective. They also oppose a balanced-budget amendment because its effects would be pro-cyclical rather than countercyclical and would reinforce recessionary or inflationary tendencies.

c. Mainstream economists also note that there has been greater stability in the macro economy since 1946, when discretionary monetary and fiscal policies were more actively used to moderate the effects of the business cycle.

5. The **disputes in macroeconomics** have led to the incorporation of several ideas from monetarism and rational expectations theories into the mainstream thinking about macroeconomics. First, monetarists have gotten mainstream economists to recognize that changes in the money supply are important in explaining long-lasting and rapid inflation. Second, mainstream economists now recognize that expectations matter because of arguments from the rational expectations theory and theories about coordination failures in the economy. There will be more price stability, full employment, and economic growth if government can create reliable expectations of those outcomes for households and businesses. In short, macroeconomics continues to develop. Table 19.1 summarizes the three alternative views of macroeconomics.

■ HINTS AND TIPS

1. The chapter may appear complex because many alternative viewpoints are presented. To simplify matters, first focus on the three questions that the chapter addresses: What causes macro instability in the economy? Does the economy self-correct? Should policymakers use rules or discretion? For each question, identify how different types of economists answer each question.

2. Review the discussions of aggregate demand and aggregate supply in Chapters 11 and 16 as preparation for the comparison of alternate views of the macro economy presented in this chapter.

3. Monetarist and mainstream views of the macro economy are two approaches of looking at the same thing. The similarities can best be seen in equations in nominal form. The monetarist equation of exchange is $MV = PQ$. The Keynesian-based mainstream equation is $C_a + I_g + X_n + G = GDP$. The MV term is the monetarist expression for the mainstream equilibrium $C_a + I_g + X_n + G$. The PQ term is the monetarist expression for GDP. Monetarists give more emphasis to the role of money and assume that velocity is relatively stable. Mainstream economists give more emphasis to the instability caused by investment spending and to influences on GDP from consumption, net exports, and government spending.

■ IMPORTANT TERMS

classical view

Keynesian view

monetarism

equation of exchange

velocity

real-business-cycle theory

coordination failures

rational expectations theory

new classical economics

price-level surprises

efficiency wage

insider–outsider theory

monetary rule

■ FILL-IN QUESTIONS

1. The aggregate supply curve of the classical economists is (horizontal, vertical) _____, and the aggregate supply curve of the Keynesian economists is _____ up to the full-employment level of output. Therefore, a decrease in aggregate demand will have no effect on price level and will decrease output and employment in the (classical, Keynesian) _____ model, but a decrease in aggregate demand will decrease the price level and have no effect on output and employment in the _____ model.

2. In the classical way of thinking, changes in the money supply shift the aggregate (demand, supply) _____ curve. If the money supply increases, then the curve will (increase, decrease) _____, and if the money supply decreases, then the curve will _____. If the nation's monetary authorities maintain a constant supply of money, this curve will be (stable, unstable) _____.

3. From the Keynesian perspective, aggregate demand is (stable, unstable) _____, even if there are no changes in the supply of money, largely because of the volatility in (investment, government) _____ spending.

4. The mainstream view is that macro instability is caused by changes in investment spending that shift the aggregate (demand, supply) _____ curve. If it increases too rapidly, then (inflation, recession) _____ can occur, but if it decreases, then the economy can experience _____. Occasionally, adverse aggregate (demand, supply) _____ shocks also cause instability.

5. Monetarists argue that capitalism is inherently (stable, unstable) _____ because most of its

markets are (competitive, noncompetitive) _____. They believe that government intervention in the economy has contributed to macroeconomic (stability, instability) _____ and has promoted (flexibility, inflexibility) _____ in wages.

6. The basic equation of the monetarists is _____ = _____. Indicate what each of the following four letters in the equation represents:

   a. *M:* _____

   b. *V:* _____

   c. *P:* _____

   d. *Q:* _____

7. Monetarists believe that *V* is relatively (stable, unstable) _____ because people have a _____ desire to hold money relative to holding other financial and real assets or for making purchases. The amount of money people will want to hold will depend on the level of (real, nominal) _____ GDP.

8. An increase in *M,* to the monetarist's way of thinking, will leave the public with (more, less) _____ money than it wishes to have, induce the public to (increase, decrease) _____ its spending for consumer and capital goods, which will result in a(n) _____ in aggregate demand and nominal GDP until nominal GDP equals *MV.*

9. Monetarists believe that the most significant cause of macroeconomic instability has been inappropriate (fiscal, monetary) _____ policy. Too rapid increases in *M* cause (recession, inflation) _____; insufficient growth of *M* causes _____.

10. The theory that changes in resource availability and technology (real factors), which alter productivity, are the main causes of instability in the macro economy is held by (real-business-cycle, rational expectations) _____ economists. In this theory, shifts in the economy's long-run aggregate (demand, supply) _____ curve change real output. As a consequence, money demand and money supply change, shifting the aggregate demand curve in the (opposite, same) _____ direction as the initial change in long-run aggregate supply. Real output thus can change (with, without) _____ a change in the price level.

11. A coordination failure is said to occur when people (do, do not) _____ reach a mutually benefi-

cial equilibrium because they lack some way to jointly coordinate their actions. In this view, there is (are) (one, a number of) _____ equilibrium position(s) in the economy. Macroeconomic instability is the result of changing (the money supply, expectations) _____ that result in changing the equilibrium position(s).

12. Monetarists and rational expectations economists view the economy as (capable, incapable) _____ of self-correction when it deviates from the full-employment level of real output. Monetarists suggest that this adjustment occurs (gradually, rapidly) _____, while rational expectations economists argue that it occurs _____.

13. Rational expectations theory assumes that with sufficient information, people's beliefs about future economic outcomes (are, are not) _____ accurate reflections of the likelihood of the outcomes occurring. It also assumes that markets are highly competitive, meaning that prices and wages are (flexible, inflexible) _____.

14. In the rational expectations theory, changes in aggregate demand that change the price level and real output are (anticipated, unanticipated) _____, while changes in aggregate demand that only change the price level and not real output are _____.

15. The view of mainstream economists is that many prices and wages are (flexible, inflexible) _____ downward for (short, long) _____ periods of time. This situation (increases, decreases) _____ the ability of the economy to automatically self-correct for deviations from full-employment output.

16. A higher wage can result in more efficiency because it results in (greater, less) _____ work effort, supervision costs that are (lower, higher) _____, and (more, less) _____ turnover in jobs. Efficiency wages (increase, decrease) _____ the downward inflexibility of wages because they make firms more reluctant to cut wages when aggregate demand declines.

17. Monetarists and rational expectations economists support a monetary rule because they believe that discretionary monetary policy tends to (stabilize, destabilize) _____ the economy. With this rule the money supply would be increased at a rate (greater than, less than, equal to) _____ the long-run growth of potential GDP; graphically, this can be shown by a shift in aggregate demand that would be _____ the shift in long-run aggregate supply resulting from economic growth.

18. Proponents of the rational expectations theory contend that discretionary monetary policy is (effective, ineffective) _____ and like the monetarists favor (rules, discretion) _____. When considering discretionary fiscal policy, most monetarists and RET economists (do, do not) _____ advocate its use.

19. Mainstream economists (support, oppose) _____ a monetary rule and a balanced-budget requirement. They view discretionary monetary policy as (effective, ineffective) _____, and think discretionary fiscal policy is _____ but should be held in reserve when monetary policy works too slowly. They say the use of discretionary monetary and fiscal policies since 1950 has produced (more, less) _____ stability in the macro economy.

20. Many ideas from alternative views of the macro economy have been absorbed into mainstream thinking about macroeconomics. There is more recognition that excessive growth of the money supply is a major cause of (recession, inflation) _____, and that expectations and coordination failures are (important, unimportant) _____ in the formulation of government policies for price stability, unemployment, and economic growth.

■ **TRUE–FALSE QUESTIONS**

Circle T if the statement is true, F if it is false.

1. The classical view is that the aggregate supply curve is vertical. **T F**

2. Classical economists consider the aggregate demand curve to be unstable. **T F**

3. Keynesians think that the aggregate supply curve is horizontal (to full-employment output). **T F**

4. Keynesians suggest that full employment is the norm in the economy. **T F**

5. The mainstream view is that macro instability is caused by the volatility of investment spending, which shifts the aggregate demand curve. **T F**

6. Monetarists argue that the market system would provide for macroeconomic stability were it not for government interference in the economy. **T F**

7. In the equation of exchange, the left side, *MV*, represents the total amount received by sellers of output, while the right side, *PQ*, represents the total amount spent by purchasers of that output. **T F**

8. Monetarists argue that *V* in the equation of exchange is relatively stable and that a change in *M* will bring about a direct and proportional change in *PQ*. **T F**

9. Most monetarists believe that an increase in the money supply has no effect on real output and employment in the short run. **T F**

10. In the monetarist view, the only cause of the Great Depression was the decline in investment spending. **T F**

11. Real-business-cycle theory views changes in resource availability and technology, which alter productivity, as the main cause of macroeconomic instability. **T F**

12. In the real-business-cycle theory, real output changes only with a change in the price level. **T F**

13. A coordination failure is said to occur when people do not reach a mutually beneficial equilibrium because they lack some way to jointly coordinate their actions to achieve it. **T F**

14. People's expectations have no effect on coordination failures. **T F**

15. New classical economists see the economy as automatically correcting itself when disturbed from its full-employment level of real output. **T F**

16. The rational expectations theory assumes that both product and resource markets are uncompetitive and wages and prices are inflexible. **T F**

17. In the rational expectations theory, a fully anticipated price-level change results in a change in real output. **T F**

18. Mainstream economists contend that many wages and prices are inflexible downward. **T F**

19. An efficiency wage is a below-market wage that spurs greater work effort and gives the firm more profits because of lower wage costs. **T F**

20. Insider–outsider theory offers one explanation for the downward inflexibility of wages in the economy. **T F**

21. Monetarists believe that a monetary rule would reduce instability in the macro economy. **T F**

22. Rational expectations economists argue that monetary policy should be left to the discretion of government. **T F**

23. Monetarists support the use of fiscal policy, especially as a means of controlling inflation. **T F**

24. Mainstream economists believe that discretionary monetary policy is an effective tool for stabilizing the economy. **T F**

25. The mainstream view of the economy since 1950 believes that the economy has become inherently less stable because of the use of fiscal policy. **T F**

■ MULTIPLE-CHOICE QUESTIONS

Circle the letter that corresponds to the best answer.

1. Classical economists suggest that full employment is
   (a) best achieved through government interventions
   (b) not possible in an unstable market economy
   (c) inversely related to the price level
   (d) the norm in a market economy

2. The aggregate supply curve of classical economists
   (a) is vertical
   (b) is horizontal
   (c) slopes upward
   (d) slopes downward

3. Classical theory concludes that the production behavior of firms will not change when the price level decreases because input costs would
   (a) rise along with product prices to leave real profits and output unchanged
   (b) fall along with product prices to leave real profits and output unchanged
   (c) fall, but product prices would rise, offsetting any change in real profits or output
   (d) rise, but product prices would rise, offsetting any change in real profits or output

4. In classical economics, a decrease in aggregate demand results in
   (a) a decrease in both the price level and domestic output
   (b) a decrease in the price level and no change in domestic output
   (c) no change in the price level and a decrease in domestic output
   (d) no change in either the price level or domestic output

5. The aggregate supply curve in the Keynesian model is
   (a) vertical at the full-employment output level
   (b) horizontal to the full-employment output level
   (c) positively sloped to the full-employment output level
   (d) negatively sloped to the full-employment output level

6. In the Keynesian model, a decrease in aggregate demand results in
   (a) a decrease in both the price level and domestic output
   (b) a decrease in the price level and no change in domestic output
   (c) no change in the price level and a decrease in domestic output
   (d) no change in either the price level or domestic output

7. The mainstream view of the economy holds that
   (a) government intervention in the economy is not desirable
   (b) product and labor markets are highly competitive and flexible

(c) changes in investment spending lead to changes in aggregate demand
(d) economic growth is best achieved through implementation of a monetary rule

8. In the monetarist perspective
   (a) discretionary monetary policy is the most effective way to moderate swings in the business cycle
   (b) government policies have reduced macroeconomic stability
   (c) macroeconomic stability results from adverse aggregate supply shocks
   (d) markets in a capitalistic economy are largely noncompetitive

9. Which is the equation of exchange?
   (a) $PQ/M + V = GDP$
   (b) $V = M + PQ$
   (c) $MV = PQ$
   (d) $V + I_g + M = GDP$

10. In the equation of exchange, if V is stable, an increase in M will necessarily increase
    (a) the demand for money
    (b) government spending
    (c) nominal GDP
    (d) velocity

11. When nominal gross domestic product (GDP) is divided by the money supply (M), you will obtain the
    (a) velocity of money
    (b) monetary multiplier
    (c) equation of exchange
    (d) monetary rule

12. Monetarists argue that the amount of money the public will want to hold depends primarily on the level of
    (a) nominal GDP
    (b) investment
    (c) taxes
    (d) prices

13. Real-business-cycle theory suggests that
    (a) velocity changes gradually and predictably; thus it is able to accommodate the long-run changes in nominal GDP
    (b) the volatility of investment is the main cause of the economy's instability
    (c) inappropriate monetary policy is the single most important cause of macroeconomic instability
    (d) changes in technology and resources affect productivity, and thus the long-run growth of aggregate supply

14. In the real-business-cycle theory, if the long-run aggregate supply increased, then aggregate demand would increase by
    (a) an equal amount, so real output and the price level would increase
    (b) less than an equal amount, so real output would increase and the price level would decrease
    (c) greater than an equal amount, so real output and the price level would increase
    (d) an equal amount, so real output would increase and the price level would be unchanged

15. If aggregate demand declined and the economy experienced a recession due to a self-fulfilling prophecy, this would be an example of

(a) real-business-cycle theory

(b) insider—outsider theory

(c) a coordination failure

(d) a change in velocity

16. In the new classical view, when the economy diverges from its full-employment output,

(a) internal mechanisms within the economy would automatically return it to its full-employment output

(b) discretionary monetary policy is needed to return it to its full-employment output

(c) discretionary fiscal policy is needed to return it to its full-employment output

(d) the adoption of an efficiency wage in the economy would return it to its full-employment output

17. The views about the speed of adjustment for self-correction in the economy suggest that

(a) monetarists think it would be gradual, and rational expectations economists think it would be quick

(b) monetarists think it would be quick, and rational expectations economists think it would be gradual

(c) monetarists and mainstream economists think it would be quick

(d) real-business-cycle theorists and rational expectations economists think it would be gradual

18. Proponents of the rational expectations theory argue that people

(a) are not as rational as monetarists assume them to be

(b) make forecasts that are based on poor information, causing economic policy to be driven by self-fulfilling prophecy

(c) form beliefs about future economic outcomes that accurately reflect the likelihood that those outcomes will occur

(d) do not respond quickly to changes in wages and prices, causing a misallocation of economic resources in the economy

19. In the rational expectations theory, a temporary change in real output would occur from a

(a) fully anticipated price-level change

(b) downward wage inflexibility

(c) coordination failure

(d) price-level surprise

20. The conclusion mainstream economists draw about the downward price and wage inflexibility is that

(a) the effects can be reversed relatively quickly

(b) efficiency wages do not contribute to the problem

(c) the economy can be mired in recession for long periods

(d) wage and price controls are needed to counteract the situation

21. According to mainstream economists, which of the following contributes to the downward inflexibility of wages?

(a) price-level surprises

(b) insider—outsider relationships

(c) adverse aggregate supply shocks

(d) inadequate investment spending

22. The rule suggested by the monetarists is that the money supply should be increased at the same rate as the

(a) price level

(b) interest rate

(c) velocity of money

(d) potential growth in real GDP

23. To stabilize the economy, monetarist and rational expectations economists advocate

(a) the use of price-level surprises and adoption of an efficiency wage

(b) a monetary rule and a balanced-budget requirement

(c) the use of discretionary fiscal policy instead of discretionary monetary policy

(d) the use of discretionary monetary policy instead of discretionary fiscal policy

24. Mainstream economists support

(a) increasing the money supply at a constant rate

(b) eliminating insider—outsider relationships in business

(c) the use of discretionary monetary and fiscal policies

(d) a balanced-budget requirement and a monetary rule

25. Which of the following would be an idea from monetarism that has been absorbed into mainstream macroeconomics?

(a) how changes in investment spending change aggregate demand

(b) the importance of money and the money supply in the economy

(c) using discretion rather than rules for guiding economic policy

(d) building the macro foundations for microeconomics

■ **PROBLEMS**

1. Assume that you are a monetarist in this problem and that **V** is stable and equal to 4. In the following table is the aggregate supply schedule: the real output **Q** which producers will offer for sale at seven different price levels **P**.

P	Q	PQ	MV
$1.00	100	$____	$____
2.00	110	____	____
3.00	120	____	____
4.00	130	____	____
5.00	140	____	____
6.00	150	____	____
7.00	160	____	____

a. Compute and enter in the table on the previous page the seven values of **PQ**.

b. Assume **M** is $90. Enter the values of **MV** on each of the seven lines in the table. The equilibrium

(1) nominal domestic output (**PQ** or **MV**) is $_____.

(2) price level is $_____.

(3) real domestic output (**Q**) is $_____.

c. When **M** increases to $175, **MV** at each price level

is $_____ and the equilibrium

(1) nominal domestic output is $_____.

(2) price level is $_____.

(3) real domestic output is $_____.

2. Indicate what perspective(s) of economics would be most closely associated with each position. Use the following abbreviations: **MAI** (mainstream economics), **MON** (monetarism), **RET** (rational expectations theory), and **RBC** (real-business-cycle theory).

a. macro instability from investment spending _____

b. macro instability from inappropriate monetary policy _____

c. macro instability from changes in resource availability and technology _____

d. equation of exchange _____

e. fiscal policy can be effective _____

f. unanticipated price-level changes _____

g. downward inflexibility of wages and prices _____

h. monetary rule _____

i. neutral fiscal policy _____

j. economy automatically self-corrects _____

k. monetary policy is effective _____

3. Following are price-level (**PL**) and output (**Q**) combinations to describe aggregate demand and aggregate supply curves: (1) **PL** and **Q₁** is **AD₁**; (2) **PL** and **Q₂** is **AD₂**; (3) **PL** and **Q₃** is **AS_LR1**; (4) **PL** and **Q₄** is **AS_LR2**.

PL	Q_1	Q_2	Q_3	Q_4
250	0	200	400	600
200	200	400	400	600
150	400	600	400	600
100	600	800	400	600
50	800	1,000	400	600

a. Use the following to graph **AD₁**, **AD₂**, **AS_LR1**, and **AS_LR2**. Label the vertical axis as the price level and the horizontal axis as real output (**Q**).

0

b. If the economy is initially in equilibrium where **AD₁** and **AS_LR1** intersect, the price level will be _____ and real output will be _____.

c. If, over time, the economy grows from **AS_LR1** to **AS_LR2**, the equilibrium price level will be _____ and real output will be _____.

d. Assume a monetary rule is adopted that increases the money supply proportionate to the increase in aggregate supply. Aggregate demand will increase from **AD₁** to **AD₂**, making the price level_____ and real output _____.

e. Mainstream economists would argue that velocity is unstable, so a constant increase in the money supply might not shift **AD₁** all the way to **AD₂**. In this case, the price level would fall below the target of _____. It might also be the case that the constant increase in the money supply might shift **AD₁** beyond **AD₂**, so the price level would rise above the target of _____.

■ **SHORT ANSWER AND ESSAY QUESTIONS**

1. What is the difference between the classical and Keynesian aggregate supply curves? Draw a graph showing the difference. What is the justification for each viewpoint?

2. What is the effect of a decrease in aggregate demand on the price level and real domestic output in the classical and Keynesian models? Show the change in a graph.

3. Why did classical economists consider the aggregate demand curve to be stable? What is the response of Keynesians to this position?

4. Why does the classical aggregate demand curve have a negative (downward) slope?

5. Explain the two causes of macroeconomic instability in the view of mainstream economists.

6. What do monetarists see as the cause of economic instability in the economy? Explain, using the equation of exchange, how a change in the money supply will affect nominal GDP.

7. Why do monetarists argue that the velocity of money is stable? If the money supply increases, how will people respond from a monetarist perspective?

8. Compare and contrast the monetarist and mainstream views on the causes of macroeconomic instability. How do monetarists explain the Great Depression?

9. Explain the real-business-cycle view of macroeconomic instability using an aggregate demand and supply graph.

10. Give a macroeconomic example of how coordination failures cause macroeconomic instability.

11. Explain the new classical view of self-correction in the macro economy. Contrast the monetarist perspective with that of rational expectations in terms of the real output, the price level, and the speed of adjustment.

12. Describe the two assumptions on which rational expectations are based. How realistic is it to expect that people will be able to accurately forecast economic outcomes?

13. Use a graph to illustrate and explain the mainstream view of self-correction in the macro economy.

14. Why would an efficiency wage lead to downward inflexibility in prices?

15. Give an example of insider–outsider relationships and explain how it affects wage flexibility.

16. What is the monetary rule? Why do monetarists suggest this rule to replace discretionary monetary policy?

17. What is the perspective of rational expectations economists on a monetary rule and the conduct of monetary policy?

18. What is the position of some monetarist and rational expectations economists on a requirement for a balanced budget? Why do they adopt such a position?

19. How do mainstream economists defend the use of discretionary monetary and fiscal policies? What interpretation do mainstream economists make of the historical evidence on the relationship between macroeconomic policy and instability?

20. What influences have monetarism and the rational expectations theory had on mainstream macroeconomic theory and policy? Give several examples of ideas that have changed mainstream thinking.

ANSWERS

Chapter 19 Disputes over Macro Theory and Policy

FILL-IN QUESTIONS

1. vertical, horizontal, Keynesian, classical
2. demand, increase, decrease, stable
3. unstable, investment
4. demand, inflation, recession, supply
5. stable, competitive, instability, inflexibility
6. $MV = PQ$; a. the money supply; b. the velocity of money; c. the average price of each unit of physical output; d. the physical volume of goods and services produced
7. stable, stable, nominal
8. more, increase, increase
9. monetary, inflation, recession
10. real-business-cycle, supply, same, without
11. do not, a number of, expectations
12. capable, gradually, rapidly
13. are, flexible
14. unanticipated, anticipated
15. inflexible, long, decreases
16. greater, lower, less, increase
17. destabilize, equal to, equal to
18. ineffective, rules, do not
19. oppose, effective, effective, more
20. inflation, important

TRUE–FALSE QUESTIONS

1. T, pp. 338–339	10. F, p. 342	19. F, pp. 346–347
2. F, p. 339	11. T, pp. 342–343	20. T, p. 347
3. T, p. 340	12. F, pp. 342–343	21. T, pp. 347–348
4. F, p. 340	13. T, p. 343	22. F, pp. 347–348
5. T, p. 340	14. F, p. 343	23. F, p. 348
6. T, p. 340	15. T, pp. 344–345	24. T, pp. 349–350
7. F, p. 341	16. F, pp. 345–346	25. F, p. 350
8. T, p. 341	17. F, pp. 345–346	
9. F, p. 341	18. T, p. 346	

MULTIPLE-CHOICE QUESTIONS

1. d, pp. 338–339	10. c, p. 341	19. d, pp. 345–346
2. a, pp. 338–339	11. a, p. 341	20. c, p. 346
3. b, pp. 338–339	12. a, pp. 341–342	21. b, p. 347
4. b, p. 339	13. d, pp. 342–343	22. d, pp. 347–348
5. b, p. 340	14. d, pp. 342–343	23. b, pp. 348–349
6. c, p. 340	15. c, pp. 343–344	24. c, pp. 349–350
7. c, p. 340	16. a, pp. 344–345	25. b, pp. 350–352
8. b, p. 341	17. a, p. 345	
9. c, p. 341	18. c, pp. 345–346	

PROBLEMS

1. a. 100, 220, 360, 520, 700, 900, 1120; b. 360, 360, 360, 360, 360, 360, 360, (1) 360, (2) 3.00, (3) 120; c. 700, (1) 700, (2) 5.00, (3) 140
2. a. MAI; b. MON, RET; c. RBC; d. MON; e. MAI; f. RET; g. MAI; h. MON, RET; i. MON, RET; j. MON, RET; k. MAI
3. a. graph similar to Figure 17.4 in the text; b. 150, 400; c. 100, 600; d. 150, 600; e. 150, 150

SHORT ANSWER AND ESSAY QUESTIONS

1. pp. 338–340	8. pp. 340–342	15. p. 347
2. pp. 338–340	9. pp. 342–343	16. pp. 348–349
3. pp. 339–340	10. p. 343	17. p. 349
4. pp. 338–339	11. pp. 344–345	18. p. 349
5. pp. 340–341	12. pp. 345–346	19. pp. 349–350
6. pp. 341–342	13. pp. 346–347	20. pp. 350–352
7. pp. 341–342	14. pp. 346–347	

CHAPTER 20

International Trade

In Chapter 6 you learned about the role of the United States in the global economy and the basic principles of international trade. Chapter 20 extends that analysis by giving you a more advanced understanding of comparative advantage. It also uses the tools of supply and demand to explain the equilibrium prices and quantities of imports and exports and the economic effects of tariffs and quotas. It examines the fallacious arguments for trade protectionism and the global efforts to liberalize trade.

After a brief review of the facts of international trade presented in Chapter 6, the text uses graphical analysis to explain why nations trade: to take advantage of the benefits of specialization. Nations specialize in and export those goods and services in the production of which they have a **comparative advantage.** A comparative advantage means that the opportunity cost of producing a particular good or service is lower in that nation than in another nation. These nations will avoid producing and will import the goods and services that other nations have a comparative advantage in producing. In this way all nations are able to obtain products that are produced as inexpensively as possible. Put another way, when nations specialize in those products in which they have a comparative advantage, the world as a whole can obtain more goods and services from its resources; each nation of the world can enjoy a standard of living higher than it would have if it did not specialize and export and import.

The principle of comparative advantage tells us why nations trade, but what determines the equilibrium prices and quantities of the imports and exports resulting from trade? To answer this question, the text uses the **supply and demand analysis,** originally presented in Chapter 3, to explain equilibrium in the world market for a product. A simplified two-nation and one-product model of trade is used to construct export supply curves and import demand curves for each nation. Equilibrium occurs where one nation's export supply curve intersects another nation's import demand curve.

Regardless of the advantages of specialization and trade among nations, people in the United States and throughout the world for well over 200 years have debated whether **free trade or protection** was the better policy for their nation. Economists took part in this debate and, with few exceptions, argued for free trade and against protection. Those who favor free trade contend that free trade benefits both the nation and the world as a whole. "Free traders" argue that tariffs, import quotas, and other barriers to international trade prevent or reduce specialization and decrease both a nation's and the world's production and standard of living.

Despite the case for trade, nations have erected and continue to erect **trade barriers** against other nations. The latter part of this chapter focuses attention on (1) what motivates nations to impose tariffs and to limit the quantities of goods imported from abroad; (2) the economic effects of protection on a nation's own prosperity and on the prosperity of the world economy; (3) the kinds of arguments those who favor protection use to support their position (on what grounds do they base their contention that their nation will benefit from the erection of barriers that reduce imports from foreign nations); and (4) how the nations of the world have responded to trade liberalization through the **World Trade Organization** (WTO).

Whether the direction of the international trade policy in the United States will be toward freer trade or more protectionism is a question that gets debated as each new trade issue is presented to the U.S. public. The decision on each issue may well depend on your understanding of the advantages of free trade and the problems with trade protection for the nation and the world economy.

■ CHECKLIST

When you have studied this chapter you should be able to

☐ Cite some key facts about international trade.
☐ State the three economic circumstances that make it desirable for nations to specialize and trade.
☐ Compute the costs of producing two commodities when given the data in a two-nation example.
☐ Determine which nation has the comparative advantage in the production of each commodity using the cost data you computed for the two-nation example.
☐ Calculate the range in which the terms of trade will occur in the two-nation example.
☐ Explain how nations gain from trade and specialization based on the two-nation example.
☐ Discuss how increasing costs affect specialization in the two-nation example.
☐ Restate the case for free trade.
☐ Construct domestic supply and demand curves for two nations that trade a product.
☐ Construct export supply and import demand curves for two nations that trade a product.

☐ Use supply and demand analysis to explain how the equilibrium prices and quantities of exports and imports are determined for two nations that trade a product.

☐ Identify the four principal types of artificial barriers to international trade and the motives for erecting these barriers.

☐ Explain the economic effects of a protective tariff on resource allocation, the price of the commodity, the total production of the commodity, and the outputs of foreign and domestic producers of the commodity.

☐ Analyze the economic effects of an import quota and compare them with the economic effects of a tariff.

☐ Enumerate six arguments used to support the case for protection and find the problems with each argument.

☐ Offer a summation of the arguments for and against trade protection.

☐ Describe the formation, purpose, and issues of the World Trade Organization.

■ CHAPTER OUTLINE

1. Some facts on international trade from Chapter 6 are worth reviewing.

   a. About 11% of the total output (GDP) of the United States is accounted for by exports of goods and services, a percentage that has doubled since 1975. The percentage of exports is much higher in other industrially advanced nations (e.g., 62% in the Netherlands, 41% in Canada), but the size of the U.S. economy means that it has the largest volume of imports and exports in the world.

   b. The United States has a trade deficit in goods, a trade surplus in services, and a trade deficit in goods and services.

   c. The major exports of the United States are computers, chemicals, semiconductors, and consumer durables. The major imports are petroleum, automobiles, computers, and household appliances. Most of the trade occurs with other industrially advanced nations. Canada is the largest trading partner for the United States.

   d. The major participants in international trade are the United States, Japan, and the nations of Western Europe. Newer participants include the Asian economies of South Korea, Singapore and Taiwan. Russia, the nations of Eastern Europe, and China have increased their international trade.

   e. International trade and finance is also a focus of economic policy as shown by issues faced by the World Trade Organization (WTO) and International Monetary Fund (IMF).

2. The **economic basis for trade** is based on several circumstances. Specialization and trade among nations is advantageous because the world's resources are not evenly distributed and efficient production of different commodities requires different technologies and combinations of resources. Also, products differ in quality and other attributes, so people might prefer imported to domestic goods in some cases.

3. The **principle of comparative advantage,** first presented in Chapter 6 to explain the gains from trade, can now be reexamined with the aid of graphical analysis.

   a. Suppose the world is composed of only two nations, each of which is capable of producing two different commodities and in which the production possibilities curves are different straight lines (the nations' opportunity cost ratios are constant but different).

   b. With different domestic opportunity cost ratios, each nation will have a comparative (cost) advantage in the production of one of the two commodities, and if the world is to use its resources economically, each nation must specialize in the commodity in the production of which it has a comparative advantage.

   c. The ratio at which one product is traded for another—the terms of trade—lies between the opportunity cost ratios of the two nations.

   d. Each nation gains from this trade because specialization permits a greater total output from the same resources and a better allocation of the world's resources.

   e. If opportunity cost ratios in the two nations are not constant (if there is increasing cost), specialization may not be complete.

   f. The basic argument for free trade among nations is that it leads to a better allocation of resources and a higher standard of living in the world. Several side benefits from trade are that it increases competition and deters monopoly, and offers consumers a wider array of choices. It also links the interests of nations and can reduce the threat of hostilities or war.

4. **Supply and demand analysis of exports and imports** can be used to explain how the equilibrium price and quantity for a product (e.g., aluminum) are determined when there is trade between two nations (e.g., the United States and Canada).

   a. For the United States, there will be *domestic* supply and demand as well as *export* supply and import demand for aluminum.

   (1) The price and quantity of aluminum are determined by the intersection of the domestic demand and supply curves in a world without trade.

   (2) In a world with trade, the export supply curve for the United States shows the amount of aluminum that U.S. producers will export at each world price above the domestic equilibrium price. U.S. exports will increase when the world price rises relative to the domestic price.

   (3) The import demand curve for the United States shows the amount of aluminum that U.S. citizens will import at each world price below the domestic equilibrium price. U.S. imports will increase when world prices fall relative to the domestic price.

   b. For Canada, there will be domestic supply and demand as well as export supply and import demand for aluminum. The description of these supply and demand curves is similar to the account of those of the United States previously described in point **a.**

   c. The equilibrium world price and equilibrium world levels of exports and imports can be determined with further supply and demand analysis. The export supply curves of the two nations can be plotted on one graph. The import demand curves of both nations can be plotted on the same graph. In this two-nation model, equilibrium will be achieved when one nation's import demand curve intersects another nation's export supply curve.

5. Nations limit international trade by erecting **trade barriers.** Tariffs, import quotas, a variety of nontariff barriers, and voluntary export restrictions are the principal barriers to trade.

   a. The imposition of a **tariff** on a good imported from abroad has both direct and indirect effects on an economy.

   (1) The tariff increases the domestic price of the good, reduces its domestic consumption, expands its domestic production, decreases its foreign production, and transfers income from domestic consumers to government.

   (2) It also reduces the income of foreign producers and the ability of foreign nations to purchase goods and services in the nation imposing the tariff, causes the contraction of relatively efficient industries in that nation, decreases world trade, and lowers the real output of goods and services.

   b. The imposition of a **quota** on an imported product has the same direct and indirect effects as that of a tariff on that product, with the exception that a tariff generates revenue for government use whereas an import quota transfers that revenue to foreign producers.

   c. Special-interest groups benefit from protection and persuade their nations to erect trade barriers, but the costs to consumers of this protection exceed the benefits to the economy.

   d. Tariffs and quotas affect the distribution of income. They act like sales or excise taxes on a product, so they are highly regressive for low-income consumers.

6. The arguments for **protectionism** are many, but often of questionable validity.

   a. The military self-sufficiency argument can be challenged because it is difficult to determine which industry is "vital" to national defense and must be protected; it would be more efficient economically to provide a direct subsidy to military producers rather than impose a tariff.

   b. Trade barriers do not necessarily increase domestic employment because

   (1) imports may eliminate some jobs, but create others, so imports may change only the composition of employment, not the overall level of employment;

   (2) the exports of one nation become the imports of another, so tariff barriers can be viewed as "beggar thy neighbor" policies;

   (3) other nations are likely to retaliate against the imposition of trade barriers that will reduce domestic output and employment; and

   (4) in the long run, barriers create a less efficient allocation of resources by shielding protected domestic industries from the rigors of competition.

   c. Using tariff barriers to permit diversification for stability in the economy is not necessary for advanced economies such as the United States, and there may be great economic costs to diversification in developing nations.

   d. It is alleged that infant industries need protection until they are sufficiently large to compete, but the argument may not apply in developed economies: It is difficult to select which industries will prosper; protectionism tends to persist long after it is needed; and direct subsidies may be more economically efficient. For advanced nations, a variant of this argument is **strategic trade policy.** It justifies barriers that protect the investment in high-risk, growth industries for a nation, but the policies often lead to retaliation and similar policies from other trading nations.

   e. Sometimes protection is sought against the "dumping" of excess foreign goods on U.S. markets. Dumping is a legitimate concern and is restricted under U.S. trade law, but to use dumping as an excuse for widespread tariff protection is unjustified, and the number of documented cases is few. If foreign companies are more efficient (low-cost) producers, what may appear to be dumping may actually be comparative advantage at work.

   f. Protection is sometimes sought because of the cheap foreign labor argument; it should be realized that nations gain from trade based on comparative advantage, and without trade, living standards will be lower.

   g. In summary, most protectionist arguments are fallacious or based on half-truths. The only points that have some validity, under certain conditions, are the infant industry and military-sufficiency arguments, but both are subject to abuse. The historical evidence suggests that free trade promotes and protectionism deters prosperity and economic growth in the world.

7. The **World Trade Organization** (WTO) is an international agency with about 145 participating nations that is charged with overseeing a 1994 trade agreement among nations. This agreement sought trade liberalization by: reducing tariffs worldwide; implementing new rules to promote trade in services; cutting domestic subsidies for agricultural products; protecting intellectual property; and phasing out quotas on textiles and apparel. The WTO oversees provisions of the agreement, rules on disputes, and meets on occasion to consider other trade policies. The work of the WTO is not without controversy. Critics wildly claim that it promotes global capitalism at the expense of labor and the environment. Economists argue that trade liberalization increases economic efficiency and output worldwide, and that these benefits can then be used to address domestic concerns.

■ **HINTS AND TIPS**

1. In the discussion of **comparative advantage,** the assumption of a constant-cost ratio means the production possibilities "curves" for each nation can be drawn as straight lines. The slope of the line in each nation is the opportunity cost of one product (wheat) in terms of the

other product (coffee). The reciprocal of the slope of each line is the opportunity cost of the other product (coffee) in terms of the first product (wheat).

2. The **export supply and import demand curves** in Figures 20.3 and 20.4 in the text look different from the typical supply and demand curves that you have seen so far, so you should understand how they are constructed. The export supply and import demand curves for a nation do not intersect. Each curve meets at the price point on the *Y* axis showing the equilibrium price for domestic supply and demand. At this point there are no exports or imports.

   a. The export supply curve is upsloping from that point because as world prices rise above the domestic equilibrium price, there will be increasing domestic surpluses produced by a nation that can be exported. The export supply curve reflects the positive relationship between rising world prices (above the domestic equilibrium price) and the increasing quantity of exports.

   b. The import demand curve is downsloping from the domestic equilibrium price because as world prices fall below the domestic equilibrium price, there will be increasing domestic shortages that need to be covered by increasing imports. The import demand curve reflects the inverse relationship between falling world prices (below the domestic price) and the increasing quantity of imports.

3. One of the most interesting sections of the chapter discusses the arguments for and against trade protection. You have probably heard people give one or more of the arguments for trade protection, but now you have a chance to use your economic reasoning to expose the weaknesses in these arguments. Most are half-truths and special pleadings.

■ IMPORTANT TERMS

labor-intensive goods	equilibrium world price
land-intensive goods	tariff
capital-intensive goods	revenue tariff
cost ratio	protective tariff
principle of comparative advantage	import quota
	nontariff barrier (NTB)
terms of trade	voluntary export restriction (VER)
trading possibilities line	
gains from trade	strategic trade policy
world price	dumping
domestic price	World Trade Organization (WTO)
export supply curve	
import demand curve	

SELF-TEST

■ FILL-IN QUESTIONS

1. Exports of goods and services account for about (11, 22) _____% of total output in the United States and since 1975 this percentage has (doubled, quadrupled)_____.

2. Other industrially advanced nations such as the Netherlands and Canada have a (larger, smaller) _____ percentage of exports than the United States. The United States' volume of exports and imports makes it the world's (largest, smallest) _____ trading nation.

3. Nations tend to trade among themselves because the distribution of economic resources among them is (even, uneven) _____, the efficient production of various goods and services necessitates (the same, different) _____ technologies or combinations of resources, and people prefer (more, less) _____ choices in products.

4. The principle of comparative advantage means total world output will be greatest when each good is produced by that nation having the (highest, lowest) _____ opportunity cost. The nations of the world tend to specialize in the production of those goods in which they (have, do not have) _____ a comparative advantage and then export them, and they import those goods in which they _____ a comparative advantage in production.

5. If the cost ratio in country X is 4 Panama hats equal 1 pound of bananas, while in country Y 3 Panama hats equal 1 pound of bananas, then

   a. in country X hats are relatively (expensive, inexpensive) _____ and bananas relatively _____,

   b. in country Y hats are relatively (expensive, inexpensive) _____ and bananas relatively _____,

   c. X has a comparative advantage and should specialize in the production of (bananas, hats) _____, and Y has a comparative advantage and should specialize in the production of _____.

   d. when X and Y specialize and trade, the terms of trade will be somewhere between (1, 2, 3, 4) _____ and _____ hats for each pound of bananas and will depend on world demand and supply for hats and bananas.

   e. When the actual terms of trade turn out to be 3 1/2 hats for 1 pound of bananas, the cost of obtaining
   (1) 1 Panama hat has been decreased from (2/7, 1/3) _____ to _____ pounds of bananas in Y.
   (2) 1 pound of bananas has been decreased from (3 1/2, 4) _____ to _____ Panama hats in X.

f. International specialization will not be complete if the opportunity cost of producing either good (rises, falls) _____ as a nation produces more of it.

6. The basic argument for free trade based on the principle of (bilateral negotiations, comparative advantage) _____ is that it results in a (more, less) _____ efficient allocation of resources and a (lower, higher) _____ standard of living.

7. The world equilibrium price is determined by the interaction of (domestic, world) _____ supply and demand, while the domestic equilibrium price is determined by _____ supply and demand.

8. When the world price of a good falls relative to the domestic price in a nation, the nation will (increase, decrease)_____ its imports, and when the world price rises relative to the domestic price, the nation will _____ its exports.

9. In a two-nation model for a product, the equilibrium price and quantity of imports and exports occur where one nation's import demand intersects another nation's export (supply, demand) _____ curve. In a highly competitive world market, there can be (multiple, only one) _____ price(s) for a standardized product.

10. Excise taxes on imported products are (quotas, tariffs) _____, whereas limits on the maximum amount of a product that can be imported are import _____. Tariffs applied to a product not produced domestically are (protective, revenue) _____ tariffs, but tariffs designed to shield domestic producers from foreign competition are _____ tariffs.

11. There are other types of trade barriers. Imports that are restricted through the use of a licensing requirement or bureaucratic red tape are (tariff, nontariff) _____ barriers. When foreign firms voluntarily limit their exports to another country, it would represent a voluntary (import, export) _____ restraint.

12. Nations erect barriers to international trade to benefit the economic positions of (consumers, domestic producers) _____ even though these barriers (increase, decrease) _____ economic efficiency and trade among nations and the benefits to that nation are (greater, less) _____ than the costs to it.

13. When the United States imposes a tariff on a good that is imported from abroad, the price of that good in the United States will (increase, decrease) _____, the total purchases of the good in the United States will _____, the output of U.S. producers of the good will (increase, decrease) _____, and the output of foreign producers will _____. The ability of foreigners to buy goods and services in the United States will (increase, decrease) _____ and, as a result, output and employment in U.S. industries that sell goods and services abroad will _____.

14. When comparing the effects of a tariff with the effects of a quota to restrict the U.S. imports of a product, the basic difference is that with a (tariff, quota) _____ the U.S. government will receive revenue, but with a _____ foreign producers will receive the revenue.

15. List the six arguments that protectionists use to justify trade barriers.

a. _____

b. _____

c. _____

d. _____

e. _____

f. _____

16. The military self-sufficiency argument can be challenged because it is difficult to determine which industry is (essential, unessential) _____ for national defense and must be protected. Rather than impose a tariff, a direct subsidy to producers would be (more, less) _____ efficient in this case.

17. Trade barriers do not necessarily increase domestic employment because: imports may change only the (level, composition) _____ of employment; trade barriers can be viewed as "beggar thy (customer, neighbor) _____" policies; other nations can (protest, retaliate) _____ against the trade barriers; and in the long run, the barriers create an allocation of resources that is (more, less) _____ efficient by shielding protected domestic industries from competition.

18. Using trade barriers to permit diversification for stability in an economy is not necessary for (advanced, developing) _____ economies such as in the United States, and there may be great economic costs to forcing diversification in _____ nations; it is also alleged that infant industries need protection until they are sufficiently large to compete, an argument that has been modified to strategic trade policy in _____ economies.

19. In sum, most arguments for protectionism are (strong, weak) _____ and are designed to benefit (consumers, domestic producers) _____. If these protectionism arguments were followed, it would create (losses, gains) _____ for protected industries and their workers at the expense of _____ for the economy.

20. The World Trade Organization is charged with overseeing trade (specialization, liberalization) _____. This approach to trade seeks to (increase, decrease) _____ tariffs, _____ agriculture subsidies distorting global trade, and _____ quotas on textiles and apparel. Other areas considered in this agenda are new rules to promote trade in (steel, services) _____ and (more, less) _____ protection of intellectual property rights.

■ TRUE–FALSE QUESTIONS

Circle T if the statement is true, F if it is false.

1. The bulk of U.S. export and import trade is with other industrially advanced nations.   **T F**

2. A factor that serves as the economic basis for world trade is the even distribution of resources among nations.   **T F**

3. People trade because they seek products of different quality and other nonprice attributes.   **T F**

4. Examples of capital-intensive goods would be automobiles, machinery, and chemicals.   **T F**

5. The relative efficiency with which a nation can produce specific goods is fixed over time.   **T F**

6. Mutually advantageous specialization and trade are possible between any two nations if they have the same domestic opportunity-cost ratios for any two products.   **T F**

7. The principle of comparative advantage is that total output will be greatest when each good is produced by that nation which has the higher domestic opportunity cost.   **T F**

8. By specializing based on comparative advantage, nations can obtain larger outputs with fixed amounts of resources.   **T F**

9. The terms of trade determine how the increase in world output resulting from comparative advantage is shared by trading nations.   **T F**

10. Increasing opportunity costs tend to prevent specialization among trading nations from being complete.   **T F**

11. Trade among nations tends to bring about a more efficient use of the world's resources and a higher level of material well-being.   **T F**

12. Free trade among nations tends to increase monopoly and lessen competition in these nations.   **T F**

13. A nation will export a particular product if the world price is less than the domestic price.   **T F**

14. In a two-country model, equilibrium in world prices and quantities of exports and imports will occur where one nation's export supply curve intersects the other nation's import demand curve.   **T F**

15. A tariff on coffee in the United States is an example of a protective tariff.   **T F**

16. The imposition of a tariff on a good imported from abroad will reduce the amount of the imported good that is bought.   **T F**

17. A cost of tariffs and quotas imposed by the United States is higher prices that U.S. consumers must pay for the protected product.   **T F**

18. The major difference between a tariff and a quota on an imported product is that a quota produces revenue for the government.   **T F**

19. To advocate tariffs that would protect domestic producers of goods and materials essential to national defense is to substitute a political-military objective for the economic objectives of efficiently allocating resources.   **T F**

20. Tariffs and import quotas meant to increase domestic full employment achieve short-run domestic goals by making trading partners poorer.   **T F**

21. One-crop economies may be able to make themselves more stable and diversified by imposing tariffs on goods imported from abroad, but these tariffs are also apt to lower the standard of living in these economies.   **T F**

22. Protection against the "dumping" of foreign goods at low prices on the U.S. market is one good reason for widespread, permanent tariffs.   **T F**

23. Most arguments for trade protection are special-interest pleas that, if followed, would create gains for protected industries and their workers at the expense of greater losses for the economy.   **T F**

24. The only argument for tariffs that has, in the appropriate circumstances, any economic justification is the increase-domestic-employment argument.   **T F**

25. The World Trade Organization was established by the United Nations to encourage purchases of products from developing nations.   **T F**

■ **MULTIPLE-CHOICE QUESTIONS**

Circle the letter that corresponds to the best answer.

1. Which nation leads the world in the volume of exports and imports?
(a) Japan
(b) Germany
(c) United States
(d) United Kingdom

2. Which group of nations dominates world trade?
(a) Saudi Arabia and other OPEC nations
(b) Singapore, South Korea, and Taiwan
(c) United States, Japan, and the nations of Western Europe
(d) China, Russia, and the nations of Eastern Europe

3. Nations engage in trade because
(a) world resources are evenly distributed among nations
(b) world resources are unevenly distributed among nations
(c) all products are produced from the same technology
(d) all products are produced from the same combinations of resources

Use the following tables to answer Questions 4, 5, 6, and 7.

NEPAL PRODUCTION POSSIBILITIES TABLE

Product	Production alternatives					
	A	B	C	D	E	F
Yak fat	0	4	8	12	16	20
Camel hides	40	32	24	16	8	0

KASHMIR PRODUCTION POSSIBILITIES TABLE

Product	Production alternatives					
	A	B	C	D	E	F
Yak fat	0	3	6	9	12	15
Camel hides	60	48	36	24	12	0

4. The data in the tables show that production in
(a) both Nepal and Kashmir are subject to increasing opportunity costs
(b) both Nepal and Kashmir are subject to constant opportunity costs
(c) Nepal is subject to increasing opportunity costs and Kashmir to constant opportunity costs
(d) Kashmir is subject to increasing opportunity costs and Nepal to constant opportunity costs

5. If Nepal and Kashmir engage in trade, the terms of trade will be
(a) between 2 and 4 camel hides for 1 unit of yak fat
(b) between 1/3 and 1/2 units of yak fat for 1 camel hide
(c) between 3 and 4 units of yak fat for 1 camel hide
(d) between 2 and 4 units of yak fat for 1 camel hide

6. Assume that prior to specialization and trade Nepal and Kashmir both choose production possibility C. Now if each specializes according to its comparative advantage, the resulting gains from specialization and trade will be
(a) 6 units of yak fat
(b) 8 units of yak fat
(c) 6 units of yak fat and 8 camel hides
(d) 8 units of yak fat and 6 camel hides

7. Each nation produced only one product in accordance with its comparative advantage, and the terms of trade were set at 3 camel hides for 1 unit of yak fat. In this case, Nepal could obtain a maximum combination of 8 units of yak fat and
(a) 12 camel hides
(b) 24 camel hides
(c) 36 camel hides
(d) 48 camel hides

8. What happens to a nation's imports or exports of a product when the world price of the product rises above the domestic price?
(a) Imports of the product increase.
(b) Imports of the product stay the same.
(c) Exports of the product increase.
(d) Exports of the product decrease.

9. What happens to a nation's imports or exports of a product when the world price of the product falls below the domestic price?
(a) Imports of the product increase.
(b) Imports of the product decrease.
(c) Exports of the product increase.
(d) Exports of the product stay the same.

10. Which one of the following is characteristic of tariffs?
(a) They prevent the importation of goods from abroad.
(b) They specify the maximum amounts of specific commodities that may be imported during a given period of time.
(c) They often protect domestic producers from foreign competition.
(d) They enable nations to reduce their exports and increase their imports during periods of recession.

11. The motive for barriers to the importation of goods and services from abroad is to
(a) improve economic efficiency in that nation
(b) protect and benefit domestic producers of those goods and services
(c) reduce the prices of the goods and services produced in that nation
(d) expand the export of goods and services to foreign nations

12. When a tariff is imposed on a good imported from abroad,
(a) the demand for the good increases
(b) the demand for the good decreases
(c) the supply of the good increases
(d) the supply of the good decreases

Answer Questions 13, 14, 15, 16, and 17 on the basis of the following diagram, where S_d and D_d are the domestic supply and demand for a product and P_w is the world price of that product.

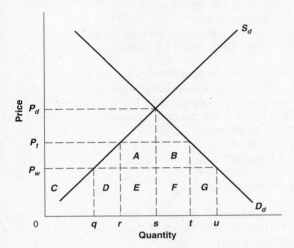

13. In a closed economy (without international trade), the equilibrium price would be
   (a) P_d, but in an open economy, the equilibrium price would be P_t
   (b) P_d, but in an open economy, the equilibrium price would be P_w
   (c) P_w, but in an open economy, the equilibrium price would be P_d
   (d) P_w, but in an open economy, the equilibrium price would be P_t

14. If there is free trade in this economy and no tariffs, the total revenue going to the foreign producers is represented by
   (a) area **C**
   (b) areas **A** and **B** combined
   (c) areas **A, B, E,** and **F** combined
   (d) areas **D, E, F,** and **G** combined

15. If a per-unit tariff was imposed in the amount of P_wP_t, then domestic producers would supply
   (a) **q** units and foreign producers would supply **qu** units
   (b) **s** units and foreign producers would supply **su** units
   (c) **r** units and foreign producers would supply **rt** units
   (d) **t** units and foreign producers would supply **tu** units

16. Given a per-unit tariff in the amount of P_wP_t, the amount of the tariff revenue paid by consumers of this product is represented by
   (a) area **A**
   (b) area **B**
   (c) areas **A** and **B** combined
   (d) areas **D, E, F,** and **G** combined

17. Assume that an import quota of **rt** units is imposed on the foreign nation producing this product. The amount of *total* revenue going to foreign producers is represented by areas

   (a) **A + B**
   (b) **E + F**
   (c) **A + B + E + F**
   (d) **D + E + F + G**

18. Tariffs lead to
   (a) the contraction of relatively efficient industries
   (b) an overallocation of resources to relatively efficient industries
   (c) an increase in the foreign demand for domestically produced goods
   (d) an underallocation of resources to relatively inefficient industries

19. Tariffs and quotas are costly to consumers because
   (a) the price of the imported good rises
   (b) the supply of the imported good increases
   (c) import competition increases for domestically produced goods
   (d) consumers shift purchases away from domestically produced goods

20. Which is a likely result of imposing tariffs to increase domestic employment?
   (a) a short-run increase in domestic employment in import industries
   (b) a decrease in the tariff rates of foreign nations
   (c) a long-run reallocation of workers from export industries to protected domestic industries
   (d) a decrease in consumer prices

21. The infant industry argument for tariffs
   (a) is especially pertinent for the European Union
   (b) generally results in tariffs that are removed after the infant industry has matured
   (c) makes it rather easy to determine which infant industries will become mature industries with comparative advantages in producing their goods
   (d) might better be replaced by an argument for outright subsidies for infant industries

22. Strategic trade policy is a modified form for advanced economies of which protectionist argument?
   (a) the increase-domestic-employment argument
   (b) the military self-sufficiency argument
   (c) the cheap foreign labor argument
   (d) the infant industry argument

23. "The nation needs to protect itself from foreign countries that sell their products in our domestic markets at less than the cost of production." This quotation would be most closely associated with which protectionist argument?
   (a) diversification for stability
   (b) increase domestic employment
   (c) protection against dumping
   (d) cheap foreign labor

24. Which is the likely result of the United States using tariffs to protect its high wages and standard of living from cheap foreign labor?
   (a) an increase in U.S. exports
   (b) a rise in the U.S. real GDP

(c) a decrease in the average productivity of U.S. workers

(d) a decrease in the quantity of labor employed by industries producing the goods on which tariffs have been levied

25. What international agency is charged with overseeing trade liberalization and with resolving disputes among nations?

(a) World Bank
(b) United Nations
(c) World Trade Organization
(d) International Monetary Fund

■ **PROBLEMS**

1. Shown below are the production possibilities curves for two nations: the United States and Chile. Suppose these two nations do not currently engage in international trade or specialization, and suppose that points **A** and **a** show the combinations of wheat and copper they now produce and consume.

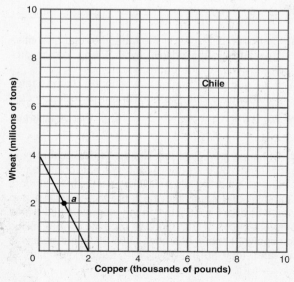

a. The straightness of the two curves indicates that the cost ratios in the two nations are (changing, constant) _____.

b. Examination of the two curves reveals that the cost ratio in

(1) the United States is _____ million tons of wheat for _____ thousand pounds of copper.

(2) Chile is _____ million tons of wheat for _____ thousand pounds of copper.

c. If these two nations were to specialize and trade wheat for copper,

(1) The United States would specialize in the production of wheat because _____

_____.

(2) Chile would specialize in the production of copper because_____

_____ .

d. The terms of trade, if specialization and trade occur, will be greater than 2 and less than 4 million tons of wheat for 1000 pounds of copper because _____

_____ .

e. Assume the terms of trade turn out to be 3 million tons of wheat for 1000 pounds of copper. Draw in the trading possibilities curve for the United States and Chile.

f. With these trading possibilities curves, suppose the United States decides to consume 5 million tons of wheat and 1000 pounds of copper while Chile decides to consume 3 million tons of wheat and 1000 pounds of copper. The gains from trade to

(1) the United States are _____ million tons of wheat and _____ thousand pounds of copper.

(2) Chile are _____ million tons of wheat and _____ thousand pounds of copper.

2. Following are tables showing the domestic supply and demand schedules and the export supply and import demand schedules for two nations (**A** and **B**).

NATION A

Price	Q_{dd}	Q_{sd}	Q_{di}	Q_{se}
$3.00	100	300	0	200
2.50	150	250	0	100
2.00	200	200	0	0
1.50	250	150	100	0
1.00	300	100	200	0

a. For nation **A**, the first column of the table is the price of a product. The second column is the quantity demanded domestically (Q_{dd}). The third column is the quantity supplied domestically (Q_{sd}). The fourth column is the quantity demanded for imports (Q_{di}). The fifth column is the quantity of exports supplied (Q_{se}).

(1) At a price of $2.00, there (will, will not) _____ be a surplus or shortage and there _____ be exports or imports.

(2) At a price of $3.00, there will be a domestic (shortage, surplus) _____ of _____ units. This domestic _____ will be eliminated by (exports, imports) _____ of _____ units.

(3) At a price of $1.00, there will be a domestic (shortage, surplus) _____ of _____ units. This domestic _____ will be eliminated by (exports, imports) _____ of _____ units.

NATION B

Price	Q_{dd}	Q_{sd}	Q_{di}	Q_{se}
$2.50	100	300	0	200
2.00	150	250	0	100
1.50	200	200	0	0
1.00	250	150	100	0

b. For nation **B,** the first column is the price of a product. The second column is the quantity demanded domestically (Q_{dd}). The third column is the quantity supplied domestically (Q_{sd}). The fourth column is the quantity demanded for imports (Q_{di}). The fifth column is the quantity of exports supplied (Q_{se}).

(1) At a price of $1.50, there (will, will not) _____ be a surplus or shortage and there _____ be exports or imports.

(2) At a price of $2.50, there will be a domestic (shortage, surplus) _____ of _____ units. This domestic _____ will be eliminated by (exports, imports) _____ of _____ units.

(3) At a price of $1.00, there will be a domestic (shortage, surplus) _____ of _____ units. This domestic _____ will be eliminated by (exports, imports) _____ of _____ units.

c. The following table shows a schedule of the import demand in Nation **A** and the export supply in Nation **B** at various prices. The first column is the price of the product. The second column is the quantity demanded for imports (Q_{diA}) in Nation **A.** The third column is the quantity of exports supplied (Q_{seB}) in Nation **B.**

Price	Q_{diA}	Q_{seB}
$2.00	0	100
1.75	50	50
1.50	100	0

(1) If the world price is $2.00, then Nation (**A, B**) _____ will want to import _____ units and Nation _____ will want to export _____ units of the product.

(2) If the world price is $1.75, then Nation (**A, B**) _____ will want to import _____ units and Nation _____ will want to export _____ units of the product.

(3) If the world price is $1.50, then Nation (**A, B**) _____ will want to import _____ units and Nation _____ will want to export _____ units of the product.

3. The following table shows the quantities of woolen gloves demanded (**D**) in the United States at several different prices (**P**). Also shown in the table are the quantities of woolen gloves that would be supplied by U.S. producers (**S_a**) and the quantities that would be supplied by foreign producers (**S_f**) at the nine different prices.

P	D	S_a	S_f	S_t	S'_f	S'_t
$2.60	450	275	475	____	____	____
2.40	500	250	450	____	____	____
2.20	550	225	425	____	____	____
2.00	600	200	400	____	____	____
1.80	650	175	375	____	____	____
1.60	700	150	350	____	____	____
1.40	750	125	325	____	____	____
1.20	800	0	300	____	____	____
1.00	850	0	0	____	____	____

a. Compute and enter in the table the total quantities that would be supplied (**S_t**) by U.S. and foreign producers at each of the prices.

b. If the market for woolen gloves in the United States is a competitive one the equilibrium price for woolen gloves is $_____ and the equilibrium quantity is _____.

c. Suppose now that the United States government imposes an 80 cent ($.80) tariff per pair of gloves on all gloves imported into the United States from abroad. Compute and enter into the table the quantities that would be supplied (**S'_f**) by foreign producers at the nine different prices. [*Hint:* If foreign producers were willing to supply 300 pairs at a price of $1.20 when there was no tariff, they are now willing to supply 300 pairs at

$2.00 (the $.80 per pair tariff plus the $1.20 they will receive for themselves). The quantities supplied at each of the other prices may be found in a similar fashion.]

d. Compute and enter into the table the total quantities that would be supplied (S'_t) by U.S. and foreign producers at each of the nine prices.

e. As a result of the imposition of the tariff the equilibrium price has risen to $_____ and the equilibrium quantity has fallen to _____.

f. The number of pairs sold by
(1) U.S. producers has (increased, decreased) _____ by _____.
(2) foreign producers has (increased, decreased) _____ by _____.

g. The total revenues (after the payment of the tariff) of
(1) U.S. producers—who do not pay the tariff—have (increased, decreased) _____ by $_____.
(2) foreign producers—who do pay the tariff— have (increased, decreased) _____ by $_____.

h. The total amount spent by U.S. buyers of woolen gloves has _____ by $_____.

i. The total number of dollars earned by foreigners has _____ by $_____, and, as a result, the total foreign demand for goods and services produced in the United States has _____ by $_____.

j. The tariff revenue of the United States government has _____ by $_____.

k. If an import quota were imposed that had the same effect as the tariff on price and output, the amount of the tariff revenue, $_____, would now be received as revenue by _____ producers.

■ **SHORT ANSWER AND ESSAY QUESTIONS**

1. Describe the quantity of imports and exports for the United States in absolute and relative terms. How has the quantity of imports and exports changed over time?

2. What are the major imports and exports of the United States? With which nations does the United States trade?

3. What role does the United States play in international trade? Who are the other major players in international trade?

4. What three factors—one dealing with the resource distribution, the second with production, and the third with the variety of product—are the basis of a rationale for trade among nations?

5. Explain
(a) the theory or principle of comparative advantage;
(b) what is meant by and what determines the terms of trade; and
(c) the gains from trade.

6. What is the case for free trade?

7. Explain how the equilibrium prices and quantities of exports and imports are determined.

8. Why will exports in a nation increase when world prices rise relative to domestic prices?

9. What motivates nations to erect barriers to the importation of goods from abroad, and what types of barriers do they erect?

10. Suppose the United States increases the tariff on automobiles imported from Germany (and other foreign countries). What is the effect of this tariff-rate increase on
(a) the price of automobiles in the United States;
(b) the total number of cars sold in the United States during a year;
(c) the number of cars produced by and employment in the German automobile industry;
(d) production by and employment in the U.S. automobile industry;
(e) German income obtained by selling cars in the United States;
(f) the German demand for goods produced in the United States;
(g) the production of and employment in those U.S. industries that now export goods to Germany;
(h) the standards of living in the United States and in Germany;
(i) the allocation of resources in the U.S. economy; and
(j) the allocation of the world's resources?

11. Explain the economic effects of a tariff and show them in a supply and demand graph.

12. Compare and contrast the economic effects of a tariff with the economic effects of an import quota on a product.

13. Critically evaluate the military self-sufficiency argument for protectionism. What industries should be protected?

14. What are four shortcomings of using tariffs or quotas to increase domestic employment in the United States?

15. What is the basis for the infant industry arguments (including strategic trade policy) for protectionism? How can it be countered?

16. Can a strong case for protectionism be made on the basis of defending against the "dumping" of products? How do you determine if a nation is dumping a product? What are the economic effects of dumping on consumers?

17. Does the economy need to shield domestic workers from competition from "cheap" foreign labor? Explain using the ideas of comparative advantage and standards of living.

18. Offer a summary of the case for protectionism. What does the historical evidence indicate? Give examples.

19. What are the trade liberalization issues that are the focus of the World Trade Organization?

20. What do critics of the World Trade Organization say about its effects on domestic economies and the global economy and what is the response from economists?

ANSWERS

Chapter 20 International Trade

FILL-IN QUESTIONS

1. 11, doubled
2. larger, largest
3. uneven, different, more
4. lowest, have, do not have
5. *a.* inexpensive, expensive; *b.* expensive, inexpensive; *c.* hats, bananas; *d.* 3, 4; *e.* (1) 1/3, 2/7, (2) 4, 3 1/2; *f.* rises
6. comparative advantage, more, higher
7. world, domestic
8. increase, increase
9. supply, only one
10. tariffs, quotas, revenue, protective
11. nontariff, export
12. domestic producers, decrease, less
13. increase, decrease, increase, decrease, decrease, decrease
14. tariff, quota
15. *a.* military self-sufficiency; *b.* support of infant industry; *c.* increase domestic employment; *d.* diversification for stability; *e.* protection against dumping; *f.* cheap foreign labor (any order for *a–f*)
16. essential, more
17. composition, neighbor, retaliate, less
18. advanced, developing, advanced
19. weak, domestic producers, gains, losses
20. liberalization, decrease, decrease, decrease, services, more

TRUE–FALSE QUESTIONS

1. T, p. 356
2. F, p. 357
3. T, pp. 357–358
4. T, p. 357
5. F, p. 358
6. F, pp. 358–359
7. F, p. 359
8. T, pp. 359–360
9. T, p. 360
10. T p. 362
11. T, pp. 362–363
12. F, p. 363
13. F, p. 363
14. T, pp. 365–366
15. F, p. 366
16. T, pp. 367–368
17. T, p. 368
18. F, p. 368
19. T, p. 369
20. T, p. 369
21. T, p. 370
22. F, p. 371
23. T, p. 372
24. F, p. 372
25. F, p. 373

MULTIPLE-CHOICE QUESTIONS

1. c, p. 356
2. c, p. 357
3. b, p. 357
4. b, p. 358
5. a, pp. 359–361
6. a, pp. 359–361
7. c, pp. 359–361
8. c, pp. 363–366
9. a, pp. 363–366
10. c, p. 366
11. b, pp. 366–368
12. d, pp. 367–368
13. b, pp. 367–368
14. d, pp. 367–368
15. c, pp. 367–368
16. c, pp. 367–368
17. c, p. 368
18. a, p. 368
19. a, p. 368
20. c, p. 369
21. d, p. 370
22. d, pp. 370–371
23. c, p. 371
24. c, p. 371
25. c, p. 373

PROBLEMS

1. *a.* constant; *b.* (1) 8, 2, (2) 4, 2; *c.* (1) it has a comparative advantage in producing wheat (its cost of producing wheat is less than Chile's), (2) it has a comparative advantage in producing copper (its cost of producing copper is less than the United States'); *d.* one of the two nations would be unwilling to trade if the terms of trade are outside this range; *f.* (1) 1, 0, (2) 1, 0
2. *a.* (1) will not, will not, (2) surplus, 200, surplus, exports, 200, (3) shortage, 200, shortage, imports, 200; *b.* (1) will not, will not, (2) surplus, 200, surplus, exports, 200, (3) shortage, 100, shortage, imports, 100; *c.* (1) A, 0, B, 100, (2) A, 50, B, 50, (3) A, 100, B, 0
3. *a.* 750, 700, 650, 600, 550, 500, 450, 300, 0; *b.* $2.00, 600; *c.* 375, 350, 325, 300, 0, 0, 0, 0, 0; *d.* 650, 600, 550, 500, 175, 150, 125, 0, 0; *e.* $2.20, 550; *f.* (1) increased, 25, (2) decreased, 75; *g.* (1) increased, $95, (2) decreased, $345; *h.* increased, $10; *i.* decreased, $345, decreased, $345; *j.* increased, $260; *k.* $260, foreign

SHORT ANSWER AND ESSAY QUESTIONS

1. pp. 356–357
2. pp. 356–357
3. pp. 356–357
4. p. 357
5. pp. 358–362
6. pp. 362–363
7. pp. 363–366
8. pp. 363–366
9. pp. 366–367
10. pp. 367–368
11. pp. 367–368
12. pp. 367–368
13. p. 369
14. p. 369
15. pp. 370–371
16. p. 371
17. p. 371
18. p. 372
19. pp. 373–374
20. p. 373

CHAPTER 21

Exchange Rates, the Balance of Payments, and Trade Deficits

In the last chapter you learned *why* nations engage in international trade and *why* they erect barriers to trade with other nations. In Chapter 21 you will learn *how* nations using different currencies are able to trade.

The means nations use to overcome the difficulties that result from the use of different currencies are fairly simple. When the residents of a nation (its consumers, business firms, or governments) wish to buy goods or services or real or financial assets from, make loans or gifts to, or pay interest and dividends to the residents of other nations, they *buy* some of the currency used in that nation. They pay for the foreign money with some of their own currency. In other words, they exchange their own currency for foreign currency.

When the residents of a nation sell goods or services or real or financial assets to, receive loans or gifts from, or are paid dividends or interest by the residents of foreign nations and obtain foreign currencies, they *sell* this foreign currency—often called foreign exchange—in return for some of their own currency. That is, they *exchange* foreign currency for their own currency.

The market in which one currency is sold and is paid for with another currency is called the **foreign exchange market.** The price that is paid (in one currency) for a unit of another currency is called the **foreign exchange rate.** And like most prices, the foreign exchange rate for any foreign currency is determined by the demand for and the supply of that foreign currency.

As you know from Chapter 20, nations buy and sell large quantities of goods and services across national boundaries. But the residents of these nations also buy and sell such financial assets as stocks and bonds and such real assets as land and capital goods in other nations, and the governments and individuals in one nation make gifts (remittances) to other nations. At the end of a year, nations summarize their foreign transactions with the rest of the world. This summary is called the nation's **balance of payments:** a record of how it obtained foreign currency during the year and what it did with this foreign currency.

Of course, all foreign currency obtained was used for some purpose—it did not evaporate—consequently the balance of payments *always* balances. The balance of payments is an extremely important and useful device for understanding the amounts and kinds of international transactions in which the residents of a nation engage. It also allows us to understand the meaning of a balance-of-payments deficit or surplus, the causes of these imbalances, and how to deal with them.

Several difficult sections of this chapter are concerned with how **flexible and fixed exchange-rate systems** handle balance-of-payments deficits and surpluses. A balance-of-payments deficit occurs when the foreign currency receipts are less than foreign currency payments and the nation must reduce its official reserves to balance its payments. Conversely, a balance-of-payments surplus occurs when foreign currency receipts are greater than foreign currency payments, and the nation must expand its official reserves to balance its payments. In these sections pay particular attention to the ways in which a flexible or floating exchange-rate system and a fixed exchange-rate system will correct balance-of-payments deficits and surpluses and the advantages and disadvantages of these two alternative systems for eliminating imbalances in international accounts.

As examples of these two types of exchange-rate systems, the next section of the chapter examines the **gold standard,** the **Bretton Woods system,** and the **managed floating exchange-rate system.** In the first two systems exchange rates are fixed, and in the third system exchange rates are fixed in the short run (to obtain the advantages of fixed exchange rates) and flexible in the long run (to enable nations to correct balance-of-payments deficits and surpluses).

The final section of the chapter examines the U.S. **trade deficits.** As you will learn, these deficits were the result of several factors—differences in national growth rates and a declining saving rate—that contributed to imports rising faster than exports. They also have several implications—increased current consumption at the expense of future consumption and increased U.S. indebtedness to foreigners.

■ CHECKLIST

When you have studied this chapter you should be able to

☐ Explain how U.S. exports create a foreign demand for dollars that in turn generates a supply of foreign currencies.

☐ Describe how U.S. imports create a domestic demand for foreign currencies that in turn generates a supply of dollars.

☐ Give a definition of a nation's balance of payments.

☐ Use the items in the current account to calculate the balance on goods, balance on goods and services, and balance on the current account when given the data.

☐ Describe how balance is achieved in the capital account.

☐ Explain the relationship between the current account, capital account, and official reserves account.

☐ Indicate how the official reserves account is used to determine whether there is a balance-of-payments deficit or surplus.

☐ Use a supply and demand graph to illustrate how a flexible exchange-rate system works to establish the price and quantity of a currency.

☐ Describe the depreciation and appreciation of a nation's currency under a flexible exchange-rate system.

☐ Identify the five principal determinants of the demand for and supply of a particular foreign currency and explain how they alter exchange rates.

☐ Explain how flexible exchange rates eventually eliminate balance-of-payments deficits or surpluses.

☐ List three disadvantages of flexible exchange rates.

☐ Use a supply and demand graph to illustrate how a fixed exchange-rate system functions.

☐ Discuss the objectives and limitations of using official reserves, trade policies, exchange controls, and domestic macroeconomic adjustments to maintain a fixed exchange rate.

☐ Identify three different exchange-rate systems used by the world's nations in recent years.

☐ List three conditions a nation had to fulfill if it was to be on the gold standard.

☐ Explain how the gold standard worked to maintain fixed exchange rates.

☐ Give reasons for the collapse of the gold standard.

☐ Explain how the Bretton Woods system attempted to stabilize exchange rates and to establish orderly changes in exchange rates for correcting balance-of-payments deficits.

☐ State reasons for the demise of the Bretton Woods system.

☐ Describe the current system of managed floating exchange rates.

☐ Discuss the pros and cons of the system of managed floating exchange rates.

☐ Describe the causes of recent trade deficits in the United States.

☐ Explain the economic implications of recent trade deficits in the United States.

■ CHAPTER OUTLINE

1. Trade between two nations differs from domestic trade because the nations use different currencies. This problem is resolved by the existence of **foreign exchange markets,** in which the currency used by one nation can be purchased and paid for with the currency of the other nation.

    a. U.S. exports create a foreign demand for dollars, and the satisfaction of this demand increases the supply of foreign currencies in the foreign exchange market.

    b. U.S. imports create a domestic demand for foreign currencies, and meeting this demand decreases the supplies of foreign currencies in the foreign exchange market.

2. The **balance of payments** for a nation is an annual record of all its transactions with the other nations in the world; it records all the payments received from and made to the rest of the world.

    a. The **current account** section of a nation's balance of payments records its trade in currently produced goods and services. Within this section

    (1) the **balance on goods** of the nation is equal to its exports of goods less its imports of goods;

    (2) the **balance on goods and services** is equal to its exports of goods and services less its imports of goods and services; and

    (3) the **balance on the current account** is equal to its balance on goods and services plus its net investment income (dividends and interest) from other nations and its net private and public transfers to other nations. This balance may be either a surplus or a deficit.

    b. The **capital account** of a nation's balance of payments records foreign purchases of real and financial assets in the United States. This item earns the United States some foreign currencies, so it is entered as a plus (+) in the capital account. U.S. purchases of real and financial assets abroad draw down U.S. holdings of foreign currencies, so this item is entered as a minus (−) in the capital account. The nation has a surplus in its capital account if foreign purchases of U.S. assets are greater than U.S. purchases of assets abroad. The nation has a deficit in its capital account if foreign purchases of U.S. assets are less than U.S. purchases of assets abroad.

    c. The **official reserves** account consists of the foreign currencies owned by the central bank. These reserves *decrease* when they are used to finance a net deficit on the combined current and capital accounts. In this case, the official reserves show as a plus (+) in the balance-of-payments account. The reserves *increase* when a nation has a net surplus on its current and capital account. In this case, they show as a minus (−) in the balance-of-payments account. The three components of the balance of payments— the current account, the capital account, and the official reserves account—must equal zero.

    d. A nation has a **balance-of-payments deficit** when imbalances in the combined current and capital accounts lead to a decrease in official reserves. A **balance-of-payments surplus** arises when imbalances in the combined current and capital accounts result in an increase in official reserves.

3. There are both a flexible or floating exchange system and a fixed exchange-rate system that nations use to correct imbalances in the balance of payments. If nations use a **flexible or floating exchange system,** the demand for and the supply of foreign currencies determine foreign exchange rates. The exchange rate for any foreign currency is the rate at which the quantity of that currency demanded is equal to the quantity of it supplied.

a. A change in the demand for or the supply of a foreign currency will cause a change in the exchange rate for that currency. When there is an increase in the price paid in dollars for a foreign currency, the dollar has *depreciated* and the foreign currency has *appreciated* in value. Conversely, when there is a decrease in the price paid in dollars for a foreign currency, the dollar has *appreciated* and the foreign currency has *depreciated* in value.

b. Changes in the demand for or supply of a foreign currency are largely the result of changes in tastes, relative incomes, relative price levels, relative interest rates, and speculation.

c. Flexible exchange rates can be used to eliminate a balance-of-payments deficit or surplus.

(1) When a nation has a payment deficit, foreign exchange rates will increase, thus making foreign goods and services more expensive and decreasing imports. These events will make a nation's goods and services less expensive for foreigners to buy, thus increasing exports.

(2) With a payment surplus, the exchange rates will increase, thus making foreign goods and services less expensive and increasing imports. This situation makes a nation's goods and services more expensive for foreigners to buy, thus decreasing exports.

d. Flexible exchange rates have disadvantages because they increase the uncertainties exporters, importers, and investors face, thus reducing international trade. This system also changes the terms of trade and creates instability in domestic economies.

4. If nations use a *fixed exchange-rate system,* the nations fix (or peg) foreign exchange rates. The governments of these nations must intervene in the foreign exchange markets to prevent shortages and surpluses caused by shifts in demand and supply.

a. One way a nation can stabilize foreign exchange rates is for its government to sell its reserves of a foreign currency in exchange for its own currency (or gold) when there is a shortage of the foreign currency. Conversely, a government would buy a foreign currency in exchange for its own currency (or gold) when there is a surplus of the foreign currency; however, currency reserves may be limited and inadequate for handling large and persistent deficits or surpluses, so it may use other means to maintain fixed exchange rates.

b. A nation might adopt trade policies that discourage imports and encourage exports.

c. A nation might impose exchange-rate controls and rationing, but these policies tend to distort trade, lead to government favoritism, restrict consumer choice, and create black markets.

d. Another way a nation can stabilize foreign exchange rates is to use monetary and fiscal policy to reduce its national income and price level and raise interest rates relative to those in other nations. These events would

lead to a decrease in demand for and increase in the supply of different foreign currencies.

5. In their recent history, the nations of the world have used three different exchange-rate systems.

a. Under the **gold standard,** each nation must define its currency in terms of a quantity of gold, maintain a fixed relationship between its gold and its money supply, and allow gold to be imported or exported without restrictions.

(1) The potential gold flows between nations would ensure that exchange rates remained fixed.

(2) Payment deficits and surpluses would be eliminated through macroeconomic adjustments. For example, if a nation had a balance-of-payments deficit and gold flowing out of the country, its money supply would decrease. This event would increase interest rates and decrease total spending, output, employment, and the price level. The opposite would happen in the other country because it would have a payments surplus. The changes in both nations would eliminate any payments deficit or surplus.

(3) During the worldwide depression of the 1930s nations felt that remaining on the gold standard threatened their recoveries, and the policy of devaluating their currencies to boost exports led to the breakdown and abandonment of the gold standard.

b. From the end of World War II until 1971, under the **Bretton Woods system,** nations were committed to the adjustable-peg system of exchange rates. The **International Monetary Fund (IMF)** was created to keep this exchange-rate system feasible and flexible.

(1) The adjustable-peg system required the United States to sell gold to other member nations at a fixed price and the other members of the IMF to define their monetary units in terms of either gold or dollars (which established fixed exchange rates among the currencies of all member nations) and required the other member nations to keep the exchange rates for their currencies from rising by selling foreign currencies, selling gold, or borrowing on a short-term basis from the IMF.

(2) The system also provided for orderly changes in exchange rates to correct a fundamental imbalance (persistent and sizable balance-of-payments deficits) by allowing a nation to devalue its currency (increase its defined gold or dollar equivalent).

(3) The other nations of the world used gold and dollars as their international monetary reserves in the Bretton Woods system. For these reserves to grow, the United States had to continue to have balance-of-payments deficits, but to continue the convertibility of dollars into gold it had to reduce the deficits, and, faced with this dilemma, in 1971 the United States suspended the convertibility of the dollar, brought an end to the Bretton Woods system, and allowed the exchange rates for the dollar and the other currencies to float.

c. Exchange rates today are allowed to float in the long term to correct balance-of-payments deficits and surpluses, but there can be short-term interventions by governments to stabilize and manage currencies. This new system of ***managed floating exchange rates*** is favored by some and criticized by others.

(1) Its proponents contend that this system has *not* led to any decrease in world trade, and has enabled the world to adjust to severe economic shocks throughout its history.

(2) Its critics argue that it has resulted in volatile exchange rates that can hurt those developing nations that are dependent on exports, has *not* reduced balance-of-payments deficits and surpluses, and is a "nonsystem" that a nation may use to achieve its own domestic economic goals.

6. The United States had large and persistent ***trade deficits*** in the past decade, and they are likely to continue.

  a. These trade deficits were the result of several factors:

  (1) more rapid growth in the domestic economy than in the economies of several major trading partners, which caused imports to rise more than exports;

  (2) the emergence of large trade deficits with China;

  (3) a decline in the rate of saving and a capital account surplus, which allowed U.S. citizens to consume more imported goods.

  b. The trade deficits of the United States have had two principal effects: They increased current domestic consumption (allowing the nation to operate outside its production possibilities frontier), and they increased the indebtedness of U.S. citizens to foreigners. A possible negative implication of these persistent trade deficits is that they will lead to permanent debt and more foreign ownership of domestic assets, or lead to large sacrifices of future domestic consumption. But, if the foreign lending increases the U.S. capital stock, then it can contribute to long-term U.S. economic growth.

■ **HINTS AND TIPS**

1. The chapter is filled with many new terms, some of which are just special words used in international economics to mean things with which you are already familiar. Other terms are new to you, so you must spend time learning them if you are to understand the chapter.

2. The terms ***depreciation*** and ***appreciation*** can be confusing when applied to foreign exchange markets.

  a. First, know the related terms. "Depreciate" means decrease or fall, whereas "appreciate" means increase or rise.

  b. Second, think of depreciation or appreciation in terms of quantities:

  (1) what *decreases* when the currency of Country A *depreciates* is the *quantity* of Country B's currency that can be purchased for *1 unit* of Country A's currency;

  (2) what *increases* when the currency of Country A *appreciates* is the *quantity* of Country B's currency that can be purchased for *1 unit* of Country A's currency.

  c. Third, consider the effect of changes in ***exchange rates:***

  (1) when the exchange rate for Country B's currency *rises*, this means that Country A's currency has

depreciated in value because 1 unit of Country A's currency will now purchase a smaller quantity of Country B's currency;

(2) when the exchange rate for Country B's currency *falls*, this means that Country A's currency has *appreciated* in value because 1 unit of Country A's currency will now purchase a larger quantity of Country B's currency.

3. The meaning of the balance of payments can also be confusing because of the number of accounts in the balance sheet. Remember that the balance of payments must always balance and sum to zero because one account in the balance of payments can be in surplus, but it will be offset by a deficit in another account. However, when people talk about a balance-of-payments surplus or deficit, they are referring to the sum of the current and capital account balances. If the total is positive, there is a balance-of-payments surplus, but if it is negative, there is a balance-of-payments deficit.

■ **IMPORTANT TERMS**

balance of payments	**fixed exchange-rate system**
current account	**purchasing-power-parity**
balance on goods and	**theory**
services	**currency interventions**
trade deficit	**exchange controls**
trade surplus	**gold standard**
balance on current account	**devaluation**
capital account	**Bretton Woods system**
balance on the capital	**International Monetary Fund**
account	**(IMF)**
official reserves	**managed floating exchange**
balance-of-payments deficit	**rate**
balance-of-payments surplus	
flexible or floating exchange-	
rate system	

SELF-TEST

■ **FILL-IN QUESTIONS**

1. The rate of exchange for the European euro is the amount in (euros, dollars) _____ that a U.S. citizen must pay to obtain 1 (euro, dollar) _____. The rate of exchange for the U.S. dollar is the amount in (euros, dollars) _____ that a citizen in the euro zone must pay to obtain 1 (euro, dollar) _____. If the rate of exchange for the euro is (1.05 euros, $0.95) _____, the rate of exchange for the U.S. dollar is _____.

2. U.S. exports create a foreign (demand for, supply of) _____ dollars and generate a

_____ foreign currencies owned by U.S. banks and available to domestic buyers; U.S. imports create a domestic (demand for, supply of) _____ foreign currencies and reduce the _____ foreign currencies held by U.S. banks and available for domestic consumers.

3. The balance of payments of a nation records all payments (domestic, foreign) _____ residents make to and receive from _____ residents. Any transaction that *earns* foreign exchange for that nation is a (debit, credit) _____, and any transaction that *uses up* foreign exchange is a _____. A debit is shown with a (+, −) _____ sign, and a credit is shown with a _____ sign.

4. If a nation has a deficit in its balance of goods, its exports of goods are (greater, less) _____ than its imports of goods, and if it has a deficit in its balance on goods and services, its exports of these items are _____ than its imports of them. The current account is equal to the balance on goods and services (plus, minus) _____ net investment income and _____ net transfers.

5. The capital account records the flow of payments from the sale or purchase of real or financial assets. Foreign purchases of real and financial assets in the United States earn foreign currencies, so they are entered as a (plus, minus) _____ in the U.S. capital account, but U.S. purchases of real and financial assets abroad draw down U.S. holding of foreign currencies, so this item is entered as a _____. If foreign purchases of U.S. assets are greater than U.S. purchases of assets abroad, the nation has a (surplus, deficit) _____ in its capital account, but if foreign purchases of U.S. assets are less than U.S. purchases of assets abroad, it has a _____.

6. A nation may finance a current account deficit by (buying, selling) _____ assets or by (borrowing, lending) _____ abroad and may use a current account surplus to (buy, sell) _____ assets or to (borrow, lend) _____ abroad.

7. The official reserves of a nation are the quantities of (foreign currencies, its own money) _____ owned by its central bank. If that nation has a deficit on the current and capital accounts, its official reserves (increase, decrease) _____, but with a surplus on the current and capital accounts, its official

reserves _____. The sum of the current, capital, and official reserves accounts must equal (0, 1) _____.

8. A nation has a balance-of-payments deficit if the sum of its current and capital accounts balances is (positive, negative) _____ and its official reserves (increase, decrease) _____. A nation has a payments surplus when the sum of its current and capital accounts balances is (positive, negative) _____ and its official reserves (increase, decrease) _____.

9. If foreign exchange rates float freely and a nation has a balance-of-payments *deficit,* that nation's currency in the foreign exchange markets will (appreciate, depreciate) _____ and foreign currencies will _____ compared to it. As a result of these changes in foreign exchange rates, the nation's imports will (increase, decrease) _____, its exports will _____, and the size of its deficit will (increase, decrease) _____.

10. What effect would each of the following have—the appreciation (**A**) or depreciation (**D**) of the euro compared to the U.S. dollar in the foreign exchange market, *ceteris paribus?*

   a. The increased preference in the United States for domestic wines over wines produced in Europe:

   _____

   b. A rise in the U.S. national income: _____

   c. An increase in the price level in Europe: _____
   d. A rise in real interest rates in the United States:

   e. The belief of speculators in Europe that the dollar will appreciate in the foreign exchange market:

   _____

11. There are three disadvantages of freely floating foreign exchange rates: the risks and uncertainties associated with flexible rates tend to (expand, diminish) _____ trade between nations; when a nation's currency depreciates, its terms of trade with other nations are (worsened, improved) _____; and fluctuating exports and imports can (stabilize, destabilize) _____ an economy.

12. To fix or peg the rate of exchange for the Mexican peso when the exchange rate for the peso is rising, the United States would (buy, sell) _____ pesos in exchange for dollars, and when the exchange rate for the peso is falling, the United States would _____ pesos in exchange for dollars.

13. Under a fixed exchange-rate system, a nation with a balance-of-payments deficit might attempt to eliminate the deficit by (taxing, subsidizing) _____ imports or by _____ exports. The nation might use exchange controls and ration foreign exchange among those who wish to (export, import) _____ goods and services and require all those who _____ goods and services to sell the foreign exchange they earn to the (businesses, government) _____.

14. If the United States has a payments deficit with Japan and the exchange rate for the Japanese yen is rising, under a fixed exchange-rate system the United States might adopt (expansionary, contractionary) _____ fiscal and monetary policies to reduce the demand for the yen, but this would bring about (inflation, recession) _____ in the United States.

15. When the nations of the world were on the gold standard exchange, rates were relatively (stable, unstable) _____. When a nation had a payments deficit, gold flowed (into, out of) _____ the nation, its money supply (increased, decreased) _____, its interest rates _____, and output, employment, income, and perhaps prices (increased, decreased) _____; thus its payments deficit _____.

16. The Bretton Woods system was established to bring about (flexible, fixed) _____ exchange rates. Under the Bretton Woods system, a member nation defined its monetary unit in terms of (oil, gold) _____ or dollars. Each member nation stabilized the exchange rate for its currency and prevented it from depreciating by (supplying, saving) _____ its official reserves of foreign currency, by (buying, selling) _____ gold, or by (borrowing from, lending to) _____ the International Monetary Fund. A nation with a deeply rooted payments deficit could (devalue, revalue) _____ its currency. The system was designed so that in the short run exchange rates would be (stable, flexible) _____ enough to promote international trade and in the long run they would be _____ enough to correct balance-of-payments imbalances.

17. The role of the dollar as a component of international monetary reserves under Bretton Woods produced a dilemma. For the dollar to remain an acceptable international monetary reserve, the U.S. payments deficits had to be (eliminated, continued) _____, but for international monetary reserves to grow to accommodate world trade, the U.S. payments deficits had to be _____. These deficits caused an acceptability problem because they resulted in (a decrease, an increase) _____ in the foreign holding of U.S. dollars and _____ in the U.S. reserves of gold, which contributed to (a decrease, an increase) _____ in the ability of the United States to convert dollars into gold and the willingness of foreigners to hold dollars as if they were as good as gold. In 1971, the United States essentially ended this system when it (adopted, suspended) _____ the convertibility of dollars into gold and allowed the value of the dollar to be determined by markets.

18. Since then the international monetary system has moved to a system of managed (fixed, floating) _____ exchange rates. This means that exchange rates of nations are (restricted from, free to) _____ find their equilibrium market levels, but nations may occasionally (leave, intervene in) _____ the foreign exchange markets to stabilize or alter market exchange rates.

19. The advantages of the current system are that the growth of trade (was, was not) _____ accommodated and that it has survived much economic (stability, turbulence) _____. Its disadvantages are its (equilibrium, volatility) _____ and the lack of guidelines for nations that make it a (bureaucracy, nonsystem) _____.

20. In recent years, the United States had large trade and current account (surpluses, deficits) _____ that were brought about by the sharp increases in its (exports, imports) _____ and the small increases in its _____. One cause was (stronger, weaker) _____ economic growth in the United States relative to _____ economic growth in Europe and Japan. Another contributing factor was a (rising, falling) _____ saving rate. One effect of the trade deficits of the United States has been (decreased, increased) _____ current domestic consumption that allows the nation to operate outside its production possibility frontier, and another effect was a (rise, fall) _____ in the indebtedness of U.S. citizens to foreigners.

■ **TRUE–FALSE QUESTIONS**

Circle T if the statement is true, F if it is false.

1. The imports of goods and services by U.S. citizens from abroad create a supply of dollars in the foreign exchange market.   **T   F**

2. The balance of payments of the United States records all the payments its residents receive from and make to the residents of foreign nations. **T F**

3. Exports are a debit item and are shown with a minus sign (−), and imports are a credit item and are shown with a plus sign (+) in the balance of payments of a nation. **T F**

4. The United States would have a balance-of-payments surplus if the balances on its current and capital accounts were positive. **T F**

5. Any nation with a balance-of-payments deficit in its current and capital accounts must reduce its official reserves. **T F**

6. The sum of a nation's current account balance, its capital account balance, and the change in its official reserves in any year is always equal to zero. **T F**

7. The purchasing-power-parity theory basically explains why there is an inverse relationship between the price of dollars and the quantity demanded. **T F**

8. The expectations of speculators in the United States that the exchange rate for Japanese yen will fall in the future will increase the supply of yen in the foreign exchange market and decrease the exchange rate for the yen. **T F**

9. If a nation has a balance-of-payments deficit and exchange rates are flexible, the price of that nation's currency in the foreign exchange markets will fall; this will reduce its imports and increase its exports. **T F**

10. Were the United States' terms of trade with Nigeria to worsen, Nigeria would obtain a greater quantity of U.S. goods and services for every barrel of oil it exported to the United States. **T F**

11. If a nation wishes to fix (or peg) the foreign exchange rate for the Swiss franc, it must buy Swiss francs with its own currency when the rate of exchange for the Swiss franc rises. **T F**

12. If exchange rates are stable or fixed and a nation has a payments surplus, prices and currency incomes in that nation will tend to rise. **T F**

13. A nation using exchange controls to eliminate a balance-of-payments surplus might depreciate its currency. **T F**

14. If country A defined its currency as worth 100 grains of gold and country B defined its currency as worth 20 grains of gold, then, ignoring packing, insuring, and shipping charges, 5 units of country A's currency would be worth 1 unit of country B's currency. **T F**

15. Under the gold standard, the potential free flow of gold among nations would result in exchange rates that are fixed. **T F**

16. In the Bretton Woods system, a nation could not devalue its currency by more than 10% without the permission of the International Monetary Fund. **T F**

17. In the Bretton Woods system, a nation with persistent balance-of-payments surpluses had an undervalued currency and should have increased the pegged value of its currency. **T F**

18. To accommodate expanding world trade in the Bretton Woods system, the U.S. dollar served as a reserve medium of exchange and the United States ran persistent balance-of-payments deficits. **T F**

19. A basic shortcoming of the Bretton Woods system was its inability to bring about the changes in exchange rates needed to correct persistent payments deficits and surpluses. **T F**

20. Using the managed floating system of exchange rates, a nation with a persistent balance-of-payments surplus should allow the value of its currency in foreign exchange markets to decrease. **T F**

21. Two criticisms of the current managed floating exchange-rate system are its potential for volatility and its lack of clear policy rules or guidelines for nations to manage exchange rates. **T F**

22. The trade deficits of the United States in recent years were caused by sharp increases in U.S. exports and slight increases in U.S. imports. **T F**

23. Improved economic growth in the major economies of the major trading partners of the United States would tend to worsen the trade deficit. **T F**

24. The decline in the saving rate in the United States contributed to the persistent trade deficit of the past decade. **T F**

25. The negative net exports of the United States have increased the indebtedness of U.S. citizens to foreigners. **T F**

■ **MULTIPLE-CHOICE QUESTIONS**

Circle the letter that corresponds to the best answer.

1. If a U.S. citizen could buy £25,000 for $100,000, the rate of exchange for the pound would be
  (a) $40
  (b) $25
  (c) $4
  (d) $.25

2. U.S. residents demand foreign currencies to
  (a) produce goods and services exported to foreign countries
  (b) pay for goods and services imported from foreign countries
  (c) receive interest payments on investments in the United States
  (d) have foreigners make real and financial investments in the United States

3. Which of the following would be a credit in the current account?
  (a) U.S. imports of goods
  (b) U.S. exports of services

(c) U.S. purchases of assets abroad

(d) U.S. interest payments for foreign capital invested in the United States

4. A nation's balance on the current account is equal to its exports less its imports of

(a) goods and services

(b) goods and services, plus U.S. purchases of assets abroad

(c) goods and services, plus net investment income and net transfers

(d) goods and services, minus foreign purchases of assets in the United States

5. The net investment income of the United States in its international balance of payments is the

(a) interest income it receives from foreign residents

(b) dividends it receives from foreign residents

(c) excess of interest and dividends it receives from foreign residents over what it paid to them

(d) excess of public and private transfer payments it receives from foreign residents over what it paid to them

6. In a flexible- or floating-exchange-rate system, when the U.S. dollar price of a British pound rises, this means that the dollar has

(a) appreciated relative to the pound and the pound has appreciated relative to the dollar

(b) appreciated relative to the pound and the pound has depreciated relative to the dollar

(c) depreciated relative to the pound and the pound has appreciated relative to the dollar

(d) depreciated relative to the pound and the pound has depreciated relative to the dollar

7. Which statement is correct about a factor that causes a nation's currency to appreciate or depreciate in value?

(a) if the supply of a nation's currency decreases, all else equal, that currency will depreciate

(b) if the supply of a nation's currency increases, all else equal, that currency will depreciate

(c) if the demand for a nation's currency increases, all else equal, that currency will depreciate

(d) if the demand for a nation's currency decreases, all else equal, that currency will appreciate

8. Assuming exchange rates are flexible, which of the following should increase the dollar price of the Swedish krona?

(a) a rate of inflation greater in Sweden than in the United States

(b) real interest rate increases greater in Sweden than in the United States

(c) national income increases greater in Sweden than in the United States

(d) the increased preference of Swedish citizens for U.S. automobiles over Swedish automobiles

9. Under a flexible exchange-rate system a nation may be able to correct or eliminate a persistent (long-term) balance-of-payments deficit by

(a) lowering the barriers on imported goods

(b) reducing the international value of its currency

(c) expanding its national income

(d) reducing its official reserves

10. If a nation had a balance-of-payments surplus and exchange rates floated freely, the foreign exchange rate for its currency would

(a) rise, its exports would increase, and its imports would decrease

(b) rise, its exports would decrease, and its imports would increase

(c) fall, its exports would increase, and its imports would decrease

(d) fall, its exports would decrease, and its imports would increase

11. Which would be a result associated with the use of freely floating foreign exchange rates to correct a nation's balance-of-payments surplus?

(a) The nation's terms of trade with other nations would be worsened.

(b) Importers in the nation who had made contracts for the future delivery of goods would find that they had to pay a higher price than expected for the goods.

(c) If the nation were at full employment, the decrease in exports and the increase in imports would be inflationary.

(d) Exporters in the nation would find their sales abroad had decreased.

12. The use of exchange controls to eliminate a nation's balance-of-payments deficit results in decreasing the nation's

(a) imports

(b) exports

(c) price level

(d) income

13. Which of these conditions did a nation have to fulfill if it was to be under the gold standard?

(a) use only gold as a medium of exchange

(b) maintain a flexible relationship between its gold stock and its currency supply

(c) allow gold to be freely exported from and imported into the nation

(d) define its monetary unit in terms of a fixed quantity of dollars

14. If the nations of the world were on the gold standard and one nation had a balance-of-payments surplus,

(a) foreign exchange rates in that nation would rise

(b) gold would tend to be imported into that country

(c) the level of prices in that country would fall

(d) employment and output in that country would fall

15. Which was the principal disadvantage of the gold standard?

(a) unstable foreign exchange rates

(b) persistent payments imbalances

(c) the uncertainties and decreased trade that resulted from the depreciation of gold

(d) the domestic macroeconomic adjustments experienced by a nation with a payments deficit or surplus

16. The objective of the adjustable-peg or Bretton Woods system was exchange rates that were
  (a) adjustable in the short run and fixed in the long run
  (b) adjustable in both the short and the long run
  (c) fixed in both the short and the long run
  (d) fixed in the short run and adjustable in the long run

17. Which is the best definition of international monetary reserves in the Bretton Woods system?
  (a) gold
  (b) dollars
  (c) gold and dollars
  (d) gold, dollars, and British pounds

18. The major dilemma created by the persistent U.S. payments deficits under the Bretton Woods system was that in order to maintain the status of the dollar as an acceptable international monetary reserve, the deficits had to
  (a) decrease, but to expand reserves to accommodate world trade, the deficits had to continue
  (b) continue, but to expand reserves to accommodate world trade, the deficits had to be eliminated
  (c) increase, but to expand reserves to accommodate world trade, the deficits had to be reduced
  (d) decrease, but to expand reserves to accommodate world trade, the deficits had to be eliminated

19. "Floating" the dollar means
  (a) the value of the dollar is determined by the demand for and the supply of the dollar
  (b) the dollar price of gold has been increased
  (c) the price of the dollar has been allowed to crawl upward at the rate of one-fourth of 1% a month
  (d) the IMF decreased the value of the dollar by 10%

20. A system of managed floating exchange rates
  (a) allows nations to stabilize exchange rates in the short term
  (b) requires nations to stabilize exchange rates in the long term
  (c) entails stable exchange rates in both the short and long term
  (d) fixes exchange rates at market levels

21. Floating exchange rates
  (a) tend to correct balance-of-payments imbalances
  (b) reduce the uncertainties and risks associated with international trade
  (c) increase the world's need for international monetary reserves
  (d) tend to have no effect on the volume of trade

22. The trade problem that faced the United States in recent years was a
  (a) deficit in its capital account
  (b) surplus in its balance on goods
  (c) deficit in its current account
  (d) surplus in its current account

23. Which was a cause of the growth of U.S. trade deficits in recent years?
  (a) protective tariffs imposed by the United States
  (b) slower economic growth in the United States
  (c) direct foreign investment in the United States
  (d) a declining saving rate in the United States

24. What would be the effect on U.S. imports and exports when the United States experiences strong economic growth but its major trading partners experience sluggish economic growth?
  (a) U.S. imports will increase more than U.S. exports
  (b) U.S. exports will increase more than U.S. imports
  (c) U.S. imports will decrease but U.S. exports will increase
  (d) there will be no effect on U.S. imports and exports

25. Two major outcomes from the trade deficits of recent years were
  (a) decreased domestic consumption and U.S. indebtedness
  (b) increased domestic consumption and U.S. indebtedness
  (c) increased domestic consumption but decreased U.S. indebtedness
  (d) decreased domestic consumption but increased U.S. indebtedness

■ **PROBLEMS**

1. Assume a U.S. exporter sells $3 million worth of wheat to an importer in Colombia. If the rate of exchange for the Colombian peso is $.02 (2 cents), the wheat has a total value of 150 million pesos.
  a. There are two ways the importer in Colombia may pay for the wheat. It might write a check for 150 million pesos drawn on its bank in Bogotá and send it to the U.S. exporter.
  (1) The American exporter would then sell the check to its bank in New Orleans and its demand deposit there would increase by $_____ million.
  (2) This New Orleans bank now sells the check for 150 million pesos to a correspondent bank (a U.S. commercial bank that keeps an account in the Bogotá bank).
  (a) The New Orleans bank's account in the correspondent bank increases by _____ million (dollars, pesos) _____; and
  (b) the correspondent bank's account in the Bogotá bank increases by _____ million (pesos, dollars) _____.
  b. The second way for the importer to pay for the wheat is to buy from its bank in Bogotá a draft on a U.S. bank for $3 million, pay for this draft by writing a check for 150 million pesos drawn on the Bogotá bank, and send the draft to the U.S. exporter.
  (1) The U.S. exporter would then deposit the draft in its account in the New Orleans bank and its demand deposit account there would increase by $_____ million.

(2) The New Orleans bank collects the amount of the draft from the U.S. bank on which it is drawn through the Federal Reserve Banks.

(a) Its account at the Fed increases by $_____ million; and

(b) the account of the bank on which the draft was drawn decreases by $ _____ million.

c. Regardless of the way used by the Colombian importer to pay for the wheat,

(1) the export of the wheat created a (demand for, supply of) _____ dollars and a _____ pesos.

(2) The number of dollars owned by the U.S. exporter has (increased, decreased) _____ and the number of pesos owned by the Colombian importer has _____.

2. The following table contains hypothetical balance-of-payments data for the United States. All figures are in billions.

Current account

(1) U.S. goods exports	$+150
(2) U.S. goods imports	−200
(3) *Balance on goods*	_____
(4) U.S. exports of services	+75
(5) U.S. imports of services	−60
(6) *Balance on services*	_____
(7) *Balance on goods and services*	_____
(8) Net investment income	+12
(9) Net transfers	−7
(10) **Balance on current account**	_____

Capital account

(11) Foreign purchases of assets in the U.S.	+80
(12) U.S. purchases of assets abroad	−55
(13) **Balance on capital account**	_____
(14) *Current and capital account balance*	_____
(15) **Official reserves**	_____
	$ 0

a. Compute with the appropriate sign (+ or −) and enter in the table the seven missing items.

b. The United States had a payments (deficit, surplus)

_____ of $ _____.

3. The following table shows supply and demand schedules for the British pound.

Quantity of pounds supplied	Price	Quantity of pounds demanded
400	$5.00	100
360	4.50	200
300	4.00	300
286	3.50	400
267	3.00	500
240	2.50	620
200	2.00	788

a. If the exchange rates are flexible

(1) what will be the rate of exchange for the pound?

$_____

(2) what will be the rate of exchange for the dollar?

£_____

(3) how many pounds will be purchased in the market?

_____

(4) how many dollars will be purchased in the market?

_____

b. If the U.S. government wished to fix or peg the price of the pound at $5.00, it would have to (buy, sell) _____ (how many) _____ pounds for $_____.

c. And if the British government wished to fix the price of the dollar at £ 2/5, it would have to (buy, sell) _____ (how many) _____ pounds for $_____.

■ SHORT ANSWER AND ESSAY QUESTIONS

1. What is the foreign exchange rate? Who are the demanders and suppliers of a particular foreign exchange, say, the British pound? Why is a buyer (demander) in the foreign exchange markets also always a seller (supplier)?

2. What is meant when it is said that "A nation's exports pay for its imports"? Do nations pay for all their imports with exports?

3. What is a balance of payments? What are the principal sections in a nation's balance of payments, and what are the principal "balances" to be found in it?

4. How can a nation finance a current account deficit, and what can it do with a current account surplus?

5. How does a nation finance a balance-of-payments deficit, and what does it do with a balance-of-payments surplus?

6. What types of events cause the exchange rate for a foreign currency to appreciate or to depreciate? How will each event affect the exchange rate for a foreign currency and for a nation's own currency?

7. How can flexible foreign exchange rates eliminate balance-of-payments deficits and surpluses? What are the problems associated with this method of correcting payments imbalances?

8. How may a nation use its international monetary reserves to fix or peg foreign exchange rates? Be precise. How does a nation obtain or acquire these monetary reserves?

9. What kinds of trade policies may nations with payments deficits use to eliminate their deficits?

10. How can foreign exchange controls be used to restore international equilibrium? Why do such exchange controls necessarily involve the rationing of foreign exchange? What effect do these controls have on prices, output, and employment in nations that use them?

11. If foreign exchange rates are fixed, what kind of domestic macroeconomic adjustments are required to eliminate a payments deficit? To eliminate a payments surplus?

12. What is the gold standard? How did the international gold standard correct payments imbalances?

13. What were the disadvantages of the gold standard for eliminating payments deficits and surpluses?

14. What did nations use as international monetary reserves under the Bretton Woods system? Why was the dollar used by nations as international money, and how could they acquire additional dollars?

15. Explain the dilemma created by the need for expanding international monetary reserves and for maintaining the status of the dollar under the Bretton Woods system.

16. Why and how did the United States shatter the Bretton Woods system in 1971?

17. Explain what is meant by a managed floating system of foreign exchange rates. When are exchange rates managed and when are they allowed to float?

18. Explain the arguments of the proponents and the critics of the managed floating system.

19. What were the causes of the trade deficits of the United States in recent years?

20. What were the effects of the trade deficits of recent years on the U.S. economy?

ANSWERS

Chapter 21 Exchange Rates, the Balance of Payments, and Trade Deficits

FILL-IN QUESTIONS

1. dollars, euro, euros, dollar, $0.95, 1.05 euros
2. demand for, supply of, demand for, supply of
3. domestic, foreign, credit, debit, −, +
4. less, less, plus, plus
5. plus, minus, surplus, deficit
6. selling, borrowing, buy, lend
7. foreign currencies, decrease, increase, zero
8. negative, decrease, positive, increase
9. depreciate, appreciate, decrease, increase, decrease
10. *a.* D; *b.* A; *c.* D; *d.* D; *e.* D
11. diminish, worsened, destabilize
12. sell, buy
13. taxing, subsidizing, import, export, government
14. contractionary, recession
15. stable, out of, decreased, increased, decreased, decreased
16. fixed, gold, supplying, selling, borrowing from, devalue, stable, flexible
17. eliminated, continued, an increase, a decrease, a decrease, suspended
18. floating, free to, intervene in
19. was, turbulence, volatility, nonsystem
20. deficits, imports, exports, stronger, weaker, falling, increased, rise

TRUE–FALSE QUESTIONS

1. T, p. 378
2. T, p. 378
3. F, pp. 378–379
4. T, pp. 378–379
5. T, p. 380
6. T, p. 380
7. F, p. 383
8. T, p. 384
9. T, pp. 384–385
10. T, p. 386
11. F, pp. 386–387
12. T, pp. 387–388
13. F, p. 387
14. F, p. 388
15. T, pp. 388–389
16. T, pp. 389–390
17. T, pp. 389–390
18. T, pp. 389–390
19. T, p. 390
20. F, pp. 390–391
21. T, p. 391
22. F, p. 392
23. F, p. 392
24. T, p. 392
25. T, p. 393

MULTIPLE-CHOICE QUESTIONS

1. c, pp. 377–378
2. b, pp. 377–378
3. b, pp. 378–379
4. c, pp. 378–379
5. c, p. 379
6. c, p. 381
7. b, pp. 382–383
8. b, p. 384
9. b, pp. 384–385
10. b, p. 385
11. d, p. 386
12. a, p. 387
13. c, p. 388
14. b, pp. 388–389
15. d, p. 389
16. d, pp. 389–390
17. c, pp. 389–390
18. a, p. 390
19. a, p. 390
20. a, pp. 390–391
21. a, pp. 384–385, 391
22. c, p. 392
23. d, p. 392
24. a, p. 392
25. b, p. 393

PROBLEMS

1. *a.* (1) 3, (2) (a) 3, dollars, (b) 150, pesos; *b.* (1) 3, (2) (a) 3, (b) 3; *c.* (1) demand for, supply of, (2) increased, decreased
2. *a.* −50, +15, −35, −30, +25, −5, +5; *b.* deficit, 5
3. *a.* (1) 4.00, (2) 1/4, (3) 300, (4) 1200; *b.* buy, 300, 1500; *c.* sell, 380, 950

SHORT ANSWER AND ESSAY QUESTIONS

1. pp. 377–378
2. pp. 377–378
3. pp. 378–380
4. pp. 378–380
5. pp. 378–381
6. pp. 382–384
7. pp. 384–386
8. pp. 386–387
9. p. 387
10. p. 387
11. pp. 387–388
12. pp. 388–389
13. p. 389
14. pp. 389–390
15. p. 390
16. p. 390
17. pp. 390–391
18. p. 391
19. p. 392
20. p. 393

The Economics of Developing Countries

Note: The bonus web chapter is available at: www.mcconnell16.com.

This chapter looks at the critical problem of raising the standards of living in **developing countries** (DVCs) of the world. The development problems in these nations, especially the poorest ones, are extensive: low literacy rates, low levels of industrialization, high dependence on agriculture, rapid rates of population growth, and widespread poverty.

There is also a growing income gap between DVCs and **industrially advanced nations** (IACs). To close this gap, there needs to be more economic growth in DVCs. To achieve that growth requires that the economic resource bases be expanded and these resources be used efficiently. As you will discover from the chapter, DVCs trying to apply these principles face **obstacles** quite different from those that limit growth in the United States and other IACs. DVCs have many problems with natural, human, and capital resources and with technology, all of which combine to hinder economic growth. Certain social, cultural, and institutional factors also create a poor environment for economic development.

These obstacles do not mean that it is impossible to increase the living standards of these DVCs. What they do indicate is that to encourage growth, the DVCs must do things that do not need to be done in the United States or other IACs. Population pressures need to be managed, and there needs to be better use of labor resources. Steps must be taken to encourage capital investment. Governments must take an active role in promoting economic growth and limiting the public sector problems for economic development. Dramatic changes in social practices and institutions are required. If these and other actions are not taken, it may not be possible to reduce the major obstacles to growth and break the **vicious circle of poverty** in the DVCs.

No matter how successful the DVCs are in overcoming these obstacles, they still will not be able to grow rapidly without more aid from IACs. This assistance can come in the form of lower trade barriers in IACs that would increase sales of products from DVCs to IACs. There can be more foreign aid in the form of government grants and loans to IACs. The banks, corporations, and other businesses in IACs can provide private capital in the form of loans or direct foreign investment in the building of new factories and businesses.

The final section of the chapter is a fitting ending to the discussion of economic problems in developing nations. It focuses on specific policies to promote economic growth in the DVCs and examines the issue from two sides. One side offers a set of policies from the perspective of DVCs, and the other side lists things IACs can do to foster economic growth in developing nations. You will have to decide after reading the chapter if any of these actions would be worthwhile.

■ **CHECKLIST**

When you have studied this chapter you should be able to

☐ Describe the extent of income inequality among nations.

☐ Classify nations based on three levels of income.

☐ Compare the effects of differences in economic growth in IACs and DVCs.

☐ Discuss the human realities of poverty in DVCs.

☐ Identify two basic avenues for economic growth in IACs and DVCs.

☐ Describe natural resource problems in DVCs.

☐ Identify the three problems related to human resources that plague the poorest DVCs.

☐ Explain the difficulties for economic growth that are created by population growth in DVCs.

☐ Compare the traditional and demographic transition views of population and economic growth in DVCs.

☐ Describe the conditions of unemployment and underemployment in DVCs.

☐ State reasons for low labor productivity in DVCs.

☐ Give three reasons for the emphasis on capital formation in the DVCs.

☐ Identify obstacles to domestic capital formation through saving.

☐ List obstacles to domestic capital formation through investment.

☐ Explain why transferring the technologies from IACs to DVCs may not be a realistic method of improving the technology in DVCs.

☐ Identify three sociocultural factors that can potentially inhibit economic growth.

☐ Describe the institutional obstacles to growth.

☐ Explain why poverty in the poor nations is a vicious circle.

☐ List five ways that governments in the DVCs can play a positive role in breaking the vicious circle of poverty.

☐ Describe the problems with the public sector in fostering economic development.

☐ Identify the three ways IACs can help the DVCs foster economic growth.

☐ Explain how reducing international trade barriers in IACs would help DVCs.
☐ Describe the two sources of foreign aid for DVCs.
☐ Give three criticisms of foreign aid to DVCs.
☐ Explain why foreign aid to DVCs has declined.
☐ Describe what groups in IACs provide private capital to DVCs.
☐ Discuss nine DVC policies for promoting economic growth.
☐ Explain five actions that IACs can take to encourage growth in DVCs.

■ **CHAPTER OUTLINE**

1. There is considerable *income inequality among nations.* The richest 20% of the world's population receives more than 80% of the world's income.

   a. Countries can also be classified into two main groups.

   (1) *Industrially advanced countries* (IACs) are characterized by well-developed market economies based on large stocks of capital goods, advanced technology for production, and well-educated workers. Among the *high-income* nations are the United States, Canada, Japan, Australia, New Zealand, and most of the nations of Western Europe. These countries averaged $26,710 per capita income in 2001.

   (2) *Developing countries* (DVCs) are a diverse group of middle-income and low-income nations. *Middle-income* nations (e.g., Brazil, Poland, Russia, South Africa, and Thailand) have per capita incomes that range from $745 to $9206, and average incomes of about $1850. There are also *low-income* nations with per capita incomes of $745 or less, and average incomes of $430. This latter group is dominated by India, Indonesia, and most of the sub-Saharan nations of Africa. These nations are not highly industrialized, are dependent on agriculture, and often have high rates of population growth and low rates of literacy. The low-income nations comprise about 41% of the world's population.

   b. There are disparities in the growth rates of nations, resulting in sizable income gaps. Some DVC have been able to improve their economic conditions over time and become IACs. Other DVCs are now showing high rates of economic growth, but still other DVCs have experienced a decline in economic growth and standards of living. If growth rates were the same for high- and low-income nations, the gap in per capita income would widen because the income base is higher in high-income nations.

   c. The human realities of extreme poverty are important. Compared with IACs, persons in DVCs have not only lower per capita incomes but also lower life expectancies, and DVCs have higher infant mortality, lower literacy rates, more of the labor force in agriculture, and fewer nonhuman sources of energy.

2. *Economic growth* requires that DVCs use their existing resources more efficiently and that they expand their available supplies of resources. The physical, human, and socioeconomic conditions in these nations are the reasons why DVCs experience different rates of economic growth.

   a. Many DVCs possess inadequate *natural resources.* This limited resource base is an obstacle to growth. The agricultural products that DVCs typically export are also subject to significant price variations on the world market, creating variations in national income.

   b. There are problems with *human resources* in DVCs.

   (1) DVCs tend to be overpopulated and have high rates of population growth. These growing populations reduce the DVCs' capacity to save, invest, and increase productivity. They also overuse land and natural resources, and the migration of rural workers to cities creates urban problems.

   (2) DVCs often experience both unemployment and underemployment, which wastes labor resources.

   (3) DVCs have low levels of labor productivity because of insufficient physical capital and lack of investment in human capital.

   c. DVCs have inadequate amounts of *capital goods,* and so find it difficult to accumulate capital. Domestic capital formation occurs through saving and investing. The potential for saving is low in many DVCs because the nations are too poor to save. There is also *capital flight* of saving from DVCs to more stable IACs. The investment obstacles include a lack of investors and entrepreneurs and a lack of incentives to invest in DVC economies. The infrastructure is poor in many DVCs.

   d. *Technological advance* is slow in DVCs. Although these nations might adopt the technologies of industrial nations, these technologies are not always appropriate for the resource endowments of the DVCs, so they must learn to develop and use their own technologies.

   e. It is difficult for DVCs to alter the *social, cultural, and institutional factors* to create a good environment for achieving economic growth.

3. In summary, DVCs face a *vicious circle of poverty.* They save little and therefore invest little in real and human capital because they are poor, and because they do not invest, their outputs per capita remain low and they remain poor. Even if the vicious circle were to be broken, a rapid increase in population would leave the standard of living unchanged.

4. There are differing views about the *role of government* in fostering economic growth in DVCs.

   a. The positive view holds that in the initial stages of economic development, government action is needed to help overcome such obstacles as the lack of law and order, of entrepreneurship, and of infrastructure. Government policies may also assist capital formation and help resolve social and institutional problems.

   b. Problems and disadvantages with the public sector in promoting growth include bureaucratic impediments, corruption, maladministration, and the importance of political objectives over economic goals. Central planning does not work because it restricts competition and individual incentives, which are important ingredients in the growth process.

5. There are several ways *IACs can help DVCs.*
a. They can lower the *trade barriers* that prevent the DVCs from selling their products in the developed countries.
b. *Loans and grants* from governments and international organizations such as the *World Bank* would also enable the DVCs to accumulate capital. This foreign aid, however, has been criticized because it increases dependency, bureaucracy, and corruption. For these reasons, and because of the end of the cold war, foreign aid to DVCs has declined.
c. DVCs can also receive flows of private capital from IACs. *Direct foreign investment* in new factories and businesses can come from banks, corporations, and financial investment companies, but such investment tends to be highly selective among nations.

6. There are several *policies for promoting growth* that DVCs and IACs might undertake. Both DVC and IAC perspectives are offered.
a. *DVC policies* for promoting growth include establishing the rule of law, opening economies to international trade, controlling population growth, encouraging direct foreign investment, building human capital, making peace with neighbors, establishing independent central banks, making realistic exchange-rate policies, and privatizing state industries.
b. *IAC policies* for encouraging economic growth in DVCs are directing foreign aid to the poorest of the DVCs, reducing tariffs and import quotas, providing debt relief to DVCs, allowing more low-skilled immigration and discouraging brain drains, and limiting arms sales to DVCs.

■ HINTS AND TIPS

1. This chapter offers a comprehensive look at the various factors affecting growth and economic development. Keep in mind that *no one factor* explains why some nations prosper and others remain poor. The chapter should give you insights into how natural, human, and capital resources together with government policies may influence a nation's economic development.

2. Several economic and demographic statistics for comparing rich and poor nations appear in the chapter's tables. You need not memorize the numbers, but you should try to get a sense of the magnitude of the differences between IACs and DVCs on several key indicators. To do this, ask yourself questions calling for *relative comparisons.* For example, how many times larger is average per capita income in IACs than in low-income DVCs? Answer: 62 times greater ($26,710/$430 = 62).

3. The chapter ends with *policy suggestions* for increasing economic growth in DVCs. Be sure to look at these policies from the perspective of both DVCs and

IACs. Identify those that you think are most important, and explain your reasoning.

■ IMPORTANT TERMS

industrially advanced countries (IACs)
developing countries (DVCs)
demographic transition view
underemployment
brain drain
capital flight
infrastructure
capital-saving technology

capital-using technology
the will to develop
capricious universe view
land reform
vicious circle of poverty
corruption
World Bank
direct foreign investment

SELF-TEST

■ FILL-IN QUESTIONS

1. There is considerable income inequality among nations. The richest 20% of the world's population receives more than (40, 80) _____% of world income, while the poorest 20% of the world's population receives less than (2, 10) _____% of world income. The poorest 60% of nations receives less than (6, 30) _____% of the world's income.

2. High-income nations can be classified as (industrially advanced, developing) _____ countries, or (IACs, DVCs) _____, and the middle- or low-income nations as _____ countries, or (DVCs, IACs) _____.

3. IACs have a (higher, lower) _____ starting base for per capita income than DVCs, so the same percentage growth rate for both IACs and DVCs means (an increase, a decrease) _____ in the absolute income gap.

4. Low per capita income in DVCs means that there are (lower, higher) _____ life expectancies, _____ adult literacy, (lower, higher) _____ daily calorie supply, _____ energy consumption, and (lower, higher) _____ infant mortality.

5. The process for economic growth is the same for IACs and DVCs. It involves (less, more) _____ efficient use of existing resources and obtaining _____ productive resources.

6. The distribution of natural resources among DVCs is (even, uneven) _____; many DVCs lack vital natural resources. Although oil resources have been used for economic growth in (OPEC nations, DVCs)

_____, IACs own or control much of the natural resources in _____. Also, exports of products from DVCs are subject to (small, large) _____ price fluctuations in the world market, and that tends to make DVC incomes (more, less) _____ stable.

7. In terms of human resources,
a. many DVCs are (under, over) _____ populated and have (higher, lower) _____ population growth rates than IACs. Rapid population growth can cause per capita income to (increase, decrease) _____.
b. In DVCs, many people are unable to find jobs, so there is (underemployment, unemployment) _____, and many people are employed for fewer hours than they desire or work at odd jobs, so there is _____.
c. In DVCs, labor productivity is very (high, low) _____, partly because these countries have not been able to invest in (stocks and bonds, human capital) _____; when the best-trained workers leave DVCs to work in IACs, there is a (demographic transition, brain drain) _____ that contributes to the decline in skill level and productivity.

8. Capital accumulation is critical to the development of DVCs. If there were more capital goods, this would improve (natural resources, labor productivity) _____ and help boost per capita output. An increase in capital goods is necessary because the (demand for, supply of) _____ arable land is limited. The process of capital formation is cumulative, investment increases the (output, natural resources) _____ of the economy, and this in turn makes it possible for the economy to save more and invest more in capital goods.

9. The formation of domestic capital requires that a nation save and invest.
a. Saving is difficult in DVCs because of (high, low) _____ per capita income, and investment is difficult because of (many, few) _____ investors or entrepreneurs, and (strong, weak) _____ incentives to invest. There is also the problem of private savings being transferred to IACs; this transfer is called (brain drain, capital flight) _____.
b. Many DVCs do not have the infrastructure or (private, public) _____ capital goods that are necessary for productive _____ investment by businesses.

c. Nonfinancial (or in-kind) investment involves the transfer of surplus labor from (agriculture, industry) _____ to the improvement of agricultural facilities or the infrastructure.

10. The technologies used in the advanced industrial countries might be borrowed by and used in the DVCs, but
a. the technologies used in the advanced countries are based on a labor force that is (skilled, unskilled) _____, labor that is relatively (abundant, scarce) _____, and capital that is relatively _____, and their technologies tend to be (labor, capital) _____-using, while
b. the technologies required in developing countries must be based on a labor force that is (skilled, unskilled) _____, labor that is relatively (abundant, scarce) _____, and capital that is relatively _____, and their technologies tend to be (labor, capital) _____-using.
c. If technological advances make it possible to replace a worn-out plow, costing $10 when new, with a new $5 plow, the technological advance is capital (saving, using) _____.

11. Other obstacles to economic growth in DVCs include those dealing with problems of national unity, religion, and customs, or (institutional, sociocultural) _____ problems, and those dealing with such issues as political corruption, poor school systems, and land reform, or _____ problems.

12. In most DVCs, there is a vicious circle of poverty. Saving is low because the income per capita is (high, low) _____, and because saving is low, investment in real and human capital is _____. For this reason the productivity of labor and output (income) per capita remain (high, low) _____.

13. List five ways that government can serve a positive role in fostering economic growth in DVCs, especially during the early phases of growth:
a. _____
b. _____
c. _____
d. _____
e. _____

14. Government involvement in the economy of DVCs can create public sector problems because government bureaucracy can (foster, impede) _____ social and economic change, government planners can give too much emphasis to (political, economic)

_____ objectives, and there can be (good, poor) _____ administration and corruption.

15. Three major ways that IACs can assist in the economic development in DVCs is by (increasing, decreasing) _____ international trade barriers, _____ foreign aid, and _____ the flow of private capital investment.

16. Direct foreign aid for DVCs generally comes from individual nations in the form of (private, public) _____ loans, grants, and programs. It can also come from the (Bank of America, World Bank), _____ which is supported by member nations. This organization is a (first, last) _____ resort lending agency for DVCs and provides (military, technical) _____ assistance for DVCs.

17. Foreign aid has been criticized in recent years because it may (increase, decrease) _____ dependency in a nation instead of creating self-sustained growth, may _____ government bureaucracy and control over a nation's economy, and may _____ the misuse of funds or corruption. These criticisms and the end of the cold war have led to a(n) _____ in the amount of foreign aid to DVCs.

18. There can also be private capital flows to DVCs in the form of direct foreign (aid, investment) _____ from IAC firms, individuals, and commercial banks, and it has increased in recent years. The reason for this change is that many DVCs have reformed their economies and adopted policies that (limit, encourage) _____ economic growth and _____ direct foreign investment. Nevertheless, the flow of private capital to DVCs is (selective, widespread) _____ among nations.

19. DVCs can adopt policies to encourage economic growth. They can (open, close) _____ economies to international trade, (encourage, discourage) _____ direct foreign investment and the development of human capital, and (expand, control) _____ population growth.

20. IACs can also adopt policies to help DVCs. They can (raise, lower) _____ trade barriers, (encourage, discourage) _____ immigration of the brightest and best-educated, and direct foreign aid to the (middle-income, low-income) _____ DVCs.

■ **TRUE–FALSE QUESTIONS**

Circle T if the statement is true, F if it is false.

1. The richest 20% of the world's population receives about 50% of the world's income while the poorest 20% receives only about 20% of the world's income. **T F**

2. Developing countries generally have high unemployment, low literacy rates, rapid population growth, and a labor force committed to agricultural production. **T F**

3. The United States has about 5% of the world's population and produces about 31% of the world's output. **T F**

4. The absolute income gap between DVCs and industrially advanced countries has decreased over the past 30 years. **T F**

5. Economic growth in both IACs and DVCs requires using economic resources more efficiently and increasing the supplies of some of these resources. **T F**

6. It is impossible to achieve a high standard of living with a small supply of natural resources. **T F**

7. DVCs have low population densities and low population growth relative to IACs. **T F**

8. The demographic transition view of population growth is that rising incomes must first be achieved, and only then will slower population growth follow. **T F**

9. A major factor contributing to the high unemployment rates in urban areas of DVCs is the fact that the migration from rural areas to cities has greatly exceeded the growth of urban job opportunities. **T F**

10. Saving in DVCs is a smaller percentage of domestic output than in IACs, and this is the chief reason total saving in DVCs is small. **T F**

11. Before private investment can be increased in DVCs, it is necessary to reduce the amount of investment in infrastructure. **T F**

12. Technological advances in DVCs will be made rapidly because the advances do not require pushing forward the frontiers of technological knowledge, and the technologies used in IACs can be easily transferred to all DVCs. **T F**

13. When technological advances are capital saving, it is possible for an economy to increase its productivity without any _net_ investment in capital goods. **T F**

14. A critical, but intangible, ingredient in economic development is the "will to develop." **T F**

15. The capricious universe view is that there is a strong correlation between individual effort and results. **T F**

16. Land reform is one of the institutional obstacles to economic growth in many developing countries. **T F**

17. The situation in which poor nations stay poor because they are poor is a description of the vicious circle of poverty. **T F**

18. The creation of an adequate infrastructure in a nation is primarily the responsibility of the private sector. **T F**

19. Governments always play a positive role in fostering the economic growth of DVCs. **T F**

20. One effective way that IACs can help DVCs is to raise trade barriers so that DVCs become more self-sufficient. **T F**

21. The World Bank is the organization to which DVCs turn for the majority of foreign aid, loans, and grants. **T F**

22. Two reasons why foreign aid is viewed as harmful are that it tends to promote dependency and generate government bureaucracy. **T F**

23. An example of direct foreign investment would be the building of an automobile factory by General Motors in Brazil. **T F**

24. In recent years, a smaller proportion of private capital flows to DVCs has been direct foreign investment rather than loans to DVC governments. **T F**

25. One policy suggested for promoting economic growth in DVCs is the establishment of independent central banks (where they do not already exist) to keep inflation in check and control the money supply. **T F**

■ **MULTIPLE-CHOICE QUESTIONS**

Circle the letter that corresponds to the best answer.

1. Data on per capita income from the nations of the world indicate that there is considerable
 (a) income equality
 (b) income inequality
 (c) stability in the income growth
 (d) deterioration in incomes for most developing nations

2. Which nation would be considered a developing nation?
 (a) India
 (b) Italy
 (c) Japan
 (d) New Zealand

3. If the per capita income is $600 a year in a DVC and $12,000 in an IAC, then a 2% growth rate in each nation will increase the absolute income gap by
 (a) $120
 (b) $228
 (c) $240
 (d) $252

4. The poorest DVCs would probably exhibit high levels of
 (a) literacy
 (b) life expectancy
 (c) infant mortality
 (d) per capita energy consumption

5. The essential paths for economic growth in any nation are expanding the
 (a) size of the population and improving agriculture

 (b) role of government and providing jobs for the unemployed
 (c) supplies of resources and using existing resources more efficiently
 (d) amount of tax subsidies to businesses and tax credits for business investment

6. Based on the rule of 70, if the United States has an annual rate of population increase of 1% and a DVC has one of 2%, how many years will it take for the population to double in each nation?
 (a) 140 years for the United States and 70 years for the DVC
 (b) 35 years for the United States and 70 years for the DVC
 (c) 70 years for the United States and 35 years for the DVC
 (d) 70 years for the United States and 140 years for the DVC

7. Assume the total real output of a developing country increases from $100 billion to $115.5 billion while its population expands from 200 to 210 million people. Real per capital income has increased by
 (a) $50
 (b) $100
 (c) $150
 (d) $200

8. An increase in the total output of consumer goods in a DVC may not increase the average standard of living because it may increase
 (a) capital flight
 (b) population growth
 (c) disguised unemployment
 (d) the quality of the labor force

9. Which best describes the unemployment found in DVCs?
 (a) the cyclical fluctuations in the nation's economy
 (b) the migration of agricultural workers from rural areas to seek jobs in urban areas
 (c) workers being laid off by large domestic or multinational corporations during periods of economic instability
 (d) the education and training of workers in the wrong types of jobs and for which there is little demand

10. Which is an obstacle to economic growth in DVCs?
 (a) the low demand for natural resources
 (b) the low supply of capital goods
 (c) the decline in demographic transition
 (d) a fall in population growth

11. Which is a reason for placing special emphasis on capital accumulation in DVCs?
 (a) the flexible supply of arable land in DVCs
 (b) the high productivity of workers in DVCs
 (c) the high marginal benefits of capital goods
 (d) the greater opportunities for capital flight

12. Which is a factor limiting saving in DVCs?
 (a) The output of the economy is too low to permit a large volume of saving.

(b) Those who do save make their savings available only to their families.

(c) Governments control the banking system and set low interest rates.

(d) There is an equal distribution of income in most nations.

13. When citizens of developing countries transfer savings to or invest savings in industrially advanced countries, this is referred to as

(a) brain drain

(b) capital flight

(c) savings potential

(d) in-kind investment

14. Which is a major obstacle to capital formation in DVCs?

(a) lack of oil resources

(b) lack of entrepreneurs

(c) lack of government price supports for products

(d) an excess of opportunities for financial investments

15. If it is cheaper to use a new fertilizer that is better adapted to a nation's topography, this is an example of

(a) a capital-using technology

(b) a capital-saving technology

(c) capital consumption

(d) private capital flows

16. Which is an example of infrastructure?

(a) a farm

(b) a steel plant

(c) an electric power plant

(d) a deposit in a financial institution

17. Which seems to be the most acute *institutional* problem that needs to be resolved by many DVCs?

(a) development of strong labor unions

(b) an increase in natural resources

(c) the adoption of birth control

(d) land reform

18. Which is a major positive role for government in the early stage of economic development?

(a) providing an adequate infrastructure

(b) conducting central economic planning

(c) improving the efficiency of tax collection

(d) creating marketing boards for export products

19. In recent years, many DVCs have come to realize that

(a) there are few disadvantages from government involvement in economic development

(b) competition and economic incentives for individuals are necessary for economic growth

(c) the World Bank is an institutional barrier to economic growth

(d) private capital is not essential for economic growth

20. Industrially advanced countries can best help DVCs by

(a) letting them raise tariffs and quotas to protect domestic markets

(b) reducing foreign grant aid but increasing loan aid

(c) increasing the flows of private capital

(d) increasing control over their capital markets

21. The major objective of the World Bank is to

(a) maximize its profits for its worldwide shareholders

(b) assist developing countries in achieving economic growth

(c) provide financial backing for the operation of the United Nations

(d) maintain stable exchange rates in the currencies of developing countries

22. A major criticism of foreign aid to developing nations is that it

(a) provides incentives for capital flight

(b) is capital using rather than capital saving

(c) encourages growth in government bureaucracy

(d) gives too much power and control to the World Bank

23. Which would be an example of direct foreign investment in DVCs?

(a) a low-interest loan from the U.S. government to Nigeria

(b) a grant from the World Bank to build a dam in Thailand

(c) the purchase of a computer business in Honduras by a U.S. firm

(d) a payment from a worker in the U.S. to a family in Iran

24. A suggested policy for DVCs to implement that promotes economic growth is

(a) reducing the control of monetary policy by central banks

(b) obtaining more low-interest loans from the World Bank

(c) encouraging more direct foreign investment

(d) expanding state industries

25. Which is a suggested policy for industrially advanced countries to adopt to foster economic growth in DVCs?

(a) increased appreciation of currencies in DVCs

(b) increased debt relief in DVCs

(c) elimination of the International Monetary Fund

(d) elimination of the OPEC oil cartel

■ **PROBLEMS**

1. Suppose that the real per capita income in the average industrially advanced country is $8000 per year and in the average DVC $500 per year.

a. The gap between their standards of living is

$_____ per year.

b. If GDP per capita were to grow at a rate of 5% during a year in both the industrially advanced country and the DVC,

(1) the standard of living in the IAC would rise to

$_____ in a year;

(2) the standard of living in the DVC would rise to

$_____ in a year; and

(3) the gap between their standards of living would

(narrow, widen) _____ to $_____ in a year.

2. While economic conditions are not identical in all DVCs, certain conditions are common to or typical of most of them. In the space after each of the following characteristics, indicate briefly the nature of this characteristic in many low-income DVCs.

  a. Standard of living (per capita income): _____

  b. Average life expectancy: _____

  c. Extent of unemployment: _____

  d. Literacy: _____

  e. Technology: _____

  f. Percentage of the population engaged in agriculture: _____

  g. Size of the population relative to the land and capital available: _____

  h. The birthrates and death rates: _____

  i. Quality of the labor force: _____

  j. Amount of capital equipment relative to the labor force: _____

  k. Level of saving: _____

  l. Incentive to invest: _____

  m. Amount of infrastructure: _____

  n. Extent of industrialization: _____

  o. Size and quality of the entrepreneurial class and the supervisory class: _____

  p. Per capita public expenditures for education and per capita energy consumption: _____

  q. Per capita consumption of food: _____

  r. Disease and malnutrition: _____

3. Suppose it takes a minimum of 5 units of food to keep a person alive for a year, the population can double itself every 10 years, and the food supply can increase every 10 years by an amount equal to what it was in the beginning (year 0).

  a. Assume that both the population and the food supply grow at these rates. Complete the following table by computing the size of the population and the food supply in years 10 through 60.

Year	Food supply	Population
0	200	20
10	_____	_____
20	_____	_____
30	_____	_____
40	_____	_____
50	_____	_____
60	_____	_____

  b. What happens to the relationship between the food supply and the population in the 30th year? _____

  _____

  c. What would actually prevent the population from growing at this rate following the 30th year? _____

  _____

  d. Assuming that the actual population growth in the years following the 30th does not outrun the food supply, what would be the size of the population in

  (1) Year 40: _____?

  (2) Year 50: _____?

  (3) Year 60: _____?

  e. Explain why the standard of living failed to increase in the years following the 30th even though the food supply increased by 75% between years 30 and 60.

  _____

■ **SHORT ANSWER AND ESSAY QUESTIONS**

  1. What is the degree of income inequality among nations of the world?

  2. How do the overall levels of economic growth per capita and the rates of economic growth compare among rich nations and poor countries? Why does the income gap widen?

  3. What are the human realities of poverty found in DVCs? (Use the socioeconomic indicators in Table 22W.1 of the text to contrast the quality of life in IACs and in DVCs.)

  4. Describe the basic paths of economic growth. Do these avenues differ for IACs and DVCs?

  5. How would you describe the natural resource situation for DVCs? In what ways do price fluctuations affect DVC exports? Is a weak natural resource base an obstacle to economic growth?

  6. Describe the implications of the high rate of growth in populations and its effects on the standard of living. Can the standard of living be raised merely by increasing the output of consumer goods in DVCs? What is the meaning of the cliché "the rich get richer and the poor get children," and how does it apply to DVCs?

  7. Compare and contrast the traditional view of population and economic growth with the demographic transition view.

  8. What is the distinction between unemployment and underemployment? How do these concepts apply to DVCs?

  9. What are the reasons for the low level of labor productivity in DVCs?

  10. How does the brain drain affect DVCs?

  11. What are the reasons for placing special emphasis on capital accumulation as a means of promoting economic growth in DVCs?

12. Why is domestic capital accumulation difficult in DVCs? Answer in terms of both the saving side and the investment side of capital accumulation. Is there capital flight from DVCs?

13. In addition to the obstacles that limit domestic investment, what other obstacles tend to limit the flow of foreign capital into DVCs? What role does infrastructure play in capital formation?

14. How might the DVCs improve their technology without engaging in slow and expensive research? Why might this be an inappropriate method of improving the technology used in the DVCs?

15. What is meant by the "will to develop"? How is it related to social and institutional change in DVCs?

16. Explain the vicious circle of poverty in the DVCs. How does population growth make an escape from this vicious circle difficult?

17. Why is the role of government expected to be a positive one in the early phases of development in DVCs? What have been the problems with the involvement of government in economic development?

18. What are three ways that IACs help DVCs?

19. How is it possible for the United States to assist DVCs without spending a penny on foreign aid? Is this type of aid sufficient to ensure rapid and substantial development in DVCs?

20. Discuss the World Bank in terms of its purposes, characteristics, sources of funds, promotion of private capital flows, and success. What are its affiliates and their purposes?

21. Discuss three criticisms of foreign aid to DVCs.

22. Describe the types of private capital flows to encourage economic growth in DVCs.

23. How have DVCs changed to accommodate encouragement of direct foreign investment? What is the problem with the selectivity of this type of investment?

24. Describe the variety of suggested policies that DVCs can adopt to promote economic growth.

25. Explain what IACs can do to assist DVCs in fostering economic growth.

ANSWERS

Chapter 22 The Economics of Developing Countries

FILL-IN QUESTIONS

1. 80, 2, 6
2. industrially advanced, IACs, developing, DVCs
3. higher, an increase
4. lower, lower, lower, lower, higher
5. more, more
6. uneven, OPEC nations, DVCs, large, less
7. *a.* over, higher, decrease; *b.* unemployment, underemployment; *c.* low, human capital, brain drain

8. labor productivity, supply of, output
9. *a.* low, few, weak, capital flight; *b.* public, private; *c.* agriculture
10. *a.* skilled, scarce, abundant, capital; *b.* unskilled, abundant, scarce, labor; *c.* saving
11. sociocultural, institutional
12. low, low, low
13. *a.* establishing effective law and order; *b.* encouraging entrepreneurship; *c.* improving the infrastructure; *d.* promoting saving and investment; *e.* dealing with the social-institutional obstacles (any order for *a–e*)
14. impede, political, poor
15. decreasing, increasing, increasing
16. public, World Bank, last, technical
17. increase, increase, increase, decrease
18. investment, encourage, encourage, selective
19. open, encourage, control
20. lower, discourage, low-income

Note: Page numbers for True–False, Multiple Choice, and Short Answer and Essay Questions refer to Bonus Web Chapter 22.

TRUE–FALSE QUESTIONS

1. F, p. 1	**10.** F, p. 8	**19.** F, p. 12
2. T, p. 3	**11.** F, pp. 8–9	**20.** F, pp. 12–13
3. T, p. 3	**12.** F, p. 9	**21.** F, pp. 13–14
4. F, p. 3	**13.** T, p. 9	**22.** T, p. 14
5. T, pp. 3–4	**14.** T, p. 9	**23.** T, p. 15
6. F, p. 4	**15.** F, p. 10	**24.** F, p. 15
7. F, pp. 4–5	**16.** T, p. 10	**25.** T, pp. 15–17
8. T, p. 6	**17.** T, pp. 10–11	
9. T, p. 7	**18.** F, p. 11	

MULTIPLE-CHOICE QUESTIONS

1. b, p. 1	**10.** b, p. 7	**19.** b, p. 12
2. a, p. 1	**11.** c, pp. 7–8	**20.** c, pp. 12, 15
3. b, p. 3	**12.** a, p. 8	**21.** b, pp. 13–14
4. c, pp. 3–4	**13.** b, p. 8	**22.** c, p. 14
5. c, pp. 3–4	**14.** b, pp. 8–9	**23.** c, p. 15
6. c, p. 5	**15.** b, p. 9	**24.** c, pp. 15–17
7. a, pp. 5–6	**16.** c, p. 9	**25.** b, pp. 17–18
8. b, p. 5	**17.** d, p. 10	
9. b, p. 7	**18.** a, pp. 11–12	

PROBLEMS

1. *a.* 7500; *b.* (1) 8400, (2) 525, (3) widen, 7875
2. *a.* low; *b.* short; *c.* widespread; *d.* low; *e.* primitive; *f.* large; *g.* large; *h.* high; *i.* poor; *j.* small; *k.* low; *l.* absent; *m.* small; *n.* small; *o.* small and poor; *p.* small; *q.* low; *r.* common
3. *a.* Food supply: 400, 600, 800, 1000, 1200, 1400; Population: 40, 80, 160, 320, 640, 1280; *b.* the food supply is just able to support the population; *c.* the inability of the food supply to support a population growing at this rate; *d.* (1) 200, (2) 240, (3) 280; *e.* the population increased as rapidly as the food supply

SHORT ANSWER AND ESSAY QUESTIONS

1. pp. 1–2	**10.** p. 7	**19.** pp. 12–13
2. p. 3	**11.** pp. 7–8	**20.** pp. 13–14
3. pp. 3–4	**12.** pp. 7–8	**21.** p. 14
4. pp. 3–4	**13.** pp. 8–9	**22.** p. 15
5. p. 4	**14.** p. 9	**23.** p. 15
6. pp. 4–6	**15.** p. 9	**24.** pp. 15–17
7. p. 6	**16.** pp. 10–11	**25.** pp. 17–18
8. p. 7	**17.** pp. 11–12	
9. p. 7	**18.** p. 12	

Transition Economies: Russia and China

Note: The bonus web chapter is available at: www.mcconnell16.com.

In the years following the Russian Revolution of 1917, many people in the United States were convinced that the economic system of the Soviet Union was unworkable and that it would break down sooner or later—proof that Marx and Lenin were unrealistic dreamers—and that the reconversion of the Soviet economy to a market system would follow. Now, some 85 years after the revolution, the Russian economy is being transformed into a market economy and a democracy.

China is also undergoing a rapid transition from a centrally planned economy to a market-based economy, but its experience differs from that of Russia. The transition in China has been longer and more gradual. The economic outcomes have also been very positive, with strong economic growth, rising productivity, and a significantly increased standard of living; however, problems remain because the Communist party retains dictatorial political control and economic development is uneven throughout the country.

This chapter provides insights into the profound turn of events in both Russia and China. The first two sections of the chapter explain the basic ideas behind **Marxian ideology,** which gave rise to these command economies. They also discuss two basic institutional features of the former Soviet Union and prereform China: These economies operated under a system of state ownership of property resources; central planning was used to set prices, restrict consumption, and direct investment to heavy industry and the military.

Although central planning served as a powerful form of economic decision making in the former Soviet Union and prereform China, it had two serious problems, as you will discover in the third section. The first problem was one of **coordination,** which resulted in production bottlenecks and managers and bureaucrats missing production targets. Central planning also created an **incentive problem** because it sent out incorrect and inadequate signals for directing the efficient allocation of an economy's resources and gave workers little reason to work hard. The lack of incentives killed entrepreneurship and stifled innovation and technological advance.

The slowing of economic growth in the Soviet economy in the 1970s and 1980s set the stage for the failure of communism and the **collapse of its command economy.** Certainly other factors contributed to the economy's deterioration, as you will discover in the fourth section of the chapter. Production was of poor quality, and there were inadequate or limited consumer goods to meet consumer

demands. The economy was overly burdened by government leaders' desire to support a large military. Agricultural inefficiencies were a drain on resources and restricted investment for other sectors of the economy.

The fifth section of the chapter explains the **five elements of market reform in the Russian economy** and its problems and prospects. The transition has led to the privatization of property resources, the promotion of competition, the decontrol of prices, and better connections to the international economy. The hyperinflation problem was solved by the establishment of a Russian central bank and the adoption of an anti-inflation monetary policy. Other problems continue to plague the economy. Real output, as well as living standards, fell significantly during the transition. Income inequality has grown, and government instability and social unrest have given organized crime the opportunity to flourish. In spite of these problems, Russia is likely to succeed in becoming an advanced market economy, but much work remains to be done.

The **market reform in China** is the focus of the sixth section of the chapter. As already noted, China's reform efforts differed significantly from those of Russia because they started earlier and have been more gradual and experimental. Partial decontrol of land and prices in agriculture unleashed the rural economy and made it more market oriented. State-owned enterprises are being consolidated and forced to become more competitive and operate like corporations. The formation of private businesses has been encouraged. New foreign investment is encouraged to help capital formation and to gain access to advanced technology.

The results from Chinese economic reforms have been impressive, as described in the final section of the chapter. The economy has grown at a 9% annual rate since 1978. The standard of living has risen fourfold and at a much faster rate than population growth. Nevertheless, China's transition to a market economy continues to face significant problems. Property rights are ill-defined. The economy has experienced periods of high inflation and is not well-integrated into the world economy. Economic development across the nation is uneven, and the average income remains low by DVC standards.

The transformations of Russian and Chinese economies into market economies are among the most important economic events of recent decades. The sweeping changes in these economies from centrally planned economies to market economies should deepen your understanding of the principles of economics and how the market system works. These dramatic developments are a fitting topic to conclude your study of economics.

■ **CHECKLIST**

When you have studied this chapter you should be able to

☐ Outline the key elements of Marxian ideology.
☐ Identify two institutional characteristics of the former Soviet Union (prior to collapse) and China (prior to its market reforms).
☐ Make seven generalizations about the central planning goals and techniques in the former Soviet Union and China.
☐ Compare how a market economy coordinates economic activity with how this works in a centrally planned economy.
☐ Explain how a market economy provides incentives and the problems with incentives in a centrally planned economy.
☐ Identify five factors that contributed to the collapse of the Soviet economy.
☐ List five factors that are important for the transition of Russia's economy to a market economy.
☐ Explain the effects of privatization in Russia.
☐ Use a supply and demand graph to discuss the difficulties that price reforms pose in the Russian transition.
☐ Describe the promotion of competition in Russia.
☐ Explain the importance of Russia joining the world economy by making the ruble fully convertible.
☐ Describe the need for price-level stabilization in Russia.
☐ Explain three other major problems the Russian economy has experienced during the transition.
☐ Evaluate the future prospects for Russia's transition to a market economy.
☐ Contrast China's path to market reforms with that of Russia.
☐ Describe agricultural and price reforms in China.
☐ Discuss the reform of urban industries and the use of special economic zones in China.
☐ Describe how the Chinese government has built supporting institutions and transformed state-owned enterprises.
☐ State the positive outcomes from the reform of the Chinese economy.
☐ Identify four significant problems in the Chinese transition to a market economy.

■ **CHAPTER OUTLINE**

1. The centrally planned economies of the former Soviet Union and prereform China were based on *Marxian ideology.* The government was viewed as a dictatorship of the proletariat (or working class) and the peasantry. Especially important was the Marxian concept of a *labor theory of value,* which held that only labor creates value in production and that profits are a *surplus value*

expropriated from workers by capitalists who, because of the institution of private property, were able to control the means of production (capital goods). The purpose of communism was to overthrow capitalism and end this exploitation of workers (and peasants) by eliminating private property and creating a classless society.

2. The two major institutional features of the precollapse Soviet and prereform Chinese economies were *state-owned enterprises* of all property resources and *central economic planning.* The command economy based most economic decisions on bureaucrats' choices rather than relying on market forces to direct economic activity.
   a. The central planning functioned differently in the former Soviet Union and prereform China.
   (1) The former Soviet Union attached great importance to rapid industrialization and military strength, whereas China emphasized rural development.
   (2) Each economy overcommitted its available resources, and often missed planning targets.
   (3) Each economy mobilized resources by increasing the quantity of resources rather than using given resources more productively.
   (4) Directives were used rather than markets and prices to allocate inputs for production in each economy.
   (5) Each government fixed and controlled prices.
   (6) Each economy emphasized self-sufficiency of the nation, viewed capitalist nations as hostile, and restricted trade.
   (7) Each economy passively used monetary and fiscal policies; unemployment was limited or disguised; the price level was controlled through government price fixing.

3. There were two basic problems with a centrally planned economy.
   a. The *coordination problem* involved the difficulty of coordinating the economy's many interdependent segments and avoiding the chain reaction that would result from a bottleneck in any one of the segments. This coordination problem became even more difficult as the economy grew larger and more complex, and more economic decisions had to be made in the production process. There were also inadequate measures of economic performance to determine the degree of success or failure of enterprises or to give clear signals to the economy.
   b. The *incentive problem* arose because in a command economy incentives are ineffective for encouraging economic initiatives and work and for directing the most efficient use of productive resources. In a market economy, profits and losses signal what firms should produce, how they should produce, and how productive resources should be allocated to best meet the wants of a nation. Central planning in the two economies also lacked entrepreneurship and stifled innovation, both of which are important forces for achieving long-term economic growth. Individual workers lacked much motivation to work hard because pay was limited and there were either few consumer goods to buy or they were of low quality.

4. The *collapse of the Soviet economy* stemmed largely from the failure of central economic planning.

 a. Economic growth declined in the 1970s and 1980s. Real output also fell sharply in the few years before the country's breakup.

 b. Technology in manufacturing lagged by western standards, and consumer goods were of poor quality.

 c. Consumers received few material benefits from years of sacrifice for rapid industrialization and the military, and consumer goods were in short supply.

 d. The large financial burden for military expenditures diverted valuable resources from the production of consumer and capital goods to military production.

 e. Agriculture acted as a drag on economic growth and hurt productivity in other sectors of the economy.

5. The *transition* of the former Soviet Union, particularly Russia, from a centrally planned to a market economy is occurring in several ways.

 a. A market economy relies on private property rights and limited government control of business. Private property rights were established to encourage entrepreneurship, and much government property was transferred to private ownership. This privatization was initially achieved through government distribution of vouchers that could be used to purchase businesses; it is now done through the direct sale of state enterprises. This change stimulated foreign investment and the flow of foreign capital to Russia; however, market reforms in agriculture have been limited.

 b. Soviet government controls on prices led to a serious misallocation of resources and poor economic incentives. Most price controls were eliminated, about 90% in 1992, so prices for goods and services were free to change and reflect relative scarcities.

 c. For a market economy to work properly, competition must be promoted by splitting up or restructuring large state-owned enterprises to reduce the potential for monopoly power from having one privatized business in an industry. Progress in this area was slow, but joint ventures and foreign investment stimulated more business competition in the Russian economy.

 d. The Soviet economy was restricted from actively participating in international trade. Action was taken to open the economy to international trade and finance by making the ruble a convertible currency.

 e. The transition to a market economy brought hyperinflation. Contributing factors included price decontrols, the ruble overhang (excess currency saved when there were few consumer goods to purchase), large government budget deficits, and the printing of money to finance the deficits. A Russian central bank was created, and an anti-inflation money policy was adopted to eliminate hyperinflation and keep prices relatively stable.

 f. Several other major problems continued to affect the transition, especially during the early years.

 (1) Real output and living standards fell during the reforms, although the decline bottomed out in 1992. Inflation, reduced international trade, bankruptcy and the closing of state enterprises, and the massive reallocation of resources and reductions in government and military spending precipitated the decline in output.

 (2) Economic inequality and social costs increased during the transition. Market reforms enriched some groups and hurt others. Economic insecurity and instability resulting from the transition raised tensions among workers and other groups, reduced the quality of life and life expectancy, and stimulated the rise of organized crime and "crony" capitalism.

 (3) The government has been weak in its enforcement of property rights and laws. It has also been unable or unwilling to collect the taxes necessary to finance basic government services.

 g. Russia has "muddled through" its first decade of a transition to a market economy. The fall in real output ended by the late 1990s and economic growth has been robust since 1999. The rate of inflation has fallen to more manageable levels. The government has turned its large budget deficits into budget surpluses, and is providing the economic institutions necessary for an effective market economy. Market reforms have taken hold and the economy is prospering.

6. The path of *market economic reforms in China* differed significantly from that in Russia. China's market reforms began earlier and were more gradual and experimental. The Communist Party in China retained dictatorial control, while in Russia the party was replaced with democratic leadership. Russia has privatized much of the economy and sold off state enterprises, whereas China has protected its state enterprises while encouraging competing private enterprises. Russia experienced a significant decline in real output; China's output has continued to grow at high rates.

 a. Agricultural reform in China began in 1978 with the leasing of land to individual farmers and permission to sell the output of the farms at competitive rather than government-controlled prices. This decollectivization and price reform provided a market basis for Chinese agriculture and the economy and released labor resources to private rural manufacturing firms (township and village enterprises).

 b. Market reforms were also established in urban industries to give *state-owned enterprises* (SOEs) more control over production and employment. Enterprises could retain profits and sell more of their output at market prices rather than government-set prices. Urban collectives were formed that operated as private firms jointly owned by managers and workers. The collectives competed strongly with state enterprises and stimulated productivity in the economy.

 c. *Special enterprise zones* were established that were open to foreign investment, private ownership, and international trade. They attracted foreign capital and increased Chinese exports. These areas undercut the support for central planning.

 d. Supporting institutions have been developed to facilitate the transition to a market economy. The Chinese central bank was established to regulate the banking system and control the money supply. The enterprise tax system replaced the profit transfer from state enterprises. Foreign exchange can be swapped as needed between enterprises. A stock market has been established.

e. State-owned enterprises have been transformed; they operate more like corporations and respond to market needs rather than to social directives. The major SOEs have been consolidated into 1000 enterprises. Government plans call for stock to be issued and for the SOEs to become shareholder owned and operate like corporations, with the government retaining control. Other SOEs will be sold or permitted to go bankrupt.

7. There are positive outcomes from China's market-based reforms, but the transition to a market economy is still incomplete.

a. China has an impressive record of growth. It has averaged 9% growth annually since 1978, among the highest percentages on record for such a period. Real output and incomes have quadrupled in less than two decades. Capital formation increased productivity, and labor resources shifted from lower areas of productivity (agriculture) to higher areas of productivity (manufacturing). International trade expanded exports and the imports of critical consumer and capital goods. Foreign investment resulted in access to new technology that can be used to further increase productivity.

b. There are continuing economic problems in China's development.

(1) Property rights are incomplete because the privatization of farmland is opposed by the Communist Party, and such a policy leads to less investment in agriculture.

(2) There have been macroeconomic problems. Until the mid-1990s, China experienced high inflation during the years of rapid economic growth because the financial and monetary control system was weak. (The central bank has been given more control over interest rates and it now has inflation under control.) The financial and banking system is weak because substantial sums are owed by state-owned enterprises to banks. There is considerable unemployment and underemployment, especially in interior regions.

(3) Economic growth is geographically uneven throughout China. Hong Kong is now part of China and has high per capita income. Although people living in enterprise zones and the coastal areas near Hong Kong have experienced substantial growth in incomes and living standards, people in poorer regions still have low incomes. Overall, China is still considered a low-income developing country.

■ HINTS AND TIPS

1. This chapter applies your knowledge of economics to explain the transformation of Russia and China from centrally planned to market-oriented economies. Throughout this chapter you will be comparing a market economy with a command economy. Review Chapter 4 before you read this chapter to make sure you have a good under-

standing of how capitalism works and its major characteristics.

2. View the chapter as a culminating exercise in your study of economics that gives you a chance to *review, apply,* and *integrate* many of the economic concepts and ideas you learned from the text. Only a few terms and concepts will be new to you in this chapter (they apply to Marxian ideology or the reforms in China or Russia).

3. Supply and demand analysis is used to explain price controls in Figure 23W.1 in the text. The figure differs from those you saw in a previous chapter (Chapter 3) because there are two supply curves. One is vertical (perfectly inelastic) because it assumes fixed government control of production and no effect on quantity supplied as price controls are lifted. The upsloping supply curve shows an increase in quantity supplied as price controls are lifted.

■ IMPORTANT TERMS

labor theory of value	state-owned enterprises (SOEs)
surplus value	urban collectives
state ownership	special economic zones (SEZs)
central economic planning	
coordination problem	
incentive problem	
township and village enterprises	

SELF-TEST

■ FILL-IN QUESTIONS

1. The ideology behind the central planning in the former Soviet Union and prereform China was that the value of any commodity is determined by the amount of

(capital, labor) _____ required to produce it. In capitalist economies, capital was (privately, publicly)

_____ owned, and capitalists exploited workers by paying them a wage that was (greater than, less

than) _____ the value of their production and

obtained (shortage, surplus) _____ value at the expense of workers.

2. In a communist economy, capital and other property resources would be (publicly, privately)

_____ owned and society would be (segre-

gated, classless) _____. The Communist Party would serve as the representative of the (capital-

ists, proletariat) _____ and peasantry and would redistribute the surplus value of workers in the form

of (tax cuts, subsidies) _____ for public and quasi-public goods. In reality, the Communist Party was

(democratic, a dictatorship) _____.

3. One major institution of the former Soviet Union and prereform China was the ownership of property resources by (the state, property owners) _____. Another institutional feature was (central, decentralized) _____ economic planning.

4. Economic planning in the former Soviet Union and prereform China functioned in several ways. In the former Soviet Union, plans sought to achieve rapid (population growth, industrialization) _____ and provision of (civilian, military) _____ goods. In China, emphasis was on (urban, rural) _____ development. In both nations, the planning policies created an (over, under) _____-commitment of the economy's resources and resulted in an _____-production of goods for consumers.

5. Economic growth was achieved by (importing, mobilizing) _____ resources and by reallocating surplus labor from (industry, agriculture) _____ to _____. The government allocated inputs among industries by (prices, directives) _____, and the government set fixed _____ for goods and services and inputs.

6. Each nation also viewed itself as a (capitalist, socialist) _____ nation surrounded by hostile _____ nations, and central plans were designed to achieve economic (freedom, self-sufficiency) _____. Macroeconomic policies were (active, passive) _____.

7. Coordination and decision making in a market economy are (centralized, decentralized) _____, but in the Soviet and prereform Chinese economies it was _____. The market system tends to produce a reasonably (efficient, inefficient) _____ allocation of resources, but in centrally planned economies it was _____ and resulted in production bottlenecks and failures to meet many production targets. Central planning became (more, less) _____ complex and difficult as each economy grew and changed over time. Indicators of economic performance were (adequate, inadequate) _____ for determining the success or failure of economic activities.

8. Another problem with central planning was that economic incentives were (effective, ineffective) _____ for encouraging work or for giving signals to planners for efficient allocation of resources in the economy. The centrally planned system also lacked the (production

targets, entrepreneurship) _____ so important to technological advance. Innovation (fostered, lagged) _____ because there was no competition.

9. A number of factors contributed to the collapse of the Soviet economy. The economy experienced a (rise, decline) _____ in economic growth in the 1970s and 1980s. Consumer goods were of (good, poor) _____ quality, and there were widespread (shortages, surpluses) _____. There was a large (consumer, military) _____ burden on the economy that diverted resources from the production of (consumer, investment) _____ goods. Agriculture was (efficient, inefficient) _____ and (helped, hurt) _____ economic growth and productivity in other sectors of the economy.

10. The Russian transition to a market economy has resulted in major reforms. Property rights have been (revoked, established) _____, and government property has been transferred to (foreign, private) _____ ownership. In Soviet Russia, the prices of goods and services were kept at low levels through price (competition, controls) _____, so the marginal cost of a product (was, was not) _____ equal to its marginal benefit. This pricing policy led to (efficient, inefficient) _____ use of resources to make products and to (surpluses, shortages) _____ of many consumer goods. Today, most prices in Russia are (still fixed, free to vary) _____.

11. Russia is also promoting competition by (forming, dismantling) _____ state-owned enterprises to reduce the potential for (rivalry, monopoly) _____. Russia has (opened, closed) _____ the economy to international trade and finance. One example of this policy is making the ruble a (fixed, convertible) _____ currency on international markets.

12. The Russian transition to a market economy was accompanied by (inflation, deflation) _____. It occurred because of price (controls, decontrols) _____, a ruble (under, over) _____ hang, and government budget (surpluses, deficits) _____. In response to this problem, the nation created an independent central (account, bank) _____ to provide control over (fiscal, monetary) _____ policy.

13. Major problems affected Russia's transition, especially in the early years. There was a (falling, rising) _____ level of real output and a _____ standard of living. Economic inequality also (increased, decreased) _____ and led to _____ economic security and (increased, decreased) _____ corruption and crime. Government provided (strong, weak) _____ enforcement of laws and was _____ in its actions to collect taxes. But in recent years the Russian economy has revived with (strong, weak) _____ levels of economic growth, (higher, lower) _____ levels of inflation, and a more effective government.

14. Compared with Russia, China's market reforms began (later, earlier) _____ and were more (rapid, gradual) _____. China asserts that communist dictatorship and markets are (incompatible, compatible) _____, while Russia views them as _____. China instituted its market reforms and experienced (growth, depression) _____, while Russia experienced _____ in its transition to a market economy. Russia (sold, protected) _____ state enterprises, while China _____ them but encouraged competing private enterprises.

15. Agricultural reform in China began in 1978 with the (selling, leasing) _____ of land to individual farmers and permission for _____ the agriculture products at (market, government) _____ prices. The reform released (capital, labor) _____ resources to private rural manufacturing firms called township and village enterprises.

16. Market reforms were also established in Chinese urban industries to give state-owned enterprises (less, more) _____ decision making about production and employment. Urban (cartels, collectives) _____ were formed that operated as private firms jointly owned by managers and workers. The competition of state and nonstate enterprises (increased, decreased) _____ productivity and innovation in the economy.

17. China created special economic zones that were (open, closed) _____ to foreign investment, private ownership, and international trade. A Chinese central bank was established to regulate the (trading, banking) _____ system and control the (import, money) _____ supply. Profit transfers from state enterprises to the central government were replaced with an enterprise (spending, tax) _____ system. Foreign exchange can be (hoarded, swapped) _____ as needed between enterprises.

18. There has been a transformation of Chinese state-owned enterprises (SOEs). They operate more like (bureaucracies, corporations) _____ and respond to (social directive, the market) _____. Plans call for the major 100 SOEs to issue (money, stock) _____ and operate more like corporations under government control. Other smaller SOEs will be (bought, sold) _____ by the government or permitted to go bankrupt.

19. The transition to a market economy in China shows positive outcomes. Economic growth in China averaged (2, 9) _____% annually since 1978. Real output and income have (doubled, quadrupled) _____ in less than two decades. China's real GDP and real income have grown much (more, less) _____ rapidly than its population.

20. Problems remain with China's transition. Privatization of farmland is (supported, opposed) _____ by the Communist Party, and this policy leads to (more, less) _____ investment in agriculture. Substantial sums are (paid, owed) _____ by state-owned enterprises to the banking system. China (is, is not) _____ fully integrated into the world economy. Economic growth is (even, uneven) _____, and China is still considered a (low, middle) _____-income developing country.

■ **TRUE–FALSE QUESTIONS**

Circle T if the statement is true, F if it is false.

1. The labor theory of value is the Marxian idea that the value of any good is determined solely by the amount of labor required for its production.　　**T F**

2. Surplus value in Marxian ideology is the value or price of a commodity at equilibrium in a competitive market.　　**T F**

3. The economies of the former Soviet Union and pre-reform China were characterized by state ownership of resources and authoritarian central planning.　　**T F**

4. The former Soviet Union was dedicated to the task of rapid industrialization and building economic self-sufficiency.　　**T F**

5. Preform China emphasized rural economic development.   **T F**

6. Economic resources tended to be undercommitted in both the former Soviet Union and prereform China.   **T F**

7. Both the former Soviet Union and prereform China actively used monetary and fiscal policies to manipulate levels of employment, output, and prices.   **T F**

8. A centrally planned economy is significantly affected by missed production targets and bottlenecks.   **T F**

9. The problems of central planning become easier and less complex as an economy grows over time.   **T F**

10. Profit is the key indicator of success and failure in a centrally planned economy.   **T F**

11. Central planning provided weak or inaccurate incentives for allocating resources to achieve economic efficiency and encourage hard work.   **T F**

12. Centrally planned economies encourage entrepreneurship and technological advance under the directive of the Communist Party.   **T F**

13. In the former Soviet Union, greater productivity and technological progress in the civilian sector were often sacrificed or limited by the demands to support a large military.   **T F**

14. As part of the transition to a market economy, Russia has taken major steps to privatize its economy and establish property rights.   **T F**

15. Price decontrol was a minor problem in the conversion of the Russian economy to capitalism because the prices the Soviet government established over the years were very similar to the economic values established in a competitive market.   **T F**

16. The transition to a market economy in Russia has required the breakup of large industries and coordinated actions to promote competition.   **T F**

17. A major accomplishment during the Russian transition to a market economy was limited inflation because of balanced budgets and a tight control of the money supply.   **T F**

18. Two major problems Russia experienced during its transition to capitalism were a decline in the standard of living and increased economic inequality.   **T F**

19. The Chinese economy used a "shock" approach to economic reform to make its transition to a market economy.   **T F**

20. Collectivization and price controls were instrumental in strengthening production incentives and moving the Chinese economy toward a market-based agriculture.   **T F**

21. The Chinese government has encouraged the formation of nonstate enterprises, called urban collectives, which are jointly owned by workers and managers.   **T F**

22. China has created special economic zones that are open to foreign investment, private ownership, and international trade.   **T F**

23. A major limitation of Chinese economic reform is the failure to create a stock market for the exchange of shares of newly created corporations.   **T F**

24. China's economic growth has declined over the past two decades because of the instability caused by its economic reforms.   **T F**

25. One continuing economic problem in China is the uneven regional economic development.   **T F**

■ **MULTIPLE-CHOICE QUESTIONS**

Circle the letter that corresponds to the best answer.

1. Which was an element in Marxian ideology?
 (a) the creation of surplus value by government
 (b) dictatorship over the business class
 (c) the private ownership of property
 (d) the labor theory of value

2. Marxian ideology was highly critical of capitalist societies because in those societies capitalists
 (a) reduced the productivity of workers by not investing their profits in new capital goods
 (b) paid workers a wage that was less than the value of their production
 (c) shared surplus value with the government
 (d) were not taxed as much as the workers

3. The institution that was most characteristic of the former Soviet Union and prereform China was
 (a) private ownership of property
 (b) authoritarian central planning
 (c) a system of markets and prices
 (d) consumer sovereignty

4. Industrialization, rapid economic growth, and military strength in the former Soviet Union and prereform China were primarily achieved by
 (a) mobilizing larger quantities of resources
 (b) joining the international economy
 (c) making currencies convertible
 (d) using an easy-money policy

5. Both the former Soviet Union and prereform China viewed themselves as socialist nations surrounded by hostile capitalist nations, and as a consequence central planning stressed the need for
 (a) hoarding gold
 (b) flexible prices
 (c) consumer sovereignty
 (d) economic self-sufficiency

6. In the former Soviet Union and prereform China, monetary policy
 (a) was active and fiscal policy was passive
 (b) was passive and fiscal policy was active
 (c) and fiscal policy were both passive
 (d) and fiscal policy were both active

7. In the system of central planning, the outputs of some industries became the inputs for other industries, but a failure of one industry to meet its production target would cause
(a) widespread unemployment
(b) inflation in wholesale and retail prices
(c) profit declines and potential bankruptcy of firms
(d) a chain reaction of production problems and bottlenecks

8. What was the major success indicator for Soviet and Chinese state enterprises?
(a) profits
(b) the level of prices
(c) production targets
(d) the enterprise tax

9. The centrally planned system in the former Soviet Union and prereform China lacked
(a) price controls
(b) entrepreneurship
(c) economic growth
(d) allocation by directives

10. In the last year or two before the Soviet economic system collapsed, real output
(a) increased slightly
(b) decreased significantly
(c) remained relatively constant
(d) increased faster than the rate of population growth

11. Which was evidence of the Soviet economy's economic failure?
(a) a tight monetary policy
(b) an oversupply of most products
(c) the poor quality of consumer goods
(d) higher productivity in agriculture than industry

12. What was the size of expenditures for the military as a percentage of domestic output in the former Soviet Union (**SU**) and the United States (**U.S.**)?

	SU %	U.S. %
(a)	26 – 30	18
(b)	21 – 25	12
(c)	15 – 20	6
(d)	10 – 14	3

13. Which was a cause of low productivity in agriculture in the former Soviet Union?
(a) inability to fertilize and weed the abundance of good farmland in the country
(b) failure to construct an effective incentive system for agriculture
(c) increase in the length of the growing season
(d) overuse of certain chemical fertilizers on crops

14. Which helped Russia make a transition to a market economy?
(a) ruble overhang
(b) price controls
(c) privatization
(d) hyperinflation

15. The effect of price controls on most consumer goods in the former Soviet Union was that
(a) surpluses developed because the quantity consumers demanded was greater than the quantity supplied at the price set by government
(b) prices fell because the quantity consumers demanded was greater than the quantity supplied
(c) prices rose because the quantity consumers demanded was less than the quantity supplied
(d) shortages developed because the quantity consumers demanded was greater than the quantity supplied at the price set by government

16. Which set of factors most likely contributed to hyper-inflation as Russia made its transition to a market economy?
(a) the breakup of state monopolies, land reform, and the poor quality of consumer goods
(b) increased military spending, investment in new technology, and the convertibility of the ruble
(c) central planning, production targets, and production bottlenecks
(d) government deficits, the ruble overhang, and price decontrols

17. Which two significant problems did Russia encounter in its transition to a market system?
(a) rising taxes and increasing life expectancies
(b) a loose monetary policy and a strict fiscal policy
(c) falling real output and declining living standards
(d) greater military spending and more environmental pollution

18. Compared with Russia, market reforms in China
(a) occurred over a longer time and were more gradual
(b) focused primarily on industry rather than agriculture
(c) relied more on monetary policy than fiscal policy
(d) were less successful and more disruptive

19. The key elements of the 1978–1984 rural economic reforms in China were
(a) passive macroeconomic policies
(b) formations of special economic zones
(c) foreign investment and loans to state-owned enterprises
(d) decollectivization and creation of a two-track price system

20. Privately owned rural manufacturing firms in China are called
(a) township and village enterprises
(b) special economic zones
(c) incentive collectives
(d) farm cooperatives

21. Chinese enterprises in urban areas that are jointly owned by their managers and workers are
(a) industrial unions
(b) urban collectives
(c) business operating units
(d) manufacturing cooperatives

22. Which would be a supporting institution for market reform in China?
    (a) a price control authority
    (b) a profit transfer system
    (c) a farm collective
    (d) a central bank

23. Since market reforms began, real output and real income in China have
    (a) doubled
    (b) tripled
    (c) quadrupled
    (d) quintupled

24. The shift of employment from agriculture toward rural and urban manufacturing in China has increased
    (a) inflation
    (b) productivity
    (c) bankruptcies
    (d) unemployment

25. One significant problem China faces in its transition to a market economy is
    (a) establishing a stock market
    (b) establishing a central bank
    (c) incomplete privatization of land
    (d) creation of special economic zones

■ PROBLEMS

1. In the following table are several major institutions and characteristics of a capitalistic economy, such as that in the United States, and a centrally planned economy, such as that in the former Soviet Union or prereform China. In the appropriate space, name the corresponding institution or characteristic of the other economy.

Capitalist institution or characteristic	Socialist institution or characteristic
a. _____	labor theory of value
b. _____	surplus value
c. private ownership of economic resources	_____
d. a market economy	_____
e. _____	state-owned enterprises
f. privately owned farms	_____
g. _____	government price controls
h. _____	passive macroeconomic policies
i. representative democracy	_____

2. Answer the following set of questions based on the table in the next column. The columns show the price, quantity demanded Q_d by consumers, and a fixed quantity supplied by government Q_{s1} for a product in the former Soviet Union. The column for Q_{s2} shows the supply curve

for the product after privatization in the industry producing the product.

Price (in rubles)	Q_d	Q_{s1}	Q_{s2}
90	25	25	55
80	30	25	50
70	35	25	45
60	40	25	40
50	45	25	35
40	50	25	30
30	55	25	25

a. When only the government supplies the product as shown in the Q_{s1} schedule, the equilibrium price will be _____ rubles and the equilibrium quantity will be _____ units.

b. If the government tries to make the product more accessible to lower-income consumers by setting the price at 30 rubles, then the quantity demanded will be _____ units and the quantity supplied will be _____ units, producing a shortage of _____ units.

c. If the government decontrolled prices but did not privatize industry, then prices would rise to _____ rubles and the government would still produce _____ units.

d. With privatization, there will be a new quantity supplied schedule (Q_{s2}). The equilibrium price will be _____ rubles and the equilibrium quantity will be _____ units. The equilibrium price has risen by _____ rubles and the equilibrium quantity by _____ units.

3. Match the terms from China's economic reform with the phrase using the appropriate number.

  1. special economic zone   **4.** town and village enterprises
  2. urban collective   **5.** enterprise tax system
  3. two-track price system   **6.** state-owned enterprise

a. Privately-owned rural manufacturing firms _____

b. Replaced the system of profit transfers from state enterprises to the central government _____

c. Areas in coastal regions that are open to foreign investment, private ownership, and international trade

    _____

d. Nonstate enterprises jointly owned by managers and their work forces in urban areas _____

e. Gives farmers ability to sell output at market-determined prices _____

f. Enterprises that are controlled by the government

    _____

■ SHORT ANSWER AND ESSAY QUESTIONS

1. What are the essential features of Marxian ideology on which the Soviet Union's command economy was based?

2. What were the two principal economic institutions of the prereform and precollapse economies of China and Russia? How do these institutions compare with those in the United States?

3. Describe how central planning functioned in the former Soviet Union and prereform China. What generalizations can you make about resource use, directives, prices, self-sufficiency, and macroeconomic policies?

4. Why does central planning result in a coordination problem? Compare the operation of central planning with the use of markets and prices for economic decision making.

5. How does central economic planning produce a significant incentive problem? What types of economic incentives for business, workers, and consumers exist in a market economy? How are those incentives different in a centrally planned economy?

6. Discuss the five factors that help explain or contributed to the collapse of the Soviet economy.

7. What action has Russia taken to privatize the economy?

8. Why was there a need for price reform in Russia in its transition to a market economy? What has been the *general* effect of this change? Use a supply and demand graph to explain the effect of the price decontrol on a specific product.

9. Discuss what is being done in Russia to promote competition. To what extent are public monopolies a problem?

10. What major problem is confronting Russia as it seeks to join the world economy?

11. How have high rates of inflation affected Russia's transition to a market economy? What has been the shift in macroeconomic policy?

12. What other major problems has Russia encountered in its transition to a market economy?

13. Evaluate the prospects for the transformation of Russia into a market economy.

14. How did China's approach to market reforms differ from that in Russia?

15. Describe how China has tried to transform agriculture and rural production.

16. What market-based changes has the Chinese government made in urban industries?

17. What actions has the Chinese government taken to encourage foreign investment and establish institutions that support a market-based economy?

18. Describe the economic transformation of state-owned enterprises in China.

19. What are the positive outcomes of China's economic reform?

20. Discuss four significant economic problems that China continues to face in its transition to a market economy.

ANSWERS

Chapter 23 Web: Transition Economies: Russia and China

FILL-IN QUESTIONS

1. labor, privately, less than, surplus
2. publicly, classless, proletariat, subsidies, a dictatorship
3. the state, central
4. industrialization, military, rural, over, under
5. mobilizing, agriculture, industry, directives, prices
6. socialist, capitalist, self-sufficiency, passive
7. decentralized, centralized, efficient, inefficient, more, inadequate
8. ineffective, entrepreneurship, lagged
9. decline, poor, shortages, military, consumer, inefficient, hurt
10. established, private, controls, was not, inefficient, shortages, free to vary
11. dismantling, monopoly, opened, convertible
12. inflation, decontrols, over, deficits, bank, monetary
13. falling, falling, increased, decreased, increased, weak, weak, strong, lower
14. earlier, gradual, compatible, incompatible, growth, depression, sold, protected
15. leasing, selling, market, labor
16. more, collectives, increased
17. open, banking, money, tax, swapped
18. corporations, the market, stock, sold
19. 9, quadrupled, more
20. opposed, less, owed, is not, uneven, low

Note: Page numbers for True–False, Multiple Choice, and Short Answer and Essay Questions refer to Bonus Web Chapter 23.

TRUE–FALSE QUESTIONS

1. T, pp. 1–2	**10.** F, pp. 4–5	**19.** F, p. 10
2. F, p. 2	**11.** T, pp. 4–5	**20.** F, pp. 10–11
3. T, p. 2	**12.** F, p. 5	**21.** T, p. 11
4. T, pp. 2–3	**13.** T, p. 6	**22.** T, p. 11
5. T, pp. 2–3	**14.** T, pp. 6–7	**23.** F, pp. 12–13
6. F, p. 3	**15.** F, p. 7	**24.** F, p. 12
7. F, p. 3	**16.** T, p. 8	**25.** T, p. 13
8. T, p. 4	**17.** F, p. 8	
9. F, p. 4	**18.** T, p. 9	

MULTIPLE-CHOICE QUESTIONS

1. d, p. 2	**10.** b, p. 6	**19.** d, pp. 10–11
2. b, p. 2	**11.** c, p. 6	**20.** a, p. 10
3. b, p. 2	**12.** c, p. 6	**21.** b, pp. 10–11
4. a, p. 3	**13.** b, p. 6	**22.** d, p. 11
5. d, p. 3	**14.** c, pp. 6–7	**23.** c, p. 12
6. c, p. 3	**15.** d, p. 7	**24.** b, p. 12
7. d, p. 4	**16.** d, p. 8	**25.** c, pp. 12–13
8. c, pp. 4–5	**17.** c, p. 9	
9. b, pp. 4–5	**18.** a, p. 10	

PROBLEMS

1. *a.* supply and demand; *b.* profit; *c.* state ownership of resources; *d.* command or centrally planned economy; *e.* corporations; *f.* collective farms or agricultural cooperatives; *g.* competitive markets and flexible prices; *h.* active or discretionary macroeconomic policies; *i.* dictatorship by the Communist Party
2. *a.* 90, 25; *b.* 55, 25, 30; *c.* 90, 25; *d.* 60, 40, 30, 15
3. *a.* 4; *b.* 5; *c.* 1; *d.* 2; *e.* 3; *f.* 6

SHORT ANSWER AND ESSAY QUESTIONS

1. pp. 1–2
2. p. 2
3. pp. 2–3
4. p. 4
5. pp. 4–5
6. pp. 5–6
7. pp. 6–7
8. pp. 7–8
9. p. 8
10. p. 8
11. p. 8
12. p. 9
13. pp. 9–12
14. p. 10
15. pp. 10–11
16. pp. 10–11
17. p. 11
18. p. 11
19. pp. 11–12
20. pp. 12–13

Glossary

Note: Terms set in *italic* type are defined separately in this glossary.

abstraction Elimination of irrelevant and noneconomic facts to obtain an *economic principle.*

actual investment The amount that *firms* do invest; equal to *planned investment* plus *unplanned investment.*

actual reserves The funds that a bank has on deposit at the *Federal Reserve Bank* of its district (plus its *vault cash*).

adjustable pegs The device used in the *Bretton Woods system* to alter *exchange rates* in an orderly way to eliminate persistent payments deficits and surpluses. Each nation defined its monetary unit in terms of (pegged it to) gold or the dollar, kept the *rate of exchange* for its money stable in the short run, and adjusted its rate in the long run when faced with international payments disequilibrium.

aggregate demand A schedule or curve that shows the total quantity of goods and services demanded (purchased) at different *price levels.*

aggregate demand–aggregate supply model The macroeconomic model that uses *aggregate demand* and *aggregate supply* to determine and explain the *price level* and the real *domestic output.*

aggregate expenditures The total amount spent for final goods and services in an economy.

aggregate expenditures–domestic output approach Determination of the equilibrium *gross domestic product* by finding the real GDP at which *aggregate expenditures* equal *domestic output.*

aggregate expenditures schedule A schedule or curve showing the total amount spent for final goods and services at different levels of *real GDP.*

aggregate supply A schedule or curve showing the total quantity of goods and services supplied (produced) at different *price levels.*

aggregate supply shocks Sudden, large changes in resource costs that shift an economy's aggregate supply curve.

aggregation The combining of individual units or data into one unit or number. For example, all prices of individual goods and services are combined into a *price level* or all units of output are aggregated into *real gross domestic product.*

allocative efficiency The apportionment of resources among firms and industries to obtain the production of the products most wanted by society (consumers); the output of each product at which its *marginal cost* and *price* or *marginal benefit* are equal.

annually balanced budget A budget in which government expenditures and tax collections are equal each year.

anticipated inflation Increases in the price level (*inflation*) that occur at the expected rate.

appreciation (of the dollar) An increase in the value of the dollar relative to the currency of another nation, so a dollar buys a larger amount of the foreign currency and thus of foreign goods.

asset Anything of monetary value owned by a firm or individual.

asset demand for money The amount of *money* people want to hold as a *store of value;* this amount varies inversely with the *interest rate.*

average propensity to consume Fraction (or percentage) of *disposable income* that households plan to spend for consumer goods and services; consumption divided by *disposable income.*

average propensity to save Fraction (or percentage) of *disposable income* that households save; *saving* divided by *disposable income.*

average tax rate Total tax paid divided by total (taxable) income, as a percentage.

balance of payments (See *International balance of payments.*)

balance-of-payments deficit The amount by which the sum of the *balance on current account* and the *balance on capital account* is negative in a year.

balance-of-payments surplus The amount by which the sum of the *balance on current account* and the *balance on capital account* is positive in a year.

balance on capital account The foreign purchases of assets in the United States less American purchases of assets abroad in a year.

balance on current account The exports of goods and services of a nation less its imports of goods and services plus its *net investment income* and *net transfers* in a year.

balance on goods and services The exports of goods and services of a nation less its imports of goods and services in a year.

balance sheet A statement of the *assets, liabilities,* and *net worth* of a firm or individual at some given time.

bank deposits The deposits that individuals or firms have at banks (or thrifts) or that banks have at the *Federal Reserve Banks.*

bankers' bank A bank that accepts the deposits of and makes loans to *depository institutions;* in the United States, a *Federal Reserve Bank.*

bank reserves The deposits of commercial banks and thrifts at *Federal Reserve Banks* plus bank and thrift *vault cash.*

barter The exchange of one good or service for another good or service.

base year The year with which other years are compared when an index is constructed; for example, the base year for a *price index.*

Board of Governors The seven-member group that supervises and controls the money and banking system of the United States; the Board of Governors of the Federal Reserve System; the Federal Reserve Board.

bond A financial device through which a borrower (a firm or government) is obligated to pay the principal and interest on a loan at a specific date in the future.

brain drain (Web chapter) The emigration of highly educated, highly skilled workers from a country.

break-even income The level of *disposable income* at which *households* plan to consume (spend) all their income and to save none of it; also, in an income transfer program, the level of earned income at which subsidy payments become zero.

Bretton Woods system The international monetary system developed after the Second World War in which *adjustable pegs* were employed, the *International Monetary Fund* helped stabilize foreign exchange rates, and gold and the dollar were used as *international monetary reserves.*

budget deficit The amount by which the expenditures of the Federal government exceed its revenues in any year.

budget surplus The amount by which the revenues of the Federal government exceed its expenditures in any year.

built-in stabilizer A mechanism that increases government's budget deficit (or reduces its surplus) during a recession and increases government's budget surplus (or reduces its deficit) during inflation without any action by policymakers. The tax system is one such mechanism.

Bureau of Economic Analysis (BEA) An agency of the U.S. Department of Commerce that compiles the national income and product accounts.

business cycle Recurring increases and decreases in the level of economic activity over periods of years; consists of peak, recession, trough, and recovery phases.

business firm (See *firm.*)

capital Human-made resources (buildings, machinery, and equipment) used to produce goods and services; goods that do not directly satisfy human wants; also called capital goods.

capital account The section of a nation's *international balance-of-payments* statement that records the foreign purchases of assets in the United States (creating monetary inflows) and U.S. purchases of assets abroad (creating monetary outflows).

capital account deficit A negative *balance on capital account.*

capital account surplus A positive *balance on capital account.*

capital flight The transfer of savings from *developing countries* to industrially advanced countries to avoid government expropriation, taxation, and high rates of inflation or to realize better investment opportunities.

capital gain The gain realized when securities or properties are sold for a price greater than the price paid for them.

capital goods (See *capital.*)

capital-intensive commodity A product that requires a relatively large amount of *capital* to be produced.

capitalism An economic system in which property resources are privately owned and markets and prices are used to direct and coordinate economic activities.

capital-saving technological advance (Web chapter) An improvement in *technology* that permits a greater quantity of a product to be produced with a specific amount of *capital* (or permits the same amount of the product to be produced with a smaller amount of capital).

capital stock The total available *capital* in a nation.

capital-using technological advance (Web chapter) An improvement in *technology* that requires the use of a greater amount of *capital* to produce a specific quantity of a product.

cartel A formal agreement among firms (or countries) in an industry to set the price of a product and establish the outputs of the individual firms (or countries) or to divide the market for the product geographically.

causation A relationship in which the occurrence of one or more events brings about another event.

CEA (See *Council of Economic Advisers.*)

central bank A bank whose chief function is the control of the nation's *money supply;* in the United States, the Federal Reserve System.

central economic planning Government determination of the objectives of the economy and how resources will be directed to attain those goals.

ceteris paribus assumption (See *other-things-equal assumption.*)

change in demand A change in the *quantity demanded* of a good or service at every price; a shift of the *demand curve* to the left or right.

change in supply A change in the *quantity supplied* of a good or service at every price; a shift of the *supply curve* to the left or right.

checkable deposit Any deposit in a *commercial bank* or *thrift institution* against which a check may be written.

checkable-deposit multiplier (See *monetary multiplier.*)

check clearing The process by which funds are transferred from the checking accounts of the writers of checks to the checking accounts of the recipients of the checks.

checking account A *checkable deposit* in a *commercial bank* or *thrift institution.*

circular flow model The flow of resources from *households* to *firms* and of products from firms to households. These flows are accompanied by reverse flows of money from firms to households and from households to firms.

classical economics The macroeconomic generalizations accepted by most economists before the 1930s that led to the conclusion that a capitalistic economy was self-regulating and therefore would usually employ its resources fully.

closed economy An economy that neither exports nor imports goods and services.

coincidence of wants A situation in which the good or service that one trader desires to obtain is the same as that which another trader desires to give up and an item that the second trader wishes to acquire is the same as that which the first trader desires to surrender.

COLA (See *cost-of-living adjustment*.)

command system A method of organizing an economy in which property resources are publicly owned and government uses *central economic planning* to direct and coordinate economic activities; command economy.

commercial bank A firm that engages in the business of banking (accepts deposits, offers checking accounts, and makes loans).

commercial banking system All *commercial banks* and *thrift institutions* as a group.

communism (See *command system*.)

comparative advantage A lower relative or comparative cost than that of another producer.

compensation to employees *Wages* and salaries plus wage and salary supplements paid by employers to workers.

competition The presence in a market of independent buyers and sellers competing with one another and the freedom of buyers and sellers to enter and leave the market.

complementary goods Products and services that are used together. When the price of one falls, the demand for the other increases (and conversely).

conglomerates Firms that produce goods and services in two or more separate industries.

consumer goods Products and services that satisfy human wants directly.

Consumer Price Index (CPI) An index that measures the prices of a fixed "market basket" of some 300 goods and services bought by a "typical" consumer.

consumer sovereignty Determination by consumers of the types and quantities of goods and services that will be produced with the scarce resources of the economy; consumers' direction of production through their dollar votes.

consumer surplus The difference between the maximum price a consumer is (or consumers are) willing to pay for an additional unit of a product and its market price; the triangular area below the demand curve and above the market price.

consumption of fixed capital An estimate of the amount of *capital* worn out or used up (consumed) in producing the *gross domestic product*; also called depreciation.

consumption schedule A schedule showing the amounts *households* plan to spend for *consumer goods* at different levels of *disposable income*.

contractionary fiscal policy A decrease in *government purchases* for goods and services, an increase in *net taxes,* or some combination of the two, for the purpose of decreasing *aggregate demand* and thus controlling inflation.

coordination failure A situation in which people do not reach a mutually beneficial outcome because they lack some way to jointly coordinate their actions; a possible cause of macroeconomic instability.

corporate income tax A tax levied on the net income (accounting profit) of corporations.

corporation A legal entity ("person") chartered by a state or the Federal government that is distinct and separate from the individuals who own it.

correlation A systematic and dependable association between two sets of data (two kinds of events); does not necessarily indicate causation.

cost-of-living adjustment (COLA) An automatic increase in the incomes (wages) of workers when inflation occurs; guaranteed by a collective bargaining contract between firms and workers.

cost-push inflation Increases in the price level (inflation) resulting from an increase in resource costs (for example, raw-material prices) and hence in *per-unit production costs;* inflation caused by reductions in *aggregate supply*.

cost ratio An equality showing the number of units of two products that can be produced with the same resources; the cost ratio 1 corn $\equiv$ 3 olives shows that the resources required to produce 3 units of olives must be shifted to corn production to produce a unit of corn.

Council of Economic Advisers (CEA) A group of three persons that advises and assists the president of the United States on economic matters (including the preparation of the annual *Economic Report of the President*).

creative destruction The hypothesis that the creation of new products and production methods simultaneously destroys the market power of existing monopolies.

credit An accounting item that increases the value of an asset (such as the foreign money owned by the residents of a nation).

credit union An association of persons who have a common tie (such as being employees of the same firm or members of the same labor union) that sells shares to (accepts deposits from) its members and makes loans to them.

crowding-out effect A rise in interest rates and a resulting decrease in *planned investment* caused by the Federal government's increased borrowing in the money market.

currency Coins and paper money.

currency appreciation (See *exchange-rate appreciation*.)

currency depreciation (See *exchange-rate depreciation*.)

currency intervention A government's buying and selling of its own currency or foreign currencies to alter international exchange rates.

current account The section in a nation's *international balance of payments* that records its exports and imports of goods and services, its *net investment income,* and its *net transfers*.

cyclical deficit A Federal *budget deficit* that is caused by a recession and the consequent decline in tax revenues.

cyclically balanced budget The equality of government expenditures and net tax collections over the course of a *business cycle;* deficits incurred during periods of recession are offset by surpluses obtained during periods of prosperity (inflation).

cyclical unemployment A type of *unemployment* caused by insufficient total spending (or by insufficient *aggregate demand*).

debit An accounting item that decreases the value of an asset (such as the foreign money owned by the residents of a nation).

deflating Finding the *real gross domestic product* by decreasing the dollar value of the GDP for a year in which prices were higher than in the *base year.*

deflation A decline in the economy's *price level.*

demand A schedule showing the amounts of a good or service that buyers (or a buyer) wish to purchase at various prices during some time period.

demand curve A curve illustrating *demand.*

demand factor (in growth) The increase in the level of *aggregate demand* that brings about the *economic growth* made possible by an increase in the production potential of the economy.

demand management The use of *fiscal policy* and *monetary policy* to increase or decrease *aggregate demand.*

demand-pull inflation Increases in the price level (inflation) resulting from an excess of demand over output at the existing price level, caused by an increase in *aggregate demand.*

dependent variable A variable that changes as a consequence of a change in some other (independent) variable; the "effect" or outcome.

depository institutions Firms that accept deposits of *money* from the public (businesses and persons); *commercial banks, savings and loan associations, mutual savings banks,* and *credit unions.*

depreciation (See *consumption of fixed capital.*)

depreciation (of the dollar) A decrease in the value of the dollar relative to another currency, so a dollar buys a smaller amount of the foreign currency and therefore of foreign goods.

derived demand The demand for a resource that depends on the demand for the products it helps to produce.

determinants of aggregate demand Factors such as consumption spending, *investment,* government spending, and *net exports* that, if they change, shift the aggregate demand curve.

determinants of aggregate supply Factors such as input prices, *productivity,* and the legal-institutional environment that, if they change, shift the aggregate supply curve.

determinants of demand Factors other than price that determine the quantities demanded of a good or service.

determinants of supply Factors other than price that determine the quantities supplied of a good or service.

devaluation A decrease in the governmentally defined value of a currency.

developing countries Many countries of Africa, Asia, and Latin America that are characterized by lack of capital goods, use of nonadvanced technologies, low literacy rates, high unemployment, rapid population growth, and labor forces heavily committed to agriculture.

direct foreign investment (Web chapter) The building of new factories (or the purchase of existing capital) in a particular nation by corporations of other nations.

direct relationship The relationship between two variables that change in the same direction, for example, product price and quantity supplied.

discount rate The interest rate that the *Federal Reserve Banks* charge on the loans they make to *commercial banks* and *thrift institutions.*

discouraged workers Employees who have left the *labor force* because they have not been able to find employment.

discretionary fiscal policy Deliberate changes in taxes (tax rates) and government spending by Congress to promote full employment, price stability, and economic growth.

discrimination The practice of according individuals or groups inferior treatment in hiring, occupational access, education and training, promotion, wage rates, or working conditions even though they have the same abilities, education and skills, and work experience as other workers.

disinflation A reduction in the rate of *inflation.*

disposable income *Personal income* less personal taxes; income available for *personal consumption expenditures* and *personal saving.*

dissaving Spending for consumer goods and services in excess of *disposable income;* the amount by which *personal consumption expenditures* exceed disposable income.

dividends Payments by a corporation of all or part of its profit to its stockholders (the corporate owners).

division of labor The separation of the work required to produce a product into a number of different tasks that are performed by different workers; *specialization* of workers.

Doha Round The latest, uncompleted (as of 2003) sequence of trade negotiations by members of the *World Trade Organization;* named after Doha, Qatar, where the set of negotiations began.

dollar votes The "votes" that consumers and entrepreneurs cast for the production of consumer and capital goods, respectively, when they purchase those goods in product and resource markets.

domestic capital formation The process of adding to a nation's stock of *capital* by saving and investing part of its own domestic output.

domestic output *Gross* (or net) *domestic product;* the total output of final goods and services produced in the economy.

domestic price The price of a good or service within a country, determined by domestic demand and supply.

double taxation The taxation of both corporate net income (profits) and the *dividends* paid from this net income when they become the personal income of households.

dumping The sale of products below cost in a foreign country or below the prices charged at home.

durable good A consumer good with an expected life (use) of 3 or more years.

earnings The money income received by a worker; equal to the *wage* (rate) multiplied by the amount of time worked.

easy money policy Federal Reserve System actions to increase the *money supply* to lower interest rates and expand *real GDP*.

economic analysis The process of deriving *economic principles* from relevant economic facts.

economic cost A payment that must be made to obtain and retain the services of a *resource;* the income a firm must provide to a resource supplier to attract the resource away from an alternative use; equal to the quantity of other products that cannot be produced when resources are instead used to make a particular product.

economic efficiency The use of the minimum necessary resources to obtain the socially optimal amounts of goods and services; entails both *productive efficiency* and *allocative efficiency.*

economic growth (1) An outward shift in the *production possibilities curve* that results from an increase in resource supplies or quality or an improvement in *technology;* (2) an increase of real output (*gross domestic product)* or real output per capita.

economic law An *economic principle* that has been tested and retested and has stood the test of time.

economic model A simplified picture of economic reality; an abstract generalization.

economic perspective A viewpoint that envisions individuals and institutions making rational decisions by comparing the marginal benefits and marginal costs associated with their actions.

economic policy A course of action intended to correct or avoid a problem.

economic principle A widely accepted generalization about the economic behavior of individuals or institutions.

economic profit The *total revenue* of a firm less its *economic costs* (which include both payments to resource suppliers and the opportunity costs of firm-owned resources); also called "pure profit" and "above-normal profit."

economic resources The *land, labor, capital,* and *entrepreneurial ability* that are used in the production of goods and services; productive agents; factors of production.

economics The social science dealing with the use of scarce resources to obtain the maximum satisfaction of society's virtually unlimited economic wants.

economic system A particular set of institutional arrangements and a coordinating mechanism for solving the economizing problem; a method of organizing an economy, of which the *market system* and the *command system* are the two general types.

economic theory A statement of a cause-effect relationship; when accepted by all economists, an *economic principle.*

economies of scale Reductions in the *per-unit cost* of producing a product as the firm expands the size of plant (its output) in the *long run;* the economies of mass production.

economizing problem The choices necessitated because society's economic wants for goods and services are unlimited but the *resources* available to satisfy these wants are limited (scarce).

efficiency factors (in growth) The capacity of an economy to combine resources effectively to achieve growth of real output that the *supply factors* (of growth) make possible.

efficiency loss (Web chapter) Reductions in combined consumer and producer surplus caused by an underallocation or overallocation of resources to the production of a good or service.

efficiency wage A wage that minimizes wage costs per unit of output by encouraging greater effort or reducing turnover.

efficient allocation of resources That allocation of an economy's resources among the production of different products that leads to the maximum satisfaction of consumers' wants, thus producing the socially optimal mix of output with society's scarce resources.

Employment Act of 1946 Federal legislation that committed the Federal government to the maintenance of economic stability (a high level of employment, a stable price level, and economic growth); established the *Council of Economic Advisers* and the *Joint Economic Committee;* and required an annual economic report by the president to Congress.

employment rate The percentage of the *labor force* employed at any time.

entrepreneurial ability The human resource that combines the other resources to produce a product, makes nonroutine decisions, innovates, and bears risks.

equation of exchange $MV = PQ$, in which M is the supply of money, V is the *velocity* of money, P is the *price level,* and Q is the physical volume of *final goods and services* produced.

equilibrium price The *price* in a competitive market at which the *quantity demanded* and the *quantity supplied* are equal, there is neither a shortage nor a surplus, and there is no tendency for price to rise or fall.

equilibrium price level The price level at which the aggregate demand curve intersects the aggregate supply curve.

equilibrium quantity (1) The quantity demanded and supplied at the equilibrium price in a competitive market; (2) the profit-maximizing output of a firm.

equilibrium real domestic output The *gross domestic product* at which the total quantity of final goods and services purchased (*aggregate expenditures)* is equal to the total quantity of final goods and services produced (the real domestic output); the real domestic output at which the aggregate demand curve intersects the aggregate supply curve.

euro The common currency unit used by 12 European nations (as of 2003) in the Euro zone, which consists of Austria, Belgium, Finland, France, Germany, Greece, Ireland, Italy, Luxembourg, the Netherlands, Portugal, and Spain.

European Union (EU) An association of 25 European nations (including 10 nations to be added in 2004) that has eliminated tariffs and quotas among them, established common tariffs for imported goods from outside the member nations, eliminated barriers to the free movement of capital, and created other common economic policies.

excess reserves The amount by which a bank's or thrift's *actual reserves* exceed its *required reserves;* actual reserves minus required reserves.

exchange control (See *foreign exchange control*.)

exchange rate The *rate of exchange* of one nation's currency for another nation's currency.

exchange-rate appreciation An increase in the value of a nation's currency in foreign exchange markets; an increase in the *rate of exchange* for foreign currencies.

exchange-rate depreciation A decrease in the value of a nation's currency in foreign exchange markets; a decrease in the *rate of exchange* for foreign currencies.

exchange-rate determinant Any factor other than the *rate of exchange* that determines a currency's demand and supply in the *foreign exchange market*.

excise tax A tax levied on the production of a specific product or on the quantity of the product purchased.

exhaustive expenditure An expenditure by government resulting directly in the employment of *economic resources* and in the absorption by government of the goods and services those resources produce; a *government purchase*.

expansionary fiscal policy An increase in *government purchases* of goods and services, a decrease in *net taxes,* or some combination of the two for the purpose of increasing *aggregate demand* and expanding real output.

expectations The anticipations of consumers, firms, and others about future economic conditions.

expected rate of return The increase in profit a firm anticipates it will obtain by purchasing capital (or engaging in research and development); expressed as a percentage of the total cost of the investment (or R&D) activity.

expenditures approach The method that adds all expenditures made for *final goods and services* to measure the *gross domestic product*.

expenditures-output approach (See *aggregate expenditures–domestic output approach*.)

exports Goods and services produced in a nation and sold to buyers in other nations.

export subsidies Government payments to domestic producers to enable them to reduce the *price* of a good or service to foreign buyers.

export supply curve An upward-sloping curve that shows the amount of a product that domestic firms will export at each *world price* that is above the *domestic price*.

export transaction A sale of a good or service that increases the amount of foreign currency flowing to a nation's citizens, firms, and government.

external debt Private or public debt owed to foreign citizens, firms, and institutions.

externality (See *spillover*.)

face value The dollar or cents value stamped on a U.S. coin.

factors of production *Economic resources: land, capital, labor,* and *entrepreneurial ability*.

fallacy of composition The false notion or assumption that what is true for the individual (or part) is necessarily true for the group (or whole).

FDIC (See *Federal Deposit Insurance Corporation*.)

Federal Deposit Insurance Corporation (FDIC) The federally chartered corporation that insures deposit liabilities (up to $100,000 per account) of *commercial banks* and *thrift institutions* (excluding *credit unions,* whose deposits are insured by the *National Credit Union Administration*).

Federal funds rate The interest rate banks and other depository institutions charge one another on overnight loans made out of their *excess reserves*.

Federal government The government of the United States, as distinct from the state and local governments.

Federal Open Market Committee (FOMC) The 12-member group that determines the purchase and sale policies of the *Federal Reserve Banks* in the market for U.S. government securities.

Federal Reserve Banks The 12 banks chartered by the U.S. government to control the *money supply* and perform other functions. (See *central bank, quasi-public bank,* and *bankers' bank*.)

Federal Reserve Note Paper money issued by the *Federal Reserve Banks*.

fiat money Anything that is *money* because government has decreed it to be money.

final goods and services Goods and services that have been purchased for final use and not for resale or further processing or manufacturing.

financial capital (See *money capital*.)

firm An organization that employs resources to produce a good or service for profit and owns and operates one or more individual *plants*.

fiscal policy Changes in government spending and tax collections designed to achieve a full-employment and noninflationary domestic output; also called *discretionary fiscal policy*.

fixed exchange rate A *rate of exchange* that is set in some way and therefore prevented from rising or falling with changes in currency supply and demand.

flexible exchange rate A *rate of exchange* determined by the international demand for and supply of a nation's money; a rate free to rise or fall (to float).

floating exchange rate (See *flexible exchange rate*.)

foreign competition (See *import competition*.)

foreign exchange control The control a government may exercise over the quantity of foreign currency demanded by its citizens and firms and over the *rates of exchange* in order to limit its *outpayments* to its *inpayments* (to eliminate a *payments deficit*).

foreign exchange market A market in which the money (currency) of one nation can be used to purchase (can be exchanged for) the money of another nation.

foreign exchange rate (See *rate of exchange*.)

foreign purchase effect The inverse relationship between the *net exports* of an economy and its price level relative to foreign price levels.

45° line A line along which the value of *GDP* (measured horizontally) is equal to the value of *aggregate expenditures* (measured vertically).

Four Fundamental Questions (of economics) The four questions that every economy must answer: what to produce, how to produce it, how to divide the total output, and how to ensure economic flexibility.

fractional reserve   A *reserve requirement* that is less than 100 percent of the checkable-deposit liabilities of a *commercial bank* or *thrift institution*.

freedom of choice   The freedom of owners of property resources to employ or dispose of them as they see fit, of workers to enter any line of work for which they are qualified, and of consumers to spend their incomes in a manner that they think is appropriate.

freedom of enterprise   The freedom of *firms* to obtain economic resources, to use those resources to produce products of the firm's own choosing, and to sell their products in markets of their choice.

free-rider problem   The inability of potential providers of an economically desirable good or service to obtain payment from those who benefit, because of *nonexcludability*.

free trade   The absence of artificial (government-imposed) barriers to trade among individuals and firms in different nations.

frictional unemployment   A type of unemployment caused by workers voluntarily changing jobs and by temporary layoffs; unemployed workers between jobs.

full employment   (1) The use of all available resources to produce want-satisfying goods and services; (2) the situation in which the *unemployment rate* is equal to the *full-employment unemployment rate* and there is *frictional* and *structural* but no *cyclical unemployment* (and the *real GDP* of the economy equals its *potential output*).

full-employment budget   A comparison of the government expenditures and tax collections that would occur if the economy operated at *full employment* throughout the year.

full-employment unemployment rate   The *unemployment rate* at which there is no *cyclical unemployment* of the *labor force;* equal to between 4 and 5 percent in the United States because some *frictional* and *structural* unemployment is unavoidable.

full production   Employment of available resources so that the maximum amount of (or total value of) goods and services is produced; occurs when both *productive efficiency* and *allocative efficiency* are realized.

functional distribution of income   The manner in which *national income* is divided among the functions performed to earn it (or the kinds of resources provided to earn it); the division of national income into wages and salaries, proprietors' income, corporate profits, interest, and rent.

functional finance   The use of *fiscal policy* to achieve a noninflationary full-employment *gross domestic product* without regard to the effect on the *public debt*.

gains from trade   The extra output that trading partners obtain through specialization of production and exchange of goods and services.

GDP   (See *gross domestic product*.)

GDP gap   Actual *gross domestic product* minus potential output; may be either a positive amount (a *positive GDP gap*) or a negative amount (a *negative GDP gap*).

GDP price index   A *price index* for all the goods and services that make up the *gross domestic product;* the price index used to adjust *nominal gross domestic product* to *real gross domestic product*.

G8 nations   A group of eight major nations (Canada, France, Germany, Italy, Japan, Russia, United Kingdom, and United States) whose leaders meet regularly to discuss common economic problems and try to coordinate economic policies.

General Agreement on Tariffs and Trade (GATT)   The international agreement reached in 1947 in which 23 nations agreed to give equal and nondiscriminatory treatment to one another, to reduce tariff rates by multinational negotiations, and to eliminate *import quotas*. It now includes most nations and has become the *World Trade Organization*.

generalization   Statement of the nature of the relation between two or more sets of facts.

gold standard   A historical system of fixed exchange rates in which nations defined their currencies in terms of gold, maintained a fixed relationship between their stocks of gold and their money supplies, and allowed gold to be freely exported and imported.

government purchases   Expenditures by government for goods and services that government consumes in providing public goods and for public (or social) capital that has a long lifetime; the expenditures of all governments in the economy for those *final goods and services*.

government transfer payment   The disbursement of money (or goods and services) by government for which government receives no currently produced good or service in return.

gross domestic product (GDP)   The total market value of all *final goods and services* produced annually within the boundaries of the United States, whether by U.S. or foreign-supplied resources.

gross private domestic investment   Expenditures for newly produced *capital goods* (such as machinery, equipment, tools, and buildings) and for additions to inventories.

guiding function of prices   The ability of price changes to bring about changes in the quantities of products and resources demanded and supplied.

household   An economic unit (of one or more persons) that provides the economy with resources and uses the income received to purchase goods and services that satisfy economic wants.

human capital   The accumulation of prior investments in education, training, health, and other factors that increase productivity.

human capital investment   Any expenditure undertaken to improve the education, skills, health, or mobility of workers, with an expectation of greater productivity and thus a positive return on the investment.

hyperinflation   A very rapid rise in the price level; an extremely high rate of inflation.

hypothesis   A tentative explanation of cause and effect that requires testing.

IMF   (See *International Monetary Fund*.)

import competition   The competition that domestic firms encounter from the products and services of foreign producers.

import demand curve A downsloping curve showing the amount of a product that an economy will import at each *world price* below the *domestic price.*

import quota A limit imposed by a nation on the quantity (or total value) of a good that may be imported during some period of time.

imports Spending by individuals, *firms,* and governments for goods and services produced in foreign nations.

import transaction The purchase of a good or service that decreases the amount of foreign money held by citizens, firms, and governments of a nation.

income A flow of dollars (or purchasing power) per unit of time derived from the use of human or property resources.

income approach The method that adds all the income generated by the production of *final goods and services* to measure the *gross domestic product.*

income effect A change in the quantity demanded of a product that results from the change in *real income (purchasing power)* caused by a change in the product's price.

income inequality The unequal distribution of an economy's total income among households or families.

increase in demand An increase in the *quantity demanded* of a good or service at every price; a shift of the *demand curve* to the right.

increase in supply An increase in the *quantity supplied* of a good or service at every price; a shift of the *supply curve* to the right.

increasing returns An increase in a firm's output by a larger percentage than the percentage increase in its inputs.

independent goods Products or services for which there is little or no relationship between the price of one and the demand for the other. When the price of one rises or falls, the demand for the other tends to remain constant.

independent variable The variable causing a change in some other (dependent) variable.

indirect business taxes Such taxes as *sales, excise,* and business *property taxes,* license fees, and *tariffs* that firms treat as costs of producing a product and pass on (in whole or in part) to buyers by charging higher prices.

individual demand The demand schedule or *demand curve* of a single buyer.

individual supply The supply schedule or *supply curve* of a single seller.

industrially advanced countries High-income countries such as the United States, Canada, Japan, and the nations of western Europe that have highly developed *market economies* based on large stocks of technologically advanced capital goods and skilled labor forces.

industry A group of (one or more) *firms* that produce identical or similar products.

inferior good A good or service whose consumption declines as income rises (and conversely), price remaining constant.

inflating Determining *real gross domestic product* by increasing the dollar value of the *nominal gross domestic product* produced in a year in which prices are lower than those in a *base year.*

inflation A rise in the general level of prices in an economy.

inflationary expectations The belief of workers, firms, and consumers that substantial inflation will occur in the future.

inflationary gap The amount by which the *aggregate expenditures schedule* must shift downward to decrease the *nominal GDP* to its full-employment noninflationary level.

inflation premium The component of the *nominal interest rate* that reflects anticipated inflation.

information technology New and more efficient methods of delivering and receiving information through use of computers, fax machines, wireless phones, and the Internet.

infrastructure The capital goods usually provided by the *public sector* for the use of its citizens and firms (for example, highways, bridges, transit systems, wastewater treatment facilities, municipal water systems, and airports).

injection An addition of spending to the income-expenditure stream: *investment, government purchases,* and *net exports.*

innovation The first commercially successful introduction of a new product, the use of a new method of production, or the creation of a new form of business organization.

inpayments The receipts of domestic or foreign money that individuals, firms, and governments of one nation obtain from the sale of goods and services abroad, as investment income and remittances, and from foreign purchases of its assets.

insider-outsider theory The hypothesis that nominal wages are inflexible downward because firms are aware that workers ("insiders") who retain employment during recession may refuse to work cooperatively with previously unemployed workers ("outsiders") who offer to work for less than the current wage.

interest The payment made for the use of money (of borrowed funds).

interest income Payments of income to those who supply the economy with *capital.*

interest rate The annual rate at which interest is paid; a percentage of the borrowed amount.

interest-rate effect The tendency for increases in the *price level* to increase the demand for money, raise interest rates, and, as a result, reduce total spending and real output in the economy (and the reverse for price-level decreases).

intermediate goods Products that are purchased for resale or further processing or manufacturing.

internally held public debt *Public debt* owed to citizens, firms, and institutions of the same nation that issued the debt.

international balance of payments A summary of all the transactions that took place between the individuals, firms, and government units of one nation and those of all other nations during a year.

international balance-of-payments deficit (See *balance-of-payments deficit.*)

international balance-of-payments surplus (See *balance-of-payments surplus.*)

international gold standard (See *gold standard.*)

International Monetary Fund (IMF) The international association of nations that was formed after the Second World War to make loans of foreign monies to nations with temporary *payments deficits* and, until the early 1970s, to administer the *adjustable pegs*. It now mainly makes loans to nations facing possible defaults on private and government loans.

international monetary reserves The foreign currencies and other assets such as gold that a nation can use to settle a *balance-of-payments deficit*.

international value of the dollar The price that must be paid in foreign currency (money) to obtain one U.S. dollar.

intrinsic value The market value of the metal within a coin.

inventories Goods that have been produced but remain unsold.

inverse relationship The relationship between two variables that change in opposite directions, for example, product price and quantity demanded.

investment Spending for the production and accumulation of *capital* and additions to inventories.

investment demand curve A curve that shows the amounts of *investment* demanded by an economy at a series of *real interest rates*.

investment goods Same as *capital* or capital goods.

investment in human capital (See *human capital investment*.)

investment schedule A curve or schedule that shows the amounts firms plan to invest at various possible values of *real gross domestic product*.

invisible hand The tendency of firms and resource suppliers that seek to further their own self-interests in competitive markets to also promote the interest of society.

Joint Economic Committee (JEC) Committee of senators and representatives that investigates economic problems of national interest.

Keynesian economics The macroeconomic generalizations that lead to the conclusion that a capitalistic economy is characterized by macroeconomic instability and that *fiscal policy* and *monetary policy* can be used to promote *full employment, price-level stability,* and *economic growth*.

Keynesianism The philosophical, ideological, and analytical views pertaining to *Keynesian economics*.

labor People's physical and mental talents and efforts that are used to help produce goods and services.

labor force Persons 16 years of age and older who are not in institutions and who are employed or are unemployed and seeking work.

labor-force participation rate The percentage of the working-age population that is actually in the *labor force*.

labor-intensive commodity A product requiring a relatively large amount of *labor* to be produced.

labor productivity Total output divided by the quantity of labor employed to produce it.

labor theory of value (Web chapter) The Marxian idea that the economic value of any commodity is determined solely by the amount of labor that is required to produce it.

labor union A group of workers organized to advance the interests of the group (to increase wages, shorten the hours worked, improve working conditions, and so on).

Laffer Curve A curve relating government tax rates and tax revenues and on which a particular tax rate (between zero and 100 percent) maximizes tax revenues.

laissez-faire capitalism (See *capitalism*.)

land Natural resources ("free gifts of nature") used to produce goods and services.

land-intensive commodity A product requiring a relatively large amount of land to be produced.

law of demand The principle that, other things equal, an increase in a product's price will reduce the quantity of it demanded, and conversely for a decrease in price.

law of increasing opportunity costs The principle that as the production of a good increases, the *opportunity cost* of producing an additional unit rises.

law of supply The principle that, other things equal, an increase in the price of a product will increase the quantity of it supplied, and conversely for a price decrease.

leakage (1) A withdrawal of potential spending from the income-expenditures stream via *saving,* tax payments, or *imports;* (2) a withdrawal that reduces the lending potential of the banking system.

learning by doing Achieving greater *productivity* and lower *average total cost* through gains in knowledge and skill that accompany repetition of a task; a source of *economies of scale*.

legal tender A legal designation of a nation's official currency (bills and coins). Payment of debts must be accepted in this monetary unit, but creditors can specify the form of payment, for example, "cash only" or "check or credit card only."

lending potential of an individual commercial bank The amount by which a single bank can safely increase the *money supply* by making new loans to (or buying securities from) the public; equal to the bank's excess reserves.

lending potential of the banking system The amount by which the banking system can increase the *money supply* by making new loans to (or buying securities from) the public; equal to the *excess reserves* of the banking system multiplied by the *monetary multiplier*.

liability A debt with a monetary value; an amount owed by a firm or an individual.

limited liability Restriction of the maximum loss to a predetermined amount for the owners (stockholders) of a *corporation*. The maximum loss is the amount they paid for their shares of stock.

limited-liability company An unincorporated business whose owners are protected by *limited liability*.

liquidity The ease with which an asset can be converted quickly into cash with little or no loss of purchasing power. Money is said to be perfectly liquid, whereas other assets have a lesser degree of liquidity.

long run (1) In *microeconomics,* a period of time long enough to enable producers of a product to change the quantities of all the resources they employ; period in which all resources and costs are variable and no resources or costs are fixed. (2) In *macroeconomics,* a period sufficiently long for *nominal wages* and other input prices to change in response to a change in the nation's *price level.*

long-run aggregate supply curve   The aggregate supply curve associated with a time period in which input prices (especially *nominal wages*) are fully responsive to changes in the *price level.*

lump-sum tax   A tax that is a constant amount (the tax revenue of government is the same) at all levels of GDP.

M1   The most narrowly defined *money supply,* equal to *currency* in the hands of the public and the *checkable deposits* of commercial banks and thrift institutions.

M2   A more broadly defined *money supply,* equal to *M1* plus *noncheckable savings accounts* (including *money market deposit accounts*), small *time deposits* (deposits of less than $100,000), and individual *money market mutual fund* balances.

M3   A very broadly defined *money supply,* equal to *M2* plus large *time deposits* (deposits of $100,000 or more).

macroeconomics   The part of economics concerned with the economy as a whole; with such major aggregates as the household, business, and government sectors; and with measures of the total economy.

managed floating exchange rate   An *exchange rate* that is allowed to change (float) as a result of changes in currency supply and demand but at times is altered (managed) by governments via their buying and selling of particular currencies.

marginal analysis   The comparison of marginal ("extra" or "additional") benefits and marginal costs, usually for decision making.

marginal benefit   The extra (additional) benefit of consuming 1 more unit of some good or service; the change in total benefit when 1 more unit is consumed.

marginal cost   The extra (additional) cost of producing 1 more unit of output; equal to the change in total cost divided by the change in output.

marginal propensity to consume   The fraction of any change in *disposable income* spent for *consumer goods;* equal to the change in consumption divided by the change in disposable income.

marginal propensity to save   The fraction of any change in *disposable income* that households save; equal to the change in *saving* divided by the change in disposable income.

marginal tax rate   The tax rate paid on each additional dollar of income.

marginal utility   The extra *utility* a consumer obtains from the consumption of 1 additional unit of a good or service; equal to the change in total utility divided by the change in the quantity consumed.

market   Any institution or mechanism that brings together buyers (demanders) and sellers (suppliers) of a particular good or service.

market demand   (See *total demand.*)

market economy   An economy in which only the private decisions of consumers, resource suppliers, and firms determine how resources are allocated; the *market system.*

market failure   The inability of a market to bring about the allocation of resources that best satisfies the wants of society; in particular, the overallocation or underallocation of resources to the production of a particular good or service because of *spillovers* or informational problems or because markets do not provide desired *public goods.*

market system   All the product and resource markets of a *market economy* and the relationships among them; a method that allows the prices determined in those markets to allocate the economy's scarce resources and to communicate and coordinate the decisions made by consumers, firms, and resource suppliers.

Medicaid   A Federal program that helps finance the medical expenses of low-income individuals and families.

Medicare   A Federal program that is financed by *payroll taxes* and provides for (1) compulsory hospital insurance for senior citizens and (2) low-cost voluntary insurance to help older Americans pay physicians' fees.

medium of exchange   Any item sellers generally accept and buyers generally use to pay for a good or service; *money;* a convenient means of exchanging goods and services without engaging in *barter.*

microeconomics   The part of economics concerned with such individual units as *industries, firms,* and *households* and with individual markets, specific goods and services, and product and resource prices.

minimum wage   The lowest *wage* employers may legally pay for an hour of work.

monetarism   The macroeconomic view that the main cause of changes in aggregate output and the price level is fluctuations in the *money supply;* espoused by advocates of a *monetary rule.*

monetary multiplier   The multiple of its *excess reserves* by which the banking system can expand *checkable deposits* and thus the *money supply* by making new loans (or buying securities); equal to 1 divided by the *reserve requirement.*

monetary policy   A central bank's changing of the *money supply* to influence interest rates and assist the economy in achieving price stability, full employment, and economic growth.

monetary rule   The rule suggested by *monetarism.* As traditionally formulated, the rule says that the *money supply* should be expanded each year at the same annual rate as the potential rate of growth of the *real gross domestic product;* the supply of money should be increased steadily between 3 and 5 percent per year. (Also see *Taylor rule.*)

money   Any item that is generally acceptable to sellers in exchange for goods and services.

money capital   Money available to purchase *capital;* simply *money,* as defined by economists.

money income   (See *nominal income.*)

money market   The market in which the demand for and the supply of money determine the *interest rate* (or the level of interest rates) in the economy.

money market deposit accounts (MMDAs)   Interest-earning accounts at banks and *thrift institutions,* which pool the funds of depositors to buy various short-term securities.

money market mutual funds (MMMFs)   Interest-bearing accounts offered by investment companies, which pool depositors' funds for the purchase of short-term securities. Depositors may write checks in minimum amounts or more against their accounts.

money supply Narrowly defined, *M*1; more broadly defined, *M*2 and *M*3.

monopoly A market structure in which the number of sellers is so small that each seller is able to influence the total supply and the price of the good or service.

most-favored-nation (MFN) status An agreement by the United States to allow some other nation's *exports* into the United States at the lowest tariff level levied by the United States, then or at any later time.

multinational corporations Firms that own production facilities in two or more countries and produce and sell their products globally.

multiple counting Wrongly including the value of *intermediate goods* in the *gross domestic product;* counting the same good or service more than once.

multiplier The ratio of a change in the equilibrium GDP to the change in *investment* or in any other component of *aggregate expenditures* or *aggregate demand;* the number by which a change in any component of aggregate expenditures or aggregate demand must be multiplied to find the resulting change in the equilibrium GDP.

multiplier effect The effect on equilibrium GDP of a change in *aggregate expenditures* or *aggregate demand* (caused by a change in the *consumption schedule, investment, government purchases,* or *net exports*).

national bank A *commercial bank* authorized to operate by the U.S. government.

National Credit Union Administration (NCUA) The federally chartered agency that insures deposit liabilities (up to $100,000 per account) in *credit unions.*

national income Total income earned by resource suppliers for their contributions to *gross domestic product;* equal to the gross domestic product minus *nonincome charges,* minus *net foreign factor income.*

national income accounting The techniques used to measure the overall production of the economy and other related variables for the nation as a whole.

natural monopoly An industry in which *economies of scale* are so great that a single firm can produce the product at a lower average total cost than would be possible if more than one firm produced the product.

natural rate of unemployment The *full-employment unemployment rate;* the unemployment rate occurring when there is no cyclical unemployment and the economy is achieving its potential output; the unemployment rate at which actual inflation equals expected inflation.

near-money Financial assets, the most important of which are *noncheckable savings accounts, time deposits,* and U.S. short-term securities and savings bonds, which are not a medium of exchange but can be readily converted into money.

negative GDP gap A situation in which actual *gross domestic product* is less than *potential output.*

negative relationship (See *inverse relationship.*)

net domestic product *Gross domestic product* less the part of the year's output that is needed to replace the *capital goods* worn out in producing the output; the nation's total output available for consumption or additions to the *capital stock.*

net export effect The idea that the impact of a change in *monetary policy* or *fiscal policy* will be strengthened or weakened by the consequent change in *net exports.* The change in net exports occurs because of changes in real interest rates, which affect exchange rates.

net exports *Exports* minus *imports.*

net foreign factor income Payments by a nation of resource income to the rest of the world minus receipts of resource income from the rest of the world.

net investment income The interest and dividend income received by the residents of a nation from residents of other nations less the interest and dividend payments made by the residents of that nation to the residents of other nations.

net private domestic investment *Gross private domestic investment* less *consumption of fixed capital;* the addition to the nation's stock of *capital* during a year.

net taxes The taxes collected by government less *government transfer payments.*

net transfers The personal and government transfer payments made by one nation to residents of foreign nations less the personal and government transfer payments received from residents of foreign nations.

network effects Increases in the value of a product to each user, including existing users, as the total number of users rises.

net worth The total *assets* less the total *liabilities* of a firm or an individual; for a firm, the claims of the owners against the firm's total assets; for an individual, his or her wealth.

new classical economics The theory that, although unanticipated price-level changes may create macroeconomic instability in the short run, the economy is stable at the full-employment level of domestic output in the long run because prices and wages adjust automatically to correct movements away from the full-employment, noninflationary output.

New Economy The label attached by some economists and the popular press to the U.S. economy since 1995. The main characteristics are accelerated *productivity growth* and *economic growth,* caused by rapid technological advance and the emergence of the global economy.

nominal gross domestic product (GDP) The *GDP* measured in terms of the price level at the time of measurement (unadjusted for *inflation*).

nominal income The number of dollars received by an individual or group for its resources during some period of time.

nominal interest rate The interest rate expressed in terms of annual amounts currently charged for interest and not adjusted for inflation.

nominal wage The amount of money received by a worker per unit of time (hour, day, etc.); money wage.

nondiscretionary fiscal policy (See *built-in stabilizer.*)

nondurable good A *consumer good* with an expected life (use) of less than 3 years.

nonexcludability The inability to keep nonpayers (free riders) from obtaining benefits from a certain good; a *public good* characteristic.

nonexhaustive expenditure An expenditure by government that does not result directly in the employment of economic resources or the production of goods and services; see *government transfer payment*.

nonincome charges *Consumption of fixed capital* and *indirect business taxes;* amounts subtracted from *GDP* (along with *net foreign factor income*) in determining *national income*.

nonincome determinants of consumption and saving All influences on consumption and saving other than the level of *GDP*.

noninterest determinants of investment All influences on the level of investment spending other than the *interest rate*.

noninvestment transaction An expenditure for stocks, bonds, or secondhand *capital goods*.

nonmarket transactions The production of goods and services excluded in the measurement of the *gross domestic product* because they are not bought and sold.

nonpriced goods (Web chapter) Goods or resources that are not priced in markets because they are owned in common by society and available for the taking on public lands.

nonproduction transaction The purchase and sale of any item that is not a currently produced good or service.

nonrivalry The idea that one person's benefit from a certain good does not reduce the benefit available to others; a *public good* characteristic.

nontariff barriers All barriers other than *protective tariffs* that nations erect to impede international trade, including *import quotas,* licensing requirements, unreasonable product-quality standards, unnecessary bureaucratic detail in customs procedures, and so on.

normal good A good or service whose consumption increases when income increases and falls when income decreases, price remaining constant.

normal profit The payment made by a firm to obtain and retain *entrepreneurial ability;* the minimum income entrepreneurial ability must receive to induce it to perform entrepreneurial functions for a firm.

normative economics The part of economics involving value judgments about what the economy should be like; focused on which economic goals and policies should be implemented; policy economics.

North American Free Trade Agreement (NAFTA) A 1993 agreement establishing, over a 15-year period, a free-trade zone composed of Canada, Mexico, and the United States.

official reserves Foreign currencies owned by the central bank of a nation.

Okun's law The generalization that any 1-percentage-point rise in the *unemployment rate* above the *full-employment unemployment rate* will increase the GDP gap by 2 percent of the *potential output* (GDP) of the economy.

OPEC (See *Organization of Petroleum Exporting Countries*.)

open economy An economy that exports and imports goods and services.

open-market operations The buying and selling of U.S. government securities by the *Federal Reserve Banks* for purposes of carrying out *monetary policy*.

opportunity cost The amount of other products that must be forgone or sacrificed to produce a unit of a product.

Organization of Petroleum Exporting Countries (OPEC) A cartel of 11 oil-producing countries (Algeria, Indonesia, Iran, Iraq, Kuwait, Libya, Nigeria, Qatar, Saudi Arabia, Venezuela, and the UAE) that controls the quantity and price of crude oil exported by its members and that accounts for 60 percent of the world's export of oil.

other-things-equal assumption The assumption that factors other than those being considered are held constant.

outpayments The expenditures of domestic or foreign currency that the individuals, firms, and governments of one nation make to purchase goods and services, for *remittances,* to pay investment income, and for purchases of foreign assets.

paper money Pieces of paper used as a *medium of exchange;* in the United States, *Federal Reserve Notes*.

partnership An unincorporated firm owned and operated by two or more persons.

patent An exclusive right given to inventors to produce and sell a new product or machine for 20 years from the time of patent application.

payments deficit (See *balance-of-payments deficit*.)

payments surplus (See *balance-of-payments surplus*.)

payroll tax A tax levied on employers of labor equal to a percentage of all or part of the wages and salaries paid by them and on employees equal to a percentage of all or part of the wages and salaries received by them.

per capita GDP *Gross domestic product* (GDP) per person; the average GDP of a population.

per capita income A nation's total income per person; the average income of a population.

personal consumption expenditures The expenditures of *households* for *durable* and *nondurable consumer goods* and services.

personal distribution of income The manner in which the economy's *personal* or *disposable income* is divided among different income classes or different households or families.

personal income The earned and unearned income available to resource suppliers and others before the payment of personal taxes.

personal income tax A tax levied on the taxable income of individuals, households, and unincorporated firms.

personal saving The *personal income* of households less personal taxes and *personal consumption expenditures; disposable income* not spent for *consumer goods*.

per-unit production cost The average production cost of a particular level of output; total input cost divided by units of output.

Phillips Curve A curve showing the relationship between the *unemployment rate* (on the horizontal axis) and the annual rate of increase in the *price level* (on the vertical axis).

planned investment The amount that *firms* plan or intend to invest.

plant   A physical establishment that performs one or more functions in the production, fabrication, and distribution of goods and services.

policy economics   The formulation of courses of action to bring about desired economic outcomes or to prevent undesired occurrences.

political business cycle   The alleged tendency of Congress to destabilize the economy by reducing taxes and increasing government expenditures before elections and to raise taxes and lower expenditures after elections.

positive economics   The analysis of facts or data to establish scientific generalizations about economic behavior.

positive GDP gap   A situation in which actual *gross domestic product* exceeds *potential output.*

positive relationship   A direct relationship between two variables.

post hoc, ergo propter hoc fallacy   The false belief that when one event precedes another, the first event must have caused the second event.

potential output   The real output *(GDP)* an economy can produce when it fully employs its available resources.

poverty   A situation in which the basic needs of an individual or family exceed the means to satisfy them.

poverty rate   The percentage of the population with incomes below the official poverty income levels that are established by the Federal government.

price   The amount of money needed to buy a particular good, service, or resource.

price index   An index number that shows how the weighted-average price of a "market basket" of goods changes over time.

price level   The weighted average of the prices of all the final goods and services produced in an economy.

price-level stability   A steadiness of the price level from one period to the next; zero or low annual inflation; also called "price stability."

price-level surprises   Unanticipated changes in the price level.

price war   Successive and continued decreases in the prices charged by firms in an oligopolistic industry. Each firm lowers its price below rivals' prices, hoping to increase its sales and revenues at its rivals' expense.

prime interest rate   The benchmark *interest rate* that banks use as a reference point for a wide range of loans to businesses and individuals.

principal-agent problem   A conflict of interest that occurs when agents (workers or managers) pursue their own objectives to the detriment of the principals' (stockholders') goals.

private good   A good or service that is individually consumed and that can be profitably provided by privately owned firms because they can exclude nonpayers from receiving the benefits.

private property   The right of private persons and firms to obtain, own, control, employ, dispose of, and bequeath *land, capital,* and other property.

private sector   The *households* and business *firms* of the economy.

producer surplus   (Web chapter) The difference between the actual price a producer receives (or producers receive) and the minimum acceptable price; the triangular area above the supply curve and below the market price.

production possibilities curve   A curve showing the different combinations of two goods or services that can be produced in a *full-employment, full-production* economy where the available supplies of resources and technology are fixed.

productive efficiency   The production of a good in the least costly way; occurs when production takes place at the output at which average cost is a minimum.

productivity   A measure of average output or real output per unit of input. For example, the productivity of labor is determined by dividing real output by hours of work.

productivity growth   The percentage change in *productivity* from one period to another.

product market   A market in which products are sold by *firms* and bought by *households.*

profit   The return to the resource *entrepreneurial ability* (see *normal profit*); *total revenue* minus total cost (see *economic profit*).

progressive tax   A tax whose *average tax rate* increases as the taxpayer's income increases and decreases as the taxpayer's income decreases.

property tax   A tax on the value of property (*capital, land, stocks* and *bonds,* and *other assets*) owned by *firms* and *households.*

proportional tax   A tax whose *average tax rate* remains constant as the taxpayer's income increases or decreases.

protective tariff   A *tariff* designed to shield domestic producers of a good or service from the competition of foreign producers.

public debt   The total amount owed by the Federal government to the owners of government securities; equal to the sum of past government *budget deficits* less government *budget surpluses.*

public good   A good or service that is characterized by *nonrivalry* and *nonexcludability;* a good or service with these characteristics provided by government.

public investments   Government expenditures on public capital (such as roads, highways, bridges, mass-transit systems, and electric power facilities) and on *human capital* (such as education, training, and health).

public sector   The part of the economy that contains all government entities; government.

purchasing power   The amount of goods and services that a monetary unit of income can buy.

purchasing power parity   The idea that exchange rates between nations equate the purchasing power of various currencies. Exchange rates between any two nations adjust to reflect the price-level differences between the countries.

pure rate of interest   An essentially risk-free, long-term interest rate that is free of the influence of market imperfections.

quantity demanded   The amount of a good or service that buyers (or a buyer) desire to purchase at a particular price during some period.

quantity supplied   The amount of a good or service that producers (or a producer) offer to sell at a particular price during some period.

quasi-public bank   A bank that is privately owned but governmentally (publicly) controlled; each of the U.S. *Federal Reserve Banks*.

quasi-public good   A good or service to which excludability could apply but that has such a large *spillover benefit* that government sponsors its production to prevent an underallocation of resources.

R&D   Research and development activities undertaken to bring about *technological advance*.

rate of exchange   The price paid in one's own money to acquire 1 unit of a foreign currency; the rate at which the money of one nation is exchanged for the money of another nation.

rate of return   The gain in net revenue divided by the cost of an investment or an *R&D* expenditure; expressed as a percentage.

rational behavior   Human behavior based on comparison of marginal costs and marginal benefits; behavior designed to maximize total utility.

rational expectations theory   The hypothesis that firms and households expect monetary and fiscal policies to have certain effects on the economy and (in pursuit of their own self-interests) take actions that make these policies ineffective.

rationing function of prices   The ability of market forces in competitive markets to equalize *quantity demanded* and *quantity supplied* and to eliminate shortages and surpluses via changes in prices.

real-balances effect   The tendency for increases in the *price level* to lower the real value (or purchasing power) of financial assets with fixed money value and, as a result, to reduce total spending and *real GDP,* and conversely for decreases in the price level.

real-business-cycle theory   A theory that *business cycles* result from changes in technology and resource availability, which affect *productivity* and thus shift *the longrun aggregate supply curve* either leftward or rightward.

real capital   (See *capital*.)

real GDP   (See *real gross domestic product*.)

real gross domestic product (GDP)   *Gross domestic product* adjusted for inflation; gross domestic product in a year divided by the GDP *price index* for that year, expressed as a decimal.

real income   The amount of goods and services that can be purchased with *nominal income* during some period of time; nominal income adjusted for inflation.

real interest rate   The interest rate expressed in dollars of constant value (adjusted for *inflation*) and equal to the *nominal interest rate* less the expected rate of inflation.

real wage   The amount of goods and services a worker can purchase with his or her *nominal wage;* the purchasing power of the nominal wage.

recession   A period of declining real GDP, accompanied by lower real income and higher unemployment.

recessionary gap   The amount by which the *aggregate expenditures schedule* must shift upward to increase the real *GDP* to its full-employment, noninflationary level.

Reciprocal Trade Agreements Act   A 1934 Federal law that authorized the president to negotiate up to 50 percent lower tariffs with foreign nations that agreed to reduce their tariffs on U.S. goods. (Such agreements incorporated the *most-favored-nation* clause.)

refinancing the public debt   Paying owners of maturing government securities with money obtained by selling new securities or with new securities.

regressive tax   A tax whose *average tax rate* decreases as the taxpayer's income increases and increases as the taxpayer's income decreases.

rental income   The payments (income) received by those who supply *land* to the economy.

required reserves   The funds that banks and thrifts must deposit with the *Federal Reserve Bank* (or hold as *vault cash*) to meet the legal *reserve requirement;* a fixed percentage of the bank's or thrift's checkable deposits.

reserve requirement   The specified minimum percentage of its checkable deposits that a bank or thrift must keep on deposit at the Federal Reserve Bank in its district or hold as *vault cash*.

resource   A natural, human, or manufactured item that helps produce goods and services; a productive agent or factor of production.

resource market   A market in which *households* sell and *firms* buy resources or the services of resources.

retiring the public debt   Reducing the size of the *public debt* by paying money to owners of maturing U.S. government securities.

revenue tariff   A *tariff* designed to produce income for the Federal government.

roundabout production   The construction and use of *capital* to aid in the production of *consumer goods*.

rule of 70   A method for determining the number of years it will take for some measure to double, given its annual percentage increase. Example: To determine the number of years it will take for the *price level* to double, divide 70 by the annual rate of *inflation*.

sales tax   A tax levied on the cost (at retail) of a broad group of products.

saving   Disposable income not spent for consumer goods; equal to *disposable income* minus *personal consumption expenditures*.

savings and loan association (S&L)   A firm that accepts deposits primarily from small individual savers and lends primarily to individuals to finance purchases such as autos and homes; now nearly indistinguishable from a *commercial bank*.

saving schedule   A schedule that shows the amounts *households* plan to save (plan not to spend for *consumer goods*), at different levels of *disposable income*.

savings deposit   A deposit that is interest-bearing and that the depositor can normally withdraw at any time.

savings institution   (See *thrift institution*.)

Say's law   The largely discredited macroeconomic generalization that the production of goods and services (supply) creates an equal *demand* for those goods and services.

scarce resources   The limited quantities of *land, capital, labor,* and *entrepreneurial ability* that are never sufficient to satisfy people's virtually unlimited economic wants.

scientific method   The procedure for the systematic pursuit of knowledge involving the observation of facts and the formulation and testing of hypotheses to obtain theories, principles, and laws.

seasonal variations Increases and decreases in the level of economic activity within a single year, caused by a change in the season.

secular trend A long-term tendency; a change in some variable over a very long period of years.

self-interest That which each firm, property owner, worker, and consumer believes is best for itself and seeks to obtain.

seniority The length of time a worker has been employed absolutely or relative to other workers; may be used to determine which workers will be laid off when there is insufficient work for them all and who will be rehired when more work becomes available.

separation of ownership and control The fact that different groups of people own a *corporation* (the stockholders) and manage it (the directors and officers).

service An (intangible) act or use for which a consumer, firm, or government is willing to pay.

shirking Workers' neglecting or evading work to increase their *utility* or well-being.

shortage The amount by which the *quantity demanded* of a product exceeds the *quantity supplied* at a particular (below-equilibrium) price.

short run (1) In microeconomics, a period of time in which producers are able to change the quantities of some but not all of the resources they employ; a period in which some resources (usually plant) are fixed and some are variable. (2) In macroeconomics, a period in which nominal wages and other input prices do not change in response to a change in the price level.

short-run aggregate supply curve An aggregate supply curve relevant to a time period in which input prices (particularly *nominal wages*) do not change in response to changes in the *price level*.

simple multiplier The *multiplier* in any economy in which government collects no *net taxes,* there are no *imports,* and *investment* is independent of the level of income; equal to 1 divided by the *marginal propensity to save.*

slope of a line The ratio of the vertical change (the rise or fall) to the horizontal change (the run) between any two points on a line. The slope of an upward-sloping line is positive, reflecting a direct relationship between two variables; the slope of a downward-sloping line is negative, reflecting an inverse relationship between two variables.

Smoot-Hawley Tariff Act Legislation passed in 1930 that established very high tariffs. Its objective was to reduce imports and stimulate the domestic economy, but it resulted only in retaliatory tariffs by other nations.

Social Security trust fund A Federal fund that saves excessive Social Security tax revenues received in one year to meet Social Security benefit obligations that exceed Social Security tax revenues in some subsequent year.

sole proprietorship An unincorporated *firm* owned and operated by one person.

special economic zones (Web chapter) Regions of China open to foreign investment, private ownership, and relatively free international trade.

specialization The use of the resources of an individual, a firm, a region, or a nation to concentrate production on one or a small number of goods and services.

speculation The activity of buying or selling with the motive of later reselling or rebuying for profit.

spillover A benefit or cost from production or consumption, accruing without compensation to nonbuyers and nonsellers of the product (see *spillover benefit* and *spillover cost*).

spillover benefit A benefit obtained without compensation by third parties from the production or consumption of sellers or buyers. Example: A beekeeper benefits when a neighboring farmer plants clover.

spillover cost A cost imposed without compensation on third parties by the production or consumption of sellers or buyers. Example: A manufacturer dumps toxic chemicals into a river, killing the fish sought by sport fishers.

SSI (See *Supplemental Security Income.*)

stagflation Inflation accompanied by stagnation in the rate of growth of output and an increase in unemployment in the economy; simultaneous increases in the *price level* and the *unemployment rate.*

startup (firm) A new firm focused on creating and introducing a particular new product or employing a specific new production or distribution method.

state bank A *commercial bank* authorized by a state government to engage in the business of banking.

state-owned enterprises (Web chapter) Businesses that are owned by the government; the major type of enterprises in Russia and China before their transitions to the market system.

stock (corporate) An ownership share in a corporation.

store of value An *asset* set aside for future use; one of the three functions of *money.*

strategic trade policy The use of trade barriers to reduce the risk inherent in product development by domestic firms, particularly that involving advanced technology.

strike The withholding of labor services by an organized group of workers (a *labor union*).

structural unemployment Unemployment of workers whose skills are not demanded by employers, who lack sufficient skill to obtain employment, or who cannot easily move to locations where jobs are available.

subsidy A payment of funds (or goods and services) by a government, firm, or household for which it receives no good or service in return. When made by a government, it is a *government transfer payment.*

substitute goods Products or services that can be used in place of each other. When the price of one falls, the demand for the other product falls; conversely, when the price of one product rises, the demand for the other product rises.

substitution effect (1) A change in the quantity demanded of a *consumer good* that results from a change in its relative expensiveness caused by a change in the product's price; (2) the effect of a change in the price of a *resource* on the quantity of the resource employed by a firm, assuming no change in its output.

supply A schedule showing the amounts of a good or service that sellers (or a seller) will offer at various prices during some period.

supply curve   A curve illustrating *supply*.

supply factor (in growth)   An increase in the availability of a resource, an improvement in its quality, or an expansion of technological knowledge that makes it possible for an economy to produce a greater output of goods and services.

supply-side economics   A view of macroeconomics that emphasizes the role of costs and *aggregate supply* in explaining *inflation, unemployment,* and *economic growth*.

surplus   The amount by which the *quantity supplied* of a product exceeds the *quantity demanded* at a specific (above-equilibrium) price.

surplus value   (Web chapter) The amount by which a worker's daily output in dollar terms exceeds his or her daily wage; the amount of the worker's output appropriated by capitalists as profit; a Marxian term.

tariff   A tax imposed by a nation on an imported good.

tax   An involuntary payment of money (or goods and services) to a government by a *household* or *firm* for which the household or firm receives no good or service directly in return.

tax incidence   The person or group that ends up paying a tax.

tax-transfer disincentives   Decreases in the incentives to work, save, invest, innovate, and take risks that allegedly result from high *marginal tax rates* and *transfer payments*.

Taylor rule   A modern monetary rule proposed by economist John Taylor that would stipulate exactly how much the Federal Reserve should change interest rates in response to divergences of real GDP from potential GDP and divergences of actual rates of inflation from a target rate of inflation.

technological advance   New and better goods and services and new and better ways of producing or distributing them.

technology   The body of knowledge and techniques that can be used to combine *economic resources* to produce goods and services.

terms of trade   The rate at which units of one product can be exchanged for units of another product; the price of a good or service; the amount of one good or service that must be given up to obtain 1 unit of another good or service.

theoretical economics   The process of deriving and applying economic theories and principles.

thrift institution   A *savings and loan association, mutual savings bank,* or *credit union*.

tight money policy   Federal Reserve System actions that contract, or restrict, the growth of the nation's *money supply* for the purpose of reducing or eliminating inflation.

till money   (See *vault cash*.)

time deposit   An interest-earning deposit in a *commercial bank* or *thrift institution* that the depositor can withdraw without penalty after the end of a specified period.

token money   Coins having a *face value* greater than their *intrinsic value*.

total demand   The demand schedule or the *demand curve* of all buyers of a good or service; also called market demand.

total demand for money   The sum of the *transactions demand for money* and the *asset demand for money*.

total product   The total output of a particular good or service produced by a firm (or a group of firms or the entire economy).

total revenue   The total number of dollars received by a firm (or firms) from the sale of a product; equal to the total expenditures for the product produced by the firm (or firms); equal to the quantity sold (demanded) multiplied by the price at which it is sold.

total spending   The total amount that buyers of goods and services spend or plan to spend; also called *aggregate expenditures*.

total supply   The supply schedule or the *supply curve* of all sellers of a good or service; also called market supply.

township and village enterprises   (Web chapter) Privately owned rural manufacturing firms in China.

trade balance   The export of goods (or goods and services) of a nation less its imports of goods (or goods and services).

trade bloc   A group of nations that lower or abolish trade barriers among members. Examples include the *European Union* and the nations of the *North American Free Trade Agreement*.

trade controls   *Tariffs, export subsidies, import quotas,* and other means a nation may employ to reduce *imports* and expand *exports*.

trade deficit   The amount by which a nation's *imports* of goods (or goods and services) exceed its *exports* of goods (or goods and services).

tradeoff   The sacrifice of some or all of one economic goal, good, or service to achieve some other goal, good, or service.

trade surplus   The amount by which a nation's *exports* of goods (or goods and services) exceed its *imports* of goods (or goods and services).

trading possibilities line   A line that shows the different combinations of two products that an economy is able to obtain (consume) when it specializes in the production of one product and trades (exports) it to obtain the other product.

transactions demand for money   The amount of money people want to hold for use as a *medium of exchange* (to make payments); varies directly with the *nominal GDP*.

transfer payment   A payment of *money* (or goods and services) by a government to a *household* or *firm* for which the payer receives no good or service directly in return.

unanticipated inflation   Increases in the price level (*inflation*) at a rate greater than expected.

underemployment   (1) The failure to produce the maximum amount of goods and services that can be produced from the resources employed; the failure to achieve *full production;* (2) a situation in which workers are employed in positions requiring less education and skill than they have.

undistributed corporate profits   After-tax corporate profits not distributed as dividends to stockholders; corporate or business saving; also called retained earnings.

unemployment The failure to use all available *economic resources* to produce desired goods and services; the failure of the economy to fully employ its *labor force*.

unemployment compensation (See *unemployment insurance*).

unemployment insurance The social insurance program that in the United States is financed by state *payroll taxes* on employers and makes income available to workers who become unemployed and are unable to find jobs.

unemployment rate The percentage of the *labor force* unemployed at any time.

unit labor cost Labor cost per unit of output; total labor cost divided by total output.

unit of account A standard unit in which prices can be stated and the value of goods and services can be compared; one of the three functions of *money*.

unlimited liability Absence of any limits on the maximum amount that an individual (usually a business owner) may become legally required to pay.

unlimited wants The insatiable desire of consumers for goods and services that will give them satisfaction or *utility*.

unplanned changes in inventories Changes in inventories that firms did not anticipate; changes in inventories that occur because of unexpected increases or decreases of aggregate spending (of *aggregate expenditures*).

unplanned investment Actual investment less *planned investment;* increases or decreases in the *inventories* of firms resulting from production greater than sales.

urban collectives (Web chapter) Chinese enterprises jointly owned by their managers and their workforces and located in urban areas.

Uruguay Round A 1995 trade agreement (to be fully implemented by 2005) that established the *World Trade Organization (WTO),* liberalized trade in goods and services, provided added protection to intellectual property (for example, *patents* and *copyrights*), and reduced farm subsidies.

utility The want-satisfying power of a good or service; the satisfaction or pleasure a consumer obtains from the consumption of a good or service (or from the consumption of a collection of goods and services).

value added The value of the product sold by a *firm* less the value of the products (materials) purchased and used by the firm to produce the product.

value judgment Opinion of what is desirable or undesirable; belief regarding what ought or ought not to be (regarding what is right or just and wrong or unjust).

value of money The quantity of goods and services for which a unit of money (a dollar) can be exchanged; the purchasing power of a unit of money; the reciprocal of the *price level*.

vault cash The *currency* a bank has in its vault and cash drawers.

velocity The number of times per year that the average dollar in the *money supply* is spent for *final goods and services;* nominal GDP divided by the money supply.

vertical intercept The point at which a line meets the vertical axis of a graph.

very long run A period in which *technology* can change and in which *firms* can introduce new products.

vicious circle of poverty (Web chapter) A problem common in some *developing countries* in which their low per capita incomes are an obstacle to realizing the levels of saving and investment requisite to acceptable rates of economic growth.

voluntary export restrictions Voluntary limitations by countries or firms of their exports to a particular foreign nation to avoid enactment of formal trade barriers by that nation.

wage The price paid for the use or services of *labor* per unit of time (per hour, per day, and so on).

wage rate (See *wage*.)

wages The income of those who supply the economy with *labor*.

wealth Anything that has value because it produces income or could produce income. Wealth is a stock; income is a flow. Assets less liabilities; net worth.

wealth effect The tendency for people to increase their consumption spending when the value of their financial and real assets rises and to decrease their consumption spending when the value of those assets falls.

"will to develop" (Web chapter) The state of wanting economic growth strongly enough to change from old to new ways of doing things.

World Bank (Web chapter) A bank that lends (and guarantees loans) to developing nations to assist them in increasing their *capital stock* and thus in achieving *economic growth;* formally, the International Bank for Reconstruction and Development.

world price The international market price of a good or service, determined by world demand and supply.

World Trade Organization (WTO) An organization of 145 nations (as of 2003) that oversees the provisions of the current world trade agreement, resolves trade disputes stemming from it, and holds forums for further rounds of trade negotiations.

WTO (See *World Trade Organization*.)

Answers to Key Questions

CHAPTER 1

1-4 Use the economic perspective to explain why someone who is normally a light eater at a standard restaurant may become somewhat of a glutton at a buffet-style restaurant which charges a single price for all you can eat.

This behavior can be explained in terms of marginal costs and marginal benefits. At a standard restaurant, items are priced individually—they have a positive marginal cost. If you order more, it will cost you more. You order until the marginal benefit from the extra food no longer exceeds the marginal cost. At a buffet you pay a flat fee no matter how much you eat. Once the fee is paid, additional food items have a zero marginal cost. You therefore continue to eat until your marginal benefit becomes zero.

1-8 Explain in detail the interrelationships between economic facts, theory, and policy. Critically evaluate this statement: "The trouble with economic theory is that it is not practical. It is detached from the real world."

Economic theory consists of factually supported generalizations about economic behavior that can be used to formulate economic policies. Economic theory enables policymakers to formulate economic policies that are relevant to real-world goals and problems that are based upon carefully observed facts.

1-10 Indicate whether each of the following statements applies to microeconomics or macroeconomics:

(a), (d), and (f) are macro; (b), (c), and (e) are micro.

1-11 Identify each of the following as either a positive or a normative statement:
  a. The high temperature today was 89 degrees.
  b. It was too hot today.
  c. Other things being equal, higher interest rates reduce the total amount of borrowing.
  d. Interest rates are too high.

(a) and (c) are positive; (b) and (d) are normative.

1-12 Explain and give an illustration of (a) the fallacy of composition; and (b) the "after this, therefore because of this" fallacy. Why are cause-and-effect relationships difficult to isolate in the social sciences?

(a) The fallacy of composition is the mistake of believing that something true for an individual part is necessarily true for the whole. Example: A single auto producer can increase its profits by lowering its price and taking business away from its competitors. But matched price cuts by all auto manufacturers will not necessarily yield higher industry profits.
(b) The "after this, therefore because of this" fallacy is incorrectly reasoning that when one event precedes another, the first event necessarily caused the second. Example: Interest rates rise, followed by an increase in the rate of inflation, leading to the erroneous conclusion that the rise in interest rates caused the inflation. Actually higher interest rates slow inflation.

Cause-and-effect relationships are difficult to isolate because "other things" are continually changing.

CHAPTER 1 APPENDIX

1-2 Indicate how each of the following might affect the data shown in Table 2 and Figure 2 of this appendix:
  a. GSU's athletic director schedules higher-quality opponents.
  b. An NBA team locates in the city where GSU plays.
  c. GSU contracts to have all its home games televised.

(a) More tickets are bought at each price; the line shifts to the right.
(b) Fewer tickets are bought at each price; the line shifts to the left.
(c) Fewer tickets are bought at each price; the line shifts to the left.

1-3 The following table contains data on the relationship between saving and income. Rearrange these data into a meaningful order and graph them on the accompanying grid. What is the slope of the line? The vertical intercept? Interpret the meaning of both the slope and the intercept. Write the equation that represents this line. What would you predict saving to be at the $12,500 level of income?

Income (per year)	Saving (per year)
$15,000	$1,000
0	−500
10,000	500
5,000	0
20,000	1,500

Income column: $0; $5,000; $10,000; $15,000; $20,000. Saving column: $−500; 0; $500; $1,000; $1,500. Slope = 0.1 (= $1,000 − $500)/($15,000 − $10,000). Vertical intercept = $−500. The slope shows the amount of saving will increase for every $1 increase in income; the intercept shows the amount of saving (dissaving) occurring when income is zero. Equation: $S = \$-500 + 0.1Y$ (where S is saving and Y is income). Saving will be $750 at the $12,500 income level.

1-7 The accompanying graph shows curve XX and tangents at points A, B, and C. Calculate the slope of the curve at these three points.

Slopes: at $A = +4$; at $B = 0$; at $C = -4$.

CHAPTER 2

2-4 Classify the following Microsoft resources as land, labor, capital, or entrepreneurial ability: code writers for software, Bill Gates, production facility for Windows CD-ROMs, "campus" on which Microsoft buildings sit, grounds crews at Microsoft campus, Microsoft corporate jet.

Land—campus where Microsoft buildings sit. *Labor*—code writers, grounds crews. *Capital*—production facility, corporate jet. *Entrepreneurial ability*—Bill Gates

2-5 Distinguish between full employment and full production as they relate to production possibilities analysis. Distinguish between productive efficiency and allocative efficiency. Give an illustration of achieving productive efficiency, but not allocative efficiency.

Full employment occurs when all available resources are utilized; full production means that all employed resources are used to provide the maximum possible satisfaction of material wants. Both are required for an economy to be producing on the production possibilities curve. An economy that is employing all available resources but which allocates labor to unproductive tasks will operate inside the curve. Likewise, putting resources to their most productive uses but failing to employ all resources will result in an economy producing inside the curve.

Allocative efficiency means that resources are being used to produce the goods and services most wanted by society. The economy is then located at the optimal point on its production possibilities curve where marginal benefit equals marginal cost for each good. Productive efficiency means the least costly production techniques are being used to produce wanted goods and services. Examples: manual typewriters produced using the least-cost techniques but for which there is no demand; cigarettes produced using least-cost techniques but for which there are "bads" created that are not accounted for by the market.

2-6 Here is a production possibilities table for war goods and civilian goods:

Type of production	Production alternatives				
	A	**B**	**C**	**D**	**E**
Automobiles	0	2	4	6	8
Missiles	30	27	21	12	0

a. Show these data graphically. Upon what specific assumptions is this production possibilities curve based?
b. If the economy is at point C, what is the cost of one more automobile? One more missile? Explain how this curve reflects increasing opportunity costs.

c. What must the economy do to operate at some point on the production possibilities curve?

(a) See curve EDCBA. The assumptions are full employment and productive efficiency, fixed supplies of resources, and fixed technology.

Question 2-6

(b) 4.5 rockets; .33 automobiles, as determined from the table. Increasing opportunity costs are reflected in the concave-from-the-origin shape of the curve. This means the economy must give up larger and larger amounts of rockets to get constant added amounts of automobiles—and vice versa.
(c) It must obtain full employment and productive efficiency.

2-11 Referring again to question 6, suppose improvement occurs in the technology of producing missiles but not in the production of automobiles. Draw the new production possibilities curve. Now assume that a technological advance occurs in producing automobiles but not in producing missiles. Draw the new production possibilities curve. Now draw a production possibilities curve that reflects technological improvement in the production of both products.

See the graph for question 2-6. PPC_1 shows improved missile technology. PPC_2 shows improved auto technology. PPC_3 shows improved technology in producing both products.

CHAPTER 3

3-2 What effect will each of the following have on the demand for product B?
  a. Product B becomes more fashionable.
  b. The price of substitute product C falls.
  c. Income declines and product B is an inferior good.
  d. Consumers anticipate the price of B will be lower in the near future.
  e. The price of complementary product D falls.

Demand increases in (a), (c), and (e); decreases in (b) and (d).

3-5 What effect will each of the following have on the supply of product B?
  a. A technological advance in the methods of producing B.
  b. A decline in the number of firms in industry B.
  c. An increase in the price of resources required in the production of B.
  d. The expectation that the equilibrium price of B will be lower in the future than it is currently.
  e. A decline in the price of product A, a good whose production requires substantially the same techniques as does the production of B.
  f. The levying of a specific sales tax upon B.

g. The granting of a 50-cent per unit subsidy for each unit of B produced.

Supply increases in (a), (d), (e), and (g); decreases in (b), (c), and (f).

3–7 Suppose the total demand for wheat and the total supply of wheat per month in the Kansas City grain market are as follows:

Thousands of bushels demanded	Price per bushel	Thousand of bushels supplied	Surplus (+) or shortage (−)
85	$3.40	72	_____
80	3.70	73	_____
75	4.00	75	_____
70	4.30	77	_____
65	4.60	79	_____
60	4.90	81	_____

a. What will be the market or equilibrium price? What is the equilibrium quantity? Fill in the surplus–shortage column and use it to explain why your answers are correct.

b. Graph the demand for wheat and the supply of wheat. Be sure to label the axes of your graph correctly. Label the equilibrium price "P" and the equilibrium quantity "Q."

c. Why will $3.40 not be the equilibrium price in this market? Why not $4.90? "Surpluses drive prices up; shortages drive them down." Do you agree?

Data from top to bottom: −13; −7; 0; +7; +14; and +21.

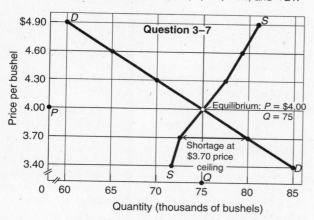

(a) $P_e = \$4.00$; $Q_e = 75,000$. Equilibrium occurs where there is neither a shortage nor surplus of wheat. At the immediately lower price of $3.70, there is a shortage of 7,000 bushels. At the immediately higher price of $4.30, there is a surplus of 7,000 bushels. (See graph above.)
(b) Quantity (thousands) of bushels.
(c) Because at $3.40 there will be a 13,000 bushel shortage which will drive the price up. Because at $4.90 there will be a 21,000 bushel surplus which will drive the price down. Quotation is incorrect; just the opposite is true.

3–8 How will each of the following changes in demand and/or supply affect equilibrium price and equilibrium quantity in a competitive market; that is, do price and quantity rise, fall, remain unchanged, or are the answers indeterminate because they depend on the magnitudes of the shifts? Use supply and demand diagrams to verify your answers.
a. Supply decreases and demand is constant.
b. Demand decreases and supply is constant.
c. Supply increases and demand is constant.

d. Demand increases and supply increases.
e. Demand increases and supply is constant.
f. Supply increases and demand decreases.
g. Demand increases and supply decreases.
h. Demand decreases and supply decreases.

(a) Price up; quantity down;
(b) Price down; quantity down;
(c) Price down; quantity up;
(d) Price indeterminate; quantity up;
(e) Price up; quantity up;
(f) Price down; quantity indeterminate;
(g) Price up, quantity indeterminate;
(h) Price indeterminate and quantity down.

3–13 Refer to the table in question 7. Suppose that the government establishes a price ceiling of $3.70 for wheat. What might prompt the government to establish this price ceiling? Explain carefully the main effects. Demonstrate your answer graphically. Next, suppose that the government establishes a price floor of $4.60 for wheat. What will be the main effects of this price floor? Demonstrate your answer graphically.

At a price of $3.70, buyers will wish to purchase 80,000 bushels, but sellers will only offer 73,000 bushels to the market. The result is a shortage of 7,000 bushels. The ceiling prevents the price from rising to encourage greater production, discourage consumption, and relieve the shortage. See the graph below.

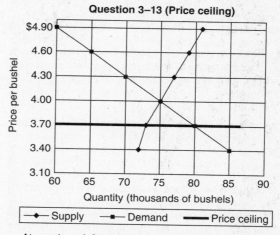

At a price of $4.60, buyers only want to purchase 65,000 bushels, but sellers want to sell 79,000 bushels, resulting in a surplus of 14,000 bushels. The floor prevents the price from falling to eliminate the surplus. See the graph below.

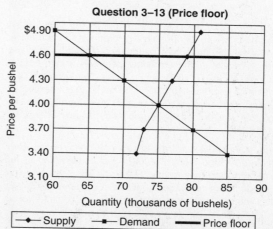

CHAPTER 4

4–7 Assume that a business firm finds that its profits will be at a maximum when it produces $40 worth of product A. Suppose also that each of the three techniques shown in the following table will produce the desired output.

Resource	Price per unit of resource	Resource Units Required		
		Technique No. 1	Technique No. 2	Technique No. 3
Labor	$3	5	2	3
Land	4	2	4	2
Capital	2	2	4	5
Entrepreneurial ability	2	4	2	4

a. With the resource prices shown, which technique will the firm choose? Why? Will production entail profits or losses? Will the industry expand or contract? When is a new equilibrium output achieved?

b. Assume now that a new technique, technique No. 4, is developed. It entails the use of 2 units of labor, 2 of land, 6 of capital, and 3 of entrepreneurial ability. Given the resource prices in the table, will the firm adopt the new technique? Explain your answers.

c. Suppose now that an increase in labor supply causes the price of labor to fall to $1.50 per unit, all other resource prices being unchanged. Which technique will the producer now choose? Explain.

d. "The market system causes the economy to conserve most in the use of those resources which are particularly scarce in supply. Resources that are scarcest relative to the demand for them have the highest prices. As a result, producers use these resources as sparingly as is possible." Evaluate this statement. Does your answer to part c, above, bear out this contention? Explain.

(a) Technique 2 because it produces the output with least cost ($34 compared to $35 each for the other two). Economic profit will be $6 (= 40 − $34), which will cause the industry to expand. Expansion will continue until prices decline to where total revenue is $34 (equal to total cost).
(b) Adopt technique 4 because its cost is now lowest at $32.
(c) Technique 1 because its cost is now lowest at $27.50.
(d) The statement is logical. Increasing scarcity causes prices to rise. Firms ignoring higher resource prices will become high-cost producers and be competed out of business by firms switching to the less expensive inputs. The market system forces producers to conserve on the use of highly scarce resources. Question 8c confirms this: Technique 1 was adopted because labor had become less expensive.

4–10 Some large hardware stores such as Home Depot boast of carrying as many as 20,000 different products in each store. What motivated the producers of those products—everything from screwdrivers to ladders to water heaters—to make them and offer them for sale? How did producers decide on the best combinations of resources to use? Who made these resources available, and why? Who decides whether these particular hardware products should continue to get produced and offered for sale?

The quest for profit led firms to produce these goods. Producers looked for and found the least-cost combination of resources in producing their output. Resource suppliers, seeking income, made these resources available. Consumers, through their dollar votes, ultimately decide on what will continue to be produced.

CHAPTER 5

5–2 Assume that the five residents of Econoville receive incomes of $50, $75, $125, $250, and $500. Present the resulting personal distribution of income as a graph similar to Figure 5.2. Compare the incomes of the lowest and highest fifth of the income receivers.

The distribution of income is quite unequal. The highest 20 percent of the residents receive 10 times more income than the lowest 20 percent.

5–4 What are the three major legal forms of business organization? Which form is the most prevalent in terms of numbers? Why do you think that is so? Which form is dominant in terms of total profits? What major advantages of this form of business organization gave rise to its dominance?

The three legal forms of business organizations are: sole proprietorship, partnership, and corporation.

Proprietorships are the most prevalent. They are easy to start (relatively low cost), often don't require a large customer base to be profitable, and provide maximum freedom for the proprietor to do what she/he thinks best.

Corporations are dominant in terms of total profits. They can access large amounts of money by issuing stocks and bonds; their limited liability is attractive to potential owners; their size and broader ownership base help ensure continuity that helps to build a large customer base and gain cost advantages (a preview for economies of scale).

5–9 What are the two characteristics of public goods? Explain the significance of each for public provision as opposed to private provision. What is the free-rider problem as it relates to public goods? Is the U.S. border patrol a public good or a private good? Why? How about satellite TV? Explain.

Public goods are nonrival (one person's consumption does not prevent consumption by another) and nonexcludable (once the goods are produced nobody—including free riders—can be excluded from the goods' benefits). If goods are nonrival, there is less incentive for private firms to produce them—those purchasing the good could simply allow others to use it without compensation. Similarly, if goods are nonexcludable, private firms are unlikely to produce them as the potential for profit is low. The free-rider problem occurs when people benefit from the public good without contributing to the cost (tax revenue proportionate to the benefit received). The U.S. border patrol is a public good—my use and benefit does not prevent yours. Satellite TV is a private good—if the dish, receiver, and service go to my residence it can't go to my neighbors. The fact that I could invite my neighbor over to watch does not change its status from being a private good.

5–10 Draw a production possibilities curve with public goods on the vertical axis and private goods on the horizontal axis. Assuming the economy is initially operating *on the curve,* indicate how the production of public goods might be increased. How might the output of public goods be increased if the economy is initially operating at a point *inside the curve?*

On the curve, the only way to obtain more public goods is to reduce the production of private goods (from *C* to *B*).

An economy operating inside the curve can expand the production of public goods without sacrificing private goods (say, from *A* to *B*) by making use of unemployed resources.

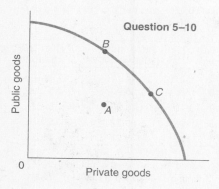

Question 5–10

5–15 Suppose in Fiscalville there is no tax on the first $10,000 of income, but a 20 percent tax on earnings between $10,000 and $20,000 and a 30 percent tax on income between $20,000 and $30,000. Any income above $30,000 is taxed at 40 percent. If your income is $50,000, how much in taxes will you pay? Determine your marginal and average tax rates. Is it a progressive tax? Explain.

Total tax = $13,000; marginal tax rate = 40%; average tax rate = 26%. This is a progressive tax; the average tax rate rises as income goes up.

CHAPTER 6

6–4 The following are production possibilities tables for South Korea and the United States. Assume that before specialization and trade the optimal product-mix for South Korea is alternative B and for the United States alternative U.

Product	South Korea's production possibilities					
	A	B	C	D	E	F
Radios (in 1000s)	30	24	18	12	6	0
Chemicals (in tons)	0	6	12	18	24	30

Product	U.S. production possibilities					
	R	S	T	U	V	W
Radios (in 1000s)	10	8	6	4	2	0
Chemicals (in tons)	0	4	8	12	16	20

a. Are comparative cost conditions such that the two areas should specialize? If so, what product should each produce?
b. What is the total gain in radio and chemical output that results from this specialization?
c. What are the limits of the terms of trade? Suppose actual terms of trade are 1 unit of radios for 1-1/2 units of chemicals and that 4 units of radios are exchanged for 6 units of chemicals. What are the gains from specialization and trade for each area?
d. Can you conclude from this illustration that specialization according to comparative advantage results in more efficient use of world resources? Explain.

(a) Yes, because the opportunity cost of radios is less (1R = 1C) in South Korea than in the United States (1R = 2C). South Korea should produce radios and the United States should produce chemicals.
(b) If they specialize, the United States can produce 20 tons of chemicals and South Korea can produce 30,000 radios. Before specialization South Korea produced alternative B and the United States alternative U for a total of 28,000 radios (24,000 + 4,000) and 18 tons of chemicals (6 tons + 12 tons). The gain is 2,000 radios and 2 tons of chemicals.
(c) The limits of the terms of trade are determined by the comparative cost conditions in each country before trade: 1R = 1C in South Korea and 1R = 2C in the United States. The terms of trade must be somewhere between these two ratios for trade to occur.
   If the terms of trade are 1R = 1-1/2C, South Korea would end up with 26,000 radios (= 30,000 − 4,000) and 6 tons of chemicals. The United States would have 4,000 radios and 14 tons of chemicals (= 20 − 6). South Korea has gained 2,000 radios. The United States has gained 2 tons of chemicals.
(d) Yes, the world is obtaining more output from its fixed resources.

6–6 True or false? "U.S. exports create a demand for foreign currencies; foreign imports of U.S. goods generate supplies of foreign currencies." Explain. Would a decline in U.S. consumer income or a weakening of U.S. preferences for foreign products cause the dollar to depreciate or appreciate? Other things equal, what would be the effects of that depreciation or appreciation on U.S. exports and imports?

The first part of this statement is incorrect. U.S. exports create a domestic *supply* of foreign currencies, not a domestic demand for them. The second part of the statement is accurate. The foreign demand for dollars (from US. exports) generates a supply of foreign currencies to the United States.
   A decline in U.S. incomes or a weakening of U.S. preferences for foreign goods would reduce U.S. imports, reducing U.S. demand for foreign currencies. These currencies would depreciate (the dollar would appreciate). Dollar appreciation means U.S. exports would decline and U.S. imports would increase.

6–10 Identify and state the significance of each of the following: (a) WTO; (b) EU; (c) euro; and (d) NAFTA. What commonality do they share?

(a) The WTO oversees trade agreements reached by member nations and arbitrates trade disputes among them. (b) The EU is a trading bloc of 25 European countries who have agreed to abolish tariffs and import quotas on most products and have liberalized the movements of labor and capital within the EU. (c) The euro is the common currency that is used by 12 of the original 15 EU countries. (d) NAFTA is a trade bloc made up of the United States, Canada, and Mexico whose purpose is to reduce tariffs and other trade barriers among the three countries.

All of the above have the goals of increasing international trade and a better allocation of the world's resources.

CHAPTER 7

7–3 Why do national income accountants include only final goods in measuring GDP for a particular year? Why don't they include the value of stocks and bonds sold? Why don't they include the value of used furniture bought and sold?

The dollar value of final goods includes the dollar value of intermediate goods. If intermediate goods were counted, then multiple counting would occur. The value of steel (intermediate good) used in autos is included in the price of the auto (the final product).

The value of stocks and bonds sold is not included in GDP because such sales and purchases simply transfer the ownership of existing assets; such sales and purchases are not themselves (economic) investment and thus should not be counted as production of final goods and services.

Used furniture was produced in some previous year; it was counted as GDP then. Its resale does not measure new production.

7–8 Below is a list of domestic output and national income figures for a given year. All figures are in billions. The questions that follow ask you to determine the major national income measures by both the expenditure and income methods. The results you obtain with the different methods should be the same.

Personal consumption expenditures	$245
Net foreign factor income earned	4
Transfer payments	12
Rents	14
Consumption of fixed capital (depreciation)	27
Social Security contributions	20
Interest	13
Proprietors' income	33
Net exports	11
Dividends	16
Compensation of employees	223
Indirect business taxes	18
Undistributed corporate profits	21
Personal taxes	26
Corporate income taxes	19
Corporate profits	56
Government purchases	72
Net private domestic investment	33
Personal saving	20

    a. Using the above data, determine GDP by both the expenditure and the income approaches. Then determine NDP.
    b. Now determine NI: first, by making the required additions and subtractions from GDP; and second, by adding up the types of income that make up NI.
    c. Adjust NI (from part b) as required to obtain PI.
    d. Adjust PI (from part c) as required to obtain DI.

    (a) GDP = $388, NDP = $361
    (b) NI = $339
    (c) PI = $291
    (d) DI = $265

7–11 Suppose that in 1984 the total output in a single-good economy was 7,000 buckets of chicken. Also suppose that in 1984 each bucket of chicken was priced at $10. Finally, assume that in 1996 the price per bucket of chicken was $16 and that 22,000 buckets were purchased. Determine the GDP price index for 1984, using 1996 as the base year. By what percentage did the price level, as measured by this index, rise between 1984 and 1996? Use the two methods listed in Table 7.6 to determine real GDP for 1984 and 1996.

X/100 = $10/$16 = .625 or 62.5 when put in percentage or index form (.625 × 100)

$$\frac{100 - 62.5}{62.5} = .60 \text{ or } 60\% \text{ (Easily calculated } \frac{16 - 10}{10} =$$

$$\frac{6}{10} = .6 = 60\%)$$

Method 1:   1996 = (22,000 × $16) ÷ 1.0 = $352,000
                1984 = (7,000 × $10) ÷ .625 = $112,000
Method 2:   1996 = 22,000 × $16 = $352,000
                1984 = 7,000 × $16 = $112,000

7–12 The following table shows nominal GDP and an appropriate price index for a group of selected years. Compute real GDP. Indicate in each calculation whether you are inflating or deflating the nominal GDP data.

Year	Nominal GDP, billions	Price index (1996 = 100)	Real GDP, billions
1960	$ 527.4	22.19	$_____
1968	911.5	26.29	$_____
1978	2295.9	48.22	$_____
1988	4742.5	80.22	$_____
1998	8790.2	103.22	$_____

Values for real GDP, top to bottom of the column: $2,376.7 (inflating); $3,467.1 (inflating); $4,761.3 (inflating); $5,911.9 (inflating); $8,516 (deflating).

CHAPTER 8

8–2 Suppose an economy's real GDP is $30,000 in year 1 and $31,200 in year 2. What is the growth rate of its real GDP? Assume that population was 100 in year 1 and 102 in year 2. What is the growth rate of GDP per capita?

Growth rate of real GDP = 4 percent [(= $31,200 − $30,000)/ $30,000]. GDP per capita in year 1 = $300 (= $30,000/100). GDP per capita in year 2 = $305.88 (= $31,200/102). Growth rate of GDP per capita is 1.96 percent = [($305.88 − $300)/300].

8–4 What are the four phases of the business cycle? How long do business cycles last? How do seasonal variations and secular trends complicate measurement of the business cycle? Why does the business cycle affect output and employment in capital goods and consumer durable goods industries more severely than in industries producing nondurables?

The four phases of a typical business cycle, starting at the bottom, are trough, recovery, peak, and recession. As seen in Table 8.2, the length of a complete cycle varies from about 2 to 3 years to as long as 15 years.

There is a pre-Christmas spurt in production and sales and a January slackening. This normal seasonal variation does not signal boom or recession. From decade to decade, the long-term trend (the secular trend) of the U.S. economy has been upward. A period of no GDP growth thus does not mean all is normal, but that the economy is operating below its trend growth of output.

Because capital goods and durable goods last, purchases can be postponed. This may happen when a recession is forecast. Capital and durable goods industries therefore suffer large output declines during recessions. In contrast, consumers cannot long postpone the buying of nondurables such as food; therefore recessions only slightly reduce nondurable output. Also, capital and durable goods expenditures tend to be "lumpy." Usually, a large expenditure is needed to purchase them, and this shrinks to zero after purchase is made.

8-6 Use the following data to calculate (a) the size of the labor force and (b) the official unemployment rate: total population, 500; population under 16 years of age or institutionalized, 120; not in labor force, 150; unemployed, 23; part-time workers looking for full-time jobs, 10.

Labor force = #230 [= 500 − (120 + 150)]; official unemployment rate = 10% [(23/230) × 100].

8-8 Assume that in a particular year the natural rate of unemployment is 5 percent and the actual rate of unemployment is 9 percent. Use Okun's law to determine the size of the GDP gap in percentage-point terms. If the nominal GDP is $500 billion in that year, how much output is being forgone because of cyclical unemployment?

GDP gap = 8 percent [= (9 − 5)] × 2; forgone output estimated at $40 billion (= 8% of $500 billion).

8-11 If the price index was 110 last year and is 121 this year, what is this year's rate of inflation? What is the "rule of 70"? How long would it take for the price level to double if inflation persisted at (a) 2, (b) 5, and (c) 10 percent per year?

This year's rate of inflation is 10% or [(121 − 110)/110] × 100.
Dividing 70 by the annual percentage rate of increase of any variable (for instance, the rate of inflation or population growth) will give the approximate number of years for doubling of the variable.
(a) 35 years (= 70/2); (b) 14 years (= 70/5); (c) 7 years (= 70/10).

CHAPTER 9

9-5 Complete the accompanying table.

Level of output and income (GDP = DI)	Consumption	Saving	APC	APS	MPC	MPS
$240	$_____	$ −4	_____	_____	_____	_____
260	$_____	0	_____	_____	_____	_____
280	$_____	4	_____	_____	_____	_____
300	$_____	8	_____	_____	_____	_____
320	$_____	12	_____	_____	_____	_____
340	$_____	16	_____	_____	_____	_____
360	$_____	20	_____	_____	_____	_____
380	$_____	24	_____	_____	_____	_____
400	$_____	28	_____	_____	_____	_____

Data for completing the table (top to bottom). Consumption: $244; $260; $276; $292; $308; $324; $340; $356; $372. APC: 1.02; 1.00; .99; .97; .96; .95; .94; .94; .93. APS: −.02; .00; .01; .03; .04; .05; .06; .06; .07. MPC: 80 throughout. MPS: 20 throughout.
  a. Show the consumption and saving schedules graphically.
  b. Find the break-even level of income. How is it possible for households to dissave at very low income levels?

c. If the proportion of total income consumed (APC) decreases and the proportion saved (APS) increases as income rises, explain both verbally and graphically how the MPC and MPS can be constant at various levels of income.

(a) See the graphs.

(b) Break-even income = $260. Households dissave borrowing or using past savings.
(c) Technically, the APC diminishes and the APS increases because the consumption and saving schedules have positive and negative vertical intercepts, respectively (Appendix to Chapter 1). MPC and MPS measure *changes* in consumption and saving as income changes; they are the *slopes* of the consumption and saving schedules. For straight-line consumption and saving schedules, these slopes do not change as the level of income changes; the slopes and thus the MPC and MPS remain constant.

9-7 Suppose a handbill publisher can buy a new duplicating machine for $500 and the duplicator has a 1-year life. The machine is expected to contribute $550 to the year's net revenue. What is the expected rate of return? If the real interest rate at which funds can be borrowed to purchase the machine is 8 percent, will the publisher choose to invest in the machine? Explain.

The expected rate of return is 10 percent ($50 expected profit/$500 cost of machine). The $50 expected profit comes from the net revenue of $550 less the $500 cost of the machine.
If the real interest rate is 8 percent, the publisher will invest in the machine as the expected profit (marginal benefit) from the investment exceeds the cost of borrowing the funds (marginal cost).

9-8 Assume there are no investment projects in the economy that yield an expected rate of return of 25 percent or more. But suppose there are $10 billion of investment projects yielding an expected rate of return of between 20 and 25 percent; another $10 billion yielding between 15 and 20 percent; another $10 billion between 10 and 15 percent; and so forth. Cumulate these data and present them graphically, putting the expected rate of net return on the vertical axis and the amount of investment on the horizontal axis. What will be the equilibrium level of aggregate investment if the real interest rate is (a) 15 percent, (b) 10 percent, and (c) 5 percent? Explain why this curve is the investment-demand curve.

See the graph that follows. Aggregate investment: (a) $20 billion; (b) $30 billion; (c) $40 billion. This is the investment-demand curve because we have applied the rule of undertaking all investment up to the point where the expected rate of return, r, equals the interest rate, i.

9-9 What is the multiplier effect? What relationship does the MPC bear to the size of the multiplier? The MPS? What will the multiplier be when the MPS is 0, .4, .6, and 1? What will it be when the MPC is 1, .9, .67, .5, and 0? How much of a change in GDP will result if firms increase their level of investment by $8 billion and the MPC is .80? If the MPC is .67?

The multiplier effect describes how an initial change in spending ripples through the economy to generate a larger change in real GDP. It occurs because of the interconnectedness of the economy, where a change in Lasslett's spending will generate

more income for Gavidia, who will in turn spend more, generating additional income for Grimes.

The MPC is directly (positively) related to the size of the multiplier. The MPS is inversely (negatively) related to the size of the multiplier.

The multiplier values for the MPS values: undefined, 2.5, 1.67, 0.

The multiplier values for the MPC values: undefined, 10, 3 (approx. actually 3.03), 2, 0.

If MPC is .80, change in GDP is $40 billion (5 × $8 = $40).

If MPC is .67, change in GDP is $24 billion (approximately) (3 × $8 = $24)

CHAPTER 10

10-2 Assuming the level of investment is $16 billion and independent of the level of total output, complete the following table and determine the equilibrium levels of output and employment in this private closed economy. What are the sizes of the MPC and MPS?

Possible levels of employment (millions)	Real domestic output (GDP = DI) (billions)	Consumption (billions)	Saving (billions)
40	$240	$244	$_____
45	260	260	$_____
50	280	276	$_____
55	300	292	$_____
60	320	308	$_____
65	340	324	$_____
70	360	340	$_____
75	380	356	$_____
80	400	372	$_____

Saving data for completing the table (top to bottom): $ − 4; $0; $4; $8; $12; $16; $20; $24; $28.

Equilibrium GDP = $340 billion, determined where (1) aggregate expenditures equal GDP (C of $324 billion + I of $16 billion = GDP of $340 billion); or (2) where planned I = S (I of $16 billion = S of $16 billion). Equilibrium level of employment = 65 million; MPC = .8; MPS = .2.

10-9 The data in columns 1 and 2 of the table below are for a private closed economy.

(1) Real domestic output (GDP = DI) billions	(2) Aggregate expenditures private closed economy, billions	(3) Exports, billions	(4) Imports, billions	(5) Net exports, private economy	(6) Aggregate expenditures, open economy, billions
$200	$240	$20	$30	$ _____	$ _____
$250	$280	$20	$30	$ _____	$ _____
$300	$320	$20	$30	$ _____	$ _____
$350	$360	$20	$30	$ _____	$ _____
$400	$400	$20	$30	$ _____	$ _____
$450	$440	$20	$30	$ _____	$ _____
$500	$480	$20	$30	$ _____	$ _____
$550	$520	$20	$30	$ _____	$ _____

a. Use columns 1 and 2 to determine the equilibrium GDP for this hypothetical economy.

b. Now open up this economy to international trade by including the export and import figures of columns 3 and 4. Fill in columns 5 and 6 to determine the equilibrium GDP for the open economy. Explain why this equilibrium GDP differs from that of the closed economy.

c. Given the original $20 billion level of exports, what would be the equilibrium GDP if imports were $10 billion greater at each level of GDP?

d. What is the multiplier in this example?

(a) Equilibrium GDP for closed economy = $400 billion.

(b) Net export data for column 5 (top to bottom): $−10 billion in each space. Aggregate expenditure data for column 6 (top to bottom): $230; $270; $310; $350; $390; $430; $470; $510. Equilibrium GDP for the open economy is $350 billion, $50 billion below the $400 billion equilibrium GDP for the closed economy. The $−10 billion of net exports is a leakage that reduces equilibrium GDP by $50 billion.

(c) Imports = $40 billion: Aggregate expenditures in the private open economy would fall by $10 billion at each GDP level and the new equilibrium GDP would be $300 billion.

(d) Since every rise of $50 billion in GDP increases aggregate expenditures by $40 billion, the MPC is .8 and so the multiplier is 5.

10–12   Refer to columns 1 and 6 of the tabular data for question 9. Incorporate government into the table by assuming that it plans to tax and spend $20 billion at each possible level of GDP. Also assume that all taxes are personal taxes and that government spending does not induce a shift in the private aggregate expenditures schedule. Compute and explain the changes in equilibrium GDP caused by the addition of government.

Before G is added, open private sector equilibrium will be at $350. The addition of government expenditures of G to our analysis raises the aggregate expenditures $(C + I_g + X_n + G)$ schedule and increases the equilibrium level of GDP as would an increase in C, I_g, or X_n. Note that changes in government spending are subject to the multiplier effect. Government spending supplements private investment and export spending $(I_g + X + G)$, increasing the equilibrium GDP to $450.

The addition of $20 billion of government expenditures and $20 billion of personal taxes increases equilibrium GDP from $350 to $370 billion. The $20 billion increase in G raises equilibrium GDP by $100 billion (= $20 billion × the multiplier of 5); the $20 billion increase in T reduces consumption by $16 billion at every level (= $20 billion × the MPC of .8). This $16 billion decline in turn reduces equilibrium GDP by $80 billion ($16 billion × multiplier of 5). The net change from including balanced government spending and taxes is $20 billion (= $100 billion − $80 billion).

10–13   Refer to the table below in answering the questions that follow:

(1) Possible levels of employment, millions	(2) Real domestic output, billions	(3) Aggregate expenditures $(C_a + I_g + X_n + G)$, billions
90	$500	$520
100	550	560
110	600	600
120	650	640
130	700	680

a. If full employment in this economy is 130 million, will there be an inflationary gap or a recessionary gap? What will be the consequence of this gap? By how much would aggregate expenditures in column 3 have to change at each level of GDP to eliminate the inflationary or recessionary gap? Explain. What is the multiplier in this example?

b. Will there be an inflationary or recessionary gap if the full-employment level of output is $500 billion? Explain the consequences. By how much would aggregate expenditures in column 3 have to change at each level of GDP to eliminate the gap? Explain. What is the multiplier in this example?

c. Assuming that investment, net exports, and government expenditures do not change with changes in real GDP, what are the sizes of the MPC, the MPS, and the multiplier?

(a) A recessionary gap. Equilibrium GDP is $600 billion, while full employment GDP is $700 billion. Employment will be 20 million less than at full employment. Aggregate expenditures would have to increase by $20 billion (= $700 billion − $680 billion) at each level of GDP to eliminate the recessionary gap. The MPC is .8, so the multiplier is 5.

(b) An inflationary gap. Aggregate expenditures will be excessive, causing demand-pull inflation. Aggregate expenditures would have to *fall* by $20 billion (= $520 billion − $500 billion) at each level of GDP to eliminate the inflationary gap. The multiplier is still 5—the level of full employment GDP does not affect the multiplier.

(c) MPC = .8 (= $40 billion/$50 billion); MPS = .2 (= 1 − .8); multiplier = 5 (= 1/.2).

CHAPTER 11

11–4   Suppose that aggregate demand and supply for a hypothetical economy are as shown:

Amount of real domestic output demanded, billions	Price level (price index)	Amount of real domestic output supplied, billions
$100	300	$450
200	250	400
300	200	300
400	150	200
500	100	100

a. Use these sets of data to graph the aggregate demand and aggregate supply curves. What is the equilibrium price level and the equilibrium level of real output in this hypothetical economy? Is the equilibrium real output also necessarily the full-capacity real output? Explain.

b. Why will a price level of 150 not be an equilibrium price level in this economy? Why not 250?

c. Suppose that buyers desire to purchase $200 billion of extra real domestic output at each price level. Sketch in the new aggregate demand curve as AD_1. What factors might cause this change in aggregate demand? What is the new equilibrium price level and level of real output?

(a) See the graph. Equilibrium price level = 200. Equilibrium real output = $300 billion. No, the full-capacity level of GDP is more likely at $400 billion, where the AS curve starts to become steeper.

(b) At a price level of 150, real GDP supplied is a maximum of $200 billion, less than the real GDP demanded of $400 billion. The shortage of real output will drive the price level up.

At a price level of 250, real GDP supplied is $400 billion, which is more than the real GDP demanded of $200 billion. The surplus of real output will drive down the price level. Equilibrium occurs at the price level at which AS and AD intersect.

(c) See the graph. Increases in consumer, investment, government, or net export spending might shift the AD curve rightward. New equilibrium price level = 250. New equilibrium GDP = $400 billion.

Question 11–4

11–5 Suppose that a hypothetical economy has the following relationship between its real output and the input quantities necessary for producing that level of output:
a. What is productivity in this economy?
b. What is the per-unit cost of production if the price of each input is $2?
c. Assume that the input price increases from $2 to $3 with no accompanying change in productivity. What is the new per-unit cost of production? In what direction did the $1 increase in input price push the economy's aggregate supply curve? What effect would this shift in aggregate supply have upon the price level and the level of real output?
d. Suppose that the increase in input price does not occur but instead that productivity increases by 100 percent. What would be the new per-unit cost of production? What effect would this change in per-unit production cost have on the aggregate supply curve? What effect would this shift in aggregate supply have on the price level and the level of real output?

Input quantity	Real domestic output
150.0	400
112.5	300
75.0	200

(a) Productivity = 2.67 (= 400/150; = 300/112.5; = 200/75.0)
(b) Per-unit cost of production = $.75 (= $2 × 112.5/300)
(c) New per-unit production cost = $1.13 (= $3 × 75/200). The AS curve would shift leftward. The price level would rise and real output would decrease.
(d) New per-unit cost of production = $0.375 (= $2 × 112.5/600). AS curve shifts to the right; price level declines, and real output increases.

11–6 What effects would each of the following have on aggregate demand or aggregate supply? In each case use a diagram to show the expected effects on the equilibrium price level and level of real output. Assume that all other things remain constant.

a. A widespread fear of depression on the part of consumers.
b. A $2 increase in the excise tax on a pack of cigarettes.
c. A reduction in interest rates at each price level.
d. A major increase in Federal spending for health care.
e. The expectation of rapid inflation.
f. The complete disintegration of OPEC, causing oil prices to fall by one-half.
g. A 10 percent reduction in personal income tax rates.
h. A sizable increase in labor productivity (with no change in nominal wages).
i. A 12 percent increase in nominal wages (with no change in productivity).
j. Depreciation in the international value of the dollar.

(a) AD curve left, output down, and price level down (assuming no ratchet effect).
(b) AS curve left, output down, and price level up.
(c) AD curve right, output and price level up.
(d) AD curve right, output and price level up (any real improvements in health care resulting from the spending would eventually increase productivity and shift AS right).
(e) AD curve right, output and price level up.
(f) AS curve right, output up, and price level down.
(g) AD curve right, output and price level up.
(h) AS curve right, output up, and price level down.
(i) AS curve left, output down, and price level up.
(j) AD curve right (increased net exports); AS curve left (higher input prices).

11–7 Other things equal, what effect will each of the following have on the equilibrium price level and level of real output?
a. An increase in aggregate demand in the steep portion of the aggregate supply curve.
b. An increase in aggregate supply with no change in aggregate demand (assume that prices and wages are flexible upward and downward).
c. Equal increases in aggregate demand and aggregate supply.
d. A reduction in aggregate demand in the flat portion of the aggregate supply curve.
e. An increase in aggregate demand and a decrease in aggregate supply.

(a) Price level rises rapidly and little change in real output.
(b) Price level drops and real output increases.
(c) Price level falls slowly and real output falls rapidly.
(d) Price level does not change, but real output declines.
(e) Price level increases, but the change in real output is indeterminate.

CHAPTER 12

12–2 Assume that a hypothetical economy with an MPC of .8 is experiencing severe recession. By how much would government spending have to increase to shift the aggregate demand curve rightward by $25 billion? How large a tax cut would be needed to achieve this same increase in aggregate demand? Why the difference? Determine one possible combination of government spending increases and tax decreases that would accomplish this same goal.

In this problem, the multiplier is 1/.2 or 5, so the increase in government spending = $5 billion.

For the tax cut question, initial spending of $5 billion is still required, but only .8 (= MPC) of a tax cut will be spent. So .8 × tax cut = $5 billion or tax cut = $6.25 billion. Part of the tax reduction ($1.25 billion) is saved, not spent.

One combination: a $1 billion increase in government spending and a $5 billion tax cut.

12–3 What are government's fiscal policy options for ending severe demand-pull inflation? Use the aggregate demand-aggregate supply model to show the impact of these policies on the price level. Which of these fiscal policy options do you think might be favored by a person who wants to preserve the size of government? A person who thinks the public sector is too large?

Options are to reduce government spending, increase taxes, or some combination of both. See Figure 12.2. If the price level is flexible downward, it will fall. In the real world, the goal is to reduce inflation—to keep prices from rising so rapidly—not to reduce the price level. A person wanting to preserve the size of government might favor a tax hike and would want to preserve government spending programs. Someone who thinks that the public sector is too large might favor cuts in government spending since this would reduce the size of government.

12–7 Define the "full-employment budget," explain its significance, and state why it may differ from the "actual budget." Suppose the full-employment, noninflationary level of real output is GDP$_3$ (not GDP$_2$) in the economy depicted in Figure 12.3. If the economy is operating at GDP$_2$ instead of GDP$_3$, what is the status of its full-employment budget? Of its current fiscal policy? What change in fiscal policy would you recommend? How would you accomplish that in terms of the G and T lines in the figure?

The full-employment budget (also call standardized) measures what the Federal deficit or surplus would be if the economy reached full-employment level of GDP with existing tax and spending policies. If the full-employment budget is balanced, then the government is engaging in neither expansionary nor contractionary policy, even if, for example, a deficit automatically results when GDP declines. The "actual" budget is the deficit or surplus that results when revenues and expenditures occur over a year if the economy is not operating at full-employment.

Looking at Figure 12.3, if the full-employment GDP level was GDP$_3$, then the full-employment budget is contractionary since a surplus would exist. Even though the "actual" budget has no deficit at GDP$_2$, fiscal policy is contractionary. To move the economy to full employment, government should cut taxes or increase spending. You would raise the G line or lower the T line or a combination of each until they intersect at GDP$_3$.

12–10 Briefly state and evaluate the problem of time lags in enacting and applying fiscal policy. Explain the notion of a political business cycle. How might expectations of a near-term policy reversal weaken fiscal policy based on changes in tax rates? What is the crowding-out effect and why is it relevant to fiscal policy? In what respect is the net export effect similar to the crowding-out effect?

It takes time to ascertain the direction in which the economy is moving (recognition lag), to get a fiscal policy enacted into law (administrative lag), and for the policy to have its full effect on the economy (operational lag). Meanwhile, other factors may change, rendering inappropriate a particular fiscal policy. Nevertheless, discretionary fiscal policy is a valuable tool in preventing severe recession or severe demand-pull inflation.

A political business cycle is the concept that politicians are more interested in reelection than in stabilizing the economy. Before the election, they enact tax cuts and spending increases to please voters even though this may fuel inflation. After the election, they apply the brakes to restrain inflation; the economy will slow and unemployment will rise. In this view the political process creates economic instability.

A decrease in tax rates might be enacted to stimulate consumer spending. If households receive the tax cut but expect it to be reversed in the near future, they may hesitate to increase their spending. Believing that tax rates will rise again (and possibly concerned that they will rise to rates higher than before the tax cut), households may instead save their additional after-tax income in anticipation of needing to pay taxes in the future.

The crowding-out effect is the reduction in investment spending caused by the increase in interest rates arising from an increase in government spending, financed by borrowing. The increase in G was designed to increase AD but the resulting increase in interest rates may decrease I. Thus the impact of the expansionary fiscal policy may be reduced.

The net export effect also arises from the higher interest rates accompanying expansionary fiscal policy. The higher interest rates make U.S. bonds more attractive to foreign buyers. The inflow of foreign currency to buy dollars to purchase the bonds drives up the international value of the dollar, making imports less expensive for the United States, and U.S. exports more expensive for people abroad. Net exports in the United States decline, and like the crowding-out effect, diminish the expansionary fiscal policy.

CHAPTER 13

13–4 What are the components of the $M1$ money supply? What is the largest component? Which of the components is legal tender? Why is the face value of a coin greater than its intrinsic value? What near-monies are included in the $M2$ money supply? What distinguishes the $M2$ and $M3$ money supplies?

$M1$ = currency (in circulation) + checkable deposits. The largest component of $M1$ is currency (52 percent), and it is the only part that is legal tender. If the face value of a coin were not greater than its intrinsic (metallic) value, people would remove coins from circulation and sell them for their metallic content. $M2$ = $M1$ + noncheckable savings deposits + money market deposit accounts + small time deposits + money market mutual fund balances. $M3$ = $M2$ + large time deposits (those of $100,000 or more). Near-monies are components of $M2$ and $M3$ not included in $M1$. $M3$ is distinguished from $M2$ by large time deposits (certificates of deposit).

13–6 Suppose the price level and value of the dollar in year 1 are 1.0 and $1.00, respectively. If the price level rises to 1.25 in year 2, what is the new value of the dollar? If instead the price level had fallen to .50, what would have been the value of the dollar? What generalization can you draw from your answer?

In the first case, the value of the dollar (in year 2, relative to year 1) is $.80 (= 1/1.25); in the second case the value is $2 (= 1/.50). Generalization: The price level and the value of the dollar are inversely related.

13–7 What is the basic determinant of (a) the transactions demand and (b) the asset demand for money? Explain how these two demands can be combined graphically to determine total money demand. How is the equilibrium interest rate in the money market determined? How might (a) the expanded use of credit cards, (b) a shortening of worker pay periods, and (c) an increase in nominal GDP each independently affect the transactions demand for money and the equilibrium interest rate?

(a) The level of nominal GDP. The higher this level, the greater the amount of money demanded for transactions. (b) The interest rate. The higher the interest rate, the smaller the amount of money demanded as an asset.

On a graph measuring the interest rate vertically and the amount of money demanded horizontally, the two demands for the money curves can be summed horizontally to get the total demand for money. This total demand shows the total amount of money demanded at each interest rate. The equilibrium interest rate is determined at the intersection of the total demand for money curve and the supply of money curve.

(a) Expanded use of credit cards: transaction demand for money declines; total demand for money declines; interest rate falls. (b) Shortening of worker pay periods: transaction demand for money declines; total demand for money declines; interest rate falls. (c) Increase in nominal GDP: transaction demand for money increases; total demand for money increases; interest rate rises.

CHAPTER 14

14–2 Why are commercial banks required to have reserves? Explain why reserves are an asset to commercial banks but a liability to the Federal Reserve Banks. What are excess reserves? How do you calculate the amount of excess reserves held by a bank? What is the significance of excess reserves?

Reserves provide the Fed a means of controlling the money supply. It is through increasing and decreasing excess reserves that the Fed is able to achieve a money supply of the size it thinks best for the economy.

Reserves are assets of commercial banks because these funds are cash belonging to them; they are a claim the commercial banks have against the Federal Reserve Bank. Reserves deposited at the Fed are a liability to the Fed because they are funds it owes; they are claims that commercial banks have against it.

Excess reserves are the amount by which actual reserves exceed required reserves: Excess reserves = actual reserves − required reserves. Commercial banks can safely lend excess reserves, thereby increasing the money supply.

14–4 "When a commercial bank makes loans, it creates money; when loans are repaid, money is destroyed." Explain.

Banks add to checking account balances when they make loans; these checkable deposits are part of the money supply. People pay off loans by writing checks; checkable deposits fall, meaning the money supply drops. Money is "destroyed."

14–8 Suppose that Continental Bank has the simplified balance sheet shown below and that the reserve ratio is 20 percent:

	Assets			Liabilities and net worth	
	(1)	(2)		(1)	(2)
Reserves	$22,000	___	___	Checkable deposits $100,000	___ ___
Securities	38,000	___	___		
Loans	40,000	___	___		

a. What is the maximum amount of new loans that this bank can make? Show in column 1 how the bank's balance sheet will appear after the bank has lent this additional amount.
b. By how much has the supply of money changed? Explain.
c. How will the bank's balance sheet appear after checks drawn for the entire amount of the new loans have been cleared against this bank? Show this new balance sheet in column 2.
d. Answer questions a, b, and c on the assumption that the reserve ratio is 15 percent.

(a) $2,000. Column 1 of Assets (top to bottom): $22,000; $38,000; $42,000. Column 1 of Liabilities: $102,000.
(b) $2,000. The bank has lent out its excess reserves, creating $2,000 of new demand-deposit money.

(c) Column 2 of Assets (top to bottom): $20,000; $38,000; $42,000. Column 2 of Liabilities; $100,000.
(d) (a) $7,000. Column 1 of Assets (top to bottom): $22,000; $38,000; $47,000. Column 1 of Liabilities: $107,000.
(b) $7,000
(c) Column 2 of Assets (top to bottom): $15,000; $38,000; $47,000. Column 1 of Liabilities: $100,000.

14–13 Suppose the simplified consolidated balance sheet shown below is for the entire commercial banking system. All figures are in billions. The reserve ratio is 25 percent.

Assets		(1)	Liabilities and Net Worth		(2)
Reserves	$ 52	___	Checkable deposits	$200	___
Securities	48	___			
Loans	100	___			

a. What amount of excess reserves does the commercial banking system have? What is the maximum amount the banking system might lend? Show in column 1 how the consolidated balance sheet would look after this amount has been lent. What is the monetary multiplier?
b. Answer question 13a assuming that the reserve ratio is 20 percent. Explain the resulting difference in the lending ability of the commercial banking system.

(a) Required reserves = $50 billion (= 25% of $200 billion); so excess reserves = $2 billion (= $52 billion − $50 billion). Maximum amount banking system can lend = $8 billion (= 1/.25 ∞ $2 billion). Column (1) of Assets data (top to bottom): $52 billion; $48 billion; $108 billion. Column (1) of Liabilities data: $208 billion. Monetary multiplier = 4 (= 1/.25).
(b) Required reserves = $40 billion (= 20% of $200 billion); so excess reserves = $12 billion (= $52 billion − $40 billion). Maximum amount banking system can lend = $60 billion (= 1/.20 ∞ $12 billion). Column (1) data for assets after loans (top to bottom): $52 billion; $48 billion; $160 billion. Column (1) data for liabilities after loans: $260 billion. Monetary multiplier = 5 (= 1/.20). The decrease in the reserve ratio increases the banking system's excess reserves from $2 billion to $12 billion and increases the size of the monetary multiplier from 4 to 5. Lending capacity becomes 5 ∞ $12 = $609 billion.

CHAPTER 15

15–2 In the table below you will find simplified consolidated balance sheets for the commercial banking system and the 12 Federal Reserve Banks. Use columns 1 through 3 to indicate how the balance sheets would read after each of transactions a to c is completed. Do not cumulate your answers; that is, analyze each transaction separately, starting in each case from the figures provided. All accounts are in billions of dollars.

Consolidated Balance Sheet: All Commercial Banks			
	(1)	(2)	(3)
Assets:			
Reserves	$ 33	___	___	___
Securities	60	___	___	___
Loans	60	___	___	___
Liabilities and net worth:			
Checkable deposits	150	___	___	___
Loans from the Federal Reserve Banks	3	___	___	___

Consolidated Balance Sheet: Twelve Federal Reserve Banks				
		(1)	(2)	(3)
Assets:				
Securities	$60	___	___	___
Loans to commercial banks	3	___	___	___
Liabilities and net worth:				
Reserves of commercial banks	$33	___	___	___
Treasury deposits	3	___	___	___
Federal Reserve Notes	27	___	___	___

a. A decline in the discount rate prompts commercial banks to borrow an additional $1 billion from the Federal Reserve Banks. Show the new balance-sheet figures in column 1 of each table.

b. The Federal Reserve Banks sell $3 billion in securities to members of the public, who pay for the bonds with checks. Show the new balance-sheet figures in column 2 of each table.

c. The Federal Reserve Banks buy $2 billion of securities from commercial banks. Show the new balance sheet figures in column 3 of each table.

d. Now review each of the above three transactions, asking yourself these three questions: (1) What change, if any, took place in the money supply as a direct and immediate result of each transaction? (2) What increase or decrease in commercial banks' reserves took place in each transaction? (3) Assuming a reserve ratio of 20 percent, what change in the money-creating potential of the commercial banking system occurred as a result of each transaction?

(a) Column (1) data, top to bottom: Bank Assets: $34, 60, 60; Liabilities: $150, 4; Fed Assets: $60, 4; Liabilities: $34, 3, 27.
(b) Column (2) data: Bank Assets: $30, 60, 60; Liabilities: $147, 3; Fed Assets: $57, 3, 30, 3, 27.
(c) Column (3) data (top to bottom): $35; $58; $60; $150; $3; (Fed banks) $62; $3; $35; $3; $27.
(d) (1) Money supply (checkable deposits) directly changes only in (b), where it decreases by $3 billion; (2) See balance sheets; (3) Money-creating potential of the banking system increases by $5 billion in (a); decreases by $12 billion in (b) (not by $15 billion—the writing of $3 billion of checks by the public to buy bonds reduces demand deposits by $3 billion, thus freeing $0.6 billion of reserves. Three billion dollars minus $0.6 billion equals $2.4 billion of reduced reserves, and this multiplied by the monetary multiplier of 5 equals $12 billion); and increases by $10 billion in (c).

15-3 Suppose that you are a member of the Board of Governors of the Federal Reserve System. The economy is experiencing a sharp and prolonged inflationary trend. What changes in **(a)** the reserve ratio, **(b)** the discount rate, and **(c)** open-market operations would you recommend? Explain in each case how the change you advocate would affect commercial bank reserves, the money supply, interest rates, and aggregate demand.

(a) Increase the reserve ratio. This would increase the size of required reserves. If the commercial banks were fully loaned up, they would have to call in loans. The money supply would decrease, interest rates would rise, and aggregate demand would decline.
(b) Increase the discount rate. This would decrease commercial bank borrowing from the Fed. Actual reserves of the commercial banks would fall, as would excess reserves and lending. The money supply would drop, interest rates would rise, and aggregate demand would decline.

(c) Sell government securities in the open market. Buyers of the bonds would write checks to the Fed on their demand deposits. When these checks cleared, reserves would flow from the banking system to the Fed. The decline in reserves would reduce the money supply, which would increase interest rates and reduce aggregate demand.

15-6 Distinguish between the Federal funds rate and the prime interest rate. In what way is the Federal funds rate a measure of the tightness or looseness of monetary policy? In 2001 the Fed used open-market operations to significantly reduce the Federal funds rate. What was the logic of those actions? What was the effect on the prime interest rate?

The Federal funds interest rate is the interest rate banks charge one another on overnight loans needed to meet the reserve requirement. The prime interest rate is the interest rate banks charge on loans to their most creditworthy customers. The tighter the monetary policy, the less the supply of excess reserves in the banking system and the higher the Federal funds rate. The reverse is true of a loose or easy monetary policy, which expands excess reserves, and the federal funds rate falls.

The Fed wanted to increase excess reserves, increase money supply growth, and lower real interest rates. In 2001 the U.S. economy was in the midst of recession, with spending in decline and stock prices falling. The terrorist attacks of September 11, 2001, added further uncertainty to the already weak economic outlook, and an easy money policy was seen as a way to boost confidence. The prime interest rate fell as a result of these actions.

15-8 Suppose the Federal Reserve decides to engage in a tight money policy as a way to reduce demand-pull inflation. Use the aggregate demand–aggregate supply model to show what this policy is intended to accomplish in a closed economy. Now introduce the open economy and explain how changes in the international value of the dollar might affect the location of your aggregate demand curve.

The intent of a tight money policy would be shown as a leftward shift of the aggregate demand curve and a decline in the price level (or, in the real world, a reduction in the rate of inflation). In an open economy, the interest rate hike resulting from the tight money policy would entice people abroad to buy U.S. securities. Because they would need U.S. dollars to buy these securities, the international demand for dollars would rise, causing the dollar to appreciate. Net exports would fall, pushing the aggregate demand curve farther leftward than in the closed economy.

CHAPTER 16

16-3 Suppose the full-employment level of real output (Q) for a hypothetical economy is $250 and the price level (P) initially is 100. Use the short-run aggregate supply schedules below to answer the questions that follow:

AS(P_{100})		AS(P_{125})		AS(P_{75})	
P	Q	P	Q	P	Q
125	280	125	250	125	310
100	250	100	220	100	280
75	220	75	190	75	250

a. What will be the level of real output in the *short run* if the price level unexpectedly rises from 100 to 125 because of an increase in aggregate demand? What if the price level falls unexpectedly from 100 to 75 because of a decrease in aggregate demand? Explain each situation, using numbers from the table.

b. What will be the level of real output in the long run when the price level rises from 100 to 125? When it falls from 100 to 75? Explain each situation.

c. Show the circumstances described in parts a and b on graph paper, and derive the long-run aggregate supply curve.

(a) $280; $220. When the price level rises from 100 to 125 [in aggregate supply schedule $AS(P_{100})$], producers experience higher prices for their products. Because nominal wages are constant, profits rise and producers increase output to $Q = 280. When the price level decreases from 100 to 75, profits decline and producers adjust their output to $Q = 75. These are short-run responses to changes in the price level.

(b) $250; $250. In the long run a rise in the price level to 125 leads to nominal wage increases. The $AS(P_{100})$ schedule changes to $AS(P_{125})$ and Q returns to $250, now at a price level of 125. In the long run a decrease in price level to 75 leads to lower nominal wages, yielding aggregate supply schedule $AS(P_{75})$. Equilibrium Q returns to $250, now at a price level of 75.

(c) Graphically, the explanation is identical to Figure 16.1b. Short-run AS: $P_1 = 100$; $P_2 = 125$; $P_3 = 75$; and $Q_1 = 250; $Q_2 = 280; and $Q_3 = 220. Long-run aggregate supply = $Q_1 = $250 at each of the three price levels.

16-4 Use graphical analysis to show how each of the following would affect the economy first in the short run and then in the long run. Assume that the United States is initially operating at its full-employment level of output, that prices and wages are eventually flexible both upward and downward, and that there is no counteracting fiscal or monetary policy.

a. Because of a war abroad, the oil supply to the United States is disrupted, sending oil prices rocketing upward.

b. Construction spending on new homes rises dramatically, greatly increasing total U.S. investment spending.

c. Economic recession occurs abroad, significantly reducing foreign purchases of U.S. exports.

(a) See Figure 16.4 in the chapter, less AD_2. Short run: The aggregate supply curve shifts to the left, the price level rises, and real output declines. Long run: The aggregate supply curve shifts back rightward (due to declining nominal wages), the price level falls, and real output increases.

(b) See Figure 16.3. Short run: The aggregate demand curve shifts to the right, and both the price level and real output increase. Long run: The aggregate supply curve shifts to the left (due to higher nominal wages), the price level rises, and real output declines.

(c) See Figure 16.5. Short run: The aggregate demand curve shifts to the left, both the price level and real output decline. Long run: The aggregate supply curve shifts to the right, the price level falls further, and real output increases.

16-6 Suppose the government misjudges the natural rate of unemployment to be much lower than it actually is, and thus undertakes expansionary fiscal and monetary policy to try to achieve the lower rate. Use the concept of the short-run Phillips Curve to explain why these policies might at first succeed. Use the concept of the long-run Phillips Curve to explain the long-run outcome of these policies.

In the short run there is probably a tradeoff between unemployment and inflation. The government's expansionary policy should reduce unemployment as aggregate demand increases. However, the government has misjudged the natural rate and will continue its expansionary policy beyond the point of the natural level of unemployment. As aggregate demand continues to rise,

prices begin to rise. In the long run, workers demand higher wages to compensate for these higher prices. Aggregate supply will decrease (shift leftward) toward the natural rate of unemployment.

In other words, any reduction of unemployment below the natural rate is only temporary and involves a short-run rise in inflation. This, in turn, causes long-run costs to rise and a decrease in aggregate supply. The end result should be an equilibrium at the natural rate of unemployment and a higher price level than the beginning level. The long-run Phillips Curve is thus a vertical line connecting the price levels possible at the natural rate of unemployment found on the horizontal axis. (See Figure 16.9.)

16-7 What is the Laffer Curve, and how does it relate to supply-side economics? Why is determining the location where the economy is on the curve so important in assessing tax policy?

Economist Arthur Laffer observed that tax revenues would obviously be zero when the tax rate was either at 0 percent or 100 percent. In between these two extremes would have to be an optimal rate where aggregate output and income produced the maximum tax revenues. This idea is presented as the Laffer Curve shown in Figure 16.10.

The difficult decision involves the analysis to determine what is the optimum tax rate for producing maximum tax revenue and the related maximum economic output level. Laffer argued that low tax rates would actually increase revenues because low rates improved productivity, saving, and investment incentives. The expansion in output and employment, and thus revenue, would more than compensate for the lower rates.

CHAPTER 17

17-1 What are the four supply factors of economic growth? What is the demand factor? What is the efficiency factor? Illustrate these factors in terms of the production possibilities curve.

The four supply factors are the quantity and quality of natural resources; the quantity and quality of human resources; the stock of capital goods; and the level of technology. The demand factor is the level of purchases needed to maintain full employment. The efficiency factor refers to both productive and allocative efficiency. Figure 17.1 illustrates these growth factors by showing movement from curve AB to curve CD.

17-5 Between 1990 and 2002 the U.S. price level rose by about 38 percent while its real output increased by about 41 percent. Use the aggregate demand–aggregate supply model to illustrate these outcomes graphically.

In the graph shown, both AD and AS expanded over the 1990–2002 period. Because aggregate supply increased as well as aggregate demand, the new equilibrium output rose at a faster pace than did the price level. P_2 is 38 percent above P_1 and GDP_2 is 41 percent greater than GDP_1.

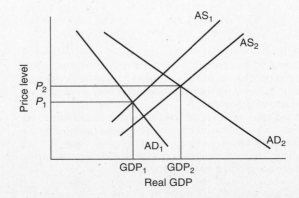

17–6 To what extent have increases in U.S. real GDP resulted from more labor inputs? From higher labor productivity? Rearrange the following contributors to the growth of real GDP in order of their quantitative importance: economies of scale, quantity of capital, improved resource allocation, education and training, technological advance.

The U.S. labor force grew by an average of about 1.7 million workers per year for each of the past 25 years, and this explains much of the growth in real GDP. From 1990–2002, higher labor productivity accounted for 68 percent of the 3 percent average annual growth. Other factors have also been important. Refer to Table 17.1. Factor importance in descending order: (1) Technological advance—the discovery of new knowledge that results in the combining of resources in more productive ways. (2) The quantity of capital. (3) Education and training. (4) Economies of scale. and (5) Improved resource allocation.

17–8 Relate each of the following to the New Economy:
  a. The rate of productivity growth
  b. Information technology
  c. Increasing returns
  d. Network effects
  e. Global competition

Each of the above is a characteristic of the New Economy. The rate of productivity growth has grown substantially due to innovations using microchips, computers, new telecommunications devices, and the Internet. All of these innovations describe features of what we call information technology, which connects information in all parts of the world with information seekers. New information products are often digital in nature and can be easily replicated once they have been developed. The start-up cost of new firms and new technology is high, but expanding production has a very low marginal cost, which leads to economies of scale—firms' outputs grow faster than their inputs. Network effects refer to a type of economy of scale whereby certain information products become more valuable to each user as the number of buyers grows. For example, a fax machine is more useful to you when lots of other people and firms have one; the same is true for compatible word-processing programs. Global competition is a feature of the New Economy because both transportation and communication can be accomplished at much lower cost and faster speed than previously, which expands market possibilities for both consumers and producers who are not very limited by national boundaries today.

CHAPTER 18

18–1 Assess the leeway for using fiscal policy as a stabilization tool under **(a)** an annually balanced budget, **(b)** a cyclically balanced budget, and **(c)** functional finance.

(a) There is practically no potential for using fiscal policy as a stabilization tool under an annually balanced budget. In an economic downturn, tax revenues fall. To keep the budget in balance, fiscal policy would require the government to reduce its spending or increase its tax rates, adding to the deficiency in spending and accelerating the downturn. If the economy were booming and tax revenues were mounting, to keep the budget balanced fiscal policy would have to increase government spending or reduce taxes, thus adding to the already excessive demand and accelerating the inflationary pressures and downs. An annually balanced budget would intensify cyclical ups and downs.
(b) A cyclically balanced budget would be countercyclical, as it should be, since it would bolster demand by lowering taxes and increasing government spending during a recession and restrain demand by raising taxes and reducing government

spending during an inflationary boom. However, because boom and bust are not always of equal intensity and duration, budget surpluses during the upswing need not automatically match budget deficits during the downswing. Requiring the budget to be balanced over the cycle may necessitate inappropriate changes in tax rates or levels of government expenditures.
(c) Functional finance pays no attention to the balance of deficits and surpluses annually or over the cycle. What counts is the maintenance of a noninflationary full-employment level of spending. Balancing the economy is what counts, not the budget.

18–3 What are the two main ways the size of the public debt is measured? Distinguish between refinancing the debt and retiring the debt. How does an internally held public debt differ from an externally held public debt? Contrast the effects of retiring an internally held debt and retiring an externally held debt.

Two ways of measuring the public debt: (1) measure its absolute dollar size; (2) measure its size as a percentage of GDP.
Refinancing the public debt simply means rolling over outstanding debt—selling "new" bonds to retire maturing bonds. Retiring the debt means purchasing bonds back from those who hold them or paying the bonds off at maturity.
An internally held debt is one in which the bondholders live in the nation having the debt; an externally held debt is one in which the bondholders are citizens of other nations. Paying off an internally held debt would involve buying back government bonds. This could present a problem of income distribution because holders of the government bonds generally have higher incomes than the average taxpayer. But paying off an internally held debt would not burden the economy as a whole—the money used to pay off the debt would stay within the domestic economy. In paying off an externally held debt, people abroad could use the proceeds of the bonds sales to buy products or other assets from the United States. However, the dollars gained could be simply exchanged for foreign currency and brought back to their home country. This would reduce U.S. foreign reserves holdings and may lower the dollar exchange rate.

18–7 Trace the cause-and-effect chain through which financing and refinancing of the public debt might affect real interest rates, private investment, the stock of capital, and economic growth. How might investment in public capital and complementarities between public and private capital alter the outcome of the cause-and-effect chain?

Cause-and-effect chain: Government borrowing to finance the debt competes with private borrowing and drives up the interest rate; the higher interest rate causes a decline in private capital and economic growth slows.
However, if public investment complements private investment, private borrowers may be willing to pay higher rates for positive growth opportunities. Productivity and economic growth could rise.

CHAPTER 19

19–1 Use the aggregate demand–aggregate supply model to compare the "old" classical and Keynesian interpretations of **(a)** the aggregate supply curve and **(b)** the stability of the aggregate demand curve. Which of these interpretations seems more consistent with the realities of the Great Depression?

(a) Classical economists envisioned the AS curve as being perfectly vertical. When prices fall, real profits do not decrease because wage rates fall in the same proportion. With constant real profits, firms have no reason to change the quantities of output they supply. Keynesians viewed the AS curve as being horizontal at outputs less than the full-employment output and vertical only at full employment. Declines in aggregate demand do not change the price level because wages and prices are assumed to be inflexible downward.

(b) Classical economists viewed AD as stable so long as the monetary authorities hold the money supply constant. Therefore inflation and deflation are unlikely. Keynesians viewed the AD curve as unstable—even if the money supply is constant—since investment spending is volatile. Decreases in AD can cause a recession; rapid increases in AD can cause demand-pull inflation.

(c) The Keynesian view seems more consistent with the facts of the Great Depression; in that period, real output declined by nearly 40 percent in the United States and remained low for a decade.

19–4 Suppose that the money supply and the nominal GDP for a hypothetical economy are $96 billion and $336 billion, respectively. What is the velocity of money? How will households and businesses react if the central bank reduces the money supply by $20 billion? By how much will nominal GDP have to fall to restore equilibrium according to the monetarist perspective?

Velocity = 3.5 or 336/96. They will cut back on their spending to try to restore their desired ratio of money to other items of wealth. Nominal GDP will fall to $266 billion (= $76 billion remaining money supply × 3.5) to restore equilibrium.

19–7 Use an AD-AS graph to demonstrate and explain the price-level and real-output outcome of an anticipated decline in aggregate demand, as viewed by RET economists. (Assume that the economy initially is operating at its full-employment level of output.) Then, demonstrate and explain on the same graph the outcome, as viewed by mainstream economists.

See the graph and the decline in aggregate demand from AD_1 to AD_2. RET view: The economy anticipates the decline in the price level and immediately moves from a to d. Mainstream view: The economy first moves from a to b and then to c. In the long run AS will shift right (as nominal wages fall), intersecting AD_2 at point d. In view of historical evidence, the mainstream view seems more plausible to us than the RET view.

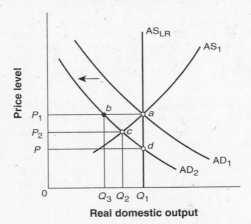

Real domestic output

19–13 Place "MON," "RET," or "MAIN" beside the statements that most closely reflect monetarist, rational expectations, or mainstream views, respectively.

a. Anticipated changes in aggregate demand affect only the price level; they have no effect on real output.

b. Downward wage inflexibility means that declines in aggregate demand can cause long-lasting recession.

c. Changes in the money supply M increase PQ; at first only Q rises because nominal wages are fixed, but once workers adapt their expectations to new realities, P rises and Q returns to its former level.

d. Fiscal and monetary policy smooth out the business cycle.

e. The Fed should increase the money supply at a fixed annual rate.

(a) RET
(b) MAIN
(c) MON
(d) MAIN
(e) MON

CHAPTER 20

20–4 Below are the hypothetical production possibilities tables for New Zealand and Spain.

New Zealand's production possibilities table (millions of bushels)				
Product	Production alternatives			
	A	**B**	**C**	**D**
Apples	0	20	40	60
Plums	15	10	5	0

Spain's production possibilities table (millions of bushels)				
Product	Production alternatives			
	R	**S**	**T**	**U**
Apples	0	20	40	60
Plums	60	40	20	0

Plot the production possibilities data for each of the two countries separately. Referring to your graphs, answer the following: (a) What is each country's cost ratio of producing plums and apples? (b) Which nation should specialize in which product? (c) Show the trading possibilities lines for each nation if the actual terms of trade are 1 plum for 2 apples. (Plot these lines on your graph.) (d) Suppose the optimum product mixes before specialization and trade were alternative B in New Zealand and S in Spain. What would be gains from specialization and trade?

(a) New Zealand's cost ratio is 1 plum = 4 apples (or 1 apple = 1/4 plum). Spain's cost ratio is 1 plum = 1 apple (or 1 apple = 1 plum). See the graphs.
(b) New Zealand should specialize in apples, Spain in plums.
(c) See the graphs.
(d) Total production before specialization and trade: 40 apples (20 + 20) and 50 plums (10 + 40). After specialization and trade: 60 apples and 60 plums. Gain = 20 apples and 10 plums.

20–6   Refer to Figure 3.5, p. 49 (Chapter 3). Assume that the graph depicts the U.S. domestic market for corn. How many bushels of corn, if any, will the United States export or import at a world price of $1, $2, $3, $4, and $5? Use this information to construct the U.S. export supply curve and import demand curve for corn. Suppose the only other corn-producing nation is France, where the domestic price is $4. Which country will export corn; which will import it?

Question 20–6

At $1: import 15,000. At $2: import 7,000. At $3: no imports or exports. At $4: export 6,000. At $5: export 10,000.
The United States will export corn; France will import it.

20–7   Draw a domestic supply and demand diagram for a product in which the United States does not have a comparative advantage. What impact do foreign imports have on domestic price and quantity? On your diagram show a protective tariff that eliminates approximately one-half the assumed imports. What are the price-quantity effects of this tariff on (a) domestic consumers, (b) domestic producers, and (c) foreign exporters? How would the effects of a quota that creates the same amount of imports differ?

Question 20–7

See the graph. The United States does not have a comparative advantage in this product so the world price P_w is below the U.S. domestic price of P_d. Imports will reduce the domestic price, increasing consumption from nontrade Q_c to Q_e, and decreasing

domestic production from Q_c to Q_a. See the graph. A tariff of P_wP_t (a) harms domestic consumers by increasing price from P_w to P_t and decreasing consumption from Q_e to Q_d; (b) aids domestic producers through the increase in price from P_w to P_t and the expansion of domestic production from Q_a to Q_b; (c) harms foreign exporters by decreasing exports from Q_aQ_e to Q_bQ_d.

An import quota of Q_bQ_d would have the same effects as the tariff, but there would be no tariff revenues to government from these imports; this revenue would effectively go to foreign producers.

CHAPTER 21

21–2   Indicate whether each of the following creates a demand for, or a supply of, European euros in foreign exchange markets:
   a. A U.S. airline firm purchases several Airbus planes assembled in France.
   b. A German automobile firm decides to build an assembly plant in South Carolina.
   c. A U.S. college student decides to spend a year studying at the Sorbonne in Paris.
   d. An Italian manufacturer ships machinery from one Italian port to another on a Liberian freighter.
   e. The United States' economy grows faster than the French economy.
   f. A United States government bond held by a Spanish citizen matures, and the loan is paid back to that person.
   g. It is widely believed that the euro will depreciate in the near future.

A demand for euros is created in (a),(c),(e), and (f), but see note below for e. A supply of euros is created in (b), (d), and (g).
   Note: Answer for (e) assumes U.S. demand for French goods will grow faster than French imports of U.S. goods.

21–3   Alpha's balance-of-payments data for 2003 are shown below. All figures are in billions of dollars. What are (a) the balance of trade, (b) the balance on goods and services, (c) the balance on current account, and (d) the balance on capital account? Does Alpha have a balance-of-payments deficit or surplus? Explain.

Goods exports	+$40	Net transfers	+$10
Goods imports	− 30	Foreign purchases of	+ 10
Service exports	+ 15	U.S. assets	
Service imports	− 10	U.S. purchases of	− 40
Net investment income	− 5	foreign assets	
		Official reserves	+ 10

Balance of trade = $10 billion surplus (= exports of goods of $40 billion minus imports of goods of $30 billion). *Note:* This is goods balance only—uses narrow definition of trade balance. Balance on goods and services = $15 billion surplus (= $55 billion of exports of goods and services minus $40 billion of imports of goods and services). Balance on current account = $20 billion surplus (= credits of $65 billion minus debits of $45 billion). Balance on capital account = $30 billion deficit (= foreign purchases of assets in the United States of $10 billion minus U.S. purchases of assets abroad of $40 billion). Balance of payments = $10 billion deficit. Therefore, U.S. must export official reserves equal to $10 billion.

21–6   Explain why the U.S. demand for Mexican pesos is downward sloping and the supply of pesos to Americans is upward sloping. Assuming a system of flexible exchange rates between Mexico and the United States, indicate whether each of the following would cause the Mexican peso to appreciate or depreciate:
   a. The United States unilaterally reduces tariffs on Mexican products.

b. Mexico encounters severe inflation.

c. Deteriorating political relations reduce American tourism in Mexico.

d. The U.S. economy moves into a severe recession.

e. The United States engages in a high interest rate monetary policy.

f. Mexican products become more fashionable to U.S. consumers.

g. The Mexican government encourages U.S. firms to invest in Mexican oil fields.

h. The rate of productivity growth in the United States diminishes sharply.

The U.S. demand for pesos is downward sloping: When the peso depreciates in value (relative to the dollar) the United States finds that Mexican goods and services are less expensive in dollar terms and purchases more of them, demanding a greater quantity of pesos in the process. The supply of pesos to the United States is upward sloping: As the peso appreciates in value (relative to the dollar), U.S. goods and services become cheaper to Mexicans in peso terms. Mexicans buy more dollars to obtain more U.S. goods, supplying a larger quantity of pesos.

The peso appreciates in (a), (f), (g), and (h) and depreciates in (b), (c), (d), and (e).

21–9 Diagram a market in which the equilibrium dollar price of one unit of fictitious currency zee (Z) is $5 (the exchange rate is $5 = Z1). Then show on your diagram a decline in the demand for zees.

a. Referring to your diagram, discuss the adjustment options the United States would have in maintaining the exchange rate at $5 = Z1 under a fixed exchange-rate system.

b. How would the U.S. balance-of-payments surplus that is created (by the decline in demand) get resolved under a system of flexible exchange rates?

See the graph illustrating the market for zees.

Question 21–9

(a) The decrease in demand for zees from D_1 to D_2 will create a surplus (*ab*) of zees at the $5 price. To maintain the $5 to Z1 exchange rate, the United States must undertake policies to shift the demand-for-zees curve rightward or shift the supply-of-zees curve leftward. To increase the demand for zees, the United States could use dollars or gold to buy zees in the foreign exchange market; employ trade policies to increase imports to the United States from Zeeonia; or enact expansionary fiscal and monetary policies to increase U.S. domestic output and income, thus increasing imports from Zeeonia and elsewhere. Expansionary monetary policy could

also reduce the *supply* of zees: Zeeons could respond to the lower U.S. interest rates by reducing their investing in the United States. Therefore, they would not supply as many zees to the foreign exchange market.

(b) Under a system of flexible exchange rates, the *ab* surplus of zees (the U.S. balance-of-payments surplus) will cause the zee to depreciate and the dollar to appreciate until the surplus is eliminated (at the $4 = Z1 exchange rate shown in the figure) because the United States would import more from Zeeonia and they would buy less from the United States since zees had lost value.

CHAPTER 22W

22W–3 Assume a DVC and an IAC presently have real per capita outputs of $500 and $5,000, respectively. If both nations have a 3 percent increase in their real per capita outputs, by how much will the per capita output gap change?

Rise in per capital output gap = $135 (= 3% × $5,000 − 3% × $500).

22W–5 Contrast the demographic transition view of population growth with the traditional view that slower population growth is a prerequisite for rising living standards in the DVCs.

Demographic transition view: Expanded output and income in developing countries will result in lower birthrates and slower growth of population. As incomes of primary family members expand, they will begin to see the marginal cost of a larger family exceeding the marginal benefit. The policy emphasis should therefore be on economic growth. Traditional view: Developing nations should reduce population growth as a first priority. Slow population growth enables the growth of per capita income.

22W–6 Because real capital is supposed to earn a higher return where it is scarce, how do you explain the fact that most international investment flows to the IACs (where capital is relatively abundant) rather than to the DVCs (where capital is very scarce)?

Capital earns a higher return where it is scarce, *other things equal*. However, when comparing investment opportunities between IACs and DVCs, other things are not equal. Advanced factories filled with specialized equipment require a productive workforce. IACs have an abundance of educated, experienced workers; these workers are scarce in DVCs. Also, IACs have extensive public infrastructures that increase the returns on private capital. Example: a network of highways makes it more profitable to produce goods that need to be widely transported. Finally, investment returns must be adjusted for risk. IACs have stable governments and "law and order," reducing the risk of capital being "nationalized" or pilfered by organized crime.

22W–12 Use Figure 22W.2 (changing the box labels as necessary) to explain rapid economic growth in a country such as South Korea or Chile. What factors other than those contained in the figure might contribute to that growth?

To describe countries such as South Korea and Chile, we would need to change labels on three boxes, leading to a change in the "results" boxes. "Rapid" population growth would change to "low" rate of population growth; "low" level of saving would change to "high" level of saving; "low" levels of investment in physical and human capital would change to "high" levels of investment in physical and human capital. These three changes would result in higher productivity and higher per capita income, which would produce a rising level of demand. Other factors: stable national government; homogeneous population; extensive investment in infrastructure; "will to develop"; strong private incentives.

CHAPTER 23W

23W−5 Use a supply and demand diagram to explain why persistent shortages of many consumer goods occurred under central planning in the Soviet Union and in prereform China. Why were black markets common in each country?

See Figure 23W.1. Because Russia and China set prices and did not allow them to change as supply or demand shifted, prices were below the equilibrium price for most goods and services. When the fixed price, P_f, is below the equilibrium price, P_e, there will be a shortage since the quantity demanded will exceed the quantity supplied.

Black markets are common where prices are fixed below equilibrium levels. People can buy goods at the fixed government prices (or pay off clerks to save such goods to sell to them), and because of the shortages at the low fixed price, resell these goods at a much higher price to those unable to find the goods in government stores at the controlled prices. This reselling is said to occur on the black market.

23W−6 What have been the major components of economic reform in Russia? What is meant when these reforms are described as "shock therapy"? How successful has Russia been thus far in its reforms?

Privatization of state-owned businesses; market-determined prices; promotion of competition; integration with the world economy; and price-level stabilization. These reforms are referred to as shock therapy because they were dramatic and quick rather than phased in over many years. Russia's reform has nominally privatized much of the economy (but property rights are still not clearly defined), establishing market-determined prices, and setting the stage for future prosperity. But the transition has resulted in declining living standards for many and increasing income inequality. Also, the government still does not have a successful program for collecting taxes.

23W−8 Relate each of the following items to the success of market reform in China: (a) leasing farmland, (b) price reform, (c) private rural and urban enterprises, (d) special economic zones, and (e) corporatization of state-owned enterprises.

(a) Leasing of land resulted in individually operated rather than collectivized farms; this greatly increased production incentives and boosted farm output.
(b) Price reform established market-based prices. These higher-than-government prices provided incentives for enterprises to expand output; they also enabled market-determined allocation of resources to replace inefficient central planning.
(c) Private rural and urban enterprises absorbed workers released by greater productivity in China's agricultural sector and established competition for China's state-owned enterprises.
(d) The special economic zones—with their private corporations, free trade, and foreign investment—established the workability and benefits of "near-capitalism."
(e) Corporatization focused the goals of state-owned enterprises on providing high-quality, minimum per-unit cost goods desired by consumers.